Thomas S. Eder

China and International Adjudication

Caution, Identity Shifts, and the Ambition to Lead

Nomos

The Deutsche Nationalbibliothek lists this publication in the Deutsche Nationalbibliografie; detailed bibliographic data are available on the Internet at http://dnb.d-nb.de

a.t.: Wien, Univ., Diss., 2020

ISBN 978-3-8487-7108-0 (Print)
978-3-7489-2562-0 (ePDF)

British Library Cataloguing-in-Publication Data
A catalogue record for this book is available from the British Library.

ISBN 978-3-8487-7108-0 (Print)
978-3-7489-2562-0 (ePDF)

Library of Congress Cataloging-in-Publication Data
Eder, Thomas S.
China and International Adjudication
Caution, Identity Shifts, and the Ambition to Lead
Thomas S. Eder
589 pp.
Includes bibliographic references and index.

ISBN 978-3-8487-7108-0 (Print)
978-3-7489-2562-0 (ePDF)

Onlineversion
Nomos eLibrary

1st Edition 2021

Acknowledgments

In considering the plentiful support I have received, I want to start with my wonderful wife Jaryna. Thank you for keeping me going throughout, inspiring me and always pushing me forward. I am grateful to my brother Andreas for being a fellow traveler who understands, and to my parents for initially setting me on this path and for their unconditional support.

I am greatly indebted to Irmgard Marboe, whose patience and guidance made this book possible. James Fry and Jerome Cohen provided me with important insights and allowed me to continue my research at Hong Kong University and NYU. I am grateful to Ursula Kriebaum, Friedl Weiss and Hans-Peter Neuhold for thoughtful comments on earlier versions of the text. All Mainland Chinese academics who graciously agreed to be interviewed by me gave this study a depth that it could not have otherwise attained. Finally, I am grateful to the University of Vienna and the Institute of Human Sciences (IWM) in Vienna for supporting my research abroad and writing phase financially.

Table of Cases

National Legislation

Table of Abbreviations

AB	Appellate Body (WTO)
AD	Anti-dumping (used in AD Agreement)
AJIL	American Journal of International Law
All ER	All England Law Reports
AoA	Agreement on Agriculture
Art(s)	Article(s)
ASEAN	Association of Southeast Asian Nations
ASIL	American Society of International Law
AsJIL	Asian Journal of International Law
BIT	Bilateral Investment Treaty
BRICS	Brazil, Russia, India, China and South Africa
CAI	Comprehensive Agreement on Investment
CETA	Comprehensive Economic and Trade Agreement (between the EU and Canada)
CJIL	Chinese Journal of International Law
CLCS	Commission on the Limits of the Continental Shelf
Co	Company
COC	Code of Conduct
Corp	Corporation
CPC	Communist Party of China
D / DS	Dispute Settlement
DOC	2002 Declaration on the Conduct of Parties in the South China Sea
DSB	Dispute Settlement Body (WTO)
DSM	Dispute Settlement Mechanism (WTO)
DSU	Dispute Settlement Understanding
EC	European Community / -ies
ECS	East China Sea
ECT	Energy Charter Treaty
ed(s)	editor(s)
edn	edition

EEZ	Exclusive Economic Zone
eg	*exempli gratia*, for example
EJIL	European Journal of International Law
EU	European Union
FDI	Foreign Direct Investment
FET	Fair and Equitable Treatment
FN	footnote(s)
FTA	Free Trade Agreement
GATS	General Agreement on Trade in Services
GATT	General Agreement on Tariffs and Trade (1947 / 1994)
G/L/	General Documents
ICJ	International Court of Justice
ICJ Rep	Reports of Judgments, Advisory Opinions and Orders of the International Court of Justice
ICSID	International Centre for the Settlement of Investment Disputes
ie	*id est*, that is
IL	international law
ILC	International Law Commission
ILM	International Legal Materials
ILR	International Law Reports
IMO	International Maritime Organization
IMS	International Minimum Standard
IP(Rs)	Intellectual Property (Rights)
IR	international relations
ISA	International Seabed Authority
ITLOS	International Tribunal for the Law of the Sea
ITLOS Rep	Reports of Judgments, Advisory Opinions and Orders of the International Tribunal for the Law of the Sea
LLC	Limited Liability Company
LNTS	League of Nations Treaty Series
Ltd	limited
MES	Market economy status
MFA	Ministry of Foreign Affairs
MFN	Most-Favored Nation
MOFCOM	Ministry of Commerce of the PRC
MoU	Memorandum of Understanding

NAFTA	North American Free Trade Agreement
NDRC	National Development and Reform Commission of the PRC
NGO	non-governmental organization
nm	nautical miles
NME	Non-market economy
No	Number
NPC	National Peoples Congress of the PRC
NPCSC	National People's Congress Standing Committee of the PRC
OUP	Oxford University Press
Para(s)	Paragraph(s)
PCA	Permanent Court of Arbitration
PCIJ	Permanent Court of International Justice
PCIJ Rep	Reports of Judgments, Advisory Opinions and Orders of the Permanent Court of International Justice
PLA	People's Liberation Army of the PRC
PRC	People's Republic of China
R	Report(s)
Res	Resolution
RCEP	Regional Comprehensive Economic Partnership Agreement (RTA in Asia)
RIAA	United Nations Reports of International Arbitration Awards
RMB	*renminbi* (Chinese currency)
RTA	Regional Trade Agreement(s)
SAR	Special Administrative Region
SCC	Stockholm Chamber of Commerce
SCM	Subsidies and countervailing measures (used in SCM Agreement)
SCO	Shanghai Cooperation Organisation
SCS	South China Sea
SEZ	Special Economic Zone
SG	Safeguards (used in SG Agreement)
S/L/	Trade in Services general documents
SOE	State-Owned Enterprise
SPC	Supreme People's Court of the PRC
SPS	Sanitary and phytosanitary measures (used in SPS Agreement)
Suppl	Supplement
TPP	Trans-Pacific Partnership Agreement (RTA in the Asia-Pacific)

TRIMS	Trade-related investment measures (used in TRIMS Agreement)
TRIPS	Trade-related intellectual property rights (used in TRIPS Agreement)
TTIP	Transatlantic Trade and Investment Partnership Agreement
UK	United Kingdom of Great Britain and Northern Ireland
UKTS	United Kingdom Treaty Series
UN	United Nations
UNC	United Nations Charter
UNCLOS	1982 United Nations Convention on the Law of the Sea
UNCITRAL	United Nations Commission on International Trade Law
UNGA	United Nations General Assembly
UNSC	United Nations Security Council
UNSG	United Nations Secretary-General
UNTS	United Nations Treaty Series
US	United States of America
USITC	United States International Trade Commission
USTR	United States Trade Representative
USTS	United States Treaty Series
VCLT	Vienna Convention on the Law of Treaties
VCST	Vienna Convention on Succession of States in respect of Treaties
vol	volume(s)
WTO	World Trade Organisation

I. Introduction – International Adjudication and China's Rise

I.1. A New Ambition – 'Guiding' International Order

When Xi Jinping started speaking on 17 February 2017 at a National Security Work Conference in Beijing,[1] most observers were already familiar with China's overall 'rise' and rhetoric of a new, responsible 'pillar' of the international order. However, things would change on this day, the ambition changed, because Xi told his surely captive audience that China was to no longer merely 'participate' and 'contribute its share.' Rather, it was to 'guide' international order – 'legal order' being implied as a part thereof – with the trade realm explicitly mentioned. The Chinese President declared the international order as clearly in need of reform to cope with the demands of a new age, and China being well qualified to take the reins of leadership. Reform efforts were thus to be led – rather than supported – by Beijing. However, the way of reform would not be to 'build a new stove,' ie to break down what is there and start anew, but rather to build from within, use existing structures and merely shape them in what China would consider a more 'just' and 'fair' direction.

Making the connection to the international legal order more explicit, some of China's most prominent international lawyers had already argued that China had to become a 'leader country' in the legal sphere to consolidate economic and political gains.[2] This would involve comprehensive engagement, including participation in international adjudication in ways that were both more active and potentially more far-reaching in breadth and depth than anything that the People's Republic's governments had previously considered acceptable.

---

1 People.cn, '习近平首提"两个引导"有深意' (Xi Jinping's first mention of the "two guides" has deeper meaning) *People.cn* (Beijing, 20 February 2017) <http://politics.people.com.cn/n1/2017/0220/c1001-29094518.html> accessed 10 January 2019.

2 Yuefeng 岳峰 Qi 齐, '中国应更积极参与国际法治进程——对话外交部国际法咨询委员会委员易显河' (China should actively participate in international rule of law processes – A conversation with member of the Foreign Ministry International Law Consultative Committee Yi Xianhe) *Oriental Outlook* (Shanghai, 28 January 2016) <http://www.lwdf.cn/article_1984_1.html> accessed 10 January 2019. See also Zhipeng 志鹏 He 何, '走向国际法强国' (Becoming a Great Power in International Law) [2015] (1) *Dangdai Faxue* 148.

Subsequently, interesting questions arise about the ways in which China engages in international adjudication, as well as the underlying factors shaping its choices.

I.2. How Nations Behave – China's Growing Impact on International Adjudication

International lawyers' preoccupation with 'how' and 'why' states embrace and comply with international legal norms, violate or seek to modify them has a long tradition, prominently represented by Louis Henkin's *How Nations Behave*.[3] In the second edition of his book, Henkin focused – for example – on the ways in which developing states were seeking to change or establish new international norms, and developed states were acting to preserve the status quo.[4]

In a related notion, Gregory Shaffer and colleagues rather recently maintained that:

> [M]ore broadly, our study suggests that one cannot fully understand international legal developments without examining dynamics within key countries, and that one cannot understand these dynamics without examining how they respond to international processes – in our case, of WTO legalization and judicialization. The two recursively and dynamically interact'.[5]

This book attempts to provide a somewhat novel approach for this kind of endeavor. It also exercises it through a case study of the state that has seen the most striking rise in importance for the international legal order since the turn of the century: the People's Republic of China (hereinafter: PRC).[6] It does so for a specific set of international legal norms, namely those related to international adjudication of investment, trade, law of the

---

3 Louis Henkin, *How Nations Behave* (Frederick Praeger 1968).

4 Louis Henkin, *How Nations Behave* (2nd edn, published for the Council on Foreign Relations, Columbia University Press 1979) 197–204.

5 Gregory C Shaffer, Michelle Ratton Sanchez Badin and Barbara Rosenberg, 'Winning at the WTO: the development of a trade policy community within Brazil' in Gregory C Shaffer and Ricardo Melendez-Ortiz (eds), *Dispute Settlement at the WTO – The Developing Country Experience* (CUP 2010) 99.

6 In the following, the term 'PRC' will only be used when referring to the respective state, its government, and official behavior. The generally used term 'China' is more open. 'Mainland China' denotes the PRC's territory without the Special Ad-

sea and territorial disputes. This is at least partly because international adjudication touches acutely on the concept of sovereignty, which has been 'at the heart of China's position in international law'.[7]

China's comprehensive relative power gains since the onset of economic reforms in 1978 are evident and recognized as such. It nonetheless bears repeating that China became the world's largest trading nation in 2013,[8] overtook the US as the world's largest economy in 2014 (with GDP measured using purchasing power parity),[9] and became the second largest investing country in 2016.[10] Since the turn of the century, China has also had a higher military budget than everyone aside from the US: in 2017, it spent more than four times the Russian budget.[11] An assertive foreign policy was adopted to go with the new capabilities in two steps, under Hu Jintao's leadership following the 2008/09 global financial crisis,[12] and after the ascension to power of Xi Jinping in 2012/13.[13]

These developments represent a major change in international relations, with potentially significant ramifications for both the PRC's behavior in the realm of international law and the international legal order as such.

---

ministrative Regions of Hong Kong and Macao, as well as the non-PRC controlled Taiwan.

7 Wim Muller, 'Beyond History and Sovereignty – China and the Future of International Law' (PhD thesis, European University Institute 2013) 31.

8 Angela Monaghan, 'China surpasses US as world's largest trading nation' *Guardian* (London, 10 January 2014) <https://www.theguardian.com/business/2014/jan/10/china-surpasses-us-world-largest-trading-nation> accessed 5 January 2019.

9 Ben Carter, 'Is China's economy really the largest in the world?' *BBC News* (London, 16 December 2014) <https://www.bbc.com/news/magazine-30483762> accessed 5 January 2019; The PRC had also significantly narrowed the gap on nominal dollar terms by 2018. While it remained somewhat far down the list on a per capita basis, China had also improved by several dozen places in that ranking in the decade up to 2018.

10 UN Conference on Trade and Development, 'World Investment Report' (2017) xi.

11 China Power Team, 'What does China really spend on its military?' *CSIS China Power* (Washington DC, 28 December 2015, updated 9 October 2018) <https://chinapower.csis.org/military-spending/> accessed 5 January 2019.

12 Rush Doshi, 'Hu's to blame for China's foreign assertiveness?' *Brookings* (Washington DC, 22 January 2019) <https://www.brookings.edu/articles/hus-to-blame-for-chinas-foreign-assertiveness/> accessed 25 January 2019.

13 Mikko Huotari and others, 'China's Emergence as a Global Security Actor – Strategies for Europe' *MERICS Papers on China no 4* (Berlin, July 2017) <https://www.merics.org/de/papers-on-china/chinas-emergence-global-security-actor> accessed 25 January 2019.

This issue 'goes to the heart of the mixed nature of international law, which has both served as a set of rules that govern the relationships between states, but has also become an instrument of change used by different actors attempting to effect change on a global level'.[14]

When deliberating about China's potential impact, it is imperative to assess its positions, how they evolved, what has influenced them, the historic roots behind Chinese legal thinking, as well as who formulates China's positions and has an influence on decision-makers.

Accordingly, the most extensive part of this book assesses the PRC's positions in the respective fields of law as they evolved throughout the research period, in which these positions both surfaced in and were influenced by case law.[15] This is the 'how' and part of the 'why' of China's engagement with international adjudication. Second, this book makes the historico-philosophical underpinning of distinct Chinese legal thought an object of critical analysis.[16] It takes this underpinning to be the prism through which Chinese scholars perceive and evaluate current international law issues, and formulate policy recommendations. Extensively discussing such inner-PRC debates,[17] it also draws on them in analyzing China's actual engagement.[18]

Preceding all of the above, the following chapter will set out the theoretical and methodological approach taken.[19] It will argue that while retaining a strong doctrinal, international legal positivist streak, an interdisciplinary approach is necessary to properly address both the PRC's *de facto* engagement and the underlying motivations.[20] Ultimately, this study aims to help to understand significant factors of China's behavior, and thereby contribute to assessing 'the conditions under which international law works [if not] to grander theoretical claims about *whether* it works'.[21]

14 Muller, 'Beyond History and Sovereignty' (n 7) 37.
15 See Chapter IV.
16 See Chapter III.
17 See Chapter V.
18 See Chapter IV.
19 See Chapter II.
20 See also Muller, 'Beyond History and Sovereignty' (n 7) 27–28.
21 Gregory Shaffer and Tom Ginsburg, 'The Empirical Turn in International Legal Scholarship' (2012) 106 AJIL 1, 44.

II. Framework – Theoretical and Methodological Approach

II.1. Introduction

This first part of the book will serve to set the stage. It will first review the focus of previous studies in terms of understanding Chinese legal thought and China's relationship with international law. The case will be made that the question of why the PRC has chosen to engage with only the forms of international adjudication that is has – including the issue of the time and (changing) intensity of engagement – has remained underexplored prior to this endeavor. Indeed, such engagement has remained underexplored in its breadth, in terms of how scholarly discourse informs it, and the way in which such discourse builds on history.

The next step will be to carefully build a theoretical and methodological framework that allows for fruitful engagement with the subject matter and deriving meaningful conclusions. A decision is made to engage in interdisciplinary research in the tradition of the school of international law and international relations. In the effort to employ international relations theory to answer questions of international law, Neoclassical Realism is drawn upon (in combination with Perception Theory). However, this research remains firmly anchored within international law and retains a strong positivistic element,[22] with an extensive focus on structured analysis of the increasingly substantive case law.

A suitable four-step methodology for this book is developed as follows. First, the history of Chinese legal thought is delineated to work out the *image* of international law in China. Second, China's concrete engagement with international adjudication on investment, trade as well as law of the sea and territorial issues from 2002 to 2018 is comprehensively discussed to clarify what *object* can be perceived in Chinese debates. Third, the contem-

---

22 Broadly in the sense of 'classical international legal positivism' where 'extra-legal considerations (economic, social, moral or political) are alien to legal analysis (…,) problems are supposed to have one correct legal answer [and the] answer is to be found in the legal system as such. See eg Andrea Bianchi, *International Law Theories – An Inquiry into Different Ways of Thinking* (OUP 2016) 21, citing Bruno Simma and Andreas L Paulus, 'The Responsibility of Individuals for Human Rights Abuses in Internal Conflict: A Positivist View' (1999) 93 AJIL 302, 304–305.

porary Chinese academic discourse on international adjudication is analyzed, and fourth conclusions are drawn, interpreting engagement through the prism of laid-out *perceptions* and the pre-formed *image*.

II.2. Previous Approaches and New Endeavor

A significant number of international studies on the PRC and international law appeared in two phases: first, around 1971, when the PRC took over the Chinese seat in the UN,[23] and throughout the 1970s with another driver of interest being the onset of economic reforms in 1978;[24] and second, research has proliferated again since the 1990s, spurred on by the PRC's WTO accession in 2001 and continuing up to the writing of this book.[25]

In the first of these phases, a strong focus was placed on the historical and philosophical origins of contemporary PRC positions on international law, the so-called 'unequal treaties',[26] and comparisons with Imperial or Republican Chinese positions,[27] as well as the issue most crucial to the PRC's approach to international law: sovereignty.[28]

In the second (and ongoing) phase, international scholars have been able to review a much longer period of PRC practice, and a much wider spectrum of engagement. Scholars have – inter alia – discussed the PRC

---

23 UNGA Res 2758 (XXVI) (25 October 1971) UN Doc A/RES/2758(XXVI)..

24 Barry Naughton, *Growing Out of the Plan: Chinese Economic Reform, 1978–1993* (CUP 1995).

25 WTO, *Protocol on the Accession of the People's Republic of China* (23 November 2001) WT/L/432 ('Accession Protocol').

26 See Chapter III.2.2.3.

27 See eg Hungdah Chiu, 'Comparison of the Nationalist and Communist Chinese Views of Unequal Treaties' in Jerome Cohen (ed), *China's Practice of International Law: Some Case Studies* (Harvard University Press 1972); Gerd Kaminski, *Chinas Völkerrecht und Außenpolitik: Historische Grundlagen* (Bastei 1972) 54–62; Daniel J Hoffheimer, 'China and the International Legal Order: An Historical Introduction' (1979) 11 Case Western Reserve Journal of International Law 251.

28 See eg Jerome Cohen, 'China and Intervention: Theory and Practice' (1973) 121 *University of Pennsylvania Law Review* 471; Suzanne Ogden, 'The Approach of the Chinese Communists to the Study of International Law, State Sovereignty and the International System' [1977] (70) *The China Quarterly* 315. See also more general titles pertinent here, such as Hungdah Chiu, 'Communist China's Attitude Toward International Law' (1966) 60 AJIL 245; Jerome Cohen (ed), *China's Practice of International Law: Some Case Studies* (Harvard University Press 1972); James C Hsiung, *Law and Policy in China's Foreign Relations – A Study of Attitudes and Practice* (Columbia University Press 1972).

and human rights post-'Tiananmen', the country's positions on international humanitarian and criminal law, and related questions of sovereignty and influence.[29] Authors have addressed participation and compliance in general,[30] and broader studies on Chinese legal reforms have also touched upon international law.[31]

On international adjudication,[32] studies have addressed the PRC's recognition of some extent of international jurisdiction in investment law from the 1980s and 1990s,[33] and some seminal work on China's investment treaties has been produced.[34] Investment arbitration awards in cases involving China were only handed down from 2011 (involving a Hong Kong investor invoking a PRC investment treaty) and 2013, with most findings

29 See eg Ann Kent, *Between Freedom and Subsistence: China and Human Rights* (OUP 1993); Muller, 'Beyond History and Sovereignty' (n 7); Björn Ahl, 'The Rise of China and International Human Rights Law' (2015) 37 *Human Rights Quarterly* 637.

30 See eg Pitman B Potter, 'China and the International Legal System: Challenges of Participation' (2007) 191 *The China Quarterly* 699.

31 See eg Stanley B Lubman, *Bird in a Cage: Legal reform in China after Mao* (Stanford University Press 1999); Randall Peerenboom, *China's Long March Toward Rule of Law* (CUP 2002).

32 On substantive studies tackling China and international adjudication in international economic law see eg Lisa Toohey, Colin B Picker and Jonathan Greenacre (eds), *China in the International Economic Order: New Directions and Changing Paradigms* (CUP 2015). On China and international adjudication overall see eg Julian Ku, 'China and the Future of International Adjudication' (2012) 27 *Maryland Journal of International Law* 154. See also Tommy Koh, 'International Law and the Peaceful Resolution of Disputes: Asian Perspectives, Contributions, and Challenges' (2011) 1 AsJIL 57; Mihaela Papa, 'Emerging Powers in International Dispute Settlement: From Legal Capacity Building to a Level Playing Field?' (2013) 4 *Journal of International Dispute Settlement* 83.

33 See Chapter IV.2.1.2.

34 See most importantly Norah Gallagher and Wenhua Shan, *Chinese Investment Treaties* (OUP 2009). See also Vivienne Bath and Luke R Nottage, *Foreign Investment and Dispute Resolution Law and Practice in Asia* (Routledge 2011); Axel Berger, 'The Politics of China's Investment Treaty-Making Program', in Tomer Broude, Marc L Busch and Amelia Porges (eds), *The Politics of International Economic Law* (CUP 2011); Lauge Skovgaard Poulsen, 'The Politics of South-South Bilateral Investment Treaties', in Tomer Broude, Marc L Busch and Amelia Porges (eds), *The Politics of International Economic Law* (CUP 2011); Axel Berger, 'Hesitant Embrace: China's Recent Approach to International Investment Rule-Making' (2015) 16 *Journal of World Investment and Trade* 843.

clustered in 2017,[35] although there has also been some notable research here.[36]

In trade law, the embrace of jurisdiction of an international judicial mechanism and the onset of actual case law went practically hand in hand with China's 2001 WTO accession.[37] Aside from a plethora of journal articles discussing individual cases involving the PRC, important publications have reviewed China's first decade within the organization.[38] On law of the sea or such dispute resolution related to territorial matters, the PRC has still only participated indirectly or under the threshold of contentious proceedings.[39] Several studies have focused on the law of the sea arbitration addressing the South China Sea – and underlying questions – which the Philippines initiated against China in 2012, and wherein awards on jurisdiction and merits were handed down in 2015 and 2016.[40]

---

35 See Chapter IV.2.1.3.

36 On investment arbitrations involving China see most notably – aside from journal articles discussing individual cases – Wenhua Shan (ed), *China and International Investment Law: Twenty Years of ICSID Membership* (Brill 2015).

37 See Chapter IV.2.2.

38 See most importantly Ka Zeng and Wei Liang (eds), *China and Global Trade Governance – China's first decade in the World Trade Organization* (Routledge 2013). See also Xiuli Han, 'China's First Ten Years in WTO Dispute Settlement' (2011) 12 *The Journal of World Investment & Trade* 49; Matthew Kennedy, 'China's role in WTO Dispute Settlement' (2012) 11 *World Trade Review* 555. See already earlier on Joseph YS Cheng, 'China's WTO membership and its concern for state sovereignty' (2004) 13 *Journal of Contemporary China* 819. See also Merit E Janow, Victoria Donaldson and Alan Yanovich (eds), *The WTO: Governance, Dispute Settlement, and Developing Countries* (Juris Publishing Inc 2008); Gregory C Shaffer and Ricardo Melendez-Ortiz, *Dispute Settlement at the WTO – The Developing Country Experience* (CUP 2010); Laura C Mahrenbach, 'Emerging powers, Domestic Politics, and WTO Dispute Settlement Reform' (2016) 21 *International Negotiation* 233.

39 See Chapters IV.3.3 and IV.3.4.

40 See eg S Jayakumar, Tommy Koh and Robert Beckman (eds), *The South China Sea Disputes and Law of the Sea* (Edward Elgar Publishing 2014); Keyuan Zou, 'The South China Sea', in Donald R Rothwell and others (eds), *The Oxford Handbook of the Law of the Sea* (OUP 2015); Keyuan Zou, 'China's Approach to UNCLOS and its Application to Disputed Issues in the South China Sea', in Jill Barrett and Richard Barnes (eds), *Law of the Sea – UNCLOS as a Living Treaty* (The British Institute of International and Comparative Law 2016); Thomas J Schoenbaum, 'The South China Sea Arbitration Decision and a Plan for Peaceful Resolution of the Disputes' (2016) 47 *Journal of Maritime Law & Commerce* 451; Stefan Talmon, 'The South China Sea Arbitration and the Finality of "Final" Awards' (2017) 8 *Journal of International Dispute Settlement* 1.

In parallel to the renewed international scholarship on the PRC and international law, Chinese scholarship also picked up and proliferated especially after WTO accession in 2001, supported by much-increased government funding. Chinese-language PRC law journals have multiplied, increased publication frequencies, and significantly improved in quality.[41] Since the early-2000s, PRC international law scholars – including (former) officials and international judges – have also started to publish more frequently on Chinese positions in English.[42] As part of this trend, the 2002-founded *Chinese Journal of International Law* (CJIL) allows greater scope for debates on China and international law, but also for voices sympathetic to PRC positions in particular, and thus an increase in Chinese influence on such debates.[43] While a self-assessment of Chinese contributions to global international law scholarship remained rather critical in 2010,[44] some contributions to international legal theory have since followed.[45]

This book contributes to the field in several respects. It comprehensively covers pertinent (sometimes very recent) case law in three fields: investment law, trade law, and law of the sea.[46] It provides a systematic English-language review of debates on engagement with international adjudication

---

41 See Chapters II.3.2 and V.

42 See eg Deming Huang, Yuan Kong and Hua Zhang, 'Symposium on China's Peaceful Development and International Law' (2006) 5 CJIL 261; Jielong Duan, 'Statement on the Rule of Law on the National and International Levels' (2007) 6 CJIL 185; Hanqin Xue, 'Chinese Observations on International Law' (2007) 6 CJIL 83; Lijiang Zhu, 'Chinese Practice of International Law: 2008' (2009) 8 CJIL 493; Bing Bing Jia, 'A Synthesis of the Notion of Sovereignty and the Ideal of the Rule of Law: Reflections on the Contemporary Chinese Approach to International Law' (2010) 53 *German Yearbook of International Law* 11; Junwu Pan, 'Chinese Philosophy and International Law' (2011) 1 AsJIL 233; Hanqin Xue, 'Meaningful Dialogue Through a Common Discourse: Law and Values in a Multi-Polar World' (2011) 1 AsJIL 13.

43 Published by Oxford University Press (OUP) in cooperation with the Chinese Society for International Law, Peking University and Wuhan University.

44 Zonglai Wang and Bin Hu, 'China's Reform and Opening-up and International Law' (2010) 9 CJIL193.

45 See eg Xianhe (Sienho) Yi (Yee), 'The International Law of Co-progressiveness: The Descriptive Observation, The Normative Position and Some Core Principles' (2014) 13 CJIL 485. Works that provide the author's name as Sienho Yee will be listed under Yi Xianhe in the bibliography – and Sienho Yee will be put in brackets in the footnotes – as this is merely a different transliteration of the same professor's name: 易显河. 'Yi Xianhe' is the Pinyin Romanization of the name, which is now the standard system in Mainland China and is also consistently used in this book.

46 See Chapter IV.

in Chinese-language PRC law journals from 2002.[47] Finally, it analyzes debates and actual engagement within a carefully-reasoned theoretical framework and within the context of the history of Chinese legal thought.[48]

II.3. Theory and Methodology

> If all this seems to suggest limits on international law as science, it signals the forceful return of international law as law, that is to say, as a disciplined craft requiring practical wisdom and sophisticated judgment. The finest practitioners of international law have less resembled chemists with equations than decision makers glimpsing through a glass darkly to guide human affairs against the brute fact of conflict and a fierce desire for cooperation. They have all operated with a keen consciousness of the primacy of power and the inevitability of conflict, yet have also skillfully developed cooperative institutions for the betterment of humanity.[49]

A theoretical and methodological framework should flow naturally (in the author's eyes) from the object of study, the questions asked about that object and the material available to draw upon in answering them. In developing such a framework, the author should at least consider the lines along which the object of study itself – should it be a (group of) person(s) – might frame and analyze a certain issue. Confines of existing approaches should be transcended where necessary and theories considered as not mutually exclusive, which they seldom are. All of these factors should lead to a coherent framework that promises to have 'explanatory power' regarding the subject matter.[50] Therefore, the reason for employing a theoretical framework at all is to seek guidance in an endeavor to select and interpret material in such a way that is most helpful to answering one's research questions.

None of the main 'methods' of international legal theory as listed eg by Ratner and Slaughter[51] – positivism, International Legal Process, the New

47 See Chapter V.
48 See Chapters II.3, III, IV, V and VI.
49 Richard H Steinberg and Jonathan M Zasloff, 'Power and International Law' (2006) 100 AJIL 87.
50 See eg Kenneth N Waltz, *Theory of International Politics* (Waveland Press 1979) 69.
51 Steven R Ratner and Anne-Marie Slaughter, 'Appraising the methods of International Law: A prospectus for readers' (1999) 93 AJIL 291, 293.

Haven School, Critical Legal Studies, feminist jurisprudence, law and economics, and international law and international relations – have delivered a 'knock-out blow'.[52] Instead, they increasingly 'lend themselves to a conscious engagement across isms, with a focus on midlevel analysis of international legal and political developments using hybrid theories'.[53] Such a hybrid theoretical model will be developed in the following sub-chapters, and employed for a mid-level analysis of the behavior of the PRC regarding the international adjudication of trade, investment, law of the sea and territorial disputes.

II.3.1. Theory – Conceptual Framework

II.3.1.1. An Interdisciplinary Approach – Questions About Both the 'Engine' and the 'Driver'

This study intends to ask different sets of questions that demand different approaches. In order to answer them, dispute resolution cannot be viewed as 'just a technical thing',[54] but neither can this side of its nature be denied. The 'engine' needs to be seriously addressed, but also the 'driver', because '[w]ho sets the destination and why and how one gets there are fundamental questions, which should not be eluded by scholars'.[55] In international law scholarship, interdisciplinarity has made deep inroads, demonstrated – inter alia – by the theme of the 10th Anniversary conference of the European Society of International Law in 2014: 'International Law and …'.[56] This book aims to provide a humble contribution to such efforts, by addressing both the 'how' and 'why' of PRC engagement with international adjudication, and drawing on different theoretical backgrounds for this purpose.

---

52 Steinberg and Zasloff (n 49) 86.

53 Ibid.

54 Thomas Schultz, 'Doing Law and Thinking about Law' (2013) 4 *Journal of International Dispute Settlement* 217, 218.

55 Bianchi (n 22) 6.

56 August Reinisch, Mary E Footer and Christina Binder (eds), *International Law and … – Select Proceedings of the European Society of International Law (Volume V 2014)* (Hart Publishing 2016).

II.3.1.1.1. Positivism – Facts of Engagement

This book aims to explore a certain state's engagement with international adjudication. One step within this endeavor will involve the screening, collection, summary, structuring and evaluation of concrete cases of such engagement.[57] On the part of the PRC, actual participation in contentious international judicial proceedings or arbitration is a recent phenomenon, although some forms of engagement below that threshold will also be relevant.

Guided by what may be called legal positivistic or 'traditional approaches',[58] this study will provide strictly intra-legal answers, applying legal interpretation to a first set of questions (mainly) in Chapter IV. Some descriptive passages are a given in answering both these and the questions laid out in Chapter II.3.1.1.2.[59] Accordingly, in the following questions this book will be interested in 'the law as it is',[60] as opposed to the diverging central research interests of other dominant theories of contemporary international legal scholarship.[61] These questions about the 'how' of China's engagement with international adjudication are:

---

57 On the value of academic analysis in the form of 'systemic description and appraisal' see eg Christoph Schreuer, 'The Development of International Law by ICSID Tribunals' (2016) 31 *ICSID Review* 728, 739.

58 Bianchi (n 22) 21–43. See also Mark Pollack, 'Political Science and International Adjudication', in Cesare PR Romano, Karen J Alter and Yuval Shany (eds), *The Oxford Handbook of International Adjudication* (OUP 2014) 360, who also talks of 'internalist, doctrinal scholarship'.

59 See also Sandesh Sivakumaran, 'The Influence of Teachings of Publicists on the Development of International Law' (2017) 66 *International and Comparative Law Quarterly* 1, 14.

60 See eg Ratner and Slaughter (n 51) 293 and Steinberg and Zasloff (n 49) 84.

61 Next to positivism, these are Critical Legal Studies (focus on the importance of language to legal development), Feminist Jurisprudence, law and economics, International Legal Process, the New Haven School and International Law and International Relations. For a somewhat different categorization see eg Bianchi (n 22) xi-xiv who termed chapters as 'Traditional Approaches', 'Constitutionalism and Global Governance', 'Marxism', 'The New Haven School', 'International Relations and Social Science Methodologies', 'Critical Legal Studies and the New Stream', 'The Helsinki School', 'Feminism', 'Third World Approaches', 'Legal Pluralism', 'Social Idealism', 'Law and Economics', and 'Law and Literature'. See also the in some ways more pertinent Cesare PR Romano, Karen J Alter and Yuval Shany (eds), *The Oxford Handbook of International Adjudication* (OUP 2014) xiii-xvi where under 'Theoretical Approaches to Studying International Adjudication' readers find 'Transnational Legal Process Theories', 'Political Science and International Adjudication', 'Sociological Approaches to International Courts',

When and in what form did the PRC recognize the jurisdiction of which international adjudicative bodies? How did the positions evolve? Which proceedings did the PRC (refuse to) participate in? What arguments did it advance, and how did tribunals decide on questions of jurisdiction and other matters deemed most relevant by this study for PRC participation in international adjudication? How do the positions taken fit within broader case law, and how does this author evaluate them overall? What likely connections between case law and relevant treaty practice can be traced? How does the PRC's practice compare with other large emerging economies?

II.3.1.1.2. International Law and International Relations – Reasons for Engagement

> In sum, although law (at a point in time) is significantly insulated from ordinary politics, it is never (except in its idealization) completely separate from politics; law remains subject to distinctive forms of legalized politics and can always be changed by politics over time. Although legalization (over time) is always political, it always occurs in the context of, and is shaped by, the existing body of law. Thus, law provides boundaries for politics yet is itself bounded by politics; politics changes those boundaries, yet is itself bounded by law.[62]

In a second step, this book aims to address litigant behavior. Herein, answers to another set of questions will be sought about the likely reasons behind the PRC's practice of (non-)engagement. Answering such questions requires extra-legal sources: in other words, an 'externalist' approach in contrast to the above-laid-out 'internalist' approach of international legal positivism.[63] In this context, political science 'promises to contribute to the

---

and 'Legal Philosophical Issues of International Adjudication: Getting Over the *Amour Impossible* between International Law and Adjudication'.

62 Kenneth W Abbott and Duncan Snidal, 'Law, Legalization, and Politics: An Agenda for the Next Generation of IL/IR Scholars', in Jeffrey L Dunoff and Mark A Pollack (eds), *Interdisciplinary Perspectives on International Law and International Relations. The State of the Art* (CUP 2013) 36.

63 For a description of an ongoing turn towards such approaches see eg Jeffrey L Dunoff and Mark A Pollack, 'International Law and International Relations: Introducing an Interdisciplinary Dialogue', in Jeffrey L Dunoff and Mark A Pollack (eds), *Interdisciplinary Perspectives on International Law and International Relations. The State of the Art* (CUP 2013) 16. See also Andreas Paulus, 'Realism and Interna-

study of international law both through its epistemological and methodological approaches and through its distinctive theories'.[64] Broadly speaking, political science follows an '"enquiry paradigm," which judges the validity of scientific claims against "external sources" [, in the context of law extra-legal sources,] of evidence'.[65]

Particularly on international adjudication and issues of 'who litigates and why',[66] recourse to International Law and International Relations (hereinafter: IL/IR) may be made to find explanations. IL/IR is open and malleable to composite theorizing.[67] It aims to make international relations theory's political science analytical tools available to international law, for examining different aspects of and causes behind the behavior of international actors regarding international law, eg through compliance studies.[68] International relations theory is particularly valuable for such an undertaking, as it is:

> primarily concerned with *explaining* political behavior – recently, at least, including law-related behavior. Especially within those schools that favor rationalist approaches, scholars seek to identify the actors relevant to an issue, the factors (material or subjective) that affect their behavior or otherwise influence events, and the "causal pathways" by which those factors have effect. These elements are typically incorporated in a model that singles out particular factors for study.[69]

---

tional Law: Two Optics in Need of Each Other' (2002) 96 *Proceedings of the ASIL Annual Meeting* 269, 272 on what 'internal' and 'external' perspectives can and cannot accomplish.

64 Pollack (n 58) 369.

65 Ibid 360.

66 See Natalie Klein, 'Who Litigates and Why', in Cesare PR Romano, Karen J Alter and Yuval Shany (eds), *The Oxford Handbook of International Adjudication* (OUP 2014) 570–571.

67 This study does not use a New Haven School approach, because it does not presuppose that all societies on earth strive towards the same eight values, and it does not support the predetermined application of a certain school of international relations theory – liberal-institutionalist – without reference to the object of study's respective context and own manner of framing pertinent questions. On this school see eg Ratner and Slaughter (n 51) 293–294; Steinberg and Zasloff (n 49) 77; Guiguo Wang, 'The New Haven School of Legal Theory from the Perspective of Traditional Chinese Culture' (2012) 20 *Asia Pacific Law Review* 214, 230; Dunoff and Pollack (n 63) 6, 8–9.

68 Ratner and Slaughter (n 51) 294.

69 Kenneth W Abbott, 'International Relations Theory, International Law, and the Regime Governing Atrocities in Internal Conflicts' (1999) 93 AJIL 361, 362.

This approach thus fits this study's focus on how international adjudication and China's role therein are perceived by Chinese international law scholars who then relay these perceptions as part of strategy formulation.[70] This study will therefore aim to use a detailed theoretical IL/IR approach – developed in the following Chapters II.3.1.2 to II.3.1.5 – and the concomitant methodology (see Chapter II.3.2) to seek answers to the following questions about the 'why' of China's engagement (mainly) via Chapters III and V:

Why did the PRC refuse or decide to become party to a regime that allows for international adjudication or even includes compulsory international adjudication? Why did it (not) issue particular reservations? Why did the PRC decide to (not) include international adjudication options in bilateral treaties that it ratified? Why did it decide to change them in new or amended treaties later on? Why did the PRC make use or refrain from making use of international adjudication when available? Why was it a rather passive or active litigant? Why did it seek to settle or refuse to do so? Why did it recognize or dispute the jurisdiction asserted by a tribunal? Why did it (not) comply with the findings? Can similar reasoning for (non-)engagement be made out in different fields of law? Are there similar patterns in (preparation for) engagement?

Whereas previously political science insights were mostly drawn upon to address litigants' behavior before courts:

> only recently [has attention turned] to understanding the behavior of states in initiating (or opting not to initiate) litigation. (…) [H]owever, the "decision to sue" is an important and under-studied question, of interest not only for its own sake but also because the cases that actually reach international courts constitute a small, and potentially biased, subset of the universe of international legal disputes.[71]

---

70 See Chapter II.3.1.2.2 for *elite perception* as an *intervening variable*. This focus on how *elite perception* and not the law itself influences decision-making makes IL/IR approaches more promising than such of International Legal Process. On the latter see eg Mary Ellen O'Connell, 'New International Legal Process' (1999) 93 AJIL 334–337; Ratner and Slaughter (n 51) 294; Steinberg and Zasloff (n 49) 78. On the presupposition that law itself does indeed influence decision-making see eg Gideon Rose, 'Neoclassical Realism and Theories of Foreign Policy' (1998) 51 *World Politics* 144, 161.

71 Pollack (n 58) 374, 384. On addressing the problem of understanding states' decisions to accept international arbitration in investment law see also Beth A Simmons, *The International Investment Regime: Sovereignty, Investor Security, and Dis-*

Such an important question can be tackled in different ways, looking – inter alia – at numbers, relative power, internal government structures, economic differences, domestic issue importance, social and political goals, and the perceived effectiveness of litigation.[72] On one representative judicial body, previous studies have not found 'clear commonalities between litigating states that could reveal which are most likely to litigate at the ICJ, except for highlighting the ever relevant dimension of national interest for the states concerned'.[73] Motivations might involve eg relieving domestic political pressure, leveling playing fields with other states, delaying (unfavorable) resolutions, protecting one's reputation, economic concerns, and attaining diverse domestic policy goals.[74] It stands to reason that case studies create 'some potential to start drawing informed conclusions on why and how states and non-state entities use international courts to achieve their goals'.[75]

This book is an attempt to provide such a case study on China. The next sup-chapters will explain this study's choice among schools of international relations theory and concomitant analytical tools and reasoning for a focus on Chinese international law scholars' debates.

II.3.1.2. Neoclassical Realism – Power, Structure, and All of Those Intervening Variables

This study will make the case for choosing a Neoclassical Realist approach among different schools of international relations theory to draw from in IL/IR answers to the 'why' of China's engagement.

---

pute Settlement Since the 1980s (Straus Institute Working Paper) (NYU School of Law 2010).

72 Klein (n 66) 570.

73 Ibid 577–578.

74 Ibid 585, 592.

75 Klein (n 66) 592.

II.3.1.2.1. A Complicated History

To date, 'realism'[76] has contributed little to IL/IR scholarship.[77] To many, this is hardly surprising. Its advent after the Second World War caused a schism between previously-interdisciplinary international law and international relations scholarship.[78] The leading proponent of 'Classical Realism' – Hans Morgenthau – relegated international law to a 'residual' role, rejecting the notion of international law's autonomy and regulatory capacity.[79] He described international relations as being governed by objective and constant 'laws' rooted in human nature, which one could only strive to understand and adapt to.[80] The first among these 'laws' was a thirst for power[81] – the ability, and perception thereof, to impose one's will on oth-

---

76 See James E Dougherty and Robert L Pfaltzgraff Jr, *Contending Theories of International Relations. A Comprehensive Survey* (5th edn, Longman 2001) 63, wherein the authors define 'realism' as an umbrella term for manifold 'realist' theories that developed after the Second World War. What 'realist' in turn means within distinct groups of such theories will be explained in the following.

77 Casper Sylvest, 'Realism and International Law: The Challenge of John H. Herz' (2010) 2 *International Theory* 410.

78 Dunoff and Pollack (n 63) 3, 8–9. Reengagement came only since the 1990s. It was initiated first by Kenneth Abbott and Anne-Marie Slaughter. See Anne-Marie Slaughter Burley, 'International Law and International Relations Theory: A Dual Agenda' (1993) 87 AJIL 205; Kenneth W Abbott, 'Modern International Relations Theory: A Prospectus for International Lawyers' (2000) 14 *Yale Journal of International Law* 335. The other side (ie international relations scholars) reciprocated calling for research on 'Legalization and World Politics' in a special issue of *International Organization* in the early 2000s. See inter alia Judith Goldstein and others, 'Introduction: Legalization and World Politics' (2000) 54 *International Organization* 385.

79 Shaffer and Ginsburg (n 21) 6 even argue that realist traditions are responsible for a general 'dearth of empirical work on international law.'.

80 Hans J Morgenthau, *Politics Among Nations. The Struggle for Power and Peace* (Knopf 1948). See also J Samuel Barkin, 'Realist Constructivism', in Hans Morgenthau, *Politics Among Nations. The Struggle for Power and Peace* (7th edn, McGraw-Hill 2006) 587; Hans J Morgenthau, *Politics Among Nations. The Struggle for Power and Peace* (7th edn, McGraw-Hill 2006) 4; Dougherty and Pfaltzgraff (n 76) 65–66, 76–77; Andreas Jacobs, 'Realismus', in Siegfried Schieder and Manuela Spindler (eds), *Theorien der Internationalen Beziehungen* (UTB 2010) 41, 48–49; Jochen von Bernstorff, 'International Legal Scholarship as a Cooling Medium in International Law and Politics' (2014) 25 EJIL 977, 987.

81 On the definition of power being contentious see Robert Gilpin, *U.S. Power and the Multinational Corporation: The Political Economy of Foreign Direct Investment* (Basic Books 1975) 24. On definitions being situational see David A Baldwin, 'Power Analysis and World Politics: New Trends Versus Old Tendencies' (1979)

ers –[82] ascribed to states as key components of and actors within an anarchic international system.[83] According to the second 'law,' all states and their respective political decision-makers act according to interests, which in turn are 'defined in terms of power' and backed by power,[84] with national survival as the greatest national interest.[85] All other factors besides these 'laws' were considered obfuscations in analyses of political actions.[86]

However, realism's relationship with international law has always been more complicated than the 'straw-man version (...) [which] makes a nice conceptual contrast – a null hypothesis backdrop – for arguments about how international law does matter'.[87] More recent authors have even redefined Morgenthau as being rather 'soft' on law, and actually 'eclectic' in considering power as well as norms when explicating international law content and developments.[88] A clearly entirely different example of a Classical Realist was John H. Herz,[89] who criticized Morgenthau's conviction that the severely limited role of international law could never change due to the 'necessity and impossibility of world government,' and instead promoted the active pragmatic development and reform of existing international law.[90]

To Herz, international law as part of the international system – just like the latter in general – was ultimately based on power. State actors would operate based on systemic pressures and relative power positions as well as

---

31 *World Politics* 161, 177; David A Baldwin, 'Interdependence and Power: A Conceptual Analysis' (1980) 34 *International Organization* 471, 499.

82 See eg Charles P Kindleberger, *Power and Money: The Politics of International Economics and the Economics of International Politics* (Basic Books 1970) 56, 65; Gilpin (n 81) 24; Dougherty and Pfaltzgraff (n 76) 72–75; Morgenthau, *Politics Among Nations* (2006) (n 80) 31; Waltz, *Theory of International Politics* (n 50) 127.

83 Morgenthau, *Politics Among Nations* (2006) (n 80) 67, FN 16; Ashley Tellis, 'Morgenthau: Politics as the Struggle for Power', in Hans Morgenthau, *Politics Among Nations. The Struggle for Power and Peace* (7th edn, McGraw-Hill 2006) 608.

84 Morgenthau, *Politics Among Nations* (2006) (n 80) 5, 10.

85 See also Dougherty and Pfaltzgraff (n 76) 63–64, 72, 76–77; Christopher C Joyner, 'International Law is, as International Relations Theory Does?' (2006) 100 AJIL 248, 252.

86 Dougherty and Pfaltzgraff (n 76) 77; Morgenthau, *Politics Among Nations* (2006) (n 80) 5.

87 Richard H Steinberg, 'Overview: Realism in International Law' (2002) 96 *Proceedings of the ASIL Annual Meeting* 260, 261.

88 Ibid.

89 Herz had his doctoral thesis supervised and was inspired by Hans Kelsen and the contribution of his 'Pure Theory of Law' to international law.

90 Sylvest (n 77) 410, 433–435.

their national interests. However, these – and the ways to realize them (ie policy choices) – were always what they were perceived to be, and perceptions could and should change. For instance, if global survival problems should come to the fore among perceived national interests, international law's position would be commensurately strengthened.[91] Herz strongly confirmed the importance of legal norms and institutions, with international law being seen as dependent on – yet not wholly determined by – power. Diplomacy's role was also underlined, albeit mainly for the sake of agreeing on additional (as well as improving existing) norms and procedures.[92]

Establishing 'Neorealism' or 'Structural Realism' in the late-1970s, Kenneth Waltz went further than Morgenthau to explicitly negate international law's autonomous impact on state behavior.[93] The international system's 'structure' – the web of relations between states as constituent 'units' – replaced the thirst for power as the most central category of analysis for state behavior.[94] Institutions manifested under international law were deemed to simply mirror such a structure and serve 'primarily national rather than international interests'.[95] Focusing on system-level analysis, sub-systemic factors (eg states' inner structure) were consciously excluded.[96]

However, only four years after Waltz's purism, Stephen Krasner modified Neorealism, including its position on international law.[97] The latter had come to be acknowledged as increasing the credibility of commitments, reducing transaction costs, facilitating cooperation, and creating incentives, ie as indeed relevant.[98] It would still be seen as 'facilitat[ing] out-

---

91 Ibid 435.

92 John H Herz, *International Politics in the Atomic Age* (Columbia University Press 1959); see also Sylvest (n 77) 410.

93 Waltz, *Theory of International Politics* (n 50) 69; Kenneth N Waltz, 'The Emerging Structure of International Politics' (1993) 18 *International Security* 44, 59. See also Kenneth N Waltz, 'Structural Realism after the Cold War' (2000) 25 *International Security* 5, 18–19; Martti Koskenniemi, *The Gentle Civilizer of Nations* (CUP 2001) 472; Niklas Schörnig, 'Neorealismus', in Siegfried Schieder and Manuela Spindler (eds), *Theorien der Internationalen Beziehungen* (UTB 2010) 66; O'Connell (n 70) 336.

94 Schörnig (n 93) 66–67.

95 Dougherty and Pfaltzgraff (n 76) 68–69; Waltz, 'Structural Realism after the Cold War' (n 93) 21.

96 Stephen D Krasner, 'Realist Views of International Law' Other' (2002) 96 *Proceedings of the ASIL Annual Meeting* 265; Schörnig (n 93) 69–70.

97 Stephen D Krasner, *International Regimes* (Cornell University Press 1983).

98 Steinberg (n 87) 261.

comes favored by powerful states (...) [but] simultaneously [as] facilitat[ing] positive-sum outcomes that would not otherwise emerge'.[99]

II.3.1.2.2. Reinventing Realism

Precise evaluations of previous strands of realism aside, the third major mold of realist thought – 'Neoclassical Realism',[100] which has been developed since the 1990s – is strikingly different in key ways.

The 'structure' of the international system and a state's (as a constituent 'unit') relative power within the system remain central, but the resulting pressures are not considered to always be dominant or directly determine policy. Such an approach could not explain different actions by states in similar positions.[101] At the same time, systemic pressures may not be neglected either, if one is to explain why states with different political systems often act alike in similar systemic positions.[102]

For Neoclassical Realists, systemic pressures always determine a range of policy options, and are considered the central and *independent variable* in shaping state behavior, making them the most important variable in the long term.[103] Nonetheless, taking on board liberal and constructivist critiques of realist thought,[104] they also became convinced that cross-fertilization with other international relations theories was necessary to make predictions at the foreign policy level,[105] and that domestic *intervening variables* (ie sub-systemic factors) determine the eventual choice among policy options.[106] In other words, '[t]he anarchic environment remains primarily

---

99 Steinberg and Zasloff (n 49) 76.

100 Gideon Rose coined the term 'Neoclassical Realism' in 1998. See Rose (n 70) 144. Among its major proponents are inter alia Thomas J Christensen, Steven E Lobell, Norrin M Ripsman, Randall Schweller, Jennifer Sterling-Folker, Jeffrey W Taliaferro, Asle Toje, and William C Wohlforth.

101 Dougherty and Pfaltzgraff (n 76) 90; Rose (n 70) 145–152.

102 Rose (n 70) 145–148.

103 Ibid 146–150.

104 See also Steven E Lobell, Norrin M Ripsman and Jeffrey W Taliaferro, *Neoclassical Realism, the State, and Foreign Policy* (CUP 2009); Norrin M Ripsman, Jeffrey W Taliaferro and Steven E Lobell, *Neoclassical Realist Theory of International Politics* (OUP 2016); Dougherty and Pfaltzgraff (n 76) 88–91.

105 Ariel Ilan Roth, 'A Bold Move Forward for Neoclassical Realism' (2006) 8 *International Studies Review* 486.

106 Peter Gourevitch, 'The Second Image Reversed: The International Sources of Domestic Politics' (1978) 32 *International Organization* 881, 900–907; Roth (n

but indirectly causal, while process remains secondarily but directly causal'.[107]

As opposed to previous realist thought, the world is not imagined as invariably conflictual, neither historically nor geographically. The contingency of history and the importance of actual foreign policy decisions are emphasized. Certain situations are considered 'ripe for rivalry,' although states will handle corresponding pressures differently depending on the *intervening variables*.[108] Like Neorealism, Neoclassical Realism allows for the rise and fall of different units within the structure. Such processes – wherein new powers start to assert themselves and challenge others – can be ripe for rivalry or friction, but only eventual policy decisions will determine whether a conflict happens.

In this new iteration, a realist approach that appreciates *intervening variables* and does not believe in an invariably conflictual world can help to comprehend both the need for international rules and the process of their production and enforcement.[109] Most contemporary realists' refusal to play that role arguably 'is both morally complacent and institutionally conservative, and it bears little resemblance to the vision of classical realists'.[110] Empirical changes to the international law-international politics-dynamic – such as the legalization process of recent decades – need to be appreciated, and a mutually-restraining relationship between power and law admitted to. A failure to do so means that realist thought is 'little more than the pure theory of law stood on its head,' and a loss of the ability to explain current states' actual behavior.[111]

International law – within a Neoclassical Realist framework – can be viewed as a part and representation of the *independent variable* of the international system. It represents the distribution of relative power at each norm's inception. Therefore, vested interests strengthen it and create a 'conservative bias' against change.[112] Bargaining around changes involves transaction costs, and international law thus influences outcomes.[113] This

---

105) 486; Jennifer Sterling-Folker, Realist Environment, Liberal Process, and Domestic Variables' (1997) 41 *International Studies Quarterly* 1, 2, 19.

107 Sterling-Folker (n 106) 22.

108 Rose (n 70) 171.

109 Sylvest (n 77) 438.

110 William E Scheuerman, *Hans Morgenthau: Realism and Beyond* (Polity 2009) 6.

111 Sylvest (n 77) 440.

112 Krasner, 'Realist Views of International Law' (n 96) 265–267.

113 Robert Howse and Ruti Teitel, 'Beyond Compliance: Rethinking Why International Law Really Matters' (2010) 1 *Global Policy* 127.

is precisely why those who seek to alter their position within the system will seek the stabilizing force of legislation, while simultaneously taking care to build on the 'stable environment' provided by existing norms.

The law also has an autonomous position, as it influences choices among policy options through its distinct influence on domestic *intervening variables*.[114] Herein, '[l]egal obligations are different in kind from obligations resulting from coercion, comity, or morality alone',[115] creating specific 'expectations that guide and shape behavior',[116] and having '"constrained", "justified" and "organized" decision makers' actions, even if it did not dictate them'.[117] The last two notions are aspects of Constructivist and International Legal Process thought that Neoclassical Realism can agree with.

Among domestic *intervening variables*, *state structure* and *elite perception* have been considered the most important.[118] The former denotes a state's strength in the sense of its capability to extract and direct resources to implement policy. If foreign policy behavior is understood as a three-stage process of *strategic assessment*, *strategy formulation* and *strategy implementation*, *state structure* will be more important in the latter phases.[119]

Elite perception relates to the fact that policies are still drafted and decided upon by actual people, whose perception of power might matter more – at least in the short to medium term – than 'simply relative quantities of physical resources or forces in being'.[120] Nonetheless, changes to the *structure* will eventually change perceptions, as eg for US threat perceptions after the Second World War, from threats to its physical territory to threats to an amorphous 'broader environment'.[121] Long-term power trends can lead to 'perceptual shocks,' when *perception* catches up with *structure* and

114 Krasner, 'Realist Views of International Law' (n 96) 266.

115 Kenneth W Abbott and others, 'The Concept of Legalization' (2000) 54 *International Organization* 401, 408.

116 Abbott and Snidal (n 62) 43–44. See also Joyner (n 85) 256.

117 O'Connell (n 70) 337.

118 Rose (n 70) 161; Randall Schweller, *Unanswered Threats: Political Constraints on the Balance of Power* (Princeton University Press 2006) 11–13; Shiping Tang, 'Taking Stock of Neoclassical Realism – A Review of: Neoclassical Realism, the State, and Foreign Policy. Edited by Steven E. Lobell, Norrin M. Ripsman, and Jeffrey W. Taliaferro' (2009) 11 *International Studies Review* 799; see also already Gourevitch (n 106) 881.

119 Shiping Tang (n 118) 799.

120 Rose (n 70) 147.

121 Ibid 156.

foreign policy behavior is suddenly realigned.[122] In any case, it is necessary to analyze how those actually drafting and deciding upon policies evaluate their situation, if concrete policy decisions are to be understood.[123] This concept – which is very much part of the first stage of *strategic assessment* – shall be further explored in the following.

II.3.1.3. Image and Perception – Structure Relayed

In order to derive value from the insight that *elite perception* shapes policy outcomes as a key *intervening variable*, it is necessary to define *perception* and *elite*. Moreover, it is also necessary to determine a way in which to capture *elite perception* and its (intended and potential) impact.

Neoclassical Realism – as explained above – is open to amalgamation. When dealing with behavioral questions, theories within the field of social sciences present themselves as a natural supplement, and herein 'Perception Theory' is perfectly suited to provide a principally structural theoretical model with the tools to analyze *perception*, as a type of unit-level factor.[124] It defines *perception* as the selective intake of others' actions based on a preconceived *image*, and *image* as the result of a selective interpretation of history and experience by the perceiving elite.[125]

Already in the 1970s, Robert Jervis supported the notion of *elite perception* influencing state behavior in *Perception and Misperception in International Politics*,[126] and Robert Putnam defined two distinct groups to be researched within such an elite in *The Comparative Study of Political Elites*.[127] The first group – the *proximate elite* – comprises actual decision-makers, ie political leaders. Data on their reasoning is often sparse, especially in authoritarian states, leading to termini for the process of interpreting their reasoning such as 'Kremlinology'. Moreover, their statements are seldom intended to inform, and always to influence, whereby they are rarely transparent about motives, and always coded. The second group – the *influential elite* – comprises those with 'substantial indirect or implicit influence;

122 Ibid 159–160.

123 Ibid 158.

124 See also Nele Noesselt, *Die Beziehungen der EU zu China und Taiwan. Hintergründe und Perzeptionen* (Kovac 2008) 33.

125 Allen S Whiting, *China Eyes Japan* (University of California Press 1989) 18.

126 Robert Jervis, *Perception and Misperception in International Politics* (Princeton University Press 1976).

127 Robert D Putnam, *The Comparative Study of Political Elites* (Prentice-Hall 1976).

those to whom decision-makers look for advice, whose opinions and interests they take into account, or from whom they fear sanctions'.[128]

Among this *influential elite* is the scholarly community, which produces rich data on its reasoning. In terms of questions regarding the emphasis on information or influence, the intended audience, and proximity to *cognitive beliefs*,[129] the situation in the particular state in question needs to be reviewed. However, in any case, published studies and interviews with members of the scholarly community provide an interesting set of data regarding choices among policy options as potentially influenced by *elite perception*.[130] Among the scholarly community, such authors 'whose full-time professional occupation it is to study and interpret' the specific issue in question should be primarily reviewed.[131] In the case of this book, this would be Mainland Chinese academics working at international law university departments and dealing with international adjudication.

If one were to seek additional intra-legal justification for the value of studying the work of eminent Chinese international law scholars, it could be highlighted that Article 38 (1) (d) ICJ Statute considers 'the teachings of the most highly qualified publicists of the various nations, as subsidiary means for the determination of rules of law'.[132] Indeed, publicists' works are frequently cited by both States in their pleadings and courts and tribunals – particularly in early case law in newer areas of the law – and they remain influential on matters of interpretation and beyond.[133] Those in the field who reject the IL/IR approach taken herein might thus still find

---

128 Ibid 11.

129 David Shambaugh, *Beautiful Imperialist: China Perceives America, 1972–1990* (Princeton University Press 1991) 5.

130 On the Soviet case see Stefan Friedrich, *China und die Europäische Union. Europas weltpolitische Rolle aus chinesischer Sicht* (Mitteilungen des Instituts für Asienkunde Hamburg Nr. 321, Verbund Stiftung Deutsches Übersee-Institut 2000) 33; Shambaugh (n 129) 22. On the Chinese case see also Shambaugh (n 129) 17 and Whiting (n 125) 18.

131 Shambaugh (n 129) 5–6.

132 Art 38 (1) (d) ICJ Statute Charter of the United Nations and Statute of the International Court of Justice (adopted 25 June 1945, entered into force 24 October 1945) 1 UNTS 16 (UN Charter) ('ICJ Statute').

133 See eg Sivakumaran (n 59) 24–29, 33 who cites inter alia Ingo Venzke, *How Interpretation Makes International Law* (OUP 2012), and notes particularly awards in investment arbitration and separate and dissenting opinions by ICJ judges as regularly referring to the teachings of publicists.

value in an analysis of PRC academic debates.[134] The analysis provided in this book covers the work of scholars who are or have been members of the International Law Commission (hereinafter: ILC) and the *Institut de Droit International* –[135] perhaps an indication of being 'most highly qualified' –[136] as well as many leading PRC government lawyers and academics. Some of the latter also frequently publish in English, (co-)edit journals, and have authored impactful monographs and journals articles. Finally, the authors considered also include most of the members of the PRC Foreign Ministry's International Law Consultative Committee.[137]

---

134 See also Sivakumaran (n 59) 14, who cites Hersch Lauterpacht, *The Development of International Law by the International Court* (Stevens and Sons 1958) 25 as having noted that '[w]hile the availability of other sources of information may have altered the nature of the function of "publicists" as recorders of the practice of States, their part as its qualified interpreters cannot always be disregarded.'.

135 Cited herein are the works of former member of the ILC (2002–2010) and current titular member of the *Institut de Droit International* (year of election 2005), ICJ Judge Xue Hanqin, as well as the works of current titular member of the *Institut de Droit International* (year of election 2009) Yi Xianhe (Sienho Yee).

136 See eg Sivakumaran (n 59) 11.

137 The PRC Foreign Ministry International Law Consultative Committee (外交部国际法咨询委员会) has twelve members, whereas this study considers the works of Ceng Huaqun, He Zhipeng, Huang Yao, Jia Bingbing, Jiang Guoqing, Yi Xianhe (Sienho Yee), Yu Minyou and Zhang Naigen (see Chapter V for comments on authors' positions) – the other members are Li Ming, Liu Huawen, Ma Chengyuan and Xiao Yongping. The Committee also has four advisors and this study considers the work of one of them: Yu Jingsong – the other advisors are former ICJ President Shi Jiuyong, PCA arbitrator Liu Nanlai, and Chairman of the China Society of Private International Law Huang Jin. See eg Jilin Province Law Society, '何志鹏教授被聘任为外交部国际法咨询委员会委员' (Professor He Zhipeng was appointed as a member of the Foreign Ministry International Law Consultative Committee) *Jilin Province Law Society* (Changchun, 8 March 2017) <http://www.jlfxhw.com/hyfc/2771.jhtml> accessed 10 January 2019.

II.3.1.4. The Chinese Case – Characteristics and Caveats

> Each civilization has its 'sources of the self' that produce varied notions of cosmos, time, society, state, and law. (...) Regional or national cultures can play an important role in how different civilizations approach international law and international institutions.[138]

II.3.1.4.1. General Notions

Approaches to explain a state's behavior should always consider the lines of thinking dominant among that state's leadership and scholarly community. Underlying theoretical perspectives will heavily influence 'assumptions, predictions, and understanding of cause and effect'.[139]

The next part of this book – Chapter III – *Image* – deals extensively with Chinese legal thought. After some 'theoretical building blocks' in pre-Imperial times, the Imperial Chinese tributary system was formulated, which has been interpreted as not only an international relations theory but also a model of international legal thought.[140] This system and its underlying theory were confronted with and ended during a century-long colonial experience with European-developed international law in the late-19th and early-20th century.[141] After a brief period of subscription to the Soviet Theory of international law, China has shifted to a pragmatist phase in which it employs various Western international legal theories, still (or rather again) marginally draws on its own earlier developments, but has not yet developed an autochthonous modern theory of international law.[142] At least one Mainland scholar has recently made a strong case for IL/IR inter-

---

138 BS Chimni, 'Asian Civilizations and International Law: Some Reflections' (2011) 1 AsJIL 40.

139 Oona Anne Hathaway and Harald Hongju Koh, *Foundations of International Law and Politics* (Foundation Press 2004); Christian Reus-Smit, *The Politics of International Law* (CUP 2004). See also Joyner (n 85) 256.

140 See eg Pan, 'Chinese Philosophy and International Law' (n 42).

141 The ominous and amorphous term 'West' will be defined here in line with Allen Carlson, 'Helping to Keep the Peace (Albeit Reluctantly): China's Recent Stance on Sovereignty and Multilateral Intervention' (2004) 77 *Pacific Affairs* 9, FN 1, as the 'shifting coalition of states (primarily located in Western Europe and North America)' that have remarkably congruent positions regarding questions of international law.

142 There are first developments in this realm, however, whereas one could point to the prominent ventures of Yi Xianhe (Sienho Yee), with his *Theory of Co-Progres-*

disciplinary research as one 'viable way' forward for the 'Chinese study of international law'.[143]

Regarding international relations theory, various forms of realist thought have been found to be prevalent among most foreign policy elites worldwide,[144] especially those of the US,[145] but also China.[146] The latter has been described as exceedingly receptive on account of its historically-developed 'strategic culture'.[147]

Chinese thought and practice in matters of both international law and international relations is certainly more complex and includes elements (eg the 'peaceful rise' model) that contradict realist thought. Such elements do not yet represent an autochthonous Chinese theory, but certainly 'theoretical building blocks'.[148] The latter largely rose as a reaction to and modification of realist assumptions and have introduced idealist and constructivist elements. They redefine *power*, whereas *image* and *perception* are seen to play a key role.[149] On account of this assumption, Chinese scholars have intensely studied Western work that often uses – and has called for the use of – perception theory, and aims to shape others' *perception* of China.[150] Correspondingly, a dominant strain of Chinese international relations research can be described as alterations of or composite models involving realist thought that often involve elements of perception theory, which is precisely what is put forward here.

On the importance of *perception* in the PRC's foreign policy, previous studies have dealt with Japan and the US, respectively considering multiple sources of data or only academic debate among international relations

---

siveness. See Xianhe (Sienho) Yi (Yee), 'The International Law of Co-progressiveness' (n 45) 485–499.

143 Liu Zhiyun, 'Interdisciplinary Research on International Relations Theory and International Law in China over the Past 10 Years' (2011) 6 *Frontiers of Law in China* 496, 522.

144 Schörnig (n 54), p. 68; Steinberg (n 87) 260.

145 Dougherty and Pfaltzgraff (n 76) 96.

146 Vitaly Kozyrev, 'China's Continental Energy Strategy: Russia and Central Asia', in Gabrielle B Collins and others (eds), *China's energy strategy: the impact on Beijing's maritime policies* (Naval Institute Press 2008) 205–206; Charles E Ziegler, 'Russia and China in Central Asia', in James Bellacqua (ed), *The Future of China-Russia Relations* (University of Kentucky Press 2010) 233.

147 See eg Alastair Ian Johnston, *Cultural Realism. Strategic Culture and Grand Strategy in Chinese History* (Princeton University Press 1995).

148 Nele Noesselt, *Alternative Weltordnungsmodelle? IB-Diskurse in China* (VS Verlag für Sozialwissenschaften / Springer Fachmedien Wiesbaden GmbH 2010) 317.

149 Ibid 317.

150 Noesselt, *Die Beziehungen der EU zu China und Taiwan* (n 124) 38–39.

scholars (ie *elite perception* of the *influential elite* variant).[151] It has even been ventured that:

> we can only understand China's increasingly complex behavior toward the United States during this period as a function of the increasingly complex images the America Watchers hold and the perceptions they articulate to those policy makers who shape and guide China's America policy.[152]

This study will argue that the same holds true for Chinese international law scholars and international law. Perceptions of various aspects of international law, as well as resulting policy prescriptions wildly differ.[153] Understanding both this and the trends that nonetheless appear is essential if we are to comprehend the PRC's behavior within the international legal system and particularly regarding international adjudication. Similarities with international relations scholars are unsurprising given that international law is seen as both part of international relations and just as sensitive by the Chinese government. International law scholars perform a role comparable to international relations scholars, constitute a part of China's foreign policy elite, and have an impact on the decision-making process. This last point appears justifiable – inter alia – in light of certain shifts in official interpretations of national interests that are in line with the academic debate.[154]

II.3.1.4.2. Articulated Perception and Cognitive Beliefs

An important caveat has to be introduced in the Chinese case with the distinction between *articulated perception* – ie publicly-accessible publications[155] – and *actual perception*, as 'communication [has previously been found to often be] instrumental and possibly multipurpose',[156] whereby a degree of uncertainty needs to be inserted.[157]

---

151 Shambaugh (n 129); Whiting (n 125).

152 Shambaugh (n 129) 35.

153 See Chapter II.3.1.4.3 for a caveat on this notion regarding the period from 2014.

154 See Chapters II.3.1.4.2 and V.

155 As opposed to so-called *neibu* ('internal materials'), which are only compiled for the political leadership and not available to researchers.

156 Whiting (n 125) 18.

157 Shambaugh (n 129) 5.

Previous studies have established that 1) *actual perception* grew less and less in line with an 'officially prescribed perception' over time, 2) and that *articulated perception* was increasingly open but had a 'double-character'.[158] Such studies found that scholars' published work certainly influences policy decisions but is in turn influenced by politics. *Proximate elite* and *influential elites* thus mutually influence each other.[159]

In the PRC, the CPC – mainly the General Secretary, Politburo, and Central Committee – defines the national interest, (partly) publicly via speeches and policy papers,[160] and in doing so draws certain red lines for scholars. At the same time, it calls on them – eg through closed 'study sessions',[161] or via state institutions' consultative committees[162] or secondments[163] – to inform its decisions, including on the matter of how to protect and further the national interest as the party has defined it. In very brief and simplified terms, the main priorities are the continued rule of the CPC, territorial integrity, economic development, fighting corruption, and gaining relative power, influence and prestige internationally.[164] Chapter V will address how PRC international law scholars suggest protecting the national interest in the context of (non-)engagement with international adjudication.

---

158 Friedrich (n 130) 36–43.

159 Shambaugh (n 129) 6.

160 See eg Sebastian Heilmann (ed), *China's Political System* (Rowman & Littlefield 2017).

161 See eg Yiyi Lu, 'The Collective Study Sessions of the Politburo: A Multipurpose Tool of China's Central Leadership' *Nottingham: China Policy Institute Briefing Series Issue 27* (Nottingham October 2007) <https://www.nottingham.ac.uk/iaps/documents/cpi/briefings/briefing-27-collective-study-sessions-of-the-politburo.pdf> accessed 1 March 2019; Alice Miller, 'Politburo Processes under Xi Jinping' *Hoover Institution China Leadership Monitor no 47* (Stanford, 14 July 2015) <https://www.hoover.org/research/politburo-processes-under-xi-jinping> accessed 1 March 2019. See also Anthea Roberts, *Is International Law International?* (OUP 2017) 122–123, who noted that four international law academics had previously been invited to give lectures to the Politburo, among them ITLOS judge Gao Zhiguo as well as trade law expert and later vice president of the Supreme People's Court Cao Jianming.

162 For example the Ministry of Foreign Affairs established an international law consultative committee, see eg Ministry of Foreign Affairs of the PRC, '外交部国际法咨询委员会召开第三次全体会议' (The Ministry of Foreign Affairs International Law Consultative Comittee convenes its third plenary meeting) (Beijing, 6 January 2016) <https://www.fmprc.gov.cn/chn//pds/wjb/zzjg/tyfls/xwlb/t1329838.htm> accessed 30 December 2018.

163 Roberts, *Is International Law International?* (n 161) 123–124.

164 See eg Heilmann, *China's Political System* (n 160).

The Chinese government – inter alia – seeks to have international relations portrayed as more favorable to Chinese interests than they are, in order to reconcile the actual situation with a certain 'target state,' and merge the identities of state and elites. In this sense, *articulated perception* continues to serve as a political device in the construction of reality.[165] More recently, scholars themselves have aimed to favorably manipulate the perception of China by other state actors and the Chinese populace, in order for the PRC to be seen as peaceful, pragmatic and responsible.[166]

Additionally, previous studies have differentiated between certain groups of Chinese international relations scholars. In the 1990s, these were a 'non-Marxist,' descriptive, policy-informing group, and a 'Marxist,' ideological, policy-sanctifying group.[167] The first group was claimed to show long-term tendencies and be less affected by short-term political whims than official statements or newspaper articles.[168]

By the late-2000s, this classification was considered outdated, due to a massive proliferation of institutions, journals and scholars leading to a greatly expanded field.[169] Grouping authors along generational lines as well as contentual and methodological orientation was deemed more useful, whereas it was considered no longer possible to assign groups of scholars to certain institutions and journals. Three age groups of scholars were noted: the first holding on to Marxist cognitive modeling and staying close to the government line, the second being very fact-driven, disinterested in theory building and rather employing exclusively Western theories, the third aiming to Sinicize Western theories, build on them and make the case for China's particularity. These age groups were not delimited, although this book's author has previously argued that it is in line with the reasoning presented to roughly consider those who graduated prior to the

---

165 Friedrich (n 130) 36–43.

166 Noesselt, *Die Beziehungen der EU zu China und Taiwan* (n 124) 178–179.

167 Shambaugh (n 129) 278–279, 288.

168 Friedrich (n 130) 45.

169 Changping 长平 Fang 方, '中国国际关系理论建设问题和思考' (Establishing a Chinese IR-Theory: Problems and Deliberations) [2005] (6) *Jiaoxue yu Yanjiu* 46; Bin 滨 Li 李, '中国的马克思主义国际关系研究' (Marxist IR-Research in China) in Yizhou 逸舟 Wang 王 (ed), *中国国际关系研究 (1995–2005) (IR-Research in China 1995–2005)* (Beijing Daxue Chubanshe 2006); Noesselt, *Alternative Weltordnungsmodelle?* (n 148) 69–80.

period of reform and opening – ie before 1978 – as belonging to the first age group.[170]

Members of the second and third groups have been found to be more professional and outspoken. They have openly criticized government interference in their work, voiced their intention to write freely and have been encouraged by subsequent statements of the CPC Central Committee.[171] The second group – which level-headedly discusses the merits of particular cases and policies without interest in theory building – has been found to be most influential on foreign policy outcomes.[172]

The tendencies laid out above are considered here to be broadly applicable to Chinese international law scholars, who long appeared on a trajectory towards more openness about their 'cognitive beliefs,' ie their real opinions and the recommendations that they would like to provide to their country's leadership. Especially since (the preparation of) China's WTO entry, and regarding international adjudication of economic issues, more fact-driven, informative and open scholarship was encouraged and carried out. Nonetheless, caveats regarding the influence of the government, political caution, tailoring of texts for different specific audiences, and self-motivated manipulation of perception remain in place.

In sum, the published work of Chinese international law (like international relations) scholars does not exclusively represent scholars' *actual perception*, but it informs policy decisions as well as indicating currently *tolerated perception*.[173] International law scholars therefore form an *influential elite* whose *perception* is an *intervening variable* relaying *structural pressures*. It can be argued that the analysis of the inner-Chinese international law discourse allows drawing inferences about the likelihood of future official positions of the Chinese government, and therefore also the likelihood of a certain political or judicial means of dispute settlement being employed in a future conflict.

---

170 Thomas Stephan Eder, *China-Russia Relations in Central Asia: Energy Policy, Beijing's New Assertiveness and 21st Century Geopolitics*, Wiesbaden, Springer, 2014, 93, FN 93.

171 Friedrich (n 130) 66–67, 77; Noesselt, *Alternative Weltordnungsmodelle?* (n 148) 74–75, 132.

172 Noesselt, *Die Beziehungen der EU zu China und Taiwan* (n 124) 32; Noesselt, *Alternative Weltordnungsmodelle?* (n 148) 70.

173 Friedrich (n 130) 42–43.

II.3.1.4.3. Published Elite Perception Since 2014

At this point, a further caveat has to be added. With ups and downs along the way, scholars indeed became increasingly candid over the two decades leading up to Xi Jinping's ascension to the highest positions in party and state in 2012 and 2013.[174] However, starting at least from 2014, the parameters for Chinese academic discourse – especially in the fields of international law and international relations – changed. Published academic discourse in this most recent period can be considered more distant from authors' cognitive beliefs, and therefore less significant for analyzing the reasons behind China's past and likely future behavior as an international legal actor.

This is mainly due to three developments that are distinct yet flow from each other. First, China's new president immediately set about centralizing power within the CPC and the Chinese state, effectively ending the previous co-existence of different power factions.[175] The constitutional reform in 2018 to remove term limits for the president signified the end of the trend of gradually institutionalizing governance.[176] Second, Xi immediately started an anti-corruption campaign on an unprecedented scale, which has partly been channeled to aid him in his power centralization efforts, and to intimidate officials, academics and businessmen who would stray too far from political orthodoxy as defined by him.[177] Third, the Philippines launched a law of the sea arbitration against China on several questions related to the South China Sea, also in 2013. This was the first time that international judicial proceedings were viewed in Beijing as

---

174 For the time up to 2008 see also Noesselt, *Die Beziehungen der EU zu China und Taiwan* (n 124) 41.

175 Sangkuk Lee, 'An Institutional Analysis of Xi Jinping's Centralization of Power' (2017) 26 *Journal of Contemporary China* 325.

176 Richard McGregor and others, 'Xi Won't Go' *China File* (New York, 25 February 2018) <http://www.chinafile.com/conversation/xi-wont-go> accessed 31 December 2018.

177 William H Overholt, 'The Politics of China's Anti-Corruption Campaign' *East Asia Forum* (Canberra, 15 September 2015) <http://www.eastasiaforum.org/2015/09/15/the-politics-of-chinas-anti-corruption-campaign/> accessed 1 March 2019; Willy Wo-lap Lam, 'China's Anti-Graft Campaign in Review' *Jamestown Foundation* (Washington DC, 7 December 2015) <https://jamestown.org/program/chinas-anti-graft-campaign-in-review/> accessed 1 March 2019; Emily Feng, 'China universities accused of ideological weakness' *Financial Times* (London, 19 June 2017) <https://www.ft.com/content/88191d36-54b4-11e7-9fed-c19e2700005f> accessed 1 March 2019.

touching on Chinese territorial claims. A nationalist wave followed, and included demands for international law scholars to more strictly focus their efforts on defending the official line.[178]

All of these developments started to take full effect in 2014. Xi's consolidation of power – combined with a strong interest in shaping and reforming the country's foreign policy –[179] also entailed a consolidation of discourse on many subjects, a narrowing of the field of what could be discussed, which positions could be taken, and where the leadership's line would have to be defended instead. The anti-corruption campaign that ensnared more than 100,000 people –[180] often indicted for practices that had become more or less commonplace – strongly instilled the notion in professionals in all sectors that very real and harsh consequences could result from a fall-out with the leadership.

In the academic realm, there has been less and less room for dissent, reversing a trend that had been going on essentially since 1978.[181] Following a period of relatively few taboos, in 2013 the CPC General Office circulated a prominent document listing 'problematic' topics in domestic discourse, including 'constitutional democracy' and 'universal rights,' calling on all levels of the party to counter such trends and strengthen work in the 'ideological sphere'.[182] In 2015, the Minister of Education warned universi-

---

178 CGTN, 'Chinese legal experts refute Philippine claim in South China Sea' (Beijing, 7 May 2016) <https://america.cgtn.com/2016/05/07/chinese-legal-experts-refute-philippine-claim-in-south-china-sea> accessed 1 March 2019.

179 Christopher K Johnson, 'Thoughts from the Chairman: Xi Jinping unveils his foreign policy vision' *CSIS* (Washington DC, 8 December 2014) <https://www.csis.org/analysis/thoughts-chairman-xi-jinping-unveils-his-foreign-policy-vision> accessed 3 October 2019.

180 Shujie Leng and David Wertime, 'China's Anti-Corruption Campaign Ensnares Tens of Thousands More – Over 100,000 cadres have now been disciplined as part of President Xi Jinping's anti-graft drive' *Foreign Policy* (Washington DC, 9 January 2015) <https://foreignpolicy.com/2015/01/09/chinas-anti-corruption-campaign-ensnares-tens-of-thousands-more/> accessed 3 October 2019.

181 Tom Philips and Ed Pilkington, 'No Country for Academics: Chinese Crackdown Forces Intellectuals abroad' *The Guardian* (London, 24 May 2016) <https://www.theguardian.com/world/2016/may/24/academics-china-crackdown-forces-intellectuals-abroad> accessed 1 March 2019; Emilie Tran, 'China: zero tolerance for academic freedom' *The Conversation* (London, 17 October 2017) <http://theconversation.com/china-zero-tolerance-for-academic-freedom-85200> accessed 30 December 2018.

182 China File, 'Document 9: A ChinaFile Translation' (New York 8 November 2013) <http://www.chinafile.com/document-9-chinafile-translation> accessed 1 March 2019.

ties against promoting 'Western values'.[183] Both steps were followed by crackdowns on lawyers, academics and journalists.[184] Already in 2014, Xi Jinping called for greater party 'ideological guidance' in universities,[185] followed by a pertinent joint CPC General Office and State Council Directive in 2015,[186] and culminating in a new campaign to 'enhance patriotism' among intellectuals in 2018, requiring – inter alia – participation in trainings and other related activities.[187] All of these developments made it less and less likely that scholars would openly contradict the government line.[188]

It soon emerged that one crucial issue was the South China Sea case, the tribunal's jurisdiction, China's potential participation, and how to deal with the (potential) award. It was therefore no real surprise that there was complete and total consensus in endorsing the government's position when the Chinese Society of International Law brought together 300 lead-

---

183 Xinhua, 'Education minister warns against "western values" in colleges' *Xinhua* (Beijing, 30 January 2015) <http://www.xinhuanet.com//english/china/2015-01/30/c_133958419.htm> accessed 30 December 2018.

184 See eg Anthony Kuhn, 'China Steps Up Crackdown On Liberal Universities' *NPR* (Washington DC, 8 September 2017) <https://www.npr.org/2017/09/08/549549998/china-steps-up-crackdown-on-liberal-universities> accessed 1 March 2019; Tran (n 175); China File, 'Document 9' (n 182).

185 Sui-Lee Wee, 'China's Xi calls for tighter ideological control in universities' *Reuters* (Beijing, 29 December 2014) <https://www.reuters.com/article/us-china-universities/chinas-xi-calls-for-tighter-ideological-control-in-universities-idUSKBN0K70TI20141229> accessed 1 March 2019. Another such call followed a two-day top-level meeting on the matter in December 2016: Xinhua, 'Xi calls for strengthened ideological work in colleges' *Xinhua* (Beijing, 9 December 2016) <http://www.xinhuanet.com//english/2016-12/09/c_135891337.htm> accessed 31 December 2018.

186 Jing Li, 'Communist Party orders a course of Marxism for China's universities' *SCMP* (Hong Kong, 20 January 2015) <https://www.scmp.com/news/china/article/1682774/communist-party-orders-course-marxism-chinas-universities> accessed 31 December 2018.

187 China Digital Times, 'CCP Launches Patriotic Education for Intellectuals' *China Digital Times* (Berkeley, 8 August 2018) <https://chinadigitaltimes.net/2018/08/ccp-launches-patriotic-education-for-intellectuals/> accessed 1 March 2019; Nectar Gan, 'China tells its intellectuals to toe the party line' *Inkstone News* (Hong Kong, 8 August 2018) <https://www.inkstonenews.com/politics/chinese-communist-party-launches-campaign-enhance-patriotism-among-intellectuals/article/2158744> accessed 1 March 2019.

188 McGregor (n 176).

ing lawyers in May 2016.[189] The tribunal was considered not to have any jurisdiction, and China to be well within its rights (and correct) not to participate in any way, and not to implement any awards resulting from these proceedings. In contrast to Russian scholars on Crimea, Chinese scholars have also published very actively in English on the South China Sea arbitration, and '[t]heir outwardly-oriented advocacy aligned with the Chinese government's worldwide public relations campaign to popularize its viewpoint on the South China Sea'.[190]

It has been noted that disagreeing with the government on the South China Sea case required an act of courage that could see one being disinvited from the next government-organized seminar, and was connected with 'fears of censorship or soft retribution in the competitive domestic academic job market'.[191] At least in private, some Chinese scholars argued in 2014 or later that China should have appeared before the tribunal to argue against jurisdiction, although they noted difficulties in publishing such arguments in Chinese journals.[192] Such limited participation would have supposedly given the PRC a better chance to win, and could have mirrored the US's approach in *Nicaragua*,[193] had China walked away from the proceedings after losing in the jurisdictional phase. As far as uniformity in opinion appears excessive and as far as Beijing may also be internally 'sur-

189 CGTN (n 178). See also Anthea Roberts, 'Crimea and the South China Sea – Connections and Disconnects among Chinese, Russian and Western International Lawyers', in Anthea Roberts and others (eds), *Comparative International Law* (OUP 2018) 111, 123, who notes similar statements by the All China Lawyers Association, the Chinese Law Society and Chinese Society of the Law of the Sea.

190 Roberts, 'Crimea and the South China Sea' (n 189) 111, 112–113.

191 Ibid 111, 130. On the first notion, Roberts quoted China specialist Jerome Cohen. On the second, she quoted Shi Jiangtao, 'Is Beijing Courting Disaster by Shunning South China Sea Tribunal?' *SCMP* (Hong Kong, 20 June 2016) <https://www.scmp.com/news/china/diplomacy-defence/article/1977418/beijing-courting-disaster-shunning-south-china-sea> accessed 1 March 2019. She also mentioned several newspaper reports about anonymous scholars' complaints. On the third notion, ie the direct quote, she referred to Julian Ku, 'China's Ridiculously Weak Legal Argument Against Complying with the South China Sea Arbitration Award' *Lawfare* (Washington DC, 6 June 2016) <https://www.lawfareblog.com/chinas-ridiculously-weak-legal-argument-against-complying-south-china-sea-arbitration-award> accessed 1 March 2019.

192 Roberts, 'Crimea and the South China Sea' (n 189) 111, 123–124.

193 *Military and Paramilitary Activities in and against Nicaragua (Nicaragua v United States of America)* (Judgment) [1986] ICJ Rep 14, para 26.

rounding itself with yes-men',[194] it risks both undermining the global discursive power of its scholars and sound strategic assessment and decision-making.

II.3.1.5. Final Remarks on Theory – Composite Approach

As argued in the preceding sub-chapters, 1) this study views the laid-out theoretical approaches as being open to amalgamation, and 2) international legal positivism, a modified realist IL/IR approach and perception theory will be part of the amalgam used in this study.

Both the need to employ a doctrinal approach seeking intra-legal answers to the 'how' of PRC engagement with international adjudication and the importance of relative power to the 'why' of such engagement are considered beyond dispute.[195] Nonetheless, relative power only leads to policy options, and the 'why' of eventual concrete policy outcomes requires analyzing *intervening variables*, whereas this book will focus on the *perceptions* of the *influential elite* of PRC international legal scholars.

The following case study accepts the described approaches' general validity and aims to concretely apply them and contribute expertise on China. It chooses to tackle the fields of trade and investment law, because there have actually been contentious proceedings with PRC participation. This study further addresses dispute resolution of law of the sea and territorial matters, because the PRC has 1) participated below the threshold of contentious proceedings in ways considered relevant (ie advisory proceedings, proceedings at the Commission on the Limts of the Continental Shelf) and has 2) indirectly participated in contentious proceedings through timely diplomatic statements explaining its legal positions (ie *Philippines v China*).[196]

Previous research has pointed to a number of assumptions concerning when governments would likely embrace international adjudication.[197] Governments might consider their relative power, their experience, the probability of winning, and the probability of establishing useful prece-

---

194 Ibid 111, 127–128.

195 See also Rose (n 70) 168.

196 *The South China Sea Arbitration (The Republic of Philippines v The People's Republic of China)*, PCA Case No 2013–19, Award (12 July 2016) ('*The South China Sea Arbitration* (Award)').

197 Pollack (n 58) 374; Klein (n 66) 583–584.

dent. They might consider a dispute so salient that substantial concessions in negotiations would be too costly in domestic political terms, and thus want to secure political cover, signal support to powerful domestic constituencies, secure either litigation or arbitration as a means considered more favorable to their desired outcome, or they might subordinate their decision to broader processes at stake.[198] This book aims to contribute to the field by reviewing the 'why' of PRC engagement, and seeking out patterns through the prism of domestic scholarly debate.

II.3.2. Methodology, Structure and Sources

This study aims to address the 'how' and 'why' of PRC engagement with international adjudication, drawing on the history of Chinese legal thought as well as PRC scholarly discourse to interpret practice. The aim is to gain a better understanding of PRC positions.

Hence, the first step – with Chapter III – will be to engage with Chinese notions of law, international law, international adjudication and sovereignty, as well as China's confrontation with a system of international law and mechanisms of international adjudication largely developed in Europe and the US. This analysis will cover a lot of ground, from the monumental civilizational struggle between Legalism and Confucianism via the long-standing Confucian Imperial system, the brief Republican period, copying of the Soviet system and Sino-Marxist legal approaches to the era of 'reform and opening' in the PRC. It will focus on the main trends, weighted towards later phases, and striving for the noted *image* to emerge through a concise but vivid analysis. This part of the book will explore secondary literature, and will not delve into the world of primary legal texts and treaties of the Imperial, Republican and Maoist eras.

In a second step – in Chapter IV – the PRC's actual participation in case law as well as pertinent treaty practice (particularly in international investment law) will be structured and analyzed, ie the *object* of Chinese scholars' *perception*. This will require extensive work with primary sources,

198 See eg Klein (n 66) 572, 583 who eg gives the example of ICTY arrest and transfer obligation compliance in return for progress in EU accession processes. She also maintains that within any realist perspective used in IL/IR research, the 'power dynamics involved in any decision to litigate,' national interests, and the perceived effectiveness of adjudication would be expected to play an important role for participation and compliance; elite perception of these matters and key definitions having to be studied.

interpretation of treaties, and evaluation of judicial findings and arbitration awards. This part of the book will first address investment law, because the PRC first embraced the jurisdiction of an international adjudicative body through its numerous BITs. It will proceed with trade law, where China first participated in international adjudication. Finally, law of the sea and territorial matters where China engaged indirectly or below the threshold of contentious proceedings will be discussed. The relevant case law will be laid out, grouped in issue areas, and analyzed against the backdrop of global case law trends and international scholarly discourse. Pertinent Chinese scholarly debates as well as policy changes will support conclusions. Regarding the research period, analysis of investment treaty practice will reach back into the 1980s, while case law analysis will start from 2002, when the PRC first participated in international adjudication, and span up to 2018, owing to the time of writing of this book.

The third step – in Chapter V – will be to discuss Chinese international law scholars' *perceptions* of concrete issues connected to participation in international adjudication in these fields (as built on the then-delineated *image* and *object*). Regarding the research period, 2002 once again appears to be a suitable starting date, as the PRC entered the WTO on 11 December 2001 and had its first case at the WTO DSM in 2002, making case law with PRC participation a possible object of debate. Scholars' *perceptions* up to 2018 will be considered. Shifts over time will be delineated, with a stronger emphasis on more recent evaluations, but also with the caveat that articles published from 2014 especially on law of the sea and territorial matters are considered less close to scholars' cognitive beliefs and thus less helpful in understanding PRC behavior.[199] The same methodology will be followed for these years, although the coverage of publications will be less complete.

This study will focus on the *articulated perception* of 'second group authors',[200] in orientation more than in age, as younger scholars shall also be included. It will become clear in the following pages in the description of core PRC law journals considered for this study that the bureaucratic position of Chinese universities quite significantly differs. Universities may be subordinated to city or provincial governments, or directly to central government ministries (mainly Education but also Science and Technology), while specific bureaucratic hierarchies for individual faculties or departments may complicate the picture. Strong differences in funding and ac-

199 See Chapter II.3.1.4.3.

200 See Chapter II.3.1.4.2.

cess may be partly connected to this issue. However, as no convincing study of this issue could be found, this book will not consider a pertinent category for the selection of scholars and journals to focus on.

Concerning the material available for this task, one can access scholars *articulated perception* via two principal routes, namely in oral or written form. The first can be through lectures that they give, statements that they make at debates, or through interviews. The second can be principally through books, scholarly articles or simplified journalistic comments. This study deems interviews and scholarly articles best suited to answer its research questions.

Interviews in a private setting and with the option of anonymity offer the promise to get closer to the *actual perception* or 'cognitive beliefs' of the scholars in question. Scholarly articles and books are likely to be closer than journalistic comments, to a careful reasoning as would be provided to political decision-makers in *strategic assessment* and *strategy formulation*. Finally, scholarly articles typically offer insights into a scholar's line of thinking that are more closely connected to a particular point in time than books compiled over a longer period, they offer a more timely option for a back and forth debate between scholars, and – due to their more limited extent – they enable reviewing a greater number of 'scholarly statements' for the type of study represented here.

Concerning the choice of scholars to interview, this author proceeded from pertinent articles already read, journals already reviewed as well as indications about qualitative international law departments in the absence of an authoritative list, and sent interview requests to scholars at ten universities in seven cities. It was possible to set up ten interviews with scholars of Wuhan, Xiamen, Tsinghua (Beijing) and NWUPL (Xi'an) Universities in the summer and fall of 2013. In the summer of 2017, repeat exchanges with two scholars at Wuhan University and another interview with a scholar at CUPL (Beijing) were arranged. This group of scholars comprises members of different generations – with an emphasis on the second group described above – with different legal foci within the research field analyzed here. These scholars work at different universities with different bureaucratic positions. Among those interviewed, most wanted to talk anonymously in order to speak more freely. The answers given by all interlocutors will therefore consistently be cited as 'Interview in [City], [Date]'.

In terms of journals, it has been explained that second group authors are not associated with specific institutions or journals, which means that one has to return to two key general demands: including the most relevant – ie the most authoritative – while also providing a broad overview of the ongoing discourse. This author chose to primarily take into account the 28 'core law journals' as defined in *A Guide to the Core Journals of China* (中文核心期刊要目总览) compiled by Peking University.[201]

Of these journals, the following 22 contained articles pertaining to the research questions posed herein (listed here in 'Pinyin' phonetics without tones, Chinese characters and English; hereinafter only the phonetical name will be given)[202]:

1. *Journal of Comparative Law* (*Bijiaofa Yanjiu* – 比较法研究, published by China University of Political Science and Law (CUPL), which is subordinated to the Ministry of Education);
2. *Contemporary Law Review* (*Dangdai Faxue* – 当代法学, published by Jilin University, which is subordinated to the Ministry of Education);
3. *Science of Law* (*Falü Kexue* – 法律科学, published by North-Western University of Political Science and Law (NWUPL), which is subordinated to the Shaanxi Province Government);
4. *Journal of Law Application* (*Falü Shiyong* – 法律适用, published by National Judges College, which is a unit of the Supreme People's Court);
5. *Studies in Law and Business* (*Fashang Yanjiu* – 法商研究, published by Zhongnan University of Economics and Law, which is subordinated to the Ministry of Education);
6. *Legal Science Monthly* (*Faxue* – 法学, published by East China University of Political Science and Law (ECUPL), which is subordinated to the Shanghai City Government);
7. *The Jurist* (*Faxuejia* – 法学家, published by Renmin University, which is subordinated to the Ministry of Education);
8. *Tribune of Law* (*Faxue Luntan* – 法学论坛, published by the 'Shandong Province Law Society', a professional association led by the CPC);
9. *Law Review* (*Faxue Pinglun* – 法学评论, published by Wuhan University, which is subordinated to the Ministry of Education);

---

201 Chinese Academy of Social Sciences, '中文核心期刊要目总览（2011 年第六版）' (A Guide to the Core Journals of China (6th edn, 2011) *Chinese Academy of Social Sciences* (Beijing, 10 December 2013) <http://www.cssn.cn/bk/bkpd_zwhxqkymzl/201312/t20131210_900382.shtml> accessed 1 March 2019.

202 The remaining journals are: *Administrative Law Review* (*Xingzheng Faxue Yanjiu* – 行政法学研究), *Criminal Science* (*Zhongguo Xingshifa Zazhi* – 中国刑事法杂志), *People's Prosecutorial Monthly* (*Renmin Jiancha* – 人民检查), *Journal of National Prosecutors College* (*Guojia Jianchaguan Xueyuan Xuebao* – 国家检查官学院学报) and *China IP Journal* (*Zhishi Chanquan* – 知识产权); *Law and Social Development* (*Fazhi yu Shehui Fazhan* – 法制与社会发展).

10. *Chinese Journal of Law* (*Faxue Yanjiu* – 法学研究, published by the Institute of Law at the Chinese Academy of Social Sciences (CASS), which is subordinated to the State Council);
11. *Law Science Magazine* (*Faxue Zazhi* – 法学杂志, published by the 'Beijing Law Society', a professional association led by the CPC);
12. *Journal of Gansu Political Science and Law Institute* (*Gansu Zhengfa Xueyuan Xuebao* – 甘肃政法学院学报, published by the Gansu Institute of Political Science and Law, which is subordinated to the Lanzhou City Government);
13. *Hebei Law Science* (*Hebei Faxue* – 河北法学, published jointly by the Hebei University of Political Science and Law (HELC), which is under the administration of the Ministry of Science and Technology and the provincial Politics and Law Committee of the CPC, as well as the 'Hebei Province Law Society', a professional association led by the CPC);
14. *Journal of Henan Administrative Institute of Political Science and Law* (*Henansheng Zhengfa Guanli Ganbu Xueyuan Xuebao* – 河南省政法管理干部学院学报) – later renamed *Journal of Henan University of Economics and Law* (*Henan Caijing Zhengfa Daxue Xuebao* – 河南财经政法大学学报, published by Henan University of Economics and Law (HUEL), which is subordinated to the Henan Province Government);
15. *Journal of East China University of Political Science and Law* (*Huadong Zhengfa Daxue Xuebao* – 华东政法大学学报, published by ECUPL);
16. *Global Law Review* (*Huanqiu Falü Pinglun* – 环球法律评论, published by the Institute of Law at CASS);
17. *Tsinghua Law Review* (*Qinghua Faxue* – 清华法学, published by Tsinghua University, which is subordinated to the Ministry of Education);
18. *Modern Law Science* (*Xiandai Faxue* – 现代法学, published by South-Western University of Political Science and Law (SWUPL), which is subordinated to the Chongqing City Government);
19. *Tribune of Political Science and Law* (*Zhengfa Luntan* – 政法论坛, published by CUPL);
20. *Journal of Politics and Law* (*Zhengzhi yu Falü* – 政治与法律, published by the Institute of Law at the Shanghai Academy of Social Sciences, which is subordinated to the Shanghai City Government);
21. *China Legal Science* (*Zhongguo Faxue* – 中国法学, published by the 'China Law Society', a professional association led by the Chinese Communist Party);

22. *Peking University Law Journal* (*Zhongwai Faxue* – 中外法学, published by Peking University, which is subordinated to the Ministry of Education).

In addition to the articles in 'core law journals,' and mainly proceeding from the authors of these articles or references therein, some articles from other journals in the catalog of the dominant *China Academic Journals* (CNKI) database have also been included.[203] The thus delimited journal articles – together with the interviews described above – serve as the main basis for this book's findings on Chinese scholarly debate.

The final step will be to draw conclusions – in Chapter VI – from the then laid-out actual engagement as well as *articulated perceptions* of the former, through the prism of the *image* of international law in the PRC. It has been argued in the preceding sub-chapters that understanding such perceptions by the *influential elite* of Chinese international law scholars means understanding an important *intervening variable* in China's behavior as an international legal actor. This assumption will be reviewed against PRC treaty practice and pertinent case law. Through the described gradual process, this book hopes to arrive at reasoned new insights into PRC decisions on engagement with international adjudication.

---

203 China Academic Journals Database <http://oversea.cnki.net/kns55/brief/result.aspx?dbPrefix=CJFD> accessed 1 March 2019.

III. Image – Historical Evolution of Chinese Positions on International Law

III.1. Introduction

> Throughout Chinese History (...) all conflicts regarding questions of law arise from the contradiction between the Confucian and Legalist schools.[204]

As argued above in Chapter II, it is both worthwhile analyzing China's scholarly community's *perception* when studying PRC legal behavior, and necessary to first gage the *image* of pertinent facets of international law that underlies such a *perception*, in the sense of a selective intake.[205] Myriad intellectual and historical processes within the long history of Chinese legal thought have formed such an *image*. This chapter traces the most important debates, corner stones and trends. It does so in two 'rounds', dealing first with law in general and then with international law, including issues of sovereignty, intervention and adjudication.

III.2. History of Chinese Legal Thought

There are three main phases of Chinese legal thought: 1) the struggle over predominance between Confucianism and Legalism in pre-Imperial times, 2) the dominance of Confucianism in the Imperial era, and 3) the Modern (Republican and Communist) period, wherein China absorbed Civil Law, Common Law and Soviet Law influences into an increasingly mixed discourse. Keeping the introductory quote from Wang Boqi in mind, continuities and recurring patterns will be highlighted.

To clarify, this book is concerned with the PRC's engagement with international adjudication, pertinent case law, Chinese-language academic discourse within the PRC on the matter, and – for the reasons laid out in

204 Robert Heuser, *Einführung in die chinesische Rechtskultur* (Institut für Asienkunde 1999) 78. For an in-depth analysis on these two schools of thought see also Karyn L Lai, *An Introduction to Chinese Philosophy* (CUP 2008) 19–54, 172–198.

205 Whiting (n 125) 18.

Chapter II – the history informing that discourse. This approach informs the choice of issues and breadth of their coverage regarding Chinese legal history. This means that – inter alia – the Republic of China (hereinafter: ROC) before 1949 is covered only briefly, while the ROC at the UN 1949–1971 is largely and legal developments on Taiwan after 1949 are fully excluded. The sub-chapters below will aim to provide supporting arguments for this choice, while one reason admittedly is this study's limited scope.

III.2.1. General Questions of Law

III.2.1.1. Roots – Confucianism Against Legalism

Every examination of China's relationship with the concept and reality of law has to start with the two philosophical schools that struggled for dominance over both government and discourse since long before the unification of the Chinese Empire in 221 BC, Confucianism (儒家) and Legalism (法家).[206]

In the 'Warring States Period' (战国时代; 475 to 221 BC), several nominal vassals of the Zhou Dynasty – a loosely overarching structure – developed into *de facto* independent states struggling for hegemony. Both the Legalist and the Confucian schools emerged as a response to the chaos and constant state of war in this period.[207] As remedies to this problem, Legalists offered formal codified laws (法 – *fa*)[208] and a centralized structure, Confucians the education of the people along the lines of an encompassing moral philosophy and code of rites (礼 – *li*).[209]

Through their champion, the king of the State of Qin, conqueror of all other Warring States and first emperor of a united China – Qin Shi

---

206 See eg Derek Bodde and Clarence Morris, *Law in Imperial China. Exemplified by 190 Ch'ing Dynasty Cases (Translated from the Hsing-an hui-lan)* (Harvard University Press 1967) 50; Heuser, *Einführung in die chinesische Rechtskultur* (n 204) 78.

207 Ernest Caldwell, 'Social Change and Written Law in Early Chinese Legal Thought' (2014) 32 *Law and History Review* 1, 4 who notes the deteriorating sociopolitical conditions requiring new methods of social control.

208 Daniel CK Chow, *The Legal System of the People's Republic of China in a Nutshell* (West Academic Publishing 2009) 42: The first written legal codes already appeared in the 6th century BC, but the oldest surviving codex dates to the 7th century AD.

209 Patrick H Glenn, *Legal Traditions of the World: Sustainable Diversity in Law* (OUP 2010) 321–322.

Huangdi (秦始皇帝) – the Legalists initially won the struggle. Under the Qin Dynasty, a 'rule by law' meant that laws were mere instruments of the ruling, and mostly directed at magistrates. Codification was strongly concentrated on administrative and criminal law. The latter involved a system of draconian punishments that turned the people against the Qin, led to their demise after only 15 years (206 BC), and lastingly damaged the standing of *fa*.[210]

The advent of the ensuing Han Dynasty meant the advent of Confucianism, which retained the upper hand until the end of the Chinese Empire in 1911.[211] Human behavior was to be modeled now according to a proclaimed rational ideal, representing conformance with a code of rites that was laid out in Confucian classics. Conflicts would then cease to arise in the first place. Moreover, it was argued that laws would only negatively influence human character regardless.[212]

Existing legal codes were not abolished, as those less convinced of the inherent goodness of human nature saw *li* and *fa* as actually complementary 'instruments for socio-political order',[213] with the possibility of resorting 'to law to maintain social order when the higher dictates of conscience failed'.[214] However, the codes were modified and reinterpreted according to Confucian moral convictions. New fields of law – especially civil and commercial law – could not be codified, as they were deemed clearly within the domain of *li*.[215] The Emperor derived his authority from the Heavens, and was thus not bound by law in any case, but rather replaced it as the ultimate authority. Accordingly, this was a 'rule of man', and one that was only in limited ways a 'rule by law'.[216]

III.2.1.2. Imperial Era – Confucian Legal Thought

The Confucian legal tradition – in line with other East Asian informal legal traditions – can be categorized as somewhere between religious and

---

210 Ibid 322–323.

211 Chow (n 208) 40–41.

212 Gerd Kaminski, *Chinesische Positionen zum Völkerrecht* (Duncker & Humblot 1973) 13–14; Peerenboom, *China's Long March* (n 31) 29–30.

213 Lai (n 197) 41.

214 Chow (n 208) 42.

215 Pitnam B Potter, *The Chinese legal system: globalization and local legal culture* (OUP 2002) 9.

216 Chow (n 208) 45–46.

positive law. It is secular, as opposed to eg Islamic law, but also eschews formal structures and sanctions, as opposed to Civil Law and Common Law.[217] Normativity rooted in religion is rejected, as it either leads to complex written legal systems – like in the Talmudic, Islamic and Hindu tradition – or diverts attention from daily life through a metaphysical occupation with an immortal soul, like in Christianity, Buddhism and Daoism. However, Confucianism shares its distaste for positive law with the latter two.[218]

Confucianism is centered on persuasion and leading by example instead of compulsion and sanctions. Constant consensus building via *li* in order to safeguard a harmonious society is presented as preferable to alleged incessant disputes over the content of codified law. *Fa* elements only serve as subordinate supplements for the inveterate, which is why legal codes consist almost exclusively of criminal law.[219] This approach to law led to an ingrained equation of law and punishment among the Chinese populace, a 2000-year continuation of a negative *image*, first formed in the Qin Dynasty. Law was mostly feared, not seen as a potential safeguard of one's civil interests;[220] although, particularly in the latter stages of the Empire, the use of contracts was widespread and legal principles from the codes also used by magistrates in their rulings on civil matters.[221]

The Confucianization of existing law meant 1) abstractions were eschewed to make the law comprehensible, 2) the system became increasingly casuistic (eg 20 distinct offenses involving the killing of a person), 3) a comprehensive mitigation of the strictness of *fa*, and most importantly 4) a reorientation along the lines of the social relations (社会关系) that are the foundation of a Confucian society.[222] These are: father-son, husband-wife, older brother-younger brother, older friend-younger friend, and ruler-sub-

217 Glenn (n 209) 326.

218 Ibid 331–333.

219 Heuser, *Einführung in die chinesische Rechtskultur* (n 204) 78–79; Peerenboom, *China's Long March* (n 31) 29.

220 Pan, 'Chinese Philosophy and International Law' (n 42) 234.

221 See eg Madeleine Zelin, 'The Rights of Tenants in Mid-Qing Sichuan: A Study of Land-Related Lawsuits in the Baxian Archives' (1986) 45 *Journal of Asian Studies* 499; Philip CC Huang, 'Codified Law and Magisterial Adjudication in the Qing', in Kathryn Bernhardt and Philip CC Huang (eds), *Civil Law in Qing and Republican China* (Stanford University Press 1994). See also Madeleine Zelin, Jonathan Ocko, and Robert Gardella (eds), *Contract and Property in Early Modern China* (Stanford University Press 2004).

222 Glenn (n 209) 334–335.

ject.[223] All of these relationships, and thus also the legal system, are thought of as necessarily hierarchical, whereas one side owes obedience and piety and the other care.[224] In practice, this leads to different penalties for crimes within or without the family, against the superior or inferior side in one of the described social relations, and against persons of different social position.[225]

The Confucian system thinks of the individual as at the same time free and inseparably connected to the relations within which it exists. As the individual can thus only be conceptualized relationally, no concept of individual rights was developed. Instead there is a system of mutual duties.[226] The latter depend on the web of relations according to the informal norms of *li*, which determine whether a particular inequality should be remedied,[227] or whether the corresponding social structure is 'essential to the orderly existence of society'.[228]

In the realm of dispute settlement, a strong preference for mediation grows out of the distrust of positive law and the longing for harmony through adherence to *li*.[229]This, in turn, led to punishments for those citizens who would 'recklessly' seek adjudication and disrupt harmony, as well as to the non-existence of professional lawyers.[230] However, particularly towards the end of the Empire, moralistic expectations increasingly diverged from the reality of more frequent civil litigation on the ground.[231] When court proceedings nonetheless took place, judgments were not only (and often not even primarily) based on *fa*, but also on *li*.[232] There was no separation of powers and no independent judiciary, but a

223 Pan, 'Chinese Philosophy and International Law' (n 42) 235.

224 Chow (n 208) 43.

225 Bodde and Morris (n 206) 50; Chow (n 208) 47; Heuser, *Einführung in die chinesische Rechtskultur* (n 204) 70–71; Potter, *The Chinese legal system* (n 215) 9.

226 Yuanshi Bu, *Einführung in das Recht Chinas: Rechtsstand: September 2008* (CH Beck 2009) 8; Chow (n 208) 47; Kaminski, *Chinesische Positionen zum Völkerrecht* (n 212) 36.

227 Glenn (n 209) 335–338.

228 Potter, *The Chinese legal system* (n 215) 8–9.

229 Ibid 9.

230 Chow (n 208) 52–53; Kaminski, *Chinesische Positionen zum Völkerrecht* (n 212) 20.

231 See eg Philip CC Huang, *Civil Justice in China: Representation and Practice in the Qing* (Stanford University Press 1996).

232 Pan, 'Chinese Philosophy and International Law' (n 42) 234.

comprehensive system of appeals did exist, and the possibility of harsh sanctions against erring judicial magistrates.[233]

Confucian legal codes hardly changed over centuries,[234] which is partly due to the Confucian Imperial examinations system and its impact on education and intellectual development. The system was meritocratic and education was valued, but the latter was constrained by having to stay in line with and focus on Confucian teachings, which do not foresee any substantial changes to the world and the societal relations that are its foundation. Intellectual development by some accounts stagnated after the 13th century.[235] The last notable piece of legislation in Imperial times was the Qing Code of 1740.[236] However, despite these limitations Confucianism was highly influential internationally, most prominently in Korea and Japan, but also in Southeast Asia, where it 'is currently being taught officially in Singapore and (…) has been recently described as "omnipotent" in family relations in (communist) Vietnam'.[237]

III.2.1.3. Modernity – Western and Soviet Influence

III.2.1.3.1. Late Qing and Republican Reforms

Shortly before the end of the last Imperial dynasty, the Qing, an attempt was made to reform the system with Western models in mind, which was then continued in the Republican Era (中华民国) (1912 to 1949; and then on Taiwan up until today). This should on the one hand afford legal stability and predictability to Western investors, and on the other hand strengthen the country and allow it to reduce the oppressive Western political presence. The ensuing codifications, which were often based on German models (sometimes indirectly through Japanese adaptations) – eg in Civil Procedure Law also on Austrian legislation – were hardly implemented in

233 Chow (n 208) 50; Glenn (n 209) 324–325.

234 They were complemented, however, by an ever more sophisticated system of sub-statutes, which prevailed in cases of conflict. Some cases were noted as having more or less precedential value, and non-binding official commentaries were published. See eg Peerenboom, *China's Long March* (n 31) 6.

235 Glenn (n 209) 338–341.

236 William C Jones, *The Great Qing Code: A New Translation* (Clarendon Press 1994); Chow (n 208) 42; Heuser, *Einführung in die chinesische Rechtskultur* (n 204) 114.

237 Glenn (n 209) 331–332.

practice.[238] Broad sections of society did not know of their existence, judges often did not heed to them, and even the founder and first president of the Republic – Sun Yat-sen – called them only practicable when in line with *li*.[239] There was considerable continuity between the late Imperial and Republican phases. For example, the Republic enacted the 1907 draft Criminal Code in 1912 and only replaced it in 1928. Moreover, the 1929/1930 Civil Code – the first in Chinese history – drew on custom and law operative during the Qing Dynasty, as well as the drafting process for such a code that had been ongoing until the Empire's fall in 1911.[240]

The 'Common Program of the Chinese People's Political Consultative Conference' adopted by Communist forces in September 1949 – shortly before the official establishment of the PRC – abrogated all laws adopted in the Republican period.[241] The radical ideological, institutional and legal break is one reason why this book will not proceed into more detail on legal developments in the Republican period. Legal developments on Taiwan after 1949 are considered entirely beyond the scope of this research.

III.2.1.3.2. Soviet Models, Sino-Marxism and Pragmatism

The ensuing PRC (中华人民共和国) era can be divided into three phases: 1) copying the Soviet model (1949–1957), 2) Sino-Marxist legal approaches (1957–1978), and 3) legal reforms, modernization and professionalization (since 1978).

---

238 Chow (n 208) 53–54; Glenn (n 209) 345–346, FN 124.

239 Kaminski, *Chinesische Positionen zum Völkerrecht* (n 212) 22–25.

240 See Constitution of the People's Republic of China (adopted 4 December 1982 by the Fifth National People's Congress) ('Constitution of the PRC 1982'); Xu, 'Law, Custom, and Social Norms: Civil Adjudications in Qing and Republican China' (2018) 36 *Law and History Review* 77, 99–100, who for the text of the Civil Code cites *Zhonghua Minguo Xianxing Fagui Daquan* (A Complete Compilation of Current Laws and Regulations of the Republic of China) (Shangwu yinshuguan 1934). See also Philip CC Huang and Kathryn Bernhardt (eds), *The History and Theory of Legal Practice in China – Towards a Historical-Social Jurisprudence* (Brill 2014) 95, who for the texts of the criminal codes cite *Zhonghua Liufa* (Six laws of China) [1913] (Shangwu Yinshuguan 1927); 'Zhonghua Minguo Xingfa' (The Criminal Code of the Republic of China), in *Liufa Quanshu (Complete Book of the Six Laws)* (Shanghai faxue bianyi she 1928).

241 Bu (n 226) 2. See also Percy R Luney Jr, 'Traditions and Foreign Influences: Systems of Law in China and Japan' (1989) 52 *Law and Contemporary Problems* 129, 132.

III.2.1.3.2.1. Soviet Influence

The first phase included the adoption of a constitution in 1954,[242] as well as a fairly extensive body of laws up until 1957. The intention was to construct a Socialist state and all its institutions based on the Soviet model. Compliance with detailed rules of conduct was a priority in a system of comprehensive normativity.[243] Legal institutions and professions, as well as law faculties were established.[244] The resulting formal law-based system was in many ways quite similar to the Western one – 'only' adding a bloated public sector including inherent corruption, collectivized land, and the parallel institutions of a party not bound by the law.[245]

That position of the Chinese Communist Party (hereinafter: CPC), above law and state, has to be taken into account after 1949. Not only codified state law is relevant, but also party statutes and the ideology of Sino-Marxism, without which interpretation and application of legal norms cannot be properly assessed. The party controls all branches of government, but creates its own kind of 'separation of powers' through the establishment of several parallel institutions in one organizational area.[246]

The three central intellectual components of this system were 1) the (ever more nationalist-leaning) proletarian positioning, 2) an ideological line that views practice as the only 'standard of truth', and thus anticipates ideological fluctuations, and 3) a methodological dialectic.[247] The party demands the adaptation of all intellectual life to and through Sino-Marxism. Within the corresponding system of societal management – very much like

---

242 Constitution of the People's Republic of China (adopted 20 September 1954 by the First National People's Congress); The 1954 PRC Constitution very heavily borrowed from the 1936 Soviet Constitution, see Jizeng Fan, 'Constitutional Transplant in the People's Republic of China: The Influence of the Soviet Model and Challenges in the Globalization Era' (2015) 2 *BRICS Law Journal* 50, 56–59.

243 Kaminski, *Chinesische Positionen zum Völkerrecht* (n 212) 25–26; Luney (n 241) 132–133.

244 Chow (n 208) 55.

245 Glenn (n 209) 348; Hanns-Georg Tanneberger, 'Das Verhältnis der Volksrepublik China zum Völkerrecht – unter besonderer Berücksichtigung der historischen Erfahrungen des Landes mit den sog. „Ungleichen Verträgen" seit dem Frieden von Nanking (1842) und der eigenen Vertragspraxis gegenüber sechs asiatischen Staaten (Afghanistan, Birma, Ceylon, Indonesien, Nepal, Pakistan)' (PhD Thesis, University of Bochum 1974) 59.

246 Harro von Senger, *Einführung in das chinesische Recht* (CH Beck 1994) 214–215.

247 Ibid 217–227.

in the traditional Chinese system – law is only one means of directing the populace. For a long time, it is not even viewed as the most important one, as it is criticized for only creating external conformity instead of internal conviction.

III.2.1.3.2.2. Sino-Marxism

During the 'Hundred Flowers Campaign' (百花运动) in 1957 the Chinese leadership asked intellectuals to roundly criticize the party, in order for it to profit from a variety of views and adjust where necessary. However, party leadership was shocked on account of the level of participation and intensity of criticism, and tilted immediately to attacking its critics through the Anti-Rightist-Campaign (反右派运动). The (partly European-educated) leading jurists of the early years of the PRC had led the criticism. They had lamented slow progress in codification, legal violations during mass campaigns of the party, as well as appointments of untrained party members to judicial positions. Now they were the ones who were most fiercely attacked.[248]

The ensuing developments constituted a hard 'anti-Legalist turn',[249] marking the beginning of the second phase of PRC legal history: Sino-Marxism. Legal education was abolished, legal professions and formalized legal norms again the objects of disdain. Between 1957 and 1978 not a single law was adopted, and between 1965 and 1974 the National People's Congress (hereinafter: NPC) (全国人民代表大会), the official legislative body, did not meet at all.[250]

Western models, including the Soviet one, were completely rejected, and informal mediation, persuasion and moral education came to the fore. This tendency, which was amplified during the Cultural Revolution (文化大革命) (1966–1976), was actually in many ways in keeping with Confucian tradition, which still had an impact on popular sentiment.[251] The two pre-1978 phases of PRC legal history can be juxtaposed as 'external system',

---

248 Kaminski, *Chinesische Positionen zum Völkerrecht* (n 212) 27–28. See also Luney (n 241) 133–134 who emphasizes the importance of the 1957 break in Sino-Soviet relations for the turn against 'more regularized legal provisions and procedures.'.

249 Glenn (n 209) 349.

250 Bu (n 226) 2.

251 Kaminski, *Chinesische Positionen zum Völkerrecht* (n 212) 28–31; Tanneberger (n 245) 61–62.

ie normative laws aiming to determine behavior from the outside, and 'internal system', ie education and social pressure aiming to determine behavior from the inside.[252] As Confucianism was still presented as a 'feudal bogeyman,' Confucian social relations were now replaced with Socialist institutions and work units, the moral code of the *li* with Mao Zedong Thought (毛泽东思想).[253] The informal legal approach was nonetheless in line with the precursor's teachings. Since the late-1970s, '[a] re-emergence of traditional Chinese teaching has [indeed] become an ally in the effort to generate loyalty and preserve structure; it has already been said that China's government is no longer a communist one but only a confucian one'.[254]

Since the 1990s, there has been a movement calling for a return to indigenous sources of law, which criticizes the allegedly chaotic transplanting of Western legal concepts and institutions, and posits that the Chinese populace simply rejects and always will reject some of them. Foreign legal influence is expected to wane once 'self regenerating capacity' is regained; such a transition supposedly led to more autonomous and confident developments in Japanese law.[255]

III.2.1.3.2.3. Pragmatism

The third phase of PRC legal thought begins with the year 1978. Two years after Mao died and the Cultural Revolution ended, Deng Xiaoping (邓小平) started his politics of 'reform and opening' (改革开放). Economic reforms and interest in foreign investment went hand in hand with legal reforms intended to provide legal certainty for both investors and the new class of domestic entrepreneurs. This trend was reinforced with the 1982 Constitution, and especially its amendment in 1999, which demands 'governing the country according to the law' (以法治国) and making it a 'Socialist country ruled by law'.[256] However, the Constitution is not centered

252 Tanneberger (n 245) 59–61.
253 Glenn (n 209) 349; Kaminski, *Chinesische Positionen zum Völkerrecht* (n 212) 31.
254 Glenn (n 209) 349.
255 Bu (n 226) 2.
256 Constitution of the PRC 1982; 1999 Amendment to the Constitution of the People's Republic of China (adopted 15 March 1999 by the Ninth National People's Congress); Robert Heuser, 'What "Rule of Law"? The Traditional Chinese Concept of Good Government and Challenges of the 21st Century' (2004) 64 *Zeitschrift für ausländisches öffentliches Recht und Völkerrecht* 723; Fusen Zhang

on guaranteeing certain rights and does not prescribe a separation of powers. Instead, it summarizes 'the results of the efforts of the Communist Party in gaining power, establishing the People's Republic and pushing for economic reforms'.[257]

Beijing was unsure about the introduction of certain Western liberal-democratic concepts, and at first marketed the described reorientation domestically as the price the country had to pay for access to global markets and economic development.[258] Nonetheless, leading cadres of the CPC had learned the dangers of tendencies towards legal nihilism at first hand during the Cultural Revolution, when the fanatics of political terror also reached their doorstep. The renewed interest in law thus also grew out of self-protection, and the desire to uphold order and avoid a repeat of those years of chaos.[259] Law schools were reopened, lawyers could exercise their profession again, and the ministry of justice and courts were re-established.[260] Legislative powers again rested with the NPC and its Standing Committee, and the State Council issued regulations based on the laws and the constitution.[261] A wave of codifications reached all fields of law, especially civil and commercial law; the quality of legislation increased along with the quantity.[262]

However, CPC political 'party lines' were still considered sources of law, custom remained important in contract law, and no case law system was introduced in the PRC.[263] The legislative process remained a highly complicated exercise of consensus building among different power and interest groups, whereby authorities could even refrain from the enforcement of already-legislated norms if the political consensus were in danger.[264]

In a sense, as both law and custom resurged, *fa* and (!) *li* saw a comeback after the years of Sino-Marxism. The result is that:

> the new socialist legislation looks in many instances just like western legislation. It doesn't, however, do the same work, nesting as it does in deeper forms of normativity and subject to the pushing and shoving of

---

and Zejun Hu, *Outlines of the Legal System of the People's Republic of China* (Falü Chubanshe 2004) 1.

257 Heuser, 'What "Rule of Law"?' (n 256) 729.

258 Potter, *The Chinese legal system* (n 215) 1.

259 Chow (n 208) 57–59.

260 Luney (n 241) 134; Chow (n 208) 61.

261 Zhang and Hu (n 249) 2–3.

262 Bu (n 226) 3.

263 Zhang and Hu (n 249) 13–14.

264 Potter, *The Chinese legal system* (n 215) 12.

> the communist party. Just as communism had to bend to deep-rooted east Asian thought, however, so too is western-style law clearly the object of confucianization, as filtered through communist authority.[265]

Chinese values and practices long remained so important that:

> despite the influences exerted by foreign legal norms, Chinese law remains dominated by local legal culture. The development of the Chinese legal system over the past twenty years has reflected a process of selective adaptation, by which borrowed foreign norms about law and legal institutions have been mediated by local legal culture.[266]

The actual effect of 'imported norms' strongly depends on it being in line with existing values. Moreover – as official declarations on the appropriate role of law in the PRC confirm – tradition strongly affects the selection process of foreign norms to be imported, blocking those too strongly associated with liberalism and individualism.[267]

Despite growing numbers of court cases in urban areas, mediation remains central and litigation sometimes frowned upon. Judges are still bound to party instructions, and the prestige of lawyers is only gradually increasing.[268] Confessions and reeducation remain crucial, as they were in Confucian and Sino-Marxist legal thought, while court proceedings are flawed from a Civil or Common Law perspective, and corruption rampant.[269]

The government still views law, as in the Imperial and Republican eras, as an instrument of rule: the achievement of political goals is to be facilitated, but no immutable norms created that would limit the room for maneuver. Law here:

> is not a limit on state power; rather, it is a mechanism by which state power is exercised, as the legal forms and institutions that comprise the Chinese legal system are established and operate to protect the Party/state's political power. (...) While Party members are subject to Party discipline for violating the law, the Party retains its authority to determine the content of law and the scope of its application.[270]

265 Glenn (n 209) 349–350.

266 Potter, *The Chinese legal system* (n 215) 2.

267 Ibid 7.

268 Hanqin Xue and Qian Jin, 'International Treaties in the Chinese Domestic Legal System' (2009) 8 CJIL 299, 322.

269 Glenn (n 209) 350–353.

270 Potter, *The Chinese legal system* (n 215) 10–11.

III.2.1.4. Conclusion

In conclusion, it can be posited that no pre-1978 (Mainland) Chinese government – be it Imperial, Republican of Communist – ever embraced a 'rule of law,' in the sense of a system wherein even the government is subject to the law, powers are separated, and the judiciary is independent. Instead, law was viewed as an instrument of power and of social control, and sometimes rejected completely as an impediment to unrestricted rule. Despite a certain ambivalence regarding the introduction of Western-inspired legal institutions, the Chinese legal system has been broadened and deepened, developed and modernized tremendously since 1978. The two dominant reasons were pragmatic: 1) upholding a stability that had been lost in the Cultural Revolution, and 2) allowing for economic development. Both lead back to one central goal: strengthening a nation under the CPC.

Official declarations have gone far now in strongly embracing the 'rule of law',[271] even declaring support for it a common international responsibility.[272] While it suits the government to make such declarations – inter alia – for reasons of foreign policy, the main conditions described above remain the same within China – reforms have even slowed down – and what exists on the ground remains a 'rule by law'.

Despite this necessary context, China still truly underwent a monumental shift. Whether this will eventually be a shift towards Civil and Common Law system conceptions of a 'rule of law' or rather a continuous effort to redefine this language remains an open question. Developments from 2012/2013 do not make it seem likely that the first path would be taken in the short to medium term. However, it remains clear that the pendulum has swung back from Confucian persuasion to Legalist 'rule by law.'

---

271 Chow (n 208) 62–66.

272 See eg the statement by China's representative at the UN General Assembly 2007 (Sixth Committee, 62nd Session): Duan, 'Statement on the Rule of Law' (n 42) 185–188.

III.2.2. International Law – Sovereignty, Intervention, Adjudication

> In other words, the loss or gain of sovereign rights by other actors was always seen through this prism of China's own sovereignty in a way that often overemphasized the possible implications of intervention elsewhere for China's own sovereignty claims.[273]

Chinese legal thought on questions of international law can be divided into five phases: 1) the development of a pre-Imperial Chinese inter-state framework before 221 BC, 2) the Chinese Imperial tributary system (朝贡制度), 3) the 'unequal treaties' (不平等条约)-period, when China was first confronted with the by then developed mainly European-shaped international legal system, 4) pre-1978 PRC adherence to the Soviet Theory of International Law, and 5) post-1978 PRC pragmatism.[274]

III.2.2.1. Pre-Imperial Times – A 'Chinese Community of Nations'?

The independent feudal states of the Eastern Zhou Dynasty-period (771 to 221 BC) had:

> [a] rough system of commonly accepted norms, institutions, and processes for the conduct of their relations. Some aspects of that system, like certain aspects of the system that regulated the interaction of the city-states of ancient Greece, bear a striking similarity to the international law that emerged from the multi-state system of fifteenth and sixteenth century Europe.[275]

---

273 Carlson, 'Helping to Keep the Peace' (n 141) 16 on the lasting effects of the 'century of humiliation'. In the cited article, Carlson also notes concrete references by Chinese international law professors at a series of conferences in 2002 as evidence of this claim.

274 Categorization on the basis of previous work such as Björn Ahl, 'China' in Rüdiger Wolfrum (ed), *Max Planck Encyclopedia of Public International Law – Volume II* (OUP 2012); Bodde and Morris (n 206); Bu (n 226); Chiu, 'Communist China's Attitude' (n 28); Chow (n 208); Carl Q Christol, 'Communist China and International Law – Strategy and Tactics' (1968) 21 *The Western Political Quarterly* 456; Cohen, *China's Practice of International Law* (n 28); Glenn (n 209); Heuser, *Einführung in die chinesische Rechtskultur* (n 204); Hsiung, *Law and Policy* (n 28); Kaminski, *Chinesische Positionen zum Völkerrecht* (n 212); Pan, 'Chinese Philosophy and International Law' (n 42) 233–248; Tanneberger (n 245); Senger (n 239).

275 Cohen, 'China and Intervention' (n 28) 474.

During this period, the Zhou Dynasty was only a powerless overarching structure, while the individual feudal states in fact represented an international law community.[276] Diplomatic relations were established and regulated,[277] and a Chinese conference of states regularly met under the chairmanship of the strongest state and conducted joint military campaigns against those violating the peace. For this purpose, treaties of alliance were concluded. A sort of customary international law regulated their form and content, and the chairman of the conference of states monitored compliance.[278] For multilateral recognition as a subject of international law in the sense of a member of the conference of states, certain ritual, administrative and economic conditions of contemporary Chinese civilization needed to be fulfilled.[279] However, regarding bilateral treaties of alliance, 'Barbarian tribes' could also have subjectivity under international law.[280] Concerning *ius ad bellum* and *ius in bello*, constraining state practice developed, but was later increasingly ignored during an ever more intense struggle for predominance.[281]

Leaders of Chinese polities:

> have been concerned with the rules governing intervention in internal affairs almost since the beginning of recorded time. (...) In pre-imperial China it was generally accepted that each of the feudal states had a right to manage its own affairs and had a corresponding duty not to interfere in the affairs of other feudal states.[282]

Sovereignty was always paired with the equality of states, which the philosopher Mengzi (孟子) (372–289 BC) identified as the central problem when establishing just international relations.[283] However, the principle was regularly violated, violations were rationalized – eg claiming that prevailing ethics would deem bowing to the 'most virtuous' desirable – and

276 Kaminski, *Chinesische Positionen zum Völkerrecht* (n 212) 38.
277 Kaminski, *Chinas Völkerrecht und Außenpolitik* (n 27) 54–62.
278 Ibid 64–75; Kaminski, *Chinesische Positionen zum Völkerrecht* (n 212) 39, 53–55.
279 Kaminski, *Chinas Völkerrecht und Außenpolitik* (n 27) 32, 46.
280 Kaminski, *Chinesische Positionen zum Völkerrecht* (n 212) 40–46.
281 Kaminski, *Chinas Völkerrecht und Außenpolitik* (n 27) 76, 93; Kaminski, *Chinesische Positionen zum Völkerrecht* (n 212) 56–57.
282 Cohen, 'China and Intervention' (n 28) 474. See also Kaminski, *Chinesische Positionen zum Völkerrecht* (n 212) 199.
283 Kaminski, *Chinesische Positionen zum Völkerrecht* (n 212) 199.

three prominent exceptions to the principle gained general acceptance: self-defense, sanctioning treaty violations, rescuing an oppressed people.[284]

All of the described rudiments of an international legal system that emerged about 2,000 years before 'traditional' European international law were discarded when China transitioned to its Imperial era, wherein questions about inter-state relations should reappear under entirely different conditions.

III.2.2.2. Imperial Era – Hierarchical Tributary System

The unification of all feudal states into one Chinese Empire in 221 BC caused a thorough re-evaluation of the framework of inter-state relations. Within the newly-developed China-centric universalistic tributary system, no other actor was considered equal to the Chinese Empire.[285] Instead, an anti-egalitarian system was organized in strict hierarchical terms.[286] This system of 'international *li*' (see Pan Junwu) played a similar role to Western international law in regional international relations.[287]

It was centered around the Chinese Emperor, the 'Son of Heaven' (天子),[288] whom all 'lower' rulers depended on. China only accepted the latter as legitimate after investiture by the Emperor. Within a complex system of ritualized contacts – just like in domestic matters, relations and conflicts were handled in accordance with the rules of *li* – they had to send tribute missions to the Emperor and received gifts and benefits in return.[289]

The intention was not to conquer, exploit or proselytize, but rather to build a web of rights and duties in line with the Confucian concept of an ideal family;[290] the tributary states of course being the younger family members to the Chinese Empire's patriarch.[291] In this 'divine world order,' the Chinese Emperor, whose superior power but more importantly moral authority was to be emphasized, was responsible for all peoples 'under the

284 Cohen, 'China and Intervention' (n 28) 474.

285 Rune Svarverud, *International Law as World Order in Late Imperial China – Translation, Reception and Discourse, 1847–1911* (Brill 2007) 8–12.

286 Kaminski, *Chinesische Positionen zum Völkerrecht* (n 212) 70–71.

287 Pan, 'Chinese Philosophy and International Law' (n 42) 235.

288 Hoffheimer (n 27) 251, 252.

289 Cohen, 'China and Intervention' (n 28) 475; Tanneberger (n 245) 17–18.

290 Tanneberger (n 245) 17–18.

291 Pan, 'Chinese Philosophy and International Law' (n 42) 235.

Heavens' (天下 – *tianxia*), his 'constitutive people' was all humanity.[292] He had to secure peace and order among them, and care for them – the value of the gifts provided to tributary delegations by the Emperor mostly exceeded that of the respective tribute by far.[293] On the other hand, this system negated any kind of sovereignty of tributary states.[294]

The consequences of this attitude – maintained until the end of the last dynasty, despite some periods of weakness wherein it only existed in theory[295] – will be elaborated on in the following sub-chapter. Neither the ruling nor intellectual elites of this period in any way discussed European international law concepts.

The Sino-centric universalism connected to the Confucian tributary system precluded any continued support for the sovereignty and equality of states,[296] which had been previously touted as the highest priority in a just international system. There was no equal to China, as it was held that 'there is only one sun in the sky and one sovereign over mankind'.[297] The Chinese emperor, as the sovereign, stood at the top of a hierarchical system wherein he was responsible for 'everything under the Heavens'. His sovereignty and rule were not limited, and rulers of any state could only be recognized after he had appointed them. China thus deemed itself entitled and responsible to intervene 'whenever and wherever she judged it necessary because the Chinese emperor was responsible for all the peoples under Heaven and because their rulers were viewed as his appointed representatives'.[298]

China only rarely made use of this self-awarded right of intervention, partly out of a conscious focus on a culturally and morally, not militarily, supported system, partly out of a lack of military options.[299] However, foreign dynasties recognized the necessity to limit their own sovereignty within the tributary system, in order to avoid interference by China in times of

292 Tanneberger (n 245) 17.
293 Kaminski, *Chinesische Positionen zum Völkerrecht* (n 212) 70–71; Tanneberger (n 245) 16–18.
294 Cohen, 'China and Intervention' (n 28) 475–476.
295 Kaminski, *Chinesische Positionen zum Völkerrecht* (n 212) 73, 90; Tanneberger (n 245) 16.
296 Hoffheimer (n 27) 251, 253.
297 Pan, 'Chinese Philosophy and International Law' (n 42) 235.
298 Cohen, 'China and Intervention' (n 28) 475.
299 Pan, 'Chinese Philosophy and International Law' (n 42) 235.

peace, and be supported (or reinstated) by it in case of a rebellion (eg in the case of the Lê-Dynasty in Vietnam in 1788).[300]

III.2.2.3. Unequal Treaties – Late Empire and Republican Period

The tributary system came to an end through several devastating blows in the so-called 'century of humiliation' (mid-19th to mid-20th century).[301] In the latter days of the Chinese Empire, a long series of wars starting with the First Opium War (1839–1842), and the constant threat of further use of blunt military power, allowed foreign powers to (in the Chinese diction) coerce China into ever more so-called 'unequal treaties,' which also sanctioned extra-territorial rights in China and straightforward territorial gains.

III.2.2.3.1. Definitional Issues

On the issue of what he termed 'forbidden treaties,' Verdross had written of *jus cogens* in the form of a general principle prohibiting treaties *contra bonos mores*, in the sense of restricting '*the liberty of one contracting party in an excessive or unworthy manner or which endanger its most important rights*'.[302] Pertinent treaty norms would have to be considered void where they would force a state party into contradiction with the '*ethical minimum* recognized by all the states of the international community'.[303] Among examples provided was eg preventing a state's courts and police from protecting life, liberty and property of citizens and aliens on its territory (ie maintenance of public order).[304] Formal voidance would be deemed unnecessary since such norms could never 'really become law,' although the other party could submit the issue to adjudication of course.[305]

The Vienna Convention on the Law of Treaties (hereinafter: VCLT) later enshrined in its Article 53, the voidance of a treaty 'conflicting with a

300 Cohen, 'China and Intervention' (n 28) 475.

301 According to the PRC's narrative, the onset of the First Opium War in 1839 marks its start, and the founding of the PRC in 1949 its end.

302 Alfred von Verdross, 'Forbidden Treaties in International Law: Comments on Professor Garner's Report on "The Law of Treaties"' (1937) 31 AJIL 571, 572, 574 (italics in the original).

303 Ibid 574 (italics in the original).

304 Ibid 574–575.

305 Ibid 577.

peremptory norm of general international law ("jus cogens")'.[306] As examples for such *jus cogens* the ILC provided unlawful use of force, genocide, slave trading and piracy.[307] The picture is less clear on other matters. The two preceding VCLT articles make clear that treaties are also void where the representative of a state was coerced to consent by (threat of) force, or the state itself was coerced by (threat of) force 'in violation of the principles of international law embodied in the Charter of the United Nations'.[308]

Returning to 'unequal treaties,' it should be underlined that this term mostly refers to a 'historical category',[309] with no clear legal consequences.[310] However, its proponents have certainly discussed it in a context similar to the above-laid-out deliberations on voidness or voidability due to the violations of peremptory norms. The doctrine builds on the natural law concept of 'fair price' (*pretium iustum*), which Grotius and Vattel wanted to see transposed to the law of treaties.[311] It came to prominent use

---

306 Art 53 Vienna Convention on the Law of Treaties (adopted 23 May 1969, entered into force 27 January 1980) 1155 UNTS 331 ('VCLT'), see also Art 64 for voidance due to the emergence of a new peremptory norm, and see Art 71 for the consequences of such invalidity of a treaty.

307 ILC, 'Report of the International Law Commission on the Work of its 18th Session' (4 May-19 July 1966) UN Doc A/6309/Rev.l.

308 Arts 51 and 52 VCLT. See also Art 69 for the consequences of invalidity in these cases.

309 The term was likely first used in publications of the Guomindang Party, which came to dominate the Republican Era. See Stefan Kroll, *Normgenese durch Re-interpretation – China und das europäische Völkerrecht im 19. und 20. Jahrhundert* (Nomos 2012) 179.

310 See, however, Darrell Moellendorf, 'Treaty Norms and Climate Change Mitigation' (2009) 23 *Ethics and International Affairs* 247, 249–253, for a discussion of 'justness' and 'equality' in burden-sharing on climate change; See also Alice de Jonge, 'From Unequal Treaties to Differential treatment: is There a Role for Equality in Treaty Relations' (2014) 4 AsJIL 125 who proposes to recognize a 'general principle in favour of remedying unacceptable levels of inequality' and 'that the persistence of inequality should provide grounds for seeking the renegotiation of a treaty'.

311 Lucius Caflisch, 'Unequal Treaties' (1992) 35 *German Yearbook of International Law* 52; see also Chiu, 'Comparison of the Nationalist and Communist Chinese Views' (n 27) 240, who notes that Pufendorf described treaties as unequal when 'the things promised by the two parties are unequal, or when either party is made inferior to the other', but adds that legal effect was either not discussed or affirmed by classical authors.

after the First World War, first in Russia (from 1922 the Soviet Union),[312] then in the Republic of China and other Asian states seeking a remedy against treaty-based restrictions to their sovereignty that had accumulated since the mid-19th century.[313] The treaties designated in this way were those concluded between Imperialist powers on the one side, and Asian or African states on the other, which were concluded following a (threat of) war and – inter alia – limited the latters' sovereignty eg by enforcing extraterritorial jurisdiction.[314] However, the inequality argument mainly remained a political and moral one, while on the legal side inequality only suggests – but does not prove – coercion.[315]

III.2.2.3.2. Late Qing (1839–1911): Confrontation and Lasting Attitudes

For China, all had begun with the First Opium War – and the peace treaty that ended it in 1842, the Treaty of Nanjing – which was ignited by China's decision to use international law to end opium imports. In line with Vattel's *Le Droit des Gens*, which had already been translated, the Imperial government declared opium contraband and demanded that British traders surrender it to the authorities. In return, the British government declared war.[316] Along with this and many following declarations, supposed legal justifications were always provided.[317] China thus experienced the mostly European-developed international law first and foremost within the framework of colonial aggression, with theory and practice in

---

312 See Stuart S Malawer, 'Imposed Treaties and International Law' (1977) 7 *California Western International Law Journal* 1, 27–29, who writes about the Soviet government designating the Treaty of Brest-Litovsk (1918) an 'imposed agreement' when trying to discredit it. Military operations had continued during treaty negotiations. In the Versailles Treaty, the legitimacy of treaties imposed by aggression was indeed questioned and the Brest-Litovsk Treaty annulled.

313 Caflisch (n 311) 52. See also Malawer (n 312) 107–108 who adds that Mexico and Brazil wanted the UN Charter to contain a provision empowering the General Assembly to recommend the termination or renegotiation of 'unjust' treaties.

314 Elena Conde Pérez and Zhaklin Valerieva Yaneva, 'Unequal Treaties in International Law' (*Oxford Bibliographies*, 30 August 2016) <http://www.oxfordbibliographies.com/view/document/obo-9780199796953/obo-9780199796953-0131.xml> accessed 8 March 2019.

315 Caflisch (n 311) 79.

316 Ahl, 'China' (n 274) 149.

317 Tanneberger (n 245) 75–76.

marked contradiction.[318] Addressing the dimension of this Sino-Western encounter, previous studies have written about 'a clash between different worldviews, different kinds of political and legal cosmologies – not merely an encounter in space and time, but an encounter between different kinds of space and time, underwriting distinctive notions of sovereignty'.[319]

Treaties like the Treaty of Nanjing – many were to follow – primarily or exclusively burdened China, partially made it into a colony, and formed an interlinked regulatory system through most-favored-nation clauses.[320] Cohen provides a vivid and arresting description of the resulting 'half-colonial' status, when he writes that '[b]esides losing substantial portions of its territory, as well as control over its tributary states, China was made to suffer an elaborate structure of extraterritorial privileges, inequitable tariff restrictions, "leased territories," foreign concessions and settlements, foreign armed forces, and foreign railway, postal, customs, wireless, and other administrative networks'.[321] However, China criticized the 'inequality of rank' even more than the perceived unfair content.[322] China saw itself excluded from the circle of 'civilized' Christian states of the West,[323] among which treaties would need to include some manner of interest balancing.[324] This is how China came to the concept of 'unequal treaties' through its own experiences.[325]

This development had three consequences with key importance for this book. First, Chinese authors started to comprehensively translate, study

318 Xue, 'Meaningful Dialogue' (n 42) 15.

319 Teemu Ruskola, 'China in the Age of the World Picture', in Anne Orford and Florian Hoffmann (eds), *The Oxford Handbook of the Theory of International Law* (OUP 2016) 138, 143.

320 Kroll (n 309) 27–28.

321 Cohen, 'China and Intervention' (n 28) 476. See also Phil CW Chan, 'China's Approaches to International Law since the Opium War' (2014) 27 *Leiden Journal of International Law* 859, 873, who notes that 19 states secured extraterritorial privileges from Imperial China in this period.

322 Tanneberger (n 245) 13.

323 Indeed, the British Empire justified demands for extraterritorial jurisdiction by holding Chinese law to be too 'arbitrary' and 'despotic' for application to British subjects, see Ruskola (n 319) 147.

324 Kaminski, *Chinesische Positionen zum Völkerrecht* (n 212) 106–108; see also Tanneberger (n 245) 69–70 who notes that leading authors of the 19th and early 20th centuries did not want to grant 'uncivilized' Afro-Asian states equality in inter-state relations inter alia due to supposedly lacking protection for foreigners in their domestic legal systems.

325 Chiu, 'Comparison of the Nationalist and Communist Chinese Views' (n 27) 241–242, 247–248.

and interpret Western international law, criticizing some aspects of theory but mainly Europeans' practice, while at the same time trying to employ the framework to China's advantage. China accepted the existing norms on diplomatic and consular relations,[326] marking the beginning of a long process of progressive selective acceptance of Western international legal norms.[327] This was later complemented, of course, by efforts to shape new and reform existing norms. Such a trend only took hold, because and as far as the Chinese side was convinced that this could help defend against Western powers. A lasting foundation for a pragmatic approach to international law was laid by these early developments,[328] as a commitment to thorough research, skeptical caution and gradually increased participation.

Second, Chinese intellectuals of the 19th and early-20th centuries became intensely occupied with the issues of sovereignty and intervention, for obvious reasons.[329] These concepts were actually something very old in China,[330] but also something strikingly new to an Empire long-accustomed to the tributary system.[331] In this period, Beijing experienced its own sovereignty as humiliatingly ignored and violated in a system that should theoretically have valued it highly.[332]

Third, a lasting anti-Western nationalism and deep mistrust towards the mostly European-developed international legal system emerged. Proponents of all political camps – be they Monarchists, Republicans or Communists – made it their utmost priority to fully recover Chinese sovereignty and establish a state that is internationally recognized to be an equal to those of the West.[333] Almost two centuries after the beginning of the First Opium War, today's governing elite still argues that recovering sovereignty

326 Kaminski, *Chinesische Positionen zum Völkerrecht* (n 212) 91–93, see also p. 115; Tanneberger (n 245) 18–19. China also established a foreign ministry – earlier the Ministry of Rites (礼部) had taken care of the tributary system – allowed first diplomatic missions in Beijing.

327 Hsiung, *Law and Policy* (n 28) 315–316.

328 Pan, 'Chinese Philosophy and International Law' (n 42) 238.

329 Cohen, 'China and Intervention' (n 28) 476.

330 See Chapter III.2.2.1.

331 See Chapter III.2.2.2. See also Byron N Tzou, *China and International Law: the boundary disputes* (Praeger 1990) 7.

332 Chiu, 'Comparison of the Nationalist and Communist Chinese Views' (n 27) 243.

333 Cohen, 'China and Intervention' (n 28) 476.

– meaning reclaiming Taiwan – is its highest priority.[334] In the mission to restore China's status, it upgraded ambitions, and seeks to be a *primus inter pares* that leads the international community.[335]

III.2.2.3.3. Republic (1912–1949): Struggle for Renegotiation

The ROC, established through the overthrow of a monarchy weakened in part by colonial powers, first merely viewed such treaties as subject to renegotiation, not as invalid.[336] Having fought on the side of the Allies in the First World War, Republican China attempted in vain to use arguments rooted in European international law traditions – such as *rebus sic stantibus* –[337] at and after the peace conferences, to achieve the revision of the 'unequal treaties,' especially the return of lost territories.[338] The 'Betrayal of Versailles', the utter disregard for Chinese interests and sovereignty at the central peace conference after the First World War,[339] led to a marked turn away from the West among Chinese intellectuals, in political as in international legal thought.[340]

---

334 Ibid 477; Robert G Sutter, *Foreign Relations of the PRC – The Legacies and Constraints of China's International Politics Since 1949* (Rowman & Littlefield 2013) 169.

335 People.cn, '习近平首提"两个引导"有深意' (Xi Jinping's first mention of the "two guides" has deeper meaning) *People.cn* (Beijing, 20 February 2017) <http://politics.people.com.cn/n1/2017/0220/c1001-29094518.html> accessed 10 January 2019.

336 Malawer (n 312) 35. See also Chiu, 'Comparison of the Nationalist and Communist Chinese Views' (n 27) 255–258 who notes that the ROC did not want to violate *rebus sic stantibus*.

337 See Pasha L Hsieh, 'Wellington Koo, International Law and Modern China' (2016) 56 *Indian Journal of International Law* 307, 317–318 who describes how the entry into the war against Germany was deemed a fundamental change of circumstances that supposedly meant that a number of so-called 'unequal treaties' could no longer be enforced; see also Art 62 VCLT which can be considered a codification of pertinent customary law.

338 Kaminski, *Chinesische Positionen zum Völkerrecht* (n 212) 128, 165.

339 The German colony of Qingdao, for example, was handed to Japan instead of returning it to China.

340 China had entered the war on the side of the Allies in 1917. It had hoped that in return (some of) the 'unequal treaties' would be annulled and Japanese claims regarding former German territories in China (mainly Tsingtao) and a host of extraterritorial rights in further Chinese regions would be rejected. None of this happened. Britain and France supported Japan's claims and did not relinquish their own positions in China.

In the following years up until the end of the Chinese Civil War in 1949, the ROC engaged in a long and never entirely successful struggle for the cancellation of the described treaties. Its priority was to end consular jurisdiction, and regain Chinese sovereignty over foreign dependencies in China, as well as full customs sovereignty.[341]

In pursuit of its goals, the ROC – a founding member of the League of Nations[342] – engaged in 'assertive legalism' (see Hsieh).[343] In 1926, it unilaterally abrogated the 1865 Sino-Belgium Treaty, which conferred unilateral privileges and only allowed for amendment by Belgium, prompting Belgium to bring a claim at the Permanent Court of International Justice (hereinafter: PCIJ).[344] Belgium settled for a new renegotiated treaty following pressure by the UK and others interested in stronger relations with the ROC.[345] After Japan's invasion of Manchuria in 1931, the ROC appealed to the League, resorting to Articles X, XI and XV of the League Covenant,[346] and achieving a supportive report by the League's General Assembly – Japan responded by quitting the League.[347]

Finally, new contractual bases for China's bilateral relations with the US and UK in 1943 marked important successes, but the task remained incomplete, alas, and in 1945 China even concluded what can be described as a new 'unequal treaty' with the Soviet Union.[348] The age of 'unequal treaties' only ended with the establishment of the PRC in October 1949, which declared all remaining such treaties null and void.[349]

In its last years on the Chinese Mainland (1945–1949), the ROC remained on an engagement trajectory with the international legal order. It

---

341 Hsiung, *Law and Policy* (n 28) 85–88; Chiu, 'Comparison of the Nationalist and Communist Chinese Views' (n 27) 244.

342 Annex I Covenant of the League of Nations (adopted 28 June 1919) 222 CTS 195.

343 Hsieh (n 337) 316.

344 *Denunciation of the Treaty of 2 November 1865 between China and Belgium (Belgium v China)* (Application Instituting Proceedings, Orders of 8 January, 15 February and 18 June 1927) PCIJ Rep Series A No 8.

345 *Denunciation of the Treaty of 2 November 1865 between China and Belgium (Belgium v China)* (Order of May 25 1929) PCIJ Series A No 18.

346 Arts X, XI and XV Covenant of the League of Nations (adopted 28 June 1919) 222 CTS 195, Art XI of the Covenant being the precursor to Chapter VII UN Charter. See also Chan, 'China's Approaches' (n 321) 872.

347 Hsieh (n 337) 320.

348 Chiu, 'Comparison of the Nationalist and Communist Chinese Views' (n 27) 255–258.

349 Ahl, 'China' (n 274) 149.

was the first among the founding members to sign the UN Charter, became a veto-holding permanent member of the UN Security Council (hereinafter: UNSC) – until the PRC took over China's UN seat in 1971 –[350] and held the Vice-Chairman position of the commission drafting the Universal Declaration of Human Rights.[351] Its delegation's proposal was key for Article 13 UN Charter on UNGA promotion of international law development and the ensuing creation of the ILC, as well as Article 76 including independence as an objective for trust territories.[352] Finally, two ROC-nominated judges served on the ICJ from 1946 to 1967,[353] and the ROC indeed even went as far as recognizing the compulsory jurisdiction of the Court.[354]

The ROC leadership's convictions on strengthening of the principles of sovereignty and non-intervention did not change after the 1949 defeat in the civil war. As long as the nationalist leadership on Taiwan held China's UN seat, ie 1971, it continued its calls in this regard.[355] However, for the reasons laid out in Chapter III.2, this book does not cover the ROC after 1949, focusing its attention on the PRC.

III.2.2.4. Maoism (1949–1978)

III.2.2.4.1. Early Years and Soviet Legal Thought (1949–1957)

Two major trends coalesced in the early PRC that determined a negative pre-disposition towards the entire international legal system. A third trend

350 The ROC lost its UN seat (and thus also its UNSC seat) to the PRC via UNGA Res 2758 (XXVI) (25 October 1971) UN Doc A/RES/2758(XXVI).

351 China also voted in favor of the declaration. See Dag Hammarskjöld Library, 'Drafting of the Universal Declaration of Human Rights – Drafting Committee Members' <http://research.un.org/en/undhr/draftingcommittee> accessed 11 December 2018; United Nations General Assembly, 'Voting History on UN Doc A/RES/217(III)[A]' <http://unbisnet.un.org:8080/ipac20/ipac.jsp?&profile=voting&uri=full=3100023~%21909326~%210&ri=1&aspect=power&menu=search&source=~%21horizon> accessed 11 December 2018.

352 Arts 13 and 76 Charter of the United Nations and Statute of the International Court of Justice (adopted 25 June 1945, entered into force 24 October 1945) 1 UNTS 16 (UN Charter); Hsieh (n 337) 321–322.

353 Hsu Mo and Vi Kuiyuin Wellington Koo as listed on ICJ, 'All Members' <https://www.icj-cij.org/en/all-members> accessed 11 December 2018.

354 Chan, 'China's Approaches' (n 321) 886.

355 Cohen, 'China and Intervention' (n 28) 476.

would compound these developments following the Sino-Soviet split and break-up of the Socialist bloc.

First, the experiences of the 'century of humiliation' left the Chinese people with a deeply cynical view of Western international law, as a mere tool in legitimizing aggressive actions.[356] It is important to highlight that all leaders of the PRC up until the 1904-born Deng Xiaoping gave up power in 1993 had personally experienced foreign domination and the struggle against it.[357] Their central mission was the restoration of Chinese sovereignty, which also dominated the Chinese international law discourse.[358] They still felt confirmed in their suspicion of potentially not being protected, by post-Second World War standard works of international law, like Oppenheim and Lauterpacht's, which continued to elaborate on the applicability of norms to 'civilized states'.[359] Moreover, the US's blocking of the Communist government's takeover of the island of Taiwan – which had been granted to China in the Allies' declarations of Cairo (1943) and Potsdam (1945) – was touted as proof of a justified fear of a hypocritical system.[360]

Second, the Marxist conviction that all existing law was to be considered and disregarded as 'bourgeois law' now also took hold in China. The international legal system was seen as an 'instrument of bourgeois nations to perpetuate their favoured positions in the world'.[361] The PRC followed early Soviet scholarship on international law (ie 1920s to 1950s), perceiving it as a means of class struggle and following the idea of a 'double superstructure: on the one hand, the legal superstructure of capitalist countries, and, on the other hand, the legal superstructure of socialist countries'.[362] International norms would be such concurrent to both superstructures

356 Tanneberger (n 245) 55; Tzou (n 331) 3.
357 Cohen, 'China and Intervention' (n 28) 477.
358 Ahl, 'China' (n 274) 151; Cohen, 'China and Intervention' (n 28) 475.
359 Chiu, 'Communist China's Attitude' (n 28) 250; Christol (n 274) 459; Tanneberger (n 245) 70–71, 75; Tzou (n 331) 9.
360 '"The Cairo Declaration," issued 26 November 1943, History and Public Policy Program Digital Archive, Foreign Relations of the United States, Diplomatic Papers, The Conferences at Cairo and Tehran, 1943' (Washington DC, United States Government Printing Office 1961) 448–449, <https://digitalarchive.wilsoncenter.org/document/122101> accessed 25 October 2019; 'Primary Source Document with Questions – "The Potsdam Declaration," issued 26 July 1945' (Columbia University, Asia for Educators 2019) <http://afe.easia.columbia.edu/ps/japan/potsdam.pdf> accessed 25 October 2019; Tanneberger (n 245) 84–85.
361 Tzou (n 331) 7.
362 Bianchi (n 22) 74.

and constitute an 'inter-class compromise', whereby Moscow took this to justify participation.[363]

Beijing classified all international organizations in their entirety as 'bourgeois-controlled' and opted for a course of complete non-cooperation;[364] going beyond the Soviet course of action. Of course, the PRC's exclusion from the UN, where the ROC continued to hold China's seat until 1971 strongly played into this. The new ideological direction and decisive break with the Republican era – denounced as 'bourgeois' and part of what was wrong with the international order – also meant that Beijing now distanced itself from all previous Chinese engagement with international law.

In line with most developing states and the Soviet Union, the PRC adopted a 'nineteenth-century notion of sovereignty'.[365] Constant threats to that sovereignty were seen manifested – inter alia – in multilateral treaties with the supposed intention of perpetuating some states' inferior positions (eg *Partial Nuclear Test Ban Treaty* of 1963),[366] and in Western 'imperialist' theories perceived as tools of American hegemony (eg mutual inter-dependence, global law and global citizenship). The US was considered to pursue pertinent goals also by establishing international organizations it could dominate and elevating international law above national law so it could interfere in the internal affairs of other countries.[367]

III.2.2.4.2. Sino-Marxism Outside the UN (1957–1971)

III.2.2.4.2.1. Divergence from the Soviet Path

From 1957, a third trend comes in, working against PRC engagement with the international legal order. Underlying the break-up of relations – Soviet economic support ended in 1960, actual military skirmishes occurred in

---

363 Ibid.

364 Tzou (n 331) 3.

365 Tanneberger (n 245) 84–85, 97, 101. Although all unequal treaties had been declared void the Soviet Union retained privileges in Manchuria well into the 1950s see Cohen, 'China and Intervention' (n 28) 475.

366 Treaty banning nuclear weapon tests in the atmosphere, in outer space and under water (opened for signature 5 August 1963, entered into force 10 October 1963) 480 UNTS 43; Chiu, 'Comparison of the Nationalist and Communist Chinese Views' (n 27) 262–263.

367 Christol (n 274) 466; Tanneberger (n 245) 101, 109.

1969 – the PRC had begun to take an independent path on issues of ideology and law. The pendulum swinging back against Legalism not only meant rejecting the previously-emulated Soviet legal system domestically, but also Soviet international law positions.[368]

International law discourse in Moscow was changing to only see one legal superstructure, made up of treaties between states of the two different camps. These would point the way towards 'peaceful coexistence' with the capitalist camp.[369] Beijing rejected this development and remained more irreconcilable with Western international law.[370] Particularly after Moscow justified the invasion of Czechoslovakia in 1968 under 'Socialist internationalism',[371] Beijing also came to categorically reject the existence of a separate Socialist international law regulating relations among Socialist states, as an instrument of Soviet hegemony.[372] The PRC now further emphasized sovereignty[373] and portrayed Soviet-dominated international organizations, Soviet-initiated treaties and Soviet imperialism as similar to US counterparts.[374]

In the years before the PRC took over the Chinese seat at the UN, existing international law was perceived as a political instrument, which – following alleged Western practice – was to be employed when useful and

368 See Chapter III.2.1.3.2.2. See also Bu (n 226) 2; Chiu, 'Communist China's Attitude' (n 28) 247; Tanneberger (n 245) 57–58, 116–119.

369 Bianchi (n 22) 74–75. See also Grigory Tunkin, 'Coexistence and International Law' (1958) 95 *Recueil des Cours* 1; WE Butler, '"Socialist International Law" or "Socialist Principles of International Relations"?' (1971) 65 AJIL 796 for specific lines of reasoning in justifying such enforcement, including via military intervention, within the Socialist camp and in order to uphold 'Socialist sovereignty'.

370 Chiu, 'Communist China's Attitude' (n 28) 266; Christol (n 274) 467.

371 Alina Cherviatsova and Oleksandr Yarmysh, 'Soviet International Law: Between Slogans and Practice' (2017) 19 *Journal of the History of International Law* 296, 321.

372 Ahl, 'China' (n 274) 150; Cohen, 'China and Intervention' (n 28) 477, 487–488 who notes that Moscow's justification that 'the interests of the community' represent a higher sovereignty than that of the individual member-states was considered 'gangster logic'.

373 China also decried the trend towards accepting the subjectivity under international law of international organizations and individual persons as an attempt to intervene in the internal affairs of weaker states, see Chiu, 'Communist China's Attitude' (n 28) 250–251.

374 Christol (n 274) 466–467; Chiu, 'Comparison of the Nationalist and Communist Chinese Views' (n 27) 262–263; Cohen, 'China and Intervention' (n 28) 477.

otherwise ignored.[375] This was not to deny the existence of international law, nor to categorically reject 'traditional' international law,[376] which was used in arguments when opportune.[377] The PRC did not put forward new form or content for international legal relations, but rather – especially regarding treaties – acted quite conventionally.[378] Indeed, it accorded them absolute priority among the sources of law as listed in Article 38 (1) of the Statute of the International Court of Justice (in the following: ICJ Statute),[379] largely relegating customary international law to the sidelines (as based on Western practice),[380] rejecting general principles, and being unclear on subsidiary means.[381]

Concerning diplomatic relations, the peculiar concept of 'people's diplomacy' was drafted in accordance with Maoist policy of the 'mass line.' Partly due to the PRC's non-recognition at the UN, unofficial so-called 'friendship delegations,' comprising representatives of different sectors of China's society and economy, accompanied or replaced official delegations.[382] In line with Chinese tradition, as well as governments' positions in most developing nations, inter-state disputes were resolved exclusively through negotiations; rejecting all of the supposedly Western-controlled international tribunals.[383]

III.2.2.4.2.2. Five Principles of Peaceful Co-Existence

The PRC, while not presenting something new, wanted to accentuate certain aspects in the international legal order. Crucial here, are the 'Five Principles of Peaceful Co-Existence,' which were first agreed upon in a bi-

375 Chiu, 'Communist China's Attitude' (n 28) 248–249; Christol (n 274) 466; Tzou (n 331) 15.
376 Hsiung, *Law and Policy* (n 28) 315–316; Tzou (n 331) 7.
377 Chiu, 'Communist China's Attitude' (n 28) 246.
378 Tanneberger (n 245) 88.
379 Art 38 (1) ICJ Statute.
380 Christol (n 274) 463–464; Diplomatic notes and Chinese literature, however, did invoke customary international law, and there was a certain implicit acceptance, see Chiu, 'Communist China's Attitude' (n 28) 258–259.
381 Chiu, 'Communist China's Attitude' (n 28) 258–259; Christol (n 274) 464.
382 Tanneberger (n 245) 78–81.
383 Ibid 119–120.

lateral treaty with India in 1954,[384] and clearly draw on the UN Charter. They are: 1) mutual respect for each other's territorial integrity and sovereignty, 2) mutual non-aggression, 3) mutual non-interference in each other's internal affairs, 4) equality and cooperation for mutual benefit, and 5) peaceful co-existence.[385] Foreign critics lampooned these principles as anyway in line with Western international law, as vague and as legally impractical. Chinese authors did not deny the validity of these criticisms, but maintained that the principles had another goal. Exactly due to their vagueness and the hinted joint experience of suffering of former colonial peoples, they were a way of strengthening China's position in this community.[386] Fittingly, the PRC also opposed the Indian view that the 1954 treaty, which had first included the principles, was binding;[387] Beijing rather used a political declaration to underline a strict view of sovereignty.

This is the context for the PRC supporting the Bandung Conference of Asian and African States in 1955, when it built on the 'Five Principles' with its 10-point 'Declaration on Promotion of World Peace and Co-operation'.[388] In 1961, the Non-Aligned Movement adopted the 'Five Principles',[389] and in 1970 the UN General Assembly incorporated them into the 'Declaration on the International Law Principles of Friendly Relations and Co-operation Among States'.[390] The resolution of bilateral conflicts on this basis has, of course, only worked where both sides showed necessary goodwill. Ironically, the peaceful settlement of the 1962 border dispute between China and India failed abysmally.[391]

384 Agreement (with exchange of notes) on trade and intercourse between Tibet Region of China and India (adopted 29 April 1954, entered into force 17 August 1954) 299 UNTS 57; Qingguo Jia, 'China', in Koji Watanabe (ed), *Humanitarian Intervention. The Evolving Asian Debate* (Japan Center for International Exchange, Brookings Institution Press 2003) 21. For quickly ensuing problems connected with said treaty see, however, Prabhakar Singh, 'Sino-Indian Attitudes to International Law: Nations, States and Colonial Hangovers' (2015) 3 *The Chinese Journal of Comparative Law* 348, 361–363.

385 Compare these eg with Art 2 (1), (2), (3), (4) and (7) UN Charter. See Senger (n 239) 45–46.

386 Tanneberger (n 245) 88, 96.

387 Singh, 'Sino-Indian Attitudes to International Law' (n 384) 363.

388 Ahl, 'China' (n 274) 150–151.

389 Miguel de Serpa Soares, 'Keynote Speech at the International Colloquium on the Five Principles of Peaceful Co-existence and the Development of International Law' (2014) 13 CJIL 481, 482.

390 UNGA Res 2625 (XXV) (24 October 1970); Xue, 'Meaningful Dialogue' (n 42) 4–5.

391 Tanneberger (n 245) 95.

The PRC connected its strict rejection of international intervention – the concept of humanitarian intervention supposedly having 'class character' – with the five principles.[392] However, its international law scholars mostly evaluated individual incidents ex post, judging the legitimacy of interventions on the invitation of an internationally-recognized government according to the malleable category of 'whether the invitation coincides with the genuine desires of the ... people'.[393] Not complying with its own (tentative) standards on interference in internal affairs, the PRC excoriated international criticism of Tibetans' treatment and the establishment of Tibet research institutes, but itself emphatically criticized South Africa's treatment of non-White citizens and allowed foreign revolutionary movements to establish 'embassies' and governments in exile in Beijing.[394] The PRC ingeniously solved this obvious contradiction by excluding 'Imperialist' states from the declared principles, because they were supposedly violating them anyway. Aware that this position did not convince a majority of states, Beijing operated covertly when supporting revolutions, and later gave the policy up altogether.[395]

III.2.2.4.3. Pre-reform PRC in the UN (1971–1978)

In a first monumental step towards integration with the international legal order, the PRC took over China's seat at the UN, and thus also in the UNSC, in 1971.[396] Over the following decade it largely observed, adjusted to its new position, and eg only used its UNSC veto powers two times.[397] In 1972, the PRC blocked Bangladesh's initial application for UN membership, out of concern over Taiwan's status and due to Beijing's close relations with Pakistan.[398] Moreover, China vetoed a draft amendment to a

392 Cohen, 'China and Intervention' (n 28) 478–481.
393 Ibid 483, 487–488, supposedly this precondition was fulfilled in Hungary 1956 (Soviet Union), but not in Czechoslovakia 1968 (Soviet Union) or Lebanon 1958 (US).
394 Ibid 489–493.
395 Ibid 495–501.
396 UNGA Res 2758 (XXVI) (25 October 1971) UN Doc A/RES/2758(XXVI).
397 Phil CW Chan, 'A Keen Observer of the International Rule of Law? International Law in China's Voting Behaviour and Argumentation in the United Nations Security Council' (2013) 26 *Leiden Journal of International Law* 875, 889.
398 Para 15 UNSC Verbatim Record (25 August 1972) UN Doc S/PV/1660. See also Chan, 'A Keen Observer' (n 397) 889.

draft resolution calling for the cessation of hostilities between Israel and Arab states, using the opportunity to position itself as a supporter of Arab developing states against supposed Israeli aggression.[399] The PRC, absorbed by the domestic Cultural Revolution, was also rather passive in the UN General Assembly (hereinafter: UNGA), abstaining almost at every third vote. Nonetheless, it gradually joined the specialized and affiliated agencies of the UN, and grew accustomed to such integration.[400]

Joining the UN also meant *ipso facto* becoming party to the ICJ Statute.[401] However, in accordance with the convictions laid out above, the PRC continued to reject the jurisdiction of any international court or arbitral tribunal, which supposedly were all Western-controlled and could not be objective on issues concerning the PRC.[402] Explicit reservations against ICJ jurisdiction were issued at every relevant treaty conclusion.[403] Beijing cited several ICJ cases as 'obvious' evidence of the court's supposed Imperialist nature – eg *Corfu Channel*.[404] Moreover, in the negotiations preceding the United Nations Convention on the Law of the Sea (in the following: UNCLOS), the Chinese delegation rejected a clause included in an earlier draft that would have provided for compulsory jurisdiction of the International Tribunal for the Law of the Sea (in the following: ITLOS) as violating China's sovereignty.[405]

---

399 Para 19 UNSC Verbatim Record (10 September 1972) UN Doc S/PV/1662. See also Chan, 'A Keen Observer' (n 397) 889.

400 Zhang Guihong and Feng Yuqiao, 'China's UN Diplomacy: 1971–2011' (2011) 35 *Strategic Analysis* 973, 975.

401 Art 93 UN Charter.

402 Tanneberger (n 245) 119–120.

403 See eg the PRC's reservation to Art 22 International Convention on the Elimination of All Forms of Racial Discrimination (signed 21 December 1965, entered into force 4 January 1969) 660 UNTS 195 (CERD): UN Treaty Collection, 'International Convention on the Elimination of All Forms of Racial Discrimination – Declarations and Reservations < https://treaties.un.org/Pages/ViewDetails.aspx?src=TREATY&mtdsg_no=IV-2&chapter=4&clang=_en#EndDec> accessed 26 October 2019. The PRC's reservation, circulated 13 January 1982, reads: 'The People's Republic of China has reservations on the provisions of article 22 of the Convention and will not be bound by it'. See also Pan, 'Chinese Philosophy and International Law' (n 42) 245.

404 *Corfu Channel (United Kingdom v Albania)* (Merits) [1949] ICJ Rep 4; Ahl, 'China' (n 274) 155.

405 United Nations Convention on the Law of the Sea (opened for signature 10 December 1982, entered into force 16 November 1994) 1833 UNTS 3 ('UNCLOS').

III.2.2.5. Pragmatism (1978-): Reform and Opening

III.2.2.5.1. A new mindset

After Deng Xiaoping took the reins in 1978, Chinese governing philosophy shifted towards pragmatism, where 'all should start from reality'. On the legal side, this meant law being a servant of policy, international law a servant of foreign policy, and since 'China's "reality" has been the need for economic development [,] (…) international law serves the country's economic development'.[406] Engagement with the international legal order would allow China to more effectively reap desired economic benefits from integration with international society (including attracting foreign investment and technology).[407]

This shift was more than a mere variation of the previous opportunistic view, because international law now attained enormous importance in the ruling elites' thinking and was indeed recognized as a framework for rule-based pragmatic international politics, which could never be completely replaced 'by a state's policy of expedience'.[408] It came to be viewed as indispensable for 'socialist modernization construction' in the sense of peaceful and sustainable development,[409] because it could provide a 'peaceful and safe outside environment, (…) an equal and impartial competition order, and (…) a legal safeguard for international co-operation'.[410] Therefore, China should also 'duly undertake its responsibility and play an active role in international legal development'.[411]

Accordingly, the PRC grew to accept the core tenets of the existing international legal system as the point of departure for any negotiation and reform. Instead of outright rejecting the entire system, the intention became to gain influence within the system and affect change in line with Chinese conceptions. By defining international law not as the *common will* of states but rather as *reconciled will*, constant changes on account of developments in international relations were expected, reassuringly for Bei-

406 Pan, 'Chinese Philosophy and International Law' (n 42) 239.
407 Ibid; Ahl, 'China' (n 274) 149.
408 Ibid 248.
409 Ahl, 'China' (n 274) 149.
410 Huang, Kong and Zhang (n 42) 262; This is why the PRC ratified more than 300 multilateral and more than 17,000 bilateral treaties (Duan, 'Statement on the Rule of Law' (n 42) 186).
411 Xue, 'Meaningful Dialogue' (n 42) 18.

jing.[412] Confidently, it has been held that 'with a greater mix of cultures in international society, the international legal order will transform and, in this regard, Asian peoples are expected to play an important role in the diversification of power and values'.[413]

The theoretical roof of these transformational impulses China purports to intend for and deem necessary remains somewhat unclear. However, it appears evident that the 'PRC's modern positions on questions of public international law have been formed rather by its desire to regain the status of a world power than by ideological principles'.[414]

Among the Chinese scholars interviewed for this book, 1) most emphasized the pragmatic nature of Chinese positions, 2) none claimed that Sino-Marxist ideology was shaping Chinese positions, 3) and only some saw Chinese tradition or Confucianism as having a degree of influence.[415] Confucianism has experienced a certain comeback – some authors call for the reestablishment of an 'international *li*,' and reject certain existing norms as violating such a system of 'harmony' –[416] but concepts remain vague. Instead, support for a supposedly needed 'trans-civilizational approach' to solve legitimacy problems of the existing international legal order, to improve feelings of 'ownership' seems to be more favored.[417] Increased PRC influence and power would fit nicely.

On their country's ongoing skepticism regarding qualifications of state sovereignty, interviewed scholars again mainly gave three types of answers.[418] First, Chinese experiences in the 'century of humiliation' are said to have created a trauma that is difficult to overcome. Second, the perception of a lack of equality in the international system is put forward as root cause for any restraint. The third and most prevalent line of argumentation holds that pragmatism is more important than anything else in terms of embracing or rejecting any type of international interaction.

412 Pan, 'Chinese Philosophy and International Law' (n 42) 239.
413 Xue, 'Meaningful Dialogue' (n 42) 19.
414 Ahl, 'China' (n 274) 158.
415 Author's interviews in Wuhan, Xiamen, Xi'an, Beijing and Singapore, June and September 2013.
416 Pan, 'Chinese Philosophy and International Law' (n 42) 236–237.
417 Edith Brown Weiss, 'International Law in a Kaleidoscopic World' (2011) 1 AsJIL 21, 24–27. See also Yasuaki Onuma, 'A Trans-Civilizational Perspective of International Law: Lectures in Public International Law at the Hague Academy of International Law' (*Lecture Readings – Peace Palace Library*, 2007) <http://www.ppl.nl/summercourses/readinglist.php?year52007&lecturer5onuma&maintopic5Public%20International%20Law> accessed 2 September 2015.
418 Author's interviews in Wuhan and Singapore, June 2013.

It follows that one needs to differentiate between abstract and concrete sovereignty: 'Whereas abstract sovereignty involves retaining ultimate control over domestic affairs and having equal status on the international stage, concrete sovereignty allows for dividing and transferring sovereign powers after making a cost-benefit analysis'.[419] The Chinese leadership assumes that through relatively minor concessions – mostly concerning economic sovereignty, and in ways viewed as inevitable – it can considerably bolster the country's position. That is why flexibility has been demonstrated, most prominently with the WTO accession in 2001.[420]

Although concessions on 'political, military and cultural sovereignty' are a different story, the overall tendency remains the same: more flexibility. Since the *United Nations Conference on the Law of the Sea* 1973, the PRC eg gradually accepted the concepts of *ius cogens* and *common heritage of mankind*.[421] Further steps were taken in the 1990s, eg on humanitarian interventions and in the ratification of UNCLOS, when the PRC needed to break out of diplomatic isolation after the quashing of protests on Tiananmen Square. At the same time, the PRC can continue to underline the centrality of the principle of sovereignty in the abstract, and present itself as representative of non-European developing nations with different historical experiences and priorities, certain apprehensions about the existing system, and another vision for the future.[422]

In line with the new approach, the PRC allowed international law back to universities (1979), and established a Chinese Society of International Law (1981).[423] Beijing focused on joining every international organization potentially relevant for economic development and social stability. Financial help through UNDP and World Bank programs was accepted, and in 2001 China joined the WTO.[424]

---

419 Ahl, 'China' (n 274) 151.

420 Ibid.

421 Ibid.

422 Xue, 'Chinese Observations on International Law' (n 42) 84–85; Senger (n 239) 45–46.

423 Ahl, 'China' (n 274) 149.

424 WTO, *Protocol on the Accession of the People's Republic of China* (23 November 2001) WT/L/432 ('Accession Protocol'); Ahl, 'China' (n 274) 155.

III.2.2.5.2. Sources of International Law and Domestic Application

Treaties remained strongly prioritized as sources of international law.[425] This is also clear from treaty norms (in the absence of a reservation) outranking domestic civil provisions, while customary international law may only be applied where pertinent domestic provisions are lacking.[426] The PRC continued to emphasize Articles 52 and 53 VCLT, and how what China termed 'unequal treaties' were such that fell under their scope.[427]

However, the PRC adopted a flexible attitude, and frequently cited UNGA resolutions,[428] terming them 'expressions of customary international law,' and demonstrating that its attitude on the latter changed with its position in the international legal order.[429] Only those UNGA resolutions were deemed to assume the quality of customary international law that 1) clarify international legal principles or norms, 2) have been adopted (almost) unanimously – to show *opinio juris* – and 3) signify an emerging global legal consciousness around new principles and norms – eg the *Friendly Relations Declaration 1970*.[430] China's UN ambassador in 1997 called for the strengthening of 'rule of law' on the international level, and for 'international treaties and principles of international customary law, as well as the binding decisions adopted by the Security Council [to] all be strictly adhered to'.[431]

---

425 Treaties are concluded according to the Law of the People's Republic of China on the Procedure of the Conclusion of Treaties (adopted 28 December 1990, entered into force 28 December 1990). Their binding force is recognized, whereas the PRC distinguishes between self-executing and non-self-executing treaties. Where domestic legislation has to be amended, the President will ratify changes upon recommendation by the NPC Standing Committee. See Arts 7 and 8 Legislation Law of the People's Republic of China (adopted 15 March 2000, entered into force 1 July 2000). See also Hungdah Chiu, 'Chinese Views on the Sources of International Law' (1987) 28 *Harvard International Law Journal* 289; Bing Bing Jia, 'The Relations between Treaties and Custom' (2010) 9 CJIL 81.

426 See Art 142 General Principles of Civil Law of the People's Republic of China (adopted 12 April 1986, entered into force 1 January 1987).

427 Arts 52 and 53 VCLT; Pan, 'Chinese Philosophy and International Law' (n 42) 242–244, who noted that although the Chinese government even considered such treaties invalid from their inception, it still used borders regulated therein as the basis of later negotiations with Russia and Myanmar.

428 Senger (n 239) 47.

429 Pan, 'Chinese Philosophy and International Law' (n 42) 242.

430 Ahl, 'China' (n 274) 150. UNGA Res 2625 (XXV) (24 October 1970).

431 Duan, 'Statement on the Rule of Law' (n 42) 187.

The PRC has rejected general principles of international law under certain conditions, especially if it considered them discriminatory (partly due to supposed European roots).[432] However, sometimes Beijing has also declared them to represent a certain common sense of justice, describing them as fundamental principles of international law or common principles of different legal traditions around the world.[433]

Domestically, the Chinese constitution does not mention international law as a source of law, and correspondingly does not provide for an explicit rank of international treaties.[434] Nonetheless, it is generally accepted that the latter may not contradict the constitution without a corresponding constitutional amendment.[435] More than 70 acts of domestic legislation deal with international treaties and determine that they prevail in the case of conflict with domestic law, as long as no reservations were made. Therefore, international treaties are certainly part of the PRC's domestic legal system.[436] Some laws even regulate that in cases where neither national legislation nor international treaties determine a certain matter, customary international law is to be adhered to.[437]

However, in practice, international treaties only take precedence where domestic laws include an explicit norm to that effect, which mostly concerns civil or commercial law issues including cross border issues.[438] As national laws do not eg reference the human rights treaties that the PRC has ratified, those do not apply in a Chinese court.[439]

III.2.2.5.3. Sovereignty and Human Rights

In another step of integration, 'modern Chinese international legal doctrine has begun to recognize (…) that the concept of State sovereignty no

---

432 Christol (n 274) 463–464; Pan, 'Chinese Philosophy and International Law' (n 42) 8–9; Tanneberger (n 245) 122–123.

433 Ahl, 'China' (n 274) 150.

434 Constitution of the PRC 1982. See also Chow (n 208) 170.

435 Xue and Jin (n 268) 301–302.

436 Ahl, 'China' (n 274) 157; Chow (n 208) 170; Senger (n 246) 43; Xue and Jin (n 268) 301–303; Zhang and Hu (n 249) 11.

437 Zhang and Hu (n 249) 13. See also eg Art 142 General Principles of Civil Law of the People's Republic of China (adopted 12 April 1986, entered into force 1 January 1987).

438 Xue and Jin (n 268) 305.

439 Ahl, 'China' (n 274) 157.

longer precludes international scrutiny of alleged human rights violations'.[440] The PRC became a member of more than 20 human rights treaties, among them six core human rights instruments,[441] and largely kept to its reporting duties within the respective frameworks.[442] However, replies to international criticism following these reports showed continuity with the previous approach to individual rights. People remained 'an object of the care of their leaders [and not a] subject of rights vis-à-vis the leadership', and constitutionally defined '"rights of citizens" [remained] totally at the discretion of the leadership'.[443]

Responding to criticism, the PRC argued with the supposed importance of a different historico-cultural background and value system as well as a different stage of economic development.[444] It termed the US hypocritical due to its non-ratification of important human rights treaties and support for successive Israeli government's policies towards Palestinians.[445] Supposedly only economic development and a stable society can allow for better human rights protection, whereas social and economic rights are empha-

440 Ibid 152–153.

441 Convention on the Elimination of all Forms of Discrimination against Women (opened for signature 1 March 1980, entered into force 3 September 1981) 1249 UNTS 13 (ratified by the PRC on 4 November 1980, with a reservation regarding Article 29 (1)); International Convention on the Elimination of All Forms of Racial Discrimination (signed 21 December 1965, entered into force 4 January 1969) 660 UNTS 195 (CERD) (ratified by the PRC on 29 December 1981, with a reservation regarding Article 22); Convention Against Torture and Other Forms of Cruel, Inhuman or Degrading Treatment or Punishment (opened for signature 10 December 1984, entered into force 26 June 1987) 1465 UNTS 85 (ratified by the PRC on 4 October 1988, with a declaration on non-recognition of the competence of the Committee against Torture under Article 20, and on not considering itself bound by Article 30 (1)); Convention on the Rights of the Child (opened for signature 20 November 1989, entered into force 2 September 1990) 1577 UNTS 3 (ratified by the PRC on 2 March 1992 with a declaration regarding the PRC's domestic norms on family planning); International Covenant on Economic, Social and Cultural Rights (opened for signature 16 December 1966, entered into force 3 January 1976) 993 UNTS 3 (ICESCR); Convention on the Rights of Persons with Disabilities (adopted 13 December 2006, entered into force 3 May 2008) 2515 UNTS 3 (ratified by the PRC on 1 August 2008). See also Ahl, 'The Rise of China and International Human Rights Law' (n 29) 638, FN 2; Muller, 'Beyond History and Sovereignty' (n 7) 172–174.

442 Ahl, 'China' (n 274) 152–153.

443 Heuser, 'What "Rule of Law"?' (n 256) 724.

444 Qingguo Jia (n 384) 25.

445 Duan, 'Statement on the Rule of Law' (n 42) 187; Senger (n 246) 159–160.

sized, and subsistence called the principal human right.[446] Human rights are seen as emanating from the state, open to reservations,[447] and only possibly functional in connection with corresponding duties defined by the state.[448] In a sustained 'counter-discourse,' the PRC focuses not on challenging rights themselves, but rather on contesting the implications they would have –[449] integration, here, does not necessarily signify socialization, but it does reflect a conscious decision to work from within.

III.2.2.5.4. Sovereignty and Intervention

After the end of the Cold War, UNSC sanctioned use of force – exception to the general prohibition on the use of force (Article 2 (4) UN Charter) in addition to self-defense –[450] increased in number and diversified in type. Peacekeeping operations of a new generation developed, including peace enforcement and peace-building operations, eg in Bosnia and Somalia.[451] Moreover, the UNSC sanctioned willing states' use of force eg in Kuwait, which had called for collective self-defense against Iraq.[452] From the late-1990s, the US and certain NATO (as well as other) allies also carried out a so-called 'humanitarian intervention' without UNSC authorization against Yugoslavia to end the war in Kosovo, and another intervention against Iraq, with the latter being unconvincingly justified by the US with a supposed breach of UNSC Res 1441 (2002).[453] Intentions were laudable at least on Kosovo, and sustained, large scale, unsanctioned violations of

---

446 Senger (n 246) 156.

447 Qingguo Jia (n 384) 25.

448 Senger (n 246) 152.

449 Ahl, 'The Rise of China and International Human Rights Law' (n 29) 639.

450 Art 2 (4) UN Charter. See eg Bruno Simma (ed), *The Charter of the United Nations* (2nd edn, OUP 2002); Natalia Ochoa-Ruiz and Esther Salamanca-Aguado, 'Exploring the Limits of International Law relating to the Use of Force in Self-defence' (2005) 16 EJIL 499.

451 See United Nations Department of Peacekeeping Operations, *United Nations Peacekeeping Operations: Principles and Guidelines* (United Nations 2008); UNSC Res 1031 (15 December 1995) UN Doc S/RES/1031 and UNSC Res 837 (6 June 1993) UN Doc S/RES/837.

452 In the absence of Art 43 UN Charter arrangements, the UNSC authorized the use of force under enforcement powers in Chapter VII UN Charter (binding due to Art 25 UN Charter). See eg, on forcing the withdrawal of Iraqi troops from Kuwait, UNSC Res 678 (29 November 1990) UN Doc S/RES/678.

453 See UNSC Res 1441 (8 November 2002) UN Doc S/RES/1441.

international humanitarian law and human rights law are indeed concerning. Nevertheless, the latter two interventions were both carried out in violation of international law.[454]

On the issue of the use of force and multilateral interventions overall, as well as concomitant sovereignty issues, the PRC criticized circumventions of the UNSC, supposed double standards, and alignment with US foreign policy interests, while deeming interventions largely counter-productive.[455] Chinese scholars advised caution in the practical application of the concepts of humanitarian intervention and 'responsibility to protect' (R2P), although they perceived some strong points in underlying theory.[456] Strong states would supposedly attempt to use the pretense of humanitarian necessity to further their own interests, violate weaker states' sovereignty, and disturb national and international order – even UN reform was supposedly necessary to avoid further instances of strong states going it alone.[457]

However, in order to end China's diplomatic isolation and regain acceptance as a responsible member of the international community after the quashing of the Tiananmen Square protests in 1989, the PRC supported numerous American and European initiatives and even took part in such UN operations.[458] It conceded that the nature of sovereignty had changed, and that the UN indeed sometimes had the right to intervene in Member State affairs.[459]

In practice, the PRC went for more active engagement, in the sense of both participation and using its veto powers. Already in the 1980s, the PRC had been both gradually more at ease and more conciliatory in the UNSC –[460] it did not use its veto. In the 1990s, it supported the United Nations Protection Force (UNPROFOR) in former Yugoslavia and the hu-

454 See eg Nico Krisch, 'Review Essay Legality, Morality and the Dilemma of Humanitarian Intervention after Kosovo' (2002) 16 EJIL 323; Sean D Murphy, 'Assessing the Legality of Invading Iraq' (2004) 92 *Georgetown Law Journal* 173.

455 Qingguo Jia (n 384) 23.

456 The PRC even endorsed R2P in the 2005 World Summit Outcome Document but remained cautious on how to implement it, see Andrew Garwood-Gowers, 'China's "Responsible Protection" Concept: Reinterpreting the Responsibility to Protect (R2P) and Military Intervention for Humanitarian Purposes' (2016) 6 AsJIL 89.

457 Qingguo Jia (n 384) 20, 31.

458 Ahl, 'China' (n 274) 151–152; Carlson, 'Helping to Keep the Peace' (n 141) 10–11.

459 Ahl, 'China' (n 274) 151; Qingguo Jia (n 384) 25.

460 Chan, 'A Keen Observer' (n 397) 890.

manitarian intervention in Timor-Leste.[461] It sent observers to Kuwait, support staff to the UN interim administration in Cambodia, and police forces to Timor-Leste.[462] Chinese observers were part of the United Nations Operation in Mozambique (ONUMOZ) and United Nations Observer Mission in Liberia.[463] Beijing did not criticize the US intervention in Somalia, and (in the early-2000s) supported the overthrow of the Taliban in Afghanistan and the 'war on terror' in general.[464] The only two Chinese vetoes in the 1990s, regarding Guatemala and Macedonia, were on countries that recognized the ROC government on Taiwan as the legitimate government of China at the time – although Beijing only mentioned Taiwan in the veto on Guatemala.[465]

Western and Chinese positions had almost converged in the mid-1990s, after a short period of enthusiasm for multilateral interventions wore off in North American and European capitals.[466] However, the intervention in Kosovo in the late-1990s signified a new break. Kosovo represented a change in the Western position rather than the PRC's, which continued to reject a non-UNSC sanctioned military intervention.[467] Beijing had earlier also criticized the expansion of mandates and did not support corresponding resolutions regarding Yugoslavia and Kuwait/Iraq, and opposed (potential) interventions in Haiti and Rwanda.[468] Later on, China opposed sanctions against and interventions in Sudan, Myanmar, and Zimbabwe,[469] and on the latter two indeed made use of its veto.[470] China ab-

461 See UNSC Res 743 (21 February 1992) UN Doc S/RES/743, which established the United Nations Protection Force (UNPROFOR) in former Yugoslavia; UNSC Res 1264 (15 September 1999) UN Doc S/RES/1264 and UNSC Res 1272 (25 October 1999) UN Doc S/RES/1272, which allowed for a humanitarian intervention in Timor-Leste; the PRC had earlier also supported UNSC Res 660 (2 August 1990) UN Doc S/RES/660, which demanded a withdrawal of Iraqi troops from Kuwait.

462 Qingguo Jia (n 384) 24.

463 Carlson, 'Helping to Keep the Peace' (n 141) 16.

464 Ibid 10; Qingguo Jia (n 384) 24.

465 UNSC Verbatim Record (10 January 1997) UN Doc S/PV/3730; UNSC Verbatim Record (25 February 1999) UN Doc S/PV/3982. See also Chan, 'A Keen Observer' (n 397) 890.

466 Carlson, 'Helping to Keep the Peace' (n 141) 17.

467 Ibid 19–21.

468 Ahl, 'China' (n 274) 151–152; Carlson, 'Helping to Keep the Peace' (n 141) 16–17; Senger (n 246) 47.

469 Zhu, 'Chinese Practice of International Law: 2008' (n 42) 494–498.

470 UNSC Verbatim Record (12 January 2007) UN Doc S/PV/5619; UNSC Verbatim Record (11 July 2008) UN Doc S/PV/5933.

stained on military intervention in Libya,[471] but then harshly criticized NATO's interpretation of the mandate, repositioned itself on R2P,[472] and changed its former practice of rare UNSC veto usage – six (!) vetoes on Syria-related resolutions followed.[473]

Drawing on the International Commission on Intervention and State Sovereignty (ICISS) 2001 conception of R2P and the Brazilian 2011 proposal of 'Responsibility while Protecting' (RwP), the PRC MFA think tank CIIS in 2012 also made a contribution to pertinent normative discussions: 'Responsible Protection' (RP).[474] The concept – it has received some degree of official PRC endorsement but has not been formally adopted – demonstrates a recognition that non-consensual military intervention may be needed, but under more restrictive conditions than followed in some previous instances.[475] Only engaging with R2P's third pillar – international community responses to a state manifestly failing to prevent mass atrocities against its population – RP is rather a contribution to the normative development of R2P than an alternative to it.[476] Compared to ICISS' R2P concept, RP limits authorization more strictly to the UNSC – excluding the UNGA also in exceptional circumstances – requires the establishment of supervision and evaluation mechanisms, and more strongly demands the exhaustion of all other means, as well as limiting the means of protection and considering consequences for regional stability.[477]

By acquiescing to or even supporting most relevant interventions in the 1990s, the Chinese government created the necessary space for a shift in inner-Chinese scholarly debate –[478] scholars even described participation in

471 UNSC Res 1973 (17 March 2011) UN Doc S/RES/1973.

472 Matthias Vanhullebusch, 'Regime Change, the Security Council and China' (2015) 14 CJIL 665, 677.

473 UNSC Verbatim Record (4 October 2011) UN Doc S/PV/6627; UNSC Verbatim Record (4 February 2012) UN Doc S/PV/6711; UNSC Verbatim Record (19 July 2012) UN Doc S/PV/6810; UNSC Verbatim Record (22 May 2014) UN Doc S/PV/7180; UNSC Verbatim Record (5 December 2016) UN Doc S/PV/7825; UNSC Verbatim Record (28 February 2017) UN Doc S/PV/7893. See also Garwood-Gowers (n 456) 90.

474 Zongze Ruan, '"Responsible Protection: Building a Safer World" (*China Institute of International Studies*, 15 June 2012) <http://www.ciis.org.cn/english/2012-06/15/content_5090912.htm> accessed 20 December 2018. See also Garwood-Gowers (n 456) 90–92.

475 See also Garwood-Gowers (n 456) 92–93.

476 Ibid 111.

477 Ibid 103–111.

478 Carlson, 'Helping to Keep the Peace' (n 141) 24–25.

'protective interventions' (that fulfill necessary conditions) as potentially contributive to China protecting national interests and attaining great power status.[479] The PRC also achieved a drastic change in terms of how it was perceived internationally. Until the recent spate of Syria-connected vetoes, China only rejected those interventions that were viewed negatively by a majority of the international community. However, even with such interventions, Beijing let others take the lead among the critics (ie Russia).[480]

III.2.2.5.5. Sovereignty and Adjudication

Finally, we get to the area of engagement with the international legal order at the heart of this book: international adjudication. The ROC had already seen a case at the PCIJ initiated and then withdrawn by Belgium, before the Chinese side needed to decide on whether to participate in the proceedings.[481] No further cases followed after the establishment of the ICJ.[482] The PRC, then, distanced itself from all steps of engagement the ROC had taken and strictly opposed any engagement with supposedly Western-controlled, 'bourgeois' international courts and arbitral tribunals[483] – including informing the UN Secretary-General in 1972 that it considered the ROC's recognition of compulsory ICJ jurisdiction to be defunct.[484]

The inner-PRC discourse on engagement with international dispute resolution mechanisms (ie international adjudication) changed in the late-1980s and early-1990s. Once again, space for debates was created through Beijing's desire to end isolation after Tiananmen, and a change in the scholarly discourse precipitated gradual policy shifts. The PRC supported the establishment of the International Criminal Tribunal for the former Yugoslavia (ICTY), Chinese international law professor Wang Tieya served as a judge there, and allowed for the establishment of the In-

---

479 Zewei 泽伟 Yang 杨, '国际社会的民主和法治价值与保护性干预' (Democratic and Rule of Law Values of International Society and Protective Intervention) (2012) 30 *Falü Kexue* 41, 46–47.

480 Carlson, 'Helping to Keep the Peace' (n 141) 14.

481 *Denunciation of the Treaty of 2 November 1865 between China and Belgium (Belgium v China)* (Order of May 25 1929) PCIJ Series A No 18.

482 See Chapter III.2.2.3.3.

483 See Chapters III.2.2.4.1 and III.2.2.4.2.

484 Pan, 'Chinese Philosophy and International Law' (n 42) 245.

ternational Criminal Tribunal for Rwanda (ICTR) by abstaining in the pertinent UNSC vote.[485]

Moreover, China signed and ratified the Convention on the Settlement of Investment Disputes between States and Nationals of Other States (hereinafter: ICSID Convention) in 1993,[486] and thereby accepted the possibility of resolving investment disputes at the World Bank's ICSID, which signified the first embrace of an institutionalized international dispute resolution mechanism that could potentially address cases with Chinese involvement.[487] Awards in investment arbitration are binding and to be enforced akin to domestic court judgments, but states have to additionally submit to ICSID jurisdiction through bilateral investment treaties (hereinafter: BITs), which China only did gradually – first in very limited ways – in the 1990s.[488] First cases appeared much later.[489] China also became a party to the Convention Establishing the Multilateral Investment Guarantee Agency (MIGA) – partly also served as dispute settlement forum.[490] Moreover, China resumed activities at the Permanent Court of Arbitration (hereinafter: PCA), nominated four experts as arbitrators, and accepted all Hague Conventions on the peaceful resolution of international conflicts.[491]

This tendency was strongly reinforced in 2001, when the PRC joined the WTO and thus submitted to its Dispute Settlement Mechanism (hereinafter: DSM); another momentous step towards engagement since the WTO DSM assumes automatic jurisdiction. The consent given through

485 UNSC Preliminary Verbatim Record (25 May 1993) UN Doc S/PV/3217; UNSC Provisional Verbatim Record (8 November 1994) UN Doc S/PV/3453. See also Duan, 'Statement on the Rule of Law' (n 42) 186.

486 Convention on the Settlement of Investment Disputes between States and Nationals of Other States (adopted 18 March 1965, entered into force 14 October 1966) 575 UNTS 159 (ICSID Convention). The convention established ICSID within the framework of the World Bank.

487 See Chapter IV.2.1.1.

488 Arts 1 (2), 53 and 54 (1) ICSID Convention; see Chapters IV.2.1.2.3 and IV.2.1.2.4.

489 See Chapter IV.2.1.3.

490 Convention Establishing the Multilateral Investment Guarantee Agency (adopted 11 October 1985, entered into force 12 April 1988) 1508 UNTS 99; MIGA, 'Member Countries' <https://www.miga.org/member-countries> accessed 30 March 2019.

491 Pan, 'Chinese Philosophy and International Law' (n 42) 245–246. The four PCA Members from the PRC listed at the end of 2018 were Xue Hanqin (since 2009), Liu Zhenmin (since 2014), Liu Daqun (since 2014) and Huang Jin (since 2017).

joining the WTO suffices.[492] The PRC first remained rather passive, and only grew more litigious after gathering a few years of experience,[493] in any case largely complying with a variety of reports.[494] In the two-level DSM system, including the Dispute Settlement Body (hereinafter: DSB) and the Appellate Body (hereinafter: AB), PRC citizens have served on DSB panels and as AB members.[495]

Aside from economic matters, China took further steps towards engagement with international adjudication by signing UNCLOS in 1982, and ratifying it in 1996. The Chinese government issued an explanatory declaration upon ratification, referencing its claim to the offshore land features in the South and East China Seas, as well as an Article 298 UNCLOS declaration later on in 2006, making use of most options in UNCLOS to exclude compulsory dispute settlement.[496] However, UNCLOS does not allow for the exclusion of compulsory dispute settlement for all matters, which means that ratification was still a dramatic step for the PRC to take, as it signified the first time that it surrendered itself to international adjudication outside of the economic realm.[497] Chinese judges have served at the International Tribunal for the Law of the Sea (hereinafter: ITLOS) since 1996.[498]

Even the icy attitude regarding the ICJ changed over time; supposedly on account of stronger participation of judges from developing nations. Discourse moved towards only issuing further reservations against ICJ jurisdiction in the case of essential national interests being affected.[499] PRC-nominated judges have served at the Court since 1985.[500] In practice, the

---

492 See Chapter IV.2.2.1.
493 See Chapters IV.2.2.2.1, IV.2.2.2.2 and IV.2.2.2.3.
494 See Chapter IV.2.2.2.3.9.
495 See Chapter IV.2.2.1.
496 See Chapter IV.3.2.1.2; Art 298 UNCLOS (n 394); United Nations Division for Ocean Affairs and the Law of the Sea, 'United Nations Convention on the Law of the Sea – Declarations made upon signature, ratification, accession or succession or anytime thereafter' <http://www.un.org/Depts/los/convention_agreements/convention_declarations.htm> accessed 30 March 2019.
497 See Chapter IV.3.2.1.2.
498 Zhao Lihai (1996–2000), Xu Guangjian (2001–2007) and Gao Zhiguo (since 2008).
499 See eg Yong 勇 Wang 王 and Zhengfeng 征峰 Guan 管, '五十五年来中国对国际法院诉讼管辖权的态度之述评' (Review of China's Attitude towards the Litigation Jurisdiction of International Courts over the last Fifty Years) [2002] (3) *Huadong Zhengfa Xueyuan Xuebao* 72, 73.
500 Ni Zhengyu (1985–1994), Shi Jiuyong (1994–2010) and Xue Hanqin (since 2010).

Chinese leadership has largely kept to its position of only seeking bilateral solutions via negotiation on law of the sea and territorial disputes, but it has grown open to engaging with dispute settlement bodies below the threshold of contentious proceedings.[501] Some Chinese international legal scholars moved much further towards engagement, pointed to the contradiction between advocating respect for international law and strengthening the UN on the one hand, and rejection of the ICJ on the other, and partly even want to submit territorial conflicts to the ICJ or ITLOS.[502]

III.2.2.6. Conclusion

Two crucial trajectories in China's relations with international legal order need to be set out. First, there was a back and forth over the millennia on the notions of equality between different polities, sovereignty, and intervention. China witnessed a community of nations emerge in the Warring States period that developed a number of rules for inter-state behavior quite similar to those that arose in sixteenth century Europe. During the Confucian-dominated Chinese Empire, and the hierarchical tributary system it established, equality and sovereignty were no longer possible, and intervention in others' affairs a potential patriarchal duty of the Emperor. Violently confronted with European-developed international legal order as a means to solidify Colonial gains against 'uncivilized' nations, the Late Empire and ROC returned to cherishing equality and sovereignty. Both the ROC and PRC eventually grew sufficiently confident to give up some elements of 'concrete sovereignty' to secure political or economic gains through integration that could bolster China's status and power on an international level (ie 'abstract sovereignty').

Second, since its confrontation with a largely European-developed international legal order in the 19th century, China has mostly pursued a path of active preparation and cautious engagement. Viewing the existing order with strong wariness, China remained keenly aware of its importance and intent on shaping its development. The early PRC constituted a detour in this regard that was due both to stringent ideology and institutional exclu-

501 See eg Zhu, 'Chinese Practice of International Law: 2008' (n 42) 504–507. Below the threshold of contentious proceedings, however, the PRC took part in advisory proceedings at the ICJ and ITLOS, and engaged with the Commission on the Limits of the Continental Shelf (CLCS), see Chapter IV.3.3.

502 See Chapter V.3.3.2.2.

sion. The ROC had already been part of the League of Nations and moved to the very core of the UN, including UNSC veto power and prominent roles in contemporary treaty drafting. It had been faced with a claim at the PCIJ and accepted compulsory ICJ jurisdiction. The PRC has over the last half-century of UN presence been growing into this role, gained confidence, and progressively engaged. It grew more active in UNSC and UNGA, ratified important treaties including reporting duties, participated in UN peacekeeping, and even accepted the jurisdiction of international adjudicative bodies from investment to trade to law of the sea matters.

The way in which the PRC engages – including its speed and manner – might not comport with what some had hoped for. It shows caution and deliberation, an unwillingness to risk premature exposure and defeat, and certainly different priorities than among liberal democracies. However, China clearly remains set on securing a seat at the table wherever possible, and willing to join organizations, ratify treaties, and even accept international adjudication where it considers itself ready and those steps necessary for relative power gains.

IV. Object – PRC Practice in International Adjudication

IV.1. Introduction

Following the exploration of the *image* of international law and adjudication that has arisen over time in China, this part of the book will address pertinent mechanisms and concrete instances of Chinese engagement. First, this will allow exploring questions about the 'how' of PRC engagement with international adjudication. Second, this history of engagement forms the *object* of Chinese scholars' *perceptions* and basis for recommendations, which will be addressed in Chapter V. The first sub-section expounds on institutions, cases, issues, Chinese government positions and treaties in the realm of economy (ie investment and trade disputes), and the second sub-section on those in the realm of territory (ie disputes concerning the law of the sea and the law of territorial acquisition). Treaties and case proceedings up until the end of 2018 will be considered.

IV.2. Economy

The post-reform PRC has been much quicker to engage with international dispute resolution mechanisms in the economic sphere, because this was deemed to be necessary for the country's economic development, and to encroach less on China's sovereignty than jurisdiction regarding law of the sea and territorial acquisition disputes would. Most importantly, the primary venues for state-state trade dispute settlement (ie the WTO DSM) and investor-state dispute settlement (hereinafter: ISDS) (ie ICSID and ad-hoc investment arbitration) have been engaged with. These will be the focus of this chapter.

Proceeding chronologically, the following remarks will first deal with China's several 'generations' of 'Bilateral Investment Treaty' (in the following: BIT) practice starting in 1982, including the evolving stance on investment arbitration, to then address the existing case law. Thereafter, the PRC's 2001 WTO accession and participation in the DSM process will be discussed. Both chapters will also include brief comparative sub-chapters, reviewing the practice of other large emerging economies. In short preliminary conclusions, the general trajectory of Chinese engagement with international adjudication in investment and trade law and its consequences will be reflected upon.

IV.2.1. Phase One – the PRC and Investment Arbitration

IV.2.1.1. China's Accession to the ICSID Convention

The ICSID has been the most important forum for settling investment disputes since the 1990s,[503] after receiving a rather modest caseload in its early years. Parties can make use of Arbitration Rules and rely on institutional support, eg ICSID staff supporting proceedings and organizing venues for hearings, while independent arbitral tribunals will consider each case.[504] Any Contracting State to the ICSID Convention or national of such a state may submit a request for the initiation of proceedings to the Secretary-General, who will register such a request, if the dispute is not 'manifestly outside the jurisdiction of the Centre'.[505] Parties may agree on one arbitrator or any uneven number of arbitrators. Where the parties do not agree on the method of appointment and number of arbitrators, they shall nominate one arbitrator each, and a third arbitrator, the president of the Tribunal, is to be appointed by agreement of the parties.[506]

The thus established arbitral tribunal will decide the dispute based on such law as agreed upon by the parties. If there is no such agreement, the tribunal shall apply the law of the Contracting State party to the dispute, as well as rules of international law that may be applicable.[507]

---

503 Meg Kinnear and others (eds), *Building International Investment Law – The First 50 Years of ICSID* (Kluwer Law International 2016) li.

504 Section 1 Chapter I, Section 3 Chapter IV, and Chapter VII ICSID Convention; ICSID Rules of Procedure for Arbitration Proceedings (10 April 2006) ('ICSID Arbitration Rules'); Christoph Schreuer, 'Investment Arbitration', in Cesare PR Romano, Karen J Alter and Yuval Shany (eds), *The Oxford Handbook of International Adjudication* (OUP 2014) 298.

505 Art 36 ICSID Convention; Christoph H Schreuer, Loretta Malintoppi, August Reinisch and Anthony Sinclair, *The ICSID Convention: A Commentary* (2nd edn, CUP 2009) 455–474.

506 Art 37 (2) ICSID Convention; Schreuer and others, *The ICSID Convention* (n 505) 478–489.

507 Art 42 (1) ICSID Convention; Schreuer and others, *The ICSID Convention* (n 505) 557–630; Schreuer, 'The Development of International Law by ICSID Tribunals' (n 54) 731–734; W Michael Reisman and Mahnoush H Arsanjani, 'Applicable Law under the ICSID Convention: The Tortured History of the Inter-

Striving to attract more foreign investors, the PRC signed the ICSID Convention on 9 February 1990 and ratified it to enter into force on 6 February 1993.[508] This was part of the Chinese government's bid to overcome international isolation after Tiananmen by actively engaging international institutions and supporting international initiatives.[509]

The PRC's first ever embrace of an international tribunal's jurisdiction was still a somewhat cautious step.[510] Jurisdiction depends on 'double-consent.' It does not suffice that both the host state and the investor's home state have ratified the ICSID Convention, as such participation does not amount to consent to jurisdiction. They have to also have specifically consented to jurisdiction, for example by stipulating ICSID jurisdiction in a treaty, a contract or domestic legislation: in other words, they have to 'consent in writing to submit [the dispute in question] to the Centre' (Article 25 (1) ICSID Convention).[511]

The PRC also submitted an Article 25 (4) ICSID Convention notification in 1993 that made clear China's intent to only submit questions of compensation in expropriation and nationalization cases to ICSID jurisdiction.[512] Such a notification does not have direct legal consequences, but may impact the interpretation of consent clauses (as might the absence of

---

pretation of Article 42', in Meg Kinnear and others (eds), *Building International Investment Law – The First 50 Years of ICSID* (Kluwer Law International 2016) 3–12.

508 ICSID, 'Database of ICSID Member States' <https://icsid.worldbank.org/en/Pages/about/Database-of-Member-States.aspx> accessed 30 March 2019. See also Justin S Hempson-Jones, 'The Evolution of China's Engagement with International Governmental Organizations: Toward a Liberal Foreign Policy?' (2005) 45 *Asian Survey* 702; Ko-Yung Tung and Rafael Cox-Alomar, 'The New Generation of China BITs in Light of Tza Yap Shum v. Republic of Peru' (2006) 17 *American Review of International Arbitration* 461, 463; Xiuwen Zhao and Lisa A Kloppenberg, 'Reforming Chinese Arbitration Law and Practices in the Global Economy' (2006) 31 *University of Dayton Law Review* 421, 434.

509 Ahl, 'China' (n 274) 151–152.

510 Tong Qi, 'How Exactly does China Consent to Investor-State Arbitration: On the First ICSID Case Against China' (2012) 5 *Contemporary Asia Arbitration Journal* 265, 268.

511 Art 25 (1) ICSID Convention; Schreuer and others, *The ICSID Convention* (n 505) 85–263; Schreuer, 'Investment Arbitration' (n 504) 302–304; Tong Qi, 'How Exactly does China Consent' (n 510) 269–270.

512 Art 25 (4) ICSID Convention; '[P]ursuant to Article 25(4) of the Convention, the Chinese Government would only consider submitting to the jurisdiction of the International Centre for Settlement of Investment Disputes disputes over compensation resulting from expropriation and nationalization' (date of notification, 7 January 1993), International Centre for Settlement of Investment Dis-

corresponding notifications).[513] Demonstrating its still limited willingness to accept international adjudication, China also included restrictive ISDS clauses in its early BITs,[514] and appears to have been wary about their interpretation. For example, in its first BIT including access to ICSID arbitration, China limited such access to disputes about the amount of compensation for expropriation (Article 9 China-Spain BIT 1992).[515]

Moreover, the mere fact of China informing other states about its limited intentions of using ICSID, through the above notification, gives some insight into the state of inner-Chinese debates on the issue at that time. For context, it is interesting to note that of the more than 150 contracting states of the ICSID Convention, only nine others submitted Art 25 (4) notifications, and Israel and Guyana have since withdrawn their notifications. The others that have not since retracted are Jamaica (submitted in 1974), Papua New Guinea (1978), Saudi Arabia (1980), Turkey (1989), Guatemala (2003), Ecuador (2007) – denunciation of the Convention in 2009, effective 2010 – and Indonesia (2012). Of these notifications, none were akin to

---

putes, 'China – Designations and Notifications' <https://icsid.worldbank.org/en/Pages/about/MembershipStateDetails.aspx?state=ST30> accessed 30 March 2019 ('PRC Art 25 (4) ICSID Convention-Notification'). See also Wei 伟 Chen 沈, '论中国双边投资协定中限制性投资争端解决条款的解释和适用' (Discussing the Interpretation and Application of the Restrictive Investment Dispute Settlement Clause in Chinese BITs) (2012) 24 *Zhongwai Faxue* 1046, 1051; Ku, 'China and the Future of International Adjudication' (n 32) 164; Tong Qi, 'How Exactly does China Consent' (n 510) 268; Wang, 'China's Practice in International Investment Law' (n 408) 577; Caixia 彩霞 Yang 杨 and Quan 泉 Qin 秦, '国际投资争端解决中的无默契仲裁初探' (First Explorations of Arbitration without Privity in International Investment Dispute Settlement) [2011] (3) *Bijiaofa Yanjiu* 108, 120; Gordon Smith, 'Chinese Bilateral Investment Treaties: Restrictions on International Arbitratio' (2010) 76 *Arbitration* 58.

513 The lack of Art 25 (4) notifications was cited in favor of ICSID jurisdiction in *Fedax NV v Republic of Venezuela*, ICSID Case No ARB/96/3(1), Decision on Jurisdiction (11 July 1997) para 33; *Ceskoslovenska Obchodni Banka, AS v Slovak Republic*, ICSID Case No ARB/97/4, Decision of the Tribunal on Objections to Jurisdiction (24 May 1999) para 65. See Schreuer and others, *The ICSID Convention* (n 505) 343–344, 346–347.

514 See Chapters IV.2.1.2.2 and IV.2.1.2.3.

515 Art 9 Acuerdo para la Proteccion y Fomento Reciprocos de Inversiones entre el Reino de Espana y la Republica Popular de China (signed 6 February 1992, entered into force 1 May 1993, terminated, new China-Spain BIT entered into force 1 July 2008) ('China-Spain BIT 1992').

China's, and most were more limited, eg Jamaica, Saudi Arabia and Ecuador intended to exclude hydrocarbon or mineral resource disputes.[516]

On the other hand, the significance of participation in ICSID arbitration should not be underestimated, as certain aspects very strongly touch on issues of sovereignty. Parties cannot avoid proceedings through non-cooperation, as the Chairman of ICSID's Administrative Council will appoint arbitrators if parties fail to do so (Article 38 ICSID Convention); tribunals have competence to decide whether they have jurisdiction (Article 41 ICSID Convention); and non-appearance or failure to make written submissions cannot block the tribunal from rendering an award (Article 45 ICSID Convention).[517]

Awards are binding and final, and not open to domestic review.[518] Annulment proceedings may be requested only on limited grounds.[519] However, Article 55 ICSID Convention stipulates that the law on state immunity from execution in any contracting state is not derogated.[520]

Pecuniary obligations due to awards by ICSID tribunals are to be executed like domestic court judgments (Articles 53 (1), 54 (1), (3) ICSID Convention).[521] Where parties fail to comply with an award, the investor's state

516 ICSID, 'Contracting States and Measures taken by them for the Purpose of the Convention' (Washington DC, February 2019) <https://icsid.worldbank.org/en/Documents/icsiddocs/ICSID%208-Contracting%20States%20and%20Measures%20Taken%20by%20Them%20for%20the%20Purpose%20of%20the%20Convention.pdf> (accessed 30 March 2019); Schreuer and others, *The ICSID Convention* (n 505) 344–345.

517 Arts 38, 41 and 45 ICSID Convention; Schreuer and others, *The ICSID Convention* (n 505) 490–497, 516–544, 708–730. For some terminological clarification see Veijo Heiskanen, 'Ménage à trois? Jurisdiction, Admissibility and Competence in Investment Treaty Arbitration' (2014) 29 *ICSID Review* 231.

518 Art 53 ICSID Convention; Schreuer and others, *The ICSID Convention* (n 505) 1096–1114; Schreuer, 'Investment Arbitration' (n 504) 298, 311–312.

519 Arts 3 and 52 ICSID Convention; Schreuer and others, *The ICSID Convention* (n 505) 15, 890–1095; Hi-Taek Shin, 'Annulment', in Meg Kinnear and others (eds), *Building International Investment Law – The First 50 Years of ICSID* (Kluwer Law International 2016) 699.

520 Arts 51 (4) and 55 ICSID Convention; Schreuer and others, *The ICSID Convention* (n 505) 887–889, 1151–1185; Martina Polasek, 'Introductory Note to the Three Decisions on the Stay of Enforcement of an ICSID Award' (2005) 20 *ICSID Review* 581; Inna Uchkunollva and Oleg Temnikov, 'Enforcement of Awards Under the ICSID Convention – What Solutions to the Problem of State Immunity' (2014) 29 *ICSID Review* 187.

521 Arts 53 (1) and 54 (1), (3) ICSID Convention; Schreuer and others, *The ICSID Convention* (n 505) 1099–1113, 1123–1144, 1148–1150; Schreuer, 'Investment

of nationality's right to diplomatic protection revives (Articles 27, 53 ICSID Convention).[522]

In addition to or instead of ICSID, investors may have the option of an investment arbitration at an institution primarily occupied with commercial arbitrations, such as the Arbitral Tribunal of the International Chamber of Commerce in Paris (hereinafter: ICC) and the Arbitration Institute of the Chamber of Commerce in Stockholm, as well as an ad hoc arbitration under UNCITRAL Arbitration Rules.[523]

China's described reticence has delayed the appearance of case law, with the first case against the PRC, *Ekran Berhad*, being filed in 2011.[524] That was also the year Prof. Chen An became the first Chinese arbitrator to be

---

Arbitration' (n 504) 312; Stephan W Schill, 'Tearing Down the Great Wall: The New Generation Investment Treaties of the People's Republic of China' (2007) 15 *Cardozo Journal of International & Contemporary Law* 73, 88.

522 Arts 27 and 53 ICSID Convention; Schreuer and others, *The ICSID Convention* (n 505) 414–430, 1096–1114; Victorino J Tejera Pérez, 'Diplomatic Protection Revival for Failure to Comply with Investment Arbitration Awards' (2012) 3 *Journal of International Dispute Settlement* 445.

523 UNGA Res 68/109 (16 December 2013) UN Doc A/RES/68/109 ('UNCITRAL Arbitration Rules'); On pertinent BITs see eg Art 9 (2) (b) and (d) Agreement on the promotion and the reciprocal protection of investments between the Government of the Republic of Cyprus and the Great Socialist People's Libyan Arab Jamahiriya (signed 30 June 2004, entered into force 13 February 2005) ('Cyprus-Libya BIT 2004'); Art 10 (2.2) Accord entre les gouvernements du Royaume de Belgique et du Grand-Duche de Luxembourg, et le Gouvernement de l'Union des Républiques Socialistes Sovietiques, concernant l'encouragementet la protection réciproques des investissements (signed 9 February 1989, entered into force 18 August 1991) ('Belgium-Luxembourg Economic Union-Soviet Union BIT 1989'); Art 6 (3) (b) Treaty with the Czech and Slovak Federal Republic concerning the reciprocal encouragement and protection of investment (signed 22 October 1991, entered into force 19 December 1992) ('Czechoslovakia-US BIT 1991'). As for pertinent case law see eg *Olin Holdings Limited v Libya*, ICC Case No 20355/MCP, Final Award (25 May 2018); *Berschader v Russian Federation*, SCC Case No V080/2004, Award (21 April 2006); *Ronald S. Lauder v Czech Republic*, UNCITRAL, Final Award (3 September 2001). See also Rudolf Dolzer and Christoph Schreuer, *Principles of International Investment Law* (2nd edn, OUP 2012) 241–244..

524 *Ekran Berhad v People's Republic of China*, ICSID Case No ARB/11/15 (registered 24 May 2011, suspended 22 July 2011, discontinued 16 May 2013, no official documents available); Tong Qi, 'How Exactly does China Consent' (n 510) 286; Jie Wang, 'Investor-State Arbitration: Where does China Stand?' (2009) 32 *Suffolk Transnational Law Review* 493, 495.

part of ICSID arbitration in two cases – he later resigned in May 2013 before awards were rendered.[525]

IV.2.1.2. China's Evolving BIT Practice

IV.2.1.2.1. Introduction

BITs are international treaties intended to attract investors by providing them with additional legal protection. They aim to reduce political risk, and generally include the provision of different forums for resolving pertinent disputes.[526]

Modern investment protection rules originate in US 'friendship, commerce and navigation treaties' (hereinafter: FCN treaties), which focused on trade, but already included provisions on compensation.[527]

Germany was the initiator of dedicated modern investment treaties, the treaty it concluded with Pakistan in 1959 being the first such BIT.[528] Other European states followed. Japan and the US only joined the European

525 Prof. Chen was appointed to two tribunals followed by conjoined proceedings, *Bernhard von Pezold and Others v Republic of Zimbabwe*, ICSID Case No ARB/10/15, Award (28 July 2015) paras 5, 25–26; *Border Timbers Limited, Border Timbers International (Private) Limited, and Hangani Development Co (Private) Limited v Republic of Zimbabwe*, ICSID Case No ARB/10/25, Award (28 July 2015) paras 5, 25–26; Teresa Cheng SC from Hong Kong even served as president of the tribunal in *Bawabet Al Kuwait Holding Company v Arab Republic of Egypt*, ICSID Case No ARB/11/6, Notice of Arbitration (18 March 2011). See Zhanghui Wu, 'International Arbitration for Chinese-Foreign Disputes: Emerging Choices in 2012' (2012) 41 *International Law News* 1, 4. *Bawabet v Egypt* was settled 9 October 2016.

526 Jeswald W Salacuse, 'The Emerging Global Regime for Investment' (2010) 51 *Harvard International Law Journal* 427, 428, 434–435; Jan Paulsson, 'The Power of States to Make Meaningful Promises to Foreigners' (2010) 1 *Journal of International Dispute Settlement* 341, 344; Philippe Kahn and Thomas Wälde, *New Aspects of International Investment Law* (Brill-Nijhoff 2007) 43, 119; Schreuer, 'Investment Arbitration' (n 504) 296–297.

527 Dolzer and Schreuer (n 523) 1–2.

528 Treaty between the Federal Republic of Germany and Pakistan for the Promotion and Protection of Investments (signed 25 November 1959, entered into force 1 July 1962) ('Germany-Pakistan BIT 1959').

practice in 1977 and 1982, and India followed in 1994.[529] In the mid-2000s new treaties between developing states were increasingly concluded, replacing the traditional scheme of treaties between developed and developing states. Interestingly, the scope and contents of the respective treaties do not differ significantly.[530]

Despite certainly a good amount of overlap, China's BIT practice can be broadly categorized in four different generations: 1) 1982 to 1989/1990, 2) 1989/1990 to 1998, 3) 1998 to 2008, and 4) 2008 to 2018. Evolution through these generations has come about as China 1) followed global practice on improving case law-tested treaty formats, and as it 2) grew into a two-way investment giant.[531]

Most previous studies have delineated two generations of Chinese BITs,[532] taking 1998 as the decisive watershed, when, in the Barbados-China BIT, China agreed to access to investor-state arbitration for all investment disputes instead of just such about the amount of compensation for arbitration.[533] Others have identified a first generation of BITs from the inception of China's BIT programme in 1982 throughout the 1980s, a second

529 Agreement between Japan and the Arab Republic of Egypt Concerning the Encouragement and Reciprocal Protection of Investment (signed 28 January 1977, entered into force 14 January 1978) ('Egypt-Japan BIT 1977'); Treaty between the United States of America and the Republic of Panama Concerning the Treatment and Protection of Investments (signed 27 October 1982, entered into force 30 May 1991) ('Panama-US BIT 1982'); Agreement between the Government of the United Kingdom of Great Britain and Northern Ireland and the Government of the Republic of India for the Promotion and Protection of Investments (signed 14 March 1994, entered into force 6 January 1995) ('India-UK BIT 1994').

530 Dolzer and Schreuer (n 523) 7–8.

531 See also Yongjie Li, 'Factors to be Considerd for China's Future Investment Treaties', in Wenhua Shan (ed), *China and International Investment Law: Twenty Years of ICSID Membership* (Brill 2015) 173.

532 See eg Nils Eliasson, 'The Chinese Investment Treaty Programme, Jurisdictional Challenges and Investment Planning: The Example of Chinese Outbound Investments in the Natural Resources Sector', in Wenhua Shan (ed), *China and International Investment Law: Twenty Years of ICSID Membership* (Brill 2015) 235; Karl P Sauvant and Michael D Nolan, 'China's Outward Foreign Direct Investment and International Investment Law' (2015) 18 *Journal of International Economic* Law 893, 914–915; Berger, 'The Politics of China's Investment Treaty-Making Program' (n 34) 171; Tong Qi, 'How Exactly does China Consent' (n 510) 269–272; Schill, 'Tearing Down the Great Wall' (n 521) 91; Yang and Qin (n 512) 120; Smith (n 498) 120.

533 Art 9 Agreement between the Government of Barbados and the Government of the People's Republic of China for the Promotion and Protection of Invest-

generation of BITs following China's signature of the ICSID Convention in 1990 (ratified in 1993) and running up until the Barbados-China BIT 1998, and a third generation thereafter.[534]

This book embraces the above three-generations-delineation, while maintaining that between first- and second-generation BITs, China's second Model BIT in 1989 and signature of the ICSID Convention in 1990 should be considered as a two-step break.[535] It also argues that China's BIT practice has further progressed since 2008. A fourth generation of treaties has gradually been taking shape since the China-Mexico BIT 2008 and the investment chapter of the China-New Zealand FTA 2008. It is largely marked by 'Americanization,' which typically means that treaties are much more comprehensive, include more detailed provisions or even separate sections on dispute settlement, and also address market access.[536] Similar approaches have been adopted in some recent studies, albeit which have proposed a three-phase delimitation,[537] or have also focused on China's selection of partner countries in delineating the phases, not only BIT content.[538]

---

ments (signed 20 July 1998, entered into force 1 October 1999) ('Barbados-China BIT 1998').

534 See eg Gallagher and Shan, *Chinese Investment Treaties* (n 34) 35; Yongjie Li (n 531) 174. For another three phase-delineation, but in the stages pre-1978, 1978–1998 and post-1998, see Ka Zeng and Yue Lu, 'Variation in Bilateral Investment Treaty Provisions and Foreign Direct Investment Flows to China, 1997–2011' (2016) 42 *International Interactions* 820, 823.

535 Chinese Model BIT II (1989) as drafted by the Directorate-General of Treaty and Law in the MOFCOM and as translated into English by Prof. Shan Wenhua and printed in Gallagher and Shan, *Chinese Investment Treaties* (n 34) 427–433.

536 See Chapter IV.2.1.2.5.

537 Shu Zhang, 'China's Approach in Drafting the Investor-State Arbitration Clause: A Review from the "Belt and Road" Regions' Perspective' (2017) 5 *The Chinese Journal of Comparative Law* 79, 82–83; Manjiao Chi, 'From Europeanization toward Americanization: the shift of China's dichotomic investment treaty-making strategy' (2017) 23 *Canadian Foreign Policy Journal* 158, 163. For China's move from the European to the American model of BITs see also Marc and Catharine Titi, 'The Evolution of EU Investment Law and the Future of EU-China Investment Relations', in Wenhua Shan (ed), *China and International Investment Law: Twenty Years of ICSID Membership* (Brill 2015) 365.

538 Berger, 'Hesitant Embrace' (n 34) 844–845.

IV.2.1.2.2. First Generation – Cautious Beginnings

China concluded its first ever BIT with Sweden in 1982 –[539] the start of its first generation of BITs. This appeared a logical step in attracting foreign investment to fuel economic development, the new overriding policy goal of the Chinese government since the onset of reforms in 1978. It followed the promulgation of a first law on foreign investment in 1979, the Chinese-Foreign Equity Joint Venture Law (EJVL), and the amendment of the Chinese Constitution in 1982 to confirm the protection of foreign investment.[540] The Chinese government realized that it needed to do more to dispel mistrust of the investment climate, focusing on attracting and protecting inward investment – most BITs in this phase are with European developed countries – but also to protect China's own incipient outward FDI.

China's first Model BIT in 1984 (China Model BIT, Version I), and first-generation BITs, remained relatively conservative and in line with contemporary practice among Communist states.[541] As a caveat on the importance of China's Model BITs, it should be mentioned that it was usually the other side's Model BITs that shaped the outcome more whenever China concluded an investment treaty with a (relative to China) capital-exporting country, as was typically the case in these early years.[542]

Aside from basic provisions on – inter alia – definitions, FET, MFN treatment, expropriation and compensation, investor-state disputes were entrusted mainly to domestic courts, with ad-hoc international arbitration

539 Agreement on the Mutual Protection of Investments between the Government of the Kingdom of Sweden and the Government of the People's Republic of China (signed 29 March 1982, entered into force 29 March 1982) ('China-Sweden BIT 1982').

540 Law on Sino-Foreign Equity Joint Ventures (adopted 1 July 1979, entered into force 1 July 1979); Art 18 Constitution of the PRC 1982 – Art 18: 'All foreign enterprises and other foreign investment located in China, as well as joint ventures with Chinese and foreign investment located in China, shall abide by the law of the People's Republic of China. Their lawful rights and interest are protected by the law of the People's Republic of China'.

541 Chinese Model BIT Version I (1984) as drafted by the Directorate-General of Treaty and Law in the MOFCOM and as reprinted in its English version in Gallagher and Shan, *Chinese Investment Treaties* (n 34) 421–425. For a list of PRC BITs see Chinese Ministry of Commerce, 'List of Bilateral Investment Treaties Concluded by China (12 December 2016)' [Chinese] <http://tfs.mofcom.gov.cn/article/Nocategory/201111/20111107819474.shtml> accessed 30 March 2019.

542 Manjiao Chi, 'From Europeanization toward Americanization' (n 537) 159.

only open for disputes regarding the amount of compensation for expropriation (if at all) (ie 'quantum cases').[543] This type of dispute resolution provision was also included in many BITs concluded by the USSR and other Communist countries,[544] and represented 'general scepticism towards foreign investment, private enterprise and international arbitration, as well as (...) general concerns related to the erosion of State sovereignty'.[545]

As far as international dispute resolution was an option, treaties included 'fork-in the-road' clauses, ie the international route was cut, if domestic courts had already been addressed.[546] The agreed-upon international dispute resolution mechanism was always ad-hoc arbitration, under UNCITRAL Arbitration Rules or otherwise, while China had not yet ratified the ICSID Convention.[547] However, soon after China concluded its first BIT, clauses began to be included – via signed and annexed protocols or exchanges of letters – that foresaw a renegotiation of the matter of dis-

543 See eg Art 7 Agreement between the Government of the United Kingdom of Great Britain and Northern Ireland and the Government of the People's Republic of China concerning the Promotion and Reciprocal Protection of Investments (signed 15 May 1986, entered into force 15 May 1987) ('China-United Kingdom BIT 1986'). See also Berger, 'The Politics of China's Investment Treaty-Making Program' (n 34) 172–174, Kenneth J Vandevelde, *Bilateral Investment Treaties: History, Policy, Interpretation* (OUP 2010) 433; Paul Peters, 'Dispute Settlement Arrangements in Investment Treaties' (1991) 22 *Netherlands Yearbook of International Law* 91, 119, 129; Shu Zhang (n 537) 87–88.

544 See eg Art 7 Abkommen zwischen der Republik Österreich und der Union der Sozialistischen Sowjetrepubliken über die Förderung und den gegenseitigen Schutz von Investitionen samt Notenwechsel (signed 8 February 1990, entered into force 1 September 1991) ('Austria-Soviet Union BIT 1990'); Art 8 Accord entre l'Union économique belgo-luxembourgeoise et la République socialiste tchécoslovaque concernant la promotion et la protection réciproques des investissements (signed 24 April 1989, entered into force 13 February 1992) ('Belgium-Luxembourg Economic Union-Czech Republic / Slovakia BIT 1989'). See also August Reinisch, 'How Narrow are Narrow Dispute Settlement Clauses in Investment Treaties?' (2011) 2 *Journal of International Dispute Settlement* 115, 117.

545 Michael Hwang and Aloysius Chang, 'Government of the Lao People's Democratic Republic v Sanum Investments Ltd – A Tale of Two Letters' (2015) 30 *ICSID Review* 506, 520.

546 See eg Art 13 (2) and (3) Agreement between the Government of the Democratic Socialist Republic of Sri Lanka and the Government of the People's Republic of China on the Reciprocal Promotion and Protection of Investment (signed 13 March 1986, entered into force 25 March 1987) ('China-Sri Lanka BIT 1986').

547 UNCITRAL Arbitration Rules (n 523); Art 7 China-United Kingdom BIT 1986.

pute resolution after both states had become parties to the ICSID Convention (see eg the China-Singapore BIT 1985).[548]

China's BITs with developing states, Thailand being the first, were more encouraging on investment in preambles, but also in terms of how clauses eg on the definition of 'investment' and consultation processes were drafted.[549] By contrast, such BITs more strongly emphasized sovereignty. Some – eg with Sri Lanka – required specific host state approval before an investment could enjoy BIT protection, and explicitly reserved determination of an expropriation's legality only for domestic courts.[550] The only first-generation BIT with a Socialist state – the China-Romania BIT – required that disputes over the amount of compensation for expropriation are reviewed by a domestic body first, and if they are not resolved, they must be settled as a state-state matter rather than an investor-state dispute.[551]

IV.2.1.2.3. Second Generation – Access to ICSID

A second generation of Chinese BITs followed China's second Model BIT in 1989 (China Model BIT, Version II) and signature of the ICSID Convention in 1990.[552] On substantive provisions, China's second Model BIT and

548 Exchanges of Letters Ib and IIb on Art 13 Agreement between the Government of the People's Republic of China and the Government of the Republic of Singapore on the Promotion and Protection of Investments (signed 21 November 1985, entered into force 7 February 1986) ('China-Singapore BIT 1985'). See also Schill, 'Tearing Down the Great Wall' (n 521) 89–91; Guiguo Wang, 'Chinese Mechanisms for Resolving Investor-State Disputes' (2011) 1 *Jindal Journal of International Affairs* 204, 214; Jie Wang (n 524) 496.

549 See Gallagher and Shan, *Chinese Investment Treaties* (n 34) 37 and Preamble, Arts 1 (3) and 9 Agreement between the Government of the Kingdom of Thailand and the Government of the People's Republic of China for the Promotion and Protection of Investments (signed 12 March 1985, entered into force 13 December 1985, terminated, [regional] ASEAN-China Investment Agreement entered into force 1 January 2010) ('China-Thailand BIT 1985').

550 Arts 2 (1) and 6 (2) China-Sri Lanka BIT 1986.

551 See Gallagher and Shan, *Chinese Investment Treaties* (n 34) 37–38 and Art 4 (3) Agreement Between the Government of the People's Republic of China and the Government of Romania Concerning the Encouragement and Reciprocal Protection of Investments (signed 10 Feburary 1983, did not enter into force) ('China-Romania BIT 1983').

552 Chinese Model BIT II (1989) as drafted by the Directorate-General of Treaty and Law in the MOFCOM and as translated into English by Prof. Shan Wenhua and printed in Gallagher and Shan, *Chinese Investment Treaties* (n 34) 427–433.

following BITs in this generation changed in adding an umbrella clause and a (qualified, 'best effort') national treatment standard.[553]

The PRC's eventual signing and ratification of the ICSID Convention in 1990 and 1993, respectively, did not immediately lead to drastic change in ISDS provisions. Nonetheless, in 1993 BITs began to explicitly refer to ICSID instead of simply ad-hoc arbitration as an option for quantum cases, with the China-Lithuania BIT the first to do so.[554] However, there were exceptions to the new type of investment treaties and three subsequent BITs with Uruguay, Azerbaijan and Ecuador eg did not make any reference to ICSID.[555]

BITs continued to include fork-in-the-road clauses stating that investors could not address international investment arbitration if they had already submitted the case to a domestic court in the host state.[556] This was in line with eg Argentina's contemporary practice and similar phrasing in the En-

553 Arts 2 (2) and 3 (3) Chinese Model BIT II (1989) as drafted by the Directorate-General of Treaty and Law in the MOFCOM and as translated into English by Prof. Shan Wenhua and printed in Gallagher and Shan, *Chinese Investment Treaties* (n 34) 427–433. For pertinent national treatment clauses see eg Art 3 (4) China-Spain BIT 1992; Art 3 (3) Agreement Between the Government of the People's Republic of China and the Government of the Republic of Iceland Concerning the Promotion and Reciprocal Protection of Investments (signed 13 March 1994, entered into force 1 March 1997) ('China-Iceland BIT 1994'). See also Berger, 'The Politics of China's Investment Treaty-Making Program' (n 34) 172–173; Sauvant and Nolan (n 532) 922–924.

554 Art 8 (2) Agreement between the Government of the Republic of Lithuania and the Government of the People's Republic of China concerning the Encouragement and Reciprocal Protection of Investments (signed 8 November 1993, entered into force 1 June 1994) ('China-Lithuania BIT 1993').

555 Art 9 Agreement Between the Government of the People's Republic of China and the Government of the Oriental Republic of Uruguay Concerning the Encouragement and Reciprocal Protection of Investments (signed 2 December 1993, entered into force 1 December 1997) ('China-Uruguay BIT 1993'); Art 9 Agreement between the Government of the People's Republic of China and the Government of the Azerbaijan Republic concerning the Encouragement and Reciprocal Protection of Investments (signed 8 March 1994, entered into force 1 April 1995) ('Azerbaijan-China BIT 1994'); Art 9 Convenio entre el Gobierno de la República del Ecuador y el Gobierno de la Republica Popular de China para el Fomento y Proteccion Reciprocos de Inversiones (signed 21 March 1994, entered into force 1 July 1997) ('China-Ecuador BIT 1994'); see also Gallagher and Shan, *Chinese Investment Treaties* (n 34) 39, FN 186.

556 See eg Art 8 (2) and (3) Agreement between the Government of the People's Republic of China and the Government of the Republic of Slovenia concerning the encouragement and reciprocal protection of investments (signed, entered into force) ('China-Slovenia BIT 1993') – Art 8:

ergy Charter Treaty, a multilateral framework formed in 1991 that covers – inter alia – trade and investment issues in the energy realm.[557] Importantly, such clauses only apply when indeed the same parties submit the same dispute on account of the same cause of action, which arbitrators rarely determine to be the case.[558] China also upheld the limitation of international arbitration cases to disputes over the amount of compensation for expropriation, maintaining that no foreign authority should be able to determine 'public necessity' concerning ownership determinations.[559]

Moreover, accession to the ICSID Convention contributed – as did intensified competition for FDI from post-Communist Eastern European states and former Soviet republics, as well as Latin American nations[560] – to China much more actively pursuing BITs. Investment treaties with every external economic partner of any importance – except the US – were concluded in the following years.[561]

'2. If the dispute cannot be settled through negotiations within six months, either party to the dispute shall be entitled to submit the dispute to the competent courtof the Contracting state accepting the investment.
3. If a dispute involving the amount of compensation for expropriation cannot be settled within six months after resort to negotiations as specified in Paragraph I of this Article, it may be submitted at the request of either party to an ad hoc arbitrary tribunal. The provisions of this Paragraph shall not apply if the investor concerned has resorted to the procedure specified in the Paragraph 2 of this Article'.

557 Art 8 (2) Accord entre le gouvernement de la République française et le gouvernement de la république Argentine sur l'encouragement et la protection réciproques des investissements (signed 3 July 1991, entered into force 3 March 1993) ('Argentina-France BIT 1991'); Art 26 (3) (b) The Energy Charter Treaty (adopted 17 December 1994, entered into force 16 April 1998) 2080 UNTS 95 ('ECT'). See also Thomas Roe, Matthew Happold and James Dingemans QC, *Settlement of Investor-State Disputes under the Energy Charter Treaty* (CUP 2011) 146–149; Kaj Hobér, 'Investment Arbitration and the Energy Charter Treaty' (2010) 1 *Journal of International Dispute* Settlement 153, 163; Thomas W Wälde, 'Investment Arbitration Under the Energy Charter Treaty – From Dispute Settlement to Treaty Implementation' (1996) 12 *Arbitration International* 429, 460.

558 See eg *Lauder* (n 523) paras 156–166; *CMS Gas Transmission Company v Argentina*, ICSID Case No ARB/01/8, Decision on Jurisdiction (17 July 2003) paras 77–82; *Toto Costruzioni Generali SpA v The Republic of Lebanon*, ICSID Case No ARB/07/12, Decision on Jurisdiction (11 September 2009) paras 203–217.

559 See eg Art 9 (3) China-Iceland BIT 1994. See also Jane Y Willems, 'The Settlement of Investor State Disputes and China: New Developments on ICSID Jurisdiction' (2011) 8 *South Carolina Journal of International Law & Business* 3.

560 Gallagher and Shan, *Chinese Investment Treaties* (n 34) 41.

561 Guiguo Wang, 'Chinese Mechanisms' (n 533) 213.

IV.2.1.2.4. Third Generation – 'Any Dispute Concerning an Investment'

The third generation of PRC BITs starts with the Barbados-China BIT 1998 and the China-Botswana BIT 2000 (signed, but not in force),[562] which in turn followed the country's third Model BIT adopted in 1997.[563] These treaties grant access to ICSID arbitration for all investor-state disputes, breaking markedly with China's previous practice.[564]

This was partly a realization of developments in modern investment law, where direct expropriations – with only the quantum of compensation in dispute – had progressively become less relevant, replaced by the issue of indirect expropriation.[565] In 2008, the PRC had already entered into more than 40 BITs with open access to international arbitration – including twelve renegotiations or added protocols[566] and two FTAs.[567]

---

562 Art 9 (2) Barbados-China BIT 1998; Art 9 (1) and (3) Agreement between the Government of the Republic of Botswana and the Government of the People's Republic of China on Promotion and Protection of Investments (signed 12 June 2000, not in force) ('Botswana-China BIT 2000').

563 Chinese Model BIT III (1997) as drafted by the Directorate-General of Treaty and Law in the MOFCOM and as reprinted in its English version in Gallagher and Shan, *Chinese Investment Treaties* (n 34) 433–437.

564 For China's shift towards broad access to international arbitration see also Berger, 'The Politics of China's Investment Treaty-Making Program' (n 34) 174–175; Tong Qi, 'How Exactly does China Consent' (n 510) 271–272; Schill, 'Tearing Down the Great Wall' (n 521) 76, 91–92; Ku, 'China and the Future of International Adjudication' (n 32) 164; Tung and Cox-Alomar (n 508) 461–463; Jie Wang (n 524) 497–498; Willems (n 559) 4; Yang and Qin (n 512) 120.

565 Hwang and Chang, 'Government of the Lao People's Democratic Republic' (n 545) 520.

566 The pertinent Amendment Protocols were such to the China-Sweden BIT 1982 (signed 27 September 2004, not in force), the Agreement Between the Government of the People's Republic of China and the Government of Romania Concerning the Encouragement and Reciprocal Protection of Investments (signed 12 July 1994, entered into force 1 September 1995, Amendment Protocol signed 16 April 2007, entered into force 1 September 2008) ('China-Romania BIT 1994'), and the Agreement Between the Government of the People's Republic of China and the Government of the Republic of Cuba Concerning the Encouragement and Reciprocal Protection of Investments (signed 24 April 1995, entered into force 1 August 1996, Amendment Protocol signed 20 April 2007, entered into force 1 December 2008) ('China-Cuba BIT 1995').

567 See 1) Chapter 9 Free Trade Agreement between the Government of the Islamic Republic of Pakistan and the Government of the People's Republic of China (signed 24 November 2006, entered into force 1 July 2007) ('China-Pakistan FTA 2006'), and 2) Chapter 11 Free Trade Agreement between the Government of New Zealand and the Government of the People's Republic of China (signed

However, once again there were exceptions to the new practice, and some BITs – like the one concluded with Qatar in 1999 – still conformed to second- or even first-generation dispute settlement provisions.[568]

The new Chinese Model BIT – just like the previous ones – followed the shorter European model, instead of the 'more prescriptive' North American one. It largely comports with the European standard also on substantive provisions, but exhibits a number of specificities.[569]

First, in the definition of 'investment' a 'subject to local law' requirement has been retained (Art 1 (1) Chinese Model BIT, Version III), wherein only investments approved through China's 'one by one' admission system are eligible for BIT protection.[570]

Second, China's incomplete transformation to a market economy leads to measures that would be incompatible with national treatment and nondiscriminatory treatment, but are factored in by making national treatment subject to local laws and regulations or through 'grandfather clauses' – stronger protection than previous 'best effort' phrasing on national treatment.[571]

Deng Xiaoping had clarified the goal of creating a 'Socialist market economy' in 1992, and the constitution was amended accordingly in 1993,

---

7 April 2008, entered into force 1 October 2008) ('New Zealand-China FTA 2008').

568 Art 9 Agreement Between the Government of the People's Republic of China and the Government of the State of Qatar Concerning the Encouragement and Reciprocal Protection of Investments (signed 9 April 1999, entered into force 1 April 2000) ('China-Qatar BIT 1999'). In the China-Qatar BIT, in line with the first generation of Chinese BITs, only ad hoc arbitration can be accessed, not ICSID, and only if the dispute is about the amount of compensation for expropriation. See also eg Agreement between the Government of Namibia and the Government of the People's Republic of China for the Promotion and Protection of Investments (signed 17 November 2005, not in force) ('China-Namibia BIT 2005'); Agreement between the Government of the Republic of Guinea and the Government of the People's Republic of China on the Promotion and Protection of Investments (signed 18 November 2005, not in force) ('China-Guinea BIT 2005').

569 See also Gallagher and Shan, *Chinese Investment Treaties* (n 34) 43–44, 433.

570 Art 1 (1) Chinese Model BIT Version III (1997).

571 Art 3 (2) and Protocol, point 3 Agreement between the People's Republic of China and the Federal Republic of Germany on the Encouragement and Reciprocal Protection of Investments (signed 1 December 2003, entered into force 11 November 2005) ('China-Germany BIT 2003'). See also Wenhua Shan, Norah Gallagher and Sheng Zhang, 'National Treatment for Foreign Investment in China: A Changing Landscape' (2012) 27 *ICSID Review* 120, 134–136.

whereby foreign-invested enterprises were to gradually receive 'national treatment.' However, the legacy of the planned economy persisted (and still does) in some ways.[572]

Since the shift in policy, national treatment clauses were included in many Chinese BITs, while investors might try to use MFN clauses in other BITs to attain national treatment. They might also try to access unqualified national treatment via corresponding clauses – first included in the China-Seychelles BIT 2007 (not in force).[573] On the domestic level, a more recent development can be seen in the government's efforts to in turn 'cut certain incentives previously enjoyed only by foreign investors', ie 'superior-national treatment'.[574]

Third, importantly, the Model BIT continued to include a fork-in-the-road clause on dispute resolution, demanding a choice between domestic courts or ICSID arbitration where the dispute cannot be settled within six months (Chinese Model BIT, Version III, Article 9 (2)).[575] A local administrative review process, which may take three months, can be required in third-generation BITs, if ICSID arbitration is chosen (Chinese Model BIT, Version III, Article 9 (2)).[576] Investors' rights concerning expropriation, transfer rights, FET, as well as full protection did not significantly change compared to earlier Chinese BITs.[577] Third-generation BITs concluded

---

572 1993 Amendment to the Constitution of the People's Republic of China (adopted 29 March 1993 by the Eighth National People's Congress). See Gallagher and Shan, *Chinese Investment Treaties* (n 34) 7–8.

573 See Shan, Gallagher and Zhang (n 571) 136, who cite Art 5 Agreement between the People's Republic of China and the Republic of Seychelles on the Promotion and Protection of Investments (signed 10 February 2007, not in force) ('China-Seychelles BIT 2007') – Art 5: 'Each Contracting Party shall apply on its territory to the investors of the other Party, with respect to their investments and activities related to the investments, a treatment not less favourable than that granted to its investors, or the treatment granted to the investors of the most favoured nation, if the latter is more favourable (…).'.

574 Shan, Gallagher and Zhang (n 571) 121 citing the example of urban maintenance and construction tax as well as educational surcharges being levied on foreign invested enterprises starting in December 2010.

575 Art 9 (2) Chinese Model BIT Version III (1997).

576 Art 9 (2) Chinese Model BIT Version III (1997); As for BIT provisions along these lines see eg Art 9 (2) and Protocol, point 6 China-Germany BIT 2003; Tung and Cox-Alomar (n 508) 462; Jie Wang (n 524) 498; Willems (n 559) 15–17.

577 See also Gallagher and Shan, *Chinese Investment Treaties* (n 34) 382.

with Cyprus, the Netherlands and Germany in the early-2000s already conform to standard treaty practice in 'all major aspects'.[578]

The sustained shift to a more liberal attitude regarding investor-state arbitration in the 2000s was mainly driven by the rise in Chinese outward foreign investment – eventually making it one of the most important home states globally. Such investment was supported by the government's 'going abroad' policy – put forward in 1998 and incorporated in the 10th Five-Year Plan in 2001 – which encouraged Chinese companies to support national development by investing abroad.[579]

IV.2.1.2.5. Fourth Generation – Americanization

China's policy of state support for outward investment was later reinforced 1) in 2008 to make use of the opportunity of cheap deals abroad following the global economic crisis,[580] and 2) in 2013 with the declaration of the 'Silk Road Economic Belt'- and 'Maritime Silk Road'-initiatives (now jointly as the 'Belt and Road-Initiative'). The latter encourage Chinese outward investment with a focus on energy, transport, industry, telecommunications and digital economy.[581] Already around the financial crisis in 2008, China achieved the status of a major investment-exporting country. At important party gatherings, such as the CPC's 18th National Congress in 2012

---

578 Agreement between the Government of the People's Republic of China and the Government of the Republic of Cyprus for the Reciprocal Promotion and Protection of Investments (signed 17 January 2001, entered into force 29 April 2002) ('China-Cyprus BIT 2001'); Agreement on encouragement and reciprocal protection of investments between the Government of the People's Republic of China and the Government of the Kingdom of the Netherlands (signed 26 November 2001, entered into force 1 August 2004) ('China-Netherlands BIT 2001'); China-Germany BIT 2003; see also Gallagher and Shan, *Chinese Investment Treaties* (n 34) 382–383..

579 Premier of the State Council Zhu Rongji, 'Report on the Outline of the Tenth Five-Year Plan for National Economic and Social Development (2001)' (Beijing, 5 March 2001) <http://www.gov.cn/english/official/2005-07/29/content_18334.htm> accessed 1 April 2018; National People's Congress, '国民经济和社会发展第十个五年计划纲要' (Tenth Five-Year Plan for National Economic and Social Development) (Beijing, 17 March 2001) <www.people.com.cn/GB/shizheng/16/20010318/419582.html> accessed 1 April 2018; Shan, Gallagher and Zhang (n 571) 123–124.

580 Eder, *China-Russia Relations* (n 170).

581 Thomas S Eder and Jacob Mardell, 'MERICS BRI Tracker' *MERICS* (Berlin, 2019) <https://www.merics.org/en/bri-tracker> accessed 30 October 2019.

and the Third Plenary Session of the 18th Central Committee in 2013, the Chinese leadership lamented sharply rising risks to outward investment, and decided to hasten its investment treaty program worldwide – no longer seeing a North-South contradiction – as well as potentially setting up funds to support investors in costly arbitrations.[582]

Against this backdrop, a fourth generation of BITs started to take shape,[583] beginning with the China-Mexico BIT 2008 and the investment chapter of the China-New Zealand FTA 2008,[584] albeit only gradually and of course again overlapping with examples of previous generations of BITs.[585] China remained very active in concluding further investment treaties, and as of the end of 2018 – second only to Germany – had concluded BITs with more than 130 states, with over 110 being in effect at the time. These treaties included sixteen of the other nineteen G20 members, and over 60 with open access to international arbitration. Next to its BITs, China also concluded further international investment and trade agree-

582 Tong 彤 Qi 漆, '论中国海外投资者对国际投资仲裁机制的利用' (Reviewing Chinese overseas investors' use of international investment arbitration) [2014] (3) *Dongfang Faxue* 89, 90, 95–96.

583 For a similar approach see also Manjiao Chi, 'From Europeanization toward Americanization' (n 537) 163.

584 Agreement between the Government of the United Mexican States and the Government of the People's Republic of China on the Promotion and Reciprocal Protection of Investments (signed 11 July 2008, entered into force 6 June 2009) ('China-Mexico BIT 2008'); Chapter 11 New Zealand-China FTA 2008. The texts of the following investment treaties are not available online China-Turkey BIT 2015, China-Congo DR BIT 2011, China-Chad BIT 2010, China-Bahamas BIT 2009, China-Costa Rica BIT 2007.

585 See eg Agreement between the Swiss Federal Council and the Government of the People's Republic of China on the Promotion and Reciprocal Protection of Investments (signed 27 January 2009, entered into force 13 April 2010) ('China-Switzerland BIT 2009'); Accord sur la promotion et la protection réciproques des investissements entre le gouvernement de la république du Mali et le gouvernement de la république populaire de Chine (signed 12 February 2009, entered into force 16 July 2009) ('China-Mali BIT 2009'); Agreement between the Government of the People's Republic of China and the Government of Malta on the Promotion and Protection of Investments (signed 22 February 2009, entered into force 1 April 2009) ('China-Malta BIT 2009'); Agreement between the Government of the People's Republic of China and the Government of Libya on the Promotion and Protection of Investments (signed 4 August 2010, not in force) ('China-Libya BIT 2010').

ments with substantive rules on investment.[586] Moreover, the Chinese government was in negotiations for BITs with both the EU and US.[587]

Chinese investment treaties of the fourth generation are – inter alia – leaving the European model behind, and are shifting to the American model. This typically means that they are much longer, detailed and self-contained, include provisions on market access – here China is most reticent – and pre-establishment protection, as well as general exceptions, and arguably have advantages in enforcement. They usually expand the European model simple ISDS clause to a more detailed one or even a separate section.[588]

---

586 Chinese FTAs with substantive rules on investment: China-Pakistan FTA 2006; New Zealand-China FTA 2008; Free Trade Agreement between the Government of the People's Republic of China and the Government of the Republic of Peru (signed 28 April 2009, entered into force 1 March 2010) ('China-Peru FTA 2009'); Free Trade Agreement between the Government of the People's Republic of China and the Government of the Republic of Costa Rica (signed 1 April 2010, entered into force 1 August 2011) ('China-Costa Rica FTA 2010'); Free Trade Agreement between the Government of the People's Republic of China and the Government of the Republic of Korea (signed 1 June 2015, entered into force 20 December 2015) ('China-Republic of Korea FTA 2015'); Free Trade Agreement between the Government of Australia and the Government of the People's Republic of China (signed 17 June 2015, entered into force 20 December 2015) ('Australia-China FTA 2015'); Investment agreements with more than one partner country: Agreement on Investment of the Framework Agreement on Comprehensive Economic Cooperation between the People's Republic of China and the Association of Southeast Asian Nations (signed 15 August 2009, entered into force 1 January 2010) ('ASEAN-China Investment Agreement 2009'); Agreement among the Government of Japan, the Government of the Republic of Korea and the Government of the People's Republic of China for the Promotion, Facilitation and Protection of Investment (signed 13 May 2012, entered into force 17 May 2014) ('Investment promotion and protection agreement between Japan, Republic of Korea and China 2012').

587 David Baron and others, 'ICSID Arbitration Initiated Against China as Negotiations Move Ahead on U.S.-China Bilateral Investment Treaty' (*The National Law Review*, 12 December 2014) <http://www.natlawreview.com/article/icsid-arbitration-initiated-against-china-negotiations-move-ahead-us-china-bilateral> (accessed 30 March 2019); UNCTAD – Investment Policy Hub, *China* <http://investmentpolicyhub.unctad.org/IIA/CountryBits/42> (accessed 30 March 2019); Chinese Ministry of Commerce, 'List of Bilateral Investment Treaties Concluded by China (12 December 2016)' [Chinese] <http://tfs.mofcom.gov.cn/article/Nocategory/201111/20111107819474.shtml> accessed 30 March 2019.

588 See also Manjiao Chi, 'From Europeanization toward Americanization' (n 537) 164–165; Manjiao Chi, 'A Long March towards Compatibility, Coherence and

Several factors may be behind the phenomenon of Americanization. First, China only began to negotiate investment treaties with North American states (including the US) in the late 2000s. These states' Model BITs could develop influence on China, where earlier there had only been European Model BITs' influence. Second, Chinese negotiators might have found European model BITs easier to handle while they remained relatively inexperienced. Third, the Chinese government grew more interested in market access for its investors as well as further improved investment protection – even vis-à-vis the most advanced economies, including the US – as China became a leading capital-exporting country.[589] The latter trend also owes to ballooning Chinese investment in risk-prone environments, partly politically incentivized in connection with China's infrastructure foreign policy as well as its drive to secure various raw materials. Regarding market access, another pertinent issue is industrialized economies barring certain Chinese enterprises from a number of investments citing national security reasons. Fourth, Chinese investment treaty negotiators have lauded elements of the American model that they deem more balanced in the sense of protecting public interest regulatory space as well as investments.[590]

Those treaties not involving a North American state party are particularly supportive of the hypothesis of a fourth generation of Chinese investment treaties.[591] Evidently, such new patterns are not merely the result of North American Model BITs being the basis of negotiations.

Examples of American model stand-alone ISDS sections or comprehensive ISDS provisions can be found in Chapter III Section 1 China-Mexico BIT 2008, Part C Canada-China BIT 2012, and Article 15 Investment promotion and protection agreement between Japan, the Republic of Korea and China 2012,[592] but also in Chapter 11 Section 2 China-New Zealand FTA 2008, Article 12.12 China-Republic of Korea FTA 2015, and Chapter

---

Consistency: the Future of China's Investment Agreements' (2015) 18 *Zeitschrift für Europarechtliche Studien* 373, 380.

589 See also Manjiao Chi, 'From Europeanization toward Americanization' (n 537) 163–164, 165–167, who cites on Chinese government strategy Chinese Ministry of Commerce, '加强对我国企业海外利益的保障' (Enhancing the protection of Chinese enterprises' overseas investment) (Beijing, 22 October 2014) <http://finance.china.com.cn/news/20141022/2742563.shtml> accessed 30 March 2019.

590 Yongjie Li (n 531) 175.

591 See eg Chapter 9 Section B Australia-China FTA 2015.

592 Chapter III Section 1 China-Mexico BIT 2008; Part C Agreement Between the Government of Canada and the Government of the People's Republic of China

9 Section B China-Australia FTA 2015.[593] Additional ISDS provisions of this generation are those in the China-Colombia BIT 2008, China-Uzbekistan BIT 2011 and China-Tanzania BIT 2013,[594] moreover in the ASEAN-China Investment Agreement 2009.[595] Such provisions are more tailored in the sense that they extensively describe certain breaches of the agreement, which can lead to investment arbitration.[596]

In contrast to most Chinese BITs, the Canada-China BIT 2012 in Article 33 also contains a general exceptions clause similar to Article XX GATT.[597] A less extensive general exceptions provision can also be found in the China-Australia FTA 2015,[598] while the China-Colombia BIT 2008, the Investment promotion and protection agreement between Japan, the Republic of Korea and China 2012 and China-Republic of Korea FTA 2015 only include security exceptions.[599]

Elements of pre-investment protection also already appeared in China's first FTA with an OECD country, the China-New Zealand FTA 2008. This was the first Chinese treaty to have the MFN and transfer clauses apply to

---

for the Promotion and Reciprocal Protection of Investments (signed 9 September 2012, entered into force 1 October 2014) ('Canada-China BIT 2012'); Art 15 Investment promotion and protection agreement between Japan, Republic of Korea and China 2012.

593 Chapter 11 Section 2 New Zealand-China FTA 2008; Art 12.12 China-Republic of Korea FTA 2015; Chapter 9 Section B Australia-China FTA 2015.

594 Art 9 Bilateral Agreement for the Promotion and Protection of Investments between the Government of the Republic of Colombia and the Government of the People's Republic of China on (signed 22 November 2008, entered into force 2 July 2013) ('China-Colombia BIT 2008'); Art 12 Agreement between the Government of the People's Republic of China and the Government of the Republic of Uzbekistan on the Promotion and Protection of Investments (signed 19 April 2011, entered into force 1 September 2011) ('China-Uzbekistan BIT 2011'); Art 13 Agreement between the Government of the People's Republic of China and the Government of the United Republic of Tanzania concerning the Promotion and Reciprocal Protection of Investments (signed 24 March 2013, entered into force 17 April 2014) ('China-Tanzania BIT 2013').

595 Art 14 ASEAN-China Investment Agreement 2009.

596 Shu Zhang (n 537) 88.

597 Art 33 Canada-China BIT 2012; Art 22 General Agreement on Tariffs and Trade (adopted 15 April 1994, entered into force 1 January 1995) 1867 UNTS 187 ('GATT 1994').

598 9.8 Australia-China FTA 2015.

599 Art 12 China-Colombia BIT 2008; Art 18 Investment promotion and protection agreement between Japan, Republic of Korea and China 2012; Chapter 12 Art 12.14 China-Republic of Korea FTA 2015.

the 'establishment of investment'.[600] Later on, similar clauses have been included in the ASEAN-China Investment Agreement 2009, the China-Uzbekistan BIT 2011, the China-Tanzania BIT 2013, and the Australia-China FTA 2015.[601]

Since 2013, the Chinese government first moved towards a cautiously liberalized 'positive list' approach somewhat 'similar to the [national treatment] obligations under GATS'[602], and then switched to a 'negative list' approach (again being gradually further liberalized), concerning how inbound investments and the pre-establishment phase are handled.[603]

At the same time, – inter alia – Article 18 Canada-China BIT 2012 has delivered on giving state parties a greater role in treaty interpretation,[604] which Chinese scholars had recommended (and therein praised Article 28.2 US Model BIT 2012).[605]

---

600 Arts 135, 139 and 142 New Zealand-China FTA 2008. See also Gallagher and Shan, *Chinese Investment Treaties* (n 34) 29, 101, 104.

601 Arts 1 (e), 5 and 10 ASEAN-China Investment Agreement 2009; Arts 1 (2) and 4 (1) China-Uzbekistan BIT 2011; Arts 1 (2) and 4 (1) China-Tanzania BIT 2013; Chapter 9 Arts 9.1 (e) and 9.4 (1) Australia-China FTA 2015. For a somewhat more cautious version see Chapter 12 Arts 12.1, 12.2 (2) and 12.4 (1) China-Republic of Korea FTA 2015.

602 Shan, Gallagher and Zhang (n 571) 144.

603 Alan Wang and others, 'China's new "negative list"' *Lexology* (Beijing, 11 July 2018) <https://www.lexology.com/library/detail.aspx?g=5f3db2d8-3bdb-40e8-a238-de41509373ee&utm_source=lexology+daily+newsfeed&utm_medium=html+email&utm_campaign=lexology+subscriber+daily+feed&utm_content=lexology+daily+newsfeed+2018-07-16&utm_term> accessed 30 March 2019. China used to follow a restrictive 'positive list-approach', where only investments in limited specifically listed sectors were open for foreign investment, with others being subject to approval requirements. Now it has reversed this logic, with investments only barred or restricted in sectors that are expressly listed.

604 Art 18 Canada-China BIT 2012.

605 See also Chapter V.2.2. See eg Yongjie Li (n 531) 178; Art 28 (2) US Model BIT 2012. For an example of an early provision on a consultation mechanism leading to non-binding joint statements that tribunals have taken into account see eg Art 9 Agreement on encouragement and reciprocal protection of investments between the Kingdom of the Netherlands and the Czech and Slovak Federal Republic (signed 29 April 1991, entered into force 1 October 1992) ('Netherlands-Czechoslovakia BIT 1991') as referred to in *CME Czech Republic BV v The Czech Republic*, UNCITRAL, Final Award (14 March 2003) paras 87–93, 437, 50.

These developments – they might be further spurred by treaty negotiations with both the EU and US[606] – point to two things. First, China's priorities are shifting, as the importance of access and protection for China's outbound investment rises, and impulses are necessary to keep inbound investments flowing. Beijing has become willing to both open up some more and grant additional protection. Second, China moves to in parallel gain additional predictability and control, by adding detail, exceptions and interpretation prerogatives for the contracting states.

IV.2.1.2.6. Comparative View – Last BRIC standing: Chinese exception to the restrictive turn

The rationale for BITs was to encourage developed country investments in developing countries. The latter were thus involved from the start, as in the aforementioned Germany-Pakistan BIT 1959. Such so-called 'North-South BITs' remained the norm for the longest time, although 'South-South BITs' also appeared early on beginning with the Kuwait-Iraq BIT 1964.[607] Included provisions have generally been very similar to such in 'North-South BITs',[608] although some nuance is warranted.[609] Especially in Latin America, governments long subscribed to the so-called 'Calvo Doctrine,' holding that aliens could not receive better treatment than nationals and would therefore only be able to seek redress through local authorities. These states were then reticent about investment arbitration. They mostly

606 European Commission, 'EU-China Investment Agreement: Report of the 16th Round of Negotiations' (Brussels, 12–15 December 2017) <http://trade.ec.europa.eu/doclib/docs/2017/december/tradoc_156520.pdf> accessed 30 March 2019; Chinese Ministry of Commerce, 'The 29th China-U.S. BIT Negotiation Held in Washington, 26 September 2016' (Beijing, 26 September 2016) <http://english.mofcom.gov.cn/article/newsrelease/significantnews/201609/20160901404077.shtml> accessed 30 March 2019. See also Bath (n 458) 239–240; Shu Zhang (n 537) 80; Eric Pekar, 'The Chinese Investment Regime and the US-China BIT Negotiations', in Wenhua Shan (ed), *China and International Investment Law: Twenty Years of ICSID Membership* (Brill 2015) 283.

607 Protocol between the Government of the State of Kuwait and the Republic of Iraq on the Promotion of the Movement of Capital and Investments between the Two Countries (signed 25 October 1964, entered into force 7 June 1966, terminated 4 February 2015, replaced by the Kuwait-Iraq BIT 2013) ('Kuwait-Iraq BIT 1964'). See also Poulsen (n 34) 186.

608 Dolzer and Schreuer (n 523) 7–8.

609 Poulsen (n 34) 198–199.

departed from such thinking in the 1990s, but the so-called 'Bolivarian Socialist' states returned to it in the 2000s, and Venezuela, Bolivia and Ecuador even denounced the ICSID Convention,[610] and partly revoked BITs.[611]

The large emerging economies grouped under the BRICS label – Brazil, Russia, India, China and South Africa – are arguably a separate group, and its other representatives are most comparable to and relevant for the Chinese experience and development.[612] These countries are (or were) the largest developing or transitioning economies in their respective continents. Moreover, they have met in formal summits since 2009 – with South Africa joining in 2010 – purported to already have congruent convictions about the nature of international relations and goals for the international order, as well as declaring to coordinate henceforth.[613] In the fol-

610 See also Daniel Tavela Luís and José Augusto Fontoura Costa, 'Repúblicas bolivarianas e o ICSID: será que o inimigo não é outro?' (2016) XVI *Anuario Mexicano de Derecho Internacional* 189, 190; Shan, Gallagher and Zhang (n 571) 122, FN 13.

611 See also Jose Gustavo Prieto Muñoz, 'Ecuador's 2017 termination of treaties: How not to exit the international investment regime' (2017) 14 *Brazilian Journal of International* Law 178. On countries taking different decisions on the matter, ie Argentina maintaining its BITs while Ecuador terminated them see Julia Calvert, 'Constructing investor rights? Why some states (fail to) terminate bilateral investment treaties' (2018) 25 *Review of International Political Economy* 75.

612 The BRICS are an association of large emerging economies. Several years after the term BRIC was coined by a Goldman Sachs manager in 2001, for the central emerging econmies of the time – Brazil, Russia, India and China – the respective governments began to meet informally. A first official summit was held in 2009, and South Africa was inducted as fifth member of the group in 2010. The annual summits have since become a fixture, and the 'New Development Bank' (multilateral development bank) and the 'BRICS Contingent Reserve Arrangement' (short-term lender) have been set up (both in force since 2015). For further literature on the BRICS see Kevin Gray and Craig N Murphy, 'Rising powers and the future of global governance' (2013) 34 *Third World Quarterly* 183; Andrew Hurrell, 'Lula's Brazil: A rising power, but going where?' (2008) 107 *Current History* 51; S Neil Macfarlane, 'The "R" in BRICs: Is Russia an emerging power?' (2006) 82 *International Affairs* 41; Amrita Narlikar, 'India rising: Responsible to whom?' (2013) 89 *International Affairs* 561; Ian Taylor, 'Is Africa Rising?' (2014) 21 *Brown Journal of World Affairs* 143.

613 See eg President of Russia, 'Joint Statement of the BRIC Countries' Leaders' (Moscow, 16 January 2009) <http://en.kremlin.ru/supplement/209> accessed 30 March 2019. See also annual summit statements and declarations since 2009 up to the Xinhua, 'BRICS Leaders Xiamen Declaration 2017' *Xinhua* (Xiamen, 4 September 2017) <http://www.xinhuanet.com/english/2017-09/04/c_136583396_2.htm> accessed 30 March 2019.

lowing, this chapter will briefly discuss whether and how the other BRICS countries fit with the above described trend lines, and highlight some similarities and differences with China.

The Russian Federation has signed but not ratified the ICSID Convention, and has seen more than 60 BITs enter into force[614] – the first being the Soviet Union's treaty with Canada in June 1991.[615] Russia has been party to more than 20 investment arbitrations as respondent (the first in 1996), while its investors initiated more than ten cases (the first in 2004).[616] Many of the country's BITs contained narrow dispute resolution clauses, limiting investment arbitration to disputes about the amount or mode of compensation for expropriation,[617] while various tribunals have differed as to whether these clauses are to be interpreted narrowly or broadly.[618] More recent BITs have included broad arbitration clauses.[619] On substantive

---

614 UNCTAD Investment Policy Hub, 'Russia – BITs' <http://investmentpolicyhub.unctad.org/IIA/CountryBits/175#iiaInnerMenu> accessed 30 March 2019.

615 Agreement between the Government of Canada and the Government of the Union of Soviet Socialist Republics for the Promotion and Reciprocal Protection of Investments (signed 20 November 1989, entered into force 27 June 1991) ('Canada-Soviet Union BIT 1989'). The Russian Federation took on the Soviet Union's rights and obligations under international treaties, once the latter was dissolved.

616 UNCTAD Investment Policy Hub, 'Russia – Investment Arbitration' <http://investmentpolicyhub.unctad.org/ISDS/CountryCases/175?partyRole=2> accessed 30 March 2019.

617 See eg Art 10 Accord entre les Gouvernements du Royaume de Belgique et du Grand-Duche de Luxembourg, et le Gouvernement de L'Union des Republiques Socialistes Sovietiques, Concernant L'Encouragement Et la Protection Reciproques des Investissements (signed 9 February 1989, entered into force 18 August 1991) ('Belgium-Luxembourg Economic Union-Soviet Union BIT 1989'); Art 10 Convenio de Fomento y Protección Recíproca de Inversiones entre España y la Unión de Repúblicas Socialistas Soviéticas (signed 26 October 1990, entered into force 28 November 1991) ('Spain-Soviet Union BIT 1990').

618 For a narrow interpretation see eg *Berschader* (n 523) para 153. For a broad interpretation see eg *Renta 4 SVSA and others v Russian Federation*, SCC Case No V024/2007, Award on Preliminary Objections (20 March 2009) para 31. See also Irmgard Marboe, 'Quasar de Valores SICAV SA and others v The Russian Federation – Another Chapter of the Yucos Affair' (2013) 28 *ICSID Review* 247, 248; Anatole Boute, 'The Protection of Russian Investments in the EU Energy Market: A Case in Support of Russia's Ratification of the Energy Charter Treaty' (2014) 29 *ICSID Review* 525, 530–531.

619 See eg Art 9 Agreement between the Government of the Russian Federation and the Government of the People's Republic of China on the Promotion and Reciprocal Protection Of Investments (signed 9 November 2006, entered into force 1 May 2009) ('China-Russia BIT 2006').

clauses, Russian BITs have tended towards international standard practice, including eg FET, national treatment, MFN, and full protection and security clauses, even if limited in certain ways.[620]

Importantly, Russia released new guidelines for future investment treaties in 2016, however, which supersede earlier Model BITs.[621] The new guidelines retain broad access to arbitration, but deviate in many important ways from previous partly liberal practice on substantive provisions. They – inter alia – require that the investor carries out 'substantial business activity' in the host state, and is a national or a company owned or controlled by nationals of the home state. Protection will only be accorded to investments in specific assets listed in an Annex to the respective BIT, while sectors like utilities are excluded.[622] Furthermore, FET clauses are to be replaced with clauses prohibiting arbitrary treatment. Full protection and security clauses are to be deleted, while umbrella clauses had not been in previous Model BITs either. State measures are listed that are not to be considered as expropriation. The guidelines also specify that MFN clauses cannot be used to import dispute resolution clauses, and introduce a statute of limitations of two years for arbitration. Finally, the guidelines introduce the option of state party consultations – which can be initiated after notice of arbitration was submitted – that 1) block the commencement

620 See eg Arts 2 and 3 Agreement between the Government of the Kingdom of Denmark and the Government of the Russian Federation concerning the Promotion and Reciprocal Protection of Investments (signed 4 November 1993, entered into force 26 August 1998) ('Denmark-Russia BIT 1993').

621 Government of the Russian Federation, 'Decision No 992 – On the conclusion of international treaties of the Russian Federation for the promotion and protection of investments (adopted 30 September 2016)' <http://pravo.gov.ru/proxy/ips/?docbody=&prevDoc=102071479&backlink=1&&nd=102412234> accessed 3 May 2018 [Russian] ('Russian Investment Treaty Guidelines 2016'). See also Model BIT (approved by Resolution of the government of the Russian Federation of 11 June 1992 No 395, as amended on 26 June 1995); Model BIT (approved by Resolution of the government of the Russian Federation of 9 June 2001 No 465, as amended on 11 April 2002 and 17 December 2010). See also Joel Dahlquist, 'Russia sets out new guidelines for contents of future investment treaties' *IAReporter* (Santa Monica, 26 October 2016) <https://www.iareporter.com/articles/russia-sets-out-new-guidelines-for-negotiation-of-future-investment-treaties/> accessed 3 May 2018.

622 See eg General Approaches II.10, III.15 and V Russian Investment Treaty Guidelines 2016.

of an arbitration or suspend an ongoing arbitration, and 2) can lead to a binding interpretation of BIT provisions raised in the dispute.[623]

Compared to China there are some similarities, such as the establishment of a large BIT network starting in the 1980s, the transition from restricted to broader arbitration clauses, and years of fairly standard practice on substantive provisions. However, there are crucial differences. First, Russia was part of investment arbitrations much sooner after its first BIT came into effect, and a much larger caseload accumulated. Second, Russia took a restrictive turn with its new guidelines on investment treaties in 2016, which includes strongly limiting or even deleting core substantive provisions. This strongly contrasts with China's fourth-generation BITs,[624] and marks a clear parting of ways in the two countries' approaches.

The Indian government opted for liberalizing the economy in 1991, and concluded India's first BIT in 1994.[625] Thereafter, a large network of BITs – more than 70 have entered into force – was nonetheless built up, and Delhi opted for liberal protection standards to attract investment.[626] India, which has not ratified the ICSID Convention, was thereafter the host state in 21 investment arbitrations (first in 2003), and the home state in four such cases (first in 2000).[627] It was thus first on the home state side, and India was still a capital-exporting country at the time of its previous Model BIT in 2003, only later receiving massive investment inflows. Case numbers picked up since 2011, and India became one of the most frequently challenged host states, whereas investors – inter alia – addressed retrospective taxes and the cancellation of telecom licenses.[628] Especially *White Industries v India* caused a major debate, wherein a large amount of compen-

---

623 See also Evgeniya Rubinina and Noah Rubins, 'Russia – Overview of Investment Treaty Programme' *Global Arbitration Review* (London, 21 October 2016) <http://globalarbitrationreview.com/jurisdiction/2000149/russia> accessed 5 May 2017.

624 See Chapter IV.2.1.2.5.

625 India-UK BIT 1994.

626 UNCTAD Investment Policy Hub, 'India – BITs' <http://investmentpolicyhub.unctad.org/IIA/CountryBits/96#iiaInnerMenu> accessed 20 April 2018.

627 UNCTAD Investment Policy Hub, 'India – Investment Arbitration' <http://investmentpolicyhub.unctad.org/ISDS/CountryCases/96?partyRole=2> accessed 20 April 2018.

628 Prabhash Ranjan, 'India and Bilateral Investment Treaties – A Changing Landscape' (2014) 29 *ICSID Review* 419.

sation was granted on account of delays in the Indian judiciary.[629] This development led the government to rethink its approach and adopt a new Model BIT 2015 that is substantially more restrictive than its precursor and India's previous BIT practice.[630] As opposed to most of India's international investment agreements, this Model BITs preamble notes securing regulatory space as one of the objectives.[631]

With its new Model BIT that will inform negotiations for BITs with the US and Canada, Delhi opted for a much longer and detailed treaty text, in that sense a more 'American' one. It narrowed the scope of 'investor' to natural persons, and legal entities 'owned or controlled' by a natural person and conducting 'real and substantial business operations' in the host state, that made, 'own' or 'control' an investment.[632] It follows that holding companies and minority shareholders are to be excluded. Required 'real and substantial business operations' were connected to long-term capital commitment, staff size, entrepreneurial risk and 'substantial contribution to the development of the host State through operations along with the transfer of technological know-how'.[633]

India also made the state's 'public purpose' defense on expropriation non-reviewable, and taxation measures non-justiciable.[634] It deleted MFN, full protection and security, and umbrella clauses, and replaced the FET clause with a narrower 'standard of treatment' clause. India's earlier Model BIT 2003 had contained an MFN clause, as many of its BITs did.[635] An MFN clause had allowed for the importation of an 'effective means' obliga-

---

629 *White Industries Australia Limited v The Republic of India*, UNCITRAL, Final Award (30 November 2011). See also Grant Hanessian and Kabir Duggal, 'The 2015 Indian Model BIT: Is This Change the World Wishes to See?' (2015) 30 *ICSID Review* 729, 730–731; Tania Voon and Andrew D Mitchell, 'Denunciation, Termination and Survival: The Interplay of Treaty Law and International Investment Law' (2016) 31 *ICSID Review* 413, 424.

630 Government of India, 'India Model BIT 2015' <https://www.mygov.in/sites/default/files/master_image/Model%20Text%20for%20the%20Indian%20Bilateral%20Investment%20Treaty.pdf> accessed 30 March 2019 ('India Model BIT 2015'). See also Aniruddha Rajput, 'India's shifting treaty practice: a comparative analysis of the 2003 and 2015 Model BITs' (2016) 7 *Jindal Global Law Review* 201.

631 Preamble India Model BIT 2015; Azernoosh Bazrafkan, 'The (R)evolution of Indian model bilateral investment treaty: escaping liability without mitigating risks' (2016) 7 *Jindal Global Law Review* 245, 246.

632 Art 1.9 India Model BIT 2015.

633 Art 1.2.1 India Model BIT 2015.

634 Arts 2.6 (iv) and 5.5 India Model BIT 2015.

635 India Model BIT 2015; Italaw, 'India Model BIT 2003' Art 4 (2) <https://www.italaw.com/sites/default/files/archive/ita1026.pdf> accessed 30 March 2019 ('India

tion in *White Industries v India*, making the issue sensitive.[636] Moreover, wide-ranging (and self-judging) 'exceptions' are introduced to emphasize sovereign prerogatives ranging from 'essential security interests' to 'improving working conditions' and 'protecting public morals or maintaining public order'.[637]

Investor-state arbitration is retained – in a separate chapter on dispute settlement such as in American model BITs – but for it to be accessible, several preconditions have to be fulfilled (which would take no less than two years to fulfill).[638] The pertinent 'claim' has to be submitted to the domestic court system within one year of when the investor was or should have been aware of the treaty breach. If not satisfied, the investor has to seek amicable resolution for at least one year, before a 'notice of dispute' can be submitted, but only if no more than eighteen months have elapsed from the conclusion of domestic proceedings, or no more than three years from acquiring knowledge of the dispute (or when it should have been acquired), whichever is later. Ninety days after the 'notice,' a claim may be filed.[639]

India's treaty practice differs in important ways from that of China. First, India concluded its first BIT much later, when China was already ratifying large numbers of (for China) second-generation BITs – although case law with Indian participation appeared several years earlier. Second, after they shared a somewhat parallel phase of liberalization – India participated in many more investment arbitrations than China – India took a sharp turn to a more restrictive approach in recent years, as exemplified by its Model BIT 2015. China's fourth generation of investment treaties,

---

Model BIT 2003'). See also eg Art 4 (2) Agreement between the Government of the Republic of India and the Government of the Republic of Slovenia on the Mutual Promotion and Protection of Investments (signed 14 June 2011, entered into force 22 March 2017) ('India-Slovenia BIT 2011'). For arguments on how MFN provisions in Indian BITs were supposedly overly broad and unqualified and thus required reform see Prabhash Ranjan, 'Most favoured nation provision in Indian bilateral investment treaties: A case for reform' (2015) 55 *Indian Journal of International Law* 39.

636 Art 4 (2) Agreement between the Government of Australia and the Government of the Republic of India on the Promotion and Protection of Investments (signed 26 February 1999, entered into force 4 May 2000) ('Australia-India BIT 1999'); *White Industries* (n 629) para 16.1.1(a). See also Hanessian and Duggal (n 629) 729–730, 735–737.

637 Preamble and Arts 16–18 India Model BIT 2015.

638 Art 14 India Model BIT 2015.

639 Arts 14.3 and 14.4 India Model BIT 2015.

meanwhile, have become Americanized, and Chinese negotiators have – inter alia – lauded as one benefit that American model treaties are supposedly better at 'balancing' investor and host state rights,[640] eg by more extensively describing the breaches that can lead to international arbitration. However, China did not depart at all from general convention like India, by deleting core provisions or drastically restricting access to international dispute settlement.

South Africa has also not ratified the ICSID Convention. It ratified more than 20 BITs,[641] starting in 1997.[642] However, South Africa only ratified two more treaties[643] after it experienced investment arbitration on the respondent side for the first and only time in 2007,[644] the same year as China's first involvement.[645] South African investors have since initiated three investment arbitrations starting in 2012.[646] The country long had fairly standard BITs and did not change its practice for years, but entered a review process in 2009 initiated by the country's Department of Trade and Industry, which eventually led to a moratorium on further agreements, a

640 Yongjie Li (n 531) 175.

641 UNCTAD Investment Policy Hub, 'South Africa – BITs' <http://investmentpolicyhub.unctad.org/IIA/CountryBits/195#iiaInnerMenu>.

642 Agreement between the Republic of South Africa and the Republic of Cuba for the Promotion and Reciprocal Protection of Investments (signed 8 December 1995, entered into force 7 April 1997) ('Cuba-South Africa BIT 1995').

643 Agreement between the Government of the Republic of South Africa and the Government of the Republic of Zimbabwe for the Promotion and Reciprocal Protection of Investments (signed 27 November 2009, entered into force 15 September 2010) ('South Africa-Zimbabwe BIT 2009'); Agreement between the Government of the Republic of South Africa and the Government of the Republic of Senegal for the Promotion and Reciprocal Protection of Investments (signed 19 June 1998, entered into force 29 December 2010) ('Senegal-South Africa BIT 1998').

644 *Piero Foresti, Laura de Carli and others v Republic of South Africa*, ICSID Case No ARB(AF)/07/1, Award (4 August 2010). A large number of African states have not yet been involved in investment arbitration, while most others only participated in a handful of cases and only as respondents. Only Tunisia (2004), Mauritius (2003), and Egypt (1998) were part of proceedings on both ends, while only Egypt was involved in a substantial number of cases (three as home state, 28 as host state).

645 *Tza Yap Shum v Republic of Peru*, ICSID Case No ARB/07/6, Award (7 July 2011) ('*Tza* (Award)')..

646 UNCTAD Investment Policy Hub, 'South Africa – Investment Arbitration' <http://investmentpolicyhub.unctad.org/ISDS/CountryCases/195?partyRole=2>.

2010 decision to not renew BITs whose validity was limited in time, and unilateral terminations of treaties starting in 2012.[647]

A particular difficulty in South Africa is how to square investment protection with black economic empowerment policies, exceptions to the protection of property rights that are part of the South African constitution, and exceptions to non-discrimination represented by the *Broad Based Black Economic Empowerment Acts* and the *Preferential Procurement Policy Framework Act*.[648]

A new *Protection of Investment Act* was adopted by parliament in December 2015,[649] to seek a more 'balanced' regime and provide 'clarity.' The developing domestic framework is supposed to gradually replace investor-state arbitration (sunset periods of ten to fifteen years are in place for the terminated BITs).[650]

Compared to China, South Africa, started its BIT program late, failed to ratify a large proportion of its investment treaties, and, most crucially, drew entirely different conclusions after its first participation in international investment arbitration. While the Chinese government went for Americanization viewed as 'balancing' provisions, for more detail in order to avoid outcomes it did not intend, its South African counterpart froze the program altogether and partly rolled back what had been built up.

---

647 See also Voon and Mitchell (n 629) 424–425. Among those countries that did not receive notices of termination are: China, the Republic of Korea, Russia, and some African partners, but also Italy, Sweden and Finland.

648 Section 25 (8) Constitution of the Republic of South Africa (adopted 8 May 1996 and amended 11 October 1996 by the Constitutional Assembly, entered into force 4 February 1997); Preferential Procurement Policy Framework Act 5 of 2000 (entered into force 3 February 2000) [South Africa]; Broad Based Black Economic Empowerment Act 53 of 2003 (entered into force 9 January 2004) [South Africa]; Broad Based Black Economic Empowerment Act 46 of 2013 (entered into force 27 January 2014) [South Africa]. See also Engela C Schlemmer, 'An Overview of South Africa's Bilateral Investment Treaties and Investment Policy' (2016) 31 *ICSID Review* 167, 172. On black economic empowerment being touted as a regional norm of customary international law by member states of the Southern African Development Community (SADC) see Ben Chigara, 'European/Southern African Development Community (SADC) states' bilateral investment agreements (BITs) for the promotion and protection of foreign investments vs post-apartheid SADC economic and social reconstruction policy' (2011) 10 *Journal of International Trade Law and Policy* 213.

649 Protection of Investment Act 22 of 2015 (entered into force 15 December 2015) [South Africa].

650 Schlemmer (n 648) 167, 189–190, 192.

Chinese authors have even addressed a supposed need on the part of China to become active and uphold 'reformism' in the face of such 'radical renunciation of existing BITs' as in South Africa's case, support the conclusion of BITs as 'embodiment of the international rule of law,' and convince Pretoria to hold on to (updated) South-South BITs.[651]

However, rather than South Africa, Brazil appears to be the most restrictive investment law actor throughout. Importantly, Brazil has not ratified the ICSID Convention, an anomaly in Latin America.[652] Adherence to the Calvo Doctrine, as well as criticism of a departure from state to state arbitration and supposed favoritism towards investors were in line with Latin American practice during World Bank consultations in the 1960s,[653] but others changed tack in the 1980s. However, Brazil was one of the last developing countries to even negotiate for BITs. It signed the first of over twenty in 1994,[654] but only ratified the first BIT, the one with Angola, in October 2017.[655]

Brazil has not yet participated in any international investment arbitration,[656] and in fact the included ISDS clauses were crucial to the Brazilian Congress never agreeing to ratify BITs.[657]

In addition to a hawkishly opposed faction in Congress, lacking prioritization on part of the Executive, and a belief that Brazil would be sufficient-

651 See eg Xiuli Han, 'The China–South Africa Bilateral Investment Treaty: National rule of law versus international rule of law' (2017) 24 *South African Journal of International Affairs* 269, 283–284.

652 ICSID, 'List of Member States' <https://icsid.worldbank.org/en/Pages/icsiddocs/List-of-Member-States.aspx> accessed 30 March 2019. In South America, Argentina, Uruguay, Paraguay, Chile, Peru, Colombia and Guyana ratified the ICSID Convention – Venezuela, Bolivia and Ecuador also did but later withdrew – as did all Central American states except Belize.

653 Jean Kalicki and Suzana Medeiros, 'Revisiting Brazil's Traditional Reluctance Towards ICSID, BITs and Investor-State Arbitration' (2008) 24 *Arbitration International* 423, 431–433.

654 Acordo para a Promoção e a Proteção Recíproca de Investimentos entre o Governo da República Portuguesa eo Governo da República Federativo do Brasil (signed 9 February 1994, not in force) ('Brazil-Portugal BIT 1994').

655 Acordo de Cooperação e Facilitação de Investimentos entre o Governo da República Federativa do Brasil e o Governo da República de Angola (signed 1 April 2015, entered into force 11 October 2017) ('Brazil-Angola BIT 2015'); UNCTAD Investment Policy Hub, 'Brazil – BITs' <http://investmentpolicyhub.unctad.org/IIA/CountryBits/27#iiaInnerMenu2018> accessed 30 March 2019.

656 In Latin America only Brazil, Suriname and Honduras were not yet involved in investment arbitration.

657 Kalicki and Medeiros (n 653) 433–434.

ly attractive to investors without BITs, all contributed to non-ratification, despite Brazil liberalizing its economy in other ways since the early-1990s.[658]

Recent BITs concluded by Brazil, eg with Angola and Mozambique, do not contain investor-state arbitration clauses, appearing to revert to traditional diplomatic protection.[659] In Latin America, Brazil has, together with its MERCOSUR partners Argentina, Uruguay and Paraguay, also put forward a new investment protocol that excludes investor-state arbitration.[660] This protocol requires investors to have a seat and substantial activity in the host state,[661] excludes FET and full protection and security standards, strongly limits national treatment and MFN standards (specifically ISDS provisions cannot be imported), excludes protection against indirect expropriation,[662] and includes a self-judging security exception.[663]

Having only just ratified its first BIT in late 2017 – and not having been part of any investment arbitration – Brazil does not share the Chinese in-

658 Daniela Campello and Leany Lemos, 'The non-ratification of bilateral investment treaties in Brazil: a story of conflict in a land of cooperation' (2015) 22 *Review of International Political Economy* 1055, 1076–1078.

659 Acordo de Cooperação e Facilitação de Investimentos entre o Governo da República Federativa do Brasil e o Governo da República de Angola (signed 1 April 2015, entered into force 11 October 2017) ('Brazil-Angola BIT 2015'); Acordo de Cooperação e Facilitação de Investimentos entre o Governo da República Federativa do Brasil e o Governo da República de Moçambique (signed 30 March 2015, not in force) ('Brazil-Mozambique BIT 2015'). See also Joaquim de Paiva Muniz and Luis Peretti, 'Brazil Signs New Bilateral Investment Treaties with Mozambique and Angola: New Approach to BITs or "Toothless Lions"?' *Global Arbitration News* (London, 7 April 2015 <https://globalarbitrationnews.com/20150407-brazil-signs-new-bilateral-investment-treaties/> accessed 10 November 2018.

660 Protocolo de Cooperación y Facilitación de Inversiones Intra-MERCOSUR (signed 7 April 2017, not in force) ('Intra-MERCOSUR Investment Facilitation Protocol 2017'). MERCOSUR is a regional block in South America, from which Venezuela has been suspended in December 2016, while Bolivia is in the process of integration. On the new MERCOSUR Protocol see also Damien Charlotin and Luke Eric Peterson, 'Analysis: In new MERCOSUR Investment Protocol, Brazil, Uruguay, Paraguay and Argentina radically pare back protections, and exclude investor-state arbitration' *IAReporter* (Santa Monica, 4 May 2017 <https://www.iareporter.com/articles/analysis-in-new-mercosur-investment-protocol-brazil-uruguay-paraguay-and-argentina-radically-pare-back-protections-and-exclude-investor-state-arbitration/> accessed 10 November 2018.

661 Art 3 (3) and (4) Intra-MERCOSUR Investment Facilitation Protocol 2017.

662 Ibid Arts 4, 5, 6 and 7.

663 Ibid Art 12.

vestment treaty experience at all.[664] In some ways, the two are in fact at two different ends of the spectrum on BIT strategies among developing countries.[665] Both have become prime FDI destinations among developing countries,[666] but have adopted opposing strategies. In contrast to China's liberalization and then Americanization of such clauses, Brazil does not allow for investor-state arbitration at all in its recent treaty practice. Like India, but unlike China, Brazil has also been willing to delete core substantive provisions.

It appears clear that among the BRICS, China has become the last one standing, in still moving forward on BIT liberalization and engagement with investment arbitration. The Chinese government was the first of this group to start building a network of international investment agreements, built the largest one, and had the most linear (and gradual) development towards liberalization and (arguably) refinement.

What marks China's distinct status, mainly, are the years of its fourth generation of BITs, ie since 2008,[667] and thus also the reaction to investment arbitrations that perhaps did not always have the desired outcome.[668] In this most recent period, all other BRICS, regardless whether they had previously pursued a somewhat liberal BIT strategy or not, took a decisive restrictive turn – for Brazil only on paper. While China merely detailed circumstances that would allow for access to international arbitration and secured regulatory space arguably in line with American model BITs, all other BRICS adopted (Model) treaties, 'guidelines,' or domestic legislation that clarified their intention to either delete core substantive protection clauses for investors, end – not start in Brazil's case – access to international arbitration, or both.

Several factors may help explain this. First, the same political party with the same basic underlying (and in its implementation gradually developing) policy approach has been in power in Beijing since the start of the Chinese BIT program in 1982. Second, China is by far the largest economy among these states, has retained the most consistent growth rates, and has most clearly developed into a strong capital-exporting country.

---

664 See Chapters IV.2.1.2.1 to IV.2.1.2.5.

665 See also Dan Wei, 'Bilateral investment treaties: an empirical analysis of the practices of Brazil and China' (2012) 33 *European Journal of Law and Economy* 663, 666–669.

666 See also World Investment Report 2017 (n 10).

667 See Chapter IV.2.1.2.5.

668 See Chapter IV.2.1.3.

Third, China entered a newly-assertive foreign policy stage – of which outward investment is a core component – in 2013, as spelled out in President Xi Jinping's speeches, party conferences and 'white papers' on everything from foreign economic to security policy.[669] The most eye-catching verbalization has been the 'Belt and Road'-Initiative (or 'One Belt, One Road'). A vehicle for multiple policy objectives, and driven by various motivations, the most relevant drivers for the purposes of this study are: finding profitable investment opportunities for Chinese currency reserves, and aiding Chinese companies to become more competitive by acquiring high-technology, innovative companies abroad.[670] These motivations have led to an astounding and unprecedented situation in 2016, when Chinese FDI flows to both the EU and the US were markedly higher than the reverse flows.[671] None of the other BRICS is in a comparable situation.[672]

IV.2.1.3. Investment Arbitration with Chinese Participation

There have been three investment arbitrations filed by foreign investors against China, and five cases where Chinese investors – including one from Hong Kong and one from Macao – initiated arbitrations under Chinese investment treaties.[673] This paucity of case law can be explained through the PRC's skepticism towards international adjudication in general,[674] and international investment arbitration in particular. The latter was expressed through China's early BIT practice on dispute settlement clauses, limiting the range of cases that may be submitted to international invest-

---

669 See Chapters I.1, I.2, II.3.1.4.3 and IV.2.1.2.5.

670 See Chapter IV.2.1.2.5; Eder and Mardell (n 581).

671 Thilo Hanemann and Mikko Huotari, 'Chinese investment in Europe: record flows and growing imbalances' *Joint report by MERICS and Rhodium Group* (Berlin, January 2017) <https://www.merics.org/en/papers-on-china/chinese-investment-europe-record-flows-and-growing-imbalances> accessed 3 November 2019; Echo Huang, 'Chinese investment in the US skyrocketed last year' *Quartz* (New York, 3 January 2017) <https://qz.com/876693/chinese-investment-in-the-us-skyrocketed-in-2016/> accessed 3 November 2019.

672 World Investment Report 2017 (n 10).

673 Only cases wherein investors relied on PRC investment treaties will be considered, ie not such building on the BITs concluded by Hong Kong, Macao, or Taiwan.

674 See Chapter III.2.

ment arbitration to such about the amount of compensation for expropriation.[675]

In the following sub-chapters, the discussion of relevant case law will be structured along four issue areas. In choosing the latter, this book is most interested in jurisdictional issues, as it seeks to explore under which circumstances the PRC embraces the jurisdiction of international adjudicative bodies, and keeps doing so after case law arises. Having '[transferred] sovereign powers after making a cost-benefit analysis' (concrete sovereignty),[676] it is imperative to assess how the Chinese government reacts when such a 'transfer' is misinterpreted in its eyes. Pertinent issues have been key to outcomes in the cases involving China thus far, have dominated Chinese scholarly discourse thereon,[677] and have thus informed policy recommendations to the government in Beijing.

Regarding central issues at the jurisdiction stage, most prominently, the question arose as to how tribunals are to deal with limited arbitration clauses in early Chinese BITs, whether these clauses should be interpreted narrowly or broadly, and whether MFN clauses might be used to import more liberal dispute resolution clauses from other BITs.[678] Moreover, whether China's BITs cover its entire sovereign territory, including the special administrative regions (hereinafter: SAR) Hong Kong and Macao.[679] Temporal issues have arisen, on interpreting when investors might rely on which of two successive BITs, and under which circumstances investors' claims may be time-barred.[680] Finally, an issue that is also included due to its salience for China's politico-economic system: the question emerged whether state-owned enterprises are protected as 'investors'.[681]

The pertinent parts of the case law will be discussed in the relevant chapter, whereas the first mention of a case will be used to also summarize the factual background and procedural history for proper context. Sub-chapters will address 'relevant case law' for the given issue jointly except where longer case summaries are included (as necessary context). On each issue, 'discussion' sub-chapters will follow that provide analysis, while drawing

675 See Chapters IV.2.1.2.2 and IV.2.1.2.3.

676 Ahl, 'China' (n 274) 151.

677 See Chapter V.2.2.

678 See Chapter IV.2.1.3.1.

679 See Chapter IV.2.1.3.3. See also Norah Gallagher, 'China's BITs and Arbitration Practice: Progress and Problems', in Wenhua Shan (ed), *China and International Investment Law: Twenty Years of ICSID Membership* (Brill 2015) 208–212.

680 See Chapter IV.2.1.3.2.

681 See Chapter IV.2.1.3.4.

on wider international case law and scholarship, as well as Chinese investment treaty practice and Chinese discourse as laid out in Chapters IV.2.1.2 and V.2.2.

IV.2.1.3.1. Limited Arbitration Clauses – Interpretation and MFN Use

The most dominant theme in investment arbitrations involving China has been the issue of its restrictive arbitration clauses in first- and second-generation BITs. Such treaties, which still exist in large numbers and are only gradually replaced or modified through Amendment Protocols, generally limit investors' access to international arbitration to disputes about the amount of compensation for expropriation. Like in wider international debates in case law and scholarship, the issue arose, as to how narrowly such clauses have to be interpreted, and whether MFN clauses can allow for the import of broader dispute settlement clauses from other BITs.

Particularly on this issue the appearance of case law was likely, due to China's liberalization drive evidenced by third- and fourth-generation BITs,[682] and its rise to prominence as both a host and home state. The Chinese government signaled openness with such a treaty practice, while previous BIT generations' restrictive arbitration clauses appeared outdated and case law developments pointed to potential workarounds: broad interpretation or reliance on MFN clauses.

Tribunal decisions on such matters would nevertheless have to be viewed as sensitive in the Chinese context, where a tentative, step-by-step engagement strategy had been behind the very intentional limitation of access to arbitration in early BITs. The preceding comparative deliberations on BRICS BIT practice have shown how unfavorable and in some cases unexpected outcomes – or the fear thereof – could be one factor behind a reversal of liberalization and engagement processes.[683] China's path has been markedly different from the other BRICS,[684] but a review of pertinent case law should be no less elucidating as to its fourth-generation BIT practice, and should provide indications regarding future engagement.

682 See Chapters IV.2.1.2.4 and IV.2.1.2.5.
683 See Chapter IV.2.1.2.6.
684 See Chapters IV.2.1.2.4 and IV.2.1.2.5.

IV.2.1.3.1.1. Broad or Narrow Interpretation

The question of how to interpret restrictive arbitration clauses in Chinese BITs has emerged in the majority of investment arbitrations with Chinese participation. These cases will thus first be noted here, including summaries of their factual background and procedural history. This will provide a necessary basis for further analysis, including on why the issue elicited heated debate among Chinese scholars. It will also help explain consequences the Chinese government drew in preparations for potential further engagement.

Both the pertinent cases and below discussion thereof should be prefaced by a very brief reiteration of treaty interpretation rules. Interpretation generally proceeds from Article 31 Vienna Convention on the Law of Treaties (hereinafter: VCLT), referencing 'ordinary meaning,' context, and object and purpose (on the latter BIT preambles have often been considered). Supplementary means in Article 32 VCLT – preparatory work and circumstances of the treaty conclusion – only come in when Article 31 does not suffice or delivers a 'manifestly absurd or unreasonable' result.[685] The PRC acceded to the VCLT on 3 September 1997.[686]

IV.2.1.3.1.1.1. Tza Yap Shum v Republic of Peru (ICSID)

The first ICSID Case ever to involve the PRC – seminal to Chinese discourse, and thus to be laid out in further detail herein – was *Tza Yap Shum v Republic of Peru*, filed by an investor from Hong Kong in 2007, invoking a second-generation Chinese BIT.[687] Mr. Tza (the 'Claimant') is a Chinese national and Hong Kong resident. He had made a sizable investment towards and was the 90 % indirect shareholder of *TSG Peru S.A.C* ('TSG'), a

685 Arts 31 and 32 VCLT.

686 United Nations Treaty Collection – Status of Treaties, 'Vienna Convention on the Law of Treaties' <https://treaties.un.org/PAGES/ViewDetailsIII.aspx?src=TREATY&mtdsg_no=XXIII-1&chapter=23&Temp=mtdsg3&clang=_en#EndDec> accessed 4 December 2018.

687 *Tza Yap Shum v Republic of Peru*, ICSID Case No ARB/07/6, Decision on Jurisdiction (19 June 2009) paras 1, 5, 30 ('*Tza* (Decision on Jurisdiction)'); Agreement between the Government of the Republic of Peru and the Government of the People's Republic of China concerning the Encouragement and Reciprocal Protection of Investments (signed 9 June 1994, entered into force 1 February 1995) ('Peru-China BIT 1994').

company incorporated in Peru (the 'Respondent') that manufactured food products from fish and exported them to Asia.[688]

The Peruvian National Superintendence of Tax Administration ('SUNAT') in 2004 conducted an audit, found that TSG had failed to accurately state its total sales volume, and in 2005 issued a series of retroactive taxation decisions on account of supposed income tax and general sales tax violations. Through preliminary precautionary measures, it froze TSG's bank accounts, attached certain assets of TSG, and had all Peruvian banks retain funds in connection with TSG transactions that would pass through them.[689] TSG's complaint before SUNAT and appeal to the Peruvian Tax Court were rejected. Being unable to use Peruvian banks, the company's sales drastically decreased, and it applied for debt restructuring to continue operating.[690] Peru maintained that the precautionary measures had been necessary to secure the recovery of tax arrears.[691]

According to Mr. Tza, the actions of the Peruvian government amounted to indirect expropriation through the destruction of his company's economic viability. He claimed that the Respondent had violated obligations on protection and FET of investments, compensation for expropriation or similar measures and allowing the transfer of capital and returns.[692]

Peru objected to jurisdiction, holding, most importantly, that Article 8 (3) Peru-China BIT limits international arbitration to disputes 'involving the amount of compensation for expropriation,' excluding the issue of whether an expropriation indeed happened and all other possible disputes.[693]

In its decision on jurisdiction, the tribunal supported a broad interpretation of the above phrase as necessary to give full meaning to all elements of the dispute resolution clause in this BIT.[694] It maintained that an 'interpretation in good faith in accordance with the ordinary meaning' (see Article 31 VCLT) of the word 'involving' – while 'limited to' could also have been used – led it to conclude that a dispute must only 'include' the determination of a quantum, but does not have to be restricted to that issue. Rather,

688 *Tza* (Decision on Jurisdiction) (n 687) paras 1, 30, 42, 88.
689 *Tza* (Award) (n 645) paras 78–81, 103–107, 108–124.
690 Ibid paras 83, 109–113, 164–170.
691 Ibid paras 86–92.
692 Arts 3–4 and 6 Peru-China BIT 1994; *Tza* (Award) (n 645) paras 74–85.
693 Art 8 (3) Peru-China BIT 1994; *Tza* (Decision on Jurisdiction) (n 687) paras 129–137. The rejection of Peru's contention that the Peru-China BIT 1994 is not applicable to Hong Kong is discussed in Chapter IV.2.1.3.3.
694 Art 8 Peru-China BIT; *Tza* (Decision on Jurisdiction) (n 687) paras 187–188.

such disputes, following expropriation, could also involve other questions 'inherent in an expropriation': whether it occurred, was in line with the public interest, complied with required procedures, and was non-discriminatory.[695] Moreover, in the context of the fork-in-the-road clause in the last sentence of Article 8 (3) – '[t]he provisions of this paragraph shall not apply if the investor concerned has resorted to the procedure specified in paragraph 2 of this Article' (ie local courts)[696] – the tribunal found that following a narrow interpretation the investor would in fact never have access to arbitration. Once it would address the local courts to ascertain the fact of expropriation, it would be fully barred from accessing arbitration, including on the quantum.[697] Finally, such a reading would supposedly go against the BIT's Preamble due to the treaty failing to attract further investments.[698]

The tribunal's award of 7 July 2011 found that the preliminary precautionary measures applied by SUNAT indeed constituted an indirect expropriation, that SUNAT had acted in an arbitrary way, and that TSG had not had adequate access to effective legal remedies to challenge the precautionary measures.[699] Based on the adjusted book value of TSG, Mr. Tza was awarded USD 786,306 in compensation (plus interest).[700]

The Peruvian government then secured a stay of enforcement, while seeking 'partial annulment of the Decision on Jurisdiction with respect to the Tribunal's conclusion that all of Claimant's expropriation claims were within the scope of Article 8(3) of the BIT'.[701] As reasons, it proffered that supposedly 1) the tribunal had 'manifestly exceeded its powers' by ignoring the plain meaning of the text, disregarding parties' intentions and China's notification to ICSID, and misrepresenting jurisprudence, that 2) the arbitrators failed to state reasons for their interpretation, and that 3) they seriously departed from a fundamental rule of procedure, by assuming ju-

695 Art 31 VCLT; Arts 4 and 8 (3) Peru-China BIT 1994; *Tza* (Decision on Jurisdiction) (n 687) paras 150–152, 188; .

696 Arts 8 (2) and 8 (3) last sentence Peru-China BIT 1994.

697 *Tza* (Award) (n 645) paras 154–161.

698 Preamble Peru-China BIT 1994; *Tza* (Award) (n 645) para 153.

699 Art 4 Peru-China BIT 1994; *Tza* (Award) (n 645) paras 170, 218, 240, 252.

700 *Tza* (Award) (n 645) paras 261–268, 279–280, 282–285, 292.

701 *Tza Yap Shum v Republic of Peru*, ICSID Case No ARB/07/6, Decision on Annulment (12 February 2015) para 4 ('*Tza* (Decision on Annulment)'); *Tza Yap Shum v Republic of Peru*, ICSID Case No ARB/07/6, Reply on Annulment (2 November 2012) para 85; Art 8 (3) Peru-China BIT 1994; Art 52 ICSID Convention; r 50 and r 54 (2) ICSID Arbitration Rules.

risdiction where it was lacking, not addressing material questions presented by the parties and not giving Peru an opportunity to express its views on important issues.[702]

The ad-hoc committee constituted to decide on annulment reminded that the arbitral tribunal had determined the meaning of Article 8 (3) Peru-China BIT through semantic interpretation,[703] and that on matters of interpretation an ad-hoc committee 'should not substitute its own decision for that of the arbitral tribunal'.[704] It maintained that interpretation 'leaves room for discussion',[705] is 'susceptible of argument one way or the other',[706] and that there was no 'manifest excess of powers' that would have to be 'manifest' in the sense of both substance and being 'textually obvious'[707] and immediately 'self-evident'[708].[709] Furthermore, the committee underlined on BIT negotiators' testimony and China's Article 25 (4)-notification that the tribunal was competent to judge the admissibility of and evaluate evidence, and that it is not the committee's task to re-evaluate

702 Arts 52 (1) (b), (d) and (e) ICSID Convention; Art 8 (3) Peru-China BIT 1994; *Tza* (Decision on Annulment) (n 701) paras 51–52, 53–57 and 58–61.

703 Art 8 (3) Peru-China BIT 1994; *Tza* (Decision on Annulment) (n 701) para 74, refers to *Tza* (Decision on Jurisdiction) (n 687) para 151.

704 *Tza* (Decision on Annulment) (n 701) para 81, citing *Industria Nacional de Alimentos, SA and Indalsa Peru, SA (formerly Empresas Lucchetti, SA and Lucchetti Peru, SA) v Peru*, ICSID Case No ARB/03/4, Decision on Annulment (5 September 2007) para 112, and also referring to *Fraport AG Frankfurt Airport Services Worldwide v Philippines*, ICSID Case No ARB/03/25, Decision on Annulment (23 December 2010) para 44.

705 *Duke Energy International Peru Invesments No. 1 Ltd v Republic of Peru*, ICSID Case No ARB/03/28, Decision on Annulment (1 March 2011) para 160.

706 *CDC Group plc v Republic of the Seychelles*, ICSID Case No ARB/02/14, Decision on Annulment (29 June 2005) para 41.

707 *Hussein Nuaman Soufraki v The United Arab Emirates*, ICSID Case No ARB/02/7, Decision on Annulment (5 June 2007) para 40.

708 *Wena Hotels Ltd v Arab Republic of Egypt*, ICSID Case No ARB/98/4, Decision on Annulment (5 February 2002) para 25.

709 *Tza* (Decision on Annulment) (n 701) paras 80–82, also refers to *Industria Nacional* (n 704) para 112; *Klöckner Industrie-Anlagen GmbH and others v United Republic of Cameroon and Société Camerounaise des Engrais*, ICSID Case No ARB/81/2, Decision on Annulment (3 May 1985) para 52(e); *Patrick Mitchell v Democratic Republic of Congo*, ICSID Case No ARB/99/7, Decision on the Application for the Annulment of the Award (1 November 2006) para 20; *M.C.I. Power Group L.C. and New Turbine, Inc. v Ecuador*, ICSID Case No ARB/03/6, Decision on Annulment (19 October 2009) para 49.

these decisions.[710] Nonetheless, it noted that an appellate body with broader powers 'might well find fault as a matter of law with some aspects of the Tribunal's application of the VCLT'.[711]

The committee also maintained that the tribunal was not required to explain itself on each piece of evidence and that it did provide adequate reasoning for its award that was neither frivolous nor insufficient.[712] Citing the decision in *MINE v Guinea*, it held that adequacy here meant enabling 'one to follow how the tribunal proceeded from Point A to Point B and eventually to its conclusion, even if it made an error in fact or law.'[713] On the supposed 'serious departure from a fundamental rule of procedure,' the ad-hoc committee found that the arbitral tribunal was free to evaluate evidence and determine its own jurisdiction, and had provided adequate reasoning.[714]

Alternatively, Peru also claimed that the tribunal had manifestly exceeded its powers by deciding on matters that had been agreed to be outside the tribunals' jurisdiction.[715] The ad-hoc committee once again referred to the arbitral tribunal's prerogative to interpret the law and provision of adequate reasoning, underlined its own nature not being that of an appeals court that may 're-decide the merits,' and ultimately dismissed Peru's Application for Annulment in its entirety and terminated the stay of enforcement on 12 February 2015[716].[717]

---

710 R 34 and r 36 ICSID Arbitration Rules; PRC Art 25 (4) ICSID Convention-Notification; *Tza* (Decision on Annulment) (n 701) paras 93 and 94–99, citing *CDC Group* (n 706) paras 46 and 77; *Rumeli Telekom A.S. and Telsim Mobil Telekomunikasyon Hizmetleri v Kazakhstan*, ICSID Case No ARB/05/16, Decision on Annulment (25 March 2010) para 96.

711 *Tza* (Decision on Annulment) (n 701) para 99.

712 Art 8 (3) Peru-China BIT 1994; Art 52 (1) (e) ICSID Convention; *Tza* (Decision on Annulment) (n 701) paras 100–113.

713 *Tza* (Decision on Annulment) (n 701) para 112; *Maritime International Nominees Establishment v Republic of Guinea*, ICSID Case No ARB/84/4, Decision on Annulment (14 December 1989) para 5.09.

714 *Tza* (Decision on Annulment) (n 701) paras 114–116, 120, 141–142, citing *Wena Hotels* (n 708) para 25; Art 41 ICSID Convention.

715 *Tza* (Decision on Annulment) (n 701) paras 143–147.

716 Ibid paras 156, 158.161, 171, 178–179, 191–193, 198, 210.

717 For analysis of this and the following cases with regard to the issue at hand see Chapter IV.2.1.3.1.1.7 ('Discussion'). On each issue, such a sub-chapter providing analysis follows sub-chapters laying out relevant cases and addresses them jointly.

IV.2.1.3.1.1.2. Ekran Berhad v People's Republic of China (ICSID)

The first case filed against the PRC by a foreign investor was *Ekran Berhad v People's Republic of China*, which was registered on 24 May 2011.[718] *Ekran Berhad* is a Malaysian construction, timber logging and property development company. Its subsidiary *Sino Malaysia Art & Culture* (SMCAC) – focused on developing cultural facilities – had the rights to a 70-year leasehold over 900 hectares of land in Hainan Province, valued at around USD 6 million.[719]

The investor filed a claim based on the China-Malaysia BIT 1988, a first-generation Chinese BIT, on account of its leasehold being revoked without compensation in 2004.[720] It had complained to local authorities and gone through several rounds of negotiations before it approached ICSID. Chinese authorities maintained that the company's right was revoked in line with PRC laws on 'idle lands.' The latter require the revocation of leaseholds, should the land not be used for more than two years.[721]

Only two months after the case had been registered – before the tribunal had been constituted – the parties filed a formal 'request for the discontinuance of the proceeding' and the ICSID Secretary-General took note of the discontinuance in a procedural order.[722]

The China-Malaysia BIT, similar to the Peru-China BIT, allows for (in this case only) ad-hoc arbitration in disputes 'relating to the amount of compensation' (as well as 'any other disputes agreed upon by both parties'), but lacks a similar fork-in-the-road clause.[723] The investor could have

718 *Ekran Berhad* (n 524).

719 See Luke Eric Peterson, 'China is sued for the first time in an ICSID arbitration; Malaysian investor, Ekran, had rights to 900 hectares of land for development in China' *IAReporter* (Santa Monica, 26 May 2011) <http://www.iareporter.com.uaccess.univie.ac.at/articles/china-is-sued-for-the-first-time-in-an-icsid-arbitration-malaysian-investor-ekran-had-rights-to-900-hectares-of-land-for-development-in-china/> accessed 25 January 2017.

720 Agreement between the Government of the People's Republic of China and the Government of Malaysia concerning the Reciprocal Encouragement and Protection of Investments (signed 21 November 1988, entered into force 31 March 1990) ('China-Malaysia BIT 1988'). See also Norah Gallagher, 'Role of China in Investment: BITs, SOEs, Private Enterprises, and Evolution of Policy' (2016) 31 *ICSID Review* 88, 95.

721 See also Gallagher, 'China's BITs and Arbitration Practice' (n 678) 209.

722 *Ekran Berhad* (n 524); r 43 (1) ICSID Arbitration Rules. See also Tong Qi, 'How Exactly does China Consent' (n 510) 267; Zhanghui Wu (n 525) 3.

723 Art 7 China-Malaysia BIT 1988.

proffered arguments along the lines of those in *Tza* in favor of broad interpretation, but might have had greater difficulty convincing the tribunal.

IV.2.1.3.1.1.3. Sanum v Lao People's Democratic Republic (ad hoc, PCA)

The second award based on a Chinese BIT was rendered in ad-hoc proceedings launched by a Macao-registered resort and hotel gambling company under the (second-generation) China-Laos BIT 1993 against Laos with a notice of arbitration dated 14 August 2013.[724] The PCA served as the registry, Singapore as the seat of arbitration, and the 2010 UNCITRAL Arbitration Rules were applied.[725] This influential case for subsequent case law took many turns, includes multiple relevant decisions, and thus will also be laid out in further detail. Two main issues arose: interpretation of the restrictive arbitration clause in the China-Laos BIT 1993 – discussed here – and applicability of the BIT to Macao.[726]

Sanum was established in Macao in 2005 – Portugal had handed Macao back to China in 1999 – and in 2007 partnered with the Laotian company *ST Group* to operate two casinos and five slot clubs through joint ven-

724 *Sanum Investments Limited v Lao People's Democratic Republic*, PCA Case No 2013–13, Award on Jurisdiction (13 December 2013) paras 1–3, 21, 25, 320 ('*Sanum* (Award on Jurisdiction)'); *Sanum Investments Limited v Lao People's Democratic Republic*, PCA Case No 2013–13, Notice of Arbitration (14 August 2012) paras 1–3; Agreement between the Government of the People's Republic of China and the Government of the Lao People's Democratic Republic concerning the Encouragement and Reciprocal Protection of Investments (signed 31 January 1993, entered into force 1 June 1993) ('China-Laos BIT 1993'). Parallel to Sanum, its Aruba, Netherlands, registered 100 % owner Lao Holdings N.V. filed for arbitration at ICSID under the Laos-Netherlands BIT. See *Lao Holdings NV v Lao People's Democratic Republic*, ICSID Case No ARB(AF)/12/6, Decision on Jurisdiction (21 February 2014); Agreement on Encouragement and Reciprocal Protection of Investments between the Lao People's Democratic Republic and the Kingdom of the Netherlands (signed 16 May 2003, entered into force 1 May 2005) ('Laos-Netherlands BIT 2003'). See also *Sanum* (Award on Jurisdiction) (n 724) paras 41–42.

725 *Sanum* (Award on Jurisdiction) (n 724) para 5. UNCITRAL Arbitration Rules (n 523). See also Dolzer and Schreuer (n 523) 243; Debby Lim, 'Case Comment: Government of the Lao People's Democratic Republic v Sanum Investments Ltd [2015] SGHC 15' *Singapore Law Blog* (Singapore, 10 March 2015) <http://www.singaporelawblog.sg/blog/article/95> accessed 30 March 2019.

726 For this see Chapter IV.2.1.3.3.

tures.[727] The investment depended on government approval, but Laotian politicians had supposedly provided explicit guarantees about the investment, the larger investment climate, and tax regime.[728] Laos, Sanum and its Laotian business partners then concluded two project development agreements on casinos giving Sanum 60 % share ownership, and committing Laos to an 'Investment Incentive Policy' specifically related to tax exemptions.[729]

In Sanum's view, the Respondent breached FET, MFN, expropriation and transfer of payments clauses in the China-Laos BIT 1993.[730] The Respondent – inter alia – allegedly deprived the Claimant 'of the benefits from its capital investment by the imposition of unfair and discriminatory taxes.'[731] Laos countered that the Claimant had not made any capital investments, but rather only provided a loan, that the main joint venture had been relieved of its obligation to pay out shareholders due to it making a loss every year, and that concerns about such joint venture's book keeping and loans had to be addressed.[732]

Laos challenged jurisdiction – inter alia – due to the restrictive arbitration clause in Article 8 (3) China-Laos BIT 1993 supposedly having to be narrowly interpreted, and thus not covering whether an expropriation occurred.[733] However, the tribunal followed the decision in *Tza Yap Shum*, and decided that 'involve' does not mean 'limited to' in terms of disputes about the amount of compensation for expropriation. Arbitrators added that in the split case law on the interpretation of similar treaty provisions, none of the cases deciding in favor of narrow interpretations involve fork-in-the-road clauses in the underlying BITs – like the one in the Peru-China BIT 1994 relevant for *Tza* and the identical one in the last sentence of Article 8 (3) China-Laos BIT 1993 – 'that would limit the investor's access to arbitration if the investor had recourse first to the local courts to deter-

727 *Sanum* (Award on Jurisdiction) (n 724) paras 18–20, 21–22, 24.

728 Ibid paras 23–24, 26–27.

729 *Sanum* (Award on Jurisdiction) (n 724) paras 28–33.

730 Arts 3 (1) and (2), 4, 5 China-Laos BIT 1993; *Sanum* (Award on Jurisdiction) (n 724) para 39.

731 *Government of the Lao People's Democratic Republic v Sanum Investments Ltd* [2015] 2 SLR 322, para 10 ('*Sanum* (Singapore High Court Judgment)').

732 *Sanum* (Award on Jurisdiction) (n 724) para 40.

733 Art 8 (3) China-Laos BIT 1993; *Sanum* (Award on Jurisdiction) (n 724) paras 144–156.

mine whether an expropriation had actually occurred'.[734] Accordingly, the tribunal assumed jurisdiction for the expropriation claims under Article 8(3) of the BIT.[735]

After the award on jurisdiction, the parties reached a settlement in June 2014, without admission as to any liabilities, leaving open the option of reviving the arbitration should certain provisions of the agreement be breached.[736] However, ahead of the settlement agreement, Laos had filed applications for proceedings and the admission of two diplomatic letters at the Singapore High Court,[737] challenging the arbitral award pursuant to Article 10 (3) (a) of Singapore's *International Arbitration Act* (Chapter 143A), which stipulates overriding court supervision and allows appeals on arbitral tribunals' rulings on jurisdiction,[738] although this case was the first time that Singapore's courts reviewed an investment treaty arbitral award.[739] Laos – inter alia – contended that Sanum's expropriation claims exceeded the scope of the arbitration clause in Article 8 (3) China-Laos BIT 1993.[740] Sanum in turn held that only issues of international law non-justiciable by the court had been raised, and that the two letters could not be admitted as evidence.[741]

The Court found that the arbitral tribunal would not have had subject-matter jurisdiction concerning the expropriation claims – aside from the BIT supposedly not being applicable to Macao –[742] holding that, would broader jurisdiction for arbitral tribunals have been intended, the phrasing of Article 8 (1) China-Laos BIT 1993, 'any dispute in connection with an investment,' could have been used in Article 8 (3) as well, instead of 'a dis-

---

734 *Sanum* (Award on Jurisdiction) (n 724) para 340, see also paras 329, 342; *Tza* (Decision on Annulment) (n 701) para 74; *Tza* (Decision on Jurisdiction) (n 687) para 151.

735 Art 8 (3) China-Laos BIT 1993; *Sanum* (Award on Jurisdiction) (n 724) para 370 (iii).

736 *Sanum Investments Limited v Lao People's Democratic Republic*, PCA Case No 2013–13, Deed of Settlement (15 June 2014) paras 1, 32.

737 See Chapter IV.2.1.3.3 for a further discussion of this issue.

738 Art 10 (3) (a) Chapter 143A International Arbitration Act (revised edition 2002) (original enactment Act 23 of 1994, revised 31 December 2002, consolidated version in force from 1 June 2012) [Singapore]; *Sanum* (Singapore High Court Judgment) (n 731) paras 2, 14–15.

739 See Hwang and Chang, 'Government of the Lao People's Democratic Republic' (n 545) 506.

740 Art 8 (3) China-Laos BIT 1993; *Sanum* (Singapore High Court Judgment) (n 731) para 17 (b).

741 *Sanum* (Singapore High Court Judgment) (n 731) para 18.

742 See Chapter IV.2.1.3.3.

pute involving the amount of compensation for expropriation'.[743] The Court added that the fork-in-the-road clause in Article 8 (3) only leaving a narrow path for arbitration did not mean that investors would not have access to arbitration at all, and that the limited scope for arbitration was to be seen in line with typical distrust of international tribunals among Communist governments.[744]

It also criticized the tribunal in *Tza Yap Shum* for placing 'undue reliance' on BITs' 'general purpose of promoting investments,' and that the PRC-Laos BIT 1993 belonging to what the Court terms China's 'first generation' of BITs supports a narrow interpretation of the clause.[745] The Court, in conclusion, found that the arbitral tribunal did not have jurisdiction, and allowed the plaintiff's (ie Laos') application.[746]

This case took yet another turn, when Singapore's Court of Appeal determined that the arbitral tribunal did have subject-matter jurisdiction after all.[747] The judges found that the ordinary meaning of 'involving the amount of compensation of expropriation' supported both a narrow and a broad interpretation,[748] but that both the context of Article 8 (3) and the BIT's object and purpose pointed to a broad reading.[749]

---

743 Art 8 (1) and (3) China-Laos BIT 1993; *Sanum* (Singapore High Court Judgment) (n 731) para 121; Gallagher, 'Role of China' (n 720) 98.

744 *Sanum* (Singapore High Court Judgment) (n 731) paras 122–123. For a similar clause not being considered a fork-in-the-road clause see *Olin Holdings* (n 523) para 38 (b). For other cases where a Communist-era treaty needed to be interepreted see eg *Austrian Airlines v The Slovak Republic*, UNCITRAL, Final Award (9 October 2009); *Berschader* (n 523); *Renta 4* (n 618). See also Gallagher, 'China's BITs and Arbitration Practice' (n 678) 210–211; Leon E Trakman, 'Geopolitics, China, and Investor-State Arbitration', in Lisa Toohey, Colin B Picker and Jonathan Greenacre, *China in the International Economic Order: New Directions and Changing Paradigms* (CUP 2015) 284. For the importance of Communist states' intention to provide only limited protection to foreign investors and the continued relevance of 'clear' and 'unambiguous' consent see also Pia Acconci, 'Most-Favoured Nation Treatment', in Peter Muchlinski, Federico Ortino and Christoph Schreuer, *The Oxford Handbook of International Investment Law* (OUP 2008) 399–400, 402.

745 *Sanum* (Singapore High Court Judgment) (n 731) paras 124–126.

746 Ibid paras 128–129.

747 *Sanum Investments Ltd v Government of the Lao People's Democratic Republic* [2016] SGCA 57, paras 123–124, 152 ('*Sanum* (Singapore Court of Appeal Judgment)').

748 Ibid para 126.

749 Ibid paras 127–147, 148–150.

Referencing *Tza Yap Shum*, the judges considered that the fork-in-the-road clause in Article 8 (3) would render access to international arbitration impossible, could arbitrators not also determine whether an expropriation has taken place.[750] According to them, the phrasing would not allow for national courts to determine liability, and the quantum of compensation to be left for an arbitral tribunal to decide; rather, any dispute brought to a national court would block further access to arbitration.[751]

On different outcomes in several previous cases, judges argued that in *Plama* there was no comparable fork-in-the-road clause to consider,[752] but rather an 'express demarcation' in Article 4 (1) of the underlying Bulgaria-Cyprus BIT on who should address the legality of and compensation for expropriation, respectively.[753] Similarly, in *Austrian Airlines v Slovakia*, the relevant Article 4 (4) Austria-Czechoslovakia BIT 1990 expressly assigned questions of 'legitimacy of the expropriation' to national courts.[754] Finally, the Germany-Bulgaria BIT 1986 relevant to *ST-AD GmbH v Bulgaria* not only contained this 'express demarcation,' but also 'expressly contemplated' that after a national court determines an expropriation's lawfulness,

750 Art 8 (3) China-Laos BIT 1993; *Sanum* (Singapore Court of Appeal Judgment) (n 747) paras 127–131; *Tza* (Decision on Jurisdiction) (n 687) para 188.

751 *Sanum* (Singapore Court of Appeal Judgment) (n 747) para 130.

752 As also in *Berschader* (n 523); *RosInvestCo UK Ltd v Russian Federation*, SCC Case No Arb V079/2005, Award on Jurisdiction (1 October 2007). In these two cases the relevant BITs were Belgium-Luxembourg Economic Union-Soviet Union BIT 1989; Agreement between the Government of the United Kingdom of Great Britain and Northern Ireland and the Government of the Union of Soviet Socialist Republics and the for the Promotion and Reciprocal Protection of Investments (signed 6 April 1989, entered into force 3 July 1991) ('United Kingdom-Soviet Union BIT 1989'). See *Sanum* (Singapore Court of Appeal Judgment) (n 747) paras 142–145.

753 *Sanum* (Singapore Court of Appeal Judgment) (n 747) paras 135–137; *Plama Consortium Limited v Republic of Bulgaria*, ICSID Case No ARB/03/24, Decision on Jurisdiction (8 February 2005) ('*Plama* (Decision on Jurisdiction)'); Art 4 (1) Agreement between the Government of the People's Republic of Bulgaria and the Government of the Republic of Cyprus on Mutual Encouragement and Protection of Investments (signed 12 November 1987, entered into force 18 May 1988) ('Bulgaria-Cyprus BIT 1987').

754 *Sanum* (Singapore Court of Appeal Judgment) (n 747) para 140; *Austrian Airlines* (n 744); Art 4 (4) Abkommen zwischen der Tschechischen und Slowakischen Föderativen Republik und der Republik Österreich über die Förderung und den Schutz von Investitionen (signed 15 October 1990, entered into force 1 October 1991) ('Austria-Czechoslovakia BIT 1990').

compensation can be addressed via international arbitration.[755] The Court of Appeal judges in *Sanum* thus concluded that the High Court judge was wrong, and affirmed the arbitral tribunal's jurisdiction.[756]

In yet another chapter of this story, initially parallel arbitral proceedings against Laos by Sanum's owner Lao Holdings NV at ICSID under the Netherlands-Laos BIT were revived – also suspended after a 2014 agreement, later found to have been breached – and consolidated with fresh claims by Sanum in 2017; the case is pending.[757]

IV.2.1.3.1.1.4. Beijing Urban v Republic of Yemen (ICSID)

The second ICSID case filed by a Mainland Chinese investor, *Beijing Urban Construction Group Co. Ltd. V Republic of Yemen*, was registered on 3 December 2014.[758] *Beijing Urban* had concluded a USD 114 million contract with Yemen's civil aviation and meteorology authority to construct an international airport in Sana'a, and started work in 2006.[759] According to the Claimant, it was deprived of its investment in breach of the China-Yemen BIT 1998.[760] The Respondent supposedly had its security forces forcibly de-

755 *Sanum* (Singapore Court of Appeal Judgment) (n 747) para 141; *ST-AD GmbH v Republic of Bulgaria*, PCA Case No 2011–06, Award on Jurisdiction (18 July 2013); Art 4 (3) Treaty between the Federal Republic of Germany and the People's Republic of Bulgaria concerning the Reciprocal Encouragement and Protection of Investments (signed 12 April 1986, entered into force 10 March 1988) ('Germany-Bulgaria BIT 1986').

756 *Sanum* (Singapore Court of Appeal Judgment) (n 747) paras 152–153.

757 *Lao Holdings NV and Sanum Investments Limited v Lao People's Democratic Republic* (ICSID Case No ARB(AF)/16/2 and ICSID Case No ADHOC/17) (registered 27 May 2016 and date of notification 14 April 2017); *Sanum Investments Limited v Lao People's Democratic Republic*, ICSID Case No ADHOC/17/1, Procedural Order No. 1 (16 May 2017); *Lao Holdings NV and Sanum Investments Limited v Lao People's Democratic Republic*, ICSID Case No ARB(AF)/16/2 and ICSID Case No ADHOC/17/1, Procedural Order No. 2 (18 September 2017); *Lao Holdings NV and Sanum Investments Limited v Lao People's Democratic Republic*, ICSID Case No ARB(AF)/16/2 and ICSID Case No ADHOC/17/1, Procedural Order No. 5 (18 May 2018).

758 *Beijing Urban Construction Group Co Ltd v Republic of Yemen*, ICSID Case No ARB/14/30, Decision on Jurisdiction (31 May 2017) para 7 ('*Beijing Urban* (Decision on Jurisdiction)')..

759 Ibid paras 1, 3, 23.

760 Agreement between the Government of the People's Republic of China and the Government of the Republic of Yemen concerning the Encouragement and Re-

ny Claimant employees access to the construction site in July 2009, and then announced that it would terminate the contract due to the Claimant not completing the works.[761] The Yemeni government contended that the tribunal lacked jurisdiction due to the limited arbitration clause in Article 10 China-Yemen BIT ('relating to the amount of compensation for expropriation'), which should be narrowly interpreted, as opposed to the decision in *Tza Yap Shum*.[762]

In its Decision on Jurisdiction, the tribunal rejected the Respondent's pertinent objection, while relying on Article 31 VCLT in its interpretation, and not considering reliance on Article 32 VCLT 'supplementary means' necessary.[763] After maintaining that the word 'or' in Article 10 (2) China-Yemen BIT contains a fork-in-the-road choice between domestic courts and ICSID arbitration, and that the principle of effective interpretation requires them to not nullify any choices granted to the investor, the arbitrators declared textual interpretation building on 'ordinary meaning' as ultimately inconclusive regarding broad or narrow interpretation of the phrase 'relating to the amount of compensation for expropriation'.[764] However, seen in the context of the entire Article 10 China-Yemen BIT, the tribunal viewed the narrow interpretation as denying the investor a real choice, because it would have to go to a domestic court to ascertain whether an expropriation had occurred – part of answering that question being addressing compensation – whenever the host state would not willingly concede so, and would then be cut off from arbitration.[765] Finally, narrow interpretation is seen as running counter to object and purpose of the BIT.[766]

Also discounting most other objections – except MFN use to import another dispute resolution clause (see below) – the tribunal found that it did have jurisdiction in May 2017.[767] However, there was no decision on the

---

ciprocal Protection of Investments (signed 16 February 1998, entered into force 10 April 2002) ('China-Yemen BIT 1998'); *Beijing Urban* (Decision on Jurisdiction) (n 758) para 2.

761 *Beijing Urban* (Decision on Jurisdiction) (n 758) para 25.

762 Art 10 China-Yemen BIT 1998; *Beijing Urban* (Decision on Jurisdiction) (n 758) paras 28, 48–52.

763 *Beijing Urban* (Decision on Jurisdiction) (n 758) paras 54, 93–97, 109.

764 Ibid paras 71–72, 77, referencing *Sanum* (Singapore Court of Appeal Judgment) (n 747) para 126; Art 10 (2) China-Yemen BIT 1998.

765 *Beijing Urban* (Decision on Jurisdiction) (n 758) paras 78–87, agrees with the tribunal in *Tza* (Decision on Jurisdiction) (n 687) paras 154, 188.

766 *Beijing Urban* (Decision on Jurisdiction) (n 758) paras 88–92.

767 Ibid para 147.

merits, as the parties came to an agreement, and the tribunal took note of discontinuance in June 2018.[768]

IV.2.1.3.1.1.5. China Heilongjiang v Mongolia (ad hoc, PCA)

In *China Heilongjiang International Economic & Technical Cooperative Corp., et al. v Mongolia*, the three (partly state-owned) Claimants initiated proceedings in February 2010 under the China-Mongolia BIT 1991, with the Permanent Court of Arbitration (hereinafter: PCA) accepting to administer proceedings.[769]

The Claimants had since 2004 held 70 % of a Mongolian corporation, Tumurtei Khuder, which in turn held a mining license for the Tumurtei iron ore deposit.[770] This license was revoked in September 2006 on account of supposed violations of licensing conditions – inter alia – related to the use of explosives and environmental regulations; challenges to this decision in the domestic court system failed.[771]

The Claimants alleged expropriation of their investments in breach of Article 4 China-Mongolia BIT 1991, and requested restitution of such a license or compensation.[772] The Respondent, in turn, among a series of jurisdictional objections, maintained that the limited arbitration clause in Article 8 (3) China-Mongolia BIT 1991 ('involving the amount of compensation for expropriation') did not extend to the issue of whether an expropriation occurred.[773]

---

768 R 43 (1) ICSID Arbitration Rules; *Beijing Urban Construction Group Co Ltd v Republic of Yemen* (ICSID Case No. ARB/14/30) (registered 3 December 2014, suspended 29 January 2018, discontinued 7 June 2018).

769 Agreement between the Government of the Mongolian People's Republic and the Government of the People's Republic of China concerning the Encouragement and Reciprocal Protection of Investments (signed 25 August 1991, entered into force 1 November 1993) ('China-Mongolia BIT 1991'); *China Heilongjiang International Economic & Technical Cooperative Corp, Beijing Shougang Mining Investment Company Ltd, and Qinhuangdaoshi Qinlong International Industrial Co Ltd v Mongolia*, PCA Case No 2010-20, Award (30 June 2017) paras 1, 5, 9, 17, 190.

770 *China Heilongjiang* (n 769) paras 90–94, 98, 144–145.

771 Ibid paras 175–177, 179–180.

772 Ibid paras 222–224; Art 4 China-Mongolia BIT 1991.

773 Art 8 (3) China-Mongolia BIT 1991; *China Heilongjiang* (n 769) paras 231 (b), 253–261.

In its Award of 30 June 2017, the tribunal upheld this objection ratione materiae and found that it did not have jurisdiction to consider the claims presented.[774] The arbitrators agreed with the Singapore Court of Appeal in *Sanum* that the word 'involve' would support both a broad and a narrow interpretation, and that contextual interpretation is necessary.[775] However, they subsequently explicitly went a different way than the tribunals in *Sanum* and *Tza Yap Shum*, when it came to resolving the matter of forks in the road in dispute resolution clauses and the principle of effet utile, arguing that Article 8 (3) China-Mongolia BIT 1991 would retain its legal effect even with a narrow interpretation.[776]

The tribunal posited that while all investment disputes could be submitted to local courts, the category of disputes to which access to arbitration was clearly limited involved those regarding whether compensation due under Article 4 (1) China-Mongolia BIT 1991 was sufficient as under Article 4 (2) China-Mongolia BIT 1991, and further maintained that during judicial proceedings on the question of whether an expropriation had occurred, this issue could be reserved for subsequent arbitral proceedings.[777] It did not view such a decision as running counter to the BIT's object and purpose,[778] and eventually found that it did not have 'jurisdiction to entertain the Claimants' claims'.[779]

On 28 September 2017, the investors submitted a petition to a US Federal Court, moving to set aside the arbitral award, which thus became public.[780]

774 *China Heilongjiang* (n 769) para 477.

775 Ibid para 439, referencing *Sanum* (Singapore Court of Appeal Judgment) (n 747) para 126.

776 Art 8 (3) China-Mongolia BIT 1991; *China Heilongjiang* (n 769) para 447–448.

777 Arts 4 (1) and (2), 8 (2) and (3) China-Mongolia BIT 1991; *China Heilongjiang* (n 769) paras 445, 449–450.

778 *China Heilongjiang* (n 769) para 451.

779 Ibid para 477.

780 Petition to vacate Arbitral Award declining to exercise arbitral jurisdiction and compel arbitration, Beijing Shougang Mining Investment Company Ltd, China Heilongjiang International Economic & Technical Cooperative Corp, and Qinhuangdaoshi Industrial Co Ltd v Mongolia, No 17 CV 7436 (SDNY).

IV.2.1.3.1.1.6. Hela Schwarz GmbH v People's Republic of China (ICSID)

This third ICSID claim against China was brought under the China-Germany BIT 2003, was registered on 21 June 2017, and the tribunal was constituted in January 2018 –[781] the Claimant's request for provisional measures was denied in August 2018.[782] The Claimant is a spice and food additive manufacturer who alleges that the compensation that it received after expropriation was wholly inadequate. One of the two law firms engaged by China is once again a Chinese firm.[783]

While this case does not involve a restrictive arbitration clause but rather a liberal one in a third-generation Chinese BIT, it is interesting for two reasons. First, a very narrow claim against China has been launched – indeed only addressing the quantum of compensation after expropriation had already been admitted by the host state and some measure of compensation paid – perhaps increasing the probability that this could be the first case China might lose as a Respondent. It will be telling how the Chinese government chooses to deal with such a development. Second, the Chinese government partly relies on domestic legal representation – a growing trend aimed at bolstering Chinese law firms experience – and it will be interesting to see how successful that strategy is.

IV.2.1.3.1.1.7. Discussion

The cases laid out above involving China or Chinese investors contributed to the development of pertinent case law. Most favored broader interpretations of limited arbitration clauses, and all of them focused on the exact

781 *Hela Schwarz GmbH v People's Republic of China* (ICSID Case No ARB/17/19) (registered 21 June 2017); *Hela Schwarz GmbH v People's Republic of China*, ICSID Case No ARB/17/19, Procedural Order No 1 (9 March 2018) ('*Hela Schwarz GmbH* (Procedural Order No 1)'); China-Germany BIT 2003.

782 *Hela Schwarz GmbH v People's Republic of China*, ICSID Case No ARB/17/19, Procedural Order No 2 (10 August 2018) ('*Hela Schwarz GmbH* (Procedural Order No 2)').

783 See also Luke Eric Peterson, 'Investment treaty claim against China is ready to proceed to provisional measures ruling, as three arbitrators are put in place' *IAReporter* (Santa Monica, 8 January 2018) <https://www-iareporter-com.uaccess.univie.ac.at/articles/bit-claim-against-china-is-ready-to-proceed-to-provisional-measures-ruling-as-three-arbitrators-are-put-in-place/> accessed 10 June 2018.

language in dispute resolution provisions, as well as how to deal with fork-in-the-road clauses.

The tribunal in *Tza Yap Shum* argued for broad interpretation pointing to the fork-in-the-road clause in the last sentence of Article 8 (3) Peru-China BIT 1994 which bars access to arbitration where local courts had already been addressed. It found that, if arbitration could not address all aspects inherent to an expropriation,[784] it would in fact always be barred from speaking to the quantum as well, because once local courts were approached to ascertain the fact of expropriation, an investor would be fully barred from accessing arbitration on any matter.[785] The arbitrators in *Sanum* found an identical phrase in Article 8 (3) China-Laos BIT 1993, went for broad interpretation as well, and rightly noted that no previous decision favoring narrow interpretation had involved an underlying BIT with a similar fork-in-the-road clause.[786] They also underlined being bound by the principle of effet utile and that narrow interpretation would render Article 8 (3) ineffective.[787] The Singapore Appeal Court later agreed, arguing that the phrasing at issue would not allow for local courts to determine liability and an arbitral tribunal to later address the quantum; access to arbitration would rather be completely cut.[788] The arbitrators in *Beijing Urban v Yemen* agreed on the effet utile principle and fork-in-the-road clauses

784 For previous decisions arguing that 'concerning the amount of compensation for expropriation' had to be read broadly – 'every aspect of its subject' – relying on 'ordinary meaning' (Art 31 (1) VCLT) see eg *European Media Ventures SA v Czech Republic* [2007] EWHC 2851 (Comm), [2007] All ER (D) 75 (Dec) paras 43–44; *European Media Ventures SA v Czech Republic*, UNCITRAL, Award on Jurisdiction (15 May 2007) paras 48–68. See also *Franz Sedelmayer v Russian Federation*, SCC, Award (7 July 1998); *Telenor Mobile Communications AS v Hungary*, ICSID Case No ARB/04/15, Award (13 September 2006); *Saipem SpA v People's Republic of Bangladesh*, ICSID Case No ARB/05/07, Decision on Jurisdiction and Recommendation on Provisional Measures (21 March 2007); *Renta 4* (n 618).

785 *Tza* (Award) (n 645) paras 154–161; Art 8 (3) Peru-China BIT 1994.

786 Art 8 (3) China-Laos BIT 1993; *Sanum* (Award on Jurisdiction) (n 724) paras 329, 340–342. For pertinent clauses and decisions favoring narrow interpretation see Article 10 (1) Belgium-Luxembourg Economic Union-Soviet Union BIT 1989 for *Berschader* (n 523); Art 4 (1) Bulgaria-Cyprus BIT 1987 for *Plama* (Decision on Jurisdiction) (n 753), Article 4 (4) Austria-Czechoslovakia BIT 1990 for *Austrian Airlines* (n 744), and Art 4 (3) Germany-Bulgaria BIT 1986 for *ST-AD GmbH* (n 755).

787 *Sanum* (Award on Jurisdiction) (n 724) para 333.

788 *Sanum* (Singapore Court of Appeal Judgment) (n 747) para 130.

and added that a local court would inevitably also address compensation to answer whether an expropriation had occurred.[789]

On the other side of the debate, the High Court of Singapore reviewing the *Sanum* award held that the scope of arbitration was intended to be very narrow. It maintained that the scope might be very limited due to the fork-in-the-road clause, but that it was certainly not non-existent, and did not necessitate broad interpretation on effet utile grounds.[790] The tribunal in *China Heilongjiang v Mongolia*, facing the same language as those in *Tza* and *Sanum*, argued that effet utile would also be upheld with narrow interpretation, because the issue of the amount of compensation could be reserved for subsequent arbitral proceedings during a court case on expropriation.[791]

Once a host state does not concede expropriation, and the investor has to address a local court on the question, he would indeed get caught up in the fork-in-the-road clause, because the court would address effective and appropriate compensation as one of the conditions for something constituting an expropriation or not. This has been convincingly argued in *Beijing Urban v Yemen* – similarly as in *Tza* and *Sanum* – with reference to the expropriation and arbitration clauses in Articles 4 and 10 China-Yemen BIT 1998.[792]

The arbitrators in *China Heilongjiang* did not explain how a local court could comply with an investor's request to reserve the issue of quantum for subsequent arbitration.[793] They seem to consider it sufficient for such disputes on the quantum to be open to international arbitration, where the host state 'formally proclaimed' an expropriation or itself submitted the matter to its domestic courts.[794] They are correct in that the scope of the clause would not be non-existent, and that contracting states may have intended to achieve such a narrow scope. The result of in effect handing host states an easy route to avoiding international arbitration also on the quantum – particularly in times where direct expropriation becomes increasingly irrelevant – is not satisfying in light of object and purpose of the

789 Art 10 (2) China-Yemen BIT 1998; *Beijing Urban* (Decision on Jurisdiction) (n 758) paras 71–72, 77, 78–87.

790 *Sanum* (Singapore High Court Judgment) (n 731) paras 122–123.

791 Arts 4 (1) and (2), 8 (2) and (3) China-Mongolia BIT 1991; *China Heilongjiang* (n 769) paras 445, 447–448, 449–450.

792 Arts 4 and 10 China-Yemen BIT 1998; *Beijing Urban* (Decision on Jurisdiction) (n 758) paras 55, 81.

793 *China Heilongjiang* (n 769) para 449.

794 Ibid para 448.

ISDS provision. At the same time, it is questionable whether it is appropriate for a tribunal to correct the meaning of such a clause.[795]

Among Chinese international lawyers, this issue has been one of the main focal points of pertinent debate.[796] There has been a lot of criticism, especially of the first case, *Tza Yap Shum*; supposedly an 'edifying' example of an investment tribunal trying to get around jurisdictional limitations and excessively relying on semantic interpretation.[797] The tribunal was supposedly 'expansionist,' its approach 'problematic,' and its reasoning 'not technically persuasive,' but on the other hand 'consistent with the BIT practice trend'.[798] Annulment proceedings on account of the tribunal supposedly 'manifestly exceeding its powers' were thought to be in order by some authors.[799] Others noted that developing countries, including China, might exhibit more caution going forward, on account of such decisions, and also referenced Bolivia's withdrawal from the ICSID Convention.[800]

Thus realizing the vulnerability of Chinese treaties to such interpretations, which China supposedly did not intend, Chinese scholars recommended and the Chinese government moved to empower the 'treaty-maker'.[801]

Two things should be made clear. First, China's fourth-generation treaties do not represent the aforementioned retrenchment. Second, the issue grew less relevant for China, since its third-generation BITs no longer included pertinent restrictive ISDS clauses, and it had already started a drive to amend or replace older treaties to – inter alia – also include broad access to arbitration. The pending *Hela Schwarz* concerns such a third-generation BIT (and China already conceded expropriation, supposedly only

795 See also Reinisch (n 544) 171–174; Hwang and Chang, 'Government of the Lao People's Democratic Republic' (n 545) 520–522.

796 See Chapter V.2.2.

797 See eg Hong 虹 Chen 沈, '论 ICSID 对涉中国投资条约仲裁的管辖权' (On the Jurisdiction of ICSID Relating to China Investment-Treaty-Based Arbitration) (2011) 32 (7) *Faxue Zazhi* 128, 130.

798 Wei Shen, 'The good, the bad, or the ugly? A critique of the decision on jurisdiction and competence in Tza Yap Shum v. The Republic of Peru' (2011) 10 CJIL 55, 74.

799 See eg Guiguo Wang, 'Chinese Mechanisms' (n 533) 230–231.

800 Wei Shen, 'The good, the bad, or the ugly?' (n 798) 95.

801 For Chinese debates on the issue see Chapter V.2.2.3.2.2. For China's fourth generation BIT practice that followed this first instance of case law see Chapter IV.2.1.2.5.

paying insufficient compensation).[802] Moreover, in the settled case *Ekran Berhad*, the tribunal could not have relied on a fork-in-the-road clause as in previous awards,[803] and would have probably – and in this case rightly – favored narrow interpretation.

The fourth-generation BITs represent a reaction, albeit a different kind, a retooling in the form of an alignment with the American model. Beijing came to consider this model as giving contracting states more control, including via much more extensive and detailed ISDS provisions, while remaining on a liberal trajectory.

These treaties also started to include provisions more explicitly giving state parties a role in treaty interpretation. Illustrating this point, Article 18 (1) and (2) Canada-China BIT 2012 allow for contracting party consultations leading to the issuance of binding treaty interpretations.[804] Such provisions remind both of Art 30 (3) US Model BIT 2012 and Articles 1131 (2) and 2001 (1) NAFTA, whereas the latter provisions establish a Free Trade Commission for the three NAFTA states, which can issue binding interpretations.[805]

IV.2.1.3.1.2. MFN Application to Procedural Provisions

The second aspect connected to restrictive arbitration clauses in early Chinese BITs has been the attempted use of MFN clauses to import clauses. This has also been the case in the majority of cases involving China, although it has never been at the forefront and never successful. Neverthe-

802 *Hela Schwarz GmbH v People's Republic of China* (ICSID Case No ARB/17/19) (registered 21 June 2017); *Hela Schwarz GmbH* (Procedural Order No 1) (n 781). See also Art 9 China-Germany BIT 2003; Peterson, 'Investment treaty claim' (n 756).

803 Art 7 China-Malaysia BIT 1988.

804 Art 18 (1) and (2) Canada-China BIT 2012. See also Arts 19 and 23 China-Mexico BIT 2008; Art 16 China-Uzbekistan BIT 2011; Art 17 China-Tanzania BIT 2013. See also Art 155 New Zealand-China FTA 2008; Art 9.18 Australia-China FTA 2015. For a less developed precursor to these clauses see Art 12 China-Russia BIT 2006. For an endorsement of such reforms by a Chinese official and negotiator who also lauds pertinent US moves see Yongjie Li (n 531) 178–179.

805 Art 30 (3) US Model BIT 2012; Arts 1131 (2) and 2001 (1) North American Free Trade Agreement between Canada, the United States and Mexico (signed 17 December 1992, entered into force 1 January 1994) (NAFTA).

less, the topic has been prominent in pertinent Chinese debates and evoked further policy recommendations heeded by the government.[806]

IV.2.1.3.1.2.1. Relevant case law

The arbitrators in *Tza Yap Shum v Republic of Peru* did not need to use the BIT's MFN clause to access the broader arbitration clause in the Peru-Colombia BIT,[807] as the Claimant had submitted, because they instead relied on a broad interpretation of the Peru-China BIT arbitration clause.[808] Nonetheless, they addressed the issue of pertinent MFN clause usage, and found that the more specific wording in Article 8 (3) Peru-China BIT 1994, should prevail over the more general MFN clause.[809]

In *Ekran Berhad v People's Republic of China*, the question did not arise due to discontinued proceedings, but the investor could have also attempted accessing broad arbitration clauses in other BITs through the China-Malaysia BIT 1988 MFN clause.[810] However, the chances would have been slim, on account of the parallels to *Tza Yap Shum*. In both cases, the arbitration clause in the pertinent BIT refers to disputes on the amount of compensation for expropriation, and 'other matters (...) if the parties to the dispute so agree' (Article 8 (3) China-Peru BIT 1994) or 'any other disputes agreed by the parties' (Article 7 (4) China-Malaysia BIT).[811] Again, this more specific wording would likely have been considered to prevail over the more general MFN clause.

In *Sanum v Laos*, as in *Tza Yap Shum*, the tribunal did not need to rely on the MFN clause in Article 3 (2) China-Laos BIT 1993 to assume jurisdiction for the question of whether an expropriation had occurred, as it already chose to broadly interpret the arbitration clause in Article 8 (3). On claims pertaining to other matters than expropriation, the tribunal held that Article 3 (2) could not be used to extend protection and add a commensurate dispute settlement clause in a way that would amount to 'a substantial re-write of the Treaty and an extension of the States Parties' consent to arbitration beyond what may be assumed to have been their inten-

806 As discussed below in Chapter IV.2.1.3.1.2.2.
807 China-Colombia BIT 2008.
808 See Chapter IV.2.1.3.1.1.
809 *Tza* (Decision on Jurisdiction) (n 687) paras 193–220; Arts 3 (2), 8 (3) Peru-China BIT 1994.
810 *Ekran Berhad* (n 524); Art 3 China-Malaysia BIT 1988.
811 Art 7 (4) China-Malaysia BIT 1988; Art 8 (3) Peru-China BIT 1994.

tion, given the limited reach of the Treaty protection and dispute settlement clauses'.[812]

In *Ansung v People's Republic of China*, the second case filed against China,[813] the Claimant – inter alia – attempted to use the MFN clause in Article 3 (3) China-Republic of Korea 2007 to access more favorable arbitration clauses in other Chinese BITs that do not contain a temporal limitation.[814] The tribunal dismissed this defense, finding that a 'plain reading of this Article' does not support the MFN clause extending to the 'State's consent to arbitrate with investors and, in particular, not to the temporal limitation period for investor-State arbitration'.[815] Moreover, the arbitrators noted that Article 3 (5) China-Republic of Korea BIT 2007 explicitly offers MFN protection regarding 'access to courts of justice and administrative tribunals and authorities',[816] while such a 'reference to international dispute resolution is conspicuously absent'.[817] Arbitrators did not consider it necessary to review past case law on MFN clause interpretation more thoroughly.[818]

Aside from arguing for broad interpretation of the arbitration clause in the China-Yemen BIT 1998, the Claimant in *Beijing Urban v Republic of Yemen* also maintained that said treaty's MFN clause in Article 3 (1) could be used to access the more liberal dispute resolution clause in the Yemen-UK BIT 1982.[819] The tribunal once again rejected such an attempt. It argued that ordinary meaning and context of the phrase 'treatment accorded

---

812 Arts 3 (2), 8 (3) China-Laos BIT 1993; *Sanum* (Award on Jurisdiction) (n 724) para 358.

813 The case is discussed more in-depth below in Chapter IV.2.1.3.2 as MFN was only a peripheral issue.

814 *Ansung Housing Co Ltd v People's Republic of China*, ICSID Case No ARB/14/25, Award (9 March 2017) paras 124–129, 136; Art 3 (3) Agreement between the Government of the People's Republic of China and the Government of the Republic of Korea on the Promotion and Protection of Investments (signed 7 September 2007, entered into force 1 December 2007) ('China-Republic of Korea BIT 2007').

815 *Ansung* (n 814) para 138.

816 Art 3 (5) China-Republic of Korea BIT 2007.

817 *Ansung* (n 814) para 139.

818 Ibid para 140.

819 *Beijing Urban* (Decision on Jurisdiction) (n 758) para 111; Art 3 (1) China-Yemen BIT 1998; Agreement between the Government of the United Kingdom of Great Britain and Northern Ireland and the Government of the Yemen Arab Republic for the Promotion and Protection of Investments (signed 25 February 1982, entered into force 11 November 1983) ('United Kingdom-Yemen BIT 1982').

to investors of the other Contracting party in its territory with respect to activities relating to investments'[820] in the pertinent MFN clause, could only refer to geographically associated substantive treatment, ie not international arbitration.[821]

IV.2.1.3.1.2.2. Discussion

As is well known, there are two lines of case law with respect to the use of MFN clauses to import procedural provisions[822].

The first line of case law follows *Maffezini*,[823] wherein the investor wanted (and indeed managed) to get around a provision in the Argentina-Spain BIT 1991 mandating an 18-month period of first attempting settlement through the domestic courts,[824] and to rather use the dispute resolution clause in the Chile-Spain BIT 1991.[825] The tribunal accepted, emphasizing

---

820 Art 3 (1) China-Yemen BIT 1998.

821 *Beijing Urban* (Decision on Jurisdiction) (n 758) paras 110, 112–121, 146.

822 For a description of a 'jurisprudential schism' where cases align with landmark precursors 'in spirit, albeit not necessarily in respect of all details' see Stephan W Schill, 'Maffezini v. Plama: Reflections on the Jurisprudential Schism in the Application of Most-Favored-Nation Clauses to Matters of Dispute Settlement', in Meg Kinnear and others (eds), *Building International Investment Law – The First 50 Years of ICSID* (Kluwer Law International 2016) 259.

823 *Emilio Agustin Maffezini v Kingdom of Spain*, ICSID Case No. ARB/97/7, Decision on Jurisdiction (25 January 2000) para 64 ('*Maffezini* (Decision on Jurisdiction)'); *Emilio Agustin Maffezini v Kingdom of Spain*, ICSID Case No. ARB/97/7, Award on Merits (13 November 2000) para 21 ('*Maffezini* (Award on Merits)'). In favor of MFN application to dispute settlement provisions see inter alia also *Siemens AG v Argentine Republic*, ICSID Case No ARB/02/8, Decision on Jurisdiction (3 August 2004); *RosInvestCo* (n 752); *Impregilo SpA v Argentine Republic*, ICSID Case No ARB/07/17, Award (21 June 2011); *Garantie Koza LLP v Turkmenistan*, ICSID Case No ARB/11/20, Decision on the objection to jurisdiction for lack of consent and dissenting opinion (3 July 2013). For cases contradicting *Maffezini* on MFN and pre-arbitration requirements see inter alia *Wintershall Aktiengesellschaft v Argentine Republic*, ICSID Case No ARB/04/14, Award (8 December 2008); *Daimler Financial Services AG v Argentine Republic*, ICSID Case No ARB/05/1, Award (22 August 2012).

824 Art X (3) (a) Acuerdo para la Promocion y la Proteccion Reciproca de Inversiones entre El Reino de Espana ya la Republica Argentina (signed 3 October 1991, entered into force 28 September 1992) ('Argentina-Spain BIT 1991').

825 Art 10 Acuerdo entra la Republica de Chile y El Reino de Espana para la Proteccion y Fomento Reciprocos de Inversiones (signed 3 October 1991, entered into force 28 March 1994) ('Chile-Spain BIT 1991').

that substantive rights and procedural enforcement under BITs were inextricably linked, and that the *ejusdem generis* rule was satisfied in light of the broad nature of the pertinent MFN clause.[826] However, it also underlined limits of MFN application, noting public policy considerations that cannot be overridden.[827]

On the other side, many tribunals followed the arbitrators in *Plama*, which held that '[a]n MFN provision in a basic treaty does not incorporate by reference dispute settlement provisions in whole or in part set forth in another treaty, unless the MFN provision in the basic treaty leaves no doubt that the Contracting Parties intended to incorporate them'.[828] The tribunal in *Telenor* further maintained that where the contracting states have both entered BITs with restrictive and such with expansive dispute resolution clauses, the parties' intentions would be subverted by allowing MFN clause invocation on the method of dispute resolution.[829]

However, strong contradiction in tribunals' reasoning to central questions,[830] 'heated disagreement' about the correct approach to interpreting MFN clauses,[831] and thus a split case law particularly on extending the scope of jurisdiction long remained.[832]

826 *Maffezini* (Decision on Jurisdiction) (n 823) paras 54–56; Art 4 (2) Argentina-Spain BIT 1991.

827 *Maffezini* (Decision on Jurisdiction) (n 823) paras 62–63, including conditions such as exhaustion of local remedies, fork-in-the-road clauses, and consent to a particular arbitration forum.

828 *Plama* (Decision on Jurisdiction) (n 753) para 223. For further decisions against MFN application to dispute settlement provisions see inter alia also *Berschader* (n 523); *Telenor* (n 784); *Renta 4* (n 618); *Kilic Insaat Ithalat Ihracat Sanayi ve Ticaret Anonim Sirketi v Turkmenistan*, ICSID Case No ARB/10/1, Award (2 July 2013); *ST-AD GmbH* (n 755). For cases contradicting *Plama* on MFN use to import access to additional issues or venues see eg *RosInvestCo* (n 752); *Garantie Koza* (n 823).

829 *Telenor* (n 784) para 95.

830 See Guido Santiago Tawil, 'Most Favoured Nation Clauses and Jurisdiction Clauses in Investment Treaty Arbitration', in Christina Binder and others (eds), *International Investment Law for the 21st Century: Essays in Honour of Christoph Schreuer* (OUP 2009) 9 where the issue is highlighted as 'one of the most controversial topics in investment treaty arbitration'. See also Schreuer, 'Investment Arbitration' (n 504).

831 Martins Paparinskis, 'MFN Clauses and International Dispute Settlement: Moving beyond Maffezini and Plama?' (2011) 26 *ICSID Review* 14, 15; Reinisch (n 544) 115, 155–172.

832 When it comes to procedural obstacles like having to resort to domestic courts within a certain time period, MFN use has mostly been accepted, while attempts to extend the scope of jurisdiction to additional issues or an additional

All pertinent cases involving China fall in the second camp, ie a narrower interpretation of the MFN clauses. Exact language has been important. The arbitrators in *Ansung* underlined that the pertinent MFN clause offered explicit protection regarding 'access to courts of justice and administrative tribunals',[833] but conspicuously not to international arbitration.[834] Interestingly, this case merely pertained to getting around a temporal limitation, not adding a forum or substantive matter of dispute, and thus could have been expected to follow the first line of case law. Colleagues in *Beijing Urban* argued that the phrase 'treatment (...) in its territory' excluded international arbitration, as it did not concern substantive treatment and was not geographically associated.[835] The tribunal in *Tza*,[836] in contextual interpretation of the MFN clause, pointed to more specific wording in the arbitration clause foreclosing broad MFN clause interpretation – '[a]ny disputes on other matters (...) may be submitted to the Center if the Parties to the dispute so agree' (Article 8 (3) Peru-China BIT 1994).[837] In *Sanum*, it was found that MFN use to expand jurisdiction to claims beyond expropriation, where the pertinent arbitration clause only talks about the quantum, would be a 'substantial re-write' of the BIT and fail to respect State Party consent.[838]

This study wants to underline several points on the MFN issue. First, outcomes, once again and rightly so, have to depend on the exact language and context in every individual case. Decisions in *Ansung*, *Beijing Urban* and *Tza* were intimately connected to particular language in pertinent MFN and arbitration clauses, and might have been quite different had cer-

venue have mostly been rejected – the specific wording of the MFN clause has been important here. See also Inna Uchkunova and Oleg Temnikov, 'Toss out the Baby and Put the Water to Bed: On MFN Clauses and the Significance of Treaty Interpretation' (2015) 30 *ICSID Review* 414, 436; Matthias Herdegen, *Principles of International Economic Law* (2nd edn, OUP 2016) 454. See also Tawil (n 830) 12–13; Smith (n 498) 68–69; Kaj Hobér, 'MFN Clauses and Dispute Resolution in Investment Treaties: Have we reached the end of the road?', in Christina Binder and others (eds), *International Investment Law for the 21st Century: Essays in Honour of Christoph Schreuer* (OUP 2009) 41.

833 Art 3 (5) China-Republic of Korea BIT 2007.

834 *Ansung* (n 814) para 139.

835 *Beijing Urban* (Decision on Jurisdiction) (n 758) paras 110, 112–121, 146; Art 3 (1) China-Yemen BIT 1998.

836 *Tza* (Decision on Jurisdiction) (n 687) paras 193–220.

837 Art 8 (3) Peru-China BIT 1994.

838 Arts 3 (2), 8 (3) China-Laos BIT 1993; *Sanum* (Award on Jurisdiction) (n 724) para 358.

tain phrases been missing. Second, a majority of cases, and *Tza*, *Sanum* and *Beijing Urban* are generally in line with the trend, reject MFN application to procedural matters in a way that adds another venue or issue. Third, on getting around procedural obstacles, such as minimum litigation periods preceding access to arbitration, *Ansung* might not herald a turn in the case law. The explicit mention of access to courts and administrative tribunals, but not international arbitration, in the underlying MFN clause makes the circumstances rather particular to this case.

Despite the rejection of an MFN clause use to import broader arbitration access in *Tza Yap Shum*, Chinese discourse on such practice, criticism as well as recommendations on how to address the issue, was lively in the years around that first case.[839] Scholars categorically rejected MFN application to dispute resolution clauses,[840] and maintained that such would generally go against contracting parties' intent, and could not reflect their consent to jurisdiction.[841]

On this issue as well, Chinese scholars (earlier on) perceived vulnerability and recommended treaty changes to explicitly exclude MFN application to procedural matters, which was heeded by the Chinese government.[842] The new Chinese BIT practice on MFN clauses can be witnessed – inter alia – in the FTAs with New Zealand, Peru, South Korea and Australia, as well as the BITs with Uzbekistan, Canada, Japan and South Korea in a trilateral agreement, and Tanzania.[843]

---

839 See Chapters V.2.2.2, V.2.2.3.2.2 and V.2.2.3.2.3.

840 See eg Shixi 世席 Huang 黄, '国际投资仲裁中最惠国条款的适用和管辖权的新发展' (New Developments Regarding the Application of the Most-Favored-Nation Clause and Jurisdiction in International Investment Arbitration) (2013) 31 (2) *Falü Kexue* 177, 184–185; Nan 楠 Wang 王, '最惠国待遇条款在国际投资争端解决事项上的适用问题' (On the Application of Most-Favored-Nation Treatment Clause to International Investment Dispute Settlement) (2010) 28 (1) *Hebei Faxue* 120.

841 See eg Tong Qi, 'How Exactly does China Consent' (n 510) 286–287; Kuiran 岿然 Liang 梁, '美国双边投资协定范本争议解决条款分析——以对 ICSID 仲裁管辖权之认可为视角' (The Dispute Settlement Article of the US 2012 BIT Model ———Its Consent Clause to ICSID Arbitration) (2016) 34 (3) *Hebei Faxue* 121, 128, 131.

842 For Chinese debates on the issue see Chapter V.2.2.3.2.2. For China's fourth generation BIT practice more broadly see Chapter IV.2.1.2.5.

843 Art 139 (2) New Zealand-China FTA 2008; Art 131 (2) China-Peru FTA 2009; Art 12.4 (3) China-Republic of Korea FTA 2015; Art 9.4 (2) Australia-China FTA 2015; Art 4 (3) China-Uzbekistan BIT 2011; Art 5 (3) Canada-China BIT 2012; Art 4 (3) Investment promotion and protection agreement between Japan, Republic of Korea and China 2012; Art 4 (3) China-Tanzania BIT 2013.

This fits with a broader international development wherein, in line with scholarly recommendations towards more detailed drafting,[844] investment treaty practice has partly changed – as for example reflected by Article 8.7 CETA – to include more detailed and restrictive MFN provisions, particularly on procedural matters.[845]

IV.2.1.3.2. Temporal Issues – Successive BITs and Time-limits

The second key theme in the case law involving China has been temporal issues. First, the Chinese government has concluded a considerable number of new BITs with countries it had already concluded older generation BITs with. Questions connected to the correct application of successive BITs arose, while investors would be understandably tempted to go for a younger more liberal BIT wherever it appears possible.[846] Second, several Chinese BITs – partly third generation – included provisions barring claims after a certain amount of time has passed since the investor acquired or should have acquired knowledge of the loss or damage in question.[847] Disagreement on the nature of that point and the issue of it having been passed would also have had to be expected.

Both sub-issues have been at the heart of only one arbitration involving China, namely *Ping An v Belgium* on successive BITs, and *Ansung v China* on time-barred claims. Particularly the question of how to maneuver situa-

844 See eg Julien Chaisse and Shintaro Hamanaka, 'The "Noodle Bowl Effect" of Investment Treaties in Asia: The Phenomenon, the Problems, the Practical Solutions' (2018) 33 *ICSID Review* 1; Tawil (n 830) 30. See also Thomas W Wälde, 'Interpreting Investment Treaties: Experiences and Examples', in Christina Binder and others (eds), *International Investment Law for the 21st Century: Essays in Honour of Christoph Schreuer* (OUP 2009) 780.

845 Art 8.7 Comprehensive Economic and Trade Agreement (CETA) between Canada, of the one part, and the European Union, of the other part (signed 30 October 2016, not yet entered into force) ('CETA'), whereas Art 8.7 (4) explicitly states that '[f]or greater certainty, the "treatment" referred to in paragraphs 1 and 2 does not include procedures for the resolution of investment disputes between investors and states provided for in other international investment treaties and other tradeagreements'. See also Andreas R Ziegler, 'Most Favoured-Nation (MFN) Treatment', in August Reinisch (ed), *Standards of Investment Protection* (OUP 2008) 85–86.

846 See also Jean Ho, 'Investment Protection under Successive Treaties' (2017) 32 *ICSID Review* 58, 61. On the evolution of Chinese investment treaty-making see Chapter IV.2.1.2.

847 Art 9 (7) China-Republic of Korea BIT 2007.

tions where two BITs have successively been adopted, have been hotly debated in China. *Ping An* was also hailed at the time as a 'signal [for] the beginning of a wave of Chinese claims',[848] because it had been preceded by years of massive Chinese outward investments, as well as a series of issues with the latter, arising from the economic and financial crisis.

IV.2.1.3.2.1. Ping An v Kingdom of Belgium (ICSID)

Ping An, a life insurance company, filed this ICSID case – the first initiated by a Mainland Chinese investor and the first to address one of China's third-generation BITs – against Belgium on 7 September 2012.[849]

Ping An had acquired EUR 2 billion or 4.81 % in shares of the Belgian-Dutch commercial and savings bank Fortis from October 2007 to July 2008.[850] During the global financial crisis, concerns about the bank's solvency led to it losing access to the overnight interbank market on 26 September 2008. Two days later, the Belgian, Dutch and Luxembourg governments decided to acquire large shares in Fortis, while the Belgian national bank provided EUR 14.8 billion in emergency liquidity assistance.[851] In a second step, in early October 2008, Belgium and the Netherlands acquired the rest of Fortis' Dutch and Belgian assets – 75 % of the Belgian banking arm of *Fortis* was immediately sold to BNP Paribas – while Luxembourg increased its share in the company's local subsidiary.[852]

The Claimant alleged that its interest was first halved, and eventually Belgium's actions constituted complete expropriation;[853] Belgium supposedly coerced Fortis to sell shares to it under market value, sold a part in a way that 'stripped enormous value' from Fortis, failed to adequately compensate Fortis and its shareholders while enriching itself in the process,[854]

---

848 Myles Neligan, 'China insurer Ping An files claim for Fortis loss' *Reuters* (London, 24 September 2012) <http://in.reuters.com/article/2012/09/24/pingan-fortis-idINL5E8KO9V520120924> accessed 30 March 2019.

849 *Ping An Life Insurance Company of China, Limited and Ping An Insurance (Group) Company of China, Limited v Kingdom of Belgium*, ICSID Case No ARB/12/29, Award (30 April 2015) para 7. See also Qing Ren, 'Ping An v Belgium – Temporal Jurisdiction of Successive BITs' (2016) 31 *ICSID Review* 129.

850 *Ping An Life Insurance* (n 849) para 57.

851 Ibid paras 58–60.

852 Ibid paras 61–62.

853 Ibid paras 60, 62.

854 Ibid paras 74–78.

and supposedly discriminated Fortis vis-à-vis the bank Dexia, which obtained sufficient interbank lending guarantees to sort out its problems.[855] Ping An sought additional compensation, or alternatively that the Belgian government pay it a *pro rata* share of its supposed unjust enrichment, arguing that the tribunal had jurisdiction under Article 8 (1) Belgium-Luxembourg Economic Union-China BIT 2005, while it alleged violations by the Respondent of Article 3 (1) and (2), each in conjunction with Article 3 (3) or Article 11, and of Article 4 Belgium-Luxembourg Economic Union-China BIT 1984 (equitable treatment and protection, MFN, and expropriation clauses).[856]

Belgium argued that the tribunal lacked jurisdiction ratione temporis, because Ping An had filed its claim based on the Belgium-Luxembourg Economic Union-China BIT 2005. However, this new BIT was not yet in force when the dispute arose. The Claimant itself claimed that the letter they sent the Belgian Ambassador in Beijing on 14 October 2009 constituted a notice of dispute under Article 8 (1) of the new BIT. However, that BIT only entered into force on 1 December 2009, and Belgium's consent to arbitration under Article 8 (1) is limited to disputes arising after the BIT entered into force.[857] The Claimant should supposedly instead have addressed the Belgian courts or invoked the older BIT under its sunset clause in Article 14 (1).[858] Belgium added that arbitration under the old BIT could not have entailed proceedings at ICSID, and was limited to disputes over the amount of compensation for expropriation.[859]

---

855 Ibid paras 66–72.

856 Arts 3 (1), (2) and (3), 4 and 11 Accord entre l'Union Economique Belgo-Luxembourgeoise et le Gouvernment de la Republique Populaire de Chine en la Matiere de l'Encouragement et de la Protection Reciproques des Investissements (signed 4 June 1984, entered into force 5 October 1986, terminated, new Belgium-Luxembourg Economic Union-China BIT entered into force 1 December 2009) ('Belgium-Luxembourg Economic Union-China BIT 1984'); Art 8 (1) Accord entre l'Union Economique Belgo-Luxembourgeoise et le Gouvernment de la Republique Populaire de Chine concernant l'Encouragement et la Protection Reciproque des Investissements (signed 6 June 2005, entered into force 1 December 2009) ('Belgium-Luxembourg Economic Union-China BIT 2005'); *Ping An Life Insurance* (n 849) paras 38, 79–89, 93–95, 97, 131–137.

857 *Ping An Life Insurance* (n 849) paras 105–111, 113–114, 138–152.

858 Ibid paras 151–152, referencing *Werner Schneider acting in his capacity as insolvency administrator of Walter Bau Ag (In Liquidation) v Kingdom of Thailand (formerly Walter Bau AG (in liquidation) v Kingdom of Thailand)*, UNCITRAL, Award (1 July 2009) para 9.5(c).

859 *Ping An Life Insurance* (n 849) para 138.

In its 2015 award, the tribunal upheld Belgium's ratione temporis objection, emphasizing that it was constituted under the new BIT, although the Claimant did not rely on substantive provisions of that treaty, and that the dispute had crystallized while the old BIT was in force.[860] They underlined the importance of the ordinary meaning approach in interpreting BITs and the non-retroactivity of substantive obligations.[861] The temporal application of jurisdictional provisions might be a different matter, but the plain meaning of the text of Article 8 (1) of the new BIT – 'when a legal dispute arises' – read in conjunction with Article 8 (2) and the transition clause in Article 10 (2) is also said to indicate non-retroactivity for jurisdiction. The transition clause explicitly excludes jurisdiction for disputes already under judicial or arbitral proceedings before the new BIT entered into force, but does not address those that have only been notified. However, arbitrators argued that assuming retroactivity would suddenly give investors access not only to ICSID arbitration but also to a very broad dispute settlement clause instead of the old restrictive one, and that the parties would not have wanted this.[862]

IV.2.1.3.2.2. Ansung v People's Republic of China (ICSID)

On 4 November 2014, a case against China was registered at ICSID, filed by a South Korean real estate developer – Ansung – under Article 9 China-Republic of Korea BIT 2007, a third-generation BIT.[863] Ansung invoked that the company had entered into an Investment Agreement – relevant approvals for the development noted as obtained – with the Communist Party of the Sheyang Harbor Industrial Zone Administration Committee (the 'Committee') on 12 December 2006 to build an eighteen-hole golf course, clubhouse and condominiums in two phases.[864] It was then allegedly held up by domestic legal changes, was denied the necessary land use rights to start the second phase, and ascertained that a Chinese company had already started operation of an eighteen-hole golf course nearby that authorities termed illegal but did nothing to stop operating.[865] An-

860 Ibid paras 129–130.

861 Ibid paras 166–173, referencing *Fraport AG* (n 704) para 340.

862 Arts 8 (1) and (2), 10 (2) Belgium-Luxembourg Economic Union-China BIT 2005; *Ping An Life Insurance* (n 849) paras 186, 223–233.

863 Art 9 China-Republic of Korea BIT 2007; *Ansung* (n 814) para 8.

864 *Ansung* (n 814) para 36.

865 Ibid paras 38–40, 41–46.

sung's Chinese subsidiary could not repay loans the Committee had arranged, and Committee officials started blockading the golf course, eventually leading Ansung to sell to a Chinese purchaser at a serious financial loss in 2011.[866]

China filed preliminary objections pursuant to ICSID Arbitration Rule 41 (5), holding that the claim was 'manifestly without legal merit'.[867] It maintained that Ansung filed for arbitration after 'more than 3 years [had] elapsed from the date on which the investor first acquired, or should have first acquired, the knowledge that the investor had incurred loss or damage,' violating Article 9 (7) China-Republic of Korea BIT 2007.[868] In their interpretation of Rule 41 (5), both the Claimant and the Respondent relied on *Trans-Global Petroleum v Jordan*, and the interpretation therein of 'manifestly' requiring the objection to be established 'clearly and obviously, with relative ease and dispatch.'[869]

The tribunal, in its award on 9 March 2017, dismissed Ansung's claims in an expedited fashion during a preliminary phase of proceedings.[870] On the temporal limit in Article 9 (7) China-Republic of Korea BIT 2007, it underlined that knowledge of the fact of the loss, not the quantum and not the liquidation of a damage, is relevant for the start date; not 'full and precise knowledge of the loss or damage', but only a 'first appreciation that loss or damage will be (or has been) incurred. It neither requires nor permits a claimant to wait and see the full extent of the loss or damage that will or may result'.[871] The arbitrators maintained that Ansung's own pleadings indicated knowledge of the competing golf course in 2007, its start of operations in 2009, Ansung's Chinese subsidiary not being able to repay a

866 Ibid paras 46–52, 53–55.

867 R 41 (5) ICSID Arbitration Rules; *Ansung* (n 814) paras 15–16.

868 Art 9 (7) China-Republic of Korea BIT 2007 – Art 9 (7): 'Notwithstanding the provisions of paragraph 3 of this Article, an investor may not make a claim pursuant to paragraph 3 of this Article if more than three years have elapsed from the date on which the investor first acquired, or should have first acquired, knowledge that the investor had incurred loss or damage'; *Ansung* (n 814) para 56.

869 *Ansung* (n 814) paras 62–69, referencing *Trans-Global Petroleum, Inc. v Hashemite Kingdom of Jordan*, ICSID Case No ARB/07/25, Decision on the Respondent's Objection Under Rule 41(5) (12 May 2008) para 88.

870 *Ansung* (n 814) paras 142–144 and X (1).

871 Art 9 (7) China-Republic of Korea BIT 2007; *Ansung* (n 814) para 111, see also paras 32, 71, 107, 110, referencing *Spence International Investments et al v Republic of Costa Rica*, ICSID Case No UNCT/13/2, Interim Award (25 October 2016) para 213.

loan in June 2011, and Ansung having to dispose of the subsidiary to avoid further losses by October 2011.[872] On the end date of the limitation period, they referred to the 'plain language' in Art 9 (7) China-Republic of Korea BIT and the decision in *Vannessa Ventures v Venezuela* indicating that deposition of the arbitration request with ICSID is decisive – 7 October 2014 in this case – and held that this happened more than three years after the start date of early October 2011 (at the latest), leading to the claim being time-barred and thus manifestly without merit.[873]

IV.2.1.3.2.3. Discussion

The tribunal in *Ping An* was in line with previous case law on disputes that had crystallized before a new BIT was in force.[874] Some critics emphasized that Article 10 (2) of the later BIT only expressly excludes disputes 'already under judicial or arbitral process',[875] not such that had merely been notified, and suggested consciously different wording in Chinese BITs on this matter. However, the arbitrators in *Ping An* have also convincingly settled on non-retroactivity for merely notified disputes. They argued that the parties would not have intended for retroactivity that suddenly gives investors access not only to ICSID, but also to a much broader ISDS clause.[876]

Chinese international law scholars have repeatedly referred to *Ping An* as an important motivation behind their recommendation for Beijing to improve drafting of transitional clauses – ie more detailed and clear, eg also referring to disputes that have only been notified ahead of the new treaty's

872 *Ansung* (n 814) para 107.

873 Art 9 (7) China-Republic of Korea BIT 2007; *Ansung* (n 814) paras 5–6, 115–116, 118, 121–122, referencing *Vannessa Ventures Ltd v Bolivarian Republic of Venezuela*, ICSID Case No ARB(AF)/04/6, Decision on Jurisdiction (22 August 2008) para 31.

874 Tribunals have generally supported non-retroactivity, especially with dispute settlement clauses differing strongly. For cases wherein a later BIT explicitly excluded disputes that had 'arisen' before its entry into force see eg *Jan de Nul NV and Dredging International NV v Arab Republic of Egypt*, ICSID Case No ARB/04/13, Award (6 November 2008); *ABCI Investments Ltd v Republic of Tunisia*, ICSID Case No ARB/04/12, Decision on Jurisdiction (18 February 2011). For cases where no comparable restrictive phrasing was included in the BIT see eg *Werner Schneider* (n 858).

875 See eg Qing Ren (n 820) 133–137; Art 10 (2) (Belgium-Luxembourg Economic Union-China BIT 2005.

876 *Ping An Life Insurance* (n 849) paras 229–230.

entry into force – so that Chinese investors would not go wrong again in their reliance on one of two successive treaties.[877]

On the issue of claims being time-barred, Article 1116 (2) NAFTA is similar to Article 9 (7) China-Republic of Korea BIT 2007, which was at issue in the only relevant case with Chinese participation, *Ansung*. The limitation period for claims is set at three years, the start date connects to when the 'investor first acquired, or should have first acquired, knowledge that the investor had incurred loss or damage'.[878] The only difference is that the NAFTA text additionally includes 'knowledge of the alleged breach'.[879]

The issue of the noted NAFTA provision was at stake in several cases, whereas the tribunal in *Grand River v US* underlined the distinction between actual and constructive knowledge, and only found the latter established, ie that the Claimant should have known about the legislation affecting its business.[880] Moreover, the arbitrators convincingly – and in line with their colleagues in *Mondev*[881] – argued that acquiring knowledge of a loss or damage does not require knowing the extent of such loss or damage.[882] This supports the findings in *Ansung*. The Claimant's evocation, in that case, of *Pope & Talbot, Inc. v Canada* as to knowledge having to be of 'actual damage, rather than predicted future damage' goes fail,[883] also because the context of the China-Republic of Korea BIT 2007 is different, given the lack of differentiation between knowledge of a 'breach' and of a 'loss or damage'.

---

877 See Chapters V. 2.2.3.2.1 and V.2.2.3.2.2; Yong 勇 Liu 刘, '"中国平安诉比利时王国投资仲裁案"——以条约适用的时际法为视角' ("China Ping An v. Kingdom of Belgium Investment Arbitration" – From the Perspectve of the Intertemporal Law on Treaty Application) (2016) 38 (4) *Huanqiu Falü Pinglun* 162, 174; Jin 劲 Sun 孙, '论构建中国全方位对外投资条约体系' (On Establishing China's Comprehensive Investment Treaty System) [2017] (2) *Guojifa Yanjiu* 3, 10. See also Dilini Pathirana, 'Making an Arbitration Claim under Chinese BITs: Some Inferences from Recent ISDS Cases' (2017) 5 *The Chinese Journal of Comparative Law* 420, 432.

878 Art 9 (7) China-Republic of Korea BIT 2007.

879 Art 1116 (2) NAFTA.

880 *Grand River Enterprises Six Nations Ltd., et al v United States of America*, UNCITRAL, Decision on Objections to Jurisdiction (20 July 2006, administered by ICSID) paras 56, 71.

881 Mondev International Ltd. v United States of America, ICSID Case No ARB(AF)/99/2, Award (11 October 2002) para 87.

882 *Grand River Enterprises* (n 880) para 78.

883 *Ansung* (n 814) para 94, citing *Pope & Talbot, Inc. v Government of Canada*, UNCITRAL, Award (24 February 2000) para 12.

There has not yet been much time for this case for debate among Chinese international lawyers, much less for policy changes. Nevertheless, and despite the claims having been rejected, the fact remains significant that *Ansung* was the first award in a case where China was the Respondent – a second may soon follow in *Hela Schwarz GmbH v China*. It has been highlighted that the US adapted its Model BIT after being the Respondent in several NAFTA cases even though it had not lost a single one of them.[884] Furthermore, the issue of limitation periods might emerge again as other Chinese investment treaties include comparable provisions,[885] forming part of a larger trend of Americanization of procedural provisions in China's (and other states') investment treaties.[886] Another interesting aspect of *Ansung* was that China was not only represented by the international law firm Dentons Europe LLP – containing a Chinese law firm merged into the company in 2015 – but also by the Chinese law firm Zhong Lun as well as by representatives of its Ministry of Commerce's Department of Treaty and Law.[887] This connects to the policy goal of bolstering domestic international law talent and reducing reliance on international law firms.[888]

---

884 Gallagher, 'Role of China' (n 720) 96–97.

885 For provisions comparable to Art 9 (7) China-Republic of Korea BIT 2007 see also Art 15 (11) Investment promotion and protection agreement between Japan, Republic of Korea and China 2012; Art 12.12 (11) China-Republic of Korea FTA 2015. For provisions comparable to Art 1116 (2) NAFTA see also Art 154 New Zealand-China FTA 2008; Art 21 (2) (f) Canada-China BIT 2012; Art 9.14 (1) Australia-China FTA 2015. For further similar provisions – knowledge of 'events which gave rise to the dispute' – see also Art 13 (7) China-Mexico BIT 2008; Art 12 (4) China-Uzbekistan BIT 2012; Art 13 (4) China-Tanzania BIT 2013.

886 See Chapter IV.2.1.2.5. See also Andrea K Bjorklund, 'Waiver of Local Remedies and Limitation Periods', in Meg Kinnear and others (eds), *Building International Investment Law – The First 50 Years of ICSID* (Kluwer Law International 2016) 244–250.

887 Luke Eric Peterson, 'China prevails as arbitrators dismiss Korean investor's ICSID claim for non-compliance with BIT's 3 year claims window; MFN argument also fails' *IAReporter* (Santa Monica, 10 March 2017) <http://www.iareporter.com.uaccess.univie.ac.at/articles/china-prevails-as-arbitrators-dismiss-korean-investors-icsid-claim-for-non-compliance-with-bits-3-year-claims-window-mfn-argument-also-fails/> accessed 11 March 2017.

888 See Chapters V.2.1.3.1 and V.2.2.3.2.

IV.2.1.3.3. Geographical Scope – Application of Chinese BITs to Hong Kong and Macao

The third prominent issue in investment arbitration with Chinese involvement was whether China's BITs (automatically) cover its Special Administrative Regions (hereinafter: SAR) Hong Kong and Macao, which have the power to also conclude their own BITs.[889]

IV.2.1.3.3.1. Relevant case law

In *Tza Yap Shum v Republic of Peru*, the tribunal rather straightforwardly rejected the Respondent's objections, and found that it 1) was satisfied that the Claimant – a Hong Kong investor – had proved his Chinese nationality, and 2) was not convinced that the PRC and Peru had the intention of excluding Hong Kong residents who also have Chinese nationality from their BIT's applicability.[890]

In *Sanum v Lao People's Democratic Republic*, the issue arose in the long-winded legal battle between the Macao investor Sanum and Laos.[891] According to Laos, Sanum (ie the 'investor') did not qualify as 'economic entit[y] established in accordance with the laws and regulations of each contracting State' (Article 1 (2) China-Laos BIT 1993), because it was constituted under Macao law, nor as an 'economic entity' (Article 1 (2) (b) China-Laos BIT 1993), because it lacked economic activities within Mainland China, its management seat in the Macao SAR gave it Macao nationality, and shell companies and investments of non-contracting States should not receive protection.[892]

The tribunal once again rejected the pertinent objections, arguing that 1) application was not expressly excluded (as in the China-Russia BIT

889 Art 31 Constitution of the PRC 1982. See also Arts 22, 116, 118 and 151 Basic Law of the Hong Kong Special Administrative Region of the People's Republic of China (adopted 4 April 1990, entered into effect 1 July 1997); Arts 22 and 136 Basic Law of the Macao Special Administrative Region of the People's Republic of China (adopted 31 March 1993, entered into effect 20 December 1999).

890 *Tza* (Decision on Jurisdiction) (n 687) paras 32, 43–48, 52–77.

891 *Sanum* (Award on Jurisdiction) (n 724) paras 51–52.

892 Art 1 (2) China-Laos BIT 1993; *Sanum* (Award on Jurisdiction) (n 724) paras 111, 119.

2009),[893] that 2) parties failed to provide affidavits from pertinent government authorities and clarify the situation,[894] and that 3) the customary international law 'moving treaty frontier' rule was to be applied.[895] They found the latter rule reflected in Article 15 Convention on the Succession of States in Respect of Treaties (hereinafter: VCST), which stipulates applicability should such not be 'incompatible with object and purpose of the treaty or (…) radically change the conditions for its operation'.[896] Second, Article 29 VCLT stipulates applicability where no intention is established that the BIT should not be 'binding upon each party in respect of its entire territory'.[897] The arbitrators found in the investor's favor.[898]

Laos challenged the award at the Singapore High Court.[899] It filed for the admission of two diplomatic letters sent after the arbitral award, wherein both governments affirm their view that the China-Laos BIT did not extend to Macao, as long as no separate future arrangements were made.[900]

The Singapore High Court disagreed with Sanum's contention of non-justiciability due to only issues of 'pure international law' being raised,[901] and admitted the diplomatic letters as fresh evidence,[902] on account of 'sufficiently strong reasons' that they could most likely not have been adduced earlier, were 'probably' of important influence on the result of the application before the Court, and were considered apparently credible.[903] The

893 China-Laos BIT 1993; Protocol to the Agreement para 1 (1) China-Russia BIT 2006; *Sanum* (Award on Jurisdiction) (n 724) para 271.

894 *Sanum* (Award on Jurisdiction) (n 724) para 232.

895 Ibid paras 219, 222.

896 Art 15 Vienna Convention on the Succession of States in Respect of Treaties (adopted 23 August 1978, entered into force 6 November 1996) 1946 UNTS 3 ('VCST'); *Sanum* (Award on Jurisdiction) (n 724) paras 225, 236, 239–269.

897 Art 29 VCLT; *Sanum* (Award on Jurisdiction) (n 724) 236, 270–300. See also Hwang and Chang, 'Government of the Lao People's Democratic Republic' (n 545) 510 on these norms' relevance as customary international law, while the two states are parties to the VCLT but not the VCST.

898 *Sanum* (Award on Jurisdiction) (n 724) paras 370.

899 See also Chapter IV.2.1.3.1.

900 *Sanum* (Singapore High Court Judgment) (n 731) paras 15, 39–40.

901 Ibid para 30.

902 Ibid para 16.

903 Ibid paras 44–50, 56. Conditions are derived from *Ladd v Marshall* [1954] 1 WLR 1489 as modified in *Lassiter Ann Masters v To Keng Lam (alias Toh Jeanette)* [2004] 2 SLR(R) 392. See also Art V (1) (a) Convention on the Recognition and Enforcement of Foreign Arbitral Awards (signed 10 June 1958, entered into force 7 June 1959) 330 UNTS 38 ('New York Convention').

Court then maintained that the letters constituted a 'subsequent agreement' on the interpretation of the BIT (Article 31 (3) (a) VCLT) – seeing them as an affirmation of the parties initial common understanding – and were sufficient to 'otherwise establish' that the parties did not intend for the BIT to apply to Macao (Article 15 VCST; Article 29 VCLT).[904] It rejected the need to explicitly discount applicability to Macao as in the China-Russia BIT 2009, considered Macao's ability to negotiate its own BITs as an additional (limited) point of evidence, and 'on a balance of probabilities' decided against applicability to Macao.[905]

However, Singapore's Court of Appeal reversed this finding in 2016.[906] It admitted two further diplomatic letters into evidence,[907] and rejected the notion that the High Court should have shown deference to the arbitral tribunal.[908] Nonetheless, the Court interpreted the parties' silence on the issue of applicability to Macao ahead of this case – despite the 1999 handover of the territory to China being foreseeable when the BIT was concluded – as a lack of intention to exclude Macao,[909] and also did not find such intention 'otherwise established'.[910] The judges discounted the initial diplomatic letters as post-critical date evidence that does not confirm pre-critical date evidence but rather attempts to advance the Claimant's position *post hoc*.[911]

---

904 Arts 29 and 31 VCLT; Art 15 VCST; *Sanum* (Singapore High Court Judgment) (n 731) paras 50, 57–64, 70, 77.

905 *Sanum* (Singapore High Court Judgment) (n 731) paras 70, 79–82, 88, 110–111.

906 *Sanum* (Singapore Court of Appeal Judgment) (n 747) paras 122, 152.

907 Ibid paras 13, 24, 27–35.

908 Ibid para 44.

909 Ibid paras 54–60.

910 Art 29 VCLT – Art 29: 'Territorial scope of treaties – Unless a different intention appears from the treaty or is otherwise established, a treaty is binding upon each party in respect of its entire territory'; *Sanum* (Singapore Court of Appeal Judgment) (n 747) paras 72–82, 83–91.

911 *Sanum* (Singapore Court of Appeal Judgment) (n 747) paras 67, 100, 105–112, referencing *Compania de Aguas del Aconquija SA and Vivendi Universal v Argentina*, ICSID Case No ARB/97/3, Decision on Jurisdiction (14 November 2005); *Mavrommatis Jerusalem Concessions (Greece v Britain)* (Judgment) PCIJ Series A No 5 [29]–[30].

IV.2.1.3.3.2. Discussion

Three key issues should be discussed regarding the above cases, wherein tribunals correctly allowed investors from Hong Kong and Macao to invoke PRC BITs. First, domestic law – in this case the laws of the PRC on nationality, applicable to Hong Kong and Macao – determines who has nationality for the purposes of a BIT if there is no explicit exclusion of a certain group, which was not the case for Hong Kong or Macao residents in the BITs underlying *Tza* and *Sanum*.[912] Double citizenship could complicate the issue in future cases. Moreover, legal persons incorporated under Hong Kong or Macao law could have been a different matter than natural persons. The latter are conferred Chinese nationality by central government-level PRC law, but eg Hong Kong companies are incorporated based on Hong Kong SAR-level legislation.[913]

The tribunal in *Tza* did not address this issue. However, the arbitrators in *Sanum* made a convincing case that Hong Kong and Macao are part of the contracting state China, part of its sovereignty, and that it was logical to assume that if the BIT was taken to apply to China's entire territory, 'an economic entity established under the laws applicable in any part of the territory of the PRC is to be considered to have been established under the laws and regulations of the PRC'.[914]

Second, the Hong Kong and Macao 'Special Administrative Regions' (SARs) have the power to conclude international treaties on trade and investment issues, including BITs, and Hong Kong has done so in a dozen cases. This book considers the argument persuasive that this autonomy being intended to benefit its residents not restrict their rights weighs in favor of them having the right to invoke their own but also China's BITs.[915]

Third, the particular issue of the two contracting states submitting notes verbales while proceedings are already underway should be commented on. Generally, unilateral statements by involved states on BIT interpretation during proceedings would be considered self-serving and of limited

912 See also Gallagher, 'China's BITs and Arbitration Practice' (n 678) 208.
913 See also Wei Shen, 'The good, the bad, or the ugly?' (n 798) 62–63.
914 Art 1 (2) (b) China-Laos BIT 1993; *Sanum* (Award on Jurisdiction) (n 724) para 303, see also paras 301–305. See also Pathirana (n 877) 426 citing Nils Eliasson, 'Chinese Investment Treaties: A Procedural Perspective', in Vivienne Bath and Luke Nottage (eds), *Foreign Investment and Dispute Resolution Law and Practice in Asia* (Routledge 2011) 105.
915 *Sanum* (Award on Jurisdiction) (n 724) para 242.

value.[916] One important facet here is that arbitrators and judges need to honor the principle of contemporaneity on treaty interpretation and the date of institution of proceedings as relevant date for determining jurisdiction. The evidentiary value of notes verbales sent later on as 'subsequent agreement' in determining jurisdiction has to be considered diminished.[917] States as parties to the respective BIT are indeed the 'owners' of the treaty, and Article 31 (3) (a) VCLT reminds that in interpretation there 'shall be taken into account, together with the context: (a) any subsequent agreement between the parties regarding the interpretation of the treaty or the application of its provisions'.[918] However, at the same time, states parties are limited by the obligation to uphold due process, equality of arms and legitimate expectations of investor-claimants as 'third-party beneficiaries.' Caution is due when procedural and substantive rights already granted to investors might be taken away.[919]

As another interesting aspect of this development, it shows that the Chinese government is an active participant in the interpretation and application process of investment treaties.[920] This fits with the overall trend of trying to further calibrate China's treaties,[921] and including provisions granting states an explicit role in treaty interpretation.[922]

Chinese international law scholars have instead been mostly critical of the pertinent findings in *Tza* and *Sanum*, maintaining that they supposedly undermine the SARs' autonomy, contracting states trust in investment arbitration, and diplomatic relations between them.[923] Chinese treaty practice has not yet changed – only the China-Russia BIT 2006 explicitly ex-

916 See eg *Aguas del Tunari SA v Republic of Bolivia*, ICSID Case No ARB/02/3, Decision on Respondent's Objections to Jurisdiction (21 October 2005) paras 47, 249–263 as cited in Dolzer and Schreuer (n 523) 31–32.

917 See also Hwang and Chang, 'Government of the Lao People's Democratic Republic' (n 545) 519.

918 Art 31 (3) (a) VCLT.

919 See also Wälde, 'Interpreting Investment Treaties' (n 844) 765–766.

920 See also Gallagher, 'Role of China' (n 720) 98–99.

921 See fourth-generation treaties in Chapter IV.2.1.2.5.

922 See Chapter IV.2.1.3.1.1.7.

923 Hong Chen (n 797) 128, 130; Shixi 世席 Huang 黄, '国际投资仲裁裁决的司法审查及投资条约解释的公正性基于"Ｓａｎｕｍ案"和"Ｙｕｋｏｓ案"判决的考察' (Inspecting the equitability of the judicial review of international arbitral awards and the interpretation of investment treaties based on the rulings in Sanum and Yukos) [2017] (3) *Faxue* 130, 144–145.

cludes the SARs.[924] However, the Chinese government has issued a statement to clarify its position, maintaining that:

> as a principle, the investment agreements between the central government and foreign countries do not apply to SARs, unless otherwise decided by the central government after seeking the views of the SAR governments and consulting with the other contracting parties of the agreement.[925]

Nonetheless, it is doubtful that this statement will have strong evidentiary value in future arbitrations.[926]

IV.2.1.3.4. Availability of the ICSID Convention to SOEs

A further issue of contention has been connected to state-owned enterprises (hereinafter: SOEs) being a dominant driver of Chinese outward investment – setting China apart from most home states.[927] Tribunals have addressed whether such entities are covered under the term 'national of another contracting state' in Article 25 (1) ICSID Convention, and disputes involving them can thus fall within the jurisdiction of the Centre.[928]

IV.2.1.3.4.1. Relevant case law

The tribunal in *Beijing Urban v Yemen* was unconvinced by jurisdictional objections by the Respondent related to the Claimant supposedly not being a 'national of another contracting state' under Article 25 (1) ICSID Convention, due to it being a state-owned enterprise.[929] The arbitrators maintained that the Claimant was publicly funded and wholly state-owned, but did not act as an agent of the Chinese government or discharge

---

924 Article 1 of the Protocol to the China-Russia BIT 2006.

925 Ministry of Foreign Affairs of the People's Republic of China, 'Foreign Ministry Spokesperson Hua Chunying's Regular Press Conference on October 21, 2016' (Beijing, 21 October 2016) <http://www.fmprc.gov.cn/mfa_eng/xwfw_665399/s2510_665401/t1407743.shtml> accessed 2 July 2018.

926 See also Pathirana (n 877) 432.

927 Sauvant and Nolan (n 532) 893, 895.

928 Art 25 (1) ICSID Convention.

929 Ibid; *Beijing Urban* (Decision on Jurisdiction) (n 758) paras 29, 147.

governmental functions when building part of a terminal at Sana'a International Airport under a commercial contract.[930]

The Respondent in *China Heilongjiang v Mongolia* objected to jurisdiction – inter alia – on the grounds that the Claimants supposedly failed to qualify as protected 'investors' under Article 1 (2) China-Mongolia BIT 1991 on account of (some of them) not constituting 'economic entities' but rather state-owned 'quasi-instrumentalities of the Chinese government'.[931] The arbitrators were not convinced, and emphasized the broad terms in which 'economic entity' was set out in the BIT, and that neither the treaty nor other evidence established that the meaning should have been a more limited one, excluding certain kinds of legal entities.[932]

IV.2.1.3.4.2. Discussion

The contention that wholly or partly government-owned entities could not be 'nationals' under Article 25 (1) has been refuted in the Convention's drafting history, pertinent scholarship and case law.[933] The decisive question instead has been whether the company at issue discharged an essentially governmental function.[934] There has been no case so far, wherein an investor would have been judged outside ICSID jurisdiction due to its non-private character. The tribunal in *CSOB v Slovakia* maintained that the Czech state agency's international banking transactions were commercial.[935] The arbitrators in *Rumeli Telekom v Kazakhstan* rejected the notion that the possibility of award proceeds flowing to Turkey's treasury would exclude the Claimant.[936] Finally, part-ownership by the Norwegian government in *Telenor v Hungary*,[937] and UK government ownership of the Claimant in *CDC v Seychelles*,[938] where a commercial loan was at issue, did

930 *Beijing Urban* (Decision on Jurisdiction) (n 758) paras 31–44.

931 *China Heilongjiang* (n 769) paras 269–276; Art 1 (2) China-Mongolia BIT 1991.

932 *China Heilongjiang* (n 769) paras 411–422.

933 Schreuer and others, *The ICSID Convention* (n 505) 161–162; Art 25 (1) ICSID Convention.

934 Aron Broches, 'The Convention on the Settlement of Investment Disputes between States and Nationals of Other States' (1972) 136 *Recueil des Cours* 331, 354–355. See also *Ceskoslovenska Obchodni Banka* (n 513) paras 16–27.

935 *Ceskoslovenska Obchodni Banka* (n 513) paras 16–27.

936 *Rumeli Telekom* (n 710) paras 325–328.

937 *Telenor* (n 784) paras 16, 18.

938 *CDC Group* (n 706) paras 6, 19, 34.

not cause Respondents to pursue objections arguing that the Claimant was not a 'national of another Contracting State'.

Case law involving China thus fits the wider trend. Going forward, similar cases will again be judged on the concrete circumstances, and Chinese SOEs will again receive protection if they act as commercial actors. However, this does not mean that China could not pose a unique challenge to the system on this matter, which future treaty partners might have to take into account. It appears that the CPC is simultaneously centralizing control over the national economy,[939] strengthening its influence on private companies through the compulsory establishment of party cells,[940] retaining the strong role of SOEs as outward investors,[941] and cementing its position as by far the most important home state among state-led economies.[942]

In Chinese academic discourse, this issue has not been prominently discussed. Nonetheless, the Chinese government has – and here it may be relevant that *China Heilongjiang* had been ongoing for a very long time[943] – adapted treaty practice somewhat.[944] Despite case law and scholarship suggesting that investments by SOEs as commercial actors are anyway protected, Article 10 (a) Canada-China BIT 2012 makes it very explicit that what is protected is 'any entity constituted or organized in accordance with the laws of a Contracting Party, such as public institutions, corporations, foundations, agencies, cooperatives, trusts, societies, associations and similar entities and private companies, firms, partnerships, establishments, joint ven-

939 Max J Zenglein and Maximilian Kärnfeldt, 'MERICS Economic Indicators Q1/2018' *MERICS* (Berlin, 24 April 2018) <https://www.merics.org/de/merics-trackers/economic-indicators-q1-2018> accessed 25 June 2018.

940 Michael Martina, 'Exclusive: In China, the Party's push for influence inside foreign firms stirs fears' *Reuters* (Beijing, 24 August 2017) <https://www.reuters.com/article/us-china-congress-companies-idUSKCN1B40JU> accessed 25 June 2018; Sebastian Heilmann, 'How the CCP embraces and co-opts China's private sector' *MERICS* (Berlin, 21 November 2017) <https://www.merics.org/de/blog/how-ccp-embraces-and-co-opts-chinas-private-sector> accessed 25 June 2018.

941 Sean O'Connor, 'SOE Megamergers Signal New Direction in China's Economic Policy', *U.S.-China Economic and Security Review Commission – Staff Report* (Washington DC, 24 May 2018) <https://www.uscc.gov/sites/default/files/Research/SOE%20Megamergers.pdf> accessed 25 June 2018.

942 World Investment Report 2017 (n 10).

943 The first point in the 'procedural history' was a so-called 'notice of dispute' to the Prime Minister of Mongolia on 26 December 2006, see *China Heilongjiang* (n 769) para 7.

944 As also in line with fourth generation BITs penchant for more detail, see Chapter IV.2.1.2.5.

tures and organizations, whether or not for profit, and irrespective of whether their liabilities are limited or otherwise'.[945] It therefore remains unlikely that ICSID would judge Chinese investors outside its jurisdiction on account of their non-private character.

IV.2.1.4. Conclusions on China and Investment Arbitration

Two comparisons can serve to elucidate the Chinese government's stance on investment arbitration over time, and give indications as to future steps.

First, in the context of its more than prominent position as an investor host and home state,[946] and compared to other similar state actors, China has been fittingly active (or more) in the conclusion of investment treaties,[947] but very little engaged in investment arbitration.[948] The latter fact has begun to change only gradually over the last few years. Such cautious, tentative engagement fits the *image* of international law among Chinese elites as expounded on in Chapter III.2.2. Since the onset of the period of reform and opening in 1978, this *image* (similar to late Imperial times) has been one of a point of departure-framework that 1) has flaws and should be engaged with caution, but that 2) is a reality that China has no choice but to engage and shape from within to defend its national interests.

The main trend line of China's investment treaty practice, which can be characterized as gradual liberalization, demonstrates an acceptance of the given forms of investment law as well as the process of its further development. One has to be engaged in drafting treaty law and increasingly open to be part of the burgeoning case law, if one is to influence the system. Nevertheless, China took its time to prepare, only gradually liberalized BITs, was happy to settle first claims (see *Ekran Berhad*), and to see in-

945 Arts 1 (2) (b) and 10 (a) Canada-China BIT 2012. For increasingly detailed provisions, focus on public institutions, and rejection of a for-profit nature being relevant, see also Art 2 (b) China-Republic of Korea BIT 2007; Art 135 New Zealand-China FTA 2008; Art 1 (f) ASEAN-China Investment Agreement 2009; Art 1 (b) China-Mexico BIT 2008; Art 2 (b) China-Uzbekistan BIT 2011; Art 1 (4) Investment promotion and protection agreement between Japan, Republic of Korea and China 2012; Art 2 (b) China-Tanzania BIT 2013; Art 12.1 (2) China-Republic of Korea FTA 2015; Art 9.1 (b) Australia-China FTA 2015.

946 World Investment Report 2017 (n 10).

947 See Chapter IV.2.1.2.

948 See Chapter IV.2.1.3.

vestors often too concerned about their future business to launch them in the first place, while Chinese investors fit the pattern of Asian investors overall as traditionally not bringing many claims.[949]

In terms of the second comparison, unlike the other BRICS states,[950] China developed the first and largest treaty network, took the most linear path towards liberalism, but also the longest time from BIT development to participation in investment arbitration. Most strikingly, actual engagement and negative outcomes did not throw it off course. While all other BRICS states took a decisively restrictive turn since the economic crisis in 2008, China merely recalibrated and gradually switched from the European to the American model that it deemed more amenable to securing regulatory space. Individual cases with Chinese participation – as Chapter IV.2.1.3 shows – were followed by concrete changes to Chinese treaty practice. Provisions were included or amended to more explicitly give state parties a role in treaty interpretation, make MFN clauses more detailed and explicitly excluding their application to procedural matters, and expressly address SOEs in 'investor' definitions.

China is most clearly set apart from other BRICS states by the fact that the interplay between its ambition and the *image* of international law that it holds does not allow for isolationism. China is to regain its status as world power and views engagement with the main institutions of the present international legal order as indispensable on this path. Whereas this meant attracting investment (and technology) in the past, it now just as importantly means enabling and protecting outward investment. Herein, 'concrete' sovereignty can be transferred following cost-benefit analyses,[951] in the service of economic strength and ultimately overall relative power gains.

In view of the Chinese leadership's transition to a more assertive foreign policy since 2013, including a redoubled emphasis on expanding external economic relations, but also going so far as to call for 'guiding' global or-

949 See also Pathirana (n 877) 422, FN 13 citing Trakman, 'Geopolitics, China, and Investor-State Arbitration' (n 744) 268; VS Vadi, 'Law, Culture, and the Politics of Chinese Outward Foreign Investment' in Paolo Farah and Elena Cima (eds), *China's Influence on Non-Trade Concerns in International Economic Law* (Routledge 2016) 98; Leon E Trakman, 'China and Foreign Direct Investment: Does Distance Lend Enchantment to the View?' (2014) 2 *Chinese Journal of Comparative Law* 1.

950 See Chapter IV.2.1.2.6.

951 See Chapter III.2.

der[952] – clearly including the international legal order – a restrictive turn in investment law like those of the other BRICS is not to be expected in the upcoming years either. China is setting explicit policy goals on increasing outward investment and directly connects them with the Belt and Road Initiative, which is intimately associated with Chinese President Xi Jinping and has been introduced into the Communist Party's constitution.[953] At the same time, policy documents call for addressing sharply rising risks and past losses with a hastened global investment treaty strategy.[954] As advertised by the party itself online,[955] leading scholars on its ideological concepts have also maintained that China needs to actively shape global investment treaty practice to reap participation and reform 'dividends', stimulate its own economy and aid domestic reforms.

Further treaty recalibrations are likely, but with continued broad access to international arbitration. At the same time, the body of case law involving China will presumably grow more quickly. Chinese investors will be able to rely on further liberal BITs, have more investment stock to protect, and gain confidence through experience. The PRC, in turn, is likely to gradually and carefully accept that some cases against it will not be averted or settled, but rather lost as 'part of the game' just as in trade law.

---

952 See eg Huang Zheping, 'Chinese president Xi Jinping has vowed to lead the "new world order"' *Quartz* (New York, 22 February 2017) <https://qz.com/916382/chinese-president-xi-jinping-has-vowed-to-lead-the-new-world-order/> accessed 24 July 2018.

953 Constitution of the Communist Party of China (revised and adopted 24 October 2017) <http://www.xinhuanet.com/english/special/2017-11/03/c_136725945.htm> accessed 20 November 2018.

954 See also Tong Qi, 'Reviewing Chinese overseas investors' use' (n 582) 89–90, 95–96 [Chinese].

955 Research Center for the Theory System of Socialism with Chinese Characteristics – Chinese Academy of Social Sciences, '争取国际投资规则制定话语权' (Strive for the right to speak on international investment rules) *CPC News* (Beijing, 2 April 2014) <http://theory.people.com.cn/n/2014/0402/c40531-24801269.html> accessed 30 March 2019.

IV.2.2. Phase Two – the PRC and the WTO DSM

IV.2.2.1. China's Accession to the WTO and the WTO DSM

China's accession to the WTO on 11 December 2001 marked a decisive further step towards engagement with international adjudication.[956] There are several key qualitative differences between ratifying the ICSID Convention and acceding to the WTO.

Most importantly, through accession a WTO Member automatically accepts the compulsory and exclusive jurisdiction of the WTO Dispute Settlement Mechanism (hereinafter: DSM),[957] without the need for further declarations of consent, and without the possibility to even notify an intention to limit the types of cases one would consider submitting. The DSM, thus the only global venue for state-state trade disputes, is regulated in the Dispute Settlement Understanding (hereinafter: DSU). The DSU is one of multiple multilateral 'WTO agreements' that are annexed to one single document, the 'Marrakesh Agreement Establishing the World Trade Organization' (hereinafter: WTO Agreement),[958] making them binding on all

956 This was actually in some ways a return to the trade regime on China's part. The Republic of China was a co-founding contracting party to the GATT in 1947, but after losing the civil war against the Communists, the Nationalist government (now in Taiwan) withdrew from the GATT in 1950. The People's Republic of China only in 1986 sought to resume China's status as a GATT contracting party and engaged in negotiations that were to take 15 years, see Liyu Han and Henry Gao, 'China's experience in utilizing the WTO Dispute Settlement Mechanism', in Gregroy C Shaffer and Ricardo Melendez-Ortiz, *Dispute Settlement at the WTO – The Developing Country Experience* (CUP 2010) 141, FN 5.

957 Art 1 Understanding on Rules and Procedures Governing the Settlement of Disputes (adopted 15 April 1994, entered into force 1 January 1995) 1869 UNTS 401 ('DSU') (Annex 2 of the WTO Agreement).

958 Marrakesh Agreement Establishing the World Trade Organization (adopted 15 April 1994, entered into force 1 January 1995) 1867 UNTS 154 ('WTO Agreement'); DSU. Further annexed is first of all the GATT 1994 which incorporated its predecessor the GATT 1947 as amended before the GATT 1994 entered into force (see Art II (4) and Annex 1A WTO Agreement). Other annexed agreements are inter alia Agreement on Agriculture (adopted 15 April 1994, entered into force 1 January 1995) 1867 UNTS 410 ('Agreement on Agriculture'); The WTO Agreement on the Application of Sanitary and Phytosanitary Measures (adopted 15 April 1994, entered into force 1 January 1995) 1867 UNTS 493 ('SPS Agreement'); Agreement on Textiles and Clothing (adopted 15 April 1994, entered into force 1 January 1995, terminated 1 January 2005) 1868 UNTS 14; Agreement on Technical Barriers to Trade (adopted 15 April 1994, entered into force 1 January 1995) 1868 UNTS 120 ('TBT Agreement'); Agreement on

Members of the WTO,[959] with no reservation being allowed.[960] The DSU applies to all of these agreements as an 'integrated dispute settlement system'.[961]

Second, short time frames distinctively mark DSM proceedings,[962] limiting the time for negotiated settlements. On a complaining Member's request – and after preceding consultations fail – the Dispute Settlement Body (hereinafter: DSB)[963] grants the establishment of an ad-hoc Panel of three (or five) persons from a roster established by the Members (in their individual capacity, not as government representatives).[964] Later, Members may (and often do) notify an appeal to be heard (on a rotational basis) by

---

Trade-Related Investment Measures (adopted 15 April 1994, entered into force 1 January 1995) 1868 UNTS 186 ('TRIMS Agreement'); Agreement on Implementation of Article VI of the General Agreement on Tariffs and Trade 1994 (adopted 15 April 1994, entered into force 1 January 1995) 1868 UNTS 201 ('AD Agreement'); Agreement on Rules of Origin (adopted 15 April 1994, entered into force 1 January 1995) 1868 UNTS 397; Agreement on Subsidies and Countervailing Measures (adopted 15 April 1994, entered into force 1 January 1995) 1869 UNTS 14 ('SCM Agreement'); Agreement on Safeguards (adopted 15 April 1994, entered into force 1 January 1995) 1869 UNTS 154 ('SG Agreement'); General Agreement on Trade in Services (adopted 15 April 1994, entered into force 1 January 1995) 1869 UNTS 183 ('GATS'); Agreement on Trade-Related Aspects of Intellectual Property Rights (adopted 15 April 1994, entered into force 1 January 1995) 1869 UNTS 299 ('TRIPS Agreement').

959 Annex 4 contains plurilateral agreements only binding on those that accepted them, whereas those that have not been terminated are the Agreement on Trade in Civil Aircraft (adopted 15 April 1994, entered into force 1995) 1186 UNTS 170; Agreement on Government Procurement (adopted 15 April 1994, entered into force 1995) 1235 UNTS 258.

960 Art XVI:5 WTO Agreement. See also Mitsuo Matsushita, Thomas J Schoenbaum and Petros C Mavroidis, *The World Trade Organization – Law, Practice and Policy* (2nd edn, OUP 2006) 7; Joseph F Dennin, *Law & Practice of the World Trade Organization – Commentary Binder 1* (OUP 2007) 29–30.

961 Arts 1, 3.2 and Appendix I DSU. Appendix I lists the 'covered agreements.'.

962 On this being a standout feature compared to other international dispute resolution mechanisms see also Peter Van den Bossche and Werner Zdouc, *The Law and Policy of the World Trade Organization* (3rd edn, CUP 2013) 246–250.

963 The DSB is an *alter ego* of the WTO's General Council, the chief decision-making and policy body composed of all Members; see Art IV (3)-(4) WTO Agreement. See also Rüdiger Wolfrum, Peter-Tobias Stoll and Karen Kaiser (eds), *WTO – Institutions and Dispute Settlement* (Martinus Nijhoff Publishers 2006) 46–47.

964 Arts 4.7, 6–8 DSU.

three members of the permanent Appellate Body (hereinafter: AB).[965] Normally, the overall timeframe for DSM cases should not exceed twelve months (15 if there is an appeal).[966]

Third, the fairly strong enforcement regime in the trade realm relies on Member-level retaliation capacities – after authorization by the DSB –[967] potentially affecting the way subsequent compliance by the Chinese government would be perceived domestically.

Participation in this system runs counter to the PRC's earlier general policy of only ratifying international agreements when it could submit reservations on the jurisdiction of dispute settlement mechanisms, eg regarding the ICJ when China ratified the VCLT,[968] or jurisdiction would still depend on a second expression of consent, eg ratification of the ICSID Convention and ensuing relevant BIT jurisdiction clauses. Chinese authors have highlighted that this was indeed an unprecedented step, as a degree of sovereignty was ceded to a 'world trade court'.[969] However, the Chinese government determined that non-accession would go against its economic, political and strategic interests,[970] which it deemed better defended through the 'relatively effective' WTO DSM.[971] This conviction held, despite the unusually strict 'Accession Protocol' China had to sign up to.[972]

---

965 The AB is composed of seven persons of 'recognized authority', appointed by the DSB for four-year terms, who are representative of the WTO membership and independent of any government, see Art 17 DSU.

966 Arts 12.9, 17.5 and 20 DSU.

967 Arts 22.2 – 22.4, 22.6, 22.7 and 23.2 DSU. Retaliation should be 'parallel' (same economic sector), but if impractical, can also be cross-sector or even cross-agreement.

968 Art 66 VCLT: UN Treaty Collection, 'Vienna Convention on the Law of Treaties – Declarations and Reservations <https://treaties.un.org/Pages/ViewDetailsIII.aspx?src=TREATY&mtdsg_no=XXIII-1&chapter=23&Temp=mtdsg3&clang=_en#EndDec> accessed 5 November 2019. The PRC's reservation reads: 'The People's Republic of China makes its reservation to article 66 of the said Convention.'.

969 See eg Manjiao Chi, 'China's Participation in WTO Dispute Settlement over the Past Decade: Experiences and Impacts' (2012) 15 *Journal of International Economic Law* 29, 30.

970 Jacques HJ Bourgeois, 'China and the WTO Dispute Settlement Mechanism' (2011) 2 *Opinio Juris in Comparatione* 1, 9.

971 Manjiao Chi, 'China's Participation' (n 969) 30.

972 WTO, *Protocol on the Accession of the People's Republic of China* (23 November 2001) WT/L/432 ('Accession Protocol'). On the accession process see Art XII:1–2 WTO Agreement.

Nonetheless, there are also some qualifications here concerning the WTO accession's significance in demonstrating the Chinese government to be willing to expose itself. First, the DSU is still geared towards caution and accommodation, with a clear preference for an amicable solution.[973] Members are reminded to exercise judgment as to whether an 'action under these procedures would be fruitful',[974] and then have to engage in good faith consultations before the matter can proceed.[975] They can voluntarily employ good offices, conciliation or mediation, which may be offered by the WTO Director-General at any time.[976] Second, the existence of an appellate body is a rarity in international dispute settlement, and an opportunity to change an unfavorable outcome that has been reassuring to some on the Chinese side. Third, Chinese officials and scholars fully expected that the Accession Protocol provision they viewed as most problematic would disappear as an issue after 15 years.[977]

China's WTO engagement nonetheless signifies a sea change, it has come a long way, and it has brought many changes within the country. In both preparing its accession and in reaction to new challenges inside the WTO, China has comprehensively overhauled domestic legislation and institutional structures, while engaging in sustained litigation capacity building.[978]

Around 3,000 laws and regulations were changed amid frantic legislative activity. The PRC introduced a 'Foreign Trade Law' in 1994 (later revised in 2004) eg liberalizing trading rights and establishing an automatic licensing system.[979] Transparency was increased and judicial review of all trade-related matters – eg administrative decisions on patents and trademarks – became possible.[980] The *Law on Administrative Review*, *Law on Legislation*,

---

973 Art 3.7 DSU. See also WTO, *Mexico: Anti-Dumping Investigation of High-Fructose Corn Syrup (HFCS) from the United States–Report of the Appellate Body after Recourse to Article 21.5 DSU* (22 October 2001) WT/DS132/AB/RW.

974 Art 3.7 DSU.

975 Art 4.3 DSU.

976 Art 5 DSU.

977 See paras 15 (a) (ii) and (d) Accession Protocol. See also Chapter V.2.1.3.2.

978 Ya Julia Qin, 'Trade, Investment and beyond: The Impact of WTO Accession on China's Legal System' (2007) 191 *The China Quarterly* 720, 721.

979 Foreign Trade Law of the People's Republic of China (adopted 12 May 1994, entered into force 1 July 1994).

980 Manjiao Chi, 'China's Participation' (n 969) 43; Ya Julia Qin, 'Trade, Investment and beyond' (n 978) 734–736; Mei-Ying Veron Hung, 'China's WTO Commitment on Independent Judicial Review: Impact on Legal and Political Reform' (2004) 52 *The American Journal of Comparative Law* 77, 78–79.

and *Law on Administrative Permissions* – all passed around the time of WTO accession – 'set boundaries for the exercise of government powers and provide[d] the legal basis for judicial review of specific administrative actions'.[981] At the same time, the Chinese government launched a 'rule of law'-campaign, and competence and independence of the Chinese judiciary were increased – albeit within bounds, of course, in the politically unreformed party-state.[982] Amendments to laws on patents, copyright and trademarks brought new judicial review procedures, and many cumbersome investment requirements were removed through eg modifications of the 'Law on Foreign-funded Enterprises'.[983]

The broad field of building litigation capacity entailed institutional reforms, including restructuring the ministry of foreign trade and economic cooperation and especially the ministry of commerce (hereinafter: MOFCOM). MOFCOM set up a Division of WTO Law in the Department of Treaty and Law, which now represents the PRC at DSM proceedings.[984] Beyond that, China 1) set up a system of close cooperation between MOFCOM, universities and think tanks, 2) established WTO-focused think tanks (eg Shanghai WTO Affairs Consultation Center, Beijing Centre for WTO Affairs, Shenzhen WTO Affairs Centre), 3) and incentivized law schools around the country to research WTO law and cases, as well as in-

981 Ya Julia Qin, 'Trade, Investment and beyond' (n 978) 736; Administrative Review Law of the People's Republic of China (adopted 29 April 1999, entered into force 1 October 1999); Legislation Law of the People's Republic of China (adopted 15 March 2000, entered into force 1 July 2000); Administrative Permission Law of the People's Republic of China (adopted 27 August 2003, entered into force 1 July 2004). See also Mei-Ying Veron Hung (n 980) 79–81.

982 Manjiao Chi, 'China's Participation' (n 969) 49; Ya Julia Qin, 'Trade, Investment and beyond' (n 978) 736; Guiguo Wang, 'Chinese Mechanisms' (n 533) p. 208.

983 Law of the People's Republic of China on Foreign-funded Enterprises (adopted 12 April 1986, amended 31 October 2000, entered into force 31 October 2000); Patent Law of the People's Republic of China (adopted 12 March 1984, entered into force 12 March 1984, amended for the second time 25 August 2000); Copyright Law of the People's Republic of China (adopted 7 September 1990, entered into force 7 September 1990, amended for the first time 27 October 2001); Trademark Law of the People's Republic of China (adopted 23 August 1982, entered into force 23 August 1982, amended for the second time 27 October 2001). See also Han and Gao (n 956) 144.

984 Manjiao Chi, 'China's Participation' (n 969) 30.

troduce WTO law courses.[985] Furthermore, the Chinese government specifically intended to give domestic law firms the opportunity to learn and build capacity. It would go on to typically hire a US or European law firm to carry the main workload when it was a principal party to a dispute, but also bring in a domestic Chinese law firm to observe the Western counterparts. The below-described massive third-party participation rate also served to provide domestic law firms, which in these cases usually played a larger role, with another opportunity to practice.[986]

The Chinese government also seeks to further Chinese citizens working at the WTO Secretariat, being nominated to the Indicative List of Panelists, and serving as members of the Appellate Body. The first Chinese member of a Panel was Zhang Yuqing, Director-General of the Department of Treaty and Law at MOFCOM, in the Article 21.5 compliance proceedings in *EC-Bananas*.[987] Zhang Yuejiao, who had previously held the same domestic position, was first to join the AB in 2008; and after two four-year terms Hong Zhao, previously Minister Counselor in charge of legal affairs at China's mission to the WTO, replaced him in 2016.[988]

Building on such groundwork, over time China has become one of the most active Members of the WTO and most frequent users of the DSM. Up to the end of 2018, it had been involved in significantly more than 200 cases – 20 as a complainant, more than 40 as a respondent, and more than 160 as a third party – which already ranked it in fourth place overall, behind the US, the EU and Japan.[989]

---

985 Han and Gao (n 956) 145–146, who note that courses have been organized by the Ministry of Justice and the Supreme People's Court, foreign experts like former AB members invited, and WTO-provided courses participated in as well as point to supposed strongest universities on WTO law as Wuhan University, the Shanghai Institute of Foreign Trade, and the University of International Business & Economics in Beijing.

986 Han and Gao (n 956) 148.

987 WTO, *European Communities: Regime for the Importation, Sale and Distribution of Bananas—Reports of the Appellate Body after Recourse to Article 21.5 DSU* (26 November 2008) WT/DS27/AB/RW/USA and WT/DS27/AB/RW2/ECU.

988 Han and Gao (n 956) 149–150; WTO, 'Appellate Body Members' <https://www.wto.org/english/tratop_e/dispu_e/ab_members_descrp_e.htm> accessed 1 November 2018.

989 WTO, 'Disputes by country/territory' <https://www.wto.org/english/tratop_e/dispu_e/dispu_by_country_e.htm> accessed 3 January 2019.

IV.2.2.2. DSM Case Law with Chinese Participation

Chinese participation in WTO dispute settlement can be divided into three phases, wherein China can be defined respectively as a 'rule-taker' (November 2001 to February 2006), 'rule-shaker' (March 2006 to August 2008), and 'rule-maker' (since September 2008).[990] The first phase begins with the entry into force of China's WTO Accession Protocol;[991] the second phase with the request for consultations in *China-Auto Parts*,[992] the first case China did not settle as a respondent; and the third phase, finally, with China's request for consultations in *US-Anti-Dumping and Countervailing Duties*,[993] which marked the beginning of China's offensive as a complainant, and of a series of complaints aimed at changing the rules, particularly Accession Protocol norms, through the DSM.

In the following, case law involving China will be discussed in the respective sub-chapter on the phase within which the request for consultations was submitted. The numbers of cases differ wildly. In the first and second phase, there were only a handful of cases. As China's behavior shall still be illustrated, discussions will be more extensive. In the third phase, case numbers explode both on the complainant and respondent side. To

990 See Henry Gao, 'China on the World Stage: A Trade Law Perspective' Other' (2010) 104 *Proceedings of the ASIL Annual Meeting* 532, 533–535. For similarly delineated phases that they call 'acceptance,' 'consolidation,' and 'activation' see Bryan Mercurio and Mitali Tyagi, 'China's Evolving Role in WTO Dispute Settlement: Acceptance, Consolidation and Activation', in C Herrmann and JP Terhechte (eds) (2012) 3 *European Yearbook of International Economic Law* 89, 91, who also refer to China at the end of their research period reaching a stage of 'aggressive legalism,' as first used to describe Japan's trade strategy in Saadia M Pekkanen, 'Aggressive Legalism: The Rules of the WTO and Japan's Emerging Trade Strategy' (2001) 24 *The World Economy* 707. For similar deliberations see also Marcia Don Harpaz, 'Sense and sensibilities of China and WTO Dispute settlement', in Ka Zeng and Wei Liang (eds), *China and Global Trade Governance – China's first decade in the World Trade Organization* (Routledge 2013) 241–245.

991 China's Accession Protocol to the WTO came into force 11 November 2001, while the 'date of membership' is 11 December 2001. See Notification of Acceptance and Entry into Force of the Protocol on Accession of the People's Republic of China done at Doha on 10 November 2001 (20 November 2001) WLI/100.

992 WTO, *China: Measures Affecting Imports of Automobile Parts–Request for Consultations* (30 March 2006) WT/DS339/1 ('*China–Auto Parts* (Request for Consultations)').

993 WTO, *United States: Definitive Anti-Dumping and Countervailing Duties on Certain Products from China–Request for Consultations* (19 September 2008) WT/DS379/1 ('*US–Anti-Dumping and Countervailing Duties (China)* (Request for Consultations)').

cover all of them extensively would go beyond the scope of this study. The discussion will therefore be oriented according to the importance of pertinent proceedings to the purposes of this study. Although third party participation has been an invaluable learning exercise for the Chinese government, pertinent cases are considered to have had rather limited impact and their discussion would also go beyond the scope of this study. Accordingly, only cases where China was a principal party will be addressed. Finally, cases that did not go beyond the consultation stage will be addressed more briefly.

Other Members raised more complaints against China then the other way around – as is the case for the US – but as China settled many disputes as a respondent, especially in earlier years, the numbers for panel proceedings are more evenly divided. As will be explained below, the differences in Chinese behavior regarding the DSM in different phases of participation were quite striking.

IV.2.2.2.1. China as a 'rule-taker' – November 2001 to February 2006

In the first phase ('rule-taker'), official statements by leading politicians as well as policy White Papers still indicated that engagement as a principal party would be altogether avoided where possible.[994] China developed into a perennial third party to familiarize itself with the DSM, which has been a common practice for developing countries to reduce start up costs in trade litigation.[995] It went as far as becoming 'an active participant as an interested third party to over half of the cases'.[996]

The cautious attitude resulted in the PRC only initiating one case (*US–Steel Safeguards*), and also only being the respondent to one complaint

994 See eg Xiaojun Li, 'Understanding China's Behavioral Change in the WTO Dispute Settlement System: Power, Capacity, and Normative Constraints in Trade Adjudication' (2012) 52 *Asian Survey* 1111, 1132–1133, who cites State Council of the PRC, 'White Paper – China's Peaceful Development Road' <http://www.china.org.cn/english/2005/Dec/152669.htm> accessed 30 March 2019, and a 2005 speech of the since disgraced former Minister of Commerce Bo Xilai.

995 Christina L Davis and Sarah Blodgett Bermeo, 'Who Files? Developing Country Participation in GATT/WTO Adjudication' (2009) 71 *The Journal of Politics* 1033, 1038.

996 Xiaojun Li (n 994) 1126.

(*China–Value-Added Tax*).[997] As for not being a respondent more often, China had actively attempted to avoid that situation by resolving matters before they reach such a 'confrontational' stage. In 2004, the Chinese government was able to strike a bilateral agreement with the EU to avoid a complaint from Brussels about Chinese coke export restrictions. In January 2006, Chinese authorities quickly repealed an anti-dumping duty on kraft linerboard, when the US was just about to file a case.[998] Both sides of a WTO dispute were first experienced with the United States being the (main) party on the other side.[999]

The Chinese government's caution was not the only reason for the paucity of cases. Indeed, other Members also showed a level of restraint.[1000] Moreover, transitional periods meant that certain accession commitments were phased in over three (trading rights, end certain non-tariff measures) or six years (certain GATS commitments), and some claims were raised with a dedicated transitional review mechanism. China, meanwhile, did make use of the option to put forward observations in the Textiles Monitoring Body under the later defunct Agreement on Textiles and Clothing against the US and Turkey in this period.[1001]

---

997 WTO, *United States: Definitive Safeguard Measures on Imports of Certain Steel Products—Request for Consultations by China* (2 April 2002) WT/DS252/1 ('*US–Steel Safeguards* (Request for Consultations)'); WTO, *China: Value-Added Tax on Integrated Circuits—Request for Consultations by the United States* (18 March 2004) WT/DS309/1 ('*China–Value Added Tax on Integrated Circuits* (Request for Consultations)').

998 Kennedy, 'China's role in WTO Dispute Settlement' (n 38) 559–560. According to Ya Julia Qin, 'Trade, Investment and beyond' (n 978) 727–728, the PRC had quickly 'risen to be one of the top users of antidumping measures in the world.' It had, only from 2001 to 2005, initiated 103 antidumping investigations, the third most after India and the US. At the same time, China remained the number one target nation of antidumping actions.

999 WTO, 'Disputes by Member' <https://www.wto.org/english/tratop_e/dispu_e/dispu_by_country_e.htm> accessed 5 November 2019.

1000 Kennedy, 'China's role in WTO Dispute Settlement' (n 38) 560.

1001 Kennedy, 'China's role in WTO Dispute Settlement' (n 38) 560; Agreement on Textiles and Clothing (adopted 15 April 1994, entered into force 1 January 1995, terminated 1 January 2005) 1868 UNTS 14.

IV.2.2.2.1.1. China on the Complainant Side – Safeguard Measures

In *US-Steel Safeguards*, China requested consultations for the first time.[1002] It did so after the EU, Japan and South Korea had already put forward their considerations on the same matter. Altogether, eight WTO Members challenged the US measures, in what was then the largest panel case regarding the volume of trade affected and the number of Members requesting consultations.[1003] Complainants' considerations were jointly evaluated, as the Panel issued one document containing eight separate panel reports,[1004] which will be addressed as one in the context of this study,[1005] due to the common set of findings.

China considered the US to have breached both the *Agreement on Safeguards* (hereinafter: SG Agreement) and the *General Agreement on Tariffs and Trade 1994* (hereinafter: GATT 1994) in multiple ways,[1006] by imposing increased import duties on a wide range of steel products as definitive safeguard measures.[1007] The Chinese side – inter alia – deemed 'unforeseen developments' and 'serious injury'[1008] – preconditions for safeguard measures – to be lacking, and the US measures to be discriminating.[1009] Additionally, China considered that its steel products should have been exempt,

1002 *US–Steel Safeguards* (Request for Consultations) (n 997).

1003 See also Yong-Shik Lee, *Safeguard Measures in World Trade* (Edward Elgar Publishing 2014) 267.

1004 WTO, *United States: Definitive Safeguard Measures on Imports of Certain Steel Products—Final Reports of the Panel* (11 July 2003) WT/DS248/R, WT/DS249/R, WT/DS251/R, WT/DS252/R, WT/DS253/R, WT/DS254/R, WT/DS258/R and WT/DS259/R [10.725] ('*US–Steel Safeguards* (Panel Reports)')..

1005 See also Kara Leitner and Simon Lester, 'WTO Dispute Settlement 1995–2016 – A Statistical Analysis' (2017) 20 *Journal of International Economic Law* 171, 177, FN 7.

1006 Arts I:1, II, X:3, XIX:1 and XIX:2 GATT 1994; Arts 2 (1) and (2), 3 (1) and (2), 4 (1) and (2), 5 (1) and (2), 7 (1), 8 (1), 9 (1) and 12 SG Agreement; *US–Steel Safeguards* (Request for Consultations) (n 997).

1007 Safeguard measures are defined as 'emergency' actions regarding increased imports of particular products resulting from 'unforeseen developments' (Art XIX GATT 1994), that happen 'under such conditions as to cause or threaten to cause serious injury to (…) domestic industry' (Art 2 SG Agreement). Such actions are temporary and can be in the form of quantitative restrictions, tariff quotas or raised bound tariff levels.

1008 Defined in Art 4 (1) SG Agreement as 'a significant overall impairment in the position of a domestic industry'.

1009 Arts 2 (1) and (2), 4 (1) and (2) SG Agreement; Arts I:1 and XIX:1 GATT 1994..

due to its status as a developing country only accounting for a small percentage of total imports.[1010]

The Panel determined all ten challenged 'measures' illegal.[1011] On unforeseen developments, it found the critical date to be the completion of the Uruguay Round, and argued that the Asian financial crisis and fall-out from the Soviet Union's dissolution could indeed be considered unforeseen developments, but that the US had failed to provide a 'reasoned and adequate explanation' as to their impact on its domestic industry.[1012]

The Panel emphasized the requirement of a 'recent' and 'sudden' rise in imports leading to an 'emergency,' and found the evidence only convincing for some of the product categories.[1013] As for the causal link between injury and imports, the Panel focused on analyses of 'coincidence' – a 'temporal relationship between the movements in imports and the movements in injury factors' –[1014] and 'conditions of competition' (eg employment, profits, production, capacity utilization, import volume changes and import market share), and considered them lacking on most categories.[1015] However, the Panel emphasized that even if there is a causal link, safeguards might still not be allowed, as it found a proper 'non-attribution' analysis lacking on several product lines. US authorities failed to adequately 'distinguish the injurious effect of the increased imports from the injurious effects of other factors',[1016] whereas safeguard measures could only be applied to remedy the former.

1010 Art 9 (1) and Footnote 2 SG Agreement – Art 9 (1): 'Safeguard measures shall not be applied against a product originating in a developing country Member as long as its share of imports of the product concerned in the importing Member does not exceed 3 per cent, provided that developing country Members with less than 3 per cent import share collectively account for not more than 9 per cent of total imports of the product concerned' (*de minimis* threshold) – Footnote 2: 'A Member shall immediately notify an action taken under paragraph 1 of Article 9 to the Committee on Safeguards'.

1011 *US–Steel Safeguards* (Panel Reports) (n 1004) [11.1 – 2].

1012 Art XIX:1 (a) GATT 1994; Art 3 (1) SG Agreement; *US–Steel Safeguards* (Panel Reports) (n 1004) [10.74], [10.80], [10.125], [10.128], [10.145]–[10.150].

1013 Art 2 (1) SG Agreement; Art XIX:1 (a) GATT 1994; *US–Steel Safeguards* (Panel Reports) (n 1004) [10.159], [10.166], [10.175], [10.205], [10.254].

1014 *US–Steel Safeguards* (Panel Reports) (n 1004) [10.299].

1015 Art 4 (2) (a) and (b) SG Agreement; *US–Steel Safeguards* (Panel Reports) (n 1004) [10.254], [10.299], [10.318], [10.376]–[10.381], [10.429]–[10.430.

1016 Arts 3 (1), 4 (2) (b) and (c), 5 (1) SG Agreement; *US–Steel Safeguards* (Panel Reports) (n 1004) [10.329] referencing WTO, *United States: Definitive Safeguard Measures on Imports of Circular Welded Carbon Quality Line Pipe from Korea—Report of the Appellate Body* (15 February 2002) WT/DS202/AB/R [X.200]–

Finally, the Panel found fault with US compliance with the requirement that safeguard measures cover all imports that led to the injury determination (ie 'parallelism'), as US authorities had instead been selective in safeguard application and mostly exempted NAFTA states, Israel and Jordan.[1017] The Panel did not deem it necessary to address several other issues, including a potential violation of the exemption of *de minimis* developing country exporters in Article 9.1 SG Agreement.[1018]

The AB affirmed the parts of the panel reports it considered necessary to address. The US's challenge to the applied 'standard of review' regarding 'unforeseen developments', which it viewed as overly strenuous, was struck down. The AB underlined that the same standard of 'reasoned and adequate explanation' elaborated on in *Argentina-Footwear* and *US-Lamb* was to be applied to obligations both under the SG Agreement and Article XIX GATT 1994.[1019] It also reaffirmed that import increases had to be sufficiently 'recent' and 'sudden', and concurred with the Panel on 'parallelism'.[1020]

The US complied with the AB decisions and withdrew the safeguards, and a trade war in light of the threatened retaliatory measures by several other Members was averted. However, both China and the EU had applied provisional safeguard measures in response to US actions 'to prevent a possible "diversion" of foreign steel products from the US market protected by the steel safeguards to theirs'.[1021] Interestingly, US President Bush's statement on ending the safeguards did not make any reference to the WTO's findings, but simply argued that the measures were not needed

---

[X.222] (US–Line Pipe). See also *US–Steel Safeguards* (Panel Reports) (n 1004) [10.338].

1017 *US–Steel Safeguards* (Panel Reports) (n 1004) [10.590]–[10.591], [10.609], [10.623], [10.633], [10.643], [10.653], [10.660], [10.670], [10.680], [10.692], [10.699] referencing WTO, *Argentina: Safeguard Measures on Imports of Footwear–Report of the Appellate Body* (14 December 1999) WT/DS121/AB/R [VI.111]–[VI.114]; Arts 2 and 4 SG Agreement.

1018 *US–Steel Safeguards* (Panel Reports) (n 1004) [10.706]; Art 9 (1) SG Agreement.

1019 WTO, *United States: Definitive Safeguard Measures on Imports of Certain Steel Products–Report of the Appellate Body* (10 November 2003) WT/DS248/AB/R, WT/DS249/AB/R, WT/DS251/AB/R, WT/DS252/AB/R, WT/DS253/AB/R, WT/DS254/AB/R, WT/DS258/AB/R and WT/DS259/AB/R [274]–[276], [330] ('*US–Steel Safeguards* (Appellate Body Report)'); *Argentina–Footwear (EC)* (n 1017) [V.81]; WTO, *United States: Safeguard Measures on Imports of Fresh, Chilled or Frozen Lamb from New Zealand–Report of the Appellate Body* (1 May 2001) WT/DS177/AB/R, WT/DS/178/AB/R [VI.103].

1020 *US–Steel Safeguards* (Appellate Body Report) (n 1019) [345]–[346], [456], [474].

1021 Lee, *Safeguard Measures* (n 1003) 275.

anymore and lauded his own administration for providing the US steel industry with '21 months of breathing space (...) to consolidate and restructure'.[1022] The measures had previously been described as mostly a political move that could not be walked back ahead of the 2004 US Presidential election. Only with the political cover provided by the AB report – and in the face of threatened EU retaliation against diverse products from several 'battleground' states for the election – did Bush feel that he could and should withdraw the safeguard measures.[1023]

A potential concern is that Members would henceforth face 'near-certain defeat',[1024] when complaints were leveled against their use of safeguards, due to two issues. First, due to stringent requirements in convincingly demonstrating unforeseen developments and their impact on increased imports, that the import surge was 'recent' and related to a 'serious injury,' and that 'other factors' did not cause such injury. Second, due to a certain lack of clarity on the part of the SG Agreement and the AB on how to accomplish all of that.[1025] Some authors have mooted that these issues could only be remedied by 1) the AB relying less on the treaty text and more on object and purpose of the treaty, and even drawing on economic theory directly, to develop 'coherent' standards, or 2) the WTO membership renegotiating the SG Agreement.[1026]

While such criticism might chime with other critiques leveled (often from an economics perspective) against the SG Agreement,[1027] the findings in *US-Steel Safeguards* are in line with previous case law (eg on interpreting the phrase 'in such increased quantities' with *Argentina–Footwear (EC)*).[1028] Moreover, US authorities could have very well addressed unforeseen devel-

---

1022 Sean D Murphy, 'WTO Decision Striking Down U.S. Steel Safeguard Measures' (2004) 98 AJIL 179, 180).

1023 Michael Ewing-Chow, Alex WS Goh and Akshay Kolse Patil, 'Are Asian WTO Members using the WTO DSU "Effectively"?' (2013) 16 *Journal of International Economic Law* 669, 690.

1024 Gene M Grossman and Alan O Sykes, 'United States – Definitive Safeguard Measures on Imports of Certain Steel Products (WT/DS259; WT/DS252; WT/DS248; WT/DS249; WT/DS251; WT/DS258; WT/DS254; WT/DS253: DSR 2003:VII, 3117)' (2006) 5 *World Trade Review* 146, 183–184.

1025 Ibid 184.

1026 Ibid 184–185.

1027 See also Simon Lester, Bryan Mercurio and Arwel Davies, *World Trade Law – Text, Materials and Commentary* (2nd edn, Hart 2012) 538–539; Alan O Sykes, 'The Fundamental Deficiencies of the Agreement on Safeguards: A Reply to Professor Lee' (2006) 40 *Journal of World Trade* 979.

1028 *Argentina–Footwear (EC)* (n 986) [VII.131].

opments for every pertinent product line,[1029] and not only described such developments, but also explained their connection to increased imports.[1030] Similarly, on 'parallelism,' they could have been more exact in their injury determination, in the sense of excluding NAFTA states, Israel and Jordan, if the intention was to not apply potential safeguards to them.[1031]

Looking at this study's research question, it is important to note that China chose to engage in its first complaint where other Members – the EU and Japan, no less – had already complained about the same matter. This fits China's cautious attitude in this phase, symbolized by an almost exclusive focus on engagement as a third party. Second, China chose a case that was very likely to be won, not yet confident in the abilities of its trade lawyers, nor comfortable with the thought of losing. Chinese scholars would only later come to view a supposed US strategy – as pointed to in the above quote by President Bush – of delaying outcomes by going through the motions of DSM cases it was likely going to lose, as a model for winning its industries time to adjust.[1032]

IV.2.2.2.1.2. China on the Respondent Side – National Treatment

In the first case launched against China, the US requested consultations in *China–Integrated Circuits* on 18 March 2004.[1033] China had partially refunded the 17 % value-added tax on integrated circuits if they were produced or designed in China. The US considered that China treated imported integrated circuits less favorably than domestically produced ones, and that it discriminated against services and service suppliers of Members that did not produce Chinese-designed integrated circuits, breaching Article XVII GATS (National Treatment), Articles I and III GATT 1994 (General MFN

1029 For this issue see *US–Steel Safeguards* (Appellate Body Report) (n 1019) [319].

1030 See also Lester, Mercurio and Davies (n 1027) 546.

1031 See also *US–Line Pipe* (n 1016) [IX.197].

1032 See eg Baihua 柏华 Gong 龚, '中国影响汽车零部件进口措施"WTO 争端解决案评析' (Evaluation of the WTO DSM Case "Measures Affecting Imports of Automobile Parts") [2006] (11) *Faxue* 101, 106; Jiaxiang 加祥 Hu 胡, '中国参与WTO 争端解决机制的实证分析' (Empirical Analysis of China's Participation in the WTO Dispute Resolution Mechanism) [2008] (11) *Faxue* 66, 73, 75. See also Chapter V.2.1.3.2.

1033 *China–Value Added Tax on Integrated Circuits* (Request for Consultations) (n 997).

Treatment and National Treatment on Internal Taxation and Regulation), and the Protocol on the Accession of the People's Republic of China (hereinafter: Accession Protocol).[1034] The EU, Japan, 'Chinese Taipei' (ie Taiwan) and Mexico requested to join the consultations.[1035]

Indicative of China's defensive attitude at the time, it did not take long until a mutually-agreed solution under Article 3.6 DSU was found to end the stand-off. The pertinent notification was circulated from 6 October 2005, although the DSB had already been informed in July 2004 about constructive consultations and a MoU on the matter, which the parties now considered successfully implemented. China had agreed to either amend or fully revoke its tax measures.[1036]

It once again fits China's cautious attitude at the onset of its WTO membership that it would find a mutually-agreed solution in the first case brought against it. However, the Chinese government also had an easier time settling this case, because Chinese firms were not really involved. Regulations on the tax rebates mandated that the respective firms had to sell 70–80 % of their integrated circuits in China. While most Chinese firms exported the majority of their production, foreign-invested firms like the US's Motorola that profited, ie the conflict of interest was between different exporting country companies.[1037]

1034 Ibid; Art XVII GATS; Arts I and III GATT 1994; Accession Protocol.

1035 Any state or customs territory with comprehensive autonomy over trade policy, ie also Taiwan, can accede to the WTO, see Art XII WTO Agreement. See also Dennin (n 960) 3. It should be noted that the separate customs territories Hong Kong and 'Chinese Taipei' have also engaged in disputes under the DSU. Hong Kong only brought one complaint, was never a respondent, but was a third party more than ten times. It had already been a participant in the GATT and founding member of the WTO. 'Chinese Taipei', meanwhile, only joined the WTO in 2002. Therafter, it became one of the most active third-party participants as well, with more than a hundred cases already. It also filed a handful of complaints, but was never a respondent.

1036 WTO, *China: Value-Added Tax on Integrated Circuits–Notification of Mutually Agreed Solution* (6 October 2005) WT/DS309/8 ('*China–Value Added Tax on Integrated Circuits* (Notification of Mutually Agreed Solution)'); WTO, *China: Value-Added Tax on Integrated Circuits–Joint Communication from China and the United States* (16 July 2004) WT/DS309/7; Art 3 (6) DSU. See also Xiuli Han, 'China's First Ten Years' (n 38) 55.

1037 Ewing-Chow, Goh and Patil (n 1023) 700–701.

IV.2.2.2.1.3. Conclusion

In the first phase of Chinese engagement with international adjudication in the trade field ('rule-taker'), the country's government remained exceedingly cautious. Put differently – and strongly reflecting the scholarly debate in China at the time[1038] – it was single-mindedly focused on patiently studying the system and preparing a more active participation later on. This went hand in hand, First, with strong participation as a third party; Second, with trying out a first complaint on a matter where the EU and Japan had already done so as well and where success was likely; and Third, with finding a mutually-agreed solution in the first case brought against China. In this period, China did not want to allow for a case launched against it to go beyond the consultation stage,[1039] and risk arguing its positions before a Panel and the AB.

As opposed to investment law, where Chinese engagement with international adjudication has been marked by a focus on jurisdictional matters, relevant WTO cases have instead centered around substantive issues with jurisdiction being more of a given. Chinese scholars largely praised the WTO DSM,[1040] but also put emphasis on their simply being no other option than WTO membership and accepting DSM jurisdiction.[1041]

IV.2.2.2.2. China as a 'rule-shaker' – March 2006 to August 2008

A host of developments contributed to the onset of the second phase ('rule-shaker'), wherein Beijing's attitude shifted from negotiation- to adjudication-leaning. Use of the DSM became more frequent and settlements a less frequent occasion.[1042] China came to occupy a large share of total dis-

1038 See Chapter V.2.1.3.1.

1039 See also Xiaojun Li (n 994) 1132–1133.

1040 See Chapter V.2.1.1. See eg Hua 华 Shi 师, '国际贸易争议解决方法的比较研究' (Comparative Study of International Trade Dispute Settlement Methods) (2002) 23 (6) *Faxue Zazhi* 54, 56; Ke 柯 Zhao 赵, 'WTO 争端解决机制述评' (Commentary on the WTO Dispute Settlement Mechanism) [2003] (7) *Dangdai Faxue* 124, 127.

1041 See eg Qingjiang 庆江 Kong 孔, '与世贸组织争端解决机制有关的几个问题' (On Certain Issues Regarding the WTO Dispute Settlement Mechanism) (2004) 25 (3) *Faxue Zazhi* 46.

1042 See also Manjiao Chi, 'China's Participation' (n 969) 32; Ya Julia Qin, 'Trade, Investment and beyond' (n 978) 739–740; Kara Leitner and Simon Lester,

putes and was a more frequent principal party participant, whereas the rise in cases involving China ran counter to a general decrease in usage of the system.[1043] The Chinese shift was officially announced through a Government Work Report published in March 2006. Later on, then-Minister of Commerce Chen Deming's speech at the National Working Conference on Commerce and Finance in January 2008 confirmed the course. The tenor was clear: the DSM was to be used increasingly actively, to, in Chen Deming's words, 'strive for the most favorable outcomes for China in responding to WTO disputes, and actively challenge policies of other members that damage Chinese interests'.[1044]

Among the reasons for Beijing's changed attitude it should first be mentioned that, after a transition period of five years, the country was more familiar with the system and had successfully increased its litigation capacity. Second, confidence increased with further economic success. Third, China's political leaders no longer viewed the 'involvement in international litigation as a political defeat'.[1045] Fourth, pure trade issues were considered less and less politically sensitive. Fifth, China's WTO 'accession package' did not give it a lot of 'wiggle room' regarding DSM engagement.[1046] Sixth, the Chinese government developed a 'desire to balance against (...) US power'.[1047]

A seventh reason was the contacts between Chinese and other states' diplomats and officials at the WTO in Geneva.[1048] Such interactions led the Chinese side to realize two things. One, among large emerging economies, Brazil and India appeared to make successful use of the DSM.[1049] Two, the US government appeared to not at all view its defeats at

---

'WTO Dispute Settlement 1995–2009 – A Statistical Analysis' (2010) 13 *Journal of International Economic Law* 205, 216–17.

1043 WTO, 'Disputes by Member' <https://www.wto.org/english/tratop_e/dispu_e/dispu_by_country_e.htm> accessed 5 November 2019.

1044 Xiaojun Li (n 994) 1133, who cites Wen Jiabao, 'Report on the Work of the Government' *Xinhua* (Beijing, 5 March 2006) <http://wto2.mofcom.gov.cn/article/bilateralvisits/200603/20060301691252.shtml> accessed 30 March 2019; Chen Deming, 'Chen Deming's Report at the National Working Conference on Commerce and Finance' *Chinese Ministry of Commerce* (Beijing, 21 January 2010) <http://chendeming.mofcom.gov.cn/aarticle/speeches/200801/20080105345233.html> accessed 30 March 2019.

1045 Manjiao Chi, 'China's Participation' (n 969) 38.

1046 Bourgeois (n 970) 4.

1047 Ibid 15.

1048 Xiaojun Li (n 994) 1132.

1049 See also Chapters IV.2.2.2.4 and IV.2.2.2.5.

the DSM as a loss of face, but rather as 'part of the game' in a process that sees major powers win *and* loose all of the time. Eighth, the PRC's trade interests continued to grow rapidly, and its desire to use the DSM as protection grew with them.[1050] Ninth, growing nationalism necessitated a more vigorous defense of Chinese positions. Tenth – and finally – the Chinese side increasingly employed the DSM to criticize other parties' allegedly overly broad interpretations of China's (in Beijing's eyes already exceedingly harsh) Accession Protocol.[1051]

The PRC's more adjudication-leaning stance was reflected in a growing number of disputes – still only one further case as a complainant, but five as a respondent – wherein China started to refuse to settle.[1052] This is the defining characteristic of this second phase, and also what sets China apart from other new WTO Members who acceded in the 2000s. To provide only some examples, 'Chinese Taipei' joined in 2002, as it could, being a separate customs territory. It was a complainant several times, but never a respondent. Vietnam requested consultations in a handful of disputes since it joined the WTO in 2007, and also never had a complaint brought against it. Finally, Ukraine, which acceded to the organization in 2008, also was a complainant more often than a respondent.[1053] China, in turn,

---

1050 See also Ku, 'China and the Future of International Adjudication' (n 32) 168–169; Xiaojun Li (n 994) 1133–1135.

1051 See also Bourgeois (n 970) 30–31.

1052 WTO, *United States: Preliminary Anti-Dumping and Countervailing Duty Determinations on Coated Free Sheet Paper from China–Request for Consultations* (14 September 2007) WT/DS368/1 ('*US–Coated Free Sheet Paper (China)* (Request for Consultations)'); *China–Auto Parts* (Request for Consultations) (n 992); WTO, *China: Certain Measures Granting Refunds, Reductions or Exemptions from Taxes and Other Payments–Request for Consultations* (2 February 2007) WT/DS358/1 ('*China–Taxes* (Request for Consultations)'); WTO, *China: Measures Affecting the Protection and Enforcement of Intellectual Property Rights–Request for Consultations* (10 April 2007) WT/DS362/1 ('*China–Intellectual Property Rights* (Request for Consultations)'); WTO, *China: Measures Affecting Trading Rights and Distribution Services for Certain Publications and Audiovisual Entertainment Products–Request for Consultations* (10 April 2007) WT/DS363/1 ('*China–Publications and Audiovisual Products* (Request for Consultations)'); WTO, *China: Measures Affecting Financial Information Services and Foreign Financial Information Suppliers–Request for Consultations* (3 March 2008) WT/DS372/1 ('*China–Financial Information Services* (Request for Consultations)').

1053 WTO, 'WTO Accessions Map' <https://www.wto.org/english/thewto_e/acc_e/acc_map_e.htm> accessed 5 November 2019; WTO, 'Disputes by Member' <https://www.wto.org/english/tratop_e/dispu_e/dispu_by_country_e.htm> accessed 5 November 2019.

did not yet become a more active complainant, but it did refuse to settle the complaints brought against it, instead frequently fighting the other side all of the way to the AB and, where deemed necessary, trying to 'shake or even bend the existing rules by aggressively making legal arguments that put its position in best light'.[1054]

IV.2.2.2.2.1 China on the Complainant Side – Countervailing & Anti-Dumping Duties

In China's only request for consultations in this period, *US–Coated Free Sheet Paper (China)*, it ventured forward alone for the first time and remained the only Member to request consultations.[1055] This signified another key step for the government in Beijing.

China considered that the US Department of Commerce's preliminary anti-dumping and countervailing duty determinations were inconsistent with WTO law. According to China, US authorities had not demonstrated specificity substantiated with positive evidence concerning the supposed subsidies (Articles 2 (1), (4) Agreement on Subsidies and Countervailing Measures (hereinafter: SCM Agreement)), had not properly determined the 'benefit' through the alleged 'government policy lending program' (Articles 1 and 14 SCM Agreement), and had failed to ensure that its measures were based on the amount of subsidy and dumping it respectively alleged to exist (Articles 17 and 19 SCM Agreement; Articles 7 and 9 Agreement on Implementation of Article VI of the General Agreement on Tariffs and Trade 1994 (hereinafter: AD Agreement)).[1056]

In November 2007, the US International Trade Commission (hereinafter: USITC) made negative injury determinations.[1057] The DSM case had concerned only provisional measures on the American side that were now ended. Accordingly, the dispute did not go further than the consultation stage.

1054 Gao, 'China on the World Stage' (n 990) 534.

1055 *US–Coated Free Sheet Paper (China)* (Request for Consultations) (n 1052); Kennedy, 'China's role in WTO Dispute Settlement' (n 38) 568.

1056 Arts 1, 2 (1) and (4), 14, 17 and 19 SCM Agreement; Arts 7 and 9 AD Agreement; *US–Coated Free Sheet Paper (China)* (Request for Consultations) (n 1052).

1057 Coated free sheet paper from China, Indonesia and Korea, Investigation Nos 701-TA-444–446 (Final) and 731-TA-1109 (Final) (USITC Publication 3965 December 2007).

The Chinese government was woken into action, in filing its first complaint since 2002, by the US's 2006 domestic policy-decision to 'apply the countervailing duty law to countries that the [US] treated as [non-market economy] countries in anti-dumping investigations, such as China. [Non-application] had been a rare positive aspect of [non-market economy] treatment for China, but was not mentioned in its terms of accession [to the WTO]'.[1058] The change of policy was potentially dramatic for China, because it could continue beyond the anticipated expiration of Paragraph 15 (a) (ii) of Part I of China's Accession Protocol, which allows for a methodology using 'surrogate values' in price comparisons for anti-dumping investigation purposes – more favorable to importing countries – if market economy conditions are not clearly demonstrated on the Chinese side.[1059] What is more, the US had just requested consultations on three different matters in quick succession, with another already pending, which might have stirred China to use the DSM to hit back – the same pattern could be observed with China's first complaint against the EU in 2009.[1060]

China had even for the first time submitted to the jurisdiction of a foreign court, the US Court of International Trade, to try and stop the pertinent countervailing duty investigation by the US Department of Commerce. However, the court held that it lacked jurisdiction, dismissed the case, and the Department of Commerce published the preliminary determinations that led to this DSM case.[1061]

IV.2.2.2.2.2. China on the Respondent Side

IV.2.2.2.2.2.1. National Treatment on Internal Taxation and Regulation

On the receiving end of consultation requests, China's changed behavior, in fact a veritable turnaround was on display in *China-Auto Parts*. Herein, the EU complained – and subsequently the US and Canada also requested consultations – about Chinese regulations to the effect that if certain combinations of imported automobile parts or such attaining 60 % of the later assembled vehicle's value were used in manufacturing vehicles in China, all imported parts would be categorized as complete vehicles and subjected

---

1058 Kennedy, 'China's role in WTO Dispute Settlement' (n 38) 568.

1059 Part I, Para 15 (a) (ii), (d) Accession Protocol.

1060 See also Kennedy, 'China's role in WTO Dispute Settlement' (n 38) 563.

1061 *Government of the People's Republic of China v United States*, 31 CIT 451 (2007).

to charges equaling the tariffs for a complete vehicle. The same was to apply to completely or semi-knocked down kits.[1062]

China's measures were deemed inconsistent with national treatment under the GATT 1994, as the 'internal charges' only applied to imported automobile parts, accompanying administrative measures incentivized purchasing domestic parts, and internal quantitative regulations on the mixture of parts were maintained.[1063] Alternatively, considered a customs duty, China's measures would be deemed in excess of tariff bindings in China's Schedule of Concessions.[1064] Brussels further claimed that the Chinese measures were inconsistent with national treatment and the elimination of quantitative measures under the Agreement on Trade-Related Investment Measures (hereinafter: TRIMS Agreement),[1065] and constituted illegal subsidies under the SCM Agreement,[1066] as they were contingent on the use of domestic over imported goods. Non-compliance with the TRIMS Agreement and the elimination of local content requirements, as well as tariffs exceeding 10 % on completely or semi-knocked down kits for motor vehicles were also considered violations of China's Accession Protocol and the Working Party Report.[1067]

The Panel, which addressed the three consultation requests together, found more generally that '[i]f the obligation to pay a charge does not accrue based on the product at the moment of its importation, it cannot be an "ordinary customs duty" (...) [, but is], instead, an "internal charge" (...), which obligation to pay accrues based on internal factors'.[1068] It then held that the Chinese measures clearly fell on the side of internal charges –

1062 *China–Auto Parts* (Request for Consultations) (n 992).

1063 Art III (2), (4) and (5) GATT 1994; *China–Auto Parts* (Request for Consultations) (n 992).

1064 Art II:1 (a) and (b) GATT 1994; Final Act Embodying the Results of the Uruguay Round of Multilateral Trade Negotiations (adopted 15 April 1994, entered into force 1 January 1995) 1867 UNTS 14 ('Final Act'); *China–Auto Parts* (Request for Consultations) (n 992).

1065 Arts 2.1 and 2.2 and Annex paras 1 (a) and 2 (a) TRIMS Agreement.

1066 Art 3 SCM Agreement.

1067 Part I, Para 1.2 and 7.3 Accession Protocol; Para 342 *Report of the Working Party on the Accession of China* (1 October 2001) WT/ACC/CHN/49 ('Working Party Report'); *China–Auto Parts* (Request for Consultations) (n 992).

1068 Arts II:1 (b), III:2 GATT 1994; WTO, *China: Measures Affecting Imports of Automobile Parts-Reports of the Panel* (18 July 2008) WT/DS339/R, WT/DS340/R and WT/DS342/R [7.204] ('*China–Auto Parts* (Panel Reports)').

with the exception of charges regarding completely or semi-knocked down kits -and found a breach of national treatment.[1069]

If the measures in question were 'ordinary customs duties,' the Panel resolved, then they would have breached China's commitments under Article II (1) (a) and (b) GATT 1994.[1070] However, once again the exception is completely or semi-knocked down kits, whereas the Panel upheld the complainant's argument that through the *de facto* imposition of duties above what was indicated in the Working Party Report, the pertinent measures breached China's accession obligations.[1071] China's actions were considered not justified by Article XX (d) GATT 1994, as China was found to have failed to demonstrate intent to circumvent higher tariff rates.[1072] The Panel did not believe it necessary to address potential violations of the TRIMs and SCM Agreements.[1073]

China appealed arguing that the Panel should have classified the measure as an ordinary customs duty. It held that the first sentence of Article II (1) (b) GATT 1994 had been erroneously interpreted, because the context of Rule 2 (a) of the General Rules for the Interpretation of the Harmonized System, which allows for the classification of product components as the finished product, was not taken into account.[1074]

However, the AB considered the question of whether car parts can be treated as complete vehicles not relevant context for the question of

1069 Art III (2) and (4) GATT 1994; *China–Auto Parts* (Panel Reports) (n 1068) [7.205]–[7.212], [7.223], [7.272].

1070 Art II:1 (a) and (b) GATT 1994; *China–Auto Parts* (Panel Reports) (n 1068) [7.523].

1071 Para 93 Working Party Report; *China–Auto Parts* (Panel Reports) (n 1068) [7.736], [7.758].

1072 Art XX (d) GATT 1994; *China–Auto Parts* (Panel Reports) (n 1068) [7.321]–[7.326], [7.365].

1073 *China–Auto Parts* (Panel Reports) (n 1068) [8.2], [8.5], [8.8].

1074 Art II:1 (b) GATT 1994; World Customs Organization, 'General Rules for the Interpretation of the Harmonized System' <http://www.wcoomd.org/en/faq/~/~/media/B7BC612CEB3B417BB5183841DA7413CB.ashx> accessed 30 March 2019; Rule 2 (a): 'Any reference in a heading to an article shall be taken to include a reference to that article incomplete or unfinished, provided that, as presented, the incomplete or unfinished article has the essential character of the complete or finished article. It shall also be taken to include a reference to that article complete or finished (or falling to be classified as complete or finished by virtue of this Rule), presented unassembled or disassembled'; WTO, *China: Measures Affecting Imports of Automobile Parts–Reports of the Appellate Body* (15 December 2008) WT/DS339/AB/R, WT/DS340/AB/R and WT/DS342/AB/R [14–18] ('*China–Auto Parts* (Appellate Body Reports)').

whether a measure is an internal charge or customs duty.[1075] Moreover, the AB confirmed that the obligations under the Chinese measures accrued only after importation due to internal factors, making them internal charges. It found that they incentivized preferences for domestic automobile parts, leading the AB to agree with the Panel that national treatment obligations under Article III (2) and (4) GATT 1994 were breached – while addressing the alternative findings was not deemed necessary.[1076] The only aspect of the report the AB disagreed with was the finding on completely or semi-knocked down kits. In the AB's view, the Chinese measures were to be considered internal charges also regarding these products, and inconsistent with WTO law on the same grounds as when applied to the other products.[1077]

Ultimately, the issue – entailing lengthy deliberations – of whether China had levied an internal charge or border charge was likely 'of no practical consequence in the present case'.[1078] China would anyway have been found in violation of its WTO obligations in this rather clear-cut case, be it on account of an internal charge unduly differentiating between imported and 'like domestic products',[1079] or a tariff in excess of China's Schedule.[1080]

Two things are interesting about this case in the context of this study's research question. First, that it was even fought out up to the AB stage. Second, how the Chinese government responded to defeat.

On the first matter, in this case, only two years after *China-Integrated Circuits*, the Chinese approach had changed markedly. China did not back down to find a mutually-agreed solution, but instead contested the com-

1075 *China–Auto Parts* (Appellate Body Reports) (n 1074) [152].

1076 Art III (2) and (4) GATT 1994; *China–Auto Parts* (Appellate Body Reports) (n 1074) [161]–[165], [182]–[184], [195]–[196], [209].

1077 *China–Auto Parts* (Appellate Body Reports) (n 1074) [222]–[245].

1078 Jasper Wauters and Hylke Vandenbussche, 'China – Measures Affecting Imports of Automobile Parts' (2010) 9 *World Trade Review* 201, 220 recounting the wording of the GATT Panel Report, *Canada – Import, Distribution and Sale of Certain Alcoholic Drinks by Provincial Marketing Agencies*, DS 17/R (adopted 18 February 1992) 39S/75–76, para 5.6.

1079 Art III (2) GATT 1994. For further deliberations on the elements of Art III (2) and (4) GATT 1994 and pertinent case law see also Lester, Mercurio and Davies (n 1027) 268–286, 287–306.

1080 Art II (1) GATT 1994. See also Lester, Mercurio and Davies (n 1027) 225–234.

plaint all of the way to the AB. It went on to lose – the first time ever in an international dispute proceeding of any sort.[1081]

One reason for China's refusal to settle was the absence of dominant production network dynamics in this case, meaning that a settlement would 'result in losses to a domestic constituency with no countervailing gains to another domestic constituency with overseas interests'.[1082] Moreover, the domestic constituency taking a hit in this case was a very powerful one, and one with broad public responsibilities at the time: State-Owned Enterprises (hereinafter: SOEs) in the automobile industry.[1083] The lobbying clout of this industry, where companies provided social services to workers' families 'from the cradle to the grave,' was an important difference to the situation in *China-Integrated Circuits*. Observing the heated competition with international companies for the supply of parts to the domestic car-making industry, the Chinese government felt it had to step in.[1084]

Second, despite some expectations to the contrary, China complied with the findings, also a first in its history of engagement with international tribunals.[1085] It notified implementation at the DSB meeting on 31 August 2009,[1086] following decrees by the powerful National Development and Reform Commission (NDRC), the Ministries of Finance, Commerce and of Industry and Information Technology, as well as the General Administration of Customs halting implementation of the pertinent measures, and repealing some underlying legal measures, effective from1 September 2009.[1087] The pace and level of coordination of the listed high-ranking Chinese institutions in the process of implementing the findings points to a

1081 See also Ku, 'China and the Future of International Adjudication' (n 32) 168–169.

1082 Ewing-Chow, Goh and Patil (n 1023) 702.

1083 Xiaojun Li (n 994) 1135, where in FN 71 she underlines that at the time more than 10 % of the auto parts industry, but only below 3 % of the semiconductor industry were state owned, as well as the direct government access of state-owned enterprises.

1084 Ewing-Chow, Goh and Patil (n 1023) 702.

1085 Ku, 'China and the Future of International Adjudication' (n 32) 168–169; Xiuli Han, 'China's First Ten Years' (n 38) 55–56.

1086 WTO, *China: Measures Affecting Imports of Automobile Parts–Notification of Implementation* (30 March 2006) WT/DS339.

1087 Xiuli Han, 'China's First Ten Years' (n 38) 56.

willingness at the highest levels in the Chinese government to clearly demonstrate compliance with decisions under the DSU.[1088]

Furthermore, the Chinese government was not provoked into any kind of backlash by broad media coverage of 'China's first major defeat at the WTO.' Instead, its Ministry of Commerce claimed success in garnering experience with the DSM and buying time for China's auto parts-industry. Implementation of the AB's findings was not questioned.[1089]

IV.2.2.2.2.2.2. TRIPS & Censorship

In *China-IP Rights*, the Panel mainly had to deal with the tension between China's censorship laws and copyright obligations under the Agreement on Trade-Related Intellectual Property Rights (hereinafter: TRIPS), TRIPS-compliant disposal of confiscated goods, and the necessity of TRIPS-compliant criminal procedures and penalties for trademark counterfeiting or copyright piracy. In short, the issue at hand was whether China had sufficiently harmonized and enforced its intellectual property (hereinafter: IP) law in accordance with WTO obligations.[1090]

The US considered that a Member has the obligation to protect the copyright of foreign products that are illegal within its borders due to censorship decisions. China's defense that such protection is a 'legal and material nullity' (or alternatively that censorship is a form of 'effective action' to enforce protection) failed, and it was determined to have breached Articles 9 (1) and 41 (1) TRIPS due to the lacking availability of proper enforcement procedures under Chinese law and failure to protect artistic works in line with the Berne Convention.[1091] The Panel found China largely compliant in terms of providing customs bodies the proper authority to dispose of confiscated goods.[1092] Moreover, the Panel underlined that the US

1088 Kennedy, 'China's role in WTO Dispute Settlement' (n 38) 581; Xiuli Han, 'China's First Ten Years' (n 38) 56.

1089 Xiaojun Li (n 994) 1134.

1090 *China–Intellectual Property Rights* (Request for Consultations) (n 1052).

1091 Arts 9.1 and 41.1 TRIPS Agreement; Berne Convention for the Protection of Literary and Artistic Works (adopted 9 September 1886, completed 4 May 1896, revised 14 July 1967) 828 UNTS 221 (Berne Convention); WTO, *China: Measures Affecting the Protection and Enforcement of Intellectual Property Rights–Report of the Panel* (26 January 2009) WT/DS362/R [7.134]–[7.139], [7.179]–[7.181] ('*China–Intellectual Property Rights* (Panel Report)').

1092 *China–Intellectual Property Rights* (Panel Report) (n 1091) [7.228]–[7.343].

had also not established that China's pertinent criminal thresholds violated Article 61 (1) TRIPS.[1093]

Arguably, this dispute can at least partly be traced back to drafting issues. The TRIPS provisions this case involves 'could have been drafted more specifically, with more precision. How can we explain the existing level of incompleteness of the WTO "contract" with respect to the establishment of minimum standards for enforcement of IPR law? What are the implications of this incompleteness?'.[1094] This fits with a view of the WTO as an 'incomplete contract,' in the sense that trade instruments are 'rigid,' but domestic instruments 'are largely left to the discretion of governments except that they have to abide by the principle of national treatment',[1095] which suggests the suitability of an 'incomplete contracts analysis' to elucidate the case.[1096] One form of pertinent incompleteness can be seen in the lacking reconciliation of WTO treaty values in the case of broad censorship rights – TRIPS incorporates Article 17 Berne Convention – and general copyright protection obligations under TRIPS that do not include a pertinent exception.[1097]

In this case, the Chinese government showed itself to be sufficiently comfortable with participation in the system to be satisfied with partial success and did not appeal. It was not only ready to commit to the implementation of a report that touched on the sensitive matter of censorship, but was likely actually relieved about the limited extent of its censorship regime's vulnerability vis-à-vis the TRIPS Agreement.[1098]

1093 Art 61.1 TRIPS Agreement; *China–Intellectual Property Rights* (Panel Report) (n 1091) [7.632]–[7.669].

1094 Kamal Saggi and Joel P Trachtman, 'Incomplete Harmonization Contracts in International Economic Law: Report of the Panel, China – Measures Affecting the Protection and Enforcement of Intellectual Property Rights, WT/DS362/R, adopted 20 March 2009' (2011) 10 *World Trade Review* 63, 66.

1095 Saggi and Trachtman (n 1094) 66, referencing Henrik Horn, Giovanni Maggi, and Robert W Staiger, 'Trade Agreements as Endogenously Incomplete Contracts' (2010) 100 *The American Economic Review* 394. For a nuanced critique of the Saggi and Trachtman-approach see Robert Howse, 'Case Comment: China – Measures Affecting the Protection and Enforcement of Intellectual Property Rights' (2011) 10 *World Trade Review* 87.

1096 Saggi and Trachtman (n 1094) 66, 81–84.

1097 Art 9 TRIPS Agreement; Art 17 Berne Convention for the Protection of Literary and Artistic Works (adopted 9 September 1886, completed 4 May 1896, revised 14 July 1967) 828 UNTS 221 (Berne Convention); Saggi and Trachtman (n 1094) 66–67.

1098 See also Manjiao Chi, 'China's Participation' (n 969) 45 referencing Joost Pauwelyn, 'The Dog That Barked But Didn't Bite: 15 Years of Intellectual

IV.2.2.2.2.2.3. GATT-GATS Relations & Systemic Position of the Accession Protocol

In *China-Publications and Audiovisual Products*, the US considered that China's restrictions on the importation and distribution of books and other print publications, sound recordings and films – partly by delegating the respective rights exclusively to certain domestic companies – were inconsistent with market access and national treatment obligations under the GATS and China's Accession Protocol, as well as the obligation to eliminate quantitative restrictions under the GATT 1994.[1099]

The Panel largely upheld the US claims.[1100] China appealed due to 1) a supposed confusion of 'goods' and 'services' (relating to measures on 'films for theatrical release'), 2) the allegedly mistaken rejection of the public morals exception under Article XX (a) GATT 1994, and 3) a supposed misreading of China's GATS Schedule (on 'sound recording distribution services').[1101]

However, the AB determined that pertinent films contain components of both a 'service' and a 'good,' while it is 'inevitable' that relevant regulations affect the 'service' and the physical 'good' through which it is expressed (if that is the case). Thus, the AB found that both GATS and GATT could apply.[1102] It granted that GATT exceptions could be used in principle to justify inconsistencies with other WTO agreements, including China's Accession Protocol, but eventually determined that China had not demonstrated the respective measures being 'necessary' to protect public

---

Property Disputes at the WTO' (2010) 1 *Journal of International Dispute Settlement* 389, 403.

1099 Arts XVI and XVII GATS; Part I, Paras 1.2, 5.1 – 5.2 Accession Protocol, in connection with Paras 83 and 84 Working Party Report; Art XI:1 GATT 1994; *China–Publications and Audiovisual Products* (Request for Consultations) (n 1052).

1100 WTO, *China: Measures Affecting Trading Rights and Distribution Services for Certain Publications and Audiovisual Entertainment Products–Report of the Panel* (12 August 2009) WT/DS363/R [VIII.1]–[VIII.4] ('*China–Publications and Audiovisual Products* (Panel Report)').

1101 WTO, *China: Measures Affecting Trading Rights and Distribution Services for Certain Publications and Audiovisual Entertainment Products–Report of the Appellate Body* (21 December 2009) WT/DS363/AB/R [14]–[23], [24]–[35], [36]–[53] ('*China–Publications and Audiovisual Products* (Appellate Body Report)').

1102 *China–Publications and Audiovisual Products* (Appellate Body Report) (n 1101) [188]–[200].

morals, excluding an Article XX GATT 1994 defense.[1103] Finally, the AB upheld the Panel's findings on China's GATS Schedule and violations of national treatment commitments under Article XVII GATS.[1104]

On the issue of distinguishing 'goods' and 'services,' it has to be highlighted that neither GATT nor GATS define the respective concepts, while the two agreements are not mutually exclusive (see *EC-Bananas*) in their applicability to one measure, and there are examples for dual applicability (eg periodicals as containing editorial content with services attributes and constituting a physical product, see *Canada-Periodicals*).[1105] As indications on the matter, it has been noted that at their core '[a] product is a tangible object, a service an observable action',[1106] and that there have been no real difficulties in the case law distinguishing the two. The difficulty lies in determining whether a particular measure applies to a good or service, whereas one should ask what the measure is 'affecting,' in the sense of 'modifying conditions of competition in respect of.'[1107]

This case is an example of the contention over 'the way in which [China's] accession commitments integrate into the WTO Agreement'.[1108] One crucial question raised here is whether pre-existing provisions in WTO agreements can be used to defend against Accession Protocol obligations.[1109] However, the AB relied on the specific wording regarding trading rights in discussing the possible use of GATT exceptions to justify inconsistencies with the Accession Protocol, and did not discuss the 'sys-

---

1103 Art XX GATT 1994; *China–Publications and Audiovisual Products* (Appellate Body Report) (n 1101) [223], [336]–[337].

1104 Art XVII GATS; *China–Publications and Audiovisual Products* (Appellate Body Report) (n 1101) [412]–[413].

1105 WTO, *European Communities: Regime for the Importation, Sale and Distribution of Bananas–Appellate Body Report* (9 September 1997) WT/DS27/AB/R [221]; WTO, *Canada: Certain Measures Concerning Periodicals–Report of the Appellate Body* (30 June 1997) WT/DS31/AB/R. See also Paola Conconi and Joost Pauwelyn, 'Trading Cultures: Appellate Body Report on China–Audiovisuals (WT/DS363/AB/R, adopted 19 January 2010)' (2011) 10 *World Trade Review* 95, 98–99.

1106 Frieder Roessler, 'Appellate Body Ruling in China–Publications and Audiovisual Products' (2011) 10 *World Trade Review* 119, 120.

1107 Ibid 123.

1108 Kennedy, 'China's role in WTO Dispute Settlement' (n 38) 580.

1109 Julia Ya Qin, 'Pushing the Limits of Global Governance: Trading Rights, Censorship and WTO Jurisprudence—A Commentary on the China–Publications Case' (2011) 10 CJIL 271, 291–299.

temic relationship between the [Protocol] and the rest of the WTO Agreement'.[1110]

In view of the Chinese government's approach towards the DSM it should, First, be noted that it was additionally motivated to challenge US allegations all of the way to the AB, because it considers the cultural sector a very sensitive issue due to its crucial role in aligning public opinion with the Communist Party's policy priorities.[1111] Limiting imports of cultural products to a few SOEs also aided the intended non-transparency and flexibility of the censorship process.[1112]

Another interesting point is that China did not invoke the public morals exception in Article XX GATT 1994 to defend against potential GATT and GATS violations, but did so regarding a potential breach of its Accession Protocol.[1113] This might indicate not only a willingness to avoid a larger free trade versus censorship collision, but also the Chinese government's focus on the correct interpretation of and compliance with the crucial document regulating China's distinct position within the WTO.[1114] In this case, this distinct position was China's obligation under paragraph 5.1 Accession Protocol to allow all enterprises to export and import all goods,[1115] in contrast to other Members, who may establish import and export monopolies.[1116] Challenging other Members' interpretations of the Accession Protocol was becoming an important policy goal for China in this period, and the issue will be further addressed below.[1117]

Finally, in light of the increased political sensitivity concerning cultural products, China for the first time asked for a 'reasonable period of time'

1110 *China–Publications and Audiovisual Products* (Appellate Body Report) (n 1101) [205]–[230]; see also Kennedy, 'China's role in WTO Dispute Settlement' (n 38) 580.

1111 Bourgeois (n 970) 21.

1112 Manjiao Chi, 'China's Participation' (n 969) 46 (for further discussion of SOE conformity with WTO agreements see also 41–42).

1113 Art XX GATT 1994; *China–Publications and Audiovisual Products* (Panel Report) (n 1100) [4.112]. See also Conconi and Pauwelyn (n 1105) 103.

1114 See also Conconi and Pauwelyn (n 1105) 116; Julia Ya Qin, 'Pushing the Limits' (n 1109) 274–277, 283–287.

1115 Para 5.1 Accession Protocol.

1116 Arts II (4), XI, XVII, and XX (d) GATT 1994; Understanding on the Interpretation of Article XVII of the General Agreement on Tariffs and Trade 1994 Final Act. See also Roessler, 'Appellate Body Ruling' (n 1106) 123–124; Dennin (n 960) 29–30.

1117 Chapters V.2.1.2 and V.2.1.3.

(Article 21 (3) DSU) for implementation.[1118] China and the US agreed on 14 months; China then delayed, while voicing its discomfort with the findings and necessary reforms via several status reports,[1119] but implementation was eventually notified without any compliance proceeding.[1120]

IV.2.2.2.2.2.4. Settled Cases

In *China-Taxes*, the US (later joined by Mexico) considered that Chinese measures connected to 1) the purchase of domestic products or 2) compliance with export performance criteria constitute illegal subsidies,[1121] and that they are inconsistent with national treatment,[1122] as well as China's accession obligations on non-tariff measures.[1123] The parties reached a settlement on 19 December 2007.[1124]

As for *China-Financial Services*, the EU – the US and Canada followed -considered that China had violated GATS and accession commitments by requiring foreign financial information suppliers to always go through *China Economic Information Enterprise*, an SOE controlled by Xinhua News Agency, and thus not an independent regulatory authority.[1125] China agreed to appropriate reform steps and implemented the agreed settlement.[1126]

1118 Art 21 (3) DSU; see also Xiuli Han, 'China's First Ten Years' (n 38) 56.

1119 See also Manjiao Chi, 'China's Participation' (n 969) 46–47; Kennedy, 'China's role in WTO Dispute Settlement' (n 38) 580–581.

1120 WTO, *China: Measures Affecting Trading Rights and Distribution Services for Certain Publications and Audiovisual Entertainment Products-Implementation notified* (24 May 2012) WT/DS363 <https://www.wto.org/english/tratop_e/dispu_e/cases_e/ds363_e.htm> accessed 5 June 2018.

1121 Art 3 SCM Agreement; Part I para 10.3 Accession Protocol.

1122 Art III (4) GATT 1994; Art 2 TRIMS Agreement.

1123 *China–Taxes* (Request for Consultations) (n 1052); Part I, Paras 7.2 – 7.3 Accession Protocol..

1124 WTO, *China: Certain Measures Granting Refunds, Reductions or Exemptions from Taxes and Other Payments-Settled* (19 December 2007) WT/DS358 <https://www.wto.org/english/tratop_e/dispu_e/cases_e/ds358_e.htm> accessed 5 June 2018.

1125 Arts XVI:2 (a) and (e), XVII, XVIII and standstill provision in China's GATS schedule of commitments GATS; Para 309 Working Party Report; *China–Financial Information Services* (Request for Consultations) (n 1052).

1126 WTO, *China: Measures Affecting Financial Information Services and Foreign Financial Information Suppliers–Settled* (4 December 2008) WT/DS372 <https://www.wto.org/english/tratop_e/dispu_e/cases_e/ds372_e.htm> accessed 5 June 2018. See also Bourgeois (n 970) 29.

IV.2.2.2.2.3. Conclusion

In the second phase of China's participation in the WTO DSM ('rule-shaker'), the country switched from passive learning to active defense. This entailed refusing a mutually-agreed solution and fight out disputes up to the AB when on the respondent side,[1127] and to for the first time in China's history risk and then accept defeat in international adjudication. Additionally, the Chinese government for the first time made use of WTO procedures allowing a Member to ask for a reasonable period of time for implementation,[1128] going yet further in using the system to protect its perceived interests. China engaged on sensitive issues such as censorship, and it began to focus on the systemic position of its Accession Protocol vis-à-vis the rest of the WTO Agreement, challenging other Members' interpretations. It was also willing to for the first time initiate a case as the single complainant, and study the system further from within.

This fits with yet stronger praise for the DSM from Chinese international law scholars,[1129] who – inter alia – termed it a shield for weaker economies,[1130] and an effective way to protect trade interests.[1131] More directly, it corresponds with recommendations to now fully and confidently engage,[1132] not only if success was likely, but rather where engagement was likely 'profitable',[1133] including in the sense of delaying probably inevitable outcomes in the way that the US supposedly did (eg in *US-Steel Safeguards*).[1134]

1127 China still settled two cases in this period, but the tide had turned, and mutually agreed solutions were now fewer than actively disputed cases.

1128 Art 21 (3) DSU.

1129 See Chapter V.2.1.1.

1130 See eg Xin 欣 Chen 陈, '论 WTO 争端解决机制对 WTO 农业体制的影响' (Review of the WTO Dispute Settlement Mechanism's Impact on the WTO Agricultural System) (2006) 20 (5) *Dangdai Faxue* 85, 85–87 who refers to WTO, *United States: Subsidies on Upland Cotton–Report of the Appellate Body* (3 March 2005) WT/DS267/AB/R ('*US–Upland Cotton* (Appellate Body Report)'); WTO, *European Communities: Export Subsidies on Sugar–Report of the Appellate Body* (28 April 2005) WT/DS265/AB/R ('*EC–Export Subsidies on Sugar* (Appellate Body Report)').

1131 See eg Jiaxiang Hu (n 1032) 68.

1132 See eg Haifeng 海峰 Zhao 赵, '中国与国际司法机构关系的演进' (Evolution of Relations between China and International Judicial Mechanisms) [2008] (6) *Faxue Pinglun* 3, 12.

1133 See eg Baihua Gong (n 1032) 106.

1134 See Chapter V.2.1.3.2.

IV.2.2.2.3. China As a 'Rule-Maker' – Since September 2008

In a third phase of PRC behavior within the WTO dispute settlement system ('rule-maker'), since September 2008 the country has 1) shifted from defense to offense, and 2) attempted to change interpretations of WTO rules via the DSM. China mostly refused to settle further cases. Moreover, the Chinese government has levied an inflationary number of complaints itself, and become involved with more disputes as a principal party than any other Member except the US.[1135]

The last reason given above for the shift of attitudes in the second phase – wanting to make use of the opportunity to criticize other Members' interpretations of the Accession Protocol – points to a crucial focal area of the Chinese government's efforts in this third phase, namely actively shaping accepted interpretations of the Accession Protocol. Beyond this core aspect, China has striven to make strategic use of the DSM to 1) obtain clarifications that might make it harder for other Members to impose trade protection measures or launch cases against China, 2) convince the AB to reverse certain definitions and other findings by various Panels (in cases with or without Chinese participation) that China disagrees with, 3) delay WTO-compliant behavior, and 4) retaliate and communicate displeasure with other Members' trade-related actions.[1136]

Aside from efforts via the DSM, China had also begun a diplomatic campaign to persuade other Members not to have recourse to paragraphs 15 (non-market economy treatment, hereinafter: NME, regarding price comparability in determining subsidies and dumping) and 16 (China-specific safeguard mechanism) Accession Protocol almost immediately after accession. This included a push for pertinent language in FTAs.[1137] The issue became more relevant later on, when China started to successfully conclude a row of FTAs, and had become a more consequential trade and investment partner for many Members.[1138] Additionally, China began to fix its gaze on

---

1135 WTO, 'Disputes by Member' <https://www.wto.org/english/tratop_e/dispu_e/dispu_by_country_e.htm> accessed 5 November 2019.

1136 Gao, 'China on the World Stage' (n 990) 533–535. See also Bourgeois (n 970) 10; Manjiao Chi, 'China's Participation' (n 969) 32. See also Ya Julia Qin, 'Trade, Investment and beyond' (n 978) 739–740.

1137 Kennedy, 'China's role in WTO Dispute Settlement' (n 38) 561; Paras 15 and 16 Accession Protocol.

1138 See also Chapter IV.2.2.2.3.7; Art 14 Agreement on Trade in Goods of the Framework Agreement on Comprehensive Economic Cooperation between the the People's Republic of China and the Association of Southeast Asian Na-

December 2016. This would be the end date of the applicability of the price comparison methodology in paragraph 15 (a) (ii) of the Accession Protocol, which would expire in any event after 15 years under paragraph 15 (d).[1139] That is how China understood the Accession Protocol, and that is one crucial interpretation of the document it wanted to gain general recognition of, especially by the US and EU, its most important trade partners and only targets of Chinese-initiated disputes – the Chinese government has made sure to never initiate a case against a developing country (or small) Member.

IV.2.2.2.3.1 Using the Accession Protocol Against China – Export Restrictions

IV.2.2.2.3.1.1 Relevant case law

The US – later also the EU and Mexico – requested consultations in *China-Raw Materials*.[1140] China had imposed what supposedly amounted to quantitative restrictions, export duties, additional administrative requirements, and minimum export prices for certain raw materials,[1141] in breach of GATT 1994 and Accession Protocol obligations.[1142] The PRC once again refused to settle.

The Panel determined that China's export duties on some materials indeed violated Accession Protocol obligations to eliminate export taxes and charges, finding no textual basis in the Accession Protocol to apply GATT 1994 'general exceptions' on the protection of human, animal and plant

---

tions (adopted 29 November 2004, entered into force 1 January 2005) ('ASEAN-China Trade in Goods Agreement') marked a first success for Beijing in this regard.

1139 Para 15 (a) (ii) and (d) Accession Protocol.

1140 WTO, *China: Measures Related to the Exportation of Various Raw Materials–Request for Consultations* (23 June 2009) WT/DS394/1 ('*China–Raw Materials* (Request for Consultations)').

1141 The complaint concerned restrictions on the export of bauxite, coke, fluorspar, magnesium, manganese, phosphate (yellow phosphorus), silicon metal, silicon carbide, and zinc.

1142 Paras 1.2, 5.1 – 2, 8.2 and 11.3 Accession Protocol (relating to trading rights, export licensing, as well as taxes and charges on exports); Paras 83, 84, 162 and 165 Working Party Report; Arts VIII, X and XI GATT 1994; *China–Raw Materials* (Request for Consultations) (n 1140).

life or resource conservation.[1143] The Panel admitted that this put China 'in a position unlike that of most other WTO Members who are not prohibited from using export duties, either via the terms of their respective accession protocols or their membership to the WTO at the time of its inception',[1144] but found itself unable to act otherwise. Moreover, it held that Chinese export quotas were not justified either as temporary exceptions to relief critical shortages, or as conservation of exhaustible natural resources, or as environmental protection, and violated GATT 1994 obligations to eliminate quantitative restrictions, administer laws impartially and uniformly, and publish pertinent decisions promptly.[1145]

Additionally, Chinese requirements concerning prior export performance and minimum registered capital were found in breach of trading rights commitments – but not such on national treatment – in the Accession Protocol and accompanying Working Party Report.[1146] Some aspects of China's export licensing system as well as supposedly coordinated minimum export prices were also found to violate the GATT 1994.[1147]

This time China was partly successful on appeal.[1148] According to the AB the complainants failed to establish 'sufficiently clear linkages' between the supposedly violated obligations and the 37 challenged measures, failing to comply with due process under Article 6 (2) DSU. Half of the Panel's findings were thrown out.[1149] The AB then concentrated on export

1143 Art 11.3 Accession Protocol; Art XX (b) and (g) GATT 1994; WTO, *China: Measures Related to the Exportation of Various Raw Materials–Reports of the Panel* (5 July 2011) WT/DS394/R, WT/DS395/R and WT/DS398/R [VII.64]–[VII.101], [VII.105], [VII.108], [VII.158]–[VII.160] ('*China–Raw Materials* (Panel Reports)').

1144 *China–Raw Materials* (Panel Reports) (n 1143) [VII.160]. .

1145 Arts X:1, X:3 (a), XI:1, XI:2 (a) and XX (b) and (g) GATT 1994; *China–Raw Materials* (Panel Reports) (n 1143) [VII.224]–[VII.225], [VII.354]–[VII.355], [VII.613], [VII.615], [VII.756], [VII.807].

1146 Paras 1.2, 5.1 and 5.2 Accession Protocol; Paras 83 and 84 Working Party Report; *China–Raw Materials* (Panel Reports) (n 1143) [VII.669]–[VII.670], [VII.676]–[VII.678].

1147 Arts X:1 and XI:1 GATT 1994; *China–Raw Materials* (Panel Reports) (n 1143) [VII.957]–[VII.959], [VII.982], [VII.1103].

1148 WTO, *China: Measures Related to the Exportation of Various Raw Materials–Reports of the Appellate Body* (30 January 2012) WT/DS394/AB/R, WT/DS395/AB/R and WT/DS398/AB/R ('*China–Raw Materials* (Appellate Body Reports)').

1149 Art 6 (2) DSU; *China–Raw Materials* (Appellate Body Reports) (n 1148) [233]–[235].

quotas and duties. It confirmed the rejection of China's attempted defenses and violation of the Accession Protocol.[1150]

China-Rare Earths, in many ways a follow-up dispute, was initiated by requests for consultations from Japan, the EU and the US.[1151] The complainants again considered that Chinese export duties, export quotas, licensing requirements, minimum export prices, and additional administrative requirements – this time on a number of rare earths[1152] – violated a similar lineup of GATT 1994 and Accession Protocol provisions.[1153]

China argued, citing *US-Stainless Steel (Mexico)*,[1154] that there were 'cogent reasons' to change course from *China-Raw Materials*, and let it justify its measures via Article XX GATT 1994, even though the AB usually (successfully) insists that Panels adhere to its prior findings, and itself aims to maintain consistency.[1155] The Panel agreed that the latter decision could run counter to object and purpose of the WTO Agreement, were it not just one policy instrument – export duties – China had signed away.[1156] According to the Panel, China was also right in claiming that the Accession Protocol was an 'integral part' of the WTO Agreement, but crucially the individual Accession Protocol provisions are said to not be integral parts of any WTO sub-agreement, including the GATT 1994, meaning there would

---

1150 Arts XI:2 (a) and XX GATT 1994; *China–Raw Materials* (Appellate Body Reports) (n 1148) [344], [362].

1151 WTO, *China: Measures Related to the Exportation of Rare Earths, Tungsten and Molybdenum–Request for Consultations* (13 March 2012) WT/DS431/1 ('*China–Rare Earths* (Request for Consultations)').

1152 'Rare earths' are 17 elements that are crucial to the manufacturing of high-tech products (including renewable energy products and weapons systems).

1153 Arts VII, VIII, X, XI:1 GATT 1994; Paras 1.2, 2 (A) 2, 2 (C) 1, 5.1 – 2, 7.2, 8.2, 11.3 and Annex 6 Accession Protocol; Paras 83, 84, 162 and 165 Working Party Report. See also Julia Ya Qin, 'Judicial Authority in WTO Law: A Commentary on the Appellate Body's Decision in China-Rare Earths' (2014) 13 CJIL 639, 640 who notes that the main issues 'are almost identical to those in *Raw Materials*.'.

1154 WTO, *United States-Final Anti-Dumping Measures on Stainless Steel from Mexico–Appellate Body Report* (20 May 2008) WT/DS344/AB/R [160–62].

1155 Art XX (b) and (g) GATT 1994; WTO, *China: Measures Related to the Exportation of Rare Earths, Tungsten and Molybdenum–Reports of the Panel* (26 March 2014) WT/DS431/R, WT/DS432/R and WT/DS433/R [7.55] ('*China–Rare Earths* (Reports of the Panel)'). See also Eric W Bond and Joel Trachtman, 'China-Rare Earths: Export Restrictions and the Limits of Textual Interpretation' (2016) 15 *World Trade Review* 189, 191–192.

1156 *China–Rare Earths* (Reports of the Panel) (n 1155) [7.111 – 117].

have to always be case-by-case analysis on such relationships.[1157] China was again found in breach of various WTO law provisions due to its export duties, but also its export quotas, and restrictions involving minimum registered capital, prior export experience and export performance.[1158]

China appealed, particularly on the question of whether paragraph 11.3 Accession Protocol on export taxes and charges is an integral part of the GATT 1994, although the AB's report confirmed the Panel's decision.[1159]

IV.2.2.2.3.1.2 Discussion

China certainly adopted a number of export-restricting measures,[1160] and it indeed did not contest using such measures. Members are not generally prohibited from applying them. However, at least concerning export duties, the Chinese government agreed in its Accession Protocol that it would 'eliminate all taxes and charges applied to exports unless specifically provided for in Annex 6 of this Protocol or applied in conformity with the provisions of Article VIII of the GATT 1994'.[1161] The annex, with only 84 tariff lines, was rather limited, and did not contain the raw materials in

1157 Para 1.2 Accession Protocol; *China–Rare Earths* (Reports of the Panel) (n 1155) [7.75], [7.82].

1158 Arts XI, XX GATT 1994; Paras 1.2, 5.1 and 11.3 Accession Protocol; Paras 83, 84, 162 and 165 Working Party Report; *China–Rare Earths* (Reports of the Panel) (n 1155) [7.99], [8.1.1 – 8.13].

1159 Para 11.3 Accession Protocol; WTO, *China: Measures Related to the Exportation of Rare Earths, Tungsten and Molybdenum–Reports of the Appellate Body* (7 August 2014) WT/DS431/AB/R, WT/DS432/AB/R and WT/DS433/AB/R [6.1] ('*China–Rare Earths* (Appellate Body Reports)').

1160 For a more detailed description of Chinese measures restricting the export of products relevant to *China-Raw Materials* (and also an elaboration on further restricted products) see Baris Karapinar, 'China's export restriction policies: complying with 'WTO plus' or undermining multilateralism' (2011) 10 *World Trade Review* 389, 397–400. For a list of Chinese institutions involved in the adoption of the pertinent measures see Manjiao Chi, 'From Ownership-Orientation to Governance-Orientation: An International Economic Law Perspective of China's Shifting Attitudes Towards Resource Sovereignty' (2013) Forschungskolleg Siegen Working Paper 2/2013, 10 <https://www.uni-siegen.de/fokos/publikationen/veroeffentlichungen/fokos_-_working_paper_2013-02_-_chi.pdf> accessed 1 March 2019.

1161 Art 11.3 and Annex 6 Accession Protocol; Art VIII GATT 1994.

question.[1162] The main drivers behind pertinent measures were presumably the intent to provide price advantages to domestic downstream producers and processors (*China-Raw Materials*),[1163] and the idea to improve conservation and environmental protection without harming domestic downstream industries (*China-Rare Earths*).[1164]

The Panelists in *Raw Materials* were right that China's sovereignty was not violated, because China 'exercised its inherent and sovereign right to regulate trade [including in natural resources] in negotiating, (...), the terms of its accession into the WTO [including paragraph 11.3 Accession Protocol]',[1165] committing to WTO-compliant abstention from pertinent raw material export restrictions. This has been described as China's 'WTO-plus' predicament on export duty elimination.[1166]

Nevertheless, the AB made a mistake in both cases, by rejecting the possibility of China appealing to Article XX GATT 1994 regarding its export duties. It does not make sense to allow such access for export quotas but not export duties, and the textual nuance in China's Accession Protocol is likely a 'drafting error',[1167] to which China should not be held in a manner

1162 Annex 6 Accession Protocol. See also Karapinar (n 1160) 398–400; Marco Bronckers and Keith E Maskus, 'China-Raw Materials: a controversial step towards evenhanded exploitation of natural resources' (2014) 13 *World Trade Review* 393, 396.

1163 Karapinar (n 1160) 405; Bourgeois (n 970) 25.

1164 Key for manufacturing high-tech goods, rare earths have special properties of strength, magnetism and luminescence, while production is highly polluting. At the time of the requests for consultations, China had a 97 % share of the global market, although it holds only 30 % of known global reserves. See also Bond and Trachtman (n 1155) 190–191. For a deeper investigation of China's export quota regime for rare earths as of June 2012 see Han-Wei Liu and John Maughan, 'China's Rare Earths Export Quotas: Out of the China Raw-Materials Gate, But Past the WTO's Finish Line?' (2012) 15 *Journal of International Economic Law* 971.

1165 *China–Raw Materials* (Panel Reports) (n 1143) [VII.156]–[VII.157]. The Panel at the same time confirmed permanent sovereignty over natural resources, referencing UNGA Res 626 (1952) UN Doc A/RES/626(VII); UNGA Res 1803 (1962) UN Doc A/RES/1803(XVII); Convention on Biological Diversity (adopted 5 June 1992, entered into force 29 December 1993) 1760 UNTS 79 ('Convention on Biodiversity').

1166 Julia Ya Qin, 'The predicament of China's "WTO-plus" obligation to eliminate export duties: A commentary on the China-Raw Materials case' (2012) 11 CJIL 237, 238–239.

1167 On bad drafting as a problematic issue concerning the Accession Protocol see also Bin Gu, 'Applicability of GATT Article XX in China-Raw Materials: A

of 'abstemious textualism',[1168] when the AB in other cases 'stretched and squeezed the accordion' to get to a 'much wiser outcome' (eg interpreting 'like products' differently within the same GATT 1994 article in *EC-Asbestos*).[1169] The AB failed to take the broader context and object and purpose into account as customary rules of interpretation would demand,[1170] did not conform with the call for 'holistic interpretation' in *EC-Chicken Cuts*,[1171] and in its reliance on effective interpretation ignores that other provisions of the Accession Protocol are quite evidently ineffective.[1172]In general, '[d]enying a member the mere right to invoke generally accepted public policies reflects badly on an organization like the WTO, and tarnishes its legitimacy',[1173] unnecessarily, including because the defense can, often does, and in this case would have failed.[1174] Treating the Accession Protocol as a 'covered agreement',[1175] while it is not defined as such in the DSU,[1176] might also cause issues for compliance proceedings and retaliation.[1177]

Under prevailing political conditions, it seems convincing that the only avenue for changing such outcomes is the AB's willingness to 'self-correct,'

Clash within the WTO Agreement' (2012) 15 *Journal of International Economic Law* 1007, 1031 who refers to Isabelle Van Damme, *Treaty Interpretation by the WTO Appellate Body* (OUP 2009) 646–647.

1168 Bond and Trachtman (n 1155) 208.

1169 Bronckers and Maskus (n 1162) 399–401; WTO, *European Communities: Measures Affecting Asbestis and Asbestos-Related Products–Report of the Appellate Body* (12 March 2001) WT/DS135/AB/R [88], [96 et seq]; Art III (2) and (4) GATT 1994. Then, in stark contrast to continued textualism on expxort duties, the AB appeared to at the same time exhibit a 'counter-textual approach' in part of its reasoning on export quotas and rejecting a defense via Article XX (g) GATT 1994, see Bond and Trachtman (n 1155) 207; Art XX (g) GATT 1994.

1170 See Arts 31 and 32 VCLT and Preamble WTO Agreement.

1171 Julia Ya Qin, 'Judicial Authority' (n 1153) 641–642 who refers to WTO, *European Communities: Customs Classification of Frozen Boneless Chicken Cuts–Reports of the Appellate Body* (12 September 2005) WT/DS269/AB/R and WT/DS286/AB/R [176].

1172 See eg paras 11.1 and 11.2 Accession Protocol, which merely call for compliance with GATT 1994. See also Bond and Trachtman (n 1155) 197. For an in-depth discussion of effective interpretation in AB case law see Van Damme (n 1132).

1173 Bronckers and Maskus (n 1162) 402.

1174 Arts XI and XX (g) GATT 1994; Karapinar (n 1160) 393.

1175 *China–Rare Earths* (Appellate Body Reports) (n 1159) [363].

1176 Appendix 1 DSU.

1177 Matthew Kennedy, 'The Integration of Accession Protocols into the WTO Agreement' (2013) 47 *Journal of World Trade* 45, 51–52.

as the possibility of the Ministerial Conference or General Council adopting interpretations under Article IX (2) WTO Agreement (thus reviewing decisions of the WTO judiciary) appears non-existent. However, the AB has never admitted to any legal error throughout its history.[1178]

From the perspective of China's engagement, the outcome is problematic. If generally-accepted public policies – in a multi-speed WTO – 'cannot be invoked by *all* WTO Members in respect of the *same* type of obligation',[1179] and other accession protocols do not contain provisions comparable to China's (eg Ukraine),[1180] the Chinese government might easily invoke a bias both against recently-acceded Members in general, and China in particular.[1181] It could also argue that such an arrangement 'amounts to permanent alienation of a Member's ownership right to claim a larger share of its natural resources for domestic use [and] is arguably inconsistent with the concept of permanent sovereignty over natural resources'.[1182]

Despite strong criticism of the decision in China[1183] for limiting a state's right to use the restriction of natural resource exports to support economic development, the government immediately declared its readiness to and indeed complied with the ruling.[1184] Importantly, the Chinese leadership's outlook on resource sovereignty was at that point anyway already changing from ownership-oriented to governance-oriented and from a developing country- to an investor-country perspective.[1185] Moreover, China remained committed to influence trade law through the DSM. The clear focus – as evidenced by the above two cases – was the Accession Protocol. Interestingly, as opposed to *Raw Materials*, the Chinese side was able to secure a dissenting opinion from the Panel in *Rare Earths* and was supported by several third parties. Argentina, Brazil, Colombia and Russia supported

1178 Julia Ya Qin, 'Judicial Authority' (n 1153) 649–650.

1179 Bronckers and Maskus (n 1162) 400 (italics in the original).

1180 Para 240 *Report of the Working Party on the Accession of Ukraine* (25 January 2008) WT/ACC/UKR/152.

1181 See also Karapinar (n 1160) 392.

1182 Julia Ya Qin, 'Reforming WTO Discipline on Export Duties: Sovereignty over Natural Resources, Economic Development and Environmental Protection' (2012) 46 *Journal of World Trade* 1147, 1186. See also Elisa Baroncini, 'The Applicability of GATT Article XX to China's WTO Accession Protocol in the Appellate Body Report of the China-Raw Materials Case: suggestions for a different interpretive approach' (2013) 1 (3–4) *China-EU Law Journal* 1, 24–26.

1183 See also Chapter V.2.1.2.

1184 *China–Raw Materials* (Request for Consultations) (n 1140).

1185 Manjiao Chi, 'From Ownership-Orientation to Governance-Orientation' (n 1160) 26.

China's position, and the Republic of Korea argued that there should at least be an examination of China's accession negotiations.[1186]

IV.2.2.2.3.2 Reversal of Obligations – Using the Accession Protocol in China's Favor

IV.2.2.2.3.2.1 Accession Protocol and Safeguards

IV.2.2.2.3.2.1.1 Relevant case law: US-Tyres

China considered that US transitional product-specific safeguard measures applied against certain passenger vehicle and truck tyres relying on China's Accession Protocol were in breach of that very document.[1187] Paragraph 16 Accession Protocol – a 'WTO-minus provision' lowering other Members' level of obligations[1188] – until mid-December 2013 (ie for twelve years) allowed remedial action that could normally not be taken under WTO law. Lower thresholds as compared to global safeguards included that there had to be a 'significant cause' (not a 'substantial cause') for 'material injury' (not 'serious injury'), and that only increased imports from one Member, China, had to be demonstrated, not overall increased imports, to then target the measure solely against China.[1189] Still, these thresholds were supposedly not met.

The Panel upheld the US measure,[1190] and the AB confirmed, that the US did in fact establish imports 'increasing rapidly' enough to cause material injury, and constituting a 'significant cause' for such material in-

1186 See also Julia Ya Qin, 'Judicial Authority' (n 1153) 639, 641.

1187 WTO, *United States: Measures Affecting Imports of Certain Passenger Vehicle and Light Truck Tyres from China–Request for Consultations* (14 September 2009) WT/DS399/1 ('*US–Tyres (China)* (Request for Consultations)'). The US allegedly breached para 16 Accession Protocol.

1188 See Cui Huang and Wenhua Ji, 'Understanding China's Recent Active Moves on WTO Litigation: Rising Legalism and/or Reluctant Response?' (2012) 46 *Journal of World Trade* 1281, 1293, FN 24 for an elaboration on WTO-plus obligations as referring eg to national treatment, and WTO-minus obligations referring eg to anti-dumping, anti-subsidy and safeguard measures. See also Ya Julia Qin, 'Trade, Investment and beyond' (n 978) 723.

1189 Para 16 Accession Protocol.

1190 WTO, *United States: Measures Affecting Imports of Certain Passenger Vehicle and Light Truck Tyres from China–Report of the Panel* (13 December 2010) WT/DS399/R [8.1] ('*US–Tyres (China)* (Panel Report)').

jury.[1191] The Panel had already struck down China's contentions that the US measure exceeded the extent and time period necessary to remedy the pertinent market disruption.[1192]

IV.2.2.2.3.2.1.2 Discussion

There are 'various vague terms' in paragraph 16 Accession Protocol, and previous case law was heavily used to 'fill in the gaps'.[1193] The AB erred by diluting the 'significant cause' standard in Article 16 (4) Accession Protocol through 'harmonious' interpretation with Article 16 (1) – refers to consultations instead of the right of action – by failing to clarify how it went about interpreting the Protocol – the VCLT normally does not apply to treaties between states and Ios – and by deciding that its paragraph 16 does not violate Article I GATT 1994 although it allows China-only safeguards.[1194] The case was also unusual, because the Panel was very deferential to domestic authorities on safeguards.[1195]

This case marked a number of important firsts. It was the first case China lost as the complaining party, the first successful use of an Accession Protocol as a defense, and the first time the AB upheld a challenged safeguard.[1196] Disputes related to the Agreement of Safeguards had all seen at least some parts of the relevant complaints substantiated, but the above described transitional 'buffering mechanism' – used for other states in the

1191 Para 16.4 Accession Protocol; WTO, *United States: Measures Affecting Imports of Certain Passenger Vehicle and Light Truck Tyres from China–Report of the Appellate Body* (5 September 2011) WT/DS399/AB/R [182]–[185], [195], [318], [339] ('*US–Tyres (China)* (Appellate Body Report)').

1192 Paras 16.3 and 16.6 Accession Protocol; *US–Tyres (China)* (Panel Report) (n 1190) [7.399], [7.415].

1193 See also Steve Charnovitz and Bernard Hoekman, 'US–Tyres: Upholding a WTO Accession Contract – Imposing Pain for Little Gain' (2013) 12 *World Trade Review* 273, 278–279, 284–285; the Safeguards Agreement also does not define key terms, eg 'unforeseen developments,' 'serious injury,' 'increased quantities,' and 'cause'.

1194 Art I GATT; Para 16 (1) and (4) Accession Protocol; Art 3 VCLT. See also Charnovitz and Hoekman (n 1193) 283, 285, 286–287, 294.

1195 Charnovitz and Hoekman (n 1193) 282, 286, who cite WTO, *Dominican Republic: Safeguard Measures on Imports of Polypropylene Bags and Tubular Fabric–Final Report of the Panel* (31 January 2012) WT/DS415/R as a contrasting example on deference to domestic authorities.

1196 See also Charnovitz and Hoekman (n 1193) 273–274, who note that previously a challenged safeguard was last upheld in a GATT ruling from 1951.

GATT era and revived for China – changed the equation,[1197] and provided evidence that 'China paid a higher price than any other country to join the WTO'.[1198]

US-Tyres also showed a Chinese government much more on the offensive, and readily so, as it responded with this complaint on the first working day after the safeguard measures had been announced – the fastest WTO complaint against a trade remedy measure ever.[1199] China demonstrated that it would actively challenge the application of WTO-minus or -plus obligations within the Accession Protocol, and alerted the US and other Members particularly on using transitional safeguards again.

IV.2.2.2.3.2.2 Accession Protocol and Anti-Dumping Duties

IV.2.2.2.3.2.2.1 Relevant case law

In *EC-Fasteners*, the Chinese government considered the EC's anti-dumping duties on iron or steel fasteners inconsistent with paragraph 15 Accession Protocol as well as a long list of AD Agreement and GATT 1994 obligations,[1200] and the Panel agreed on most accounts.[1201]

The AB also found the EC in breach, 'because it conditions the determination of individual dumping margins for and the imposition of individual anti-dumping duties on NME exporters or producers to the fulfilment of

1197 See also Lester, Mercurio and Davies (n 1027) 539, who refer to Michelle Q Zang, 'The WTO Contingent Trade Instruments Against China: What Does Accession Bring?' (2009) 58 *International and Comparative Law Quarterly* 321, 321–322.

1198 See also Charnovitz and Hoekman (n 1193) 282.

1199 Wenhua Ji and Cui Huang, 'China's Experience in Dealing with WTO Dispute Settlement: A Chinese Perspective' (2011) 45 *Journal of World Trade* 1, 10.

1200 Arts VI:I and X:3 (a) GATT 1994; Arts 2 (4), 4 (1), 6 (2), (4), (5), (10), and 9 (2) AD Agreement; WTO, *European Communities: Definitive Anti-Dumping Measures on Certain Iron or Steel Fasteners from China–Request for Consultations* (31 July 2009) WT/DS397/1 ('*EC–Fasteners (China)* (Request for Consultations)'); para 15 Accession Protocol.

1201 WTO, *European Communities: Definitive Anti-Dumping Measures on Certain Iron or Steel Fasteners from China–Reports of the Panel* (3 December 2010) WT/DS397/R [VII.82]–[VII.92], [VII.291]–[VII.311], [VIII.2]–[VII.3] ('*EC–Fasteners (China)* (Panel Reports)').

the [individual treatment] test',[1202] imposing countrywide duties outside of the legitimate cases listed in the AD Agreement without the Accession Protocol providing justification.[1203] On burden of proof questions, the AB found that it was only with the exporting Chinese company on 'normal value',[1204] but not on whether individual export prices can be used, the Protocol's paragraph 15 being a limited exception.[1205] It also held that the EC violated the AD Agreement with its definition of 'domestic industry' and by failing to disclose information on the product types used for price comparison in dumping determination.[1206] After the AB's decision compliance procedures followed, which broadly went in China's favor.[1207]

In *EU-Footwear*, which addressed similar issues, China considered EU anti-dumping duties on Chinese leather footwear also inconsistent with para-

1202 Arts 6 (10) and 9 (2) AD Agreement; WTO, *European Communities: Definitive Anti-Dumping Measures on Certain Iron or Steel Fasteners from China–Reports of the Appellate Body* (15 July 2011) WT/DS397/AB/R [385] ('*EC–Fasteners (China)* (Appellate Body Reports)'). The EC's pertinent regulation being in breach of the preceding norms 'as such,' also meant violations of Art XVI:4 WTO Agreement and Art 18 (4) AD Agreement.

1203 *EC–Fasteners (China)* (Appellate Body Reports) (n 1202) [310], [328]–[329], [353]–[354], [370], [384]–[385], [401], [409], [624].

1204 See Art 2 (1) AD Agreement: 'For the purpose of this Agreement, a product is to be considered as being dumped, ie introduced into the commerce of another country at less than its *normal value*, if the export price of the product exported from one country to another is less than the *comparable price, in the ordinary course of trade, for the like product when destined for consumption in the exporting country*' [emphasis added]; on 'normal value' and 'export price' see also Lester, Mercurio and Davies (n 1027) 481–484.

1205 *EC–Fasteners (China)* (Appellate Body Reports) (n 1202) [363]–[366]; Para 15 Accession Protocol.

1206 *EC–Fasteners (China)* (Appellate Body Reports) (n 1202) [624]; Arts 4 (1), 6 (2) and (4) AD Agreement..

1207 WTO, *European Communities: Definitive Anti-Dumping Measures on Certain Iron or Steel Fasteners from China-Report of the Panel after Recourse to Article 21.5 DSU* (7 August 2015) WT/DS397/RW [8.1]–[8.4] ('*EC–Fasteners (China) (Article 21.5)* (Panel Report)'); WTO, *European Communities: Definitive Anti-Dumping Measures on Certain Iron or Steel Fasteners from China–Report of the Appellate Body after Recourse to Article 21.5 DSU* (18 January 2016) WT/DS397/AB/RW [6.1]–[6.2] ('*EC–Fasteners (China) (Article 21.5)* (Appellate Body Report)'); WTO, *European Communities: Definitive Anti-Dumping Measures on Certain Iron or Steel Fasteners from China-Report(s) adopted, with recommendation to bring measure(s) into conformity* (12 February 2016) WT/DS397. See also Ilaria Espa and Philip I Levy, 'The Analogue Method Comes Unfastened – The Awkward Space between Market and Non-Market Economies in EC–Fasteners (Article 21.5)' (2018) 17 *World Trade Review* 313.

graph 15 Accession Protocol, and a long list of AD Agreement and GATT provisions.[1208] On the Accession Protocol, China contended that Members 'accepted commitments under both China's Accession Protocol and China's Accession Working Party Report'.[1209] The Panel's report again found that the EU could not require Chinese producers to bear the burden of proof as to their entitlement to individual dumping margins, and country-wide duties were found in breach of the AD Agreement, but not the Accession Protocol.[1210] Brussels did not appeal.

IV.2.2.2.3.2.2.2 Discussion

In all of the above three cases (*US–Tyres*, *EC–Fasteners*, *EU–Footwear*), China alleged that the EU and US had violated its Accession Protocol. It did not necessarily win on all accounts, but the hope was that '[a]s the [panel and AB had] not been particularly fond of trade remedy measures, there [was] a good chance that the ambiguous terms used in the Accession Protocol [would] be interpreted in a way that would restrict the utility of these provisions in the future'.[1211] China was able to secure some victories, but *EC-Fasteners* – probably most consequential – also opened up the possibility of treating China as a NME beyond the 15-year period mentioned in paragraph 15 (d) Accession Protocol (ie beyond 2016).[1212] China argued and prevailed mainly on the notion that 'China's treatment as a [NME] en-

1208 Para 15 (a) (ii) Accession Protocol; Arts 2 (2), (4) and (6), 4 (1), 6 (10), 9 (2), (3) and (4), 12.2 (2), 18 (4) AD Agreement; Arts VI:1, X:3 (a) GATT 1994; WTO, *European Union: Anti-Dumping Measures on Certain Footwear from China–Request for Consultations* (31 July 2009) WT/DS405/1 ('*EU–Footwear (China)* (Request for Consultations)').

1209 WTO, *European Union: Anti-Dumping Measures on Certain Footwear from China–Reports of the Panel* (3 December 2010) WT/DS405/R [7.170]–[7.171] ('*EU–Footwear (China)* (Panel Reports)'), referring inter alia to the application of product-specific safeguards, as well as due process.

1210 Arts 6 (10), 9 (2) and 18 (4) AD Agreement; *EU–Footwear (China)* (Panel Reports) (n 1209) [7.88], [7.179]–[7.185], [7.193]–[7.197], [7.205], [VIII.2]–[VIII.4]; WTO, *European Union: Anti-Dumping Measures on Certain Footwear from China–Implementation notified by respondent* (17 December 2012) WT/DS405 <https://www.wto.org/english/tratop_e/dispu_e/cases_e/ds405_e.htm> accessed 5 June 2018.

1211 Gao, 'China on the World Stage' (n 990) 534.

1212 *EC–Fasteners (China)* (Appellate Body Reports) (n 1202) [624]. See also Chad P Bown and Petros C Mavroidis, 'One (Firm) Is Not Enough: A Legal-Economic Analysis of EC-Fasteners' (2013) 12 *World Trade Review* 243, 254.

tailed specific consequences, and did not amount to a licence to impose AD duties on presumptions rather than on hard facts'.[1213] As for treatment as NME broadly, it was unclear whether Members that did not have pertinent domestic law criteria at the point of China's accession in 2001 could treat China as such. When benefiting from the option of treating China as an NME, the different price comparison methodology was to be notified to the WTO Anti-dumping Committee, and guided by – there was no definitive determination on such methodology – paragraph 151 Working Party Report, ie use:

> to the extent possible, and where necessary cooperation was received, the prices or costs in one or more market economy countries that were significant producers of comparable merchandise and that either were at a level of economic development comparable to that of China or were otherwise an appropriate source for the prices or costs to be utilized in light of the nature of the industry under investigation.[1214]

NME status-related claims had to be considered 'of transitional value [though] as far as China is concerned since, by virtue of the explicit wording of Article 15 of China's Protocol of Accession, China cannot be treated as an NME after 2016, that is 15 years after its succession to the WTO'.[1215]

Crucially, *EC-Fasteners* might have altered this situation. Already in *Korea-Certain Paper*, the Panel had gone beyond the exceptions in Article 6.10 AD Agreement on possibilities to not calculate individual dumping margins. This was regarding companies constituting a 'single [economic] entity'.[1216] The term had not been explained, and this is where *EC-Fasteners* comes in. While the option of imposing countrywide dumping margins for NMEs in the way that the EU did was excluded, the AB explained – while not decisive in this case, but holding central importance for cases beyond 2016 – that the following 'single entity'-situations can allow foregoing individual dumping margins:

> (i) the existence of corporate and structural links between the exporters, such as common control, shareholding and management; (ii)

1213 Bown and Mavroidis (n 1212) 243.

1214 Para 151 *Report of the Working Party on the Accession of Ukraine* (25 January 2008) WT/ACC/UKR/152.

1215 Bown and Mavroidis (n 1212) 254; Para 15 Accession Protocol.

1216 WTO, *Korea: Anti-Dumping Duties on Imports of Certain Paper from Indonesia–Report of the Panel* (28 November 2005) WT/DS312/R; Art 6 (10) AD Agreement.

> the existence of corporate and structural links between the State and the exporters, such as common control, shareholding and management; and (iii) control or material influence by the State in respect of pricing and output [which is to say situations where there is] evidence of State control or instruction of, or material influence on, the behaviour of certain exporters in respect of pricing and output. These criteria could show that, even in the absence of formal structural links between the State and specific exporters, the State in fact determines and materially influences prices and output.[1217]

This is a fairly broad understanding of 'single entity' and – via demonstrating 'State influence' – a major window to avoiding individual dumping margins,[1218] which might have dramatic consequences (especially for China and Vietnam), including strong potential for abuse.

On the broader issue of the relationship between the multilateral WTO Agreement and bilateral Accession Protocol of China, none of the disputes provided clear guidance as explicitly requested by Japan (third party) in *EC-Fasteners*.[1219]

The Chinese government demonstrated that it had learned its lessons form previous cases, and had become an aggressive but also sophisticated litigant,[1220] albeit with a mixed record on dispute outcomes. Especially *EU-Footwear* showed China willing to elaborate a much more extensive list of specific complaints covering a broad swath of issues. A large number of individual complaints were rejected, but Brussels was found in breach of several provisions (and was presumably quite occupied with its defense). The Chinese government would likely build on that approach in the future.[1221] Similar to China's first complaint without co-complainants against the US, its first action against the EU followed the initiation of three disputes by the other side. The Chinese government also elaborated on the failure of its previous strategy of bilateral negotiations and perceived necessity to

1217 *EC–Fasteners (China)* (Appellate Body Reports) (n 1202) [376], [381].

1218 See also Bown and Mavroidis (n 1212) 268, 270.

1219 *EC–Fasteners (China)* (Panel Reports) (n 1201) [7.63]. See also Mitali Tyagi, 'Flesh on a Legal Fiction: Early Practice in the WTO on Accession Protocols' (2012) 15 *Journal of International Economic Law* 391, 405, 412.

1220 See also Mercurio and Tyagi (n 990) 121–122.

1221 See also Jeffrey L Dunoff and Michael O Moore, 'Footloose and duty-free? Reflections on European Union – Anti-Dumping Measures on Certain Footwear from China' (2014) 13 *World Trade Review* 149, 178.

make stronger use of the WTO DSM instead.[1222] Success here led Chinese scholars to praise the system and call for more frequent usage.[1223]

IV.2.2.2.3.3 Double Remedies

Another area of third-phase case law connected to China's interest in systemic influence concerns supposed double remedies (ie parallel anti-dumping and countervailing duty measures). Interestingly, a sort of 'ping pong' of cases developed, wherein China served first and the tables then turned back and forth.

The US had decided in the 1980s that countervailing measures could not be applied to NMEs (see Interpretative Note ad Article VI GATT 1994) like the Soviet Union, because in these countries it was not companies that received subsidies, but rather the government shifting funds between units it all owns or controls.[1224] This decision was reversed in 2007 with respect to economically developed NMEs like China and Vietnam – such duties could now overlap with anti-dumping duties against NME exports.[1225]

1222 See eg MOFCOM as cited in Huang and Ji (n 1188) 1295–1297.

1223 See also Chapter V.2.1.3. See eg Yanyan 彦彦 Li 李, '欧盟反倾销法修改案与WTO 多边规则的适用' (The case of the EU anti-dumping law amendment and the application of WTO multilateral rules) [2017] (11) *Falü Shiyong* 55, 60–61.

1224 See also Thomas J Prusa and Edwin Vermulst, 'United States – Definitive Anti-Dumping and Countervailing Duties on Certain Products from China: Passing the Buck on Pass-Through' (2013) 12 *World Trade Review* 197, 197–198. For an explanation of NME status under WTO law see Annex I, Interpretative Note on Art VI, Para 1 GATT 1994 – '1. Hidden dumping by associated houses (that is, the sale by an importer at a price below that corresponding to the price invoiced by an exporter with whom the importer is associated, and also below the price in the exporting country) constitutes a form of price dumping with respect to which the margin of dumping may be calculated on the basis of the price at which the goods are resold by the importer; 2. It is recognized that, in the case of imports from a country which has a complete or substantially complete monopoly of its trade and where all domestic prices are fixed by the State, special difficulties may exist in determining price comparability for the purposes of paragraph 1, and in such cases importing contracting parties may find it necessary to take into account the possibility that a strict comparison with domestic prices in such a country may not always be appropriate.'.

1225 Prusa and Vermulst, 'United States – Definitive Anti-Dumping and Countervailing Duties' (n 1224) 198.

IV.2.2.2.3.3.1 Relevant case law

In *US-Anti-Dumping and Countervailing Duties (China)*, China complained against concurrent application of anti-dumping duties according to surrogate-country NME methodology and countervailing duties on the same products.[1226] US measures were supposedly in breach of the SCM and AD Agreements and the Accession Protocol – inter alia – as 'double remedy' – ie applying a second measure to the same target after inconsistent behavior had already been offset by a first measure – hindering a 'fair comparison between export price and normal value'.[1227]

The AB, reversing the Panel's findings, determined that the imposition of double remedies is indeed inconsistent with Article 19.3 SCM Agreement.[1228] However, the AB held that adjusting the US methodology could help to avoid further run-ins.[1229] On the definition of 'public body' in the SCM Agreement the AB also went against the Panel, focused on whether the entity in question exercises 'governmental authority' – instead of government control through majority state ownership – and found US measures in violation of Articles 1.1 (a) (1), 10 and 32.1 SCM Agreement.[1230] The AB mostly found in the respondent's favor on the US's use of out-of-country benchmarks to measure the benefit of a subsidy.[1231] The US re-

1226 *US–Anti-Dumping and Countervailing Duties (China)* (Request for Consultations) (n 993).

1227 Art 2.4 AD Agreement; WTO, *United States–Definitive Anti-Dumping and Countervailing Duties on Certain Products from China–Request for the Establishment of a Panel by China* (12 December 2008) WT/DS379/2 [7]–[8] ('*US–Anti-Dumping and Countervailing Duties (China)* (Request for the Establishment of a Panel by China)').

1228 Art 19.3 SCM Agreement; WTO, *United States: Definitive Anti-Dumping and Countervailing Duties on Certain Products from China–Reports of the Appellate Body* (18 October 2012) WT/DS379/AB/R [VIII.611] ('*US–Anti-Dumping and Countervailing Duties (China)* (Appellate Body Reports)'); WTO, *United States: Definitive Anti-Dumping and Countervailing Duties on Certain Products from China–Reports of the Panel* (22 October 2010) WT/DS379/R [14.67]–[14.75], Annex A-1 [29]–[32] ('*US–Anti-Dumping and Countervailing Duties (China)* (Panel Reports)').

1229 *US–Anti-Dumping and Countervailing Duties (China)* (Appellate Body Reports) (n 1228) [VII.599].

1230 Arts 1.1 (a) (1), 10 and 32.1 SCM Agreement; *US–Anti-Dumping and Countervailing Duties (China)* (Appellate Body Reports) (n 1228) [VIII.607]; *US–Anti-Dumping and Countervailing Duties (China)* (Panel Reports) (n 1228) [VII.1].

1231 Art 14 (b) and (d) SCM Agreement; *US–Anti-Dumping and Countervailing Duties (China)* (Appellate Body Reports) (n 1228) [VIII.611].

ported implementation, but China noted at the DSB that it did not consider it to have fully complied.[1232]

The US in turn requested consultations in *China-GOES*, considering that anti-dumping and countervailing duties imposed on US grain-oriented flat-rolled electrical steel (hereinafter: GOES) by China's MOFCOM violated SCM and AD Agreements, – inter alia – through some aspects of its injury determination and disclosure of essential facts.[1233] The Panel and AB agreed on nearly all points, eg faulty price effects analysis behind MOFCOM's injury determination and failure to demonstrate causation of injury (Articles 3.1, 3.2 and 3.5 AD Agreement; Articles 15.1, 15.2 and 15.5 SCM Agreement).[1234] A reasonable period of time for implementation was set through an Article 21.3 (c) DSU proceeding.[1235] Parties disagreed on implementation, the US initiated the first compliance dispute under Article 21.5 DSU in a case involving China, and the Panel determined that Chinese measures were still in breach – but at that point the measures had already expired.[1236]

The US was not quite done with returning the favor, and *China-Broiler Products* touched on many of the same issues, involving alleged multiple violations of the AD and SCM Agreements (including on proper injury de-

1232 WTO, *United States: Definitive Anti-Dumping and Countervailing Duties on Certain Products from China-Implementation notified by respondent* (31 August 2012) WT/DS379 <https://www.wto.org/english/tratop_e/dispu_e/cases_e/ds379_e.htm> accessed 5 June 2018.

1233 Arts 10, 11, 12, 15 and 22 SCM Agreement; Arts 1, 3, 6, 12 and Annex II AD Agreement; WTO, *China: Countervailing and Anti-Dumping Duties on Grain Oriented Flat-rolled Electrical Steel from the United States–Request for Consultations* (15 September 2010) WT/DS414/1 ('*China–GOES* (Request for Consultations)').

1234 Arts 3.1, 3.2, 3.5 AD Agreement; Arts 15.1, 15.2, 15.5 SCM Agreement; WTO, *China: Countervailing and Anti-Dumping Duties on Grain Oriented Flat-rolled Electrical Steel from the United States–Report of the Panel* (15 June 2012) WT/DS414/R [VIII] ('*China–GOES* (Panel Report)'); WTO, *China: Countervailing and Anti-Dumping Duties on Grain Oriented Flat-rolled Electrical Steel from the United States–Report of the Appellate Body* (18 October 2012) WT/DS414/AB/R [268] ('*China–GOES* (Appellate Body Report)').

1235 Art 21.3 (c) DSU; WTO, *China: Countervailing and Anti-Dumping Duties on Grain Oriented Flat-rolled Electrical Steel from the United States–Arbitration under Article 21.3 (c) DSU* (3 May 2012) WT/DS414/12 [4.1] ('*China–GOES* (Arbitration under Article 21.3 (c))').

1236 Art 21 (5) DSU; WTO, *China: Countervailing and Anti-Dumping Duties on Grain Oriented Flat-rolled Electrical Steel from the United States–Report of the Panel after Recourse to Article 21.5 DSU* (31 July 2015) WT/DS414/RW [8.2] ('*China–GOES (Article 21.5)* (Panel Report)').

termination and not imposing countervailing duties in excess of the subsidy found to exist).[1237] The Panel again mostly agreed with the allegations.[1238] This time, China did not appeal, parties again disagreed on implementation, and Article 21.5 DSU proceedings had the same result of China being found in continued breach despite adapting its measures.[1239]

In yet another similar case, *China-Autos (US)*, the US complained against anti-dumping and countervailing duties imposed by China on certain automobiles imported from the US.[1240] The Panel decided mostly in the US's favor, faulting – inter alia – China's injury determination (price effects and causation analyses), non-disclosure of essential facts behind its anti-dumping duties to US company respondents, and reliance on facts available without notifying unknown exporters in calculating residual anti-dumping and countervailing duty rates.[1241] Rather minor changes to MOFCOM's practice could address the issue, and the case was resolved without the need for further action within a month from the panel report.[1242]

China, in turn, filed another similar complaint, *US-Countervailing and Anti-Dumping Measures (China)*, following the above series of US-initiated cases.[1243] Without appeal, the Panel confirmed that the US's failure to investigate and avoid double remedies in a large number of investigations and reviews between 2006 and 2012 had led to violations of Articles 10,

1237 Arts 2–4, 6 and 12 AD Agreement; Arts 15–16, 19 and 22 SCM Agreement; WTO, *China: Anti-Dumping and Countervailing Duty Measures on Broiler Products from the United States–Request for Consultations* (20 September 2011) WT/DS427/1 ('*China–Broiler Products* (Request for Consultations)').

1238 WTO, *China: Anti-Dumping and Countervailing Duty Measures on Broiler Products from the United States–Report of the Panel* (2 August 2013) WT/DS427/R [VIII] ('*China–Broiler Products* (Panel Report)').

1239 Art 21 (5) DSU; *China–GOES (Article 21.5)* (Panel Report) (n 1236) [8.2].

1240 WTO, *China: Anti-Dumping and Countervailing Duties on Certain Automobiles from the United States–Request for Consultations* (5 July 2012) WT/DS440/1 ('*China–Autos (US)* (Request for Consultations)').

1241 Arts 3.2, 3.5, 6.8, 6.9 and Annex II para 1 AD Agreement; Arts 12.7, 15.2 and 15.5 SCM Agreement; WTO, *China: Anti-Dumping and Countervailing Duties on Certain Automobiles from the United States–Report of the Panel* (23 May 2014) WT/DS440/R [8.1] ('*China–Autos (US)* (Panel Report)').

1242 WTO, *China: Anti-Dumping and Countervailing Duties on Certain Automobiles from the United States-Report(s) adopted, no further action required*, WT/DS440.

1243 WTO, *United States: Countervailing and Anti-dumping Measures on Certain Products from China–Request for Consultations* (17 September 2012) WT/DS449/1.

19.3 and 32 SCM,[1244] and the US received recommendations to go back and bring them into conformity with the Agreement.[1245] Regarding additionally complained against new US legislation, Panel and AB disagreed on some matters of publication and administration of trade regulations, but neither found the US in violation.[1246] After the agreed reasonable amount of time for implementation, the parties informed the DSB of Agreed Procedures under Articles 21 and 22 DSU.[1247]

IV.2.2.2.3.3.2 Discussion

US-Anti-Dumping and Countervailing Duties (China) marked an important step in case law development – also touching on issues of crucial systemic importance to the Chinese economy – on the double-remedies issue, the contentious definition of 'public body' within the Article 1.1 (a) (1) SCM Agreement definition of subsidy, and the use out-of-country benchmarks to calculate the benefit accruing through a subsidy.[1248]

The AB reports showed that on such issues 'China's positions have begun to influence the interpretation of the covered agreements in certain respects [as] China sought and obtained a different interpretation of a term on which a previous panel (but not the Appellate Body) had already ruled'

1244 Arts 10, 19.3 and 32 SCM Agreement; WTO, *United States: Countervailing and Anti-dumping Measures on Certain Products from China–Report of the Panel* (27 March 2014) WT/DS449/R [8.1] ('*US–Countervailing and Anti-Dumping Measures (China)* (Panel Report)').

1245 *US–Countervailing and Anti-Dumping Measures (China)* (Panel Report) (n 1244) [7.355], [8.3]; WTO, *United States: Countervailing and Anti-dumping Measures on Certain Products from China–Report of the Appellate Body* (7 July 2014) WT/DS449/AB/R [5.2] ('*US–Countervailing and Anti-Dumping Measures (China)* (Appellate Body Report)')..

1246 Art X:2 GATT 1994; *US–Countervailing and Anti-Dumping Measures (China)* (Panel Report) (n 1244) [8.1]; *US–Countervailing and Anti-Dumping Measures (China)* (Appellate Body Report) (n 1245) [5.1].

1247 Arts 21 and 22 DSU; WTO, *United States: Countervailing and Anti-dumping Measures on Certain Products from China–Report(s) adopted, with recommendation to bring measure(s) into conformity*, WT/DS449 <https://www.wto.org/english/tratop_e/dispu_e/cases_e/ds449_e.htm> accessed 16 August 2018.

1248 Art 1.1 (a) (1) SCM Agreement. See also Prusa and Vermulst, 'United States – Definitive Anti-Dumping and Countervailing Duties' (n 1224) 197.

–[1249] here referring to 'public body.' On this issue, the emphasis on an entity exercising 'governmental authority' – rather than government control – was obviously a very promising ruling for China looking forward. On double remedies in simultaneous anti-dumping and countervailing duty investigations, China in *US-Anti-Dumping and Countervailing Duties (China)* managed to make use of a wider context reading to get an affirmative legal obligation for the respondent Member recognized that is not expressly in the WTO agreements: the obligation to avoid double remedies.[1250]

The following US-initiated double-remedies cases against China in turn led to multiple findings underlining MOFCOM's inadequacy mainly on injury determination (eg faulty price effects analysis), the demonstration of causation, disclosure of essential facts and reliance on facts available.[1251]

However, China might have been the hidden 'winner', and provoking these cases could very well have been a motivating factor behind adopting pertinent measures. In part, China was actually more regularly on the receiving end of practices found in breach of WTO law, being the subject of about half of all countervailing duty investigations worldwide in the five years leading up to *China–GOES*, while itself 'underusing' the measures. Clarification of the applicable rules – eg regarding sufficient evidence – would make it more difficult for other Members to 'aggressively' adopt duties on Chinese products, eg 'often heavily based on facts available'.[1252]

1249 Kennedy, 'China's role in WTO Dispute Settlement' (n 38) 578, see also 568–569, 579, referring to WTO, *Korea: Measures Affecting Trade in Commercial Vessels–Report of the Panel* (7 March 2005) WT/DS273/R, which was still endorsed in *US–Anti-Dumping and Countervailing Duties (China)* (Panel Reports) (n 1228) [VIII.3]–[VIII.18], [VIII.71]–[VIII.83]; *US–Anti-Dumping and Countervailing Duties (China)* (Appellate Body Reports) (n 1228) [282]–[322].

1250 *US–Anti-Dumping and Countervailing Duties (China)* (Appellate Body Reports) (n 1228) [103]–[123], [545], [547]–[583]. See also Kennedy, 'China's role in WTO Dispute Settlement' (n 38) 578–579, who notes that China argued with the 'collective operation' of Art VI:3 GATT 1994 and Art 10 SCM Agreement, 'read in light of' Arts 19.1, 19.3, and 19.4 SCM Agreement. The AB connected this with the requirement for a countervailing duty to be levied in the 'appropriate' amount (19.3 SCM Agreement).

1251 Arts 10, 11, 12, 15 and 22 SCM Agreement; Arts 1, 3, 6, 12 and Annex II AD Agreement; *China–GOES* (Appellate Body Report) (n 1234) [268]; *China–Broiler Products* (Panel Report) (n 1238) [VIII]; *China–Autos (US)* (Panel Report) (n 1241) [8.1].

1252 Thomas J Prusa and Edwin Vermulst, 'China – Countervailing and Anti-dumping Duties on Grain Oriented Flat-rolled Electrical Steel from the United States: exporting US AD/CVD methodologies through WTO dispute settlement?' (2014) 13 *World Trade Review* 229, 253, 263–266.

The measures complained against in *China–GOES* – targeting a niche but highly profitable steel product – were likely a message to the US in retaliation to its high-level duties on Chinese products.[1253] The way in which it pursued the case again demonstrated the strategy – according to Chinese authors copied from the US – of using DSM procedures to delay a WTO-compliant situation for the benefit of domestic industries. This includes the Article 21 (5) DSU compliance procedures it provoked by only adjusting respective duty rates instead of changing pertinent legal measures, up until a point when the measures had already expired.[1254] Moreover, preemptive compliance in *China–Autos* showed that China is willing to impose duties in a tit-for-tat with US measures as a sort of saber rattling instead of being convinced of their appropriateness under WTO law.[1255] The option for WTO members – motivated by short-term political gain – to use 'potentially WTO-consistent' measures for two to three years and then repeal them with practically no repercussions is very much part of the current order. This may be considered unfortunate, although it also serves as a pressure valve that allows more states to make their peace with the system.

The measures behind *China–Broiler Products* similarly appear intended as political signaling, showing the US that China can retaliate to comparable economic effect, in this instance to preceding US measures on Chinese tyres – and across sectors.[1256]

Chinese scholars had complained about the supposed lack of a clear definition of 'public body' in Article 1.1 (a) (1) SCM Agreement, but then reacted very positively to the AB findings in *US–Anti-Dumping and Countervailing Duties*.[1257] Confident that further case law – not only such involving China – was also strengthening China's position on this issue as well as

1253 See also Prusa and Vermulst, 'China – Countervailing and Anti-dumping Duties' (n 1252) 263.

1254 *China–GOES (Article 21.5)* (Panel Report) (n 1236) [8.2]; Julia Qin and Hylke Vandenbussche, 'China–GOES (Article 21.5): Time to Clarify the Standard for Price Suppression and Price Depression in AD/CVD Investigations' (2017) 16 *World Trade Review* 203, 203–204.

1255 Andrew D Mitchell and Thomas J Prusa, 'China–Autos: Haven't We Danced this Dance Before?' (2016) 15 *World Trade Review* 303, 324–325.

1256 Zhou Weihuan and Zhang Shu, 'Anti-dumping practices and China's implementation of WTO rulings' (2017) 230 *The China Quarterly* 512, 520.

1257 See also Chapter V.2.1.2. Art 1.1 (a) (1) SCM Agreement; *US–Anti-Dumping and Countervailing Duties (China)* (Appellate Body Reports) (n 1228) para 607. See also eg Yewei 业伟 Shi 时, WTO 补贴协定中"公共机构"认定标准研究 —— —以 DS379 案为例 (Identification Standards for "Public Body" at SCM: Taking Case DS379 for Example) [2016] (6) *Bijiaofa Yanjiu* 135, 145.

on double remedies, they counseled proactive and full engagement with the DSM.[1258]

IV.2.2.2.3.4 Countervailing Duties

IV.2.2.2.3.4.1 Relevant case law: US-Countervailing Measures (China)

Aside from cases concerning potential double remedies, China filed another complaint against US countervailing duties, including on solar panels and wind turbines, considering them not only in violation of the SCM Agreement, but also the Accession Protocol.[1259] The Panel – inter alia – again found the US in breach due to overly broad interpretation of 'public body,' and in this case also for not properly reviewing evidence before initiating an investigation (merely relying on the existence of export restraints).[1260] The AB reversed some findings of the Panel and – inter alia – determined that the US could not from the outset reject in-country private prices in China as benchmarks in its benefit analysis.[1261] Article 21.3 DSU arbitration and Article 21.5 DSU proceedings ensued, whereas the pertinent Panel report was again appealed by the US.[1262]

1258 See eg Weidong 卫东 Chen 陈, 中美围绕国有企业的补贴提供者身份之争- 以WTO 相关案例为重点 (China-US dispute about the identity of the provider of subsidies to state-owned enterprises – focusing on pertinent WTO cases) (2017) 31 (3) *Dangdai Faxue* 21.

1259 Arts 1, 2, 10, 11, 12, 14, and 32 SCM Agreement; Para 15 Accession Protocol; WTO, *United States: Countervailing Duty Measures on Certain Products from China–Request for Consultations* (25 May 2012) WT/DS437/1.

1260 Arts 1.1 (a) (1) and 11.3 SCM Agreement; WTO, *United States: Countervailing Duty Measures on Certain Products from China–Report of the Panel* (14 July 2014) WT/DS437/R [8.1]..

1261 Arts 1.1 (b) and 14 (d) SCM Agreement; WTO, *United States: Countervailing Duty Measures on Certain Products from China–Report of the Appellate Body* (18 December 2014) WT/DS437/AB/R [4.29]–[4.107], [5.1].

1262 Arts 21.3 and 21.5 DSU; WTO, *United States: Countervailing Duty Measures on Certain Products from China-Compliance proceedings ongoing*, WT/DS437 <https://www.wto.org/english/tratop_e/dispu_e/cases_e/ds437_e.htm> accessed 20 August 2018.

IV.2.2.2.3.4.2 Discussion

China, the US, and the EU had applied domestic trade remedies on various types of the respective others' environmental products in a tit-for-tat 'trade war' following the mutual subsidization of renewable energy.[1263] With this case, China managed to make the application of out-of-country benchmarks for countervailing duty purposes, and thus the imposition of higher countervailing duties, more difficult, while solidifying a more limited interpretation of 'public body'.[1264] Related decisions by the AB in this and the above cases on double remedies visibly contributed to the Chinese academic community's endorsement of strong engagement and confirmed the government's strategy.[1265]

IV.2.2.2.3.5 Anti-dumping Duties

IV.2.2.2.3.5.1 Relevant case law

Apart from the above disputes concerning double remedies, or countervailing duties alone, several further cases revolved around anti-dumping duties. *US-Shrimp and Sawblades* centered on the US's practice of 'zeroing,' an anti-dumping margin calculation methodology where non-dumped sales are not offset against dumped sales,[1266] which China considered led to multiple AD Agreement and GATT 1994 violations.[1267] The Panel agreed on the breach through 'zeroing,' and the US did not appeal.[1268]

1263 See also Rachel Brewster, Claire Brunel and Anna Maria Mayda, 'Trade in Environmental Goods: A Review of the WTO Appellate Body's Ruling in US–Countervailing Measures (China)' (2016) 15 *World Trade Review* 327, 327–328.

1264 See also Brewster, Brunel and Mayda (n 1263) 348.

1265 See Chapter V.2.1.3.2.

1266 See also Lester, Mercurio and Davies (n 1027) 484–492.

1267 Articles VI:1 and VI:2 GATT 1994; Arts 1, 2.1, 2.4, 2.4.2, 5.8, 9.2, 9.3 and 9.4 AD Agreement; WTO, *United States: Anti-Dumping Measures on Shrimp and Diamond Sawblades from China–Request for Consultations* (28 February 2011) WT/DS422/1.

1268 Art 2.4.2 AD Agreement; WTO, *United States: Anti-Dumping Measures on Shrimp and Diamond Sawblades from China–Report of the Panel* (8 June 2012) WT/DS422/R [VIII]; WTO, *United States: Anti-Dumping Measures on Shrimp and Diamond Sawblades from China–Implementation notified by respondent*, WT/422 <https://www.wto.org/english/tratop_e/dispu_e/cases_e/ds422_e.htm> accessed 17 May 2017.

With *US-Anti-Dumping Methodologies (China)*, China initiated another similar dispute, joined by Japan, Russia and Ukraine, alleging a list of AD Agreement breaches,[1269] and the Panel – inter alia – reminded the US of it being in breach of Article 2.4.2 AD Agreement due to the practice of 'zeroing'.[1270] It also deemed the practice of 'single rate presumption,' the treatment of multiple NME exporters as a single NME-wide entity, a violation of Articles 6.10 and 9.2 AD Agreement.[1271] China appealed on some questions of law and legal interpretation, seeking clarifications and a more 'complete' victory, but was only partly successful.[1272]

China, in turn, was also the target of three complaints regarding anti-dumping duties. Following the EU's complaint in *China-X-Ray Equipment*,[1273] the Panel faulted MOFCOM's injury determination due to deficient economic effects analysis, state of the industry determination, and causation analysis, while the Ministry also failed to disclose essential facts – the Panel partly relied on *China-GOES*.[1274] China did not appeal.[1275]

In the similar case *China-HP-SSST*, Japan (and later the EU) complained about Chinese anti-dumping duties on high-performance stainless steel

1269 Arts 2.4.2, 6.1, 6.8, 6.10, 9.2, 9.3, 9.4 and Annex II AD Agreement; WTO, *United States: Certain Methodologies and their Application to Anti-Dumping Proceedings Involving China–Request for Consultations* (3 December 2013) WT/DS471/1.

1270 Arts 2.4.2, 6.10 and 9.2 AD Agreement; WTO, *United States: Certain Methodologies and their Application to Anti-Dumping Proceedings Involving China–Report of the Panel* (19 October 2016) WT/DS471/R [8.1] ('*US–Anti-Dumping Methodologies (China)* (Panel Report)').

1271 Arts 2.4.2, 6.10 and 9.2 AD Agreement; *US–Anti-Dumping Methodologies (China)* (Panel Report) (n 1270) [8.1].

1272 WTO, *United States: Certain Methodologies and their Application to Anti-Dumping Proceedings Involving China–Report of the Appellate Body* (11 May 2017) WT/DS471/AB/R [6.1]–[6.11].

1273 WTO, *China: Definitive Anti-Dumping Duties on X-Ray Security Inspection Equipment from the European Union–Request for Consultations* (25 July 2011) WT/DS425/1.

1274 Arts 3.1, 3.2, 3.4, 3.5 and 6.9 AD Agreement; WTO, *China: Definitive Anti-Dumping Duties on X-Ray Security Inspection Equipment from the European Union–Report of the Panel* (26 February 2013) WT/DS425/R [VII.459]–[VII.464], [VIII].

1275 WTO, *China: Definitive Anti-Dumping Duties on X-Ray Security Inspection Equipment from the European Union–Implementation notified by respondent*, WT/DS425 <https://www.wto.org/english/tratop_e/dispu_e/cases_e/ds425_e.htm> accessed 17 May 2017.

seamless tubes ('HP-SSST').[1276] Despite disagreeing on some issues, the Panels and AB largely sided with the complainants on familiar issues with China's injury determination (eg causation analysis) and disclosure of essential facts.[1277] China promised to implement within a reasonable period of time.[1278]

Finally, Canada initiated *China-Cellulose Pulp*,[1279] and the Panel delivered a mixed result with somewhat of a MOFCOM learning curve on procedural matters visible. Nonetheless, inconsistencies with injury determination requirements in Article 3 AD Agreement (price effects, causation) were still found.[1280] China notified implementation, but Canada later requested consultations under Article 21.5 DSU.[1281]

IV.2.2.2.3.5.2 Discussion

In contrast to the EU, the US has not categorically rejected the practice of 'zeroing' after serial rulings since *EC-Bed Linen* declared it inconsistent

---

1276 WTO, *China: Measures Imposing Anti-Dumping Duties on High-Performance Stainless Steel Seamless Tubes ("HP-SSST") from Japan–Request for Consultations* (20 December 2012) WT/DS454/1; WTO, *China: Measures Imposing Anti-Dumping Duties on High-Performance Stainless Steel Seamless Tubes ("HP-SSST") from the European Union–Request for Consultations* (13 June 2013) WT/DS460/1.

1277 Arts 3.1, 3.5 and 6.9 AD Agreement; WTO, *China: Measures Imposing Anti-Dumping Duties on High-Performance Stainless Steel Seamless Tubes ("HP-SSST") from Japan / the European Union–Reports of the Panels* (14 February 2015) WT/DS454/R and WT/DS460/R [8.1]–[8.11]; WTO, *China: Measures Imposing Anti-Dumping Duties on High-Performance Stainless Steel Seamless Tubes ("HP-SSST") from Japan / the European Union–Report of the Appellate Body* (14 October 2015) WT/DS454/AB/R and WT/DS460/AB/R [6.1]–[6.4].

1278 WTO, *China: Measures Imposing Anti-Dumping Duties on High-Performance Stainless Steel Seamless Tubes ("HP-SSST") from Japan–Report(s) adopted, with recommendation to bring measure(s) into conformity*, WT/DS454 <https://www.wto.org/english/tratop_e/dispu_e/cases_e/ds454_e.htm> accessed 18 May 2017.

1279 WTO, *China: Anti-dumping Measures on Imports of Cellulose Pulp from Canada–Request for Consultations* (15 October 2014) WT/DS483/1.

1280 WTO, *China: Anti-dumping Measures on Imports of Cellulose Pulp from Canada–Report of the Panel* (25 April 2017) WT/DS483/R [8.1]–[8.3]; Arts 3.1, 3.2 and 3.5 AD Agreement.

1281 WTO, *China: Anti-dumping Measures on Imports of Cellulose Pulp from Canada–Implementation notified by respondent*, WT/DS483 https://www.wto.org/english/tratop_e/dispu_e/cases_e/ds483_e.htm> accessed 21 September 2018.

with WTO law.[1282] The US has been strongly criticized for making other Members individually resort to the DSM and complicated implementation mechanisms to rectify its illegal anti-dumping practices based on the method, and *US-Shrimp and Sawblades* has even been described as highlighting 'systemic non-compliance problems in the WTO dispute settlement system'.[1283]

The disagreement concerns the question of whether dumping should be calculated by comparing individual sales or based on an average of all sales, and pertinent interpretations of Article 2.4.2 AD Agreement. The AB and most Members have supported the latter position, several Panels and the US the former. Seeing as its arguments have not convinced the WTO's judicial decision-makers – as also evidenced by *US-Anti-Dumping Methodologies (China)* – the US has taken to pushing for an amendment of the AD Agreement allowing for 'zeroing' in the now defunct Doha Round negotiations.[1284] China, in turn, appears on the clearly victorious side concerning interpretation of the current text.

Despite being a rather pedestrian dispute highlighting procedural inadequacies on the Chinese side, *China-X-Ray Equipment* is a good example of how incumbent market champions can deploy anti-dumping measures against new foreign competitors buoyed by state industrial policy.[1285] *China–HP-SSST* and *China–Cellulose Pulp* delivered mixed results, and in the first of these two disputes some striking Chinese successes then reversed by the AB.[1286] Together, they showed a learning curve on the side of Chinese

---

1282 WTO, *European Communities: Anti-Dumping Duties on Imports of Cotton-type Bed Linen from India–Report of the Appellate Body* (1 March 2001) WT/DS141/AB/R.

1283 Dukgeon Ahn and Patrick Messerlin, 'United States – Anti-Dumping Measures on Certain Shrimp and Diamond Sawblades from China: never ending zeroing in the WTO?' (2014) 13 *World Trade Review* 267, 268.

1284 Lester, Mercurio and Davies (n 1027) 490. On the disagreements between major emerging economies, especially India, and the US, particularly on final details in agricultural matters leading to a breakdown of Doha Round negotiations on trade law reform in 2008 (and them being 'de facto' called off in 2015) see also JP Singh, 'Introduction: Emerging Powers and the WTO' (2016) 21 *International Negotiation* 201, 202. See also Kristen Hopewell, 'The BRICS – merely a fable? Emerging power alliances in global trade governance' (2017) 93 *International Affairs* 1377, 1394.

1285 Michael O Moore and Mark Wu, 'Antidumping and Strategic Industrial Policy: Tit-for-Tat Trade Remedies and the China–X-Ray Equipment Dispute' (2015) 14 *World Trade Review* 239, 239–240.

1286 Dukgeon Ahn and Maurizio Zanardi, 'China–HP-SSST: Last Part of Growing Pains?' (2017) 16 *World Trade Review* 159.

authorities, and could possibly represent 'the last part of growing pains for Chinese authorities to learn about [antidumping] legal procedures'.[1287]

IV.2.2.2.3.6 Remaining Cases – National Treatment, MFN & Non-discriminatory Administration of Quantitative Restrictions

IV.2.2.2.3.6.1 Relevant case law

In *China-Electronic Payment Services*, the US considered that Chinese government measures restricting the supply of electronic payment services for payment card transactions denominated and paid in Chinese renminbi, namely to one Chinese entity ('China UnionPay'), were inconsistent with market access and national treatment obligations due to advantages on payment card processing device compatibility and access to merchants.[1288] The Panel, unappealed, ruled that the measures largely did not violate market access commitments, but – following logic developed partly in *China-Publications and Audiovisual Products* – determined that they were inconsistent with national treatment obligations on account of how they changed the conditions of competition.[1289] China notified full implementation, but the US was not satisfied and announced that it would further monitor and review compliance.[1290]

In *US-Poultry (China)*, China complained about a host of supposed SPS Agreement, Agreement on Agriculture and GATT 1994 violations through US measures relating to the import of Chinese poultry products.[1291] The unappealed Panel report indeed found inconsistencies with MFN and quantitative restrictions provisions in the GATT 1994, and no justification

---

1287 Ibid 159.

1288 Arts XVI and XVII GATS; WTO, *China: Certain Measures Affecting Electronic Payment Services–Request for Consultations* (15 September 2010) WT/DS413/1.

1289 WTO, *China: Certain Measures Affecting Electronic Payment Services–Report of the Panel* (16 July 2012) WT/DS413/R [VIII.1]; *China–Publications and Audiovisual Products* (Panel Report) (n 1100); *China–Publications and Audiovisual Products* (Appellate Body Report) (n 1101).

1290 WTO, *China: Certain Measures Affecting Electronic Payment Services–Implementation notified by respondent* (23 July 2013) WT/DS413 <https://www.wto.org/english/tratop_e/dispu_e/cases_e/ds413_e.htm> accessed 21 August 2018.

1291 Art 4.2 Agreement on Agriculture; WTO, *United States: Certain Measures Affecting Imports of Poultry from China–Request for Consultations* (17 April 2009) WT/DS392/1 ('*US–Poultry (China)* (Request for Consultations)'); Arts 2.1 – 2.3, 3.1, 3.3, 5.1 – 5.7 and 8 SPS Agreement.

through Article XX (b) due to a number of SPS Agreement violations, – inter alia – relating to the lack of proper risk assessment and sufficient scientific evidence, as well as discrimination against China.[1292] No recommendations followed due to the measures already having expired.[1293]

Finally, in *EU-Poultry Meat (China)*, China alleged that the EU had acted inconsistently with a number of GATT 1994 provisions through its tariff rate quotas on poultry products.[1294] The EU had negotiated new tariff concessions under Article XXVIII GATT 1994 in respect of tariff rate quotas with Brazil and Thailand, after determining that only they had the required legal interest.[1295] Unappealed, the Panel determined that tariff rate quotas for some tariff lines were indeed inconsistent with Article XIII:2 (d) and the chapeau of Article XIII:2 GATT 1994 – China's increased export ability after certain SPS measures were relaxed should have been considered as a 'special factor' when determining 'substantial interest' in supplying pertinent products, and a greater 'all others' share of quotas should have been allocated – while it rejected the rest of China's long list of claims.[1296]

IV.2.2.2.3.6.2 Discussion

China-Electronic Payment Services was interesting in demonstrating certain peculiarities about the design and interpretation of GATS, because Unionpay – clearly the sole supplier in a certain segment of the market – could not be defined as a 'monopoly' or 'exclusive supplier' by the Panel (Arti-

---

1292 Arts 1, 2.2 – 2.3, 5.1 – 5.2 and 5.5 SPS Agreement; Arts I:1, XI:1 and XX (b) GATT 1994; WTO, *United States: Certain Measures Affecting Imports of Poultry from China–Report of the Panel* (29 September 2010) WT/DS392/R [VIII.1]–[VIII.4] ('*US–Poultry (China)* (Panel Report)').

1293 *US–Poultry (China)* (Panel Report) (n 1292) [VIII.7]; WTO, *United States: Certain Measures Affecting Imports of Poultry from China–Report(s) adopted, no further action required* (25 October 2010) WT/DS392.

1294 WTO, *European Union: Measures Affecting Tariff Concessions on Certain Poultry Meat Products–Request for Consultations* (8 April 2015) WT/DS492/1 ('*EU–Poultry Meat (China)* (Request for Consultations)'). See inter alia Arts I:1, II:1, chapeau of XIII:2, XIII:1, XIII:2(d), XIII:4 and XXVIII:1-XXVIII:2 GATT 1994.

1295 Art XXVIII:1 GATT 1994; WTO, *European Union: Measures Affecting Tariff Concessions on Certain Poultry Meat Products–Report of the Panel* (28 March 2017) WT/DS492/R [II.2]–[II.3] ('*EU–Poultry Meat (China)* (Panel Report)').

1296 Art XIII:2 GATT 1994; *EU–Poultry Meat (China)* (Panel Report) (n 1295) [VIII.1].

cles XVI (2) (a) and VIII GATS).[1297] Both the complaint and China refraining from an appeal were mostly due to Unionpay's expansion outside of China. Market leaders were riled by the company's explosive internationalization. On the other hand, Unionpay 'is likely to want to avoid its growth abroad being foreclosed by actions that are argued to be justified because its domestic market is closed to competition'.[1298] In the context of international expansion, leaderships both on the Unionpay company- and Chinese government-level, would likely judge this case an overall success due to the decision on defining 'monopoly.'

Even though the measure complained against in *US–Poultry (China)* was limited to a few months and it was clear that it would expire ahead of a panel report, China not only went ahead with the request for consultations, but also retaliated with countervailing duties against US chicken imports,[1299] one month after newly-inaugurated US President Obama signed off on the measure in March 2009.[1300] The purpose was to demonstrate China's new readiness to quickly and strongly engage on all levels. China appeared to seek maximum effect by aligning the timing of the dispute with a pertinent legislative process in the US Congress.[1301] Moreover, prioritizing GATT 1994 claims over SPS Agreement claims would fit Chinese interest in having a rather lean case and establishing a general precedent that may shape US Congress behavior, instead of delving into the intricacies of the SPS Agreement on an only temporarily relevant US measure.[1302]

Finally, *EU-Poultry Meat (China)* again showed that China may be satisfied with very partial victories, wherein it shapes certain definitions – in this case 'special factor' and 'substantial interest' in Article XIII:2 (d) GATT 1994 – and refrain from appeals.[1303]

1297 Arts VIII and XVI (2) (a), Annex on Financial Services of the GATS; Bernard Hoekman and Niall Meagher, 'China – Electronic Payment Services: discrimination, economic development and the GATS' (2014) 13 *World Trade Review* 409, 410–411. See also Dennin (n 960) 275–276, 278.

1298 Hoekman and Meagher (n 1297) 440–441.

1299 Mercurio and Tyagi (n 990) 121.

1300 Ji and Huang (n 1199) 8–9.

1301 Kennedy, 'China's role in WTO Dispute Settlement' (n 38) 582.

1302 Jan Bohanes, 'United States – Certain measures affecting imports of poultry from China: the fascinating case that wasn't' (2012) 11 *World Trade Review* 307, 309.

1303 Art XIII:2 GATT 1994; *EU–Poultry Meat (China)* (Panel Report) (n 1295) [VIII.1]. See also Chapter IV.2.2.2.3.6.1.

IV.2.2.2.3.7 Cases at the Consultation Stage

A large number of consultation requests filed in the third phase of China's engagement with the DSM remained at the stage of consultations or panel proceedings in December 2018. Nonetheless, some had been for a long time, with the likelihood of an eventual panel report in question. These were mainly cases filed by other Members against China[1304] and only one such dispute initiated by China.[1305]

More recent disputes also remain at the consultation or panel proceedings stages. For the years 2016 to 2018 they still include more complaints filed against China,[1306] but also two crucial cases filed by China on the question of an automatic end to the applicability of the price comparison

1304 WTO, *China: Grants, Loans and other Incentives–Request for Consultations* (19 December 2008) WT/DS387/1; WTO, *China: Provisional Anti-Dumping Duties on Certain Iron and Steel Fasteners from the European Communities–Request for Consultations* (7 May 2010) WT/DS407/1; WTO, *China: Measures concerning wind power equipment–Request for Consultations* (22 December 2010) WT/DS419/1; WTO, *China: Certain Measures Affecting the Automobile and Automobile-Parts Industries–Request for Consultations* (17 September 2012) WT/DS450/1; WTO, *China: Measures Relating to the Production and Exportation of Apparel and Textile Products–Request for Consultations* (15 October 2012) WT/DS451/1; WTO, *China: Measures Related to Demonstration Bases and Common Service Platforms Programmes–Request for Consultations* (11 February 2015) WT/DS489/1 (agreement reached in the form of a MoU, but no notification of its successful implementation yet); WTO, *China: Tax Measures Concerning Certain Domestically Produced Aircraft–Request for Consultations* (8 December 2015) WT/DS501/1.

1305 WTO, *European Union and certain Member States: Certain Measures Affecting the Renewable Energy Generation Sector–Request for Consultations* (5 November 2012) WT/DS452/1.

1306 WTO, *China: Export Duties on Certain Raw Materials–Request for Consultations* (13 July 2016) WT/DS508/1 (panel established but not yet composed); WTO, *China: Duties and other Measures concerning the Exportation of Certain Raw Materials–Request for Consultations* (19 July 2016) WT/DS509/1 (panel established but not yet composed); WTO, *China: Domestic Support for Agricultural Producers–Request for Consultations* (13 September 2016) WT/DS511/1 (outside this study's research period, a Panel Report was issued on 28 February 2019 that found China in violation of Articles 3.2 and 6.3 of the Agreement on Agriculture); WTO, *China: Tariff Rate Quotas for Certain Agricultural Products–Request for Consultations* (15 December 2016) WT/DS517/1 (outside this study's research period a Panel Report was circulated on 18 April 2019); WTO, *China: Subsidies to Producers of Primary Aluminium–Request for Consultations* (12 January 2017) WT/DS519/1; WTO, *China: Certain Measures Concerning Imports of Sugar–Request for Consultations* (16 October 2018) WT/DS568/1.

methodology in paragraph 15 (a) (ii) of the Accession Protocol in 2016 ('market economy status').[1307]

A recent trend is that other Members than the US and the EU (ie Japan, Canada and Brazil) also put forward solo requests for consultations with China. The requests contain some familiar issues on subsidies violating the SCM agreement, and tariff quotas and export duties violating China's Accession Protocol, but the latter is also considered as breached through other measures such as particular tax regimes.

The escalating overarching trade dispute between China and the United States in 2018 has shown yet another step in the development laid out above over three phases. Rising Chinese confidence, as well as familiarity with and belief in the necessity to always keep using the system and operating from within were at display when three complaints by the US[1308] were answered by five Chinese complaints.[1309]

IV.2.2.2.3.8 Market Economy Status – 'D-Day' Gone Wrong & China's Controlled Frustration

As noted at the beginning of the preceding sub-chapter, China had concentrated most strikingly on two things during the third phase of its WTO membership and DSM participation (ie from 2008, 'rule-maker'). First, go-

---

1307 See Chapter IV.2.2.2.3.8; Para 15 (a) (ii) Accession Protocol; WTO, *United States: Measures Related to Price Comparison Methodologies–Request for Consultations* (12 December 2016) WT/DS515/1 ('*US–Measures Related to Price Comparison Methodologies* (Request for Consultations)'); WTO, *European Union: Measures Related to Price Comparison Methodologies–Request for Consultations* (12 December 2016) WT/DS516/1 ('*EU–Price Comparison Methodologies* (Request for Consultations)') (panel composed and report to be issued in 2019).

1308 *China–Intellectual Property Rights* (Request for Consultations) (n 1052); WTO, *China: Certain Measures on the Transfer of Technology–Request for Consultations* (1 June 2018) WT/DS549/1; WTO, *China: Additional Duties on Certain Products from the United States–Request for Consultations* (16 July 2018) WT/DS558/1.

1309 WTO, *United States: Tariff Measures on Certain Goods from China–Request for Consultations* (4 April 2018) WT/DS543/1; WTO, United *States: Certain Measures on Steel and Aluminium Products–Request for Consultations* (5 April 2018) WT/DS544/1; WTO, *United States: Safeguard Measure on Imports of Crystalline Silicon Photovoltaic Products–Request for Consultations* (14 August 2018) WT/DS562/1; WTO, *United States: Certain Measures Related to Renewable Energy–Request for Consultations* (14 August 2018) WT/DS563/1; WTO, *United States: Tariff Measures on Certain Goods from China II–Request for Consultations* (23 August 2018) WT/DS565/1.

ing on the offense at the DSM, China tried to use trade disputes to influence the interpretations of WTO rules, especially the provisions of its own Accession Protocol. Second, the Chinese government intensified a parallel diplomatic campaign to get other Members to no longer apply NME treatment to it, by using the lure of FTAs. This second pillar of China's strategy can be considered an insurance policy of sorts, should other Members refuse to recognize the automatic end to the applicability of the price comparison methodology in paragraph 15 (a) (ii) of the Accession Protocol in 2016.[1310] Despite the insurance, the Chinese political and academic elite was largely convinced that other Members would comply with these provisions as it interpreted them. Aspects of the WTO experience perceived critically by the Chinese side caused less of a reaction on account of this conviction.[1311]

FTAs had already been ratified with ASEAN (framework agreement in 2003), Chile (2006), and Pakistan (2007). In the third phase, New Zealand (2008), Singapore (2009), Peru (2010), Costa Rica (2011), Iceland (2014), Switzerland (2014), the Republic of Korea (2015), Australia (2015), Georgia (2018) and the Maldives (not yet in force) followed.[1312] For example, the treaty with Georgia brought an agreement to no longer consider China an NME.[1313] However, not every country accepting an end to China's NME status necessarily gives up third-country comparisons in anti-dumping calculations, with Australia being a prominent example. Canberra already granted market economy status in 2005, but still attempts to retain special price calculation methodologies via reference to 'particular market situations' and non-existence of 'ordinary course of trade'.[1314] Negotiations

---

1310 Para 15 (a) (ii), (d) Accession Protocol.

1311 See Chapters V.2.1.2 and V.2.1.3.

1312 Chinese Ministry of Commerce, 'China FTA Network' <http://fta.mofcom.gov.cn/english/> accessed 30 March 2019.

1313 Art 7.1 (3) Free Trade Agreement between the Government of Georgia and the Government of the People's Republic of China (signed 13 May 2017, entered into force 1 January 2018) ('China-Georgia FTA 2017'). See also Yan 艳 Bao and Riming 日明 Cui 崔, '"丝绸之路经济带"框架下中国 – 格鲁吉亚 自由贸易区建设研究' (Studying the Establishment of the China-Georgia Free Trade Area under the Framework of the "The Silk Road Economic Belt") (2017) 45 (1) *Liaoning Daxue Xuebao* 51, 56.

1314 Mikko Huotari, Jan Gaspers and Olaf Böhnke, 'Asserting European interests – How Europe should deal with the question of China's Market Economy Status' *MERICS China Policy Brief* 8, 10–11 (Berlin, January 2016) <http://www.merics.org/en/press-contact/press-releases/asserting-european-interests.html> accessed 15 March 2017.

for further FTAs are ongoing with Israel, Mauritius, Moldova, Norway, Panama, Sri Lanka, the Gulf Cooperation council (GCC), and Japan (via a trilateral FTA with the Republic of Korea).[1315]

A still much larger (but far off) success would be the conclusion of the 'Regional Comprehensive Economic Partnership' (RCEP) Agreement, negotiations for which also include India (next to China, Japan, the Republic of Korea, ASEAN, Australia, and New Zealand). New Delhi has certainly been the most reticent participant in these talks. Indian authors have voiced general concerns about regional trade agreements such as RCEP, but also TPP and TTIP, and their potentially drastic negative impact on South Asian countries that are not party to them (eg on account of preferential tariff arrangements).[1316]

However, China's most important trade partners – the EU and the US – have not yet been realistic targets for FTA talks. With them, there was only one pillar of Chinese strategy then, to convince them that the correct interpretation of the Accession Protocol means an automatic end to China's NME status.

When the day that the Chinese side had been holding out and attempting to strategically prepare the ground for – 12 December 2016 – came, both the EU and the US refused to comply with China's expectations. The US had provisions on market economy criteria in its national law when China acceded to the WTO, as relevant under paragraph 15 (d) Accession Protocol. It stuck to the principles laid out therein – needless to say China did not fulfill the requirements – disregarded the fifteen-year deadline, and continued to apply the analog country method with case-by-case modifications.[1317] By contrast, EU law did not contain such criteria at the time of

1315 Chinese Ministry of Commerce, 'China FTA Network' <http://fta.mofcom.gov.cn/english/> accessed 30 March 2019.

1316 Mohammad Masudur Rahman and Laila Arjuman Ara, 'TPP, TTIP and RCEP: Implications for South Asian Economies' (2015) 16 *South Asia Economic Journal* 27.

1317 Terence P Stewart and others, 'Any Change to China's Non-Market Economy Status Must Be Based on the Criteria Specified under U.S. Antidumping Law' (2005) A Position Paper Prepared for the U.S.-China Economic and Security Review Commission by the Trade Lawyers Advisory Group 18 August 2005 <https://www.uscc.gov/Research/any-change-china%E2%80%99s-non-market-economy-status-must-be-based-criteria-specified-under-us> accessed 5 March 2019; Gary Clyde Hufbauer and Cathleen Cimino-Isaacs, 'Trump Says China Is Not a Market Economy. That's a Big Deal', *Peterson Institute for International Economies – Trade & Investment Policy Watch* (Washington DC, 11 April 2016)

Chinese accession.[1318] However, the EU attempted to side-step the problem by announcing that it would and eventually indeed amending its basic Anti-Dumping Regulation to no longer explicitly mandate NME treatment for certain countries, while continuing to use an NME-like methodology where it considers it not 'appropriate to use domestic prices and costs in the exporting country due to the existence in that country of significant distortions' (Article 1 Regulation (EU) 2017/2321 amending Art 2 Regulation (EU) 2016/1036 by inserting paragraph 6a (a)).[1319]

China acted – and indeed was – disappointed and somewhat surprised, at least by the EU's decision, with its last-ditch diplomatic offensive also having been for nothing.[1320] However, China's reaction has been one that both confidently operates within the system, and appears as a calm continuation of long-standing strategy: initiate cases under the DSU.

The Chinese government immediately requested consultations with the US and EU on 12 December 2016, in *US-Measures Related to Price Comparison Methodologies* (DS515) and *EU-Measures Related to Price Comparison Methodologies* (DS516).[1321] It alleged that regulations 'pertaining to the determination of normal value for "non-market economy" countries in antidumping proceedings involving products from China' were inconsistent with Articles 2.1 – 2.2, 9.2, 18.1 and 18.4 AD Agreement and Arts I:1, VI:1

<https://piie.com/blogs/trade-investment-policy-watch/outlook-market-economy-status-china> accessed 22 May 2017; Chad P Bown, 'The Outlook for Market Economy Status for China', *Peterson Institute for International Economies – OpEds* (Washington DC, 12 December 2016) <https://piie.com/commentary/op-eds/trump-says-china-not-market-economy-thats-big-deal> accessed 22 May 2017; Para 15 (d) Accession Protocol.

1318 Hufbauer and Cimino-Isaacs (n 1317).

1319 Regulation (EU) 2017/2321 of the European Parliament and of the Council of 12 December 2017 amending Regulation (EU) 2016/1036 on protection against dumped imports from countries not members of the European Union and Regulation (EU) 2016/1037 on protection against subsidised imports from countries not members of the European Union [2017] OJ L338/1.

1320 Robin Emmott, 'China, EU Commission edge towards deal on market economy status' *Reuters* (Brussels, 27 May 2016) <https://uk.reuters.com/article/uk-china-eu-trade-idUKKCN0YI1G0> accessed 8 November 2019; Shawn Donnan, Lucy Hornby and Arthur Beesley, 'China challenges EU and US over market economy status' *Financial Times* (London, 12 December 2016) <https://www.ft.com/content/6af8da62-bf5d-11e6-9bca-2b93a6856354> accessed 8 November 2019.

1321 *US–Measures Related to Price Comparison Methodologies* (Request for Consultations) (n 1307); *EU–Price Comparison Methodologies* (Request for Consultations) (n 1307).

and VI:2 GATT 1994 on the US side, and Articles 2.1 – 2.2 AD Agreement and Articles I:1 and VI:1 GATT 1994 on the side of the EU.[1322] Viet Nam, Australia, Canada, Japan, Russia, and Mexico requested to join the consultations with both the EU and US. The US and the EU also requested to join China's consultations with the respective other importer. In the case with the EU, a panel was established and composed in 2017, which later informed the DSB that it would seek to publish its report until the end of 2018, but did not do so.[1323]

Chinese scholars have argued that China never admitted to being an NME,[1324] and that *EC–Fasteners* authoritatively demonstrated paragraph 15 (a) Accession Protocol to not state whether China is an NME.[1325] They uniformly contended that China merely agreed to the temporary usage of specific price calculations that could run out earlier than but had run out on 11 December 2016.[1326]

IV.2.2.2.3.9 Conclusion

Although China has not settled further cases in its long and ongoing third phase of DSM engagement,[1327] the overall picture is still one of unusually conciliatory practice. A mutually-agreed solution was found in about a fifth of the cases where China was a principal party. Moreover, the PRC

1322 Arts 2.1 – 2.2, 9.2, 18.1 and 18.4 AD Agreement and Arts I:1, VI:1-VI:2 GATT 1994; *US–Measures Related to Price Comparison Methodologies* (Request for Consultations) (n 1307); *EU–Price Comparison Methodologies* (Request for Consultations) (n 1307).

1323 WTO, *United States: Measures Related to Price Comparison Methodologies–In consultations* (12 December 2016) WT/515; WTO, *European Union: Measures Related to Price Comparison Methodologies–Panel Composed* (10 July 2017) WT/DS516.

1324 See eg Minyou 敏友 Yu 余 and Jian 健 Guan 管, 论《中国加入议定书》第15条到期后的法律效力 (On the Legal Effect of the Expiration of Article 15 of China's Accession Protocol) (2016) 23 (6) *Shanghai Duiwai Jingmao Daxue Xuebao* 29, 39.

1325 See eg Zhaomin 兆敏 Zhu 朱, '论世界贸易组织与中国的市场经济地位' (The WTO and China's Market Economy Status) [2015] (9) *Faxue* 88, 96 citing *EC–Fasteners (China)* (Appellate Body Reports) (n 1202) [147].

1326 See Chapter V.2.1.3.2.

1327 In one case an agreement was reached in the form of an MoU, but there has been no notification of its successful implementation yet: WTO, *China: Measures Related to Demonstration Bases and Common Service Platforms Programmes–Request for Consultations* (11 February 2015) WT/DS489/1.

has made less use of the DSM than comparable trade powers, and the ratio of cases as a respondent and complainant is rather lop-sided.[1328]

The reasons for these patterns include other states' concern regarding PRC compliance, which has led to China being eg the largest target of US anti-dumping investigations.[1329] Second, several important other Members have been more adjudication-leaning than China and sooner, which is – third – also due to China's lagging litigation capacity.[1330] Generally, 'high startup costs for using trade litigation [are] a barrier to developing country use of the dispute settlement process'.[1331] On the other hand, Vietnam – as a much smaller trading power, with weaker retaliatory power, and less human, legal and financial resources – did not lack confidence and brought its first case as a solo complainant after three years, while the PRC waited six.[1332] However, the Vietnamese, government only brought four further cases since then, and was never a respondent, ie it likely defused potential disputes where it would have been a respondent in other ways, instead of 'fighting them out' at the DSM.[1333]

Fourth, as laid out in the Chapter III of this book, China is traditionally both inclined towards non-adversarial dispute resolution and distrustful of the international system; tendencies that are more pronounced regarding mechanisms the country's institutions are still rather unfamiliar with. As has been explained in Chapter IV.2.1, it was also increased engagement and familiarization that changed the PRC's initially very cautious BIT practice.[1334] The traditional Confucian aversion to litigation on account of it disrupting relationships has been explained above. Several authors have underlined its continued relevance in Chinese trade relations.[1335] Fifth, post-1978 Chinese governments have focused their energies on economic

1328 WTO, 'Disputes by Member' <https://www.wto.org/english/tratop_e/dispu_e/dispu_by_country_e.htm> accessed 5 November 2019. See also Bourgeois (n 970) 8, 33.

1329 Bourgeois (n 970) 7.

1330 Manjiao Chi, 'China's Participation' (n 969) 32–33; Tong Qi, 'How Exactly does China Consent' (n 510) 224.

1331 Davis and Blodgett Bermeo (n 995) 1033. See also Guiguo Wang, 'China's FTAs: Legal Characteristics and Implications' (2011) 105 AJIL 493, 503.

1332 Xiaojun Li (n 994) 1112, 1115.

1333 WTO, 'Disputes by Member' <https://www.wto.org/english/tratop_e/dispu_e/dispu_by_country_e.htm> accessed 5 November 2019.

1334 See Schill, 'Tearing Down the Great Wall' (n 521) 82.

1335 Bourgeois (n 970) 11; Xiaojun Li (n 994) 1129–1130; Guiguo Wang, 'Chinese Mechanisms' (533) 222–223.

growth and evaluated officials along GDP parameters, which engendered a fear of risking growth by being litigious.[1336]

Sixth, normative constraints and reputational concerns held back engagement.[1337] China settled its first case as a respondent, although Members usually continue disputed practices during WTO proceedings, because its central concern was 'for potential reputation costs associated with defending its protectionist measures in the formal WTO dispute resolution system, amid a global free trade community'.[1338] Being sued, even losing a case, and being branded a protectionist power could all have meant a loss of face within a multilateral forum that was deemed to amplify reputational risks.[1339]

However, China did not give in to domestic reputational concerns regarding the enforcement of negative rulings by the DSM. When several media outlets led with the headline 'China's first major defeat at the WTO' after *China-Auto Parts*, the government marketed the proceedings as valuable learning experience and as successfully buying time for the domestic auto industry.[1340] It noted that the ruling was unfortunate yet – surprisingly to many in the West – committed to implementation 'within a reasonable period of time'.[1341] After the defeat in *US – Tyres (China)* some scholars wondered whether China should not step back to wait and observe before initiating more disputes, as the outcomes could rather make things worse,[1342] but once again the overarching strategy was retained. On compliance, it has been cautioned that 'there are no well-defined domestic procedures for implementing' Panel and AB rulings, while it is rather political decisions that ensure implementation.[1343] Nonetheless, China by now demonstrates a level of 'compliance with reports of the WTO DSB [that] is equivalent to other leading members'.[1344]

1336 Guiguo Wang, 'Chinese Mechanisms' (533) 224.

1337 Xiaojun Li (n 994) 1113, 1128–1129.

1338 Ibid 1129; *China–Value Added Tax on Integrated Circuits* (Request for Consultations) (n 997); *China–Value Added Tax on Integrated Circuits* (Notification of Mutually Agreed Solution) (n 1036).

1339 Xiaojun Li (n 994) 1130–1131.

1340 Ibid 1134; *China–Auto Parts* (Request for Consultations) (n 992); *China–Auto Parts* (Panel Reports) (n 1068); *China–Auto Parts* (Appellate Body Reports) (n 1074).

1341 Bourgeois (n 970) 5 FN 16; Xiaojun Li (n 994) 1134.

1342 Huang and Ji (n 1188) 1300.

1343 Manjiao Chi, 'China's Participation' (n 969) 39–40.

1344 Ku, 'China and the Future of International Adjudication' (n 32) 168–169.

Even after so much anticipation had been connected to the fifteen-year deadline in paragraph 15 (d) Accession Protocol, and China was then utterly disappointed in 2016, accumulated confidence, familiarity with the system, and satisfaction with outcomes thus far, allow for continued Chinese calls to stay the course. First, there are good arguments to expect that the Panel in *EU-Measures Related to Price Comparison Methodologies* (DS516) will find the EU in breach of Articles 2.2.1.1 and 2.2 AD Agreement and Article VI:1 GATT 1994 where it discards producers' costs as distorted and replaces them with out-of-country undistorted prices and costs when applying the new non-standard methodology.[1345]

Second, it is likely that many on the Chinese side would interpret the EU's new legislation as a deliberate stalling effort, gaining EU industry a couple of years respite before the inevitable happens, and understandably employing a tactic that they long recommended their own government learn from the US.[1346] Chinese scholars indeed counsel patience, confidently recall China's rising clout within the WTO, and argue that after the 'Multi Fibre Arrangement' ran out in 2014, it also took a while before that fact was eventually accepted.[1347] Additionally, during interviews with Chinese international law scholars in 2017, the clear policy recommendation was to remain committed to using the DSM for further related disputes even if the current cases were lost.[1348] No retrenchment, but rather patient work within the system.

There is a further upward tendency now in the frequency of Chinese DSM cases. Arguably, this only makes sense, as it would be 'economically and politically to the detriment of China to abstain from using the mechanism, even if it could contribute to the improvement of its position in the organisation (sic!)'.[1349] This last notion is another crucial point. China does indeed participate in international dispute resolution where 1) it feels

1345 Andrei Suse, 'Old Wine in a New Bottle: The EU's Response to the Expiry of Section 15 (a) (ii) of China's WTO Protocol of Accession' (2017) 20 *Journal of International Economic Law* 951, 951–953.

1346 See eg Baihua Gong (n 1032) 106.

1347 See eg Min 敏 Zhao 赵, '从 WTO 的法律规则看中国如何应对市场经济地位的"非市场"阻力' (Reviewing how China should respond to the 'non-market' barrier to market economy status through WTO legal rules) [2017] (2) *Jingji Luntan* 119, 145; Arrangement Regarding International Trade in Textiles (opened for signature 20 December 1973, entered into force 3 January 1975) 25 USTS 1001 ('Multi Fibre Arrangement').

1348 Author's interviews in Beijing in July 2017.

1349 Bourgeois (n 970) 33.

ready to be successful, 2) participation appears beneficial to its economy, and 3) change to interpretations or norms themselves might be brought about. But, the Chinese government also participates to aid coalition building and grow political influence. At the DSM, China only raised disputes against the US and the EU. Japan, Canada, Mexico and Guatemala have also requested consultations with China over the years, but China never 'returned the favor'. While this might change regarding Japan and Canada, China will likely refrain from tarnishing its record of never initiating a dispute against a developing country Member.

IV.2.2.2.4. Comparative View – BRICS Lessons: Some Learn, Some Don't

IV.2.2.2.4.1. Introduction

In many years since 2000, developing country Members have actually initiated more DSM disputes than developed country Members.[1350] They have been successful with complaints against the economic superpowers US and EU – one story of 'David v Goliath' being *US-Gambling* launched by Antigua and Barbuda[1351] – and have also locked horns among each other.[1352] Examples for the latter situation are eg *Turkey-Textiles* initiated by India, and *Thailand-Cigarettes*, where the Philippines were the complainant.[1353]

1350 See David Evans and Gregory C Shaffer, 'Introduction', in Gregroy C Shaffer and Ricardo Melendez-Ortiz, *Dispute Settlement at the WTO – The Developing Country Experience* (CUP 2010) 1–2 for a discussion of problems such as Members self-determining their status as developing countries, and the statistical issue of what to count: consultations, panels established, AB reports adopted, dispute matters (ie not counting several consultation requests on the same matter). On the latter issue, the authors settle on counting consultations requests, which will be done here as well; see also Van den Bossche and Zdouc (n 962) 299.

1351 WTO, *United States: Measures Affecting the Cross-Border Supply of Gambling and Betting Services–Report of the Appellate Body* (7 April 2005) WT/DS285/AB/R.

1352 See also Van den Bossche and Zdouc (n 962) 299. For further literature on developing country experiences see Rorde Wilkinson, 'Conclusions: Emerging Powers in the WTO – Beware the Glass Ceiling' (2016) 21 *International Negotiation* 327; Singh, 'Introduction: Emerging Powers and the WTO' (n 1284) 201; Mahrenbach (n 38) 233–266; Papa (n 32) 83.

1353 WTO, *Turkey: Restrictions on Imports of Textile and Clothing Products–Report of the Appellate Body* (22 October 1999) WT/DS34/AB/R; WTO, *Thailand: Customs and Fiscal Measures on Cigarettes from the Philippines–Report of the Appellate Body*

However, interestingly, no African country ever launched a DSM case.[1354] This kind of engagement has generally also not happened from the side of least-developed countries, where there is only *India-Anti-Dumping Measure on Batteries from Bangladesh* on the active side – a case that did not progress beyond the consultation stage – and no case where a least-developed country was the respondent. The latter fact should not be considered as particularly surprising, as Article 24 (1) DSU calls on Members to 'exercise due restraint' vis-à-vis such countries.[1355]

This new activity on the part of developing country Members built on an overall strengthened commitment to the trading system. This commitment, in turn, grew out of many developing countries' successful economic diversification, rapid growth, and accordingly changed interests.[1356]

The following run-down of the experiences of BRICS countries other than China will confirm that only those that are able and willing to dedicate the appropriate human and financial resources can profit by making regular effective use of the system. Of these countries, Brazil, India and South Africa were already participants of GATT and then founding Members of the WTO. Brazil, India and China have all been among the five most active developing country complainants. In terms of the other two BRICS states, Russia only joined in 2012 and has launched seven cases as a complainant to date, while South Africa has never initiated a DSM case.[1357]

The large emerging economies with which China should be compared here have also not shied away from engaging as a respondent instead of quickly rescinding complained against measures or finding some other negotiated solution. India has been a respondent more than 20 times, and Brazil more than fifteen times. However, in this direction, the marked difference in China's importance as a global economic and trade actor as

---

(17 June 2011) WT/DS371/AB/R; WTO, *India: Anti-Dumping Measure on Batteries from Bangladesh–Request for Consultations* (28 January 2004) WT/DS306/1.

1354 WTO, 'Disputes by Member' <https://www.wto.org/english/tratop_e/dispu_e/dispu_by_country_e.htm> accessed 5 November 2019.

1355 See also Van den Bossche and Zdouc (n 962) 299–300; Art 24 (1) DSU.

1356 Patrick Low, 'Developing Countries in the World Trade Organization: What are the Issues?' in Merit E Janow, Victoria Donaldson and Alan Yanovich (eds), *The WTO: Governance, Dispute Settlement, and Developing Countries* (Juris Publishing Inc 2008) 193–197.

1357 WTO, 'Disputes by Member' <https://www.wto.org/english/tratop_e/dispu_e/dispu_by_country_e.htm> accessed 5 November 2019. See also Van den Bossche and Zdouc (n 962) 299.

well as other countries' sensitivity to the impact of China's growing presence is clearly visible. Despite only joining in 2001, China has been a respondent more than 40 times, far beyond the number for second-placed India. Russia and South Africa have only been respondents nine and five times, respectively.[1358]

Regarding participation as a third country – in some ways a learning exercise – one which developing countries typically engage with heavily before venturing forward more confidently as a principal party, India and Brazil have shown the way, starting earlier than China, and racking up around 130 and 120 cases, respectively. However, China has moved past them, with more than 150 cases. Russia already reached 50 cases in its short period of membership, while South Africa remained below ten.[1359]

IV.2.2.2.4.2. Brazil

Brazil has been not only one of the most frequent but also one of the most sophisticated and successful users of the DSM – regardless whether developing or developed[1360] – marking a stark contrast to Brazil's investment law isolationism. It has won on most complaints, settlements were largely satisfactory, and it has been cited as a model for developing country Members.[1361] Even in strategically crucial cases against the most powerful WTO Members, the US and the EU, it has prevailed, like on agricultural subsidies in *EC-Export Subsidies for Sugar* and *US-Subsidies on Upland Cotton*.[1362] Brazil played a leading role in the Doha Round. It teamed up with India in the 2000s to lead pressure on the US and EU to reform their agricultural sectors, in what has been called a 'precedent set for shared structural lead-

1358 WTO, 'Disputes by Member' <https://www.wto.org/english/tratop_e/dispu_e/dispu_by_country_e.htm> accessed 5 November 2019.

1359 Ibid.

1360 See also Davis and Blodgett Bermeo (n 995) 1034 who noted at the time that Brazil filed 'more WTO complaints […] than many countries with twice its income'.

1361 Shaffer, Badin and Rosenberg, 'Winning at the WTO' (n 5) 21–22; see also Evans and Shaffer, 'Introduction' (n 1350) 4, 6. See also Dan Wei, 'Antidumping in Emerging Countries in the Post-Crisis Era: A Case Study on Brazil and China' (2013) 16 *Journal of International Economic Law* 923.

1362 *EC–Export Subsidies on Sugar* (Appellate Body Report) (n 1130); *US–Upland Cotton* (Appellate Body Report) (n 1130).

ership beyond [the US and EU] at the very heart of the international trade negotiating process'.[1363]

In order to make this possible, the Brazilian government, driven by a shift towards an export-oriented economy and catalyzed by several cases where it was the defendant (eg *Brazil-Aircraft*),[1364] has engaged in massive institutional reorganization. It created a dedicated inter-ministerial body to prepare filings.[1365] Additionally, it set up 'three-pillar coordination' between a specialized WTO DSM unit in the capital, an enlarged diplomatic mission in Geneva, and the Brazilian private sector.[1366] Brasilia also pushed to collect, enhance, and diffuse know-how while reaching out to business consultancies, trade associations, academics, civil society and media outlets. It used a lot of international law firms but also actively supported the development of domestic firms (eg with training at the Geneva Mission).[1367] This system led to more transparency and openness to dialog regarding trade policy, and frequent participation in the DSM has allowed for refining the system amid constant experience gathering.[1368]

Brazil was more often the respondent in the first five years of the WTO – despite experience gained in GATT dispute settlement – and only thereafter launched more complaints. It then linked its active litigation efforts to its negotiation strategy (including under the Doha Round), as well as ongoing US legislative processes, and its successes eg against US subsidies for cotton producers bolstered the legitimacy of its demands.[1369]

Many of the important lessons for other developing countries probably only apply to large emerging economies able to emulate the kind of investments Brazil made in trade law and policy.[1370] One particular lesson drawn by this book is that the other factors of Brazil's success – such as bottom-up

---

1363 Shaffer, Badin and Rosenberg, 'Winning at the WTO' (n 5) 22.

1364 WTO, *Brazil: Export Financing Programme for Aircraft–Report of the Appellate Body* (2 August 1999) WT/DS46/AB/R, wherein Canada challenged Brazilian patent and industrial policy.

1365 Shaffer, Badin and Rosenberg, 'Winning at the WTO' (n 5) 42–44, 90, the 'Chamber of Foreign Trade' (CAMEX) is said body; for Brazil's institutional setup see also Dan Wei, 'Antidumping in Emerging Countries' (n 1361) 927–928.

1366 Shaffer, Badin and Rosenberg, 'Winning at the WTO' (n 5) 44–46, the 'General Dispute Settlement Unit'.

1367 Papa (n 32) 94.

1368 Shaffer, Badin and Rosenberg, 'Winning at the WTO' (n 5) 46, 90.

1369 Papa (n 32) 92, 94–95.

1370 Shaffer, Badin and Rosenberg, 'Winning at the WTO' (n 5) 98–99.

initiatives, a real role for civil society, and democratic exchange – are difficult to copy in authoritarian developing countries.

Despite Brazil having a different trade law history as a GATT contracting party and founding Member of the WTO – as well as different economic interests eg due to the importance of agricultural and other raw material exports – its DSM engagement is similar to China's in several ways. Like China, Brazil did not yet level a large number of complaints in the first years of its DSM participation. After several years of engagement, both became more forward-leaning eg in aggressively complaining against foreign anti-dumping measures: Brazil reduced the share of its affected exports from 3 % to 1 % between 2000 and 2011, while for China it was 5 % in 2011.[1371]

Providing a blueprint (incompletely) followed by China on how to become active and successful within the system, Brazil reformed competent institutions, pushed WTO law education and training, used international but also supported domestic law firms,[1372] linked relevant domestic actors, ramped up participation to gather experience and linked litigation to international negotiations as well as third state domestic legislation processes to optimize outcomes.[1373] China has been lagging in inter-ministerial coordination, and particularly in enterprise participation in trade disputes.[1374] Both countries have for a long time played rather 'pragmatic/acquiescent' roles in reform negotiations, in Brazil driven by pro-trade agricultural and manufacturing interests, compared eg with a more confrontational India.[1375] In using the DSM, both have sought to shape WTO law through certain interpretation outcomes.[1376]

China's strong focus on its Accession Protocol as an often problematized parallel regime in general, as well as the issue of a deadline for NME treatment in price calculation methodologies in particular, are an important difference to the founding Member Brazil. Moreover, China has been a respondent twice as often as a complainant, while the opposite applies for Brazil. The different makeup of its economy as well as its size has made

1371 Dan Wei (n 1361) 950.

1372 China, however, has been most consistent in supporting domestic law firms, which was facilitated by a continually growing caseload. See Papa (n 32) 98.

1373 See also Chapters IV.2.2.1 and IV.2.2.2.5.

1374 Dan Wei (n 1361) 954.

1375 Singh, 'Introduction: Emerging Powers and the WTO' (n 1284) 203, 205.

1376 Dan Wei (n 1361) 951 citing WTO, *European Communities: Antidumping Duties on Malleable Cast Iron Tube or Pipe Fittings–Appellate Body Report* (22 July 2003) WT/DS219/AB/R.

China the main target of eg US complaints, making it more difficult to turn the statistics around.[1377]

IV.2.2.2.4.3. India

India's experience is similar to Brazil's in some ways, although it had to assume a more defensive position. Where Brazil was clearly more often the complainant, India's statistics are almost balanced with a light overhang for cases where it was the defendant.[1378] The Indian central government has not succeeded in engineering effective stakeholder participation on trade policy, which shows in its performance in the DSM. At least in part, this is connected with a reticence to share information.[1379] India often preferred to settle, which is in line with DSU objectives, but also a consequence of less than optimal performance in Panel and AB proceedings.[1380] New Delhi's success when on the offensive has been more mixed than Brazil's. *EC-Tariff Preferences* was in some respects a cautionary tale. Even if a case is won, neither does that guarantee better market access, nor does it mean that there are no risks of interpretations by the Panel and AB having systemic implications that the complainant did neither expect nor wish for.[1381]

In *EC-Tariff Preferences*, India complained against some aspects of the new 'General System of Preferences' (hereinafter: GSP) scheme introduced by the EU in 2001. While India itself profited from tariff preferences under

1377 For conclusions on China's experience in the DSM see Chapters IV.2.2.2.1.3, IV.2.2.2.2.3 and IV.2.2.2.3.9, and for pertinent discourse among Chinese international lawyers see inter alia Chapters V.2.1.1, V.2.1.3.1 and V.2.1.3.2.

1378 WTO, 'Disputes by Member' <https://www.wto.org/english/tratop_e/dispu_e/dispu_by_country_e.htm> accessed 5 November 2019.

1379 Biswajit Dhar and Abhik Majumdar, 'Learning from the India-EC GDP dispute: the issues and the process' in Gregroy C Shaffer and Ricardo Melendez-Ortiz, *Dispute Settlement at the WTO – The Developing Country Experience* (CUP 2010) 182–185, 203.

1380 Ernst-Ulrich Petersmann, 'Review – Abhijit Das and James J. Nedumpara (eds.), *WTO Dispute Settlement at Twenty: Insiders' Reflections on India's Participation*, New Delhi, Centre for WTO Studies, and Singapore, Springer, 2016' (2016) 19 *Journal of International Economic Law* 893, 893–894.

1381 WTO, *European Communities: Conditions for the Granting of Tariff Preferences to Developing Countries–Appellate Body Report* (7 April 2004) WT/DS246/AB/R ('*EC–Tariff Preferences* (Appellate Body Report)'); Evans and Shaffer, 'Introduction' (n 1350) 11–12.

the 'General Arrangements,' one component part of the GSP, twelve other countries enjoyed even greater tariff reductions under the 'Drug Arrangements,' for their contributions in fighting drug production and trafficking. New Delhi considered these measures inconsistent with MFN provisions (Article I:1 GATT 1994 and paragraphs 2 (a), as well as 3 (a) and (c) of the Enabling Clause).[1382] India's exports, especially in the important textiles and clothing sector, were hit, while – inter alia – Pakistan was able to grow market share.[1383]

The case went up to the AB, and arbitration under Article 21.3 DSU followed, fixing a reasonable period for implementation, after an eventual Indian victory.[1384] Three years and three months after the request for consultations, the EU repealed the measure in June 2005, when introducing a new GSP scheme. In the meantime, India had lost considerable market share. Moreover, the new scheme once again introduced 'GSP-plus' provisions from which India did not profit. It also included a 'graduation rule,' whereunder 15 % plus market share meant losing preferential tariffs. India did not gain better access, while its lawyers voiced concerns about AB argumentation – inter alia – on matters of burden of proof allocation.[1385]

The situation has improved over recent years, as India's legal capacity and public-private coordination have substantially improved. New Delhi has also been able to markedly reduce reliance on foreign lawyers.[1386] Over the years, the Indian government used adverse rulings to hasten domestic trade law reforms, all of the while maintaining an unchallenged compliance record.[1387] Moreover, through its cases at the DSM, India has contributed to the clarification of provisions such as the concept of 'public body' in WTO subsidy rules, 'fair price comparisons' under the AD Agreement, and 'non-discrimination' in the 1979 'Enabling Clause'. The Indian government had aimed at this outcome with a strategy of influencing ju-

---

1382 WTO, *European Communities: Conditions for the Granting of Tariff Preferences to Developing Countries–Request for Consultations* (5 March 2002) WT/DS246/1 ('*EC–Tariff Preferences* (Request for Consultations)'); Art I:1 GATT 1994; paras 2 (a), 3 (a) and (c) Enabling Clause; Dhar and Majumdar (n 1379) 174–175.

1383 Dhar and Majumdar (n 1379) 176–182.

1384 *EC–Tariff Preferences* (Appellate Body Report) (n 1381); WTO, *European Communities: Conditions for the Granting of Tariff Preferences to Developing Countries —Arbitration under Article 21.3 (c) DSU* (20 September 2004) WT/DS246/14 ('*EC–Tariff Preferences* (Arbitration under Article 21.3 (c))').

1385 Dhar and Majumdar (n 1379) 190–192, 204–205.

1386 Petersmann (n 1380) 894–896. See also Papa (n 32) 95–96.

1387 Petersmann (n 1380) 894–895.

risprudence through active participation in the early years of the still young WTO dispute settlement system.[1388] Ultimately, India has become another role model on developing country Member DSM participation.

Like Brazil, India shares many similarities with China – and also served as inspiration – despite its different GATT/WTO history. India also focused on gaining experience and influence through participation, on taking an active role in reform negotiations, and on (later than Brazil) upgrading domestic litigation capabilities. Looking at its more frequent role as the respondent and mixed record of success, its early readiness to settle disputes, greater difficulties in domestic reforms and less complete domestic coordination including private actors,[1389] in some ways India's experience has been even more in line with China's than that of Brazil.[1390] China's focus on the Accession Protocol as a parallel regime is again a defining difference between the two Members. As a further factor setting it apart, the overall number of cases involving India has declined over the years,[1391] and finally, India has been a more confrontational actor in Doha Round negotiations.[1392]

IV.2.2.2.4.4. South Africa

Despite being an English-speaking common law country, contracting party of GATT and Member of the WTO, as well as an active participant in Doha Round negotiations, to date South Africa has barely participated at the DSM. It has never initiated a case, and was a respondent or third party in only a handful of cases. Requests for consultations by other Members mostly concentrated on South African anti-dumping duties.[1393]

1388 Ibid 894–895. On India having brought cases that were 'crucial for the evolution of WTO jurisprudence' see also Papa (n 32) 96. On India seeking influence on 'future rules' through DSB participation, a prominent seat at the table in reform negotiations, and overall status within the WTO see also Mahrenbach (n 38) 237–239.

1389 Papa (n 32) 95.

1390 See also Chapters IV.2.2.1 and IV.2.2.2.5.

1391 Papa (n 32) 92.

1392 Singh, 'Introduction: Emerging Powers and the WTO' (n 1284) 205.

1393 WTO, 'Disputes by Member' <https://www.wto.org/english/tratop_e/dispu_e/dispu_by_country_e.htm> accessed 5 November 2019; Gustav Brink, 'South Africa's experience with international trade dispute settlement', in Gregory C Shaffer and Ricardo Melendez-Ortiz, *Dispute Settlement at the WTO – The Developing Country Experience* (CUP 2010) 254–256.

South Africa has been hamstrung by the lack of a central coordinating point in the country, a strong mission in Geneva, and coordination between government departments and groups outside the government. The division within the Ministry of Trade and Industry responsible, and accordingly staffed, for disputes under the DSU, has been repeatedly sidelined. Moreover, the involvement of private sector experts was not realized, and the whole process was poorly coordinated.[1394] South Africa has also failed to adequately train officials, institutionalize knowledge, and gather experience through deeper engagement with the DSM beyond the consultations stage.[1395] South Africa is the only BRICS state that has not even embraced frequent third-party participation as an important learning exercise.

Additionally, South African governments wanted to refrain from potentially upsetting FTA prospects with large trade partners through WTO complaints. The question of quotas on certain Chinese products in the clothing and textiles sector was resolved outside the DSM through a MoU. The latter was the result of lengthy negotiations, from which all stakeholders were excluded. The eventual document allowed for the imposition of quotas on some of the imports in question, in return for refraining from any special safeguards investigation, agreeing to cooperate on anti-dumping investigations, and, crucially, granting China market economy status.[1396]

In short, South Africa lags behind in confidence, institutional preparedness, awareness and knowledge levels and diffusion, as well as public-private coordination.[1397] What domestic experts therefore propose, is exactly the kind of institutional restructuring and discipline, as well as all around capacity building, knowledge diffusion, and experience gathering that has made developing countries like Brazil successful.[1398]

Compared to China, South Africa has been an entirely different actor in the WTO DSM. It became a contracting party to the GATT in 1948, and a founding Member of the WTO in 1995, but still has extraordinarily limited dispute settlement experience. Nor did South African governments succeed in significantly advancing domestic litigation capabilities and general training. Far from ever transitioning to an offensive stance, where it would launch cases to defend its interests, South Africa never even fought

---

1394 Ibid 256–265, 268–269, 272; Evans and Shaffer, 'Introduction' (n 1350) 15.
1395 Brink (n 1393) 267.
1396 Ibid 265–267.
1397 Evans and Shaffer, 'Introduction' (n 1350) 15.
1398 Brink (n 1393) 272–273.

out a case beyond the consultations stage as a respondent. It may have been an active participant in Doha Round negotiations, but only as a supportive actor.

IV.2.2.2.4.5. Russia

Russia, meanwhile, is a different story for several reasons. The Russian government only achieved accession to the WTO in 2012, eleven years after China. Its international engagement comes from a different place, because it arguably 'has been driven by an attempt to manage its decline rather than facilitate its rise'.[1399] However, Russia has only been a principal participant in a handful of cases on each side, whereas the other party in all but one case has been the EU, US or Ukraine (the latter only after the Russian invasion of Ukraine).[1400] Only a few Panel reports have been issued. The EU appealed, and Russia cross-appealed in *EU–Energy Package*,[1401] Ukraine appealed in *Ukraine–Ammonium Nitrate (Russia)*,[1402] and Ukraine appealed and Russia cross-appealed in *Russia–Railway Equipment*.[1403] The Russian government agreed to implement adverse rulings in *Russia-Tariff Treatment*, *Russia-Pigs (EU)*, and *Russia–Commercial Vehicles*.[1404]

1399 Papa (n 32) 91; Macfarlane (n 612) 41; As for other Eastern European countries that rather recently joined the WTO Ukraine (joined 2008) has demonstrated a similar level of participation (five, three, sixteen) – see: WTO, 'Disputes by Member' <https://www.wto.org/english/tratop_e/dispu_e/dispu_by_country_e.htm> accessed 5 November 2019. Another emerging economy to be added here is Turkey, which was a complainant four times, a respondent nine times, and a third party seventy-five times.

1400 WTO, 'Disputes by Member' <https://www.wto.org/english/tratop_e/dispu_e/dispu_by_country_e.htm> accessed 5 November 2019.

1401 WTO, *European Union and its Member States: Certain Measures Relating to the Energy Sector–Report of the Panel* (10 August 2018) WT/DS476/R.

1402 WTO, *Ukraine: Anti-Dumping Measures on Ammonium Nitrate–Report of the Panel* (20 July 2018) WT/DS493/R.

1403 WTO, *Russian Federation: Measures affecting the importation of railway equipment and parts thereof–Report of the Panel* (30 July 2018) WT/DS499/R.

1404 WTO, *Russian Federation: Tariff Treatment of Certain Agricultural and Manufacturing Products–Report of the Panel* (12 August 2016) WT/DS485/R; WTO, *Russian Federation: Measures on the Importation of Live Pigs, Pork and Other Pig Products from the European Union–Report of the Appellate Body* (23 February 2017) WT/DS475/AB/R; WTO, *Russian Federation: Anti-Dumping Duties on Light Commercial Vehicles from Germany and Italy–Report of the Appellate Body* (22 March 2018) WT/DS485/R.

Russia is the only other BRICS state that acceded to the WTO after its foundation, and negotiated an Accession Protocol.[1405] In its DSM practice since, it has exhibited signs of wanting to follow the path China (and before it Brazil and India) took, in using third-party participation as a learning experience. It also took a few years to, as a respondent, let cases escalate to the panel stage. On the other hand, Russia was quicker than China in initiating several disputes itself. It has not focused on NME treatment while comparable provisions were not included in its Accession Protocol (only China's protocol includes elaborate provisions on the matter),[1406] and the EU and US had already granted such status long before Russia's WTO accession.[1407] Finally, Russia could not play a role in Doha Round negotiations as it joined the WTO too late.

IV.2.2.2.4.6. Concluding Remarks on BRICS Experiences in the WTO DSM

The more 'legalized' dispute resolution system of the WTO, as compared to the GATT, has leveled the playing field to a good degree, but also requires the dedication of more resources for effective use. Large economies and trade powers still have to be willing and able to develop adequate legal capacity and institutional structures – including dedicated units, interdepartmental coordination, and strong missions in Geneva – in order to succeed. They have to study the experiences of others, and be ready to take risks in making their own (first as third parties,[1408] then as principals). Finally, governments have to realize the crucial role of coordination and cooperation with academia, the private sector and civil society.[1409]

1405 WTO, *Protocol on the Accession of the Russian Federation* (17 December 2011) WT/L/839.

1406 Petros C Mavroidis and Merit E Janow, 'Free Markets, State Involvement, and the WTO: Chinese State-Owned Enterprises in the Ring' (2017) 16 *World Trade Review* 571, 575.

1407 Rui Pan, 'China in the WTO – A Chinese Perspective' in Ka Zeng and Wei Liang (eds), *China and Global Trade Governance – China's first decade in the World Trade Organization* (Routledge 2013) 37.

1408 Heavy participation as third party can also be witnessed with many developed states. Japan was the most prolific with more than 180 cases, the EU follows right behind, then the US above 140, Canada and the the Republic of Korea above 120, and Australia above 100.

1409 Evans and Shaffer, 'Introduction' (n 1350) 342–348.

Brazil, India and China have all joined the 'inner circle of power' within the WTO; cooperating in many regards, and in light of partly conflicting interests remarkably durably,[1410] during the Doha Round negotiations, challenging the US, EU and others especially on agricultural governance and on large emerging countries' access to 'special and differential treatment' (SDT).[1411]

On its path, China has evidently followed some best practices observed watching Brazil and India engage the DSM.[1412] It has invested enormous resources into legal capacity building and restructured its pertinent institutions, been an exceedingly active third-party participant, and then moved to garnering more risky but crucial experience as a principal party. Nonetheless, China long understaffed eg the WTO Division in MOFCOM's Department of Treaty and Law, and did not manage intergovernmental coordination in the same way as Brazil.[1413] Business chambers' and industry associations' lobbying efforts are hampered by Chinese law not providing sufficient legal clarity on how they may fulfill their role on protecting industry interests on trade questions.[1414] Many Chinese exporters are SOEs. Civil society and (really) private enterprises have lacked the necessary strength to play a relevant part in government considerations, while

---

1410 On one example of developing country-China contentions in the WTO see Ka Zeng, 'The political economy of developing country antidumping actions against China' in Ka Zeng and Wei Liang (eds), *China and Global Trade Governance – China's first decade in the World Trade Organization* (Routledge 2013) 261–284.

1411 Hopewell (n 1284) 1378, 1380, 1383, 1386–1387, noted that with Brazil and India displacing Japan and Canada in 2004 to join the US and EU as the dominant 'Quad' – the 'new Quad' replacing the 'old Quad' – in WTO negotiations, and China joining that high table of decision-making in 2008. For an in-depth exploration of China in the Doha Round process see Xinquan Tu, 'China's position and role in the Doha Round negotiations' in Ka Zeng and Wei Liang (eds), *China and Global Trade Governance – China's first decade in the World Trade Organization* (Routledge 2013) 167–188; Xiaodong Wang and Ka Zeng, 'China and the Doha Round non-agricultural market access (NAMA) negotiations' in Ka Zeng and Wei Liang (eds), *China and Global Trade Governance – China's first decade in the World Trade Organization* (Routledge 2013) 189–210; Wei Liang, 'China, developing countries, and the Doha agricultural negotiations' in Ka Zeng and Wei Liang (eds), *China and Global Trade Governance – China's first decade in the World Trade Organization* (Routledge 2013) 211–232.

1412 See also Chapters IV.2.2.1 and IV.2.2.2.5.

1413 Han and Gao (n 956) 163–164.

1414 Ibid 146–147.

a lack of transparency has additionally hindered input from their side.[1415] Nonetheless, China has indeed made much progress in how effective its use of the DSM has become.

Distinguishing it from all other BRICS states, China has strongly concentrated on a detailed and exacting Accession Protocol to the WTO. Furthermore, among the actively engaging BRICS states – ie all except South Africa – China is the only one with a lop-sided principal actor table clearly leaning to the respondent side. However, other than Brazil and India, China has become much more active as a complainant in recent years, and has – as in investment law – taken a more linear path towards active engagement than other BRICS countries. Much of this can again be led back to political continuity in China, as well as sheer economic size and continuous growth.[1416] What has to be added is a trade structure transitioning towards high-value exports, while export dependence remains relatively high despite efforts to bolster domestic consumption in a large market.[1417]

Underlining its political ambition to garner favor and assume a leadership role – and avoid an emerging-developing country dichotomy in the WTO –[1418] China has been the only BRICS state to never bring a complaint against a developing state.[1419] Even more, it has never done so regarding any other Member than the US and EU, not even Japan or Canada. This points to a continued reticence to litigate as it could damage relations, only overcome when considered necessary regarding the two largest trade partners and largest economic (and political) competitors, as well as China's greater concern with not being branded a protectionist power.[1420]

Finally, as with investment law, China's *image* of international law and ambition to begin 'guiding' international order do not allow for isolationism. Instead, actively engaging with the DSM (and reform negotiations), and portraying oneself as an essential pillar of the WTO, is part of the same

1415 Ibid 164–165.

1416 See also Chapter IV.2.1.4 on investment law.

1417 Tom Hancock, 'China's relentless export machine moves up the value chain' *Financial Times* (Shanghai, 23 September 2018) <https://www.ft.com/content/cdc53aee-bc2e-11e8-94b2-17176fbf93f5> accessed 9 November 2019; Stella Qiu and Tony Monroe, 'China exports grow despite U.S. tariffs, but import slump most in nearly three years' *Reuters* (Beijing, 10 June 2019) <https://www.reuters.com/article/us-china-economy-trade/china-exports-grow-despite-u-s-tariffs-but-import-slump-most-in-nearly-three-years-idUSKCN1TB040> accessed 9 November 2019.

1418 Hopewell (n 1284) 1386.

1419 Not counting South Africa, because it has never filed any complaints.

1420 Xiaojun Li (n 994) 1130–1131.

effort as China's FTA strategy,[1421] which is to help the country not only benefit economically, but to gain regulatory influence.

IV.2.2.2.5. Conclusion – China and the WTO DSM

As in investment law, China was a fairly passive actor in the first years of engagement with international adjudication in the trade field ('rule taker').[1422] Once again – in line with pertinent discourse viewing the DSM as something rather positive but also forced on China –[1423] the PRC government was cautious, focused on learning and preparing itself for later more active participation, and ready to find mutually-agreed solutions to avoid decisions being handed down by an adjudicative body. It gathered experience as a third party and as a respondent sought to compromise to not risk a case going beyond the consultation stage.

Readying itself through legislative and institutional reform, as well as comprehensive capacity building,[1424] and gaining greater influence in reform negotiations,[1425] China gradually became more active at the DSM. After five years it started to actively defend its positions as the respondent ('rule shaker'),[1426] for the first time in the PRC's history accepting defeat in international adjudication, and put a focus on challenging other Members' interpretations of its Accession Protocol. Participation in and defeats at the DSM were normalized, as China engaged to gather more in-depth experience, to obtain certain interpretations, and to simply delay outcomes for its industry, even if overall success was unlikely in a given case. Only two years later, China took the next step and began to frequently file complaints to actively shape accepted interpretations, particularly of the Accession Protocol, gain reversal of previous Panel findings, retaliate and communicate displeasure to other Members ('rule maker').[1427]

1421 Chinese Ministry of Commerce, '新形势下中国发力编织自贸区网络' (Under new circumstances, China's weaving of an FTA network gains momentum) (Beijing, 12 June 2017) <http://chinawto.mofcom.gov.cn/article/e/s/201706/20170602589908.shtml> accessed 20 October 2018.

1422 See Chapter IV.2.2.2.1.

1423 See Chapter V.2.1.3.1.

1424 See Chapter IV.2.2.1.

1425 See Chapter IV.2.2.2.4.

1426 See Chapter IV.2.2.2.2.

1427 See Chapter IV.2.2.2.3.

As with investment law, such cautious gradual engagement is in line with the *image* of international law that arose in China over time.[1428] China needs to face and work with this point of departure-framework, while trying to shape it from within. Overall, China was still relatively conciliatory, being traditionally inclined to non-adversarial dispute resolution, unfamiliar with adjudication of trade disputes and lacking litigation capacity in the early years of engagement, and afraid of disrupting trade relationships crucial to economic growth (also by acquiring a protectionist reputation). However, having gone on the offense later on, China stayed the course, despite being lopsidedly on the receiving end of complaints, domestic reputational concerns about lost cases, and even very prominent expectations about the fifteen-year deadline on alternative anti-dumping price calculation in paragraph 15 (d) Accession Protocol being disappointed.

China has been further accelerating its filing of complaints, and has complied with reports on a level with other leading Members, selling defeats domestically as valuable learning experiences. It is showing patience on NME treatment, confident in litigation capabilities, growing influence within the WTO – even the US appears to fear that China has grown too powerful to cope with under current rules – but also parallel diplomatic efforts and a burgeoning strategy to obtain commitments in bilateral FTAs to no longer use alternative anti-dumping price calculation. All the while, China remains ready to leverage these factors should substantive multilateral reform negotiations resume.[1429]

It is likely that China will stay on this path – including a proliferating caseload –, which is exactly what Chinese international law scholars have recommended.[1430] Moreover, reform stagnation in the WTO (ie paralysis of the 'rule-making' branch) also further increases the importance of the DSM, as Members attempt to use the 'judicial branch' of the WTO to shape rules.[1431]

Within the BRICS group of states, China learned a lot from especially Brazil but also India, in how to improve litigation capacity, and was motivated by seeing them succeed. Russia, in turn, follows in the footsteps of all three, while South Africa remains disengaged. However, China is distinct in its more or less linear escalation of engagement, its necessary focus

1428 See Chapters III.2.2 and IV.2.1.4.
1429 See also Dan Wei (n 1361) 957.
1430 See Chapters V.2.1.3 and V.2.3.
1431 Evans and Shaffer, 'Introduction' (n 1350) 3; Van den Bossche and Zdouc (n 962) 304.

on a severe Accession Protocol, and its DSM statistics' strong slant towards the respondent role. Additionally, China's sheer size as a trade power, its trade structure changing towards exports higher up the value chain, its political ambition to assume a comprehensive leading role in shaping the international legal order, and its strategic decision to only ever file DSM complaints against the US and EU to help it grow influence and build coalitions with other Members, set it clearly apart.

The domestic impact of China's engagement with the WTO DSM has been profound and manifold. The applicability of the WTO Agreement and the norms of the Additional Protocol amounted to tremendous external pressure, which the Chinese government was able to harness to 1) overcome domestic resistance to several economic reforms, and 2) expose the state sector to a higher level of competition.[1432] As laid out in Chapter IV.2.2.1, the PRC also enthusiastically sought to remedy the issue of lacking litigation capacity by introducing new legislation, restructuring institutions, incentivizing pertinent research and teaching at universities, establishing think tanks, and setting up close coordination and cooperation between all actors.[1433]

All of these steps have led to a growing 'rights-consciousness' among Chinese companies, which have started to lobby the government to submit WTO cases to defend them.[1434] WTO engagement has also had a domestic impact via 'spill over' effects on the PRC's overall socio-political system, as Chinese authorities accepted the obligation to implement Panel and AB findings even if sensitive issues like censorship or criminal law were touched upon[1435] – even though they might qualify compliance efforts with reference to a case's supposed special nature and complexity.[1436]

There have been further 'spill over' effects on the overall population, which has come to embrace WTO 'macro-norms' like market economy, non-discrimination and transparency, due to both the Chinese govern-

---

1432 Donald C Clarke, 'The Chinese Legal System since 1995: Steady Development and Striking Continuities' (2007) 191 *The China Quarterly* 555, 563; Ya Julia Qin, 'Trade, Investment and beyond' (n 978) 721, 723–724.

1433 For an indepth discussion of the more general question whether this aspect matters see Marc L Busch and Eric Reinhardt and Gregory Shaffer, 'Does Legal Capacity Matter? A Survey of WTO Members' (2009) 8 *World Trade Review* 559.

1434 Manjiao Chi, 'China's Participation' (n 969) 33.

1435 Ibid 44–46; eg *China–Intellectual Property Rights* (Panel Report) (n 1091).

1436 Manjiao Chi, 'China's Participation' (n 969) 47. See eg *China–Publications and Audiovisual Products* (Appellate Body Report) (n 1101).

ment and academic circles portraying the WTO 'as mostly a progressive force for China'.[1437] However, Chinese international lawyers have cautioned that later on the PRC might have the same misgivings about the WTO – eg on globalization, environmental and labor issues – that other Members voice. Moreover, a further proliferation of lost cases might eventually lead to a more contentious discussion on implications for China's sovereignty.[1438]

IV.3. Territory

IV.3.1. Chinese Territory and the People's Republic of China

In the aftermath of the Chinese Civil War (1945–1949), the victorious Communist side established the PRC on 1 October 1949, and gained control over Hainan, Tibet and Xinjiang in 1950. The UK and Portugal handed over Hong Kong and Macao in 1997 and 1999, respectively. However, in Beijing's eyes, the reunification of China will only be complete after the issue of Taiwan – until this day still governed by the losing side in the Civil War, the Republic of China – is resolved.[1439] Following the demise and dissolution of the British, French and Soviet Empires, the PRC came to share land borders with fourteen sovereign states: Russia, Kazakhstan, Kyrgyzstan, Tajikistan, Afghanistan, Pakistan,[1440] India, Nepal, Bhutan, Myanmar, Laos, Vietnam, North Korea and Mongolia. Moreover, it shares (or purports to share) maritime borders with five to eight sovereign states: North Korea, South Korea, Japan, the Philippines, Malaysia, Brunei, Indonesia and Vietnam,[1441] which brings the total number of neighboring states to 17 or 20, depending on one's legal position. Progress in border de-

---

1437 Ya Julia Qin, 'Trade, Investment and beyond' (n 978) 721, 737, 741.

1438 See Chapter V.2.1.

1439 Ben Blanchard, 'China's defence minister says resolving 'Taiwan question' is national priority' *Reuters* (Beijing, 21 October 2019) <https://www.reuters.com/article/us-china-defence-taiwan/chinas-defence-minister-says-resolving-taiwan-question-is-national-priority-idUSKBN1X003H> accessed 9 November 2019.

1440 De-facto control is considered here. The Pakistani-controlled part of Kashmir is also claimed by India. Would the territorial dispute between Delhi and Islamabad be resolved entirely in the former's favor, China and Pakistan would not have a common border.

1441 Vietnam and the Philippines dispute that the PRC indeed shares maritime borders with Malaysia, Brunei and Indonesia.

marcation has generally been easier 1) regarding land borders, and 2) with somewhat ideologically related (recently post-) Communist or Non-Aligned Movement states, and has exclusively been achieved through negotiations.

IV.3.1.1. Land Borders

The Chinese leadership has now successfully completed the demarcation of most of the PRC's land borders, generally settling the issue with twelve of its fourteen land neighbors. It concluded comprehensive treaties with Burma (Myanmar) in 1960 and Nepal in 1961, with Pakistan and Afghanistan in 1963 and with Laos in 1993, as well as partial treaties with North Korea and Mongolia in 1961 and 1963.[1442]

Negotiations with Burma, interestingly, proceeded from the respective 'unequal treaties' between China and Burma's former colonial master, the British Empire, whereas then Prime Minister Zhou Enlai stated in 1957 'that the border claimed upon the recognized treaties shall be respected in accordance with the general international practice, but this does not exclude the possibility that the governments of two friendly states come to a fair and reasonable settlement for both sides through peaceful negotia-

1442 Boundary Treaty between the Union of Burma and the People's Republic of China (adopted 1 October 1960, entered into force 4 January 1961) 1010 UNTS 135; Boundary Treaty between the People's Republic of China and the Kingdom of Nepal (adopted 5 October 1961, entered into force 5 October 1961) (1961) 4 (42) *Peking Review* 5–8; Boundary Treaty between the People's Republic of China and the Government of Pakistan (adopted 2 March 1963, entered into force 2 March 1963) (1963) 6 (10–11) *Peking Review* 70–71; Boundary Treaty between the People's Republic of China and the Kingdom of Afghanistan (adopted 22 November 1963, entered into force 22 November 1963) (1963) 6 (48) *Peking Review* 7–8; National People's Congress of the People's Republic of China, '中华人民共和国政府和老挝人民民主共和国政府边界制度条约' (Boundary Treaty between the People's Republic of China and the People's Democratic Republic of Laos) (adopted 3 December 1993, entered into force 12 August 1994) <http://www.npc.gov.cn/wxzl/gongbao/2001-01/02/content_5003197.htm> accessed 1 March 2019; Wikisource, '中华人民共和国和朝鲜民主主义人民共和国边界条约' (Border Treaty between the People's Republic of China and the Democratic People's Republic of Korea (adopted 12 October 1962, entered into force 20 March 1964) <https://goo.gl/icjLjn> accessed 1 March 2019; Border Treaty between the People's Republic of China and the People's Republic of Mongolia (adopted 25 December 1962, entered into force 25 March 1963) 984 UNTS 415.

tions.'[1443] Furthermore, the parties drew on Chinese-British exchanges of notes discussing the issue based on borders drawn in 'unequal treaties.' According to Pan Junwu, it was these treaties themselves, ie their nature and the process of how they were drafted, and not so much their content, that was rejected by the Chinese.[1444]

For a long time, the PRC's longest border was with the Soviet Union. After the Sino-Soviet split, a drawn-out gradual breakdown of relations from 1956 to 1963, this border became highly contentious. Both sides amassed military personnel and machinery on an enormous scale and violently clashed several times in 1969. Rapprochement only came under General Secretary Gorbachev starting in 1986, and reinforced with the Soviet leader's visit to Beijing in 1989. Both sides gradually withdrew their troops from the border, and achieved a major settlement with the 1991 Sino-Soviet Eastern Border Agreement, which mostly delimited the part of the border east of Mongolia.[1445]

In 1994, when Jiang Zemin became the first Chinese president to visit Moscow since 1957, and the two states elevated their relations to a 'constructive partnership', the part of the Russian-Chinese border west of Mongolia was also delimited.[1446] In 1996, the declaration of a 'strategic partnership' at President Yeltsin's visit to Beijing and the establishment of the *Shanghai Five* (since 2001: *Shanghai Cooperation Organisation*, SCO) together with Kazakhstan, Kyrgyzstan and Tajikistan signified a further upgrade

1443 As quoted in Pan, 'Chinese Philosophy and International Law' (n 42) 243.

1444 Ibid.

1445 National People's Congress of the People's Republic of China, '中华人民共和国和苏维埃社会主义共和国联盟关于中苏国界东段的协定' (Agreement between the People's Republic of China and the Union of Soviet Socialist Republics on the Eastern Section of the Sino-Soviet Border) (adopted 16 May 1991, entered into force 16 March 1992 after ratification by the Supreme Soviet of the Russian Federation) <http://www.npc.gov.cn/wxzl/wxzl/2000-12/14/content_2679.htm> accessed 1 March 2019 ('Sino-Soviet Eastern Border Agreement'). For points made on the history of this relationship see also Eder (n 166) 24.

1446 National People's Congress of the People's Republic of China, '中华人民共和国和俄罗斯联邦关于中俄国界西段的协定' (Agreement between the People's Republic of China and the Russian Federation on the Western Section of the Sino-Russian Border) (adopted 3 September 1994, entered into force 17 October 1995) <http://www.npc.gov.cn/wxzl/wxzl/2001-01/02/content_3265.htm> accessed 1 March 2019 ('Sino-Russian Western Border Agreement'). See also Eder (n 166) 26.

of relations.[1447] Marked progress in border demarcation with all SCO members followed.

The course of the Sino-Russian border was further clarified through the 2001 *Treaty of Good-Neighbourliness and Friendly Co-operation Between the People's Republic of China and the Russian Federation*,[1448] and an additional agreement in 2004 settled the last disputed areas in the East, partly concerning islands in the Amur river.[1449] A treaty with Kazakhstan was concluded in 1994 (with supplemental agreements in 1997 and 1998).[1450] An agreement with Kyrgyzstan was struck in 1996 (supplemented in 1999).[1451] The PRC and Tajikistan achieved an agreement in 1999 (supplemented in 2002).[1452] 2011 brought a very peculiar development, wherein Tajikistan – in the process of resolving the border question once and for all – ceded al-

1447 Shanghai Cooperation Organisation, 'Shanghai Declaration on the Establishment of the Shanghai Cooperation Organisation' (signed 15 June 2001) <http://eng.sectsco.org/documents/> accessed 1 March 2019); Charter of the Shanghai Cooperation Organisation (adopted 7 June 2002, entered into force 19 September 2003) 2896 UNTS 38. Uzbekistan, which does not share a border with China and was not part of the Shanghai Five, also co-founded the SCO. India and Pakistan joined the organization in 2017.

1448 Ministry of Foreign Affairs of the People's Republic of China, '中俄签署睦邻友好合作条约' (Treaty of Good-Neighbourliness and Friendly Co-operation Between the People's Republic of China and the Russian Federation) (signed 16 July 2001) <http://www.mfa.gov.cn/chn//pds/ziliao/tytj/t11111.htm> accessed 1 March 2019. See also Pan, 'Chinese Philosophy and International Law' (n 42) 244.

1449 National People's Congress, '中华人民共和国和俄罗斯联邦关于中俄国界东段的补充协定' (Supplementary Agreement of the People's Republic of China and the Russian Federation on the Eastern Section of the Sino-Russian Border) (adopted 14 October 2004, entered into force 25 May 2005) <http://www.npc.gov.cn/wxzl/wxzl/2005-07/28/content_341693.htm> accessed 1 March 2019; Eder (n 166) 32..

1450 National People's Congress, '中华人民共和国和哈萨克斯坦共和国关于中哈国界的协定' (Agreement between the People's Republic of China and the Republic of Kazakhstan on the Sino-Kazakh Border) (adopted 26 April 1994, entered into force 15 June 1995) <http://www.npc.gov.cn/wxzl/wxzl/2001-01/02/content_3261.htm> accessed 1 March 2019.

1451 National People's Congress of the People's Republic of China, '中华人民共和国和吉尔吉斯共和国关于中吉国界的协定' (Agreement between the People's Republic of China and the Republic of Kyrgyzstan on the Sino-Kyrgyz Border) (adopted 4 July 1996, entered into force 30 April 1998) <http://www.npc.gov.cn/wxzl/wxzl/2000-12/06/content_3660.htm> accessed 1 March 2019.

1452 National People's Congress of the People's Republic of China, '中华人民共和国和塔吉克斯坦共和国关于中塔国界的协定' (Agreement between the People's Republic of China and the Republic of Tajikistan on the Sino-Tajik Bor-

most 1 % of its territory to the PRC. Tajik opposition politicians as well as Tajik and Russian analysts criticized the supposed trading of territory for Chinese investment and debt forgiveness.[1453]

Despite the fact that China and Vietnam are hotly contesting (part of) their maritime borderline as well as sovereignty over certain islands, they have already resolved disputes regarding their land border in 1999.[1454] The unresolved disputes about land borders, which are to be expounded in the next chapter, are those with India and Bhutan.

IV.3.1.2. Maritime Borders

The PRC's maritime borders remain largely unsettled. The country's territorial conflicts currently most fraught with tension revolve around demarcation in the South and East China Seas, which is why they are discussed in further detail by the Chinese scholarly community and shall also receive greater attention here. The other littoral states are South Korea, Japan, the Philippines, Malaysia, Brunei, Indonesia and Vietnam. There has also been some success in this area. Aside from the aforementioned treaty on their land border, China and Vietnam also concluded a treaty demarcating their territorial seas, 'Exclusive Economic Zones' (in the following: EEZ) and continental shelves in the Gulf of Tonkin (Chinese: *beibu wan* 北部湾, Vietnamese: *Vinh Bac Bo*, both meaning 'Northern Bay').[1455] Importantly,

---

der) (adopted 13 August 1999, entered into force 1 March 2000) <http://www.npc.gov.cn/wxzl/gongbao/2001-01/04/content_5008910.htm> accessed 1 March 2019.

1453 Alexander Sodiqov, 'Tajikistan Cedes Disputed Land to China' *Jamestown* (Washington DC, 24 January 2011) <http://www.jamestown.org/single/?tx_ttnews%5Btt_news%5D=37398&no_cache=1#.VaEc5a3tmko> accessed 30 March 2019.

1454 National People's Congress of the People's Republic of China, '中华人民共和国和越南社会主义共和国陆地边界条约' (Land Border Treaty between the People's Republic of China and the Socialist People's Republic of Vietnam) (adopted 30 December 1999, entered into force 29 April 2000) <http://www.npc.gov.cn/wxzl/gongbao/2000-12/17/content_5008962.htm> accessed 1 March 2019; Ramses Amer and Clive H Schofield, 'The Sino-Vietnamese Approach to Managing Border Disputes' (2002) 5 *Maritime Briefings* 29, 29–32.

1455 National People's Congress of the People's Republic of China, '中华人民共和国和越南社会主义共和国关于两国在北部湾领海、专属经济区和大陆架的划界协定' (Demarcation Agreement on Territorial Seas, Exclusive Economic Zones, and Continental Shelves in the Gulf of Tonkin between the People's Republic of China and the Socialist People's Republic of Vietnam) (adopted

this is only a partial agreement, Sino-Vietnamese disputes concerning sovereignty over Paracel and Spratly Islands as well as maritime borders in the wider South China Sea continue.

IV.3.2. Ongoing Territorial and Law of the Sea Disputes

IV.3.2.1. South China Sea – Of Rocks and Frontiers

IV.3.2.1.1. Background to the Dispute

Arguably the most complicated of the PRC's unresolved territorial disputes, the one that initially motivated this study and is to be mainly focused on in the following, is the South China Sea dispute(s).[1456] Multiple states are involved and their overlapping claims appear mostly irreconcilable.[1457] As they dispute both the sovereignty over a multitude of offshore features and the delimitation of maritime zones – depending on the sovereignty over these features and otherwise – the law of territorial acquisition and law of the sea are both strongly relevant.

However, first the countries involved already trade diplomatic barbs over geographical names. The Chinese have termed the waters to their south *nanhai* – 南海 (South Sea), the Vietnamese speak of the *Biên Dông* (East Sea), and the Philippine government, although the second name is a rather recent trend, call these waters *Dagat Luzon* or *Dagat Kanlurang Pilipinas* (Sea of Luzon / West Philippine Sea). The conflict involves five states – the PRC, Vietnam, the Philippines, Malaysia and Brunei – and one further claimant that is not a member of the UN and holds positions (mostly) identical to those of the PRC: Taiwan. Moreover, Indonesia holds a small

---

25 December 2000, entered into force 30 June 2004) <http://www.mfa.gov.cn/chn//pds/ziliao/tytj/t556665.htm> accessed 1 March 2019. The Gulf of Tonkin is a body of water between the coasts of Northern Vietnam and the Chinese provinces Guangxi, Guangdong and Hainan that is part of the South China Sea.

1456 As noted below, the different littoral states use different terms for the South China Sea and the various offshore features therein. For reasons of convenience, this book will employ the terms predominantly used in English language literature: South China Sea, Paracel Islands, Spratly Islands, and Scarborough Shoal.

1457 See eg Banyan, 'The South China Sea: Troubled Waters' *Economist* (London, 6 August 2012) <http://www.economist.com/blogs/analects/2012/08/south-china-sea> accessed 1 March 2019.

part of the South China Sea, regarding which it is not entirely clear whether there is a dispute with China – no other littoral state disputes Indonesia's position. As all pertinent states – except the PRC – are members of ASEAN, this regional organization also factors in importantly.

The littoral countries dispute sovereignty over several (groups of) offshore features, most prominently: 1) the Paracel Islands (Chinese: *xisha* – 西沙, Vietnamese: *Hoang Sa*), which are only disputed between the PRC and Vietnam;[1458] 2) the Spratly Islands (Chinese: nansha – 南沙, Vietnamese: Truong Sa, Tagalog: *Kapuluan ng Kalayaan*), which are disputed between all countries involved; and 3) Scarborough Shoal (Chinese: *huangyan dao* – 黄岩岛, Tagalog: *Bajo de Masinloc* or *Kulumpol ng Panatag*) which is only disputed between the PRC and the Philippines.

The disputed (groups of) features comprise a multitude of mostly very small 'islands', 'rocks' and low-tide elevations. Many of these features' nature is disputed. This is highly relevant as only fully-entitled 'islands' under Article 121 (1) United Nations Convention on the Law of the Sea (in the following: UNCLOS or 'the Convention') can have EEZs and continental shelves. Meanwhile, 'rocks' under Art 121 (3) UNCLOS, small features that are above water at high tide but 'cannot sustain human habitation or economic life of their own,' are only entitled to a narrow territorial sea.[1459] Where it is within the territorial sea of a coastal state's mainland or an island, a low-tide elevation can be used to measure the breadth of the pertinent territorial sea (Article 13 (1) UNCLOS). However, should it be located at a greater distance from a high-tide elevation, a low-tide elevation will not have a territorial sea of its own (Article 13 (2) UNCLOS).[1460]

All maritime zones listed above are measured from 'baselines' along land features' coasts. The low-water lines along the coast are to be used as 'normal baselines' (Article 5 UNCLOS).[1461] In certain cases, eg where the

---

1458 Michael Strupp, 'Paracel Archipelago' in Wolfrum R (ed), *Max Planck Encyclopedia of Public International Law – Volume VIII* (OUP 2012).

1459 Art 121 (1), (2) and (3) UNCLOS (n 394) – Art 121: '1. An island is a naturally formed area of land, surrounded by water, which is above water at high tide. 2. Except as provided for in paragraph 3, the territorial sea, the contiguous zone, the exclusive economic zone and the continental shelf of an island are determined in accordance with the provisions of this Convention applicable to other land territory. 3. Rocks which cannot sustain human habitation or economic life of their own shall have no exclusive economic zone or continental shelf.'.

1460 Art 13 (1) and (2) UNCLOS.

1461 Art 5 UNCLOS.

coastline is deeply indented, where there is a fringe of islands along the coast or the low-water line is highly unstable on account of a delta, 'straight baselines' may be drawn between appropriate fixed points (Article 7 UNCLOS).[1462] Another regime is applicable for archipelagic states, such that are 'constituted wholly by one or more archipelagos' (Article 46 (a) UNCLOS). An 'archipelago' under UNCLOS is a 'group of islands, including parts of islands, interconnecting waters and other natural features which are so closely interrelated that such islands, waters and other natural features form an intrinsic geographical, economic and political entity, or which historically have been regarded as such' (Article 46 (b) UNCLOS).[1463] Such states can use straight 'archipelagic baselines,' which join 'the outermost points of the outermost islands and drying reefs of the archipelago provided that within such baselines are included the main islands and an area in which the ratio of the area of the water to the area of the land, including atolls, is between 1 to 1 and 9 to 1' (Article 47 UNCLOS).[1464]

As for the extent and legal relevance of these maritime zones, the territorial sea only extends to twelve nautical miles from the baseline (Article 3 UNCLOS),[1465] and is covered by a coastal state's sovereignty 'subject to this Convention and to other rules of international law' (Article 2 UNCLOS).[1466] EEZs extend to 200 nautical miles from the 'baseline' (Article 57 UNCLOS), and entail – inter alia – sovereign rights to the exploitation of living and non-living natural resources in the waters superjacent to the seabed, seabed and subsoil within the zone (Article 56 UNCLOS).[1467] Continental shelves, which may not extend beyond 350 nautical miles (Article 76 (5) and (6) UNCLOS), are seabed and subsoil areas:

> that extend beyond its territorial sea throughout the natural prolongation of its land territory to the outer edge of the continental margin, or to a distance of 200 nautical miles from the baselines (…) where the outer edge of the continental margin does not extend up to that distance (Article 76 (1) UNCLOS).[1468]

1462 Art 7 UNCLOS.
1463 Art 46 UNCLOS.
1464 Art 47 UNCLOS.
1465 One nautical mile converts to 1.852 kilometers.
1466 Arts 2 and 3 UNCLOS.
1467 Arts 56 and 57 UNCLOS.
1468 Art 76 UNCLOS. A definition of 'continental margins' and further explanation of seabed topography can inter alia be found in Art 76 (3), (4) and (6).

They involve 'sovereign rights for the purpose of exploring [the continental shelf] and exploiting its natural resources' (Article 77 UNCLOS).[1469]

As for waters superjacent to the seabed, outside of any states' EEZ, they form the 'high seas' (Article 86 UNCLOS).[1470] The high seas are 'open to all States, whether coastal or land-locked' (Article 87 UNCLOS),[1471] who therein enjoy – inter alia – freedom of navigation, overflight, fishing, research, and such to construct artificial islands or lay cables and pipelines, in keeping with UNCLOS and other international law rules. Moreover, seabed and subsoil areas outside of any states' continental shelf, ie beyond any state's jurisdiction, form part of the 'Area' (Article 1 (1) UNCLOS).[1472] Resources within the 'Area' are viewed as 'common heritage of mankind' (Article 136 UNCLOS), and may only be exploited in line with UNCLOS norms, as well as the rules and procedures of the International Seabed Authority (Article 137 (2) UNCLOS).[1473]

All concerned offshore features in the South China Sea had been uninhabited until territorial disputes between the various listed states erupted after the Second World War. There were violent clashes between the PRC and Vietnam in 1974 and 1988, and between the PRC and the Philippines in 1995.[1474] All parties eventually started to develop the 'islands' and 'rocks' in their possession to strengthen their respective positions in potential future confrontations, negotiations or legal proceedings. They constructed weather-, radio- and research stations, as well as small military bases and runways, lighthouses and barracks for soldiers, personnel and fishermen.[1475] At present, China controls the entirety of the Paracel Islands. In the Spratly Islands group, China, Vietnam, the Philippines, Malaysia, and Taiwan all occupy certain features. While there has so far been no construction work on Scarborough Shoal, the Chinese side took control of it after a series of incidents involving fishing boats and coast guard vessels in 2012.[1476]

1469 Art 77 UNCLOS.

1470 Art 86 UNCLOS.

1471 Art 87 UNCLOS.

1472 Art 1 (1) UNCLOS.

1473 Arts 136 and 137 UNCLOS.

1474 Strupp, 'Paracel Archipelago' (n 1458) 52; Michael Strupp, 'Spratly Islands' in Rüdiger Wolfrum (ed), *Max Planck Encyclopedia of Public International Law – Volume IX* (OUP 2012) 449.

1475 Strupp, 'Spratly Islands' (n 1474) 449–450.

1476 CSIS – Asia Maritime Transparency Initiative, 'Occupation and Island Building' (Washington DC) <https://amti.csis.org/island-tracker/> accessed 9

The question of whether the pertinent features are to be judged as 'low-tide elevations' also decides whether the law of territorial acquisition comes into play, because such features are not open to appropriation and 'treated, in effect, as part of the seabed'.[1477]

Nonetheless, the law of the sea will be relevant in any case. Therein, the central document is the aforementioned UNCLOS, which was concluded in 1982 and came into force in 1994.[1478] All above-listed littoral states have ratified it – Philippines (1984), Vietnam (1994), Malaysia, Brunei and PRC (1996).[1479] It is thus instructive to review how UNCLOS deals with overlapping claims to maritime zones.

Article 15 UNCLOS on territorial sea delimitation includes references to 'equidistance' as well as 'special circumstances' (including historic title) that may lead to modifications. Articles 74 and 83 UNCLOS on EEZ and continental shelf delimitation call for agreements geared towards achieving 'equitable solutions',[1480] while leaving open the question of criteria and method to be applied.

A rich body of case law developed on the issue.[1481] An emphasis on equitability for continental shelf delimitation could be found pre-UNCLOS in

---

November 2019, where photographic evidence of all Claimants' land reclamation and construction activity in the South China Sea is presented; Geoff Dyer and Demetri Sevastopolu, 'US strategists face dilemma over Beijing claim in South China Sea' *Reuters* (Washington DC and Hong Kong, 9 July 2014) <https://www.ft.com/content/b2176dea-0732-11e4-81c6-00144feab7de> accessed 9 November 2019.

1477 Art 13 UNCLOS. See also Clive Symmons, 'Article 13 – Low-tide elevations' in Alexander Proelss (ed), *United Nations Convention on the Law of the Sea – A Commentary* (CH Beck 2017) 134; *The South China Sea Arbitration* (Award) (n 196) para 309; *Territorial and Maritime Dispute (Nicaragua v Colombia)* (Judgment) [2012] ICJ Rep 624, [641] para 26 ('*Territorial and Maritime Dispute (Nicaragua v Colombia)* (Judgment)').

1478 UNCLOS.

1479 United Nations Division for Ocean Affairs and the Law of the Sea, 'Chronological lists of ratifications of, accessions and successions to the Convention and the related Agreements' <http://www.un.org/depts/los/reference_files/chronological_lists_of_ratifications.htm> accessed 1 March 2019. All parties to the South China Sea dispute have, moreover, ratified the Agreement relating to the implementation of Part XI of the United Nations Convention on the Law of the Sea of 10 December 1982 (with annex) (adopted 28 July 1994, entered into force 28 July 1996) 1836 UNTS 41 ('1994 Implementation Agreement').

1480 Arts 15, 74 (1) and 83 (1) UNCLOS.

1481 See also Malcolm D Evans, 'Maritime Boundary Delimitation' in Donald R Rothwell and others (eds), *The Oxford Handbook of the Law of the Sea* (OUP 2015) 256–261; Shunji Yanai, 'International Law Concerning Maritime

the *North Sea Continental Shelf* cases,[1482] and around the adoption of UNCLOS in *Tunisia v Libya*, *Gulf of Maine* and *Libya v Malta*.[1483] Ensuing cases have also confirmed that in getting to an equitable solution, equidistance as a starting point then modified due to special circumstances is part of customary international law; for delimitations of territorial seas,[1484] continental shelves, EEZs and regarding single delimitation lines.[1485]

The ICJ and ITLOS developed a 'three-stage'-delimitation methodology.[1486] Equidistance was to deliver a 'provisional line,' which was to be adjusted in case there were 'factors calling for' it to achieve an equitable result.[1487] Finally, the resulting line was to be reviewed again as to whether it led to an 'inequitable result' due to 'marked disproportion between the ratio of the respective coastal lengths and the ratio between the relevant maritime area of each State by reference to the delimitation line'.[1488] However, judges maintained that the 'three-stage test' was only 'usually' to be em-

Boundary Delimitation', in David Joseph Attard, Malgosia Fitzmaurice and Norman A Martínez Guttiérez (eds), *The IMLI Manual on International Maritime Law – Volume I: The Law of the Sea* (OUP 2014) 313–316.

1482 *North Sea Continental Shelf (Federal Republic of Germany v Denmark; Federal Republic of Germany v The Netherlands)* (Judgment) [1969] ICJ Rep 3, [54] para 101.

1483 *Continental Shelf (Tunisia v Libyan Arab Jamahiriya)* (Judgment) [1982] ICJ Rep 18; *Delimitation of the Maritime Boundary in the Gulf of Maine Area (Canada v United States of America)* (Judgment) [1984] ICJ Rep 246; *Continental Shelf (Libyan Arab Jamahiriya v Malta)* (Judgment) [1985] ICJ Rep 13.

1484 *Territorial and Maritime Dispute between Nicaragua and Honduras in the Caribbean Sea (Nicaragua v Honduras)* (Judgment) [2007] ICJ Rep 659, [720 et seq] paras 262–298.

1485 *Arbitration between Guyana and Suriname* (2007) 30 RIAA 1, [376] – [392]; *Maritime Delimitation in the Black Sea (Romania v Ukraine)* (Judgment) [2009] ICJ Rep 61, [116]; *Territorial and Maritime Dispute (Nicaragua v Colombia)* (Judgment) (n 1477) [139]; *Maritime Dispute* (Peru v Chile) (Judgment) [2014] ICJ Rep 3, [179].

1486 *Maritime Delimitation in the Black Sea (Romania v Ukraine)* (n 1485); *Delimitation of the Maritime Boundary in the Bay of Bengal* (Bangladesh v Myanmar) (Judgment) [2012] ITLOS Rep 4; *Territorial and Maritime Dispute (Nicaragua v Colombia)* (Judgment) (n 1477).

1487 *Maritime Delimitation in the Black Sea (Romania v Ukraine)* (n 1485) [116], [120].

1488 *Maritime Delimitation in the Black Sea (Romania v Ukraine)* (n 1485) [122]. See also *Delimitation of the Maritime Boundary in the Bay of Bengal* (Bangladesh v Myanmar) (n 1486) [477] – [499].

ployed where there were no 'compelling reasons preventing that' (see *Peru v Chile*),[1489] and not in 'mechanical fashion' (see *Nicaragua v Colombia*).[1490]

Among 'special circumstances' that may impact delimitation, tribunals have mainly identified 1) the length or shape of coastlines (eg *Continental Shelf (Libya v Malta)*,[1491] 2) the existence of offshore features (eg *Eritrea v Yemen (Phase Two: Maritime Delimitation)*),[1492] and 3) possible encroachment on the natural prolongation of other coast lines restricting maritime projection (such as enclosing islands) (eg *Delimitation of Maritime Areas between St. Pierre et Miquelon (Canada v France)*).[1493]

Should contracting parties be in disagreement regarding such delimitation (or other issues of UNCLOS interpretation or application), they are to turn to Chapter XV UNCLOS for rules on dispute settlement. The underlying principle is to solve all disputes by peaceful means in line with Article 2 (3) UN Charter (Article 279 UNCLOS).[1494] The corresponding means are those listed in Article 33 UN Charter, ie negotiation, enquiry, mediation, conciliation, arbitration, judicial settlement, resorting to regional agencies or arrangements, or other peaceful means of the parties' own choice. In case of parties' failure to resolve the dispute, Section 2 Chapter XV provides for compulsory procedures entailing binding decisions.[1495]

IV.3.2.1.2. Significance and Limits of Jurisdiction

The ratification of UNCLOS in 1996 signified the first time the PRC accepted international adjudication outside the economic realm, and thus a momentous step towards engagement. The Chinese government was still issuing reservations to ICJ jurisdiction in every pertinent treaty, and had only rather recently ended rhetorical vilification of international courts. However, at this point, Beijing was ready to ratify a treaty that included

---

1489 *Maritime Dispute* (Peru v Chile) (n 1485) [180].

1490 *Territorial and Maritime Dispute (Nicaragua v Colombia)* (Judgment) (n 1477) [194].

1491 *Continental Shelf (Libyan Arab Jamahiriya v Malta)* (n 1483) [5], para 79.

1492 *Award of the Arbitral Tribunal in the second stage of the proceedings between Eritrea and Yemen (Maritime Delimitation) (Eritrea v Yemen)* (1999) 22 RIAA 335, [337] ('*Eritrea v Yemen (second stage)*').

1493 *Delimitation of Maritime Areas between St. Pierre et Miquelon (Canada v France)* (Award) (1992) 21 RIAA 265, [341] para 66.

1494 UN Charter; Art 279 UNCLOS.

1495 Arts 279, 286 UNCLOS; Art 33 UN Charter.

compulsory dispute resolution methods, which could not entirely be excluded through reservations. Still, the significance of the PRC's agreement to such compulsory procedures has to be qualified to a certain degree, due to the way in which it happened and the nature of UNCLOS' dispute settlement.

First, on UNCLOS' dispute settlement, it is relevant that parties may choose among several different dispute resolution mechanisms: the ICJ, ITLOS, arbitration under Annex VII UNCLOS, and arbitration under Annex VIII UNCLOS (Article 287 UNCLOS).[1496] They may issue a corresponding declaration when signing the Convention, when ratifying it or at any later point in time. Second, the applicability of Section 2 Chapter XV on compulsory dispute settlement is limited to certain cases (Article 297 UNCLOS).[1497] Third, states may issue declarations under Articles 298 UNCLOS that further limit compulsory procedures, by excluding issues such as questions of maritime delimitation according to Articles 15, 74 and 83 (Article 298 (1) (a) (i) UNCLOS).[1498]

In the case of the PRC, it added an explanatory declaration upon ratification, highlighting that it would pursue an 'equitable solution' to all its territorial disputes via bilateral negotiations based on international law, instead of availing itself of international adjudication. Additionally, it referenced its claim to the offshore land features in the South China Sea, and its claim that they constitute archipelagos. The full text of the PRC's statement reads:

> In accordance with the decision of the Standing Committee of the Eighth National People's Congress of the People's Republic of China at its nineteenth session, the President of the People's Republic of China has hereby ratified the United Nations Convention on the Law of the Sea of 10 December 1982 and at the same time made the following statement:

1496 Art 287, Annexes VII and VIII UNCLOS.

1497 Art 297 UNCLOS.

1498 Art 298 (1) (a) (i) UNCLOS – '1. When signing, ratifying or acceding to this Convention or at any time thereafter, a State may, without prejudice to the obligations arising under section 1, declare in writing that it does not accept any one or more of the procedures provided for in section 2 with respect to one or more of the following categories of disputes:
(a) (i) disputes concerning the interpretation or application of articles 15, 74 and 83 relating to sea boundary delimitations, or those involving historic bays or titles [...]'.

1. In accordance with the provisions of the United Nations Convention on the Law of the Sea, the People's Republic of China shall enjoy sovereign rights and jurisdiction over an exclusive economic zone of 200 nautical miles and the continental shelf.
2. The People's Republic of China will effect, through consultations, the delimitation of the boundary of the maritime jurisdiction with the States with coasts opposite or adjacent to China respectively on the basis of international law and in accordance with the principle of equitability.
3. The People's Republic of China reaffirms its sovereignty over all its archipelagos and islands as listed in article 2 of the Law of the People's Republic of China on the territorial sea and the contiguous zone, which was promulgated on 25 February 1992.
4. The People's Republic of China reaffirms that the provisions of the United Nations Convention on the Law of the Sea concerning innocent passage through the territorial sea shall not prejudice the right of a coastal State to request, in accordance with its laws and regulations, a foreign State to obtain advance approval from or give prior notification to the coastal State for the passage of its warships through the territorial sea of the coastal State.[1499]

Additionally – and more importantly – China exploited every option to limit Section 2 Part XV UNCLOS-applicability provided for in Article 298, with its declaration of 25 August 2006:

> The Government of the People's Republic of China does not accept any of the procedures provided for in Section 2 of Part XV of the Convention with respect to all the categories of disputes referred to in paragraph 1 (a) (b) and (c) of Article 298 of the Convention.[1500]

The 'categories of disputes' listed in the referenced Article 298 UNCLOS are – inter alia – such 'relating to sea boundary delimitations, or those involving historic bays or titles,' 'any dispute that necessarily involves the concurrent consideration of any unsettled dispute concerning sovereignty or other rights over continental or insular land territory,' and 'disputes concerning military activities (…) and disputes concerning law enforcement activities in regard to the exercise of sovereign rights or jurisdiction

1499 United Nations Division for Ocean Affairs and the Law of the Sea, 'UNCLOS Declarations' (n 496).

1500 Ibid.

excluded from the jurisdiction of a court or tribunal under article 297, paragraph 2 or 3'.[1501]

The Chinese government was convinced at the time that these exceptions to jurisdiction would suffice to avoid any compulsory dispute settlement proceedings that could reduce the possible scope of China's claims, most importantly in the South China Sea. It considered that any dispute about rights or infringement thereof in the South China Sea, would involve sovereignty questions regarding offshore land features, the delimitation of maritime zones (partly building on sovereignty over islands), or would involve China's claim to 'historic rights' in South China Sea waters.[1502] This is to say that the PRC did not want to submit to international adjudication under the law of the sea as broadly as UNCLOS allows, and to a degree that it still considered would intolerably impinge upon its sovereignty.

Of the other countries involved in the South China Sea conflict, only Brunei did not issue a declaration upon UNCLOS signature or ratification. The Philippines, Vietnam and Malaysia all did so. The Philippines – inter alia – emphasized its sovereignty over offshore features in the South China Sea, which it groups under the term 'Kalayaan Islands,' as well as the treaty law underlying its sovereign rights as successor to the US. Manila did not exclude any types of disputes under Article 298 UNCLOS, but merely declared that submitting to peaceful resolution through any UNCLOS procedures was not to be taken as a derogation of its sovereignty.[1503]

The government of Vietnam also underlined its sovereignty over South China Sea offshore features, which it terms the 'Hoang Sa and Truong Sa archipelagoes,' and voiced a preference for resolving South China Sea-related disputes through negotiations while maintaining stability and the status quo on the ground during the process. Hanoi also did not avail itself of Article 298 UNCLOS.[1504]

Malaysia, once again not excluding any types of disputes under Article 298 UNCLOS, – inter alia – declared its preference for an equidistance or median line-approach in maritime boundary delimitation, and a single

1501 Art 298 (1) UNCLOS.

1502 See Chapter IV.3.4 for an in-depth discussion of China's pertinent positions.

1503 United Nations Division for Ocean Affairs and the Law of the Sea, 'UNCLOS Declarations' (n 496).

1504 Ibid.

maritime border for EEZ and continental shelf should relevant areas not extend further than 200 nautical miles from the baseline.[1505]

In sum, all countries involved with the exception of Brunei issued declarations upon signature or ratification of UNCLOS. However, only China excluded certain types of dispute resolution. By contrast, the other states mainly reiterated sovereignty claims to offshore features in the South China Sea and pertinent legal arguments, but appeared to have placed greater faith in UNCLOS' dispute settlement.

IV.3.2.1.3. Respective Claims and Legal Steps Taken

Only the Philippines has initiated pertinent proceedings, *Philippines v China*,[1506] and there made known its official positions. China chose to not participate in that case, and merely released a position paper and sent diplomatic notes. It outlined some positions while making clear that its statements should not be construed as accepting the jurisdiction of the arbitral tribunal in *Philippines v China*.[1507] Other littoral states were involved partly through observers sent to the tribunal, partly by receiving documents from the tribunal informing them about the proceedings, but did not join the proceedings.[1508] The following rough categorization of complainant types therefore additionally draws on diplomatic statements as well as prevalent discourse among respective international law communities. Positions will only be briefly sketched to give an impression of the dispute's intricacy, while the respective validity of claims will not be judged.

Concerning their respective claims, the parties can be located on a scale from emphasizing the law of territorial acquisition to emphasizing the law of the sea. Those employing the law of territorial acquisition in the South

1505 Ibid.

1506 *The South China Sea Arbitration (The Republic of Philippines v The People's Republic of China)* (Award on Jurisdiction and Admissibility) (2015) 170 ILR 1 ('*The South China Sea Arbitration* (Award on Jurisdiction and Admissibility) (n 1506)'); *The South China Sea Arbitration* (Award) (n 196).

1507 Ministry of Foreign Affairs of the People's Republic of China, 'Position Paper of the Government of the People's Republic of China on the Matter of Jurisdiction in the South China Sea Arbitration Initiated by the Republic of the Philippines' (Beijing, 7 December 2014) <http://www.fmprc.gov.cn/mfa_eng/zxxx_662805/t1217147.shtml> accessed 1 March 2019 ('PRC Position Paper on the South China Sea').

1508 See Chapter IV.3.4.

China Sea draw on several types of title: discovery and occupation of *terra nullius*, effective administrative exercise of jurisdiction (*effectivités*), and cession through treaty law.[1509]

The PRC is clearly on the former end of the scale. The Chinese government claims discovery and occupation of all offshore features within the so-called 'nine-dash line', encompassing almost the entire South China Sea, as well as hundreds or even thousands of years of various forms of commercial use and related administrative action (eg mapping, naming, subsuming under higher-level administrative units, visits by officials).[1510] The nine-dash line has been marked on official Chinese maps since the 1940s and is also used to claim 'historic rights' to all waters circumscribed by it.[1511] At the same time, but in a rather secondary role, China has drawn on various treaties, such as the *Convention Concerning the Delimitation of the Border Between China and Tonkin* (1887)[1512] and the *Treaty of Peace Between the Republic of China and Japan* (1952), to bolster its claim to sovereignty over respective land features.[1513]

For its maritime claims, China does, although its position is not entirely clear, likely build on the assessment that 1) groups of offshore land features, including the Paracels and Spratlys, form 'archipelagos' under Article 46 UNCLOS, around which straight baselines can be drawn and territorial seas, EEZs and continental shelves claimed, which is connected to

---

1509 See inter alia PRC Position Paper on the South China Sea (n 1507) para 4; *The South China Sea Arbitration (The Republic of Philippines v The People's Republic of China)*, PCA Case No 2013–19, Memorial of the Philippines – Volume I (30 March 2014) paras 3.3, 5.99, 6.55 ('*The South China Sea Arbitration* (Philippines Memorial – Volume I)'); Hong Thao Nguyen, 'Vietnam's Position on the Sovereignty over the Paracels & the Spratlys: Its Maritime Claims' (2012) 1 *Journal of East Asia and International Law* 165, 186–187.

1510 Strupp, 'Paracel Archipelago' (n 1458) 50–52; Strupp, 'Spratly Islands' (n 1474) 449–450; PRC Position Paper on the South China Sea (n 1507) para 4.

1511 See Chapter IV.3.4.

1512 This treaty was concluded between Imperial China and France in order to delimit French Indochina's borders with China. *Convention relative à la délimitation de la frontière entre la Chine et le Tonkin, Signée à Pékin la 26 juin 1887*, in *Treaties between China and Foreign States* (by order of the Inspector General of Customs, vol 1, Shanghai 1908) 721–724.

1513 *Treaty of Peace* (adopted 28 April 1952, entered into force 5 August 1952) 138 UNTS 3 ('Treaty of Peace Between the Republic of China and Japan'). See also Ministry of Foreign Affairs of the People's Republic of China, 'International Recognition Of China's Sovereignty over the Nansha Islands' (Beijing, 17 November 2000) <http://www.fmprc.gov.cn/mfa_eng/topics_665678/3754_666060/t19232.shtml> accessed 1 March 2019.

the assessment that 2) at least some of the offshore features are 'islands' entitled to a full set of maritime zones under Article 121 (1) UNCLOS.[1514] However, it also claims the respective waters as 'historic waters', and until recently did not prioritize geographical claims under UNCLOS.[1515]

Discovery, occupation and ensuing centuries of commercial and administrative activity are also invoked by Vietnam, ie title through occupation and *effectivités*. Nonetheless, the Vietnamese government focuses on the 19th and 20th centuries, positing that French Indochina's occupation of several features should now benefit its legal successor Vietnam. The Vietnamese government also makes rather secondary use of treaty law, where it invokes the *Treaty of Peace with Japan* (*San Francisco Peace Treaty*). The Vietnamese claim, although much less comprehensive than that of the PRC, is the second most extensive, encompassing the entirety of the Paracel and Spratly Islands.[1516]

For its maritime claims, Vietnam mostly builds on geographic proximity to its mainland coast and natural prolongation as arguments under the law of the sea, instead of relying on 'historic rights'. This is most clearly illustrated by its joint submission with Malaysia to the *Commission on the Limits of the Continental Shelf* (hereinafter: CLCS or 'the Commission') under Article 76 (8) UNCLOS.[1517] The CLCS was set up under Annex II UNCLOS. States claiming a continental shelf of more than 200 nautical miles from

---

1514 See Chapter IV.3.4.4.2; Arts 7, 46 (b), 121 (1) UNCLOS. See also Xianhe (Sienho) Yi (Yee), 'The South China Sea Arbitration Decisions on Jurisdiction and Rule of Law Concerns' (2016) 15 CJIL 219, 225.

1515 See also Ying 莹 Yao 姚, 2014 年孟加拉国与印度孟加拉湾划界案评述 ——— 兼论对中菲南海仲裁案的启示 (Comments on the 2014 Bangladesh v India Bay of Bengal border delimitation case – On inspiration for the China v Philippines South China Sea arbitration) (2015) 29 (4) *Dangdai Faxue* 149, 159; Anthony Carty and Fozia Nazir Lone, 'Some New Haven International Law Reflections on China, India and Their Various Territorial Disputes' (2011) 19 *Asia Pacific Law Review* 95, 98.

1516 *Treaty of Peace with Japan* (adopted 8 September 1951, entered into force 28 April 1952) 136 UNTS 45 ('San Francisco Peace Treaty'); Consulate of the Socialist Republic of Viet Nam in New York, 'Position Paper on the Sovereignty of Viet Nam over the Hoang Sa Archipelago' (New York, 7 July 2014) <http://vietnamconsulate-ny.org/news/2014/07/position-paper-sovereignty-viet-nam-over-hoang-sa-archipelago> accessed 1 March 2019. See also Strupp, 'Paracel Archipelago' (n 1458) 51–52; Carty and Lone (n 1515) 98–99.

1517 Receipt of the joint submission made by Malaysia and the Socialist Republic of Viet Nam to the Commission on the Limits of the Continental Shelf (7 May 2009) CLCS. 33.2009.LOS ('Joint Submission by Malaysia and Vietnam to the CLCS'); Art 76 (8) UNCLOS.

their baselines shall submit such claims to the Commission. The Commission will then make recommendations on the outer limits of the coastal state's continental shelf, and the state's delimitation following such recommendations will be binding. The goal is to satisfy 'equitable geographical representation'.[1518]

The Philippines asserts title to offshore features through occupation and *effectivités* by former Spanish colonial authorities, cession to US colonial authorities – via the *Treaty of Peace Between the United States and Spain* (1898), the *Treaty Between the Kingdom of Spain and the United States of America for Cession of Outlying Islands of the Philippines* (1900), and the *San Francisco Peace Treaty* – and succession to pertinent US sovereign rights by the Philippines at the latter's independence.[1519] Maritime claims rely on UNCLOS EEZ and continental shelf provisions, not 'historic rights.' UNCLOS maritime zones are seen to be extending mostly unencumbered from the Philippine mainland, as South China Sea land features are assessed as either low-tide elevations appertaining to the seabed or 'rocks' with only a twelve nautical mile territorial sea. The pertinent arbitration against China on various UNCLOS matters will be discussed at length in the following.[1520]

For the Malaysian government, no other state has acquired sovereignty over any offshore features within its claimed area in the South China Sea, regardless which state occupies them, if any. The clear emphasis is on maritime claims under UNCLOS, as with its Article 76 (8) UNCLOS joint sub-

---

1518 Annex II UNCLOS; United Nations Division for Ocean Affairs and the Law of the Sea, 'Commission on the Limits of the Continental Shelf (CLCS) – Purpose, functions and sessions' <http://www.un.org/depts/los/clcs_new/commission_purpose.htm> accessed 21 November 2018. See also Myron H Nordquist and others (eds), *United Nations Convention on the Law of the Sea – A Commentary – Volume II: Articles 1 to 85, Annexes I and II, Final Act, Annex II* (Martinus Nijhoff Publishers 1993) 882.

1519 *The South China Sea Arbitration* (Philippines Memorial – Volume I) (n 1509) paras 2.28, 2.33, 2.35 – 2.37, Annex LA-69 (*Treaty of Peace Between the United States and the Kingdom of Spain (Treaty of Paris)* (adopted 10 December 1898, entered into force 11 April 1899) Art III MP, Vol XI), Annex LA-70 (*Treaty Between the United States of America and the Kingdom of Spain for the Cession to the United States of Any and All Islands of the Philippine Archipelago Lying Outside of the Lines Described in Article III of the Treaty of Peace of December 10, 1898 (Treaty of Washington)* (adopted 7 November 1900) MP, Vol XI); San Francisco Peace Treaty (n 1516).

1520 See Chapter IV.3.4.

mission with Vietnam on the limits of their continental shelves.[1521] Brunei also claims an EEZ and continental shelf that overlap with other littoral states' claims, while at least one high-tide feature, Louisa Reef, falls within that area. Official pronouncements have been contradictory as to whether Brunei's government claims sovereignty over the feature.[1522]

All other constellations aside, it shall suffice here to clarify that all other littoral states' claims conflict with the Chinese position. Together with all other member states of the *Association of South East Asian Nations* (hereinafter: ASEAN),[1523] the South-East Asian littoral states signed a joint *Declaration on the Conduct of Parties in the South China Sea* with the PRC in 2002, wherein all parties agreed that they should resolve their conflicts through peaceful negotiations in accordance with UNCLOS, to exercise general restraint, to refrain from complicating the disputes – inter alia – by inhabiting as of then uninhabited land features, and to work towards the adoption of a binding 'code of conduct'.[1524]

In terms of the question of an actual resolution to the multi-faceted dispute, the Chinese government has exclusively relied on bilateral negotiations. Moreover, it has declared its readiness for joint development of disputed areas until a permanent resolution can be achieved.[1525] The other countries involved consider bilateral negotiations inevitably lop-sided and

1521 Joint Submission by Malaysia and Vietnam to the CLCS (n 1517); Carty and Lone (n 1515) 99.

1522 National Bureau of Asian Research – Maritime Awareness Project, 'Brunei' (Seattle, 2019) <http://maritimeawarenessproject.org/profiles/brunei/> accessed 1 March 2019; Carty and Lone (n 1515) 99.

1523 Asean.org, 'The ASEAN Declaration (adopted 8 August 1967)' <http://asean.org/the-asean-declaration-bangkok-declaration-bangkok-8-august-1967/> accessed 1 March 2019; *Agreement on the Establishment of the ASEAN Secretariat* (adopted 24 February 1976, entered into force 21 May 1976) 1331 UNTS 243.

1524 Asean.org, 'Declaration on the Conduct of Parties in the South China Sea (adopted by the Foreign Ministers of ASEAN and the People's Republic of China at the 8th ASEAN Summit in Phnom Penh, Cambodia on 4 November 2002, no binding force)' <http://asean.org/?static_post=declaration-on-the-conduct-of-parties-in-the-south-china-sea-2> accessed 28 July 2017 ('*Declaration on the Conduct of Parties in the South China Sea*').

1525 Ministry of Foreign Affairs of the People's Republic of China, 'China Adheres to the Position of Settling Through Negotiation the Relevant Disputes Between China and the Philippines in the South China Sea' (Beijing, 13 July 2016) <https://www.fmprc.gov.cn/nanhai/eng/snhwtlcwj_1/t1380615.htm> accessed 10 November 2019.

instead propose multilateral negotiations (eg using the ASEAN framework) or international adjudication or arbitration.[1526]

Malaysia and Vietnam have taken action in the form of the aforementioned May 2009 joint (partial) submission to the CLCS –[1527] informing the CLCS of their views regarding the extent of their respective outer continental shelves beyond 200 nautical miles from the respective baselines in the southern part of the South China Sea. They did explicitly not prejudice future delimitation between their two countries, but defined a limited area under dispute. However, the Commission may not consider submissions where there are maritime disputes with other states,[1528] which was highlighted by the PRC.

The Philippines has also taken action with its own (partial) submission to the CLCS, as well as the filing of an UNCLOS arbitration case, *Philippines v China*, which will be discussed in the following.[1529] Malaysia, Vietnam and the Philippines have already reached agreements on continental shelf or EEZ delimitation with Indonesia.[1530]

1526 Euan Graham, 'The bolt from The Hague' *The Interpreter* (Sydney, 13 July 2016) <https://www.lowyinstitute.org/the-interpreter/debate/south-china-sea-ruling> accessed 10 November 2019.

1527 See Chapter IV.3.3.2 for a more detailed discussion.

1528 Para 5 (a) Annex I *Rules of Procedure of the Commission on the Limits of the Continental Shelf* (distributed 17 April 2008) CLCS/40/Rev.1 ('CLCS Rules of Procedure').

1529 See Chapter IV.3.4; Receipt of the submission made by the Republic of the Philippines to the Commission on the Limits of the Continental Shelf (21 April 2009) CLCS. 22.2009.LOS ('Submission by the Philippines to the CLCS').

1530 *Agreement between the Government of Malaysia and the Government of the Republic of Indonesia on the Delimitation of the Continental Shelf between the Two Countries* (adopted 27 October 1969, entered into force 7 November 1969), US Department of State, 'International Boundary Study, Series A, Limits in the Seas, No 1' (21 January 1970); *Agreement between the Government of the Socialist Republic of Vietnam and the Government of the Republic of Indonesia concerning the delimitation of the continental shelf boundary* (adopted 26 June 2003, entered into force 29 May 2007) 2457 UNTS 155; Official Gazette of the Republic of the Philippines, *Agreement between the Government of the Republic of the Philippines and the Government of the Republic of Indonesia Concerning the Delimitation of the Exclusive Economic Zone Boundary* (adopted 23 May 2014) <http://www.officialgazette.gov.ph/2014/05/23/agreement-between-the-government-of-the-republic-of-the-philippines-and-the-government-of-the-republic-indonesia-concerning-the-delimitation-of-the-exclusive-economic-zone-boundary/> accessed 1 March 2019.

IV.3.2.2. East China Sea – Same, Same, But Different

The East China Sea Dispute again involves both the law on territorial acquisition and the law of the sea. First, both China and Japan claim sovereignty over a group of offshore features – once again the nature of some of these features under UNCLOS is disputed – which they call *diaoyu dao* (钓鱼岛) (Diaoyu Islands) or *senkaku-shoto* (尖閣諸島) (Senkaku Islands), respectively.[1531]

The Chinese government claims sovereignty on account of discovery, occupation and *effectivités*, arguing that these islands were ceded to Japan together with Taiwan under the coerced 'unequal' *Treaty of Shimonoseki* (1895), which ended the First Sino-Japanese War. After the Second World War, Japan would supposedly have had to return the islands to China together with Taiwan according to its obligations under the *San Francisco Peace Treaty* and *Treaty of Peace Between the Republic of China and Japan* (1952).[1532]

However, the US took control of the Senkaku/Diaoyu Islands and administered them together with Okinawa until 1971, when it handed them to Japan. The latter claims that these offshore features were *terra nullius* when occupied by Japan in 1895, purportedly ahead of and not connected to the signing of the *Treaty of Shimonoseki*. Thereafter, it is maintained that Japan exercised effective control, did not include the island group in the territory to be ceded under the aforementioned post-war treaties, and did not receive any Chinese protests up until the 1970s.[1533]

1531 In this case, the parties do not dispute the name of the body of water in question, though. The Chinese, Japanese and Korean governments all use the term 'East China Sea'. In English, there is no clear dominant terminology for the island group that will thus be termed 'Senkaku/Diaoyu Islands' in this book.

1532 *Treaties between China and Foreign States* (2nd edn by order of the Inspector General of Customs, vol 2, Shanghai 1917) 590–596; San Francisco Peace Treaty (n 1516); Treaty of Peace Between the Republic of China and Japan (n 1464); State Council Information Office of the People's Republic of China, 'Diaoyu Dao, an Inherent Territory of China' (Beijing, 26 September 2012) <http://www.fmprc.gov.cn/mfa_eng/topics_665678/diaodao_665718/t973774.shtml> accesssed 1 March 2019.

1533 Ministry of Foreign Affairs of Japan, 'Senkaku Islands Q&A' (Tokyo, 13 April 2016) <http://www.mofa.go.jp/region/asia-paci/senkaku/qa_1010.html#q1> accessed 1 March 2019; *Treaties between China and Foreign States* (2nd edn by order of the Inspector General of Customs, vol 2, Shanghai 1917) 590–596. See

Mirroring the situation regarding the Paracel Islands in the South China Sea, one party controls the entire island group and negates that there even is a dispute to adjudicate. However, in this case it is not the Chinese side but Japan.[1534]

The respective claims to EEZs and continental shelves of the PRC, Japan and South Korea overlap.[1535] Regarding its continental shelf in the East China Sea, the Chinese government has made a (partial) submission to the CLCS in December 2012, without prejudicing future maritime delimitation.[1536] It interprets geomorphologic and geological features as supporting a Chinese claim to natural prolongation up to the Okinawa Trough as a natural cut-off, which should be taken into account in reaching an equitable delimitation.[1537] This would mean that almost the entire seabed and subsoil of the East China Sea would be granted to the PRC. The only comparable situation to that of the East China Sea and the Okinawa Trough would be that of Australia and Indonesia regarding the Timor Trough. They negotiated a delimitation wherein Australia's continental shelf extends to a point already well under Indonesia's EEZ – ie there are two separate maritime borders for the water superjacent to the seabed on the one hand and the seabed and subsoil on the other.[1538]

Japan responded by underlining the necessity to reach an agreement on delimitation under Article 83 UNCLOS, and the impossibility of unilateral

---

also Masahiko Asada, 'Diaoyu/Senkaku Islands' in Rüdiger Wolfrum (ed), *Max Planck Encyclopedia of Public International Law – Volume III* (OUP 2012) 90–91.

1534 China controls the Paracels and wants to ignore Vietnam's claim. Japan controls the Senkaku/Diaoyu Islands and wants to ignore China's claim. Moreover, South Korea controls Dokdo/Takeshima Island in the Sea of Japan and wants to ignore Japan's claim. All of these features had been uninhabited until disputes led some of those in control of features to start construction work to bolster their claims.

1535 See eg The Economist, 'China, Japan and Taiwan: Profit over Patriotism – A new geographical discovery in Asia: a "sea of peace and co-operation"' (London, 19 June 2008) <http://www.economist.com/node/11591458> accessed 1 March 2019.

1536 See Chapter IV.3.3.2 for a discussion of this CLCS submission.

1537 Receipt of the submission made by the People's Republic of China to the Commission on the Limits of the Continental Shelf (14 December 2012) CLCS. 63.2012.LOS ('Submission by the PRC to the CLCS').

1538 *Treaty between the Government of Australia and the Government of the Republic of Indonesia establishing an Exclusive Economic Zone Boundary and Certain Seabed Boundaries* (adopted 14 March 1997) 1997 ATNIF 4. See also Deniz Tas, 'Oil and Gas in the East China Sea: maritime boundaries, joint development and the rule of capture' [2011] (2) *International Energy Law Review* 48, 54.

delimitation of the outer limits of one state's continental shelf where the distance between two states' opposite coasts is less than 400 nautical miles, because delimitation may not be prejudiced.[1539] Accordingly, as China did in the case of the Malaysian-Vietnamese joint submission, Japan asked the Commission to not consider the Chinese submission on account of an existing dispute. Moreover, the Japanese government maintains the position that delimitation of the EEZ should follow the median line between the respective coasts, and that it is also entitled to a 200 nautical mile-continental shelf.[1540]

In its dispute with Japan, the Chinese government has shown certain hints of openness to international adjudication that is otherwise missing. As elaborated on in Chapter IV.3.3.2 on China's engagement with the CLCS, Beijing appears willing to use the 'inquiry'-like CLCS proceedings under certain conditions;[1541] mainly when it perceives itself in the weaker position on the ground, as the other side holds offshore features in the area, and when the underlying UNCLOS norms appear to favor its claims. Going even further, Chinese scholars have favorably discussed the potential option of compulsory conciliation under Annex V Section II UNCLOS, whereas findings would not be binding, but are considered a contribution to an eventual settlement.[1542]

1539 See para 5 (a) Annex I CLCS Rules of Procedure (n 1528); Art 83 and Art 9 Annex II UNCLOS.

1540 Permanent Mission of Japan to the United Nations New York, 'Communication with regard to the submission made by China to the Commission on the Limits of the Continental Shelf' (28 December 2012) SC/12/372 ('Japan Communication on PRC's CLCS Submission'); Permanent Mission of Japan to the United Nations New York, 'Communication with regard to the submission made by China to the Commission on the Limits of the Continental Shelf' (13 August 2013) SC/13/293 ('Second Japan Communication on PRC's CLCS Submission').

1541 See also Ki Beom Lee, 'Should the Invocation of Paragraph 5(a) of Annex I to the CLCS Rules of Procedure Result in an Automatic *Deferral* of the Consideration of a Submission' (2014) 13 CJIL 605, 619.

1542 Annex V Section II UNCLOS. See also Jianjun Gao, 'The Okinawa Trough Issue in the Continental Shelf Delimitation Disputes within the East China Sea' (2010) 9 CJIL 143, 176–177.

IV.3.2.3. Sino-Indian Border Disputes – Himalayas from Kashmir to Arunachal Pradesh

As noted above, China has successfully resolved almost all land border issues. With Bhutan, China has long been engaged in regular talks towards an eventual peaceful settlement of the disputed parts of the border. In 2016, the two states held the 24th round of talks on the issue.[1543] One issue that remains a source of tension is China's interest in Bhutan ceding the Chumbi Valley. However, this concerns tension between China and India, as the latter would consider the transfer a threat to its national security. This is because the valley is very close to the narrow Siliguri Corridor, which connects to its northeastern provinces.[1544]

The only neighbor with whom a direct ongoing land border dispute is not yet on its way of being resolved through negotiations is India.[1545] First, India claims sovereignty over Aksai Chin as part of the state of Jammu and Kashmir. The territory is now administered mostly as part of the PRC's Xinjiang Autonomous Region. Second, the PRC claims sovereignty over Arunachal Pradesh as part of the Tibet Autonomous Region, whereas it is currently a province of India. Moreover, smaller areas along the border of the Tibet Autonomous Region and India are also disputed (especially the border areas between Tibet and Sikkim near Bhutan).[1546]

Both parties base their claims on superior title. India refers to cession via the *Convention Between (China), Great Britain and Tibet, signed at Simla, 3*

1543 Ministry of Foreign Affairs of the People's Republic of China, 'China and Bhutan Hold 24th Round of Talks on Boundary Issue' (Beijing, 15 August 2016) <http://www.fmprc.gov.cn/mfa_eng/wjbxw/t1389633.shtml> accessed 1 March 2019.

1544 The Economist Intelligence Unit, 'Bhutan-China border talks offer no progress on broader ties' (London, 23 August 2016) <https://goo.gl/wVn1V8> accessed 1 March 2019.

1545 See eg The Economist, 'Indian, Pakistani and Chinese Border Disputes: Fanatsy Frontiers' (London, 8 February 2012) <https://www.economist.com/node/21517168/all-comments?page=1> accessed 1 March 2019.

1546 Ministry of Foreign Affairs of the People's Republic of China, 'The Facts and China's Position Concerning the Indian Border Troops' Crossing of the China-India Boundary in the Sikkim Sector into the Chinese Territory' (Beijing, 2 August 2017) <http://www.fmprc.gov.cn/mfa_eng/zxxx_662805/P020170802542676636134.pdf> accessed 1 March 2019; Ministry of External Affairs of India, 'Recent Developments in Doklam Area' (New Delhi, 30 June 2017) <http://www.mea.gov.in/press-releases.htm?dtl/28572/Recent_Developments_in_Doklam_Area> accessed 1 March 2019. See also Zorawar Daulet Singh, 'After the Hiatus: India-China Border Diplomacy since the 1970s' (2011) 47 *China Report* 83.

July 1914 – and the PRC being the legal successor to Tibet. China rejects that argument on account of Tibet not being considered a sovereign state at that point in history. The Chinese government therefore holds that the Tibetan authorities were in no position to cede their territory. Instead, the PRC still views the lands in question as part of Tibet, which in turn it claims to have controlled (*effectivités*) since the Middle Ages and still controls.[1547]

IV.3.3. Interactions With Dispute Settlement Bodies Below the Threshold of Contentious Proceedings

As long as cases were not such wherein an adverse decision against China itself could have been taken, the leadership in Beijing already opted some time ago to also engage with international adjudicative bodies beyond trade and investment law.

In the following, this sub-chapter will discuss four advisory proceedings, two at the ICJ and two at ITLOS (requested in 2008, 2010, 2013 and 2017), which China participated in.[1548] Additionally four instances of Chinese engagement with the CLCS will be addressed: comments on submissions by Japan on the Western Pacific (2008), Vietnam on the Northern South China Sea (2009), and a joint submission by Vietnam and Malaysia regarding the Southern part of the South China Sea (2009), as well as the PRC's own partial submission on the East China Sea (2012).[1549]

1547 *Convention Between (China), Great Britain and Tibet, signed at Simla, 3 July 1914 (UK-China-Tibet)* (adopted 3 July 1914 by Great Britain and Tibet (China withdrew), no ratification, published officially in 1938) 220 CTS 144. See also Carty and Lone (n 1515) 95–97.

1548 *Accordance with International Law of the Unilateral Declaration of Independence in Respect of Kosovo* (Advisory Opinion) [2010] ICJ Rep 403 ('*Kosovo* (Advisory Opinion)'); *Responsibilities and Obligations of States Sponsoring Persons and Entities with Respect to Activities in the Area* (Advisory Opinion of 1 February 2011) [2011] ITLOS Rep 10 ('*Activities in the Area* (Advisory Opinion)'); *Request for an advisory opinion submitted by the Sub-Regional Fisheries Commission (SRFC)* (Advisory Opinion of 2 April 2015) [2015] ITLOS Rep 4 ('*Sub-Regional Fisheries Commission* (Advisory Opinion)'); *Legal Consequences of the Separation of the Chagos Archipelago from Mauritius in 1965* (Advisory Opinion) [2019] General List No 169 ('*Chagos* (Advisory Opinion)').

1549 Permanent Mission of the People's Republic of China to the United Nations New York, 'Communication with regard to the submission made by Japan to the Commission on the Limits of the Continental Shelf' (6 February 2009)

The Chinese government chose to engage in such ways in cases particularly important to national security and territorial integrity (*Kosovo*, *Chagos*, *Sub-Regional Fisheries Commission*, CLCS comments and submission), and in rather recently regulated areas where all states are comparatively devoid of experience (*Activities in the Area*), with economic motivations often playing an additional role. Beijing follows a strategy of testing the waters and feeling its way forward, which strongly chimes with the way in which it approached participation in trade and investment dispute resolution. However, what differs is the timetable.

As a side note, it can be added here that China's behavior concerning international criminal law has also been more nuanced than commonly assumed. The Chinese leadership has not ruled out eventually becoming a party to the International Criminal Court Statute, supported the establishment of the International Criminal Tribunal for the former Yugoslavia (hereinafter: ICTY) – its nationals served as judges there – and lent its vote to the creation of an international court to prosecute piracy.[1550]

CML/2/2009 ('PRC Communication on Japan's CLCS Submission'); Permanent Mission of the People's Republic of China to the United Nations New York, 'Communication with regard to the submission made by Japan to the Commission on the Limits of the Continental Shelf' (3 August 2011) CML/59/2011; Permanent Mission of the People's Republic of China to the United Nations New York, 'Communication with regard to the submission made by Viet Nam to the Commission on the Limits of the Continental Shelf' (7 May 2009) CML/18/2009 ('PRC Communication on Vietnam's CLCS Submission'); Permanent Mission of the People's Republic of China to the United Nations New York, 'Communication with regard to the submission made by Viet Nam to the Commission on the Limits of the Continental Shelf' (14 April 2011) CML/8/2011 ('Second PRC Communication on Vietnam's CLCS Submission'); Joint Submission by Malaysia and Vietnam to the CLCS (n 1517); Submission by the PRC to the CLCS (n 1537).

1550 UNSC Res 827 (25 May 1993) UN Doc S/RES/827; United Nations Security Council, 'Voting Records – S/RES/827' <http://unbisnet.un.org:8080/ipac20/ipac.jsp?profile=voting&index=.VM&term=sres827> accessed 1 March 2019; UNSC Res 2125 (18 November 2013) UN Doc S/RES/2125; United Nations Security Council, 'Voting Records – S/RES/2125' <http://unbisnet.un.org:8080/ipac20/ipac.jsp?profile=voting&index=.VM&term=sres2125> accessed 1 March 2019. See also Harriet Moynihan, 'China's Evolving Approach to International Dispute Settlement' *Chatham House Briefing – International Law Programme* (London, March 2017) 9 <https://www.chathamhouse.org/sites/files/chathamhouse/publications/research/2017-03-29-chinas-evolving-approach-international-dispute-settlement-moynihan-final.pdf> accessed 1 March 2019.

IV.3.3.1. Advisory Proceedings

IV.3.3.1.1. ICJ Advisory Opinion on Kosovo

Through Resolution 63/3, the UNGA requested an advisory opinion by the ICJ on the legality of Kosovo's declaration of independence in late 2008.[1551] The ICJ indeed delivered an opinion on 22 July 2010. According to the judges, with a vote of ten to four, Kosovo's action did not violate international law.[1552] However, the Court did not determine the scope of the right to self-determination, as it considered 'that it is not necessary to resolve these questions in the present case'.[1553] The General Assembly had only asked whether (the act of) Kosovo's declaration of independence was prohibited by international law.

The case was very attentively watched by the authorities in China, not least due to the question mark hanging over the future of Taiwan, as well as discontent among minorities in Tibet and Xinjiang. Among the many UN member states to submit written statements during the advisory proceedings was therefore, for the first time ever, the People's Republic of China –[1554] albeit with a rather brief submission.[1555] This was also the first Advisory Opinion proceeding ever in which every permanent member of the UN Security Council participated in both written and oral proceedings.[1556]

The Chinese government emphasized that UNSC Resolution 1244 (1999) explicitly pointed to a solution equipping Kosovo with 'substantial autonomy within the Federal Republic of Yugoslavia,' and underlined the importance of state sovereignty as a 'fundamental principle of international law,' citing the UN Charter and *Paramilitary Activities (Nicaragua v US)*.[1557] The Chinese statement describes self-determination as a 'basic

1551 Request for an advisory opinion of the ICJ on whether the unilateral declaration of independence of Kosovo is in accordance with international law, UNGA Res 63/3 (8 October 2008) UN Doc A/RES/63/3.

1552 *Kosovo* (Advisory Opinion) (n 1548) paras 122–123.

1553 Ibid para 83.

1554 Written Statement of the People's Republic of China to the International Court of Justice on the Issue of Kosovo (16 April 2009) <https://www.icj-cij.org/en/case/141> accessed 1 April 2019 ('*Kosovo* (PRC Written Statement)').

1555 Less than 2,500 words of text compared to the US's almost 40,000.

1556 See also Xianhe (Sienho) Yi (Yee), 'Notes on the International Court of Justice (Part 4): The Kosovo Advisory Opinion' (2010) 9 CJIL 763.

1557 UNSC Res 1244 (10 June 1999) UN Doc S/RES/1244, para 10 and Annex 2, para 5; Art 2 UN Charter; *Military and Paramilitary Activities in and against*

principle of international law,' but limited to 'situations of colonial rule or foreign occupation.' Other situations would only allow for secession, which 'is not recognized by international law.' The statement then notes that 'colonial rule ended in the world,' only to cite UNGA resolutions, which indeed reaffirm 'the right to self-determination of peoples which remain under colonial domination and foreign occupation'.[1558]

For the first and only time, China was also represented at the ICJ during oral proceedings. The honor of heading the Chinese delegation went to then Ambassador to ASEAN and current ICJ Judge Xue Hanqin.[1559] Madame Xue stressed the 'direct impact on international law as well as on the authority of the Security Council' that the ICJ advisory opinion would unfold, while lamenting 'an attitude [that] lacks sufficient respect for the rule of law in international relations' on the part of some states.[1560] She mainly criticized arguments put forward in other states' written statements. According to her, the preambular clause in Resolution 1244 was not to be treated as a mere considerandum, and the 'political process' demanded had not run its course just because the UNSC could not endorse the 'Ahtisaari Plan'.[1561] Others supposedly did not pay sufficient attention to the need for case-by-case analysis of the legality of unilateral secessions in the absence of a general prohibition.[1562] Finally, she underlined the need to decide 'by reference to the nature of the [unilateral declaration of independence] at the time it was issued,' while subsequent recognitions of independence by a great number of states could not have an effect.[1563]

The Chinese government was not satisfied with the eventual opinion delivered by the Court, but, in rather terse fashion, declared that it 'does not hinder the parties involved from properly solving the issue through negotiations'.[1564] Neither did it hinder China from continually voicing its respect for the Court and the international rule of law more generally.

Nicaragua (n 193) paras 202, 213, 263; *Kosovo* (PRC Written Statement) (n 1554) 1–3.

1558 *Kosovo* (PRC Written Statement) (n 1554) 3–7; UNGA Res 55/2 (8 September 2000) UN Doc A/RES/55/2, sec 1, para 4; UNGA Res 60/1 (16 September 2005) UN Doc A/RES/60/1, sec 1, para 5.

1559 *Accordance with International Law of the Unilateral Declaration of Independence in Respect of Kosovo* Verbatim Record 2009/29 (7 December 2009).

1560 Ibid 36, para 28.

1561 Ibid 29, para 4 and 32, para 10.

1562 Ibid 34, para 17.

1563 Ibid 36, para 27.

1564 Ministry of Foreign Affairs of the People's Republic of China, 'Foreign Ministry Spokesperson Qin Gang's Response to the International Court of Justice's

The Chinese government's experimentation with participation in the ICJ advisory proceedings on Kosovo is strongly in line with an overarching trend of Beijing inching towards engagement, which is viewed by Chinese decision-makers as the more promising route to protect national interests. This conclusion is confirmed by China's subsequent participation in further advisory proceedings, as discussed in the following sub-chapters. Such gradually increased participation in mind, Beijing might not be satisfied with the outcome of one particular case, but it will not turn towards overt and generalized criticism of the Court. Such could worsen relations with the ICJ itself, render positioning as proponent of international rule of law less convincing to other states, and in turn hurt efforts to grow Chinese influence. Moreover, should Beijing turn Chinese domestic public opinion against the Court, further steps towards engagement would be complicated.

IV.3.3.1.2. ITLOS Advisory Opinion on Activities in the Area

The Council of the International Seabed Authority filed a request with ITLOS' Seabed Disputes Chamber on 11 May 2010 to issue its first advisory opinion (Article 191 UNCLOS). It asked the Chamber about 'the legal responsibilities and obligations of States Parties to the Convention with respect to the sponsorship of activities [ie especially mining] in the Area,' 'the extent of liability of a State Party for any failure to comply with [UNCLOS] by an entity whom it has sponsored,' and the 'measures that a sponsoring State must take in order to fulfil its responsibility'.[1565] The Chamber delivered its unanimous opinion on 1 February 2011.[1566]

The 'Area' is the 'seabed and ocean floor and subsoil thereof, beyond the limits of national jurisdiction' (Article 1 (1) UNCLOS), and is governed by Part XI of UNCLOS. An International Seabed Authority – with an Assembly, Council and Secretariat as principal organs – was set up by the Convention in Kingston, Jamaica, as the organization through which the States

Advisory Opinion on the Kosovo Case' (Beijing, 23 July 2010) <http://www.fmprc.gov.cn/ce/cemd/eng/fyrth/t719113.htm> accessed 1 March 2019.

1565 Art 191 UNCLOS; *Activities in the Area* (Advisory Opinion) (n 1548); Decision of the Council of the International Seabed Authority requesting an advisory opinion pursuant to Article 191 of the United Nations Convention on the Law of the Sea (6 May 2010) ISBA/16/C/13.

1566 *Activities in the Area* (Advisory Opinion) (n 1548) para 242.

Parties control activities in the Area (Articles 156–158 UNCLOS).[1567] A State Party to UNCLOS may sponsor 'state enterprises or natural or juridical persons which possess [its] nationality (...) or are effectively controlled by [it] or [its] nationals' in exploiting resources in the Area (Article 153 (2) (b) UNCLOS).[1568]

In its written statement of 18 August 2010, China voiced its support for the Seabed Disputes Chamber's jurisdiction.[1569] After laying out its case in greater detail, the statement summarized that in judging a sponsoring State Party's 'necessary and appropriate measures' – in Annex III Article 4 (4) UNCLOS it says 'reasonably appropriate' – legislative and administrative, 'account shall be taken of the particular characteristics of [its] legal system'. In China's words, obligations 'shall be reasonable and appropriate,' in a way that is sufficient to allow supervision of the contractor, while not creating 'undue burdens on the sponsoring State'.[1570]

The advisory opinion describes indirect 'due diligence' as well as certain direct obligations on sponsoring States, the latter sometimes tempered for developing states through the phrase 'according to their capabilities.' It requires a causal link between an already occurred damage and a sponsoring State's failure to carry out its responsibilities. Moreover, pertinent domestic laws on environmental protection 'cannot be less stringent' than international rules, and obligations on a sponsored contractor have to be enforceable.[1571] Some of the language from China's written statement overlaps with that in the advisory opinion, eg on taking into account the 'particular characteristics of [a sponsoring State's legal] system'.[1572]

On 6 December 2011, China's Deputy Permanent Representative to the UN commented that through this advisory opinion ITLOS 'has entered a new stage in which it is fulfilling the comprehensive responsibilities entrusted to it by the Convention. The Chinese Government values and sup-

1567 Arts 1 (1), 156–158 and Part XI UNCLOS.

1568 Art 153 (2) (b) UNCLOS.

1569 Written Statement of the People's Republic of China on Responsibilities and obligations of States sponsoring persons and entities with respect to activities in the Area (18 August 2010), para 8 <https://www.itlos.org/fileadmin/itlos/documents/cases/case_no_17/Statement_China.pdf> accessed 1 March 2019) ('*Activities in the Area* (PRC Written Statement)').

1570 Annex III Art 4 (4) UNCLOS; *Activities in the Area* (PRC Written Statement) (n 1569) paras 34–36, 39.

1571 *Activities in the Area* (Advisory Opinion) (n 1548) para 242.

1572 Ibid para 229.

ports the important role of the Tribunal in the peaceful settlement of maritime disputes and the maintenance of international maritime order'.[1573]

Chinese companies are among the most active in concluding contracts with the International Seabed Authority, are making technological strides, and are gearing up for effective exploitation of polymetallic nodules and cobalt-rich ferromanganese crusts.[1574] The Chinese leadership has an interest in securing effective access for its resource-hungry industry, and clear and reasonable liability standards for itself. In this case, China's openness to embracing the jurisdiction of an international adjudicative body thus also has economic reasons. However, beyond that, another relevant aspect is that the Chinese government sees a lot of open regulatory space regarding deep seabed mining and aims to engage further in the future. Other states do not have an advantage in experience and expertise comparable to other fields of law. Moreover, the US is not a party to UNCLOS, and thus not a party to these regulatory processes, which therefore leaves a void that Beijing can use to grow influence while portraying itself as a responsible stakeholder.

IV.3.3.1.3. ITLOS Advisory Opinion on Illegal Fishing

China again submitted a written statement in the second advisory proceedings at ITLOS –[1575] the first for the Tribunal, as opposed to its Seabed Disputes Chamber. This time the Sub-Regional Fisheries Commission (hereinafter: SRFC), which comprises seven West African member states and is located in Dakar, Senegal, filed the request on 28 March 2013. The SRFC relied on Article 138 of the Rules of the Tribunal (ie ITLOS) – advisory opinion requests specifically provided for by an international agreement

---

1573 Wang Min, 'Statement by H.E. Ambassador Wang Min, Deputy Permanent Representative of China to the United Nations At the 66th Session of the UN General Assembly On Agenda Item 76: Oceans and the law of the sea' *Permanent Mission of the People's Republic of China to the UN* (New York, 6 December 2011) <http://www.china-un.org/eng/gdxw/t884956.htm> accessed 1 March 2019.

1574 International Seabed Authority, 'Deep Seabed Minerals Contractors' <https://www.isa.org.jm/deep-seabed-minerals-contractors> accessed 1 March 2019.

1575 Request for Advisory Opinion, with as annex the Resolution of the Conference of Ministers of the Sub-Regional Fisheries Commission (SRFC) (27 March 2013) No 437 CSRP/SP <https://www.itlos.org/fileadmin/itlos/documents/cases/case_no.21/Request_eng.pdf> accessed 1 March 2019 ('*Sub-Regional Fisheries Commission* (Request for Advisory Opinion)').

related to the purposes of UNCLOS – and Article 33 of the *Convention on the Determination of the Minimal Conditions for Access and Exploitation of Marine Resources within the Maritime Areas under Jurisdiction of the Member States of the Sub-Regional Fisheries Commission (SFRC)* (hereinafter: MCA Convention) to approach ITLOS for such an opinion.[1576]

The questions were about the nature of flag State responsibilities 'in cases where illegal, unreported and unregulated (IUU) fishing activities are conducted within the Exclusive Economic Zones of third party States,' the extent of flag State liability, and the 'rights and obligations of the coastal State in ensuring the sustainable management of shared stocks and stocks of common interest'.[1577]

The Chinese government had argued in its written statement that 'there is much room for enhanced cooperation' on IUU fishing concerns, while it at the same time does not see a basis in UNCLOS 'for the advisory competence of the full bench of the ITLOS'. Such a competence, it adds, should only be conferred by agreement of the state parties to amend UNCLOS.[1578]

In its advisory opinion of 2 April 2015, ITLOS unanimously assumed jurisdiction confined to the EEZs of SRFC Member States, which it saw satisfied through said Article 138 Rules of Procedures, and Annex VI Articles 16 and 21 UNCLOS. The latter two provisions state that the Tribunal 'shall frame rules for carrying out its functions' (ie rules of procedure), and that its jurisdiction – inter alia – comprises 'all matters specifically provided for in any other agreement which confers jurisdiction on the Tribunal.' 'Matters' is viewed as encompassing advisory opinions.[1579]

In response to the questions posed to it, ITLOS held that flag States have a 'due diligence' obligation to 'take necessary measures (…) to ensure com-

1576 Art 138 International Tribunal for the Law of the Sea – Rules of the Tribunal, ITLOS/8 (17 March 2009) ('ITLOS Rules'); *Convention on the Determination of the Minimal Conditions for Access and Exploitation of Marine Resources within the Maritime Areas under Jurisdiction of the Member States of the Sub-Regional Fisheries Commission (SFRC)* (adopted 8 June 2012, entered into force 16 September 2012) <https://www.itlos.org/fileadmin/itlos/documents/cases/case_no.21/Convention_CMA_ENG.pdf> accessed 1 March 2019.

1577 *Sub-Regional Fisheries Commission* (Request for Advisory Opinion) (n 1575).

1578 Written Statement of the People's Republic of China on Request for an advisory opinion submitted by the Sub-Regional Fisheries Commission (SRFC) (26 November 2013) para 94 <https://www.itlos.org/fileadmin/itlos/documents/cases/case_no.21/written_statements_round 1/C21_8_China_orig_Eng.pdf> accessed 1 March 2019.

1579 Annex VI Arts 16 and 21 UNCLOS; Art 138 ITLOS Rules; *Sub-Regional Fisheries Commission* (Advisory Opinion) (n 1548) paras 38–63, 219 (1).

pliance' with SRFC Member State regulations and to prevent IUU fishing by vessels flying its flag (Article 58 (3), 62 (4) and 192 UNCLOS), have an obligation to cooperate with SRFC Member States in IUU-related cases, and an obligation to investigate SRFC Member State allegations against vessels flying its flag.[1580] Liability arises not from the respective vessel's violations, but only from a 'due diligence'-failure of the flag State.[1581] On shared stocks, SRFC Member States have 'due diligence' obligations 'to seek to agree' among each other on coordination measures, and cooperate on ensuring conservation and development (Articles 63 (1), 64 (1) and 300 UNCLOS). On tuna species, SRFC Member States can require non-member States to cooperate (Article 64 (1) UNCLOS).[1582]

Following the publication of the advisory opinion there have been Chinese voices in support of the Separate Opinion of Judge Lucky, who argued that 'for the avoidance of doubt in future requests for advisory opinons, (...) article 21 should be amended to clear up any questions of jurisdiction'.[1583]

China has one of the largest fishing fleets worldwide. It has a giant population, a lack of arable land, and opposing coastlines of other states within 400 nautical miles from its coast make it difficult to claim maritime zones up to the full extent allowed under UNCLOS. China's fishing fleet often ventures far, and conflicts with local authorities around the world are common.[1584] It follows that the Chinese government is highly concerned with the operating conditions for globally operating fishing fleets.

As with the preceding advisory proceedings on seabed mining, one of the reasons for China getting involved is economic interest. Additionally, due to food security concerns, and frequent incidents between Chinese fishermen and local authorities around the East and South China Seas, national security motivations also encourage engagement. Here again, it is

1580 Arts 58 (3), 62 (4) and 192 UNCLOS; *Sub-Regional Fisheries Commission* (Advisory Opinion) (n 1548) para 219 (3).

1581 *Sub-Regional Fisheries Commission* (Advisory Opinion) (n 1548) para 219 (4).

1582 Arts 63 (1), 64 (1) and 300 UNCLOS; *Sub-Regional Fisheries Commission* (Advisory Opinion) (n 1548) para 219 (6).

1583 *Sub-Regional Fisheries Commission* (Advisory Opinion) (n 1548) Separate Opinion of Judge Lucky, para 28; See eg Jianjun Gao, 'The ITLOS Advisory Opinion for the SRFC' (2015) 14 CJIL 735, 754–755.

1584 Reuters, 'From Africa to South America, China's fishing fleet outstrips the competition' *SCMP* (Hong Kong, 23 February 2018) <https://www.scmp.com/news/china/society/article/2134438/chinas-fishing-industry-dwarfs-rest-worlds-study-suggests> accessed 15 March 2019.

important to note that the US not being a party to UNCLOS lets Beijing view the regulatory playing field as potentially easier to operate than other fields of international law, such as trade law, where the US is heavily engaged. The goal is to shape an important field of law over decades, which means it is necessary to gradually become involved, although quick success is not required.[1585]

IV.3.3.1.4. ICJ Advisory Opinion on Chagos

At a point when many observers might have expected the PRC to refrain from further engagement – after the *South China Sea Arbitration*, ie *Philippines v China*[1586] – the Chinese government demonstrated its commitment to stay the course by again submitting written comments to further ICJ advisory proceedings. On 22 June 2017 the UNGA had requested an ICJ Advisory Opinion on whether the decolonization of Mauritius had been lawfully completed with independence in 1968 following the separation of the Chagos Archipelago from Mauritius, and what the consequences of the UK's continued administration of the Chagos Archipelago were.[1587] In its Advisory Opinion, the Court found with thirteen votes to one that decolonization had not been lawfully completed, and that the UK 'is under an obligation to bring to an end its administration of the Chagos Archipelago as rapidly as possible'.[1588]

In China's written comments – which, as in *Kosovo*, were again comparatively short,[1589] and also not followed by comments on other states' submissions – the government first recalled that it had abstained from the pertinent UNGA vote.[1590] While it reaffirmed support for decolonization, China called on the two sides to reach a negotiated solution, and for the

---

1585 See also Chapters V.3.1. and V.3.3.

1586 See Chapter IV.3.4.

1587 Request for an advisory opinion of the International Court of Justice on the legal consequences of the separation of the Chagos Archipelago from Mauritius in 1965, UNGA 71/292 (22 June 2017) UN Doc A/71/L73.

1588 *Chagos* (Advisory Opinion) (n 1548) para 183.

1589 Less than 3,000 words of text compared to the more than 20,000 words of richly footnoted text submitted by the US.

1590 Written Statement of the People's Republic of China on Legal Consequences of the Separation of the Chagos Archipelago from Mauritius in 1965 (1 March 2018) para 3 <https://www.icj-cij.org/files/case-related/169/169-20180301-WRI-03-00-EN.pdf> accessed 3 March 2019.

ICJ to 'pay due regard' to the principle of consent to the judicial resolution of bilateral disputes not being circumvented.[1591]

China thus affirmed apprehensiveness towards (potential) ways to redraw borders and possible border claims via international adjudication apart from contentious proceedings both sides specifically consented to. Surely, the *South China Sea Arbitration* reinforced such apprehensiveness. Nevertheless, the PRC also demonstrated that it would continue on its incremental path of engagement below the threshold of contentious proceedings. It is certainly not inconceivable that a next step might be to participate in such as well, just to argue against jurisdiction – something many Chinese international lawyers would have wanted to do in *Philippines v China* already.[1592]

IV.3.3.2. Engagement with the CLCS

The Commission on the Limits of the Continental Shelf (hereinafter: CLCS) comprises 21 experts in pertinent natural sciences – ie not lawyers – elected by the UNCLOS States Parties (Article 2 (1) Annex II UNCLOS).[1593] If States Parties want to claim limits of their continental shelves extending further than 200 nautical miles from their baselines, they have to submit relevant information to the CLCS, which will study them and make recommendations based upon which 'final and binding' limits may be drawn (Article 76 (8) and Article 3 (1) Annex II UNCLOS).[1594]

However, in so doing, the CLCS may not prejudice maritime delimitation, given that this would be beyond its jurisdiction, and thus it cannot consider submissions where a land or maritime dispute exists (Article 76 (10) and Article 9 Annex II UNCLOS; Paragraphs 2 and 5 (a) of Annex I Rules of Procedure of the Commission).[1595]

1591 Ibid paras 12–14, 18–19.

1592 See Chapter V.3.3.2.2.3.

1593 Annex II Art 2 (1) UNCLOS.

1594 Art 76 (8) and Annex II Art 3 (1) UNCLOS.

1595 Art 76 (10) and Annex II Art 9 UNCLOS; Paras 2 and 5 (a) Annex I CLCS Rules of Procedure (n 1528) – 'In case there is a dispute in the delimitation of the continental shelf between opposite or adjacent States, or in the cases of unresolved land or maritime disputes, related to the submission, the Commission shall be: (a) Informed of such disputes by the coastal States making the submission; and (b) Assured by the coastal States making the submission to the extent

All States parties for whom UNCLOS entered into force before 13 May 1999, had to submit at least preliminary information on their outer continental shelf claims until 13 May 2009.[1596] This deadline led to a host of submissions in the months preceding it, including in East Asia. Those for whom the Convention entered into force only later also had to submit within respective ten-year periods.

The Chinese government submitted written comments on the partial submission of Japan, the partial submission of Vietnam, and the joint partial submission of Vietnam and Malaysia to the CLCS in 2009 – the latter will also be discussed in Chapter IV.3.4 – while in 2012, China filed its own (partial) submission to the CLCS.[1597] As already mentioned above in Chapters IV.3.2.1 and IV.3.2.2, the latter three submissions concerned the South China Sea and East China Sea, respectively. The CLCS deferred consideration so as not to prejudice existing maritime disputes.[1598]

Regarding the Japanese submission, the issue was not overlapping maritime claims, but rather supposedly excessive Japanese claims infringing upon the Area and thus the common heritage of mankind. The Chinese government held – as did the South Korean government in its written comments – that Okinotorishima in the Western Pacific was to be considered 'obviously' a 'rock' under Article 121 (3) UNCLOS without any claim to a continental shelf – according to 'available scientific data' – and that it was outside the Commission's mandate to make any recommendations on the relevant portions of Japan's submission.[1599] In its partial consideration, the Commission indeed decided to refrain from making recommendations on the relevant Southern Kyushu-Palau Ridge Region until the matters

possible that the submission will not prejudice matters relating to the delimitation of boundaries between States'.

1596 Para (a) Decision regarding the date of commencement of the ten-year period for making submissions to the Commission on the Limits of the Continental Shelf set out in article 4 of Annex II to the United Nations Convention on the Law of the Sea (29 May 2001) SPLOS/72 ('Decision on Deadline for CLCS Submissions'); Art 4 Annex II UNCLOS.

1597 PRC Communication on Japan's CLCS Submission (n 1549); *The South China Sea Arbitration* (Award) (n 196) paras 181–183, Figure 2, Annex 192; PRC Communication on Vietnam's CLCS Submission (n 1549); Joint Submission by Malaysia and Vietnam to the CLCS (n 1517); Submission by the PRC to the CLCS (n 1537).

1598 Para 5 (a) Annex I CLCS Rules of Procedure (n 1528); Art 83 and Art 9 Annex II UNCLOS.

1599 PRC Communication on Japan's CLCS Submission (n 1549).

brought up by both China and South Korea in pertinent notes verbales have been resolved.[1600]

In May 2009, Vietnam and Malaysia made a joint (partial) submission regarding respective outer continental shelves in the southern part of the South China Sea – Vietnam also made a separate partial submission on the northern part of the South China Sea –[1601] wherein they admitted to the existence of disputes, but claimed that their submission would not prejudice pertinent delimitation.[1602] In the description of the relevant area,[1603] both governments note that they already settled their continental shelf boundaries with Indonesia.[1604] Both only measured their continental shelves from their mainland coasts, essentially taking the position that all offshore land features in the South China Sea are at most 'rocks' under Article 121 (3) UNCLOS without entitlement to continental shelves.[1605]

Both China and the Philippines submitted notes verbales underlining that there are land and maritime disputes in the South China Sea and that they object to the CLCS considering the joint submission – the Chinese note verbale constituted the first time a Chinese government officially sub-

1600 Statement by the Chairman of the Commission on the progress of work in its twenty-ninth session (30 April 2012) CLCS/74 para 19; Summary of Recommendations of the Commission on the Limits of the Continental Shelf in Regard to the Submission mady by Japan on 12 November 2008 (adopted 19 April 2012) para 20.

1601 See Figure 1 Executive Summary Receipt of the submission made by the Socialist Republic of Viet Nam to the Commission on the Limits of the Continental Shelf (11 May 2009) CLCS. 37.2009.LOS ('Submission by Vietnam to the CLCS').

1602 Executive Summary Part I Paras 4.1 – 4.3 Joint Submission by Malaysia and Vietnam to the CLCS (n 1517).

1603 See Figure 1 Joint Submission by Malaysia and Vietnam to the CLCS (n 1517).

1604 Executive Summary Part I Para 5.1 Joint Submission by Malaysia and Vietnam to the CLCS (n 1517); *Agreement between the Government of Malaysia and the Government of the Republic of Indonesia on the Delimitation of the Continental Shelf between the Two Countries* (adopted 27 October 1969, entered into force 7 November 1969), US Department of State, 'International Boundary Study, Series A, Limits in the Seas', No. 1, 21 January 1970; *Agreement between the Government of the Socialist Republic of Vietnam and the Government of the Republic of Indonesia concerning the delimitation of the continental shelf boundary* (adopted 26 June 2003, entered into force 29 May 2007) 2457 UNTS 155.

1605 Robert Beckman, 'South China Sea: Worsening Dispute or Growing Clarity in Claims?' *RSIS Commentaries no 90* (Singapore, 16 August 2010) 2 <https://cil.nus.edu.sg/publication/south-china-sea-worsening-dispute-or-growing-clarity-in-claims/> accessed 15 March 2019.

mitted a map containing the 'nine dash line' to support its claims.[1606] The CLCS indeed decided to 'defer further consideration' and did not establish a subcommission or adopt recommendations on these two submissions regarding the South China Sea.[1607] In response to the Philippine note verbale, Beijing issued another such document in April 2011, further emphasizing its claims and putting forward several arguments to explain and support them.[1608]

Some scholars evidently believed that the PRC's notes verbales in response to the joint submission by Malaysia and Vietnam, the attachment of the map including the nine-dash-line and the explanation of China's claim, could bolster the Chinese position in a future settlement of the territorial and maritime disputes in the South China Sea. The map could supposedly produce 'important legal force' as a 'physical expression of the will of the state' through its inclusion on official communication, and the explanations serve to provide a necessary clear definition of the Chinese claim.[1609] Such deliberations point to at least a certain vague openness to third-party settlement at some point in the future, which would have to be preceded by putting China in the most favorable position possible.

1606 *The South China Sea Arbitration* (Award) (n 196) paras 181–183, Figure 2, Annex 191, Annex 192; Permanent Mission of the People's Republic of China to the United Nations New York, 'Communication with regard to the joint submission made by Malaysia and Viet Nam to the Commission on the Limits of the Continental Shelf' (7 May 2009) CML/17/2009 ('PRC Communication on the Joint CLCS Submission of Malaysia and Vietnam'); PRC Communication on Vietnam's CLCS Submission (n 1549); Permanent Mission of the Republic of the Philippines to the United Nations New York, 'Communication with regard to the joint submission made by Malaysia and Viet Nam to the Commission on the Limits of the Continental Shelf' (4 August 2009) No 000819.

1607 Statement by the Chairman of the Commission on the progress of work in its twenty-fourth session, CLCS/64 (1 October 2009) para 74. Some scholars problematize the issue of 'automatic deferral', and differences between considering (parts) of a submission, deferral, deciding not to consider or qualify a submission and not taking action, see Lee, 'Should the Invocation' (n 1541) 605; Qiu Jun, 'The CLCS Modalities for Handling Submissions Involving Disputes and Their Possible Application to the South China Sea' (2015) 14 CJIL 135.

1608 Second PRC Communication on Vietnam's CLCS Submission (n 1549).

1609 Keyuan Zou, 'China's U-Shaped Line in the South China Sea Revisited' (2012) 43 *Ocean Development & International Law* 18, 23, citing *Sovereignty Over Pulau Ligitan and Pulau Sipadan (Indonesia v Malaysia)* [2002] ICJ Rep 625, para 88. On the notes verbales supposedly clarifying China's claims see also Beckman (n 1605) 2.

Beijing's own submission to the CLCS in 2012 – aiming to make use of favorable geographical circumstances in the East China Sea vis-à-vis Japan – shows that it is strongly willing to employ such tools established by UNCLOS. This submission was preceded by preliminary information submitted in May 2009, which the Japanese government objected to.[1610] China then made its partial submission in December 2012, claiming to not prejudice future delimitation therewith, and making use of geomorphological and geological conditions in the East China Sea to claim an outer continental shelf based on and advocate an equitable delimitation taking account of natural prolongation up to the Okinawa Trough in the close vicinity of the Japanese Okinawa Islands.[1611] In its two responding notes verbales, Japan in turn pointed to an existing dispute on maritime delimitation, which may not be prejudiced, and thus asked the Commission – also successfully – to not consider the Chinese submission. Tokyo also made clear its position that EEZ delimitation should follow the median line between the respective coasts, and that it is also entitled to a 200 nautical mile-continental shelf.[1612]

Chinese international lawyers are mostly confident about their country's position regarding East China Sea continental shelf delimitation. In the context of the CLCS likely being precluded from making recommendations – inter alia – on the nature of the Okinawa Trough and the consequences of such a determination, even the potential use of compulsory conciliation under Annex V Section II UNCLOS has been suggested. A conciliation commission's findings would not be binding, but are described as contributing to a settlement of the dispute.[1613] Australia and Timor-Leste underwent such proceedings, which culminated in a new treaty on their maritime boundaries.[1614]

1610 People's Republic of China, Preliminary Information Submission to the Commission (May 2009); Letter to the UN Secretary-General, Doc SC/09/246 (23 July 2009).

1611 See Chapter IV.3.2.2; Figure 1 Executive Summary Submission by the PRC to the CLCS (n 1537). For a preceding discussion of China's position see also Jianjun Gao, 'The Okinawa Trough Issue' (n 1542) 143.

1612 Para 5 (a) Annex I CLCS Rules of Procedure (n 1528); Art 83 and Art 9 Annex II UNCLOS; Japan Communication on PRC's CLCS Submission (n 1540); Second Japan Communication on PRC's CLCS Submission (n 1540).

1613 Jianjun Gao, 'The Okinawa Trough Issue' (n 1542) 176–177; Annex V Section II UNCLOS.

1614 *Conciliation between The Democratic Republic of Timor-Leste and The Commonwealth of Australia* (Concluded) PCA Press Release No 14 (6 March 2018) <https://pcacases.com/web/sendAttach/2303> accessed 1 April 2019.

The Chinese government's written comments on other states' submissions to the CLCS and later decision to make a partial submission itself demonstrate a progressively increasing willingness to engage with the Commission. This in turn shows growing openness to a third-party authority addressing the existence of territorial and maritime disputes and potentially determining the geographical extent of Chinese sovereign rights, which is a remarkable development. Herein, the CLCS proceedings may be considered akin to 'inquiry' among methods of international dispute settlement.[1615] Chinese scholars have repeatedly praised the 'highly effective' work of the CLCS along an 'established set of modalities' that includes deferring consideration of submissions involving unresolved disputes.[1616] The Commission was said to deserve better working conditions including monetary benefits for its 'positive contribution' in 'maintaining a balance between the legitimate rights and interests of coastal States and the overall interests of the entire international community'.[1617]

IV.3.4. The First Case – Philippines v China on the South China Sea

IV.3.4.1. Background

The PRC has not yet directly participated in any contentious proceedings on law of the sea or territorial matters. However, seeking to clarify certain law of the sea questions regarding the South China Sea, the Philippines submitted a dispute – registered at the PCA on 22 January 2013 – and Annex VII UNCLOS arbitral proceedings did ensue.[1618] The Philippines

1615 Lee, 'Should the Invocation' (n 1541) 619.

1616 Qiu Jun (n 1607) 148.

1617 Lijiang Zhu, 'Chinese Practice in Public International Law: 2013' (2014) 13 CJIL 395, 413–414 citing a Chinese representative's statement at the 68th Session of the UNGA, see A/68/PV.63, 7–8. For a similar statement see also Xiaohui Wu, 'Chronology of Practice: Chinese Practice in Public International Law in 2016' (2017) 16 CJIL 547, 580 citing Wu Haitao, 'Statement by Ambassador WU Haitao at the Plenary of the 71st General Assembly under the Agenda Item 73: Oceans and the Law of the Sea' *Permanent Mission of the People's Republic of China to the UN* <www.china-un.org/eng/lhghyywj/smhwj/2016doc/t1422387.htm> accessed 1 March 2018. On the CLCS having successfully balanced states' interests see also Qiu Jun (n 1607) 135.

1618 *The South China Sea Arbitration* (Philippines Memorial – Volume I) (n 1509) para 1.1; *The South China Sea Arbitration* (Award on Jurisdiction and Admissibility) (n 1506) para 26, Annex 1 (Notification and Statement of Claim of the

mainly requested an Award determining that Parties' pertinent rights and obligations are governed by UNCLOS and that such based on China's 'nine-dash line' 'are inconsistent with the Convention and therefore invalid';[1619] moreover, whether certain land features are 'islands,' rocks,' or 'low tide elevations';[1620] and an Award, finally, that 'enables [it] to exercise and enjoy the rights within and beyond its economic zone and continental shelf that are established in the Convention'.[1621]

Instead of a formal reply to the Philippines' Notification and Statement of Claim, the PRC presented notes verbales to the Philippines,[1622] as well as the PCA, wherein it stated that 'it does not accept the arbitration initiated by the Philippines [, while the note verbale] shall not be regarded as China's acceptance of or participation in the proceedings'.[1623] The Philippines then appointed Judge Rüdiger Wolfrum (Germany) as arbitrator. Since China refused to participate, the President of ITLOS Shunji Yanai (Japan) appointed the remaining arbitrators.[1624] The PCA was agreed as Registry, and The Hague as seat of the arbitration.[1625] The arbitral tribunal

---

Republic of the Philippines, 22 January 2013); Arts 286 and 287 and Art 1 Annex VII UNCLOS.

1619 *The South China Sea Arbitration* (Award on Jurisdiction and Admissibility) (n 1506) para 26 (1).

1620 Ibid para 26 (2).

1621 Ibid para 26 (3).

1622 Ibid para 27, Annex 3 (Note Verbale from the Embassy of the People's Republic of China in Manila to the Department of Foreign Affairs of the Republic of the Philippines, No (13) PG-039, 19 February 2013); *The South China Sea Arbitration (The Republic of Philippines v The People's Republic of China)* (Concluded) PCA Press Release No 1 (27 August 2013) <https://pcacases.com/web/sendAttach/227> accessed 1 April 2019.

1623 *The South China Sea Arbitration (The Republic of Philippines v The People's Republic of China)*, PCA Case No 2013–19, Memorial of the Philippines – Volume III (30 March 2014) Annex 4 – *Note Verbale* from the Embassy of the People's Republic of China in The Hague to the Permanent Court of Arbitration, No (013)-117 (29 July 2013) 1 ('*The South China Sea Arbitration* (Philippines Memorial – Volume III)').

1624 He appointed Stanislaw Pawlak (Poland) as the second arbitrator, as the remaining arbitrators Judge Jean-Pierre Cot (France) and Professor Alfred H. A. Soons (Netherlands), and as the President of the Tribunal Ambassador M.C.W. Pinto (Sri Lanka). Ambassador Pinto withdrew subsequently, whereafter Judge Thomas A. Mensah (Ghana) was appointed as replacement. See *The South China Sea Arbitration* (Award on Jurisdiction and Admissibility) (n 1506) paras 28–31; Annex VII Art 3 (b)-(e) UNCLOS.

1625 *The South China Sea Arbitration* (Award on Jurisdiction and Admissibility) (n 1506) paras 32–34.

requested and received a supplemental written submission by the Philippines, and bifurcated proceedings to first deal with objections to jurisdiction as preliminary questions.[1626]

In the following sub-chapters the rest of the proceedings, including China's indirect participation via the issuance of a position paper and diplomatic statements as well as the two awards rendered by the tribunal, will be summarized, with this author adding only a couple of short comments. A more in-depth discussion on legal implications and criticism of the awards will follow in Chapter IV.3.4.4.2.

IV.3.4.2. Award on Jurisdiction and Admissibility

On 29 October 2015, the tribunal rendered a first award on jurisdiction and admissibility. It mostly found in the Philippines' favor or reserved pertinent consideration to the merits phase, because not only exclusively preliminary issues were involved.[1627] As China's main contention with respect to these proceedings was that the tribunal lacked jurisdiction in the first place, related matters will be laid out in detail below.

IV.3.4.2.1. China's Non-Participation

The PRC underlined its non-acceptance and non-participation in this arbitration – inter alia – in an extensive position paper published by its MFA.[1628] The tribunal decided to treat the paper, issued eight days ahead of the deadline for submitting a Counter-Memorial, as a plea concerning jurisdiction, but also to go beyond the matters raised there, request further written arguments on jurisdiction from the Philippines, and pose further

1626 *The South China Sea Arbitration* (Award on Jurisdiction and Admissibility) (n 1506) paras 59, 67–68, 92, 96; *The South China Sea Arbitration (The Republic of Philippines v The People's Republic of China)*, PCA Case No 2013–19, Supplemental Written Submission of the Philippines – Volume I (16 March 2015); *The South China Sea Arbitration (The Republic of Philippines v The People's Republic of China)* (Concluded) PCA Press Release No 4 (22 April 2015) <https://pcacases.com/web/sendAttach/1298> accessed 1 April 2019.

1627 *The South China Sea Arbitration* (Award on Jurisdiction and Admissibility) (n 1506) para 413.

1628 *The South China Sea Arbitration* (Award on Jurisdiction and Admissibility) (n 1506) paras 10, 64, 83; PRC Position Paper on the South China Sea (n 1507).

questions to its representatives at the oral hearing.[1629] The position paper mainly argues against jurisdiction due to 1) 'the essence of the subject-matter' being territorial sovereignty questions beyond the scope of UNCLOS, 2) international agreements binding the Philippines to a negotiated solution, and 3) if the subject matter were truly concerned with the interpretation and application of UNCLOS, it being an integral part of maritime delimitation as covered by China's Article 298 UNCLOS reservation.[1630]

The tribunal emphasized that a party's non-participation necessitates special scrutiny of submitted claims. However '[a]bsence of a party or failure of a party to defend its case shall not constitute a bar to the proceedings'.[1631] China would remain party to the case, and bound by any subsequent awards. To comply with its duty to assure 'each party a full opportunity to be heard and to present its case',[1632] the tribunal provided China with daily transcripts of the hearings and all submitted documents, gave it opportunity to comment, and reminded it of the possibility to join the proceedings at any stage.[1633] At the same time, the tribunal was also required to 'avoid unnecessary delay and expense and to provide a fair and efficient process for resolving the Parties' dispute',[1634] entailing the duty to protect the Philippines against disadvantage due to China's non-appearance.[1635]

1629 *The South China Sea Arbitration* (Award on Jurisdiction and Admissibility) (n 1506) paras 13–15, 52, 55–56, 59, 122–123; *The South China Sea Arbitration (The Republic of Philippines v The People's Republic of China)*, PCA Case No 2013–19, Procedural Order No 4 (21 April 2015) para 1.1; PRC Position Paper on the South China Sea (n 1507).

1630 Art 298 UNCLOS; *The South China Sea Arbitration* (Award on Jurisdiction and Admissibility) (n 1506) paras 14, 133–139; PRC Position Paper on the South China Sea (n 1507) paras 3–4, 8, 10–13, 16–17, 22, 25–27, 29, 66–69, 75.

1631 Art 9 Annex VII UNCLOS; *The South China Sea Arbitration* (Award on Jurisdiction and Admissibility) (n 1506) paras 11–12, 113–115.

1632 Art 5 Annex VII UNCLOS.

1633 *The South China Sea Arbitration* (Award on Jurisdiction and Admissibility) (n 1506) paras 15, 18, 117.

1634 *The South China Sea Arbitration (The Republic of Philippines v The People's Republic of China)*, PCA Case No 2013–19, Rules of Procedure (27 August 2013) Art 10 (1) ('*The South China Sea Arbitration* (Rules of Procedure)').

1635 *The South China Sea Arbitration* (Award on Jurisdiction and Admissibility) (n 1506) para 118. Herein the tribunal cited *"Arctic Sunrise" (Kingdom of the Netherlands v Russian Federation)* (Provisional Measures, Order of 22 November 2013) [2013] ITLOS Rep 230, para 56 ('*"Arctic Sunrise"* (Provisional Measures)').

IV.3.4.2.2. The Tribunal's Jurisdiction

The tribunal maintained that it had been correctly approached and constituted,[1636] that there was a dispute (or 'positive opposition') between the parties regarding all matters raised, and that all of them concerned the interpretation and application of UNCLOS.[1637]

On the existence of a dispute, arbitrators, First, took the view that a dispute was evident from diplomatic exchanges, on the source of maritime entitlements, namely whether 'historic rights' 'arising under another body of law were or were not preserved by the Convention'.[1638] Whereas China referred to such 'historic rights,' the Philippines related their claims only to rights emanating from land features under UNCLOS.[1639] The arbitrators noted that 'deliberate ambiguity' by one party would not be allowed to 'frustrate the resolution of a genuine dispute through arbitration',[1640] which referred to China's refusal to clarify 'the nature or scope of its claimed historic rights [and] the meaning of the "nine-dash line" [or express] a view on the status of particular maritime features'.[1641]

Second, the tribunal was convinced that there was a dispute on the status of maritime features, even though there might not have been 'granular exchanges' on the specific features in question. China considered the Spratly Islands as entitled to an EEZ and continental shelf, while the Philippines saw land features there at most entitled to a territorial sea. Views on individual features were rarely set out, and could even turn out to coincide on some of them,[1642] but the tribunal supported the ICJ's notion in *Land and Maritime Boundary (Cameroon v Nigeria)* that '[even if] the exact scope

1636 Arts 287, 288, 298, Annex VII UNCLOS; *The South China Sea Arbitration* (Award on Jurisdiction and Admissibility) (n 1506) paras 106–107, 109–111.

1637 Art 288 UNCLOS; *The South China Sea Arbitration* (Award on Jurisdiction and Admissibility) (n 1506) para 178.

1638 *The South China Sea Arbitration* (Award on Jurisdiction and Admissibility) (n 1506) para 168.

1639 Ibid paras 164–168.

1640 Ibid para 163.

1641 Ibid para 160. In the following paras 161 and 162 the tribunal cited in support of its arguments *Application of the International Convention on the Elimination of All Forms of Racial Discrimination (Georgia v Russian Federation)* (Preliminary Objections) [2011] ICJ Rep 70, [84]–[85] para 30; *Applicability of the Obligation to Arbitrate under Section 21 of the United Nations Headquarters Agreement of 26 June 1947 (Advisory Opinion)* [1988] ICJ Rep 12, [28] para 38.

1642 *The South China Sea Arbitration* (Award on Jurisdiction and Admissibility) (n 1506) paras 169–171.

of this dispute cannot be determined at present; a dispute nevertheless exists between the two Parties'.[1643]

Third, the arbitrators considered diplomatic correspondence to demonstrate disputes about the lawfulness of Chinese law enforcement activities, military presence, installations, (interference with) fishing, and interference with hydrocarbon exploration.[1644]

Addressing the allegation in China's Position Paper that the Philippines had abused UNCLOS procedures, the tribunal cited *Barbados v Trinidad and Tobago* to underline that 'unilateral invocation of the arbitration procedure cannot by itself be regarded as an abuse of right contrary to Article 300 of UNCLOS [on "good faith"] or an abuse of right contrary to general international law [as] Article 286 confers a unilateral right'.[1645]

The tribunal then considered whether the Philippines could be precluded from having recourse to compulsory dispute resolution by an agreement to resolve the dispute through negotiations.[1646] It found that the largely permissive language of the DOC – often referred to as a 'political document' – the circumstances of its adoption, and subsequent efforts to reach a binding Code of Conduct, point to it not constituting a binding 'agreement' as required by Articles 281 and 282 UNCLOS.[1647] For completeness, the award adds that 'agreed means' do not have to be pursued indefinitely – 'years of discussions' were not successful – and that the DOC does not exclude Part XV dispute settlement, as also required by Article 281 UNCLOS.[1648]

The tribunal continued that the Treaty of Amity, while a binding agreement, requires an additional specific agreement for dispute settlement procedures in Articles 13 to 15 (negotiations, using the good offices of a 'High

1643 Ibid paras 171–172; *Land and Maritime Boundary between Cameroon and Nigeria (Cameroon v Nigeria)* (Preliminary Objections) [1998] ICJ Rep 275, [316]–[317] para 93.

1644 *The South China Sea Arbitration* (Award on Jurisdiction and Admissibility) (n 1506) para 173.

1645 Arts 286, 300 UNCLOS; *The South China Sea Arbitration* (Award on Jurisdiction and Admissibility) (n 1506) paras 124–126; *Arbitration between Barbados and Trinidad and Tobago* (2006) 27 RIAA 147, [207]–[208].

1646 *The South China Sea Arbitration* (Award on Jurisdiction and Admissibility) (n 1506) paras 190, 192, 196.

1647 Arts 281, 282 UNCLOS; Declaration on the Conduct of Parties in the South China Sea (n 1524); *The South China Sea Arbitration* (Award on Jurisdiction and Admissibility) (n 1506) paras 195, 212–218, 302.

1648 Art 281 UNCLOS; *The South China Sea Arbitration* (Award on Jurisdiction and Admissibility) (n 1506) paras 219–229.

Council') to be binding.[1649] Article 282 UNCLOS was not seen to apply, – inter alia – because the dispute resolution procedures in the Treaty of Amity 'do not entail a "binding decision",' only (potentially) a recommendation by the High Council.[1650] The arbitrators also found that Article 22 (1) 'Convention on Biological Diversity' preserves UNCLOS rights including access to compulsory dispute resolution.[1651] Finally, the tribunal described a series of aspirational political statements by the Philippines that could not be seen as binding legal agreements.[1652] Citing *Land and Maritime Boundary (Cameroon v Nigeria)*, it added that grounds for estoppel could not be found, as the Philippines 'had [not] "consistently made it fully clear" that it had agreed to settle the dispute by bilateral dialogue "alone"'.[1653]

On the two parties having exchanged views before arbitral proceedings commenced, the arbitrators cited *Chagos Marine Protected Area* and *Arctic Sunrise* to underline the two necessary elements for Article 283 requirements to be satisfied: 'a dispute [having] arisen with sufficient clarity that the Parties were aware of the issues in respect of which they disagreed',[1654] and '[p]arties [exchanging] views regarding the means by which a dispute that has arisen between them may be settled';[1655] subject-matter negotiations are not required.[1656] Looking back at bi- and multilateral exchanges between 1995 and 2012, the arbitrators were 'convinced that the Parties have unequivocally exchanged views regarding the possible means of [settlement, and that] China was aware of the issues in respect of which the

---

1649 Arts 13–16 *Treaty of Amity and Cooperation in Southeast Asia* (opened for signature 24 February 1976, entered into force 15 July 1976) 1025 UNTS 319; *The South China Sea Arbitration* (Award on Jurisdiction and Admissibility) (n 1506) paras 252–269.

1650 Art 282 UNCLOS; *The South China Sea Arbitration* (Award on Jurisdiction and Admissibility) (n 1506) paras 307–310.

1651 Convention on Biodiversity (n 1165); *The South China Sea Arbitration* (Award on Jurisdiction and Admissibility) (n 1506) paras 288–289.

1652 *The South China Sea Arbitration* (Award on Jurisdiction and Admissibility) (n 1506) paras 230–233, 241–248, 302.

1653 Ibid paras 230–233, 249–251; *Land and Maritime Boundary between Cameroon and Nigeria (Cameroon v Nigeria)* (Preliminary Objections) [1998] ICJ Rep 275, [303], para 57.

1654 *Chagos Marine Protected Area (Mauritius v United Kingdom)* (Award of 18 March 2015) 31 RIAA 359, paras 382–383.

1655 *Arctic Sunrise (Kingdom of the Netherlands v Russian Federation)* (Merits, Award of 14 August 2015) (2016) 55 ILM 5, para 151 ('*Arctic Sunrise* (Merits)').

1656 Art 283 UNCLOS; *The South China Sea Arbitration* (Award on Jurisdiction and Admissibility) (n 1506) paras 322–325, 331–333.

Parties disagreed'.[1657] Moreover, they argued that parties are not obliged to further negotiate if they consider possibilities to be exhausted in this regard, and that they are best suited to judge whether that is the case.[1658]

Finally, the tribunal considered several objections to jurisdiction not 'exclusively preliminary', and reserved pertinent decisions for the merits stage.[1659] According to the arbitrators, China's 2006 Article 298-declaration meant that jurisdiction could be barred for several of the Philippines' submissions, if 1) any Chinese-claimed feature in the Spratly Islands were an 'island' under Article 121 UNCLOS, producing overlapping maritime zones that would have to first be delimited, 2) China had historic rights in the South China Sea, or 3) certain Chinese activities were of a military nature.[1660] Whether jurisdiction might be partly barred under Article 297 UNCLOS – eg Article 297 (3) on fisheries – also depended on Spratlys features' 'island' status, and the potential of Chinese claims.[1661]

Accordingly, the award reserved decisions on jurisdiction for consideration in conjunction with the merits regarding historic rights, Chinese law enforcement and military activities, and certain land features being part of the Philippines' EEZ and continental shelf. The tribunal at the same time affirmed jurisdiction over questions of island status, traditional fishing rights within territorial seas, protection and preservation of the marine environment, and coastal and flag state duties related to innocent passage.[1662]

1657 *The South China Sea Arbitration* (Award on Jurisdiction and Admissibility) (n 1506) paras 342–343.

1658 *The South China Sea Arbitration* (Award on Jurisdiction and Admissibility) (n 1506) para 350, where the tribunal cites *Land Reclamation In and Around the Straits of Johor (Malaysia v Singapore)*, (Provisional Measures) ITLOS Reports 2003, 10, para 47 ('*Straits of Johor* (Provisional Measures)'); *Mavrommatis Palestine Concessions* (Objection to the Jurisdiction of the Court, Judgment) PCIJ Series A No 2 [15].

1659 *The South China Sea Arbitration* (Award on Jurisdiction and Admissibility) (n 1506) paras 379–383; *Territorial and Maritime Dispute (Nicaragua v Colombia)* (Preliminary Objections) [2007] ICJ Rep 832, [850] para 46; *The South China Sea Arbitration* (Rules of Procedure) (n 1634) Art 20 (3).

1660 Arts 121, 298 UNCLOS; *The South China Sea Arbitration* (Award on Jurisdiction and Admissibility) (n 1506) paras 365–371, 392–396; United Nations Division for Ocean Affairs and the Law of the Sea, 'UNCLOS Declarations' (n 496).

1661 Art 297 UNCLOS; *The South China Sea Arbitration* (Award on Jurisdiction and Admissibility) (n 1506) para 359.

1662 *The South China Sea Arbitration* (Award on Jurisdiction and Admissibility) (n 1506) paras 398–412.

IV.3.4.2.3. The Chinese Government's Reaction

The Chinese Ministry of Foreign Affairs issued a statement on 30 October 2015 calling the award 'null and void' and without binding effect on China. It again accused Manila and the tribunal of having 'abused relevant procedures,' violated China's rights under UNCLOS, 'completely deviated from the purposes and objectives of the UNCLOS, and eroded the integrity and authority of the UNCLOS,' and finally called 'upon all parties concerned to work together to safeguard the integrity and authority of the UNCLOS'.[1663]

Beijing thus attempted to utterly turn around narrative and perception as to who was damaging the international legal order regarding the law of the sea. It ignored the tribunal's authority to determine its own jurisdiction, exclaiming that the tribunal 'manifestly' could not have such jurisdiction, and decrying that China's 2006 Article 298 UNCLOS declaration had been 'maliciously' evaded to 'obstinately [force] ahead with the arbitration.' The Chinese position would never change, the statement assured, and the Philippines were called upon to 'return to the right track'.[1664]

IV.3.4.3. Award on the Merits

Unperturbed, the tribunal issued its unanimous award on the merits on 12 July 2016. It delivered an almost complete victory to the Philippines. It threw out China's claims to historic rights based on the 'nine-dash line,' determined that there is no EEZ-entitled 'island' in the Spratlys, and found that China had violated UNCLOS in multiple ways.[1665]

1663 *The South China Sea Arbitration* (Award) (n 196) 61; Ministry of Foreign Affairs of the PRC, 'Statement of the Ministry of Foreign Affairs of the People's Republic of China on the Award on Jurisdiction and Admissibility of the South China Sea Arbitration by the Arbitral Tribunal Established at the Request of the Republic of the Philippines' (Beijing, 30 October 2015) <https://www.fmprc.gov.cn/mfa_eng/zxxx_662805/t1310474.shtml> accessed 1 April 2019.

1664 *The South China Sea Arbitration* (Award) (n 196) 61; PRC MFA Statement on the Award on Jurisdiction and Admissibility in the South China Sea Arbitration (n 1663).

1665 *The South China Sea Arbitration* (Award) (n 196) paras 1202–1203. See paras 78–80, 112–113 for the final, somewhat amended and clarified list of Philippine submissions.

IV.3.4.3.1 China's Non-participation

The arbitrators reiterated that in response to China's non-participation they had 'been particularly vigilant with respect to establishing whether the Philippines' claims are well founded in fact and law'.[1666] They retained independent experts on technical questions, went into many potential defenses proprio motu, posed additional questions, and provided China with daily transcripts and all written materials.[1667] They also considered information in the public domain on relevant positions of the 'Taiwan Authority of China' – a government position paper and a study by the island's international law society – which were especially focused on the supposed 'island' status of Taiwanese-controlled Itu Aba, the largest island in the Spratlys.[1668] Not being a party to UNCLOS, Taiwan could not officially submit documents or otherwise participate in the proceedings, but it nevertheless let its positions be known. It even very publicly invited the members of the tribunal to a site visit on Itu Aba, to which Beijing strongly objected. The arbitrators did not accept the invitation, with one of the reasons being the consideration that historical conditions before 'significant human modification' would be determinative for island status.[1669]

IV.3.4.3.2 Historic Rights and the Nine-Dash Line

The arbitrators noted that China had referred to historic rights in the South China Sea – inter alia – in Article 14 of its *Law on the Exclsuive Economic Zone and the Continental Shelf*, enacted in 1998, where it says that the 'provisions in this Law shall not affect the rights that the People's Republic of China has been enjoying ever since the days of the past'.[1670]

1666 *The South China Sea Arbitration* (Award) (n 196) para 15, a reference to Art 9 Annex VII UNCLOS.

1667 *The South China Sea Arbitration* (Award) (n 196) paras 15, 69, 121, 130–142.

1668 Ibid paras 89, 92, 139; Ministry of Interior of Taiwan – Maritime Information Service Center, 'Position Paper on ROC South China Sea Policy' (Taipeh, 21 March 2016) <http://maritimeinfo.moi.gov.tw/marineweb/UpLoad/UFile/0000001997/Position%20Paper%20on%20ROC%20South%20China%20Sea%20Policy.pdf> accessed 15 July 2017.

1669 *The South China Sea Arbitration* (Award) (n 196) para 142.

1670 Law on the Exclusive Economic Zone and the Continental Shelf of the People's Republic of China (adopted 26 June 1998, entered into force 26 June 1998) <www.npc.gov.cn/englishnpc/Law/2007-12/11/content_1383573.htm> <www.un.org/depts/los/legislationandtreaties/pdffiles/chn_1998_eez_act.pdf>

According to the tribunal, China never expressly clarified the nature of these supposed historic rights. A first official Chinese map including a then 'eleven-dash line,' marking most of the South China Sea as an area of Chinese historic rights, was unilaterally published by the Republic of China in 1948. Later on, the People's Republic of China removed two dashes in the Gulf of Tonkin in 1953, producing the since then maintained – although coordinates are said to be unclear – 'nine-dash line'.[1671] A new map containing the dashes was appended to China's Notes Verbales sent to the UN Secretary-General following the Joint Submission to the CLCS by Malaysia and Vietnam in 2009.[1672]

The members of the tribunal elaborate that parties may exclude compulsory jurisdiction for disputes involving 'historic bays or titles' – but not other historic rights – according to Article 298 (1) (a) (i) UNCLOS (see also Articles 10 and 15). However, in their eyes, 'as a matter of plain geography,' the South China Sea cannot be understood as a 'historic bay.' Concerning whether China claimed 'historic title,' the arbitrators professed not to have found any specific indication by China, and to thus have to evaluate its pertinent conduct. They remind that 'historic title' refers to sovereignty over land or maritime areas – the latter as internal waters or territorial sea – while the more generic 'historic rights' can also be much more limited, such as historic fishing rights.[1673]

In the arbitrators' view, China's explicit respect for freedom of navigation and overflight (going beyond innocent passage) in these waters means that it claims 'a constellation of historic rights short of title,' ie the pertinent exception in Article 298 (1) (a) (i) UNCLOS was not seen to apply and the tribunal assumed jurisdiction.[1674]

The tribunal further concluded that China had made a historic rights claim to fisheries and petroleum resources within the nine-dash line inde-

---

accessed 25 June 2017; *The South China Sea Arbitration* (Award) (n 196) paras 178–179.

1671 *The South China Sea Arbitration* (Award) (n 196) para 181, Figure 1; Boundary Department of the Ministry of Interior of the Republic of China, *Map Showing the Location of the Various Islands in the South Sea* (1948).

1672 *The South China Sea Arbitration* (Award) (n 196) paras 181–183, Figure 2, Annex 191, Annex 192; PRC Communication on the Joint CLCS Submission of Malaysia and Vietnam (n 1606); PRC Communication on Vietnam's CLCS Submission (n 1549).

1673 Arts 10, 15, 298 (1) (a) (i) UNCLOS; *The South China Sea Arbitration* (Award) (n 196) paras 205–206, 225.

1674 Arts 298 (1) (a) (i) UNCLOS; *The South China Sea Arbitration* (Award) (n 196) paras 212–214, 229.

pendent of UNCLOS. It saw this evidenced by Chinese tenders for petroleum exploration blocks beyond 200 nautical miles from any Chinese-claimed land feature or 'any possible extended continental shelf,' and frequent pertinent references in connection with 'summer fishing bans' and objections to other littoral states' fishing and hydrocarbon exploration.[1675]

On the preservation of pre-established rights to resources at variance with UNCLOS, the arbitrators held that such could remain unaffected where they are expressly preserved or are not incompatible with the Convention,[1676] while UNCLOS will prevail where such independently arisen rights are incompatible with it.[1677] They underlined that no UNCLOS article permits that historic rights to living and non-living resources of the EEZ, continental shelf, high seas or Area could continue to exist.[1678]

The tribunal concluded that China's claims are incompatible with the Convention, viewed against text and context of UNCLOS as well as pertinent case law. It emphasized the comprehensive nature of UNCLOS, citing the consensus-oriented history of negotiations – wherein China had led developing countries in lobbying for stronger EEZ and continental shelf resource jurisdiction – the language of the Preamble ('all issues related to the law of the sea'), and limited options to make reservations. It further maintained that provisions on the EEZ and continental shelf exclusively accord sovereign rights to living and non-living resources therein to the coastal state, with limited rights of other states under certain circumstances including traditional fishing rights. Finally, they cited *Gulf of Maine* as the most relevant previous instance of a claim to historic (fisheries) rights in another state's EEZ, noting that the US was considered to have lost its traditional access to Canadian fishing grounds after both states declared exclusive fishery zones.[1679]

In the arbitrators' view, China did not relinquish historic rights in the South China Sea by ratifying UNCLOS, but rather freedoms of the high seas. They argued that historic rights could only arise where international law does not already permit pertinent activities, and that before UNCLOS all maritime areas beyond narrow territorial seas were viewed as part of the

1675 *The South China Sea Arbitration* (Award) (n 196) paras 208–211.
1676 Art 311 (2) and (5) UNCLOS.
1677 Art 293 UNCLOS; Art 30 (3) VCLT.
1678 *The South China Sea Arbitration* (Award) (n 196) paras 235–239.
1679 Preamble and Arts 56, 58, 62, 77, 81 and 309 UNCLOS; *The South China Sea Arbitration* (Award) (n 196) paras 231, 240–262; *Gulf of Maine* (n 1483) [341]–[342] para 235.

high seas, whereby everybody could freely fish and explore the seabed there. Additionally they held there was a lack of evidence of the notion that China historically restricted others from using high seas freedoms, which would have been necessary to support a claim to exclusive jurisdiction.[1680]

The tribunal thus declared that maritime entitlements in the South China Sea may not extend beyond UNCLOS, and that China's claims to historic rights within the 'nine-dash line' are 'without lawful effect' where they do.[1681] All of this, it is emphasized, neither prejudices the question of sovereignty over land features, nor does it inhibit the possibility of claiming maritime zones extending from them.[1682]

IV.3.4.3.3 Status of Maritime Features

IV.3.4.3.3.1 Low-tide Elevations

On Manila's contention that Mischief Reef, Second Thomas Shoal and Subi Reef, as well as Gaven Reef and McKennan Reef (including Hughes Reef) are low-tide elevations, the arbitrators agreed except for McKennan Reef (apart from Hughes Reef) and the (distinct) northern part of Gaven Reef. Some of these land features are considered within twelve nautical miles of a 'rock' or 'island' (Hughes Reef, the (distinct) southern part of Gaven Reef, and Subi Reef), and to thus be able to serve as basepoints for the territorial seas of those high-tide features.[1683] Not having physical access to the Chinese controlled features, the tribunal in its decision process valued nautical survey charts (more than satellite imagery) as produced be-

---

1680 *The South China Sea Arbitration* (Award) (n 196) paras 268–271.

1681 Ibid paras 277–278.

1682 Ibid para 272.

1683 Art 13 UNCLOS; *The South China Sea Arbitration* (Award) (n 196) paras 352–366, 382–384. For photographs of land features in question before and after land reclamation see also *The South China Sea Arbitration* (Award) (n 196) Annex 789 Figures 22 and 23, Annex 791 Figures 26 and 27, Annex 792 Figure 31, Annex 795 Figures 28 and 29. For data on and photographs of Second Thomas Shoal, where no major land reclamation has taken place, see also CSIS – Asia Maritime Transparency Initiative, 'Second Thomas Shoal' (Washington DC) <https://amti.csis.org/second-thomas-shoal/> accessed 1 March 2019.

fore man-made changes to land features' natural state could complicate evaluations.[1684]

According to the members of the tribunal, low-tide elevations cannot be appropriated, but rather the coastal state may have sovereignty or sovereign rights over them as part of the submerged landmass of the territorial sea or continental shelf.[1685]

IV.3.4.3.3.2 'Islands' or 'Rocks'?

The tribunal found in favor of the Philippines' contentions that Scarborough Shoal, Johnson Reef, Cuarteron Reef and Fiery Cross Reef are 'rocks', and that the low-tide elevations Mischief Reef and Second Thomas Shoal are part of the Philippine EEZ and continental shelf. Arbitrators maintained that all other features in the Spratly Islands are no more than 'rocks' either, that no potential Chinese EEZ or continental shelf entitlement can reach Mischief Reef and Second Thomas Shoal – both within 200 nautical miles from the Philippines' coast – and that there can thus not be any overlapping entitlements that would call for prior delimitation, blocking the tribunal's jurisdiction.[1686]

1684 *The South China Sea Arbitration* (Award) (n 196) paras 326–332, 352–358. While the arbitrators considered charts as old as 150 years – also independently seeking additional materials from UK and Japanese archives – they preferred more recent charts, including such by Chinese authorities ('waves' of surveys were carried out in the 1860s (British Royal Navy), 1920s and 1930s (UK, Japan, France and US), recent decades (littoral states)). Interestingly, Chinese charts' depictions were sometimes in line with Philippine positions, eg on Hughes Reef, but could also be decisive where they were not, eg on McKennan Reef.

1685 *The South China Sea Arbitration* (Award) (n 196) paras 303–306, 308–309, 508–511, referencing *Territorial and Maritime Dispute (Nicaragua v Colombia)* (Judgment) (n 1477) [641] para 26.

1686 *The South China Sea Arbitration* (Award) (n 196) paras 385–387, 628–633, 643–647. For photographs of land features in question before and after land reclamation see also *The South China Sea Arbitration* (Award) (n 196) Annex 787 Figures 18 and 19, Annex 788 Figures 20 and 21, Annex 790 Figures 24 and 25, Annex 792 Figures 31 and 32. For data on and photographs of Scarborough Shoal and Second Thomas Shoal, where no major land reclamation has taken place, see also CSIS – Asia Maritime Transparency Initiative, 'Scarborough Shoal' (Washington DC) <https://amti.csis.org/scarborough-shoal/> accessed 1 March 2019; CSIS – Asia Maritime Transparency Initiative, 'Second Thomas

On Article 121 (3) UNCLOS – '[rocks] which cannot sustain human habitation or economic life of their own shall have no exclusive economic zone or continental shelf'[1687] – the arbitrators considered clear that economic activities fully dependent on external resources, mere extractive activities, or sole reliance on adjacent waters, do not suffice, and that 'the most reliable evidence (…) will usually be the historical use to which [a feature] has been put'.[1688] The purpose of the norm was seen in supporting the EEZ objective of subsistence for 'non-transient' 'natural populations' as well as the international seabed by 'disabl[ing] tiny features from unfairly and inequitably generating enormous entitlements to maritime space that would serve not to benefit the local population, but to award a windfall to the (potentially distant) State to have maintained a claim to such a feature'.[1689] In other words, the norm should 'forestall a provocative and counterproductive effort to manufacture entitlements' – inter alia – via establishing 'artificial populations'.[1690]

The award declares the land features addressed by the Philippines' submissions 'obviously' incapable of sustaining human habitation or economic life of their own, terming them 'minuscule,' and lacking of fresh water, vegetation and living space, with reclamation and construction work irrelevant to their status.[1691]

As to the remaining high-tide features relevant due to potential overlapping entitlements, the arbitrators noted on the one with the potentially strongest claim to 'island' status, Itu Aba, that it has a freshwater lens – but of fluctuating, questionable and limited quality, regeneration capacity, and volume – some vegetation including fruit trees planted by commercial fleets, and a small vegetable patch that 'would not suffice, on its own, to support a sizeable population'.[1692] The tribunal described small groups of fishermen historically having used the Spratly islands – with intermittent external supplies – but considered their efforts extractive and for the bene-

Shoal' (Washington DC) <https://amti.csis.org/second-thomas-shoal/> accessed 1 March 2019.

1687 Arts 121 (3) UNCLOS.

1688 *The South China Sea Arbitration* (Award) (n 196) paras 478–505, 508–511, 543, 549–550.

1689 Ibid para 516, see also paras 512–514, 535, 542 and the Declaration on the Maritime Zone, signed at Santiago, 18 August 1952 (Chile, Ecuador and Peru) 1976 UNTS 326.

1690 *The South China Sea Arbitration* (Award) (n 196) para 621.

1691 Ibid paras 554–570.

1692 Ibid paras 580–596.

fit of littoral states rather than Spratlys inhabitants.[1693] On the capacity to 'sustain human habitation,' the arbitrators ultimately decided on the negative, emphasizing that fishermen 1) were never referred to as eg 'from Itu Aba,' but rather as eg 'from Hainan,' 2) that they apparently did not bring their families, and 3) did not construct shelter and facilities commensurate with the intention of permanent residence. In short, the Spratlys did not become 'home' and thus no 'stable human community' ever formed.[1694]

The members of the tribunal also noted that China's statements could be understood to constitute a claim to archipelagic or straight baselines around the Spratly Islands, taken as a single unit entitled to maritime zones, but that the Spratly Islands fulfill none of the pertinent criteria.[1695] They noted that archipelagic baselines can only be used by archipelagic states – 'constituted wholly by one or more archipelagos'[1696] – encompassing 'the main islands and an area in which the ratio of the area of the water to the area of the land, including atolls, is between 1 to 1 and 9 to 1'.[1697] Straight baselines, finally, are limited by Article 7 UNCLOS to deep indents in the coastline and 'a fringe of islands along the coast in its immediate vicinity'.[1698]

IV.3.4.3.4 Lawfulness of Chinese Actions

First, the Philippines claimed that China prevented its 'enjoyment and exercise of the sovereign rights' connected to its EEZ and continental shelf by interfering with oil and gas exploration and fishing.[1699] China's earlier public statements had made clear that China considers it is the one with sovereign rights over the respective fisheries and petroleum resources.[1700] The tribunal assumed jurisdiction and determined violations through interference with a seismic survey vessel on the Philippine continental shelf, and the adoption of a fishing moratorium – as a domestic regulation with

1693 Ibid paras 597–614.

1694 Art 121 (3) UNCLOS; *The South China Sea Arbitration* (Award) (n 196) paras 615–626.

1695 *The South China Sea Arbitration* (Award) (n 196) paras 571–575.

1696 Art 46 UNCLOS.

1697 Art 47 UNCLOS.

1698 Art 7 UNCLOS.

1699 *The South China Sea Arbitration* (Award) (n 196) paras 649–680, 716.

1700 Ibid paras 687–689.

deterrent effect due to 'realistic prospects' of punitive measures – encompassing parts of the Philippine EEZ.[1701]

Second, the Philippines alleged violations through '[failing] to prevent [Chinese] nationals and vessels from exploiting the living resources' in its EEZ, referencing fishing at Mischief Reef and Second Thomas Shoal under escort by PLA naval and China Marine Surveillance ships in 2013.[1702] In earlier public statements, Beijing had rejected Philippine sovereign rights in these areas and explicitly claimed sovereignty over Mischief Reef.[1703] The arbitrators affirmed their jurisdiction and determined flag state due diligence violations due to close government coordination with private fishing operations equipped with Chinese licenses for areas considered within the Philippine EEZ, and under non-compliance with coastal state licensing and other obligations.[1704]

Third, the Philippine government complained that its fishermen were unlawfully prevented from accessing their traditional fishing grounds within the territorial sea of Scarborough Shoal after an escalatory chain reaction in 2012, supposedly set off by Chinese fishermen engaging in destructive fishing methods. In contemporaneous statements Beijing had claimed sovereignty over Scarborough Shoal as well as traditional fishing rights there. The tribunal was satisfied that China had intermittently blocked off access to the lagoon of the shoal violating Philippine traditional fishing rights, viewed traditional fishing by both parties (and Vietnam) as evident, and sovereignty over the feature as immaterial to the violation in question.[1705]

The award held that what was to be protected was only simple and small-scale traditional or 'artisanal' fishing – as opposed to 'industrial fishing' (citing *Eritrea v Yemen*) – in the territorial sea, where the exercise of sovereignty is subject to 'other rules of international law' (see Article 2 (3) UNCLOS) including customary international law (citing *Chagos*). The arbitrators underlined that the introduction of EEZs as redistribution of rights had been markedly different from previous maritime jurisdiction expansions akin to land border changes where 'acquired rights' were consid-

1701 Art 56, 77 UNCLOS; *The South China Sea Arbitration* (Award) (n 196) paras 691–694, 697, 705, 708, 712, 714–715.

1702 *The South China Sea Arbitration* (Award) (n 196) paras 717–721, 757.

1703 Ibid paras 729–732.

1704 Arts 58 (3), 61 and 62 UNCLOS; *The South China Sea Arbitration* (Award) (n 196) paras 733–756.

1705 *The South China Sea Arbitration* (Award) (n 196) paras 758, 761–769, 786–791, 793, 805–807, 810–812, 814.

ered protected, and argued that *Eritrea v Yemen* could only reach a different decision because the parties empowered it to also 'apply factors other than' UNCLOS.[1706]

Fourth, the tribunal was satisfied that Chinese construction and artificial island-building activities on the low-tide elevation Mischief Reef violated Philippine sovereign rights in EEZ and continental shelf.[1707] China had previously insisted on all steps taken being within its sovereign rights and on the purposes of construction being mainly civilian.[1708] The arbitrators accepted China's own affirmations, and rejected the jurisdictional exception on military matters (Article 298 (1) (b) UNCLOS).[1709]

Fifth, the Philippines complained that China violated its duties to exercise 'jurisdiction and control,' ensure safety and compliance with international regulations, as a flag state, by creating a 'serious risk of collision and danger' with its law enforcement operations in the territorial sea of Scarborough Shoal. The submission concerned two incidents on 28 April and 26 Ma 2012 at which Chinese government vessels almost caused collisions with Philippine vessels to bar them from supplying ships stationed at the shoal. China had responded to diplomatic protests with the reiteration that the Philippines should respect its sovereignty over the area. However, the tribunal found China to be in conscious and 'total disregard of good

1706 Art 2 (3) UNCLOS; *The South China Sea Arbitration* (Award) (n 196) paras 794, 798–799, 802–804, 808, citing *Eritrea v Yemen (second stage)* (n 1492) [359]–[360], [374], [Art 2 (3) Annex I – The Arbitration Agreement], as well as *Questions relating to Settlers of German Origin in Poland (Germany v Poland)* (Advisory Opinion) PCIJ Series B No 6 [36]; *Abyei Arbitration (Government of Sudan v Sudan People's Liberation Movement/Army)* (Final Award of 22 June 2009) 30 RIAA 145, 412, para 766; *Award between the United States and the United Kingdom relating to the Rights of Jurisdiction of United States in the Bering's Sea and the Preservation of Fur Seals (United Kingdom v United States)* (Award of 15 August 1893) 28 RIAA 263, 271.

1707 Arts 56 (1) (b), 60, 80 UNCLOS; *The South China Sea Arbitration* (Award) (n 196) paras 994, 1031–1038, 1040, 1043.

1708 *The South China Sea Arbitration* (Award) (n 196) paras 996–1009, 1020–1023, the tiny low-tide elevation was, from 1995 but especially since 2015, built into an artificial island of over five million squaremetres, complete with a 250-metre-wide channel into the lagoon, fortified seawalls, loading piers, cement plants, and (what has since become) an airstrip.

1709 Art 298 (1) (b) UNCLOS; *The South China Sea Arbitration* (Award) (n 196) paras 1024–1028.

seamanship,' with its vessels having assumed unsafe speeds and not upheld safe distances.[1710]

Sixth, the Philippines submitted that China had violated several environmental protection provisions, and noted ongoing violations. This concerned fishing with cyanide, explosives and propellers (to break up coral), harvesting endangered giant clams and sea turtles, and island-building activities particularly destructive to coral reefs.[1711] According to Chinese diplomatic statements, fishing activities were within Chinese sovereign rights and violations would be punished under Chinese law, and all construction activities only proceeded after rigorous scientific assessment ensuring environmental protection.[1712]

The tribunal again rejected the jurisdictional exception on military activities.[1713] It was satisfied that Chinese vessels had harvested endangered species and that the PRC had violated due diligence obligations, partly even encouraging fishermen through protection by government vessels.[1714] Evidence was deemed lacking on possible violations due to fishing with cyanide and explosives.[1715] The arbitrators argued that Chinese construction activities had violated several environmental protection provisions, and that Beijing had failed to cooperate on a regional basis on marine environmental protection.[1716] They maintained that within less than three years from late 2013, China had 'create[d] more than 12.8 million square metres of new land',[1717] that pre-existing installations grew to several hundred times their 2012 size, and that several large artificial islands were

1710 Art 94 UNCLOS; Rules 2, 6, 7, 8, 15, and 16 Convention on the International Regulations for Preventing Collisions at Sea (COLREGS) (1972) 1050 UNTS 16; *The South China Sea Arbitration* (Award) (n 196) paras 1044–1045, 1047–1058, 1078–1079, 1081–1108, 1109.

1711 *The South China Sea Arbitration* (Award) (n 196) paras 815–820, 826–890, 992–993.

1712 Ibid paras 913–920.

1713 Ibid paras 931–932, 935–938.

1714 Arts 192, 194 (5) UNCLOS; *The South China Sea Arbitration* (Award) (n 196) paras 950–953, 958–964, practices in the harvesting of endangered giant clams using propellers were described by one of the consulted experts as 'more thoroughly damaging to marine life than anything he had seen in four decades of investigating coral reef degradation' (para 958).

1715 *The South China Sea Arbitration* (Award) (n 196) para 975.

1716 Arts 123, 192, 194 (1) and (5), 197, 206 UNCLOS; *The South China Sea Arbitration* (Award) (n 196) paras 983–986, 991.

1717 *The South China Sea Arbitration* (Award) (n 196) paras 823–825, 853–855.

equipped with harbors, airstrips, radar, defensive and administrative facilities.[1718]

IV.3.4.3.5 Aggravation of the Dispute and Future Conduct

The tribunal confirmed that China had 'aggravated and extended the dispute' through its construction and artificial island-building activities after the arbitration was initiated,[1719] but considered jurisdiction lacking on whether China's interference with the rotation and resupply of Philippine military personnel at Second Thomas Shoal had also done so.[1720] It argued on island-building that such had permanently destroyed evidence on pertinent features' natural state and damaged coral reefs irreparably, aggravating disputes on island status, entitlements, and environmental obligations, in contravention to Articles 279 and 300 UNCLOS, Article 26 VCLT, and 'extensive jurisprudence'.[1721]

On the Philippines' submission asking for confirmation that China would have to comply with UNCLOS environmental protection duties and have due regard to the Philippines' rights and freedoms, the tribunal was not convinced that any dispute existed, presumed good faith, and that the parties had merely proceeded from different understandings of their now clarified rights under the law of the sea.[1722]

1718 Ibid paras 863–890, 1008, figures 18–32 on pages 341, 343, 347, 351, 353, 405.

1719 Ibid paras 1110–1111, 1181.

1720 Art 298 (1) (b) UNCLOS; *The South China Sea Arbitration* (Award) (n 196) paras 1110–1111, 1153–1162.

1721 Arts 279, 300 UNCLOS; Art 26 VCLT; *The South China Sea Arbitration* (Award) (n 196) paras 1166–1173, 1181; *Electricity Company of Sofia and Bulgaria (Belgium v Bulgaria)* (Interim Measures of Protection) PCIJ Rep Series A/B No 79, [199]; *LaGrand (Germany v United States of America)* (Judgment) [2001] ICJ Rep 466, [503] paras 102–103; *Delimitation of the Maritime Boundary between Ghana and Côte D'Ivoire in the Atlantic Ocean* (Provisional Measures, Order of 25 April 2015) ITLOS Reports 2015, 146, para 108(1)(e).

1722 *The South China Sea Arbitration* (Award) (n 196) paras 1182–1184, 1191–1201.

IV.3.4.4. Implications and Aftermath

IV.3.4.4.1. Political Reactions and Outlook

Unsurprisingly, on the day the award was issued, the Chinese MFA 'solemnly declare[d] that the award is null and void and has no binding force. China neither accepts nor recognizes it'.[1723] It reiterated that China was the party upholding international law, while others were undermining it. The MFA spokesperson Lu Kang scolded 'two or three countries,' explicitly Japan, for 'poking [their] nose[s] into' the issue, ie calling for compliance, and ventured that the Chinese position was 'the just position held by the majority of the international community'.[1724]

According to Article 296 (1) UNCLOS the award has to be considered final and binding.[1725] This study will also argue that the tribunal made serious efforts to evaluate every potential argument against its jurisdiction, and to apply additional scrutiny and care on account of China's non-participation and in keeping with Article 9 Annex VII UNCLOS.[1726] Future disputes may result from non-compliance, particularly regarding violating the Philippines' sovereign rights in its EEZ and continental shelf.

However, the question of potential further legal proceedings or a possible escalation on the ground receded for the time being, soon after the award was rendered. The new Philippine president Rodrigo Duterte initiated a diplomatic charm offensive towards China and made clear that he would not push for implementation of the award.[1727]

1723 Ministry of Foreign Affairs of China, 'Statement on the Award of 12 July 2016 of the Arbitral Tribunal in the South China Sea Arbitration Established at the Request of the Republic of the Philippines' (Beijing, 12 July 2016) <http://www.fmprc.gov.cn/nanhai/eng/snhwtlcwj_1/t1379492.htm> accessed 1 March 2019.

1724 Ministry of Foreign Affairs of the PRC, 'Spokesperson Lu Kang's Remarks on Japanese Foreign Minister's Statement on the Award of South China Sea Arbitration Initiated by the Philippines' (Beijing, 12 July 2016) <http://www.fmprc.gov.cn/mfa_eng/xwfw_665399/s2510_665401/t1380245.shtml> accessed 1 April 2019; Ministry of Foreign Affairs of the PRC, 'Foreign Ministry Spokesperson Lu Kang's Remarks' (Beijing, 28 July 2016) <http://www.fmprc.gov.cn/mfa_eng/xwfw_665399/s2510_665401/2535_665405/t1385371.shtml> accessed 1 April 2019.

1725 Art 296 (1) UNCLOS.

1726 Art 9 Annex VII UNCLOS.

1727 Harry Krejsa, 'Rodrigo Duterte's Turn in the South China Sea – Will the Philippines' new president snatch defeat from the jaws of victory?' *The Diplo-*

Duterte had assumed office on 30 June 2016. Despite contradictory foreign policy statements, his rapprochement with Beijing and distancing from Washington has remained a constant. The two governments have since discussed joint resource development in 'disputed' areas again – attempted, but not achieved since 1986 – all areas having been clearly assigned to the Philippines in the arbitral award.[1728] Philippine fishermen were allowed into the Scarborough Shoal's territorial sea, but not into the lagoon inside the atoll.[1729] As long as the government in Manila is not voted out, a real push – diplomatic and otherwise – for implementing the arbitration's outcome, is unlikely. The regional body the Philippines is part of, ASEAN, which was anyway split on the issue,[1730] will not champion the Philippine position, if the country itself fails to do so. Whether the Trump administration will meaningfully do so remains difficult to predict.

Domestically, the Chinese president seeks to project strength after cementing his power in the 19th National Congress of the Chinese Communist Party and First Session of the 13th National Peoples's Congress, and to bolster and centralize loyalty in party, state and armed forces leading up to the centennial of the foundation of the Chinese Communist Party in

---

mat (Tokyo, 15 July 2016) <http://thediplomat.com/2016/07/rodrigo-dutertes-turn-in-the-south-china-sea/> accessed 15 March 2019; Ben Blanchard, 'Duterte aligns Philippines with China, says U.S. has lost' *Reuters* (Beijing, 20 October 2016) <http://www.reuters.com/article/us-china-philippines-idUSKCN12K0AS> accessed 15 March 2019; Manolo Serapio and Martin Petty, 'Philippines' Duterte says pointless discussing South China Sea woes at summit' *Reuters* (Manila, 27 April 2017) <http://www.reuters.com/article/us-asean-summit-idUSKBN17T11J> accessed 15 March 2019.

1728 Nestor Corrales, 'PH, China to have joint venture in West Philippine Sea – Duterte' *Inquirer.net* (Manila, 25 July 2017) <http://globalnation.inquirer.net/159003/ph-china-joint-venture-west-philippine-sea-duterte> accessed 15 March 2019; Manuel Mogato, 'China backs joint energy development with Philippines in disputed sea' *Reuters* (Manila, 25 July 2017) <http://www.reuters.com/article/us-philippines-china-idUSKBN1AA10L> accessed 15 March 2019.

1729 CSIS – Asia Maritime Transparency Initiative, 'Updated: Imagery suggests Philippine fishermen still not entering Scarborough Shoal' *CSIS* (Washington DC, 27 October 2016) <https://amti.csis.org/china-scarborough-fishing/> accessed 15 March 2019.

1730 Manuel Mogato, Michael Martina and Ben Blanchard, 'ASEAN deadlocked on South China Sea, Cambodia blocks statement' *Reuters* (Vientiane, 25 July 2016) <https://www.reuters.com/article/us-southchinasea-ruling-asean/asean-deadlocked-on-south-china-sea-cambodia-blocks-statement-idUSKCN1050F6> accessed 10 November 2019.

2021.[1731] As a tense localized stand-off with Indian forces near the trilateral border with Bhutan also demonstrated,[1732] no concessions on territorial issues can be expected in the short term, ie the next few years are unlikely to see a change in attitude on embracing the jurisdiction of any international tribunal on a territorial dispute.

Meanwhile, China has continued its island-building and construction activities in the South China Sea, despite the tribunal's findings. Land reclamation in the Spratly Islands appears to have been completed, for the time being, before the tribunal rendered its award on the merits, but was then continued in the Paracel Islands further north, which Vietnam also claims. However, construction also appears to have continued on the Spratly Islands, eg regarding radar facilities and underground storage areas, as several air and naval bases are becoming operational.[1733]

Interestingly, in what might be a reaction to the award, China has lately downplayed the importance of historic rights, rather emphasizing its supposed sovereignty over what it still insists on calling four South China Sea 'island groups' (ie 'archipelagos'), which in turn are said to be entitled to a full set of maritime zones.[1734] Resulting claims would more or less equal the extent of the nine-dash line. Other aspects of Chinese behavior would point to its claims to seabed resources being indeed exclusive as via EEZ

1731 The Economist, 'The loyal family – Xi Jinping wants officials to declare allegiance to himself' *The Economist* (London, 6 April 2017) <https://www.economist.com/news/china/21720315-why-it-so-important-him-xi-jinping-wants-officials-declare-allegiance-himself> accessed 15 March 2019; Chris Buckley and Keith Bradsher, 'China Moves to Let Xi Stay in Power by Abolishing Term Limit' *New York Times* (New York, 25 February 2018) <https://www.nytimes.com/2018/02/25/world/asia/china-xi-jinping.html> accessed 15 March 2019.

1732 Japan Times, 'India and China face off in border standoff as fears of all-out military conflict grow' *Japan Times* (Tokyo, 25 July 2017) <http://www.japantimes.co.jp/news/2017/07/25/asia-pacific/india-china-face-off-border-standoff-fears-military-conflict-grow/#.WYcfGNPyhE4> accessed 26 July 2017.

1733 CSIS – Asia Maritime Transparency Intitiative, 'Update: China's Continuing Reclamation in the Paracels' *CSIS* (Washington DC, 9 August 2017) <https://amti.csis.org/paracels-beijings-other-buildup/> accessed 15 March 2019; CSIS – Asia Maritime Transparency Initiative, 'A Constructive Year for Chinese Base Building' *CSIS* (Washington DC, 14 December 2017) <https://amti.csis.org/constructive-year-chinese-building/> accessed 15 March 2019.

1734 Julian Ku and Christopher Mirasola, 'The South China Sea and China's "Four Sha" Claim: New Legal Theory, Same Bad Argument' *Lawfare Blog* (Washington DC, 25 September 2017) <https://www.lawfareblog.com/south-china-sea-and-chinas-four-sha-claim-new-legal-theory-same-bad-argument> accessed 15 March 2019.

and continental shelf sovereign rights, as eg Vietnam has decided to pull back from hydrocarbon exploration in disputed areas after alleged threats from the Chinese government.[1735]

IV.3.4.4.2. Criticism, Evaluation, and Legal Implications

In the following, *Philippines v China* will be reviewed along the lines of prominent points of criticism in English-language literature, whereas Chinese-language scholarly debate will be addressed in Chapter V. Comments on important legal implications of the case will be made. However, this sub-chapter will focus on issues upon which the decision might influence China's future engagement with international adjudication.

IV.3.4.4.2.1. Criticism Relating to Jurisdiction

Criticism of the award – often but certainly not always coming from Chinese authors or publications – has been intense. Aside from a long list of Chinese scholars expressing their disbelief at the tribunal's findings in Chinese-language journals,[1736] the English-language *Chinese Journal of International Law* dedicated much space to lining up mostly international authors that find fault with the awards, as discussed in the following. To be sure, voices sympathetic to different aspects of the Chinese position can certainly also be found elsewhere too.[1737]

1735 Ankit Panda, 'Vietnam Requests Spain's Repsol Suspend Work in Disputed South China Sea Oil Block' *The Diplomat* (Tokyo, 25 March 2018) <https://thediplomat.com/2018/03/vietnam-requests-spains-repsol-suspend-work-in-disputed-south-china-sea-oil-block/> accessed 15 March 2019; Bill Hayton, 'The Week Donald Trump Lost the South China Sea' *Foreign Policy* (Washington DC, 31 July 2017) <http://foreignpolicy.com/2017/07/31/the-week-donald-trump-lost-the-south-china-sea/> accessed 15 March 2019.

1736 See Chapter V.3.2.2.

1737 On the problem of arguing without opposition due to China's non-participation and criticism of jurisidictional decisions see eg Schoenbaum, 'The South China Sea Arbitration Decision' (n 40) 452–454, 459 On both jurisdictional questions and the interpretation of Article 121 (3) UNCLOS on 'rocks,' including on the size of land features playing a role, see eg Talmon, 'The South China Sea Arbitration and the Finality of "Final" Awards' (n 40) 388–401 who inter alia mentions Jan Mayen and *Maritime Delimitation in the Area between Greenland and Jan Mayen (Denmark v Norway)* (Judgment) [1993] ICJ Rep 38,

On the issue of there even being a dispute the tribunal could have had jurisdiction to speak on, some authors negate the existence of a dispute about the status of the individual maritime features. China supposedly 1) only addressed the Spratly Islands' entitlements 'as a single unit' (and Scarborough Shoal as part of Macclesfield Bank as a supposed second archipelago) and 2) did not specifically address the entitlements of the individual features, while 3) Philippine diplomatic correspondence left open the possibility of fully-entitled islands.[1738]

The tribunal can indeed be faulted with not devoting more space to the issue of the existence of a dispute regarding each and every Philippine submission. Arbitrators should have – the evidence of China's position surely paints a picture that is more vague than critics of the tribunal make it out to be – delved more into 1) the question of whether the proper reading is that China ignored the status of all land features and only claimed maritime zones from the Spratlys as an archipelago, and into 2) evidence of a dispute about the status of each feature.

However, the members of the tribunal rightly made clear that China failed to deliver a much-called-for response to the Philippine position that no pertinent feature is an EEZ-entitled 'island,' and inferences may be made, while granular exchanges on the status of each feature could not have been required. If this had not been the case, China's intentional ambiguity and refusal to expressly discuss matters – or discuss them in more legal terms – would have been sufficient to bar a case, although available evidence indeed makes a dispute plain. Moreover, the relevant and clear

---

73, para 79; Conciliation Commission on the Continental Shelf Area between Iceland and Jan Mayen *Report and Recommendations to the Governments of Iceland and Norway* (1981) 20 ILM 797, 801–803. On the contentious scholarly debates regarding the meaning of Article 121 (3) UNCLOS see also Erik Franckx, 'The Regime of Islands and Rocks', in David Joseph Attard, Malgosia Fitzmaurice and Norman A Martínez Guttiérez (eds), *The IMLI Manual on International Maritime Law – Volume I: The Law of the Sea* (OUP 2014) 113–117. On the retention of historic rights in other states' EEZ see eg Sophia Kopela, 'Historic Titles and Historic Rights in the Law of the Sea in the Light of the South China Sea Arbitration' (2017) 48 *Ocean Development & International Law* 181, 192–196.

1738 Michael Sheng-ti Gau, 'The Agreements and Disputes Crystalized by the 2009–2011 Sino-Philippine Exchange of Notes Verbales and their Relevance to the Jurisdiction and Admissibility Phase of the South China Sea Arbitration' (2016) 15 CJIL 417, 424–426; Xianhe (Sienho) Yi (Yee), 'The South China Sea Arbitration' (n 1514) 225; Stefan Talmon, 'The South China Sea Arbitration: Observations on the Award on Jurisdiction and Admissibility' (2016) 15 CJIL 309, 313–348.

Philippine position is the one taken in this case: that no feature in the Spratlys is more than a 'rock'.[1739]

One aspect that critics miss with the scenario of China only claiming maritime zones for the Spratlys as a 'unit' and there thus not being a dispute is that China indirectly took a position on island status even through the claim to an EEZ and continental shelf for the Spratlys as a unit, ie archipelago. In defining 'archipelago' under UNCLOS, Article 46 (b) speaks of 'a group of islands' – ie Article 121 (1) high-tide features – but does not explicitly require any of them to be more than Article 121 (3) 'rocks'. For dependent archipelagos, if they indeed constitute such, a continental state such as China might have been considered allowed under nascent international customary law to use straight or archipelagic baselines, although not fulfilling requirements under Article 7 and Part IV UNCLOS.[1740] However, these archipelagos would not automatically be entitled to an EEZ and continental shelf. By claiming such, China infers that there are fully-entitled 'islands' in the Spratlys. China might even interpret its positions as claims it makes as an archipelagic state, although it could only do so and enjoy concomitant rights after having declared itself an archipelagic state (see *Qatar v Bahrain*),[1741] which it has not done.

1739 *The South China Sea Arbitration* (Award on Jurisdiction and Admissibility) (n 1506) paras 159–163, 169–172; See also *ICERD Application (Georgia v Russia)* (n 1641) [84]–[85], para 30.

1740 For pertinent state practice see eg Spain (Balearic Islands), Portugal (Azores Islands), Denmark (Faroe Islands), United Kingdom (Falkland Islands), Ecuador (Galapagos Islands), Canada (Canadian Arctic Islands). The practice has been embraced by other states, for example with regard to the Faroe Islands.

1741 Arts 7, 46 (b), 121 (1) and (3) UNCLOS; *Maritime Delimitation and Territorial Questions Between Qatar and Bahrain (Qatar v Bahrain)* (Merits) [2001] ICJ Rep 40, paras 180–183; Arif Havas Oegroseno, 'Archipelagic States: From Concept to Law', in David Joseph Attard, Malgosia Fitzmaurice and Norman A Martínez Guttiérez (eds), *The IMLI Manual on International Maritime Law – Volume I: The Law of the Sea* (OUP 2014) 129–132. See also Kai Trümpler, 'Article 7 – Straight baselines' in Alexander Proelss (ed), *United Nations Convention on the Law of the Sea – A Commentary* (CH Beck 2017) 65–84; Till Markus, 'Article 46 – Use of Terms' in Alexander Proelss (ed), *United Nations Convention on the Law of the Sea – A Commentary* (CH Beck 2017) 334–352; Stefan Talmon, 'Article 121 – Regime of Islands' in Alexander Proelss (ed), *United Nations Convention on the Law of the Sea – A Commentary* (CH Beck 2017) 858–880; Nordquist and others (eds), *A Commentary – Volume II* (n 1518) 95–103, 407–415; Myron H Nordquist and others (eds), *United Nations Convention on the Law of the Sea – A Commentary – Volume III: Articles 86 to 132 and Documentary Annexes* (Martinus Nijhoff Publishers 1995) 324–339.

Second, the composition of the tribunal supposedly influenced decisions including on jurisdiction. Four of the five arbitrators being EU citizens, the tribunal was critized for not being representative of principle legal systems around the world and geographical groups, nor including a Chinese national. Such is not required for an Annex VII UNCLOS arbitral tribunal, though, nor did China make use of the option to participate and appoint one arbitrator. Perhaps the tribunal should have taken some pertinent steps akin to what is laid out in Article 2 of the Statute of ITLOS (Annex VI UNCLOS) in a case as sensitive as this one, to let the tribunal appear more 'representative' and 'impartial'.[1742] Nevertheless, it is not legally required nor convincing that only arbitrators from Asia could have gained a proper understanding of intended legal consequences of East Asian international agreements. Additionally, it is highly questionable whether any qualified Chinese national would have been willing to serve as arbitrator after the Chinese government strictly rejected any participation in the proceedings.

However, the tribunal cannot escape intimations by some scholars of a 'whiff of unfairness,' because the (particularly from a common law perspective) 'lawyer's dream' of being in a position to argue without an opponent came about.[1743] However, once again this situation was not produced by the Philippines nor the tribunal. China could have taken part in the proceedings.

Some authors allege that the members of the arbitral tribunal engaged in 'an ingenious, if suspect, interpretive flurry' on jurisdictional questions, followed by an 'incorrect and unwise' decision on the nine-dash line.[1744] That roundly misses the mark. The majority of the tribunal's findings had to be expected, China's case on most law of the sea claims, not on sovereignty over land features, was weak to begin with, but it was not even made. A chance to change the outcome was missed by non-participation.

A third point of more concrete criticism was that the arbitrators supposedly overlooked the Chinese argument that the DOC and bilateral agree-

---

1742 Art 2 of Annex VI UNCLOS; Patrick Vrancken, 'Annex VI Article 2 – Composition' in Alexander Proelss (ed), *United Nations Convention on the Law of the Sea – A Commentary* (CH Beck 2017) 2337–2339; Myron H Nordquist and others (eds), *United Nations Convention on the Law of the Sea – A Commentary – Volume V: Articles 279 to 320, Annexes V, VI, VII, VIII and IX, Final Act, Annex I, Resolutions I, III, IV* (Martinus Nijhoff Publishers 1989) 341–343; Xianhe (Sienho) Yi (Yee), 'The South China Sea Arbitration' (n 1514) 222–224.

1743 Schoenbaum, 'The South China Sea Arbitration Decision' (n 40) 452–454.

1744 Ibid 459.

ments with the Philippines *cumulatively* constituted a binding decision to make negotiations the only available form of dispute resolution.[1745] This appears a novel and creative, yet fruitless line of argument. If separate non-binding agreements do not bind Manila, these agreements do not bind it as a collective either.

Fourth, critics claimed that the necessary 'exchange of views' did not take place in the required specificity, with *North Sea Continental Shelf* cited in support of this view.[1746] However, the call for earnest negotiations towards a resolution in that case once again leads back to the Chinese government, which must be considered to have failed the obligation for parties 'so to conduct themselves that the negotiations are meaningful, which will not be the case when either of them insists upon its own position without contemplating any modification of it (...)'.[1747] Moreover, the wording in Article 283 UNCLOS – referencing an 'exchange of views regarding [a dispute's] settlement by negotiation or other peaceful means'[1748] – does not indicate a requirement for negotiations on the substance of a dispute.[1749]

Fifth, the members of the tribunal purportedly did not deal with China's position that 'whether or not low-tide elevations are subject to appropriation is itself a territorial sovereignty question beyond the scope of UNCLOS'.[1750] Two things should be mentioned here. The determination of whether something is a low-tide elevation has indeed been a problem in

---

1745 Xianhe (Sienho) Yi (Yee), 'The South China Sea Arbitration' (n 1514) 225.

1746 Sreenivasa Rao Pemmaraju, 'The South China Sea Arbitration (The Philippines v. China): Assessment of the Award on Jurisdiction and Admissibility' (2016) 15 CJIL 265, 282–287; Chris Whomersley, 'The South China Sea: The Award of the Tribunal in the Case Brought by Philippines against China – A Critique' (2016) 15 CJIL 239, 261.

1747 *North Sea Continental Shelf Cases* (n 1482) [47] para 85.

1748 Art 283 UNCLOS.

1749 Philippe Gautier, 'The Settlement of Disputes', in David Joseph Attard, Malgosia Fitzmaurice and Norman A Martínez Guttiérez (eds), *The IMLI Manual on International Maritime Law – Volume I: The Law of the Sea* (OUP 2014) 541–542; Andrew Serdy, 'Article 283 – Obligation to exchange views' in Alexander Proelss (ed), *United Nations Convention on the Law of the Sea – A Commentary* (CH Beck 2017) 1830–1838; Nordquist and others (eds), *A Commentary – Volume V* (n 1742) 28–31.

1750 Xianhe (Sienho) Yi (Yee), 'The South China Sea Arbitration' (n 1514) 225, on low-tide elevations being supposedly open to appropriation beyond the territorial sea see *Award of the Arbitral Tribunal in the First Stage of the Proceedings (Territorial Sovereignty and Scope of the Dispute) (Eritrea v Yemen)* (1998) 114 ILR 1, [para 527], treating low-tide elevations as part of an island group. On at-

the past, because international practice varies on the exact tidal datum to be used for such determination, and UNCLOS is silent on that specific matter. In *Anglo-French Continental Shelf*, the parties debated whether to use the highest tide in the year or mean high-water springs, while the tribunal did not consider a finding on this matter necessary.[1751] However, it has been clear in ICJ case law that low-tide elevations cannot be appropriated, and will be 'treated, in effect, as part of the seabed'.[1752] The Court found in *Minquiers and Ecrehos Case*, that land outside territorial waters needs to be 'permanently above high tide, thus not a drying rock' to be open to appropriation.[1753] It also rejected appropriation of such extra-territorial sea low-tide elevations in *Qatar v Bahrain*.[1754]

A seventh point of criticism was that the members of the tribunal fell short in their analysis on whether the disputes in question touch on delimitation and thus lie outside the scope of jurisdiction. Several Chinese authors viewed a textual interpretation of the word 'concerning' as particularly lacking in the Article 298 (1) (a) (i) UNCLOS optional exception to jurisdiction for 'disputes concerning the interpretation or application of articles 15, 74 and 83',[1755] which would supposedly have had to deliver a sufficiently broad meaning to cover island status determinations' effects on delimitation.[1756] Nonetheless, the notion that the Philippines and China

---

tributing sovereignty over low-tide elevations beyond the territorial sea, see W Michael Reisman, 'The Government of the State of Eritrea and the Government of the Republic of Yemen' (1999) 93 AJIL 668, 680.

1751 Yoshifumi Tanaka, *The International Law of the Sea* (2nd edn, CUP 2015) 71–73; *Arbitration between the United Kingdom of Great Britain and Northern Ireland and the French Republic on the Delimitation of the Continental Shelf* (1979) 18 ILM 397, paras 122–130; John E Noyes 'In Re Arbitration Between the Philippines and China. PCA Case No. 2013–19. Jurisdiction and Admissibility. At http://www.pca-cpa.org. UN Convention on the Law of the Sea Annex VII Arbitral Triubunal, October 29, 2015' (2016) 110 AJIL 102, 107.

1752 Symmons (n 1477) 134, 136–137, 147.

1753 *The Minquiers and Ecrehos Case (France v United Kingdom)* (Judgment) [1953] ICJ Rep 47, [53].

1754 *Maritime Delimitation and Territorial Questions Between Qatar and Bahrain* (n 1741) [104], paras 136, 138, 144, 202, 245, 248. See also *Territorial and Maritime Dispute between Nicaragua and Honduras in the Caribbean Sea* (n 1484), [720 et seq] paras 202, 219, 245, 248.

1755 Arts 15, 74, 83, 298 (1) (a) (i) UNCLOS.

1756 Xianhe (Sienho) Yi (Yee), 'The South China Sea Arbitration' (n 1514) 227–231. See also Keyuan Zou and Qiang Ye, 'Interpretation and Application of Article 298 of the Law of the Sea Convention in Recent Annex VII Arbitrations: An Appraisal' (2017) 0 *Ocean Development and International Law* 1, 5–6.

would have had to be declared states with adjacent or opposite coasts and overlapping claims seems to be at the heart of this line of criticism. Island status of features in between would have then been part of a delimitation process.

Finally, creatively it is argued that the tribunal should have considered a sui generis claim to historic title within the nine-dash line as excluding jurisdiction under Article 298 (1) (a) (i) UNCLOS. Supposedly, China's claim was to be read as one to sovereignty modified by the granting of freedom of navigation and overflight, excluding jurisdiction for the Annex VII tribunal.[1757] Here, the tribunal's emphasis on UNCLOS' comprehensive nature and specific content of 'historic bay' and 'historic title' should be reiterated,[1758] whereas this author is not convinced that an exception in the Chinese case, and recognition of a sui generis claim, would be justified.

In this authors' view, none of the above arguments can defeat jurisdiction. Where sovereignty over the concerned land features does play a role, but does not lead to an exclusion of jurisdiction, is regarding the reasons for the illegality of Chinese interference with Philippine traditional fishing in the Scarborough Shoal territorial sea.[1759] These depend on whether the Philippines have sovereignty over this 'rock,' or only have traditional fishing rights there. However, not knowing which it is does not exclude the possibility of determining illegality, because an argumentum a minori ad maius from interference in traditional fishing can be made.

IV.3.4.4.2.2. Criticism Relating to the Merits

Some points of criticism on the merits are less important for this study but still hold consequences for whether or not China might be willing to engage with potential future adjudication on law of the sea matters, especially concerning the South China Sea.

Herein, the arbitrators have been accused of erring on the issue of a possible claim and retention of non-exclusive Chinese historic rights in the Philippine EEZ.[1760] However, in the view of this author, the criticism mis-

---

1757 Xianhe (Sienho) Yi (Yee), 'The South China Sea Arbitration' (n 1514) 232–233; Art 298 (1) (a) (i) UNCLOS.

1758 *The South China Sea Arbitration* (Award) (n 196) paras 205–206, 225, 231, 240–262.

1759 Noyes, 'In Re Arbitration' (n 1751) 107.

1760 Schoenbaum, 'The South China Sea Arbitration Decision' (n 40) 461–465; Kopela (n 1737) 192–196.

reads 1) Article 62 UNCLOS, 2) the nature of China's claim, and 3) the distinction between artisanal and industrial fishing.[1761]

First, Article 62 (3) UNCLOS calls for taking into account 'the need to minimize economic dislocation in States whose nationals have habitually fished in the zone',[1762] but only in the context of a coastal state 'giving access to other States to its exclusive economic zone under this article'.[1763] This refers to paragraphs 2 and 4 of Article 62, which hold that coastal states not capable of harvesting the entire allowable catch shall give other states access, after they themselves determine their capacity to be lacking, and then only pursuant to relevant agreements and in line with the laws of the coastal state.[1764] This is something entirely different than rights to 'traditional fishing' that remained unchanged by the introduction of the UNCLOS system, thus not being contingent on a coastal state granting access due to its lacking capacity.

Second, Chinese fishing activities were decidedly not conducted in line with Philippine laws and according to pertinent agreements, nor had the Philippines determined its lacking harvesting capacity and thereupon granted access. Instead the Chinese authorities, by adopting domestic regulations – notably a fishing moratorium –[1765]with probable deterrence effects on Philippine fishermen, demonstrated that their claim is not to non-exclusive traditional fishing.

Third, traditional fishing rights in other states' territorial waters have been recognized by international tribunals only in the form of artisanal fishing, ie rather small scale and unsophisticated.[1766] It would not make sense to, in extending such rights geographically to the much larger areas of other states' EEZs, suddenly also expand them qualitatively to include industrial fishing. All indications point to the fact that the Chinese practice falls in the latter category.

1761 Art 62 UNCLOS. See also James Harrison and Elisa Morgera, 'Article 62 – Utilization of the living resources' in Alexander Proelss (ed), *United Nations Convention on the Law of the Sea – A Commentary* (CH Beck 2017) 493–506; Nordquist and others (eds), *A Commentary – Volume II* (n 1518) 612–638.

1762 Art 62 (3) UNCLOS.

1763 Art 62 (3) UNCLOS.

1764 Art 62 (2) and (4) UNCLOS.

1765 See *The South China Sea Arbitration* (Award) (n 196) para 712, FN 735: "People's Republic of China, Ministry of Agriculture, South China Sea Fishery Bureau, *Announcement on the 2012 Summer Ban on Marine Fishing in the South China Sea Maritime Space* (10 May 2012) (Annex 118)."

1766 See also Chapter IV.3.4.3.4.

Finding differently on the specific question of whether China made non-exclusive traditional fishing rights claims, and has such rights, in the Philippine EEZ might have made political sense, as it could have potentially been more conducive to Beijing's future willingness to negotiate. However, this is a completely different issue from whether or not the tribunal's legal judgment was correct.

Such thinking might still be a useful pointer on China's future behavior. Potentially, the Philippine government and other Southeast Asian claimants might be able to negotiate an agreement where they continue to refrain from pressing Beijing on implementing the award, nor launch new cases, and the Chinese government reformulates its claims to living and non-living resources within the nine-dash line as explicitly non-exclusionary – also in the sense that they can fall in a maritime zone where China does not have sovereign rights.[1767] However, to date there have been no indications that the Chinese government is indeed moving in that direction.

One additional complication for finding a compromise is the fact that there can be no (non-exclusive) traditional rights to seabed resources – aside from sedentary species belonging to the continental shelf and living in moderate depths. The previous lack of adequate technology makes it impossible for commensurate traditions to exist. Additionally, all (exclusive) historic title or bays claims regarding seabed resources within another state's continental shelf would be defeated, because the central purpose of the inherent (ie *ipso facto, ab initio*) right to a continental shelf is exactly to trump possible rival claims based in history.[1768] In other words, China could only claim non-exclusive rights to fish stocks, but not to a piece of the suspected impending oil and gas bonanza.

IV.3.4.4.2.3. Criticism Relating to the International Rule of Law

Outrage with supposed rule of law violations by the tribunal, arising from the sum of the above criticized steps, even led to the suggestion that 'in the face of serious violations of fundamental rule of law principles, a treaty [ie

1767 See also George K Ndi, 'Philippines v China: assessing the implications of the South China Sea arbitration' (2016) 8 *Australian Journal of Maritime and Ocean Affairs* 269, 283.

1768 See also Ted L McDorman, 'Rights and Jurisdiction over Resources in the South China Sea: UNCLOS and the "nine-dash line"' in S Jayakumar, Tommy Koh and Robert Beckman (eds), *The South China Sea Disputes and Law of the Sea* (Edward Elgar Publishing 2014) 159–161.

UNCLOS] making no provision for an effective appellate process may run afoul of *jus cogens*',[1769] as under Article 53 VCLT.[1770] Theoretical challenges under Articles 29 and 35 (a) and (c) 1958 ILC Model Rules of Arbitral Procedure are mooted and the lack of actionability lamented,[1771] because the tribunal supposedly exceeded its power and did not provide sufficient reasoning for its findings and the alleged 'serious departure from a fundamental rule of procedure.' The idea is that this – or 'a level below that of *jus cogens*' – could 'lead to the invalidity of the award and its lack of binding force'.[1772] *Fisheries Jurisdiction* and *Nicaragua* are cited as precedents for states considering 'that a (…) clear wrongful exercise of jurisdiction would be sufficient to render the judgments [in those cases] of the ICJ ineffective'.[1773] Some scholars evidently want China to follow that line of action.

A second line of attack against the award's binding force, is arguing that it is 'not generally acceptable,' a requirement supposedly clearly arising from the drafting history of the UN Charter. It is ventured that more states align with China's position, and more strongly, than the other way around. Supposedly this demonstrates that the award is 'not generally acceptable'.[1774]

Neither of the above two avenues is convincing, but they indicate how non-compliance might be justified. Potentially, a Chinese case for reform might also be – inter alia – based on such building blocks.

IV.3.4.4.2.4. Legal Implications

The tribunal's decisions and clarifications on 1) historic rights, 2) island status, 3) traditional fishing rights, and 4) archipelagic baselines have potentially far-reaching consequences. Many states have made claims quite

1769 Xianhe (Sienho) Yi (Yee), 'The South China Sea Arbitration' (n 1514) 234.

1770 Art 53 VCLT.

1771 Arts 29, 35 (a) and (c) ILC, 'Draft on arbitral procedure adopted by the Commission at its fifth session: report by Georges Scelle, Special Rapporteur (with a model draft on arbitral procedure annexed)' (6 March 1958) A/CN.4/113, in II *Yearbook of the International Law Commission* 1, 12.

1772 Xianhe (Sienho) Yi (Yee), 'The South China Sea Arbitration' (n 1514) 234–235.

1773 Ibid 235; *Fisheries Jurisdiction (United Kingdom v Iceland)* (Merits, Judgment) [1974] ICJ Rep 3; *Military and Paramilitary Activities in and against Nicaragua* (n 193) 14.

1774 Xianhe (Sienho) Yi (Yee), 'The South China Sea Arbitration' (n 1514) 235–236, citing the United Nations Conference on International Organization (UNCIO) in 1945, 13 UNCIO 710.

similar to those of China – eg the US, Japan and France – regarding EEZ claims from high-tide features that will in all likelihood have to be categorized as mere 'rocks'.[1775] Due to the combined impact, the award can indeed be considered 'the most important set of jurisprudential rulings in the modern history of the international law of the sea'.[1776]

There certainly are issues with some provisions in UNCLOS that need clarification – it being a 'package deal' involving 'vague compromise formulae' on 'several controversial issues'.[1777] The tribunal in *Philippines v China* took important steps to do just that. For example, this was the first law of the sea tribunal to clearly set out the difference between a fully-entitled 'island' and a mere 'rock' under Article 121 (3) UNCLOS. Should its requirements for 'islands' be respected worldwide – naturally formed, sustaining for a longer period of time either a stable and sizable human community or economic life of their own that is not purely extractive or externally dependent – the number of overlapping claims and thus maritime boundary disputes could be significantly reduced. Moreover, coastal states will benefit from larger areas for the sustenance of their population, as they are less diminished by claims extending from small islands held by other states. Finally, the high seas – free to be exploited by all, and thus beneficial to landlocked states worldwide – will grow.

IV.3.4.4.3. Conclusions – the Way(s) Forward

The tribunal in *Philippines v China* has spoken on substantive matters of general importance, such as the definition of a 'rock,' 'human habitation,' and 'economic life of its own' under Article 121 (3) UNCLOS.[1778] It has done so in an award that 'shall be final and without appeal' (Article 11 Annex VII UNCLOS).[1779]

Given China's commitment to non-compliance and even to undermining the award, further deliberations on this finality are in order. First of all, the award has 'no binding force except between the parties and in respect

1775 Lucy Reed and Kenneth Wong, 'Marine Entitlements in the South China Sea: The Arbitration Between the Philippines and China' (2016) 110 AJIL 746, 760.
1776 Schoenbaum, 'The South China Sea Arbitration Decision' (n 40) 451.
1777 See eg Pemmaraju (n 1746) 285.
1778 Art 121 (3) UNCLOS.
1779 Art 296 (1) and Art 11 Annex VII UNCLOS.

of that particular dispute' (Article 296 (2) UNCLOS).[1780] A potential future Annex VII arbitral tribunal, eg in a case initiated by Vietnam regarding the island status of various offshore features in the Paracel Islands, could apply a narrower definition of 'rocks' in Article 121 (3). A lack of substantive finality in international adjudication can be found most strikingly in investment arbitration,[1781] but also eg in the ICJ using an 'effective control' test to attribute non-State actor acts to a State in *Nicaragua* (1986) while the ICTY used an 'overall control' test in *Tadic* (1999).[1782] However, to date no other littoral state appears interested in a further case.

Aside from another ruling, negotiations could be pursued. In a potential substantive negotiation process, the Philippines and other Southeast Asian claimants could offer to recognize non-exclusive Chinese historic fishing rights within their EEZs as circumscribed by the nine-dash line – although the arbitral tribunal in *Philippines v China* rejected such rights – as long as China in return recognizes their EEZs.[1783] A negotiated solution for sovereignty over the respective high-tide features should actually be easier if their status as 'rocks' without entitlement to an EEZ is embraced. Moreover, all claimants around this semi-enclosed sea could create a multilateral organization to manage resources and protect the environment as under Articles 122 and 123 UNCLOS.[1784] However, to date Beijing has not shown any inclination to make substantive concessions to reach a negotiated compromise.

More likely, China will mount a renewed sustained initiative to reach 'implementation agreements' – treaties in their own right that are 'binding only on States that have consented to be bound in the manner specified by

1780 Art 296 (2) UNCLOS. See also Pablo Ferrara, 'Article 296 – Finality and binding force of decisions' in Alexander Proelss (ed), *United Nations Convention on the Law of the Sea – A Commentary* (CH Beck 2017) 1903–1906; Nordquist and others (eds), *A Commentary – Volume V* (n 1742) 82–84.

1781 See Chapter IV.2.1.3.

1782 Talmon, 'The South China Sea Arbitration and the Finality of "Final" Awards' (n 40) 4–6.

1783 See also Schoenbaum, 'The South China Sea Arbitration Decision' (n 40) 474.

1784 Ibid (n 40) 476; Arts 122, 123 UNCLOS; Ingo Winkelmann, 'Article 122 – Definition' in Alexander Proelss (ed), *United Nations Convention on the Law of the Sea – A Commentary* (CH Beck 2017) 881–886; Ingo Winkelmann, 'Article 123 – Cooperation of States bordering enclosed or semi-enclosed seas' in Alexander Proelss (ed), *United Nations Convention on the Law of the Sea – A Commentary* (CH Beck 2017) 886–892; Nordquist and others (eds), *A Commentary – Volume III* (n 1741) 346–353, 354–370.

that treaty'.[1785] Such agreements could address eg Article 121 (3), Article 281 (1) UNCLOS – procedure where no settlement has been reached by the parties – Article 298 (1) on certain optional exceptions to jurisdiction, or the status of dependent archipelagos of continental states and the definition of an archipelago through a certain spectrum of allowed water to land ratios (1:1 to 9:1).[1786] Such separate agreements were previously struck with the 1994 Implementation Agreement and the 1995 Straddling Fish Stock Agreement, in order to complement the Convention where the States parties perceived inadequacies.[1787] A constantly evolving area of law, the law of the sea would probably already require further regulation also eg on the genetic resources of the sea, Arctic and Antarctic issues, as well as human rights and the law of the sea.[1788] The Chinese government could lobby other governments to support additional agreements, which could then override some of the tribunal's interpretations in *Philippines v China*. However, states' interests diverge, thus making the task appear quite daunting.

Although UNCLOS does not grant 'necessary' meetings of States Parties (hereinafter: SPLOS) that can be convened under Article 319 (e) the power to interpret or amend the Convention, some SPLOS decisions have nevertheless had such an effect (eg modification of Article 4 Annex II by extending the deadline for CLCS submissions).[1789] 'General agreement,' ie consensus, is required for such SPLOS decisions, which are 'also supported by

---

1785 Jill Barrett, 'UNCLOS: A "Living" Treaty?' in Jill Barrett and Richard Barnes (eds), *Law of the Sea – UNCLOS as a Living Treaty* (British Institute of International and Comparative Law 2016) 17.

1786 Arts 121 (3), 281 (1), 298 (1) UNCLOS; Andrew Serdy, 'Article 281 – Procedure where no settlement has been reached by the parties' in Alexander Proelss (ed), *United Nations Convention on the Law of the Sea – A Commentary* (CH Beck 2017) 1820–1824; Nordquist and others (eds), *A Commentary – Volume V* (n 1742) 22–24. For a description of possible lacunae in UNCLOS on archipelagos see Tara Davenport, 'The Archipelagic Regime', in Donald R Rothwell and others (eds), *The Oxford Handbook of the Law of the Sea* (OUP 2015) 154–157.

1787 1994 Implementation Agreement (n 1479); The United Nations Agreement for the Implementation of the Provisions of the United Nations Convention on the Law of the Sea of 10 December 1982 relating to the Conservation and Management of Straddling Fish Stocks and Highly Migratory Fish Stocks (adopted 4 August 1995, entered into force 11 December 2001) 2167 UNTS 3.

1788 Norman A Martínez Gutiérrez, 'Introduction', in David Joseph Attard, Malgosia Fitzmaurice and Norman A Martínez Guttiérez (eds), *The IMLI Manual on International Maritime Law – Volume I: The Law of the Sea* (OUP 2014) lxx-lxxi.

1789 Barrett (n 1785) 17–18, who cites Alex Oude Elferink (ed), *Stability and Change in the Law of the Sea: The Role of the LOS Convention* (Martinus Nijhoff 2005);

the practice of States Parties to other treaties in effectively amending the provisions of the treaty by "subsequent agreement", of the kind referred to in Article 31 (3) (a) of the Vienna Convention on the Law of Treaties 1969'.[1790] Such actions have previously only concerned administrative matters,[1791] but might nonetheless be an avenue Beijing keeps in mind.

State practice could thus be relevant and could be focused on as evidence of a 'subsequent agreement' (Article 31 (3) (a) VCLT) or as contributing towards 'subsequent practice in the application of the treaty which establishes the agreement of the parties regarding its interpretation' (Article 31 (3) (b) VCLT).[1792] Even the practice of only some states might be relevant as a supplementary means of interpretation.[1793] The Chinese government could eg attempt to build on state practice regarding claiming EEZs from features that would likely not fulfill the pertinent criteria as judged by the tribunal in *Philippines v China*. There are a great many 'offenders'. Japan's Okinotorishima was mentioned in the award, which clearly hints at the feature (in line with Chinese claims) only being a 'rock' and Japanese claims thus being excessive.[1794] The US would not pass the test with its EEZs around eg Palmyra Atoll and Kingman Reef, nor would Australia regarding eg Heard Island, or France with eg Clipperton and Amsterdam Islands. Then there is Norway with Bouvet Island, Portugal with the Ilhas Selvagens, Mexico with the Clarion Islets, and the list goes on. Suffice it to say, if the tribunal's decision is to shape future state practice, it will have to overcome a great deal of resistance.

An attempt to amend UNCLOS according to the procedure in Article 312 would be even more ambitious, although it is certainly not unimaginable that China could convince 'not less than one half of the States Parties to reply favorably' on merely convening a conference that would then discuss amendments. The decision-making procedure at such a conference

---

Decision on Deadline for CLCS Submissions (n 1596); Arts 319 (e) and Art 4 Annex II UNCLOS.

1790 Barrett (n 1785) 18, who cites *Whaling in the Antarctica (Australia v Japan: New Zealand intervening)* (Merits) [2014] ICJ Rep 226, para 83; Art 31 (3) (a) VCLT.

1791 Barrett (n 1785) 18.

1792 Art 31 (3) (a) and (b) VCLT.

1793 Art 32 VCLT; Barrett (n 1785) 30–31, who cites eg US, Chinese and Australian practice regarding intelligence gathering on other states' EEZ as potentially aready having influenced the interpretation of Articles 58 and 59 UNCLOS, which is discussed in more detail by Douglas Guilfoyle, 'Maritime Security', in Jill Barrett and Richard Barnes (eds), *Law of the Sea – UNCLOS as a Living Treaty* (British Institute of International and Comparative Law 2016) 329–362.

1794 *The South China Sea Arbitration* (Award) (n 196) paras 451–452, 457–458.

would then be the same as at the Third United Nations Conference on the Law of the Sea. Parties 'should make every effort to reach agreement on any amendments by way of consensus and there should be no voting on them until all efforts at consensus have been exhausted'.[1795] A simplified procedure without a conference (Article 313) appears excluded, because not even one state party could object.[1796] Scholars might dismiss the notion of a first usage of UNCLOS amendment provisions as unrealistic, as the State party in question would risk being worse off than before – due to its amendment not passing or not entering into force for a long time, or others adding different amendments that contravene its interests.[1797] Nonetheless, China has already suggested it at least once, in its written submission on the SRFC Request for an Advisory Opinion.[1798]

In whatever exact form, a pertinent diplomatic and potentially legislative offensive by China is to be expected.[1799] This book will argue that the most prominent Chinese reaction to the South China Sea case, following its strong misgivings, has not been to demand leaving the UNCLOS system, or vowing to never engage in the future, but rather to lean in, and to push for supposedly much needed reform. It has been opined that:

> the appointing authority [of Annex VII arbitral tribunals] and the arbitral tribunals cannot be left to their own devices. Some monitoring is in order. It behooves the world to divine a more perfect system, probably with an appellate mechanism having direct power to correct mistakes.[1800]

1795 Art 312 UNCLOS; Patrick Vrancken, 'Article 312 – Amendment' in Alexander Proelss (ed), *United Nations Convention on the Law of the Sea – A Commentary* (CH Beck 2017) 2019–2022; Nordquist and others (eds), *A Commentary – Volume V* (n 1742) 244–266.

1796 Art 313 UNCLOS; Patrick Vrancken, 'Article 313 – Amendment by simplified procedure' in Alexander Proelss (ed), *United Nations Convention on the Law of the Sea – A Commentary* (CH Beck 2017) 2023–2025; Nordquist and others (eds), *A Commentary – Volume V* (n 1742) 267–269.

1797 Barrett (n 1785) 9, 16.

1798 Written Statement of the People's Republic of China on Request for an advisory opinion submitted by the Sub-Regional Fisheries Commission (SRFC) (26 November 2013) paras 62 and 64 <https://www.itlos.org/fileadmin/itlos/documents/cases/case_no.21/written_statements_round 1/C21_8_China_orig_Eng.pdf> accessed 3 March 2019.

1799 See also Chapter V.3.3.1.2.

1800 Xianhe (Sienho) Yi (Yee), 'The South China Sea Arbitration' (n 1514) 237.

Finally, aside from comparing China to the other BRICS states, which will be done in the following sub-chapter, it should be mentioned that around the South China Sea, some countries already resorted to international adjudication to resolve their territorial disputes. Indonesia and Malaysia addressed the ICJ in *Sovereignty over Pulau Ligitan and Pulau Sipadan*, and Malaysia and Singapore in *Sovereignty over Pedra Branca/Pulau Batu Puteh, Middle Rocks and South Ledge*.[1801] The two latter countries also conducted an Annex VII UNCLOS arbitration in *Case concerning Land Reclamation by Singapore in and around the Straits of Johor* – here, a settlement agreement set out the terms for the eventual award.[1802] Moreover, they concluded arbitration at the PCA concerning Malaysian Railway Land in Singapore.[1803]

IV.3.5. Comparative View – Last BRIC to Be Touched, Three Choices Ahead

IV.3.5.1. The BRICS Experience – Stocktake and Comparison

Developing countries have accepted the jurisdiction and made use of the ICJ, ITLOS and the PCA, including on questions of sovereignty and border delimitation, more or less since these institutions took up pertinent work.[1804] The story is more mixed for the large emerging economies within the BRICS group of states.

Brazil was only subject to one ICJ Application by Honduras in 2009, which was withdrawn one year later, without Brasilia having in any way participated in the proceedings.[1805] The Brazilian government continues to refuse issuing an Article 36 (2) ICJ Statute-declaration embracing mandato-

1801 *Sovereignty over Pulau Ligitan and Pulau Sipadan* (n 1609); *Sovereignty over Pedra Branca/Pulau Batu Puteh, Middle Rocks and South Ledge (Malaysia/Singapore)* (Judgment) [2008] ICJ Rep 12.

1802 *Straits of Johor* (Provisional Measures) (1658); *Land Reclamation by Singapore In and Around the Straits of Johor (Malaysia v Singapore)* (Award on Agreed Terms) (2005) 27 RIAA 133.

1803 *Railway Land Arbitration (Malaysia v Singapore)* (2014) 162 ILR 588.

1804 PCA, 'PCA Case registry' <http://www.pcacases.com/web/allcases/> accessed 1 March 2019; ICJ, 'List of all cases' <http://www.icj-cij.org/en/list-of-all-cases> accessed 1 March 2019; ITLOS, 'List of cases' <https://www.itlos.org/cases/list-of-cases/> accessed 1 Mrch 2019.

1805 *Certain Questions concerning Diplomatic Relations (Honduras v Brazil)* (Order of 12 May 2010) [2010] ICJ Rep 303.

ry jurisdiction, despite some lobbying in its expert community.[1806] Brazil has ratified UNCLOS,[1807] but was not party to any past cases.

Interestingly, the leaderships in Brasilia and Beijing display important similarities on the question of whether to engage with these mechanisms of international adjudication. Importantly, Brazil, as China in the South China Sea arbitration, chose to refuse any participation, when Honduras wanted to use the ICJ to settle a case.

Post-apartheid South Africa has not yet been a participant in inter-state proceedings at any of the listed mechanisms. However, the apartheid regime had earlier had to deal with a number of cases – contentious and advisory – at the ICJ concerning former South West Africa (now Namibia), which South Africa governed until 1990. The South African government disputed jurisdiction – in vain, but the Court decided in its favor on the merits – when Liberia and Ethiopia launched contentious proceedings (1960), and did not comply with the ICJ advisory opinion delivered in 1971.[1808] South Africa never declared in favor of mandatory ICJ jurisdiction. It did ratify UNCLOS,[1809] but never participated in dispute settlement thereunder.

While many aspects are obviously in line with Chinese behavior, the one important difference is that apartheid South Africa chose to contest jurisdiction before the Court instead of rejecting any kind of participation.

Although India also tried to insulate itself from these types of international adjudication, it was the first to be involved in contentious proceedings and garnered the broadest experiences.[1810] The Indian government re-

1806 Juliette Robichez and André Lamartin Montes, 'A Corte Internacional de Justiça e o Brasil: uma necessária reconciliação' (2016) 9 *Anuario Colombiano de Derecho Internacional (acdi)* 51, 52–53.

1807 United Nations Division for Ocean Affairs and the Law of the Sea, 'UNCLOS ratifications' (n 1479).

1808 *International status of South-West Africa* (Advisory Opinion) [1959] ICJ Rep 128; *South-West Africa–Voting Procedure* (Advisory Opinion) [1955] ICJ Rep 67; *Admissibility of hearings of petitioners by the Committee on South West Africa* (Advisory Opinion) [1956] ICJ Rep 23; *South West Africa (Second Phase) (Ethiopia v South Africa; Liberia v South Africa)* (Judgment) [1966] ICJ Rep 6; *Legal Consequences for States of the Continued Presence of South Africa in Namibia (South-West Africa) notwithstanding Security Council Resolution 276 (1970)* (Advisory Opinion) [1971] ICJ Rep 16.

1809 United Nations Division for Ocean Affairs and the Law of the Sea, 'UNCLOS ratifications' (n 1479).

1810 Venkatachala G Hegde, 'India and international settlement of disputes' (2016) 56 *Indian Journal of International Law* 1, 24–26.

placed a reservation to the jurisdiction of the PCIJ from colonial times, with a new reservation to ICJ jurisdiction in 1956. The reason was a case filed against it by Portugal in 1955, *Right of Passage over Indian Territory (Portugal v India)*. To India's disappointment, the Court did affirm its jurisdiction, but on the merits would eventually decide in India's favor in 1960.[1811]

Intriguingly, in what might have served as inspiration to current Chinese lawyers during *Philippines v China*, the Indian side issued a position paper while the Court was deliberating the merits in *Right of Passage*.[1812] Complaints about the respective other side's actions also show similarities. China viewed the Philippines as bound to resolve the dispute via negotiations due to earlier agreements between the parties. Back in the 1950s, India had argued that Portugal was bound by customary international law to attempt negotiations before addressing the Court.[1813]

However, further cases followed after the Indo-Pakistani War of 1971, as India gradually reevaluated its position.[1814] New Delhi indeed issued a declaration accepting compulsory ICJ jurisdiction in 1974, but included broad exceptions, crucially including all current or former Members of the Commonwealth of Nations (ie also Pakistan).[1815]

No other BRICS country, including China, has issued an Article 36 (2) ICJ Statute-declaration, regardless how many exceptions could be made in the text.

India launched a first ICJ case, and lost (*Jurisdiction of the ICAO Council*), when trying to contest the assumption of jurisdiction by the International Civil Aviation Organisation Council in a preceding dispute. Pakistan withdrew a further case in favor of negotiations (*Pakistani Prisoners of War*), after India had refused to make a formal appearance at the Court as it objected to jurisdiction. More than two decades later, the Court found that it did not have jurisdiction to judge another case launched by Pakistan (*Aerial In-*

1811 *Case concerning Right of Passage over Indian Territory (Portugal v India)* (Merits) [1960] ICJ Rep 6.

1812 Singh, 'Sino-Indian Attitudes to International Law' (n 384) 356–357, FN 56 citing Ministry of External Affairs of India, *Goa and the Charter of the United Nations* (Government of India Press 1960) 1.

1813 Ibid 356–357; *Case Concerning Right of Passage over Indian Territory (Portugal v India)* (Preliminary Objections) [1957] ICJ Rep 125.

1814 Hegde (n 1810) 1.

1815 ICJ, 'Declarations recognizing the jurisdiction of the Court as compulsory – India' <http://www.icj-cij.org/en/declarations/in> accessed 1 April 2019.

cident of 10 August 1999).[1816] Finally, in 2014, the Marshall Islands filed Applications against India, Pakistan and the UK, accusing them of not fulfilling obligations towards nuclear disarmament. The ICJ upheld India's objection to jurisdiction on account of the absence of a dispute between the parties.[1817]

In the last decade, India has become ready, to engage with other mechanisms of international adjudication. Pakistan instituted arbitral proceedings at the PCA in 2010, based on the Indus Water Treaty concerning the development and operation of hydroelectric plants on the Indus, particularly the Kishenganga plant in India-administered Kashmir (*Indus Waters Kishenganga Arbitration*). India was found obligated to maintain a specified minimum water flow, to be reconsidered in the future as environmental circumstances may change.[1818]

With the above case alone, India has gone further than China, by engaging in a judicial dispute on a matter considered very sensitive by both parties, and with the country deemed most hostile to Indian interests no less.

Furthermore, India, which ratified UNCLOS in 1995, is part of Annex VII UNCLOS proceedings instituted by Italy (*The "Enrica Lexie" Incident*), because two members of its military had been arrested and put on trial in India after they allegedly shot and killed two Indian fishermen while guarding an oil tanker. The event allegedly occurred in the contiguous zone – and thus also the EEZ – of India. Questions of jurisdiction and sovereign immunity emerged.[1819] The Italian government requested provisional measures at ITLOS under Article 290 (5) UNCLOS before the An-

---

1816 *Appeal Relating to the Jurisdiction of the ICAO Council (India v Pakistan)* (Judgment) [1972] ICJ Rep 46; *Trial of Pakistani Prisoners of War (Pakistan v India)* (Removal from the list) [1973] ICJ Rep 347; *Aerial Incident of 10 August 1999 (Pakistan v India)* (Judgment on Jurisdiction) [2000] ICJ Rep 12; Hegde (n 1810) 26.

1817 *Obligations concerning Negotiations relating to the Cessation of the Nuclear Arms Race and to Nuclear Disarmamant (Marshall Islands v India)* (Judgment on Jurisdiction) [2016] ICJ Rep 255.

1818 *Indus Waters Kishenganga Arbitration (Pakistan v India)* (Final Award of 20 December 2013) 31 RIAA 1, paras 117–122, Part V (A)-(B); *Indus Waters Treaty 1960 between the Government of India, the Government of Pakistan and the International Bank for Reconstruction and Development* (signed 19 September 1960, entered into force 12 January 1961 with retroactive effect from 1 April 1960) 419 UNTS 126; Hegde (n 1810) 19–23; John R Crook, 'In re Indus Waters Kishenganga Arbitration (Pakistan v. India). Final Award. At http:// www.pca-cpa.org. Arbitral Tribunal, December 20, 2013' (2014) 108 AJIL 308.

1819 See also Utpal Kumar Raha and KD Raju, 'The Enrica Lexie case at the permanent court of arbitration: an analysis' (2016) 56 *Indian Journal of International*

nex VII tribunal had been constituted. In August 2015, the parties were ordered to 'suspend all court proceedings which might aggravate or extend the dispute submitted to the Annex VII arbitral tribunal'.[1820] The arbitration is registered at the PCA and pending. In April 2016, the Annex VII tribunal ordered further provisional measures under Article 290 (1) UNCLOS. India had to relax bail conditions, and let the one soldier still in the country return to Italy during the proceedings. However, he would remain 'under the authority of the Supreme Court of India' and had to surrender his passport to the Italian authorities.[1821]

Most remarkably, India accepted the 2014 award in the *Bay of Bengal Maritime Boundary Arbitration*. This Annex VII UNCLOS arbitration had been launched by Bangladesh in 2009, comprehensively dealt with the delimitation of territorial sea, EEZ, and continental shelf within and beyond 200 nautical miles, and handed much of the Bay of Bengal to Bangladesh. The Tribunal largely followed ICJ case law, and the ITLOS judgment on the border between Bangladesh and Myanmar, holding that in line with transparency, predictability and equitability case law is to be emphasized as 'a source of international law under article 38(1)(d) of the Statute of the International Court of Justice, and should be read into articles 74 and 83 of the Convention.' India did not contest jurisdiction, agreed to comprehensive site visits during the proceedings, and later focused on how the award would 'enhance mutual goodwill'.[1822]

Law 221, 238, who opine that UNCLOS and international customary law point to flag state jurisdiction, but hope that pertinent case law could still deliver greater clarity on how to deal with criminal activities in the EEZ under UNCLOS.

1820 *"Enrica Lexie" (Italy v India)* (Provisional Measures, Order of 24 August 2015) [2015] ITLOS Rep 182, para 141 (1); Art 290 (5) UNCLOS; Tullio Treves, 'Article 290 – Provisional Measures' in Alexander Proelss (ed), *United Nations Convention on the Law of the Sea – A Commentary* (CH Beck 2017) 1866–1878; Nordquist and others (eds), *A Commentary – Volume V* (n 1742) 52–59.

1821 Permanent Court of Arbitration, *Case View – "Enrica Lexie" (Italy v India)*, PCA Case No 2015–28 <http://www.pcacases.com/web/view/117> accessed 1 March 2019; *"Enrica Lexie" (Italy v India)*, PCA Case No 2015–28, Order – Request for the Prescription of Provisional Measures (29 April 2016) paras 125, 132; Art 290 (1), Annex VII UNCLOS.

1822 *The Bay of Bengal Maritime Boundary Arbitration (Bangladesh v India)*, PCA Case No 2010–16, Award (7 July 2014) para 339, 509 ('*The Bay of Bengal Maritime Boundary Arbitration (Bangladesh v India)* (n 1822)'); *Delimitation of the Maritime Boundary in the Bay of Bengal* (Bangladesh v Myanmar) (n 1486); Hegde (n 1810) 34–35; Marcin Kaldunski, 'A Commentary on Maritime Boundary Ar-

Earlier on, India had already successfully negotiated an agreement to delimit its maritime border with Myanmar.[1823] After the award on the Bay of Bengal, India also ratified a Land Boundary Agreement with Bangladesh to comprehensively settle outstanding border issues to its East.[1824]

The difference in openness to international adjudication of border issues on the part of India and China can perhaps be partly led back to their relationship with colonial delimitation. While China 'sees itself as an ancient civilization that ought to recover its ancient territories to construct its sovereignty in a Westphalian sense, (...) [India] thinks of itself not only as an ancient nation but also as a modern sovereign, albeit cartographed by colonialism'.[1825] This also relates to territorial disputes between the two nations, wherein New Delhi draws on and Beijing discounts British imperial maps.[1826]

In the Russian case, the Tsarist government lost a dispute at the PCA in 1912 related to Turkish indemnity payments after the war of 1877/1878.[1827] There was no engagement with pertinent international adjudication during the Soviet period and the first decade of the Russian Federation.

However, a series of cases subsequently commenced that makes Russia – which ratified UNCLOS in 1997 – one of the most frequently-seen parties at ITLOS. The Russian government initiated one 'prompt release' (Article 292 UNCLOS) case against Australia in 2002 to free the vessel *"Volga"*.[1828]

---

bitration between Bangladesh and India Concerning the Bay of Bengal' (2015) 28 *Leiden Journal of International Law* 799.

1823 *Burma-India: Agreement on the Delimitation of the Maritime Boundary in the Andaman Sea, the Coco Channel and the Bay of Bengal* (signed 23 September 1986, entered into force 14 September 1987) 27 ILM 1144.

1824 Agreement between the Government of the Republic of India and the Government of the People's Republic of Bangladesh Concerning the Demarcation of the Land Boundary Between India and Bangladesh and Related Matters (signed 16 May 1974, amended by the Protocol to the Agreement signed 6 September 2011, entered into force 6 June 2015) <https://www.mea.gov.in/TreatyDetail.htm?2547> accessed 1 April 2019.

1825 Singh, 'Sino-Indian Attitudes to International Law' (n 384) 353.

1826 See Chapter IV.3.2.3.

1827 *Russian Claim for Interest on Indemnities (Russia v Turkey)* (Final Award) (1912) 11 RIAA 421.

1828 *"Volga" (Russian Federation v Australia)* (Prompt Release, Judgment) [2002] ITLOS Rep 10; Art 292 UNCLOS; Tullio Treves, 'Article 292 – Prompt release of vessels and crews' in Alexander Proelss (ed), *United Nations Convention on the Law of the Sea – A Commentary* (CH Beck 2017) 1881–1892; Nordquist and others (eds), *A Commentary – Volume V* (n 1742) 66–71.

In the other direction, Japan initiated two prompt release cases against the Russian Federation in 2007 (*"Hoshinmaru"* and *"Tomimaru"*).[1829] The Tribunal respectively ordered the release of the detained vessels except in *"Tomimaru"* where proceedings before the domestic Russian courts had already ended and the ship had been confiscated.

Certainly most remarkably so far, the Netherlands initiated an Annex VII UNCLOS arbitration against Russia due to the detention of – and requested provisional measures regarding – the Netherlands-registered Greenpeace vessel *Arctic Sunrise*. The activists were trying to stage a protest on an oilrig, which some of them boarded. Initial charges of 'piracy' – rare grounds for detaining foreign ships on the high seas – were soon changed to 'hooliganism.' Russia chose to openly reject the proceedings on jurisdictional grounds, refused any participation, and ignored the decision on provisional measures of 22 November 2013 ordering it to release the vessel. Nonetheless, the vessel was released, supposedly unrelated to the Tribunal's order, in June 2014.[1830]

In this dispute, as in *Philippines v* China, one party had argued in vain (in diplomatic communication not at the tribunal) that an Article 298 UNCLOS declaration, here pertaining to 'law-enforcement activities,' would exclude jurisdiction. ITLOS explained that Russia failed to read the limitation to such an exception to compulsory jurisdiction at the end of the paragraph in Article 298 (1) (b) UNCLOS – only law enforcement on research and fisheries can be excluded (Article 297 (2) and (3) UNCLOS).[1831]

Proceedings on the merits of whether the seizure of the vessel had been lawful were brought to a close by an arbitral tribunal registered at the PCA

1829 *"Hoshinmaru" Case (Japan v Russian Federation)* (Prompt Release, Judgment) [2005–2007] ITLOS Rep 18; *"Tomimaru" Case (Japan v Russian Federation)* (Prompt Release, Judgment) [2005–2007] ITLOS Rep 74.

1830 *"Arctic Sunrise"* (Provisional Measures) (n 1635) paras 23, 68, 106; *"Arctic Sunrise" (Kingdom of the Netherlands v Russian Federation)*, ITLOS Case No 22, Note verbale of the Embassy of the Russian Federation in Berlin (22 October 2013); Ministry of Foreign Affairs of the Russian Federation, 'Comment by the Information and Press Department of the Russian Ministry of Foreign Affairs regarding the situation around the Arctic Sunrise' (Moscow, 23 October 2013) <http://www.mid.ru/en/web/guest/kommentarii_predstavitelya/-/asset_publisher/MCZ7HQuMdqBY/content/id/91266> accessed 25 August 2017; Eugene Kontorovich, 'In re Arctic Sunrise (Netherlands v. Russia). PCA Case No. 2014–02. Merits. At http://www.pca-cpa.org. UN Convention on the Law of the Sea Annex VII Arbitral Tribunal, August 14, 2015' (2016) 110 AJIL 96.

1831 *"Arctic Sunrise"* (Provisional Measures) (n 1635) para 45; Arts 297 (2), (3) and 298 (1) (b) UNCLOS.

in August 2015. Some time before the award, the Russian government, in an increasingly clear BRICS pattern, issued a position paper outlining its legal arguments. Moscow continued to refuse participation at the tribunal. After the tribunal earnestly went through the arguments the Russian Foreign Ministry had put forward in the position paper, it decided against Russia and ordered it to pay compensation to the Netherlands. The tribunal ruled out 'piracy' (Article 101 (a) UNCLOS), which requires a ship to be boarded not an oilrig, and 'hot pursuit' (Article 111 UNCLOS), as the coast guard's action was found to not have been 'continuous.' It found that Russia had failed to ensure the prompt release and departure of ship and crew.[1832] Still without any comments from the Russian government, the case proceeded and another award determined the quantum of compensation at over EUR 5 million in July 2017. Once again, the Russian government refused to acknowledge the legitimacy of the findings and vowed non-compliance.[1833]

This case foreshadowed the South China Sea arbitration, in that Russia provided a model and precedent for non-participation without suffering clear negative consequences, which might have inspired China. This does not change, just because Russia lost. Both tribunals in *Arctic Sunrise* 'often appeared to put Russia's potential positions in the best possible light',[1834] and Russia's non-compliance with both the ITLOS orders and arbitral awards was not even directly mentioned at the next Meeting of State Par-

1832 *Arctic Sunrise* (Merits) (n 1655) paras 238, 271–272, 350, 357–358; Arts 101 (a), and 111 UNCLOS; Douglas Guilfoyle, 'Article 101 – Definition of piracy' in Alexander Proelss (ed), *United Nations Convention on the Law of the Sea – A Commentary* (CH Beck 2017) 737–744; Douglas Guilfoyle, 'Article 111 – Right of hot pursuit' in Alexander Proelss (ed), *United Nations Convention on the Law of the Sea – A Commentary* (CH Beck 2017) 772–779; Nordquist and others (eds), *A Commentary – Volume III* (n 1741) 196–202, 247–260; Ministry of Foreign Affairs of the Russian Federation, 'The Ministry of Foreign Affairs of the Russian Federation on certain legal issues highlighted by the action of the Arctic Sunrise against Prirazlomnaya platform' (Moscow, 5 August 2015) <http://www.mid.ru/en/web/guest/foreign_policy/news/-/asset_publisher/cKNonkJE02Bw/content/id/1639745> accessed 25 August 2017; Kontorovich (n 1830) 98–100.

1833 *"Arctic Sunrise"* (Award on Compensation of 10 July 2017) (2018) 57 ILM 556; Ministry of Foreign Affairs of the Russian Federation, 'Briefing by Deputy Director of the Information and Press Department Artyom Kozhin' (Moscow, 20 July 2017) <http://www.mid.ru/en/press_service/spokesman/briefings/-/asset_publisher/D2wHaWMCU6Od/content/id/2818579> accessed 25 August 2017.

1834 Kontorovich (n 1830) 100–101.

ties of UNCLOS.[1835] On the other hand, to be sure, the ITLOS judges in their separate opinions on provisional measures, had rather harshly criticized Russia's behavior as complicating their task, contrary to the object and purpose of the UNCLOS dispute settlement system, not serving the international rule of law, and potentially weakening its own position.[1836]

Perhaps, Russia could have indeed obtained a better result on certain points, had it chosen to participate and contest the Dutch submissions. This might lead the Russian government to compare its actions in *Arctic Sunrise* unfavorably with the above-listed cases – and the ICJ case against Georgia noted below – in which it chose to engage and gained better outcomes.[1837] Such deliberations might also set in within the Chinese leadership over time.

In September 2016, Ukraine launched a second Annex VII UNCLOS arbitration against Russia focusing on the legality of certain actions taken by Russia in the maritime zones around Crimea. This time, the Russian government has chosen to participate, argue its case, and hire a strong team of (mostly) Western lawyers including Prof. Tullio Treves, who was an ITLOS judge from 1996 to 2011. The tribunal has been constituted, the rules of procedure released, and the case is pending.[1838]

Russia has so far been party to one case at the ICJ, which was launched by Georgia in the aftermath of the Russian-Georgian War of 2008 and consolidation of Russian control over the secessionist Georgian territories of South Ossetia and Abkhazia. Georgia alleged that Russia had violated the International Convention on the Elimination of All Forms of Racial Discrimination (hereinafter: CERD) 'on and around the territory of Georgia' through 'ethnic cleansing.' However, the ICJ found that it lacked jurisdiction to address the claims. It upheld the Russian contention that requirements under Article 22 CERD were not fulfilled, to first resort to CERD

1835 UNCLOS, Report of the Twenty-Fourth Meeting of States Parties, UN Doc. SPLOS/277 (July 14, 2014).

1836 "*Arctic Sunrise*" (Provisional Measures) (n 1635), Declaration of Judge Ad Hoc Anderson, para 2, Joint Separate Opinion of Judges Wolfrum and Kelly, para 5.

1837 Douglas Guilfoyle and Cameron A Miles, 'Provisional Measures and the MV Arctic Sunrise' (2014) 108 AJIL 271, 286.

1838 *Dispute Concerning Coastal State Rights in the Black Sea, Sea of Azov, and Kerch Strait (Ukraine v the Russian Federation)*, PCA Case No 2017–6, Order on the Rules of Procedure (18 May 2017); Permanent Court of Arbitration, *Case View – Dispute Concerning Coastal State Rights in the Black Sea, Sea of Azov, and Kerch Strait (Ukraine v the Russian Federation)*, PCA Case No 2017–06, <http://www.pcacases.com/web/view/149> accessed 25 August 2017.

procedures and negotiations before the ICJ can be addressed.[1839] Contrary to the decision in *Croatia v Serbia*, the ICJ emphasized formalism in this case regarding the conditions of jurisdiction.[1840]

IV.3.5.2. Relevance for China's Future Path

A few conclusions can be drawn from the past behavior of the large emerging economies grouped together as BRICS regarding ICJ, ITLOS and PCA inter-state proceedings.

All of them have been reticent about engagement, like China, but contrary to some smaller developing nations. All of them were confronted with cases launched by others before China was, so the Chinese government could learn from their experience. The only cases initiated by them were *ICAO Council*, wherein India sought to use the ICJ to defeat another instution's jurisdiction, and *"Volga"*, a prompt release case at ITLOS launched by Russia.

India (*Pakistani Prisoners of War*), Brazil (*Certain Questions concerning Diplomatic Relations*), and Russia (*Arctic Sunrise*) all chose to refuse any participation in at least one case, as China did in *Philippines v China*. Another similarity to Chinese behavior in the latter case is the issuance of a diplomatic position paper while judicial proceedings were ongoing, as India did during *Right of Passage* and Russia during *Arctic Sunrise.*

For the path ahead, three choices emerge. Brazil and South Africa appear set on avoiding pertinent proceedings, and refusing participation when others persist in initiating them. Russian and Indian representatives have both become more familiar sights at international tribunals in recent years, but the countries' approaches appear to differ. Moscow seems ambivalent, in the course of testing out what works best, sometimes rejecting and sometimes embracing participation. India, meanwhile, is engaging head on now, and has become ready to resolve the most sensitive issues,

---

1839 *ICERD Application (Georgia v Russia)* (n 1641) paras 1, 16–17, 187; Art 22 International Convention on the Elimination of All Forms of Racial Discrimination (signed 21 December 1965, entered into force 4 January 1969) 660 UNTS 195 (CERD).

1840 Kate Parlett, 'The International Court of Justice's Decision on Preliminary Objections in Georgia v. Russia: Towards Formalism' (2012) 71 *The Cambridge Law Journal* 56, 56–58; *Application of the Convention on the Prevention and Punishment of the Crime of Genocide (Croatia v Serbia)* (Preliminary Objections, Judgment) [2008] ICJ Rep 412, [438] para 81.

even maritime border delimitation, through international adjudication. This book will argue that the Chinese path will lead from Brazil to Russia to India. The discussion of the evolving discourse among Chinese international law scholars in the following part (ie Chapter V) will make clear why and how this development can be expected.

IV.3.6. Conclusions – Territorial and Law of the Sea Disputes

The Chinese government and the expert community advising it on international law issues have taken crucial conceptual and practical steps towards engagement with international adjudication in these most sensitive areas.

The 1980s saw a major change in the PRC's attitude towards pertinent international adjudication. A first judge from the PRC served at the ICJ, and it assumed a very active part in the latter stage of the UNCLOS negotiations. In the 1990s, China ratified UNCLOS, sent a first judge to ITLOS, and influential voices supported only making further reservations against ICJ jurisdiction when essential national interests are at stake.

Another phase started in 2008. Since then, the PRC has been willing to engage with pertinent bodies of international adjudication in this field in substantive ways, albeit below the threshold of contentious proceedings. From 2008 to 2013, the Chinese leadership for the first time opted to support making written and oral comments to ICJ advisory proceedings in *Kosovo*, as well as written comments to ITLOS advisory proceedings in *Activities in the Area* and *Sub-Regional Fisheries Commission*. Moreover, the Chinese government commented on submissions to the Commission on the Limits of the Continental Shelf by Japan (2008) and Vietnam (2009) and a joint submission by Vietnam and Malaysia (2009), and even filed its own (partial) submission in 2012.

In 2013, China was for the first time confronted with contentious proceedings in the law of the sea, as the Philippines filed for Annex VII UNCLOS arbitration on South China Sea-related issues. The Chinese side was shocked, frustrated, and outraged. It refused any participation, or recognition of the awards on jurisdiction (2015) and merits (2016), and has promised non-compliance.

Contrary to some threats and premature discussions of this being a viable path for Beijing,[1841] China has not opted to denounce UNCLOS after the awards in *Philippines v China*, nor is a general isolationary trend visible. The case apparently went against the Chinese government's timetable. It was not ready yet for this next step. However, this does not mean that the timetable and underlying thinking necessarily changed. Beijing might have hit the pause button after the findings were published, or it might simply be doing what it would have done in any case.

It appears likely that further advisory proceedings at ICJ and ITLOS will again find Chinese participation – as in *Chagos* –[1842] if they are considered sufficiently important to national interests and promising enough as tools for increasing Chinese influence.[1843] The Chinese government might even decide to initiate such proceedings itself.

Contentious proceedings will still have to wait. The Chinese leadership apparently does not want to be rushed, and is willing to offend if necessary. The award in *Philippines* will be ignored. China will attempt to go around it, emphasize and maybe even encourage contradicting state practice, eg on island status, and potentially attempt to leverage new international influence into bringing about a new UNCLOS implementation agreement or even an amendment conference.

Official statements point the way towards a country that wants to be seen as upholding and even building the international legal order. The tension with China's behavior in *Philippines* is obvious and will persist for some time. However, the apparent plan, is to eventually sufficiently influence both international treaties (eg via implementation agreements) and international customary law (via state practice) to bring China's practice into line with its rhetoric.

Governments around the world should not expect a China that retreats and refuses participation. Instead, they should prepare for a China that goes on the offense. Chinese judges already serve at pertinent adjudicative bodies. China has integrated with the system's 'hardware.' In the coming

1841 See eg Stefan Talmon, 'Denouncing UNCLOS remains option for China after tribunal ruling' *Global Times* (Beijing, 3 March 2016) <http://www.globaltimes.cn/content/971707.shtml> accessed 11 November 2019; Steve Mollman, 'China is threatening to leave a major UN sea treaty – and there's nothing the US can say about it' *Quartz* (New York, 21 June 2016) <https://qz.com/712170/china-is-threatening-to-leave-a-major-un-sea-treaty-and-theres-nothing-the-us-can-say-about-it/> accessed 11 November 2019.

1842 See Chapter IV.3.3.1.4.

1843 See Chapter IV.3.3.

years, the Chinese government will refocus and concentrate on further shaping its 'software,' the legal bases underlying judicial work on territorial and law of the sea disputes. At the same time, slowly and gradually, but in a mutually-reinforcing development, China will also increasingly participate.

V. Perception – Academic Debates on Engagement with International Adjudication: Chinese International Law Scholars

V.1. Introduction

The ensuing section will discuss Chinese international law scholars' *perceptions* of the now delineated 'object'. The first sub-section will deal with economic (ie trade and investment) disputes at the WTO DSM and international investment arbitration tribunals including at ICSID. The second sub-section will consider debates about advisory and contentious proceedings on law of the sea and territorial matters at the ICJ, ITLOS, and arbitral tribunals. It will be attempted to work out chronologies, discursive trends, and the relative strength and composition of different groups of authors.[1844] The debates regarding international adjudication in the pertinent fields – trade, investment, as well as law of the sea and territorial acquisition – will all be structured along the same basic lines: general attitude, criticism, and policy recommendations.

As described in the second part of this book,[1845] the period of academic discourse covered in the following is 2002 to 2018. Analysis is built on articles published in the PRC's 28 core law journals, as well as two series of interviews with Mainland Chinese international law professors in 2013 and 2017. Starting from 2014, coverage of articles will be increasingly less complete, because published academic discourse in this last period is considered more distant from authors' cognitive beliefs, and therefore less significant for analyzing the reasons behind China's past and likely future behavior as an international legal actor.[1846]

1844 All positions and job titles of Chinese international law scholars provided in this study are those, which they held at the time of publication of the pertinent articles referred to herein. English titles of Chinese language articles are given as in the articles themselves, if provided, or were translated by this author. Direct quotations from Chinese-language articles were also translated by this author.

1845 See Chapter II.3.2.

1846 See Chapter II.3.1.4.3.

V.2. Economy

V.2.1. Participation in the WTO DSM

Recalling the three phases of China's WTO DSM engagement[1847] as a 'rule-taker' (November 2001 – February 2006), 'rule-shaker' (March 2006 – August 2008), 'rule-maker' (since September 2008), respectively, it is possible to make a series of observations referring to chronology when reviewing Chinese international law scholars' discourse on this subject.

It should be kept in mind that the first phase was one wherein the PRC almost exclusively participated as a third party and tried to settle all disputes, that it became more adjudication-leaning in the second phase, and that it started to strive for favorable Accession Protocol interpretations through the DSM in the third phase. Especially in the most recent publications, Chinese authors have a strong focus on paragraph 15 (d) of China's Accession Protocol with its fifteen-year deadline, what they think its ramifications under WTO law should be, and how they view the steps taken by the EU and US.[1848]

What will be attempted, for the most part, in the following sub-chapters is to draw out dominant themes of Chinese academic praise and criticism of the WTO DSM, as well as pertinent policy recommendations, not to engage with the discussion of every case China has been a part of. This is due to the sheer amount of relevant case law and the confines of this study. Moreover, working out broader themes is seen to be in line with the selected research questions concerning why China participated in the forms of international adjudication that it did at the time – including in terms of how it did so – and not in others. Hopefully these can serve as indicators for both past and future behavior of the PRC in this field.

V.2.1.1. General Attitude – From Stockholm Syndrome to Confident Offense

The overwhelming majority of Mainland international law professors has consistently been in favor of recognizing WTO DSM jurisdiction – ie be a Member of the WTO, as there is automatic jurisdiction – and portrayed the mechanism largely positively throughout the entire research period.

1847 See Chapter IV.2.2.2.
1848 Para 15 (d) Accession Protocol.

The interviews conducted for this study at Mainland Chinese universities strongly confirm the broad consensus on this point.[1849] Nonetheless, a certain shift in lines of argumentation can be detected.

During the first phase ('rule-taker', 2001–2006), ie the early post-accession years, many authors appeared to rely on the notion that to fight inevitable decisions made no sense, and that the best should be made of the situation. Kong Qingjiang[1850] probably distilled well the initial sentiment among Chinese international lawyers at the time of the PRC's accession to the WTO. There was simply no choice for China, if it wanted to develop further economically. The new situation had to be accepted as soon as possible.[1851] According to Yu Minyou[1852] and Xi Jing[1853], a trade power like China 'cannot avoid' participation,[1854] while Jin Xiaochen[1855] posited that within the process of globalization, states cannot but cede sovereignty on this issue, with WTO accession being termed the 'embodiment of sovereignty transfer'.[1856]

Scholars considered options as constrained by a globalized economic system wherein China already was a major trade power and wanted to further grow in strength, and did not argue for participation on the mechanism's merits alone. On the other hand, while they did not necessarily sing the DSM's praises, authors also certainly did not want their government to leave the WTO to wrest their country from DSM jurisdiction.

1849 Author's interviews in Wuhan, Xiamen, Singapore and Xi'an in June and September 2013, as well as in Beijing in July 2017.

1850 Kong Qingjiang, Professor at Hangzhou College of Commerce at Zhejiang Gongshang University.

1851 Qingjiang Kong (n 1041) 46.

1852 Yu Minyou, Deputy Director of the Wuhan University International Law Research Institute and Professor at Wuhan University Law School.

1853 Xi Jing, graduate student at Wuhan University International Law Research Institute.

1854 Minyou 敏友 Yu 余 and Jing 晶 Xi 席, '论 WTO 争端解决机制中的证据规则（下）' (Discussing Rules of Evidence at the WTO Dispute Settlement Mechanism (Second Part)) [2003] (6) *Faxue Pinglun* 92, 106.

1855 Jin Xiaochen, Associate Professor at Capital University of Economics and Business in Beijing.

1856 Xiaochen 晓晨 Jin 金, '国家主权让渡在 WTO 争端解决机制中的发展 - 兼评外经贸部、最高人民法院关于贸易壁垒、反补贴、反倾销的三个规定' (Relinquishing Sovereignty in the Development of the WTO Dispute Settlement Mechanism – Discussion of Three Provisions by the Ministry of Foreign Trade and Economic Cooperation and the Supreme People's Court on Trade Barriers, Anti-Subsidy, and Anti-Dumping) [2003] (2) *Zhengzhi yu Falü* 92, 92–93.

Such praises of the DSM appear early, but definitely grow in numbers and intensity in later phases. Accordingly, the 'rule-shaker' (2006–2008) and 'rule-maker' (2008-) phases see the discourse shifting from an embrace out of necessity to an embrace out of conviction. Already in 2002, Yu Minyou and Chen Xifeng[1857] already held that the 'expansion of global trade requires for the WTO multilateral trade system to be continually strengthened and improved,' and that the DSM is crucial to the system's functioning.[1858] In the same year, Shi Hua[1859] praised the DSM for strengthening the 'stability' and 'reliability' of the global trade system, and thus also China's trade relations.[1860] Later on, Chen Lihu and Zhou Min[1861], Wang Chenyu and He Zhipeng[1862], as well as Yu Minyou echoed this praise in the second and third phases of WTO DSM engagement.[1863] Jiang Zuoli added that Panel and AB interpretation crucially makes up for some supposed shortcomings in the agreements,[1864] and Shi Yewei lauded

---

1857 Chen Xifeng, graduate student at Wuhan University.

1858 Minyou 敏友 Yu 余 and Xifeng 喜峰 Chen 陈, '论解决 WTO 法内部冲突的司法解释原则（下）' (Discussing Judicial Interpretation Principles on How to Solve Internal Conflicts in WTO Law (Second Part)) [2002] (6) *Faxue Pinglun* 105, 112. See also Minyou 敏友 Yu 余, 'WTO 争端解决活动——中国表现及其改进建议' (WTO Dispute Settlement Activities – Some Recommendations for Improvement Put Forward by China) [2008] (4) *Faxue Pinglun* 82.

1859 Shi Hua, Associate Professor at Tongji University Law School in Shanghai.

1860 Hua Shi (n 1040) 56. For a description of the DSM as 'effective,' 'enforceable' – 'laws with enforceability are good laws' – successful in so far as 'most losing parties reform measures in question,' and 'convincing' through exhaustive DSB and AB reports see also Guohua 国华 Yang 杨, 为什么 WTO 是模范国际法 (Why the WTO is Model International Law) [2016] (6) *Guoji Shangwu Yanjiu* 28, 28–29.

1861 Chen Lihu, Professor at Suzhou University Law School, and Zhou Min, graduate student at Suzhou University Law School.

1862 Wang Chenyu, PhD Candidate at Jilin University Law School, and He Zhipeng, Professor at Jilin University Law School.

1863 Lihu 立虎 Chen 陈 and Min 敏 Zhou 周, '非 WTO 法在 WTO 争端解决中的适用' (Application of Non-WTO Law in WTO Dispute Settlement) (2006) 20 (3) *Dangdai Faxue* 75, 82; Chenyu 晨于 Wang 王 and Zhipeng 志鹏 He 何, '国际守法文化及近期发展：国际关系司法化' (International Culture of Legal Compliance and recent developments: The Judicialization of International Relations) (2010) 24 (6) *Dangdai Faxue* 133, 138; Minyou Yu, 'WTO Dispute Settlement Activities' (n 1858) 82 [Chinese].

1864 Zuoli 作利 Jiang 姜, 评 WTO 争端解决程序中法律解释的适用法 ———发展中国家的视角 (Reviewing the applicable law in WTO dispute settlement procedures – from a developing country perspective) (2014) 28 (4) *Dangdai Faxue* 131, 141.

the 'important platform for safeguarding the legitimate rights and interests of the state and industry'.[1865]

Shi Hua also commended the inclusion of special procedural norms for developing states,[1866] to which according to Zhao Ke[1867] the DSM may serve as an important shield against stronger economies.[1868] Chen Xin[1869] pointed to *US Upland Cotton* and *European Community Sugar* as two exemplary cases.[1870] Zhao Haifeng[1871] added in 2008 that the position of developing nations at international tribunals had been significantly augmented, and the justness of these judicial mechanisms acknowledged.[1872] Yu Fei[1873] and Ma Guo'an[1874] issued another early accolade, maintaining that the introduction of the DSM had led to better outcomes for weaker states, because its structure was better suited to restrict large states' unilateral sanctions, and its binding side made the WTO the most effective international organization. The DSM was said to have already gained Members' trust, as evidenced by rising case numbers.[1875] According to Zuo Haicong[1876], the DSM re-established a balance of interests.[1877] Later on, Chen Xin, and Zhao Haifeng supported such evaluations.[1878] In a recent article, Yang Guohua maintained that more than half the DSM cases are initiated by developing states and that 'laws that protect the weak are good laws'.[1879]

1865 Yewei Shi (n 1257) 146.

1866 Hua Shi (n 1040) 56.

1867 Zhao Ke, lecturer at Jilin University Law School in Changchun, Jilin Province.

1868 Ke Zhao (n 1040) 124–127.

1869 Chen Xin, postdoc at East China University of Politics and Law in Shanghai.

1870 Xin Chen (n 1130) 85, 85–87; *US–Upland Cotton* (Appellate Body Report) (n 1130); *EC–Export Subsidies on Sugar* (Appellate Body Report) (n 1130).

1871 Zhao Haifeng, Dean of Harbin Institute of Technology Law School.

1872 Haifeng Zhao (n 1132) 3, 12.

1873 Yu Fei, lecturer at Shanghai University of Finance and Economics Law School.

1874 Ma Guo'an, Associate Professor at Shanghai University of Finance and Economics Law School.

1875 Fei 菲 Yu 余 and Guo'an 国安 Ma 麻, 'WTO 争端解决机制的司法化历程及我国的对策' (DSM in WTO: Judicial System and China's Countermeasure) (2002) 20 (2) *Hebei Faxue* 26, 27–29.

1876 Zuo Haicong, Professor at the Wuhan University International Law Research Institute.

1877 Haicong 海聪 Zuo 左, '论 GATT/WTO 争端解决机制的性质' (Discussing the Nature of the GATT/WTO Dispute Settlement Mechanism) [2004] (5) *Faxuejia* 152, 160.

1878 Xin Chen (n 1130) 85–87; Haifeng Zhao (n 1132) 3, 12.

1879 Guohua Yang, 'Why the WTO is Model International Law' (n 1860) 29 [Chinese].

Already in 2003, Zhang Xiaojian wrote approvingly of the new era in international trade dispute resolution, heralded by the introduction of the DSM, which is described as a marked improvement on the GATT mechanisms. The latter supposedly left too much room for negotiation, put off decisions that often were not implemented regardless, and which were overall 'a diplomat's jurisprudence'.[1880] Zhao Ke agreed with that judgment.[1881] Huang Jianqiu and Feng Bing[1882] – who called the new judicial review system nearly complete and perfect in comparison to the GATT predecessor – confirmed the latter statement still in the 'rule-taker' phase, and later on Xiao Wei[1883] did so mainly referring to Articles 21 and 22 DSU and the new supervision of enforcement.[1884] Further early positive evaluations came from Zhang Naigen[1885], who described the DSM as at the core of the entire WTO system and essentially accommodating all WTO Members' demands.[1886] Yang Guohua even described WTO law as 'model international law,' lauding – inter alia – that protracted negotiations can be avoided, and Members can trust that rules will be enforced.[1887]

Yu Minyou already maintained in the first phase that globalization demands 'global governance' as represented by a mechanism like the DSM, which would restrict 'unipolarism' and hegemonism. While China becomes a 'true great power', it also acquires 'great responsibilities', demand-

1880 Xiaojian 潇剑 Zhang 张, 'WTO 争端解决机制之利弊得失' (Advantages and Disadvantages of the WTO Dispute Settlement Mechanism) (2003) 15 *Zhongwai Faxue* 222, 222–224.

1881 Ke Zhao (n 1040) 124–127.

1882 Huang Jianqiu and Feng Bing, Associate Professors at Suzhou University Law School.

1883 Xiao Wei, lecturer at Nanjing Normal University Law School.

1884 Jianqiu 涧秋 Huang 黄 and Bing 兵 Feng 冯, '用尽当地救济与 GATT / WTO 争端解决' (Exhaustion of Local Remedies in GATT/WTO Dispute Resolution) [2005] (6) *Faxue Pinglun* 76, 81; Wei 威 Xiao 肖, 'WTO 争端胜诉方"申请授权报复"的程序问题研究' (A Study on the Procedures of WTO Winning Party's Application for Authorization of Retaliation) (2008) 26 (1) *Hebei Faxue* 148; Arts 21 and 22 DSU.

1885 Zhang Naigen, Professor at Fudan University Law School.

1886 Naigen 乃根 Zhang 张, '论中国利用 WTO 争端解决机制的对策' (Reviewing China's Policies Regarding the Use of the WTO Dispute Settlement Mechanism) [2003] (1) *Zhengzhi yu Falü* 61, 61–62.

1887 Guohua Yang, 'Why the WTO is Model International Law' (n 1860) 30–31 [Chinese].

ing its participation.[1888] Approvingly terming it an 'international court', Zuo Haicong praised the DSM's flexibility and sequencing, calling it special for its focus on reestablishing balance in a way acceptable to both sides instead of judging who is right and punishing the other side.[1889] Li Xianbo and Zhong Yuehui[1890] described the DSM as the key to the entire global trade system's functioning, which was later reiterated by Xiao Wei.[1891] In a more recent article, Ma Ran[1892] argued with reference to the TRIPS agreement that DSM protection stimulates innovation through the effective protection of creative rights.[1893]

Among advantages that were only touted in the second and third phases, is that the use of the DSM constitutes an 'effective path,' as Hu Jiaxiang[1894] put it, in the protection of trade interests.[1895] In an article by Chen Xin, it is said to be helpful in combating the misuse of negotiations, the example being developed states' behavior regarding the liberalization of the agricultural sector.[1896] Wang Chenyu and He Zhipeng highlighted the DSM's contribution to Members' compliance with WTO law through effective mutual monitoring.[1897] For them, as well as Jin Xiaochen, the positive atti-

1888 Minyou 敏友 Yu 余, 中国和平崛起与全球治理 (China's Peaceful Rise and Global Governance) [2004] (6) *Faxuejia* 17, 21–22. For a more recent confirmation that the image of a responsible big power demands participations see Haifeng 海峰 Zhao 赵 and Chundong 春栋 Wang 王, 中国参与国际司法的路径选择 (China's choice to participate in international adjudication) [2014] (3) *Xueshu Jiaoliu* 76, 79.

1889 Haicong Zuo (n 1877) 152, 160.

1890 Li Xianbo, Professor at Hunan Normal University Law School in Changsha, Hunan Province, and Zhong Yuehui, graduate student at Hunan Normal University Law School.

1891 Xianbo 先波 Li 李 and Yuehui 月辉 Zhong 钟, 'WTO 争端解决机制权力的扩张 - 几类 WTO 争端解决机构管辖的特殊事项' (Aggressive Power Exercised by the WTO Dispute Settlement Mechanism: Several Special Issues Resolved by the DSB) (2005) 19 (6) *Dangdai Faxue* 140; Xiao Wei (n 1821) 148.

1892 Ma Ran, Associate Professor at Zhengzhou University Law School.

1893 Ran 冉 Ma 马, TRIPS 协定之文化思考 ——以文化多样性为视角 (Cultural Thoughts on TRIPS: From the Perspective of Cultural Diversity) (2015) 37 (6) *Xiandai Faxue* 154, 158.

1894 Hu Jiaxiang, lecturer at Shanghai Jiaotong University Law School.

1895 Jiaxiang Hu (n 1032) 68.

1896 Xin Chen (n 1130) 85–87, 89–90: *US–Upland Cotton* (Appellate Body Report) (n 1130); *EC–Export Subsidies on Sugar* (Appellate Body Report) (n 1130). Both cases are cited as exemplary cases. The prior practice to be stopped is developed states 'buying off' developing ones by granting them concessions in other sectors they can hardly refuse.

1897 Wang and He (n 1863) 138.

tude towards the trade law dispute resolution system explicitly included the DSM's compulsory jurisdiction, which Jin called the most important new contribution of the WTO system.[1898]

The fact that the system is two-tiered, encompassing an appellate instance, ie the AB, in general, as well as the concrete work of the AB have been viewed very positively. Ren Yuanyuan[1899] lauded the body's role in correcting misjudgments by Panels and bringing about lasting legal resolutions.[1900] Among others, Chen Weidong[1901] praised the AB's interpretation of terms such as 'public body' in contrast to initial Panel Reports.[1902]

According to Chi Manjiao[1903], China's overall attitude in trade law has been drifting towards an increasingly liberal, free-market stance. Especially regarding cases related to resource sovereignty, a shift in perspective from ownership-oriented to governance-oriented, from that of a developing nation to that of an investor country can be observed.[1904]

In a sense, this is a shift in identity for the PRC, which may be confirmed by two trend lines sketched out above. First, scholars first argued for DSM participation on account of a lack of other options, but then based on the mechanism's merits. Second, such merits were earlier mainly perceived in the strengthening of trust and stability, but later also in providing an effective path for the protection of trade interests and furthering compliance.

1898 Xiaochen Jin, 'Relinquishing Sovereignty' (n 1856) 95–96 [Chinese].

1899 Ren Yuanyuan, PhD Candidate at Fudan University Law School.

1900 Yuanyuan 媛媛 Ren 任, '论国际仲裁在 WTO 争端解决机制中的嬗变' (On the Evolution of International Arbitration in WTO Dispute Settlement System) (2012) 34 (3) *Faxue Luntan* 126, 129. Ren cautions, however, that the AB blurs the line between international adjudication and international arbitration, while corresponding norms are allegedly scattered throughout the DSU and unclear.

1901 Chen Weidong, Professor at the University of International Business and Economics Law School in Beijing.

1902 Weidong Chen (n 1258) 30.

1903 Chi Manjiao, Associate Professor at Xiamen University Law School.

1904 Manjiao Chi, 'From Ownership-Orientation to Governance-Orientation' (n 1160) 26. For liberalization and globalization as dominant, irresistable trends see also Ziping 子平 Liu 刘, 论 GATT 与 GATS 项下义务的累加性 (On the Accumulation of Duties under GATT and GATS) [2015] (1) *Huadong Zhengfa Daxue Xuebao* 35, 42.

V.2.1.2. Criticism – Jurisdictional Issues, Protection of Developing States and Implementation

V.2.1.2.1. General Points of Criticism

Regarding critical notions put forward by Chinese international lawyers, one can find general misgivings spanning different phases of engagement, and phase-dependent criticisms that show a change in priorities. Ongoing sore points will be dealt with first, whereas there are two prominent problem areas.

First, the WTO DSM supposedly favors Western, developed, and large states. In any case, not China. According to Jin Xiaochen, smaller states often choose to forego filing a claim to protect their lawful interests on account of their dependence on good relations with large states that are in violation of WTO law.[1905] When they do choose to avail themselves of such protection, Zhao Haifeng and Zuo Haicong maintained that they find a mechanism where developing states' citizens are not appropriately represented – or, in Wu Jiangong's[1906] words, the US, EU and Japan have an outsize influence[1907] – although improvements are acknowledged.[1908] A number of those interviewed for this book noted the issue of potential bias against China among Western members of Panels and the AB, and pointed to the supposedly suspiciously disproportionate win-lose balance, with one professor also calling for further research into respective individuals' voting records.[1909] Yin Deyong[1910] suggested the introduction of permanent expert panels to remedy the perceived problem concerning independence and impartiality.[1911]

1905 Xiaochen Jin, 'Relinquishing Sovereignty' (n 1856) 93 [Chinese]. See also Ke Zhao (n 1040) 124–127.

1906 Wu Jiangong, PhD Candidate at Hunan Normal University Law School in Changsha, Hunan Province.

1907 Jiangong 建功 Wu 吴, 'WTO 争端解决机制中的不公正性：以发展中国家成员为视角' (Analysis about the Unjust Character of WTO Disputes – Solving System) (2010) 31 (1) *Faxue Zazhi* 142, 143.

1908 Haifeng Zhao (n 1132) 12; Haicong Zuo (n 1877) 160.

1909 Author's interviews in Wuhan, June 2013.

1910 Yin Deyong, PhD Candidate at Chinese University of Politics and Law in Beijing.

1911 Deyong 德永 Yin 尹, '试论 WTO 争端解决机构的法律解释权' (On the Power of Legal interpretation of the WTO Dispute Settlement Body) (2004) 22 (4) *Hebei Faxue* 24, 28.

Should the composition of Panels not be an issue, there is still the legal basis, which supposedly fails to sufficiently differentiate between developed and developing states in important respects. Wu Jiangong cited supposedly much too easily adopted protectionist measures in developed states as harming development in poorer states.[1912] Moreover, Wu continued, the practice of both compensation and retaliatory measures supposedly goes against fairness due to entirely different capabilities on the side of developing and developed nations, rooted in old politico-economic power structures. Implementation is seen as slow and often intentionally delayed.[1913] More technically, Yang Guohua[1914] lamented that norms on Panel establishment and timetables for panel work do not sufficiently take developing states' situation into account (see Articles 6 (1) and Art 12 (a) Appendix 3 DSU).[1915] However, on this imbalance in general, in an article ending on a more positive note, Qi Qianqian[1916] commended the introduction of 'cross-retaliation' as a 'significant breakthrough',[1917] encouraging its use.

Within the context of legal bases supposedly favoring developed states, in the interviews conducted for this study another frequent point of criticism was that the conditions of the Additional Protocol China had to sign with its accession to the WTO are hindering a level playing field.[1918] Zhang Naigen also lamented early on that the application of NME standards to China on dumping and subsidies block more successful participation.[1919] Zhou Yanyun[1920] and Zhou Zhongxue[1921] recently alleged a 'legit-

---

1912 Jiangong Wu (n 1907) 142.

1913 Ibid 142–144.

1914 Yang Guohua, Professor at Hunan Normal University in Changsha, Hunan Province.

1915 Guohua 国华 Yang 杨 and others, 'WTO 争端解决机制中的专家组程序研究（下）' (Research of the Expert Panel Procedure at the WTO DSM (Second Part)) [2004] (4) *Faxue Pinglun* 69, 82; Appendix 6 Arts 6 (1) and 12 (a) DSU.

1916 Qi Qianqian, PhD Candidate at the University of International Business and Economics Law School in Beijing.

1917 Qianqian 倩倩 Qi 齐, '确定 WTO 贸易报复形式的法律标准和仲裁实践' (Determining Legal Standards of and Arbitration Practice regarding Modes of WTO Trade Retaliation) [2013] (4) *Bijiaofa Yanjiu* 96, 105.

1918 Author's interviews in Wuhan and Xiamen in June 2013.

1919 Naigen Zhang (n 1886) 61, 63.

1920 Zhou Yanyun, professor at Southeast University Law School.

1921 Zhou Zhongxue, lecturer at Changzhou University Law School.

imacy crisis' of such Member-specific WTO-plus or -minus rules.[1922] On domestic policy goals, Ma Ran recently argued that Article 10 (2) Accession Protocol on subsidies for SOEs – in the context of Articles 1 (2), 2 and 21 SCM Agreement – unduly constrains Beijing regarding its cultural industry.[1923]

Second, authors criticized supposed issues with ambiguity in WTO law. The main issue in the first phase of engagement was the perceived ambiguity of norms on Panel and AB jurisdiction, – inter alia – highlighted by Li Xianbo and Zhong Yuehui, who referred to the national security exception in Article 21 GATT and the effects of its supposed ambiguity in cases such as *Nicaragua–Imports from Honduras and Colombia*.[1924] Yin Deyong also described the supposed problem of multiple Panels as well as the AB moving to exploit this ambiguity to extend their own jurisdiction to cover cases that the author would consider otherwise outside DSM jurisdiction due to unclear norms (eg Article 21 GATT), 'institutional balance' issues or 'political sensitivity'.[1925] Yin called for monitoring Panels so powers are not exceeded, and a further judicialization of the WTO DSM leading to stronger adherence to interpretations and decisions without introducing a formal case law system.[1926]

A prominent recent complaint is centered on 'public body' in Article 1.1 (a) (1) SCM Agreement. Shi Yewei[1927] lamented the absence of a clear definition of the term, and supported the AB's position in *US–Anti-Dumping*

1922 Yanyun 艳云 Zhou 周 and Zhongxue 忠学 Zhou 周, "WTO 国家特定规则"的合法性危机及其化解路径 ——基于中国入世议定书中的超 WTO 和负 WTO 规则的思考 (The Legitimacy Crisis of WTO National Specific Rules and its Solution – Reflections on the Rules of "WTO-plus" Rules and "WTO-minus" Rules in Accession Protocol of China) (2018) 33 (2) *Henan Caijing Zhengfa Daxue Xuebao* 160, 166.

1923 Ran 冉 Ma 马, WTO 补贴规则视角下中国文化产业财税政策措施探析 (A Study on China's Cultural Industry Financial Measures and Tax Policies in the Framework of WTO Subsidy Rules) (2016) 31 (5) *Henan Caijing Zhengfa Daxue Xuebao* 158, 165; Para 10 (2) Accession Protocol; Arts 1 (2), 2 and 21 SCM Agreement.

1924 Art 21 GATT 1994; WTO Documents, *Nicaragua: Measures Affecting Imports from Honduras and Colombia -Statements by Nicaragua* (30 May 2000) WT/DSB/COM/5/Rev 1; Li and Zhong (n 1891) 140–141; Li 丽 Yu 余, 'WTO 执行争端次序问题：双边解决和多边完善' (The Issue of Implementing WTO Dispute Sequencing: Bilateral Solutions and Multilateral Improvement) [2007] (2) *Falü Shiyong* 45, 49.

1925 Deyong Yin (n 1911) 24.

1926 Ibid 24, 28.

1927 Shi Yewei, PhD Candidate at Peking University Law School.

and Countervailing Duties that besides government control, empowerment to fulfill government functions is necessary.[1928] Chen Weidong also lauded the AB for demanding further evidence than formal features of government control to identify a 'public body,' and was optimistic that case law including *US – Carbon Steel (India)* would bolster the Chinese position in future cases against the US.[1929]

Different priorities in later phases of engagement shine through in Li Xiaoling's[1930] complaint about the DSU supposedly neither setting clear standards for compensation nor procedures for establishing the amount of compensation.[1931] In Jiang Zuoli's view, WTO law also lacks definitive provisions on evidentiary standards, and Panel and AB use of the common law prima facie instead of the civil law preponderance standard in determining a shift in the burden of proof has disadvantaged mostly civil law-adherent developing nations.[1932]

As for further complaints on supposed legal uncertainty, Liu Ziping added that accumulative obligations through GATT 1994 and GATS may create uncertainty, and, due to 'omnidirectional non-discrimination protection,' even forcibly open up cultural industries in a way Members had not agreed to.[1933] Chen Yayun[1934] criticized a supposed lack of clarity on the relationship between WTO law and general international law in DSM

1928 Yewei Shi (n 1257) 135, 145; *US–Anti-Dumping and Countervailing Duties (China)* (Appellate Body Reports) (n 1228) para 607; Art 1.1 (a) (1) SCM Agreement.

1929 Weidong Chen (n 1258) 30; WTO, *United States: Countervailing Measures on Certain Hot-Rolled Carbon Steel Flat Products from India–Report of the Appellate Body* (8 December 2014) WT/DS436/AB/R [4.55].

1930 Li Xiaoling, Associate Professor at the China Youth University of Political Studies Law School.

1931 Xiaoling 晓玲 Li 李, WTO 补偿实践的动向及其改革启示 (Trend of WTO Compensation Practices and Its Enlightenment on Reform) (2014) 36 (6) *Xiandai Faxue* 157, 158.

1932 Zuoli 作利 Jiang 姜, 试论 WTO 争端解决程序中适用盖然性优势证明标准的合理性 (On the Justification of the Evidential Preponderance Standard to Be Applied in WTO Dispute Settlement Proceedings) [2014] (6) *Bijiaofa Yanjiu* 137.

1933 Ziping Liu (n 1904) 35.

1934 Chen Yayun, lecturer at Henan University Law School.

proceedings, and Ye Bo[1935] highlighted an insufficient definition of Art 11 DSU's 'objective evaluations'.[1936]

According to Xiao Bing[1937] and Jiang Zuoli, other facets of this problem are allegedly very inconsistent norm application by Panels and the AB, as well as the use of supposedly not entirely suited VCLT interpretation (instead of amending WTO law to create separate interpretation rules).[1938] The Chinese authors herein of course contradict Article 3 (2) DSU, which explicitly states that the provisions of the WTO Agreements are to be clarified in DSM procedures 'in accordance with the customary rules of interpretation of public international law.' Those customary rules are exactly what is codified in the VCLT.[1939]

Ma Zhongfa[1940] criticized the Panels' supposed failing to properly use systematic interpretation in *Rare Earths*. In Ma's opinion, Article 11 (3) Accession Protocol should have been viewed as an indispensable part of the GATT 1994, leading to the applicability of the Article XX GATT 1994, and export restrictions of rare earths should have been recognized as in line with the sustainable development goal in the Marrakesh Agreement.[1941] According to Liu Ying[1942] and Du Lei[1943] the supposedly not clearly defined relationship between the Accession Protocol and WTO multilateral agreement is a larger problem that should be remedied via an Article IX (2)

1935 Ye Bo, PhD Candidate at Wuhan University International Law Research Institute.

1936 Art 11 DSU; Yayun 亚芸 Chen 陈, WTO 争端解决机构法律适用范围争议及原因探析 (Comment on Disputes of Range of WTO Dispute Settlement Mechanism Applicable Law and Reason Analysis) (2015) 33 (6) *Hebei Faxue* 86, 95. On this issue see already Chen and Zhou (n 1863) 82; Bo 波 Ye 叶, 'WTO 健康和安全争端中的审查标准' (Examination Standards in WTO Health and Security Disputes) [2009] (2) *Faxue Pinglun* 90, 94.

1937 Xiao Bing, lecturer at Nanjing University Law School.

1938 Zuoli Jiang, 'Reviewing the applicable law' (n 1864) 131, 140 [Chinese]; Bing 冰 Xiao 肖, 'WTO 争端案件中的规则应用差异分析' (Analysis of Differences in Norm Application in WTO Disputes) [2010] (9) *Faxue* 58, 68.

1939 Art 3 (2) DSU; VCLT as customary international law codification.

1940 Ma Zhongfa, Professor at Fudan University.

1941 Zhongfa 忠法 Ma 马, 论条约的整体解释法 ——以美日欧诉中国稀土等产品出口措施案为例 (On systematic interpretation of treaties – taking the case measures related to the export of rare earths and other products wherein the US, Japan, and EC sued China as an example) (2014) 28 (4) *Dangdai Faxue* 142, 142–143, 152; *China–Rare Earths* (Reports of the Panel) (n 1155) [8.1]–[8.3.3]; Art XX GATT 1994; Para 11 (3) Accession Protocol.

1942 Liu Yin, Associate Professor at Wuhan University.

1943 Du Lei, Master Student at Wuhan University.

Marrakesh Agreement-interpretation of the Agreement's Article XII by the WTO Ministerial Conference and General Council. The latter should in their view underline that the Accession Protocol has multilateral character, is an integral part of the Marrakesh Agreement, and that all rights and obligations of the Marrakesh Agreement are prima facie applicable to China unless explicitly excluded in the Accession Protocol.[1944]

V.2.1.2.2. Phase-Dependent Criticism – From Defense to Offense

On phase-dependent criticism, three clusters of issues shall be mentioned.

The first phase of DSM participation saw Chinese authors take a defensive posture. In the preceding paragraphs it was already laid out how the system's supposed bias against developing states was a prominent point of discussion – later on it was rather a bias against China specifically – and how Panels and the AB allegedly exploited ambiguous norms to expand their jurisdiction. Yang Guohua also lamented third-party rights being too weak. This can be called defensive, as the conclusion is that such rights should be strengthened, not that China should be the complainant more often. The focus on third-party rights is strongly in line with the PRC's practice in the first phase, which in turn comports with scholars' recommendations at the time.[1945] Reticence to use the 'trade court' fully is also represented in Yang's censure that states often do not make earnest attempts to use the consultation procedures provided for.[1946] Moreover, such caution is evident in expressions of doubt regarding both transparency[1947]

1944 Ying 瑛 Liu 刘 and Lei 蕾 Du 杜, 论《中国入世议定书》与 WTO 多边贸易协定的关系——从"中国稀土案"上诉机构报告切入 (Relations between 'China's WTO Accession Protocol' and WTO Multilateral Agreements – Cutting in from the 'China Rare Earts Case' Appellate Body Report) [2015] (1) *Huadong Zhengfa Daxue Xuebao* 25, 33–34; Arts IX (2) and XII WTO Agreement; Accession Protocol.

1945 See Chapter IV.2.2.2.1 and Chapter V.2.1.3.1. See also Guohua Yang and others, 'Research of the Expert Panel Procedure (Second Part)' (n 1915) 82 [Chinese]. Yang also wants Art 10 (2) DSU to include the phrase 'within ten days,' though, ie add a time limit. See also Dennin (n 960) 311–312.

1946 Guohua 国华 Yang 杨 and others, 'WTO 争端解决机制中的磋商程序研究' (Research on the Consultation Procedures in the WTO Dispute Settlement Mechanism) [2003] (2) *Faxue Pinglun* 71, 77.

1947 Deyong Yin (n 1911) 28.

and discretion[1948]. On the latter point, Yin Deyong worried about the protection of industry secrets in evidence procedures. Zhang Xinjun still referred to transparency issues harming trust in the institution in 2007.[1949]

In the second, 'rule-shaker' phase, Chinese scholars began to take the offensive. They started to discuss problems with enforcement and implementation. In Hu Jiaxiang's as well as Yu Minyou's evaluation, compensation and retaliatory measures were both granted their respective advantages, whether opening up markets for the former, or aiding enforcement and acting as a deterrent for the latter, although they were both also criticized. Compensation was seen as problematic for its reliance on voluntary cooperation, and considered to likely cause further disputes. The notion that retaliatory measures go against free markets was now highlighted as a negative aspect, while they were also said to be self-injurious, follow the wrong sequencing and be difficult to adopt.[1950] Both Hu Jiaxiang and Yu Minyou saw frequent 're-violations' and evasion tactics as well as renewed complaints as indictments of the current system.[1951] Yu Minyou demanded stronger enforcement by managing to enforce the immediate cessation of illegal behavior through corresponding legislative changes.[1952] Chen

---

1948 Ibid 28. See also Yu and Xi, 'Discussing Rules of Evidence (Second Part)' (n 1854) 86–98, 106 [Chinese].

1949 Xiaojian 潇剑 Zhang 张, 'WTO 争端解决机制中的专家决策与公众参与' (Expert Decision and Public Participation in the WTO Dispute Settlement Mechanism) (2007) 25 (3) *Hebei Faxue* 39, 44. On the transparency in other parts of the WTO system, such as Heads of Delegations' (HOD) decision-making, see eg Jianming 建明 Sheng 盛 and Ying 楹 Zhong 钟, 关于 WTO"协商一致"与"一揽子协定"决策 原则的实证分析及其改革路径研究 (An Empirical Study of the Principles of Consensus and Single Undertaking in the WTO Decision-making Mechanism and the Path of Reform) (2015) 33 (8) *Hebei Faxue* 45, 55.

1950 Jiaxiang Hu (n 1032) 74–75: It is inter alia questioned whether Art 21 (5) DSU is a general or special procedure and how long, if it is determined that 90 days are not enough time for a report, said procedure can be extended; Minyou 敏友 Yu 余, '终止不法行为——世贸组织争端解决机制提供的首要救济' (Stopping Illegal Behavior – Principle Remedies Provided by the WTO Dispute Settlement Mechanism) [2006] (6) *Faxue Pinglun* 85, 89–90. See also Jun 军 Wang 王 and Sa 撒 Su 粟, WTO 争端解决机制中的救济体系框架及改革问题实证研究 (Empirical Study of the Relief System Framework in the WTO Dispute Settlement Mechanism and Reform Issues) (2014) 28 (3) *Dangdai Faxue* 27, 33–34.

1951 Jiaxiang Hu (n 1032) 74–75; Minyou 敏友 Yu 余, '论世贸组织法律救济的特性' (Characteristics of Legal Remedies Provided by the WTO Dispute Settlement Mechanism) (2006) 28 (6) *Xiandai Faxue* 14.

1952 Minyou Yu, 'Stopping Illegal Behavior' (n 1950) 90.

Rudan,[1953] finally, pointed to the 'time cost' in enforcement, and likely upcoming problems due to US protectionism under the Trump administration.[1954]

Moreover, in the second and third phases of engagement, the shift towards an 'offensive' posture is also exemplified by constructive 'technical' criticism on diverse issue items, while authors professed to want to 'perfect' the system.

One prominent topic here was competing dispute resolution jurisdictions. Chen Rudan as well as Ji Wenhua[1955] and Huang Cui[1956] wrote about the relationship between WTO and various FTAs.[1957] The latter two, as well as Shi Xiaoli[1958], Xu Yunliang[1959] and Zhang Xinyu[1960], all discussed potential jurisdictional competition between WTO DSM and the respective instruments of various regional trade agreements (RTAs),[1961]

1953 Chen Rudan, lecturer at East China University of Politics and Law in Shanghai.

1954 Rudan 儒丹 Chen 陈, WTO 裁决执行与国家利益实现的潜在背离研究 (On the implementation of WTO findings and potential deviations from the realization of national interests) (2017) 39 (5) *Huanqiu falü pinglun* 177, 191.

1955 Ji Wenhua, Ministry of Commerce's (MOFCOM) Department of Treaty and Law.

1956 Huang Cui, researcher at Qinghua University Institute for Public Administration in Beijing.

1957 Rudan 儒丹 Chen 陈, '非 WTO 协议"在 WTO 争端解决中的适用' (The Use of 'Non-WTO Agreements' in WTO Dispute Resolution) [2009] (2) *Faxue* 117, 126; Wenhua 文华 Ji 纪 and Cui 萃 Huang 黄, 'WTO 与 FTA 争端解决管辖权的竞合与协调' (Competition, Cooperation and Coordination between WTO and FTA Dispute Resolution Jurisdictions) [2006] (7) *Faxue* 37, 42.

1958 Shi Xiaoli, Professor at Chinese University of Politics and Law International Law Research Institute in Beijing.

1959 Xu Yunliang, PhD Candidate at Xiamen University Law School and Associate Professor at the Open University of Fujian in Fuzhou, Fujian Province.

1960 Zhang Xinyu, PhD Candidate at Southwestern University of Politics and Law in Chongqing and lecturer at Sichuan Foreign Language Studies Institute.

1961 Wenhua 文华 Ji 纪 and Cui 萃 Huang 黄, '从案例看 WTO 如何处理 RTA 争端管辖权问题' (Analysis on the Jurisdiction Coincidence between the WTO and RTA: Case Study) (2006) 24 (11) *Hebei Faxue* 65, 65–67; Xiaoli 晓丽 Shi 史, '区域贸易协定争端解决机制中的"场所选择条款"探析' (Analysis of the "Choice of Forum Article" in Regional Trade Agreement Dispute Resolution Mechanisms) (2008) 26 (2) *Zhengfa Luntan* 104; Yunliang 运良 Xu 徐, '论协调 WTO 争端解决机制与 RTAs 争端解决机制管辖权冲突的原则' (On Rules About Coordinating Conflicts Between WTO Disputes Solving System And RTAs Disputes Solving System Competence) (2009) 30 (3) *Faxue Zazhi* 136; Xinyu 昕宇 Zhang 张, '中国—东盟自由贸易区仲裁机制研究' (Research on

while Fu Jun[1962] analyzed the relationship between WTO and IMF.[1963] Shi, Ji and Huang recommended in the late 2000s that the WTO study and endorse 'forum selection clauses' in various RTAs, while Zhang Xinjun held that RTA dispute settlement systems should, like the WTO DSM, allow for the possibility of repealing awards on account of certain important issues and within a certain time frame.[1964] Xu Yunliang described the three principles for solving jurisdictional disputes between the WTO DSM and RTA dispute settlement mechanisms as autonomy of will, self-discipline and non bis in idem.[1965] One interviewee ventured in 2013 that China could conclude an RTA and introduce a corresponding dispute settlement mechanism within the SCO.[1966]

Moreover, in the second and third phases, Chen Lihu and Zhou Min, as well as Ceng Wei[1967] debated how to best apply non-WTO law in DSM proceedings,[1968] Han Liyu[1969] the correct use of the burden of proof in Panel and AB proceedings,[1970] and Lü Xiaojie[1971] and Jiang Zuoli[1972] that

---

the Arbitration System of China-ASEAN Free-trade Area) (2010) 28 (6) *Hebei Faxue* 175, 180.

1962 Fu Jun, Associate Professor at University of International Business and Economics Law School in Beijing.

1963 Jun 军 Fu 伏, 'WTO 外汇争端祖管辖安排：模糊性及其现实理性角' (WTO's Jurisdiction over Exchange Disputes: Vagueness and Rationality) (2007) 29 (5) *Xiandai Faxue* 128, 134–135.

1964 Xiaoli Shi (n 1961) 104; Ji and Huang, 'Analysis on the Jurisdiction Coincidence' (n 1961) 65–67 [Chinese]; Xinyu Zhang (n 1898) 180.

1965 Yunliang Xu (n 1961) 136.

1966 Author's interview in Wuhan, June 2013.

1967 Ceng Wei, Professor at Guizhou Nationalities University Law School.

1968 Wei 炜 Ceng 曾, 论国际习惯法在 W T O 争端解决中的适用 ———以预防原则为例 (On the use of international customary law in WTO dispute resolution – taking the precautionary principle as an example) [2015] (4) *Faxue Pinglun* 109, the author considers customary international law as too conservatively applied; Chen and Zhou (n 1863) 82. See also Ran Ma, 'Cultural Thoughts' (n 1893) 154 [Chinese] with a call to take the *Convention on Cultural Diversity* into account when interpreting TRIPS to allow for sustainable development in the cutltural industries.

1969 Han Liyu, Associate Professor at Renmin University in Beijing.

1970 Liyu 立余 Han 韩, 'WTO 争端解决程序中的举证责任' (Burden of Proof in WTO Dispute Settlement) (2007) 29 (3) *Xiandai Faxue* 79.

1971 Lü Xiaojie, lecturer at Qinghua University Law School.

1972 Jiang Zuoli, Professor at Shandong University Law School in Jinan, Shandong Province.

of the principles of 'good faith' and judicial economy, respectively.[1973] Wang Chao[1974] expounded the relationship between GATT 1994, DSU and Safeguard Measures Agreement in the context of 'unforeseen developments'.[1975]

V.2.1.3. Policy Recommendations – The Art of War

V.2.1.3.1. Observe, Study, Shape – General Approaches and Early Recommendations from the WTO Accession 2001 to 2006

V.2.1.3.1.1. Research, Training and Cautious Engagement

The most prominent among all policy recommendations regarding trade dispute resolution is actually independent of the phases of engagement. Nonetheless, it is worth noting that it is particularly prevalent in the first phase, fits neatly with other recommendations that will also be expounded here, and was connected with different suggestions regarding behavior vis-à-vis the DSM at the time. The recommendation was to study and train, while holding off on full engagement.

A plethora of proponents of Chinese academia exhorted their government early on to actively devise a system of specialized research into, and teaching and training of WTO law, DSM case law and compliance practices. Feng Bing and Huang Jianqiu[1976], Gong Baihua[1977], Guo Li[1978],

---

1973 Zuoli 作利 Jiang 姜, '诚信原则在 WTO 争端解决机制中的适用评析' (On Application of Good Faith in the WTO Dispute Settlement Mechanism) (2010) 32 (1) *Xiandai Faxue* 108; Xiaojie 晓杰 Lü 吕, '对 WTO 争端解决机制中司法经济原则功能的再思考' (Further Reflections on the Function of the Judicial Economy Principle in the WTO Dispute Settlement Mechanism) (2008) 30 (6) *Huanqiu Falü Pinglun* 81.

1974 Wang Chao, researcher at China University of Mining and Technology in Beijing.

1975 Chao 超 Wang 王, '评 WTO 争端解决机构对保障措施中"未预见的情况"的判断' (Reviewing WTO DSM Decisions on Safeguard Measures and "Unforeseen Developments") [2006] (9) *Faxue* 131.

1976 Bing 兵 Feng 冯 and Jianqiu 涧秋 Huang 黄, '论 WTO 争端解决活动中的法律解释' (Discussing Legal Interpretation in WTO Dispute Resolution Activities) (2002) 20 (1) *Falü Kexue* 76.

1977 Gong Baihua, lecturer at Fudan University Law School in Shanghai.

1978 Guo Li, PhD Candidate at Peking University Law School.

Kong Qingjiang[1979], Xiong Li[1980], Yu Fei and Ma Guo'an, Yu Minyou and Chen Xifeng, Yu Minyou and Xi Jing, Zhang Naigen, as well as Zhao Ke all penned papers on this.[1981] In the 'rule-shaker' phase, further articles were put out by Han Liyu, Hu Jiaxiang, Yu Minyou again, Zhao Haifeng, and Zhu Guangdong[1982].[1983]

Feng Bing and Huang Jianqiu underlined that Panel and AB interpretations might not create precedent, but do still have important influence.[1984] According to Zhu Guangdong, Panel and AB practice can be used to push proceedings in the desired direction when China is either complainant or respondent in the case in question.[1985] Zhao Haifeng wanted Chinese legal education to also be internationalized and internationally integrated.[1986] Qiao Sheng[1987], Zhang Naigen, Ji Wenhua[1988] and Jiang Liyong[1989] added that the country's government, academia, specialized law firms and industry needed to coordinate better on trade matters, while the latter two authors reminded that the public should be better informed and mobilized

1979 Qingjiang Kong (n 1041) 46.

1980 Xiong Li, graduate student at Wuhan University Law School.

1981 Baihua Gong (n 1032) 101; Li 雳 Guo 郭, 'WTO 争端解决的个案剖析与启示——以美国、印度药品及农用化学品专利保护'纠纷为例 (Case Study and Message on WTO Dispute Resolution – Taking the US-India Pharmaceutical and Agricultural Chemical Products Patent Protection Dispute as an Example) [2002] (4) *Faxue Pinglun* 83, 90; Li 丽 Xiong 熊, '对 WTO 争端解决机制专家组程序的几点反思' (Some Thoughts on the WTO DSM's Expert Panel Procedure) [2002] (2) *Bijiaofa Yanjiu* 49, 56; Yu and Ma (n 1875) 26, 29; Yu and Chen, 'Discussing Judicial Interpretation (Second Part)' (n 1858) 112; Yu and Xi, 'Discussing Rules of Evidence (Second Part)' (n 1854) 106; Naigen Zhang (n 1886) 61–62, 64; Ke Zhao (n 1040) 127.

1982 Zhu Guangdong, Associate Professor at Yancheng Normal University.

1983 Liyu 立余 Han 韩, 'WTO 争端解决中的案例法方法' (The Case Law Applied in the WTO Settlement) (2008) 30 (3) *Xiandai Faxue* 123, 132; Jiaxiang Hu (n 1032) 66; Minyou Yu, 'WTO Dispute Settlement Activities' (n 1858) 95 [Chinese]; Haifeng Zhao (n 1132) 12; Guangdong 广东 Zhu 朱, '论 WTO 争端解决中的司法克制思想' (On Judicial Restraint in WTO Dispute Settlement) [2007] (1) *Gansu Zhengfa Xueyuan Xuebao* 67, 69–70.

1984 Feng and Huang (n 1976) 76.

1985 Guangdong Zhu, 'On Judicial Restraint' (n 1983) 69–70 [Chinese].

1986 Haifeng Zhao (n 1132) 12.

1987 Qiao Sheng, researcher at Nanjing University of Finance and Economics.

1988 Ji Wenhua, PhD Candidate at Peking University Law School and staff at the Ministry of Commerce (MOFCOM).

1989 Jiang Liyong, official in China's delegation at the WTO.

to reinforce these efforts.[1990] For Ji Wenhua and Jiang Liyong, as well as Zhu Guangdong, participating in DSM proceedings as a third party allows expanding one's understanding of the institution through hands-on experience.[1991] Han Liyu summed this debate up with a Chinese proverb, positing that China would be like 'a blind man sizing up an elephant', were it not to properly study and 'master (…) the rules of the game'.[1992]

Indeed actively filing claims, or not settling and having it come to proceedings wherein China would be a respondent, was not yet the favored course in the early years. Zhao Ke and Qiao Sheng touted negotiations as primary way of dispute resolution.[1993] Right after the PRC's accession to the WTO, Yang Guohua also encouraged deliberations on how to make consultation procedures more effective and increase the number of honest attempts to use them.[1994] However, Qiao Sheng and Zhao Ke already maintained in 2002 and 2003, respectively, that the government should not hesitate to defend them at the DSM, should interests demand it.[1995] Generally, international lawyers tie their recommendations to the national interest, and this topic is no exception. For example, Yu Minyou and Chen Xifeng, as well as Zhang Naigen argued that research into WTO law served a more successful protection of China's legal interests.[1996] When discussing the need to study other Members' positions, Zhang quoted Sun Zi – the author of *The Art of War* (5th century BC) – and summed up his recommendations to the Chinese government in the following way: 'know the

1990 Wenhua 文华 Ji 纪 and Liyong 丽勇 Jiang 姜, '中国对和平争端解决的充分参与 - WTO 争端解决中的第三方与中国的参与' (China's Full Participation in Peaceful Dispute Resolution – the Third Party in WTO Dispute Resolution and China's Participation) [2004] (6) *Faxuejia* 27, 30; Sheng 生 Qiao 乔, 'WTO 争端解决机制与我国之因应对策' (WTO's DSM and China's Countermeasures) (2002) 20 (6) *Hebei Faxue* 17, 20–21; Naigen Zhang (n 1886) 64.

1991 Ji and Jiang (n 1990) 30; Guangdong 广东 Zhu 朱, 'WTO 争端解决中的司法克制及其对我国的启示' (Judicial Restraint in WTO Dispute Resolution and Lessons for China) (2007) 25 (1) *Falü Kexue* 134, 141.

1992 Liyu Han, 'The Case Law Applied' (n 1983) 132 [Chinese]. For Han, it was particularly case law and especially common law countries' practice that had to be researched.

1993 Sheng Qiao (n 1990) 20–21; Ke Zhao (n 1040) 126.

1994 Guohua Yang and others, 'Research on the Consultation Procedures' (n 1946) 77.

1995 Sheng Qiao (n 1990) 20–21; Ke Zhao (n 1040) 126.

1996 Yu and Chen, 'Discussing Judicial Interpretation (Second Part)' (n 1858) 112; Naigen Zhang (n 1886) 61–62, 64.

enemy and know yourself, and you can fight a hundred battles without defeat'.[1997]

In conjunction with research and gathering third-party participation experience, Yu Minyou and Xi Jing advised strategic and circumspect collection of evidence,[1998] Xiong Li wanted the government to set up rapid reaction mechanisms, ie competence centers, to gather evidence and draft appeals (in case of a negative ruling).[1999] Gong Baihua, Hu Jiaxiang, Qiao Sheng, Yu Minyou and Zhao Ke counseled the improvement of domestic legislation and strengthening of domestic institutions.[2000]

Following such counsel would supposedly allow Chinese officials, elites and the Chinese public to gain an entirely new level of confidence in China's abilities, confirmed by previously unheard successes at the DSM. This, in turn, would supposedly lead to greater usage of the mechanism and better protection of Chinese interests.[2001]

V.2.1.3.1.2. Demonstrating Compliance

Another general, phase-independent recommendation aside from gaining a better understanding of the DSM and popularizing the knowledge, was to keep within the system and show compliance, something called for in unison. Cai Xue'en[2002] and Zhang Fakun[2003] already counseled strict ful-

1997 Naigen Zhang (n 1886) 64.

1998 Yu and Xi, 'Discussing Rules of Evidence (Second Part)' (n 1854) 106. See also Minyou 敏友 Yu 余 and Jing 晶 Xi 席, '论 WTO 争端解决机制中的证据规则（上）' (Discussing Rules of Evidence at the WTO Dispute Settlement Mechanism (First Part)) [2003] (5) *Faxue Pinglun* 86.

1999 Li Xiong (n 1981) 56.

2000 Baihua Gong (n 1032) 106: referring to an expected defeat in *China-Auto Parts* on account of badly worded domestic legislation; Jiaxiang Hu (n 1032) 68; Sheng Qiao (n 1990) 20–21; Minyou Yu, 'WTO Dispute Settlement Activities' (n 1858) 95 [Chinese]; Ke Zhao (n 1040) 127. See also Yunting 运婷 Zhang 张, Hao 皓 Wang 王 and Longxiang 龙祥 Shi 史, 欧美承认中国市场经济地位问题及中国的对策 (The Issue of EU and US recognition of Chinese Market Economy Status and Chinese Countermeasures) [2016] (6) *Guoji Shangwu Yanjiu* 89, 93.

2001 Line of thinking confirmed by author's interview in Xi'an, September 2013.

2002 Cai Xue'en, lawyer in the PRC.

2003 Zhang Fakun, Professor at Jianghan University in Wuhan, Hubei Province.

fillment of WTO agreements and compliance with the DSM in 2003.[2004] In 2005, Jiang Liyong added that the US implementation of Panel Reports was relatively proactive, and that this was the only way to then hold others to the same standard and protect trade interests. However, it is noted that certain difficulties in compliance remain, on account of the power relationship between the American President and Congress, which leads to other parties of trade disputes sometimes having to adopt retaliatory measures.[2005] Later on, Wang Chenyu and He Zhipeng confirmed the notion of compliance being the only path to making others comply,[2006] and Han Yichou underlined the connection to China's reputation and crucial soft power gains.[2007] Responding to the aforementioned implementation issues perceived by Chinese scholars, Jin Xiaochen as well as Na Li[2008] and Zhong Xinxin[2009] supported early on, the further judicialization and transfer of sovereignty, if necessary, to ensure compliance.[2010] The interviews conducted for this study in 2013 and 2017 confirmed the Chinese view that compliance needs to be upheld. Interviewees were also asked whether they would stick to that view, if China were to lose the ongoing cases against the EU and US on the meaning of the fifteen-year deadline in Article 15 (d) Accession Protocol, and all of them unequivocally said 'yes'.[2011]

2004 Xue'en 学恩 Cai 蔡 and Fakun 发坤 Zhang 张, '论 WTO 争端解决机制中的举证责任' (Discussing the Burden of Proof in the WTO Dispute Settlement System) [2003] (6) *Faxue Pinglun* 107, 112.

2005 Liyong 丽勇 Jiang 姜, '美国在 WTO 争端解决活动中的实践考察和立场研究' (Research on the Positions and Investigation of the Practice of the United States in WTO Dispute Settlement Activities) [2005] (2) *Faxue Pinglun* 134, 139.

2006 Wang and He (n 1863) 138.

2007 Yichou 逸畴 Han 韩, 中国遵守 WTO 不利裁决的策略及其对国家声誉的影响研究 (Study on China's Strategy of Complying with Unfavorable WTO Rulings and its Impact on National Reputation) (2018) 32 (6) *Dangdai Faxue* 123, 135–136.

2008 Na Li, Professor at Jilin University in Changchun, Jilin Province.

2009 Zhong Xinxin, graduate student at Jilin University in Changchun, Jilin Province.

2010 Xiaochen Jin, 'Relinquishing Sovereignty' (n 1856) 95–96 [Chinese]; Li 力 Na 那 and Xinxin 欣欣 Zhong 仲, '论 WTO 争端解决机制的"司法化"趋势' (Discussing the Trend of "Judicialization" of the WTO's Dispute Settlement Mechanism) (2002) 16 (4) *Dangdai Faxue* 9, 13.

2011 Author's interviews with Chinese scholars in Wuhan, Xiamen, Beijing and Xi'an in June and September 2013; author's interviews with Chinese international law scholars in Beijing in July 2017; *US–Measures Related to Price Comparison Methodologies* (Request for Consultations) (n 1307); *EU–Price Comparison Methodologies* (Request for Consultations) (n 1307).

V.2.1.3.1.3. Participating in Reform Negotiations

Third, Chinese scholars generally did not want their government to accept the system as it is, and did not perceive it as static anyway. As international law in general is considered to be the product of constant renegotiations reflecting changing relative power positions in international relations, so are legal norms regulating the DSM. Reviewing this within the context of a larger strategic framework, active participation in WTO reform negotiations – as well as keeping those negotiations perpetually ongoing – was portrayed as the crucial policy recommendation by Xu Chongli[2012], Yang Guohua, Yu Li[2013] and Zhu Guangdong.[2014] Within such reform processes, Chinese influence should be expanded, supported by concrete parallel steps such as – according to Xiong Li – having more Chinese experts enter WTO expert panels wherever possible.[2015] Swift and radical change might not be possible, Xu Chongli wrote in the first phase of engagement, but the important thing was to keep negotiations open while China's weight grows. This is why the PRC – unlike other developing countries – did not advocate ending Doha Round negotiations on account of developed countries' agriculture subsidies, but rather – together with other G20 nations – determined to keep negotiating.[2016]

The broader strategic choice the government supposedly made, and which these authors embrace, is to work to change the existing economic order's development from within,[2017] and engage pragmatically with international tribunals where it is considered to be beneficial to China's economic development.[2018]

In the context of reform, Yu Minyou posited that new responsibilities also demanded of China that it contribute more to global international law scholarship with the goal of achieving a truly global international legal

2012 Xu Chongli, Professor at Xiamen University Law School.

2013 Yu Li, lecturer at Wuhan University.

2014 Chongli 崇利 Xu 徐, '国际经济法律秩序与中国的"和平崛起"战略——以国际关系理论分析的视角' (The International Economic Law System and China's "Peaceful Rise" Strategy – From an International Relations Theory Viewpoint) [2005] (2) *Bijiaofa Yanjiu* 79, 94; Guohua Yang and others, 'Research of the Expert Panel Procedure (Second Part)' (n 1915) 82 [Chinese]; Li Yu (n 1924) 49; Guangdong Zhu, 'On Judicial Restraint' (n 1983) 69 [Chinese].

2015 Li Xiong (n 1981) 56.

2016 Chongli Xu, 'The International Economic Law' (n 2014) 94 [Chinese].

2017 Ibid 90–94. According to Xu, this choice can be justified on the basis of international relations theory and analysis of the international economic order.

2018 Haifeng Zhao (n 1132) 12.

theory that benefits the development of all humankind.[2019] However, Wu Jiangong cautioned that a myriad of previous reform proposals had not been heeded, and that it was very difficult to reform the system while in his view it was controlled by developed states.[2020]

According to Jiang Zuoli, the judicialization process was to be considered normal as 'rapid development of economic globalization has already led to the economies and legal systems of all countries worldwide fusing together, all countries worldwide have already reached a consensus: no country ever has a free dinner in cooperation, if one wants to secure bigger benefits, each member needs to compromise and transfer an appropriate part of its sovereignty. The WTO system is the outcome of just such a concession.'[2021] Moreover, according to Jiang, gains in efficiency and developments towards an even more mutually-beneficial system would allow for further sovereignty transfers.[2022]

In a way, this recommendation could also be read as a reassurance that improvement is possible, has happened before, and is likely to happen again. In some scholars' accounts, it may also to a certain degree have been an invitation to wait. When lamenting the application of NME standards to the PRC, Zhang Naigen already in 2003 qualified his criticism by noting that this would only be an issue until the end of the Accession Protocol's applicability in 2016.[2023] An interview conducted for this study in 2013 confirmed this optimism that most problems the Chinese side had with certain aspects of dispute settlement within the WTO would fall away, case statistics become more balanced, and Chinese trust grow, with the end of what authors perceived as the most egregious parts of the 'special regime' instituted by the Accession Protocol.[2024]

V.2.1.3.1.4. Using China's Position As a Developing State

A further prominent notion, prevalent in earlier years, but still repeated less frequently later on, is that the Chinese government should do its utmost to exploit the existing, if insufficient, special norms protecting devel-

2019 Minyou Yu, 'China's Peaceful Rise and Global Governance' (n 1888) 21–22 [Chinese].
2020 Jiangong Wu (n 1907) 144.
2021 Zuoli Jiang, 'On application of good faith' (n 1973) 118 [Chinese].
2022 Ibid 118.
2023 Naigen Zhang (n 1886) 63.
2024 Author's interview in Wuhan, June 2013.

oping states. For example, shortly after China's accession, Zhang Xiaojian underlined the importance of the 'Principle of Preferential Treatment of Developing Countries,' seen represented in Article 24 DSU on 'Special Procedures Involving Least-Developed Country Members' (eg more time to submit evidence).[2025] Hu Jiaxiang, Shi Hua, Wu Jiangong, Xiong Li, Yu Fei and Ma Guo'an, as well as Zhao Ke all recommended this strategy, in conjunction with lobbying for further such norms, and effective South-South cooperation to offset supposed advantages for developed states, particularly in compensation and retaliatory measures.[2026] Early on, Shi Hua still called for conflict avoidance wherever possible, and generally careful selection of dispute settlement methods.[2027]

V.2.1.3.1.5. The Role of Individuals

Finally, during the first phase of participation several Chinese academics deliberated on the possibility of somehow strengthening individuals' position in international trade law, possibly even granting them the right to file claims. Jin Xiaochen maintained in 2003 that this could help to depoliticize DSM proceedings and increase predictability.[2028] It was deemed problematic that governments may decide to not file a suit to protect their citizens' rights at the DSM. Small countries' governments would supposedly tend to not want to risk their relationship with major powers on behalf of a few citizens' interests.[2029] Chen Huihua[2030] agreed and added that international corporations might not always have a clear home country, and if they had one that did take up their cause, it might not pursue the case as

2025 Art 24 DSU; Xiaojian Zhang, 'Advantages and Disadvantages' (n 1880) 226–227 [Chinese].

2026 Jiaxiang Hu (n 1032) 71, 75–76; Hua Shi (n 1040) 56; Jiangong Wu (n 1907) 142–143; Li Xiong (n 1981) 56; Yu and Ma (n 1875) 29; Ke Zhao (n 1040) 124–127.

2027 Hua Shi (n 1040) 56.

2028 Xiaochen 晓晨 Jin 金, 'WTO 争端解决机制霞私人诉权的探讨' (Inquiry into Individuals Right to Sue under the WTO Dispute Settlement Mechanism) (2003) 24 (2) *Faxue Zazhi* 31; Xiaochen Jin, 'Relinquishing Sovereignty' (n 1856) 93–94 [Chinese].

2029 Xiaochen Jin, 'Relinquishing Sovereignty' (n 1856) 93 [Chinese].

2030 Chen Huihua, lecturer at Xiamen University.

the investor would.[2031] Liang Kaiyin[2032] in 2009 expected individuals to get access to the WTO DSM – referring to regional experiences in NAFTA and EC – and echoed the depoliticization argument.[2033] According to Liang and Chen Huihua, the DSM and ICSID systems should even be joined up eventually, to protect investors' interests even better by giving them more of a choice in dispute settlement. Hints of such a future development were seen eg in the text of the 'Agreement of Preshipment Inspection'.[2034] On the other hand, Jin Xiaochen noted the issue of large differences in domestic norms on disputes between the state and individuals,[2035] and Xu Quan[2036] argued against direct private right of action in the DSM, as China should support the 'state right of action' theory.[2037]

V.2.1.3.2. Engage, Defend, Shape – Recommendations Since the Shift to Active Participation in 2006

V.2.1.3.2.1. Confidence, Pragmatism and More Active Participation

The pragmatism represented in policy proposals on gradual engagement, participating vigorously in reform negotiations, and waiting for time to heal perceived flaws – until late 2016 – is also evident in later recommendations. Zhao Haifeng posited in 2008 that pragmatism in China's engagement with international tribunals should and will continue.[2038]

2031 Huihua 慧骅 Chen 沈, '国家和私人间投资争端解决机制的冲突和协调——兼比较 WTO 与 ICSID 争端解决机制的冲突和协调' (Conflict and Coordination of State-Private Investment Dispute Resolution Mechanisms – Comparing WTO and ICSID Dispute Settlement Mechanisms, Conflicts and Coordination) (2003) 17 (3) *Dangdai Faxue* 104, 107.

2032 Liang Kaiyin, PhD candidate at Hunan Normal University.

2033 Kaiyin 开银 Liang 梁, 论 ICSID 与 WTO 争端解决机制的冲突及选择——以国家和私人投资争议解决为视角 (On Conflicts And Choice of Disputes Solving Systems Between ICSID And WTO) (2009) 30 (8) *Faxue Zazhi* 90, 93.

2034 Agreement on Preshipment Inspection (signed 15 April 1994, entered into force 1 January 1995) 1868 UNTS 368; Huihua Chen (n 2031) 107.

2035 Jin Xiaochen, 'Inquiry into Individuals Right to Sue' (n 2028) 31 [Chinese].

2036 Xu Quan, Associate Professor at Southwestern University of Politics and Law.

2037 Quan 泉 Xu 徐, 'WTO 争端解决机制下私人诉权之审视' (A Jurisprudential Study of Private Right of Action in WTO Dispute Settlement Framework) (2007) 29 (3) *Xiandai Faxue* 72.

2038 Haifeng Zhao (n 1132) 12.

Second- and third-phase recommendations exhibit the change in priorities. The need to study the system and gain experience is still mentioned. However, at this point, as China had already gained some practice and expertise, several scholars counseled full and confident participation including frequent appeals[2039] – according to Zhu Guangdong the only way to master the system, win cases and protect interests.[2040] Liang Yong and Yu Minyou in 2010 called for courage in protecting interests through bringing more complaints and responding better to such at the 'trade court'.[2041] In 2017, Li Yanyan[2042] wrote that Beijing should take heart in the fact that victories against the EU and US were not uncommon, and sue more, citing *EC-Fasteners* in praising both the opportunity to sue and win again, if reports are not correctly implemented, and the AB in general.[2043] Shi Yewei was especially optimistic about 'double remedy' and 'public body' cases.[2044] Yang Guohua lamented the excessive workload the AB was under, and called for more resources to continue work that is deemed very successful.[2045]

2039 Rudan Chen, 'On the implementation' (n 1954) 177; Weidong Chen (n 1258) 21; Yewei Shi (n 1257) 145–146; Guohua Yang, 'Why the WTO is Model International Law' (n 1860) 29 [Chinese]; Haifeng Zhao (n 1132) 12. For a recent article urging further study of the rules see Nei 内 Zhang 张 and Bing 冰 Xiao 肖, 论《中国加入 WTO 议定书》第 15 条"自动终止条款"的法律效应 (On the Legal Effect of Automatic Terminating Clause of Article 15 in China's Accession Protocol) (2016) 38 (5) *Xiandai Faxue* 141, 147. For a call to also strengthen personnel training to no longer depend on European and American lawyers see Zhao and Wang, 'China's choice to participate' (n 1888) 79 [Chinese].

2040 Guangdong Zhu, 'Judicial Restraint in WTO Dispute Resolution' (n 1991) 141 [Chinese]. On the need to be better at using trade rules see also Zhongfa Ma (n 1941) 152.

2041 Yong 咏 Liang 梁, 'WTO 框架下碳关税可能引致的贸易争端与解决' (Trade Disputes Possibly Brought About by Carbon Taxes under the WTO Framework and Solutions) [2010] (7) *Faxue* 76, 84, who thinks that the PRC should for example be vigilant regarding carbon taxes on imported products; Minyou Yu, 'WTO Dispute Settlement Activities' (n 1858) 82 [Chinese].

2042 Li Yanyan, PhD at Beijing Normal University Law School and member of the MOFCOM Trade Remedy and Investigation Bureau.

2043 Yanyan Li (n 1223) 60–61; *EC–Fasteners (China)* (Appellate Body Reports) (n 1202).

2044 Yewei Shi (n 1257) 145–146.

2045 Guohua 国华 Yang 杨, WTO 上诉机构的产生与运作研究 (On the Creation and Operation of the WTO Appellate Body) (2018) 40 (2) *Xiandai Faxue* 147, 155–156.

Hu Jiaxiang posited at the onset of the 'rule-maker' phase that more active participation was indispensable, necessitated by protectionism's resurgence, and beneficial to Chinese rule of law building and economic development. China was said to need to go through the whole process as a complainant and respondent, concerning more than simply the few issues that had typically been at stake, and with more than just the usual few counterparts.[2046] In Peng Delei's[2047] view, the Chinese side needed to up its level of legal argumentation at the DSM;[2048] Liu Yichun saw a lack of specialized personnel.[2049] Adding specific points to study in recent articles, Han Yichou[2050] emphasized litigation experience on using the 'relief gap' between negative ruling and authorization of retaliation, Liu Ziping[2051] research on the impact of accumulative obligations through GATT 1994 and GATS,[2052] and Li Dongdong[2053] studying technical trade barriers as an issue that had not yet been the subject matter of China's DSM cases but was growing in importance.[2054]

Compliance and domestic reforms were also still urged, but increasing nuance showed China's growing maturity. Zhang Nei and Xiao Bing, citing *EU–Cost Adjustment Methodologies (Russia)*, noted in 2016 that in the long-term only market-oriented reforms could insulate China against spe-

2046 Jiaxiang Hu (n 1032) 66–68. For a call to make full use of the DSM see also Zhang, Wang and Shi (n 2000) 93. For simply showing up being half the battle, ie complainants high rate of DSM victories see Zhao and Wang, 'China's choice to participate' (n 1888) 77 [Chinese].

2047 Peng Delei, lecturer at the East China University of Science and Technology.

2048 Delei 德雷 Peng 彭, 论 WTO"疑难案件"的裁判进路:法律原则 (Discussing the WTO's path to judging 'difficult cases': legal principles) [2015] (1) *Huadong Zhengfa Daxue Xuebao* 6.

2049 Yichun 怡纯 Liu 刘, 利用 WTO 争端解决机制维护中国权益探讨 (Discussion on Maintaining China's Rights and Interests by Using the WTO Dispute Settlement Mechanism) (2018) 36 (5) *Zhengfa Luntan* 112, 113.

2050 Han Yichou, Researcher at ECUPL.

2051 Liu Ziping, PhD Candidate at Beijing University Law School.

2052 Yichou 逸畴 Han 韩, WTO "免费通行" 现象研究 (On the phenomenon of 'free riding' in the WTO) (2016) 30 (3) *Dangdai Faxue* 138; Ziping Liu (n 1904) 42.

2053 Li Dongdong, PhD Candidate at Xiamen University Law School.

2054 Dongdong 冬冬 Li 李, WTO 国民待遇原则在《TBT 协定》适用中的新发展 (The New Development of WTO National Treatment Principle in the Application of TBT Agreement) (2017) 39 (2) *Faxue Luntan* 151, 159.

cial price calculation methods.[2055] In further third-phase articles, Chen Binbin[2056] called for WTO law-aligned reforms to China's domestic agricultural subsidy system, Liu Ziping and Ma Ran for the phased abolition of export subsidies for cultural products, and Ma Zhongfa for clarifying domestic norms on rare earth management and their relation to environmental protection.[2057] Providing slightly more nuance on the compliance picture in the WTO DSM, Han Yichou emphasized that the system's flexibility meant that international obligations could also be met, and reputational costs avoided, by paying compensation or accepting retaliation. He praised the room to maneuver this provides in the context of sovereignty as well as motivation to participate.[2058]

In the 'rule-shaker' phase, Gong Baihua and Hu Jiaxiang saw their government as up to then applying the wrong standard for deciding whether or not China should engage. Gong noted that 'WTO dispute resolution cannot be based on the precondition of whether or not there is an absolute guarantee [of success], but it should be deliberated whether it is worth it (profitable) or not.'[2059] The argument was explained by reference to US practice, which allegedly showed a penchant to engage in DSM proceedings in cases that would very likely be lost, only to have the whole process serve to delay particular outcomes for American industries, granting them time to adjust to the new circumstances (eg in *US–Steel Safeguards*). This, the authors wrote, was an example worth considering.[2060]

2055 Zhang and Xiao (n 2039) 147–148; WTO, *European Union: Cost Adjustment Methodologies and Certain Anti-Dumping Measures on Imports from Russia–Request for Consultations* (23 December 2013) WT/DS474/1.

2056 Chen Binbin, Associate Professor at Huaqiao University Law School.

2057 Binbin 斌彬 Chen 陈, 'WTO"蓝箱"规则改革的新进展及我国的对策' (The Recent Advances in 'Blue Box' Rules of WTO and the Countermeasures of China) (2014) 36 (2) *Xiandai Faxue* 138, 150–151; Ziping Liu (n 1904) 42; Ran Ma, 'A Study on China's Cultural Industry' (n 1923) 158, 164–165, wherein Ma also underlines GATS-compatible tax incentive options for cultural services; Zhongfa Ma (n 1941) 152. For a recommendation to reform domestic laws to reduce even the likelihood of potential violations of the TBT Agreement see Dongdong Li (n 2054) 160. For a further voice in favor of domestic reforms see also Yichun Liu (n 2049) 113.

2058 Yichou 逸畴 Han 韩, WTO 争端解决机制及其对国家声誉的影响研究 (On the influence of the WTO dispute settlement mechanism on national reputation) (2015) 29 (2) *Dangdai Faxue* 95, 107.

2059 Baihua Gong (n 1032) 106 (translation by this author).

2060 Ibid 106; *US–Steel Safeguards* (Appellate Body Report) (n 1019); Jiaxiang Hu (n 1032) 73, 75.

Authors also still recommended that China take an active part in trade law reform negotiations in the second and third phases of engagement.[2061] Success might be difficult – the US and the EU are seen as partly circumventing the process with large regional FTAs – but Chinese scholars have been urging patience in a gradual, long-term process that allows Beijing to contribute to the international rule of law.[2062] Hong Dongying called on his government to take up a role commensurate with China's new position in the international economic order.[2063] According to Qi Qianqian international economic relations will continue to become ever more complicated in this era of globalization, and will have to be developed but also 'tamed' within the WTO system.[2064] Yu Minyou explicitly supported strengthening the DSM, described as rule-based, de-politicized dispute resolution.[2065] In 2010, Jiang Zuoli did not expect strong resistance by states against another little transfer of sovereignty, as long as there is an efficient solution to disputes and a mutually-beneficial system that benefits global economic growth.[2066]

Recommended reforms included Zhang Xiaojian's[2067] suggestion to have an amendment to the DSU passed allowing for greater public participation in the form of eg technological experts in the Expert Panel phase – supposedly adding transparency and being conducive to greater trust in the system.[2068] Jiang Zuoli proposed to amend the DSU to regulate the issue of non-WTO norms application building on Article 38 ICJ Statute, and prevent the 'abuse of rights by expert panels and the appellate body'.[2069] To Wang Jun[2070] and Su Sa,[2071] reforms were needed to achieve faster imple-

2061 See eg Yewei Shi (n 1257) 146; Yichun Liu (n 2049) 113.

2062 Rudan Chen, 'On the implementation' (n 1954) 191–192; Guohua Yang, 'Why the WTO is Model International Law' (n 1860) 31–32 [Chinese].

2063 Dongying 冬英 Hong 洪, '以法院文化建设推动司法的改革与发展' (Promoting Judicial Reform and Development through Building Court Culture) [2012] (11) *Faxue* 19.

2064 Qianqian Qi (n 1917) 105.

2065 Minyou Yu, 'WTO Dispute Settlement Activities' (n 1858) 94–95 [Chinese].

2066 Zuoli Jiang, 'On application of good faith' (n 1973) 118 [Chinese].

2067 Zhang Xiaojian, Associate Professor at Peking University.

2068 Xiaojian Zhang, 'Expert Decision' (n 1949) 44 [Chinese].

2069 Zuoli Jiang, 'Reviewing the applicable law' (n 1864) 140 [Chinese]; Art 38 ICJ Statute.

2070 Wang Jun, Professor at the University of International Business and Economics Law School.

2071 Su Sa, PhD Candidate at the University of International Business and Economics Law School.

mentation. In their view, proposals to determine the level of damage during the performance review stage of Article 21 (5) DSU proceedings to avoid Article 22 (6) DSU arbitration, went too far, but incremental or partial retaliation as well as collective retaliation options had to be considered.[2072] On compensation, Li Xiaoling positively remarked on a EU proposal in Doha Round negotiations to improve the attractiveness of compensation. She suggested that MFN treatment had reduced motivation, and that in the event of DSU reform an 'independent procedure' for determining the extent of the damage suffered as well as strengthened implementation supervision should be introduced.[2073]

In a display of how pragmatism leads to different approaches once conditions change, Chen Rudan delivered an interesting analysis of DSM practice in 2012. He distinguished between questions of law and questions of fact as a factor concerning the scope of appellate review. It is first held that current practice is favorable to the complainant, and thus to developed states as they are more prolific complainants. However, the policy recommended is in fact support for the ongoing practice, albeit negative for China up to that point, because going forward the future largest economy had the largest growth potential in complaints and would therefore eventually profit from it.[2074]

V.2.1.3.2.2. Continued NME Treatment and Chinese Responses

Since around 2016, recommendations have trended further towards multifaceted activism and away from previous hope for future solutions arriving on their own. This is strongly linked with the crucial role of the fifteen-year deadline up to December 2016 in Paragraph 15 (d) Accession Protocol, and its interpretation by the Chinese side and other Members. The norm itself reads as follows:

> Once China has established, under the national law of the importing WTO Member, that it is a market economy, the provisions of subparagraph (a) shall be terminated provided that the importing Member's national law contains market economy criteria as of the date of acces-

2072 Wang and Su (n 1950) 36–37; Arts 21 (5) and 22 (6) DSU.

2073 Xiaoling Li (n 1931) 157, 164–165.

2074 Rudan 儒丹 Chen 陈, '世界贸易组织争端解决实践中的识别冲突问题' (The Problem of Distinguishing Conflicts in WTO Dispute Resolution Practice) [2012] (7) *Faxue* 50, 59.

> sion. In any event, the provisions of subparagraph (a)(ii) shall expire 15 years after the date of accession. In addition, should China establish, pursuant to the national law of the importing WTO Member, that market economy conditions prevail in a particular industry or sector, the non-market economy provisions of subparagraph (a) shall no longer apply to that industry or sector.[2075]

Paragraph 15 (d) thus refers to different parts of Article 15 (a) Accession Protocol, which shall also be provided here in full:

> In determining price comparability under Article VI of the GATT 1994 and the Anti-Dumping Agreement, the importing WTO Member shall use either Chinese prices or costs for the industry under investigation or a methodology that is not based on a strict comparison with domestic prices or costs in China based on the following rules:
> (i) If the producers under investigation can clearly show that market economy conditions prevail in the industry producing the like product with regard to the manufacture, production and sale of that product, the importing WTO Member shall use Chinese prices or costs for the industry under investigation in determining price comparability;
> (ii) The importing WTO Member may use a methodology that is not based on a strict comparison with domestic prices or costs in China if the producers under investigation cannot clearly show that market economy conditions prevail in the industry producing the like product with regard to manufacture, production and sale of that product.[2076]

Increasingly intense Chinese diplomatic efforts failed to convince the EU and US to outright declare the PRC a market economy in 2016.[2077] As described in Chapter IV.2.2.2.3.7, US national law had included standards on pertinent status at the time of China's WTO accession. Washington continues to see these unfulfilled and to apply the analog country method with case-by-case modifications.[2078] EU law did not include such norms at the time. In 2016 and 2017, EU institutions settled on new legislation that in-

---

2075 Para 15 (d) Accession Protocol.

2076 Ibid.

2077 Financial Times, 'China fights for market economy status – Beijing had thought trade advantage would come automatically at end of this year' (London, 9 May 2016) <https://www.ft.com/content/572f435e-0784-11e6-9b51-0fb5e65703ce> accessed 30 December 2017.

2078 Stewart and others (n 1317); Hufbauer and Cimino-Isaacs (n 1317); Bown (n 1317).

troduced a mechanism for determining price comparability that deletes the issue of whether a state is a market economy, but allows foregoing the use of domestic prices or costs in cases of 'significant distortions'.[2079]

Chinese international law scholars have, in a broad consensus, posited that other Members can no longer use alternative price calculation methodology in anti-dumping cases since 11 December 2016.[2080] In the eyes of several authors, the EU and US wrongly focus only on the first sentence of Paragraph 15 (d) Accession Protocol, and thus 'market economy status'. To them, there is a need to differentiate between 1) the conditional termination clause referring to market economy status under Members' national laws, and 2) the unconditional termination clause in the paragraph's second sentence referring only to an international law obligation to end 'non-market methodologies' after 11 December 2016. The 'in any event' at the beginning of the second sentence supposedly lifts the conditionality of the first sentence, ie China does not need to prove anything under the national law of another Member. In their view, the rest of Paragraph 15 could not suffice to justify the continued application of 'non-market methodologies'.[2081]

Yu Minyou and Guan Jian[2082] added that China may have allowed for the temporary usage of such methodology, but never admitted to being a non-market economy or would it be categorized as such by any WTO norm.[2083] According to Zhu Zhaomin[2084], who cited *EC-Fasteners* as having provided the authoritative interpretation of Paragraph 15 Accession Protocol, Paragraph 15 (a) does not state whether China is a market economy or not. It supposedly merely allows other Members to make specific price calculations until 1) the industry in question or 2) the Chinese economy as a whole have been recognized as operating under market conditions, or, if the first two scenarios did not materialize, until 3) 11 Decem-

2079 Regulation (EU) 2017/2321 of the European Parliament and of the Council of 12 December 2017 amending Regulation (EU) 2016/1036 on protection against dumped imports from countries not members of the European Union and Regulation (EU) 2016/1037 on protection against subsidised imports from countries not members of the European Union [2017] OJ L338/1.

2080 See inter alia Yanyan Li (n 1223) 60; Min Zhao (n 1347) 145.

2081 Minyou Yu and Jian Guan (n 1286) 29; Zhang and Xiao (n 2039) 141, 143, 145, 148.

2082 Guan Jian, PhD Candidate at Wuhan University Law School.

2083 Minyou Yu and Jian Guan (n 1286) 39.

2084 Zhu Zhaomin, lecturer at Shanghai International Studies University Law School.

ber 2016.[2085] Zhu contended that such unilateral temporary arrangements did not become permanent part of general WTO law.[2086]

As for the rest of Article 15 Accession Protocol besides subparagraph (a) (ii), Zhang Nei[2087] and Xiao Bing[2088] ventured that in line with the ILC principle of giving full effect to norms in Article 31 and 32 VCLT interpretation subparagraph (a) (i) should still apply where China has not been recognized as a market economy. The term 'Chinese prices' should be interpreted as 'Chinese retail prices,' or, if interpreted broadly, has to include 'Chinese costs'.[2089]

Returning to a hopeful note, in a recent article Zhao Min[2090] referred to the previous case of the 'Multi Fibre Arrangement,' which was applicable until 2014 (from 1974). Supposedly, eventual acceptance of the agreement having run its course also took a while. Zhao also counseled patience, considering that the US's importance to China's economy is supposedly decreasing, while China's position within the WTO is seen as ascending.[2091]

Despite the end of the fifteen-year period set out in Article 15 of the Accession Protocol not delivering the degree of salvation China had hoped for, scholars have not changed their general thrust of argument on participation.[2092]

However, Chinese trade law scholars make additional recommendations, such as increasing diplomatic efforts to convince governments worldwide to abandon analog country and constructed value methodolo-

2085 Para 15 (a) Accession Protocol; Zhaomin Zhu (n 1325) 96 citing *EC–Fasteners (China)* (Appellate Body Reports) (n 1202) [147].

2086 Zhaomin Zhu (n 1325) 96.

2087 Zhang Nei, PhD Candidate at Nanjing University Law School.

2088 Xiao Bing, Professor at Southeast University Law School.

2089 Para 15 (a) (i) and (ii) Accession Protocol; Arts 31 and 32 VCLT; Zhang and Xiao (n 2039) 144. See also Zhang and Xiao (n 2039) 147, where the authors remark that China should advocate with general WTO anti-dumping rules on MES, as they are supposedly less stringent than domestic ones in the EU and US, and argue that the standard of proof in Art 15 (a) is lower than that in subparagraph (d).

2090 Zhao Min, lecturer at the Shanghai Lixin University of Accounting and Finance.

2091 Min Zhao (n 1347) 145; Arrangement Regarding International Trade in Textiles (opened for signature 20 December 1973, entered into force 3 January 1975) 25 USTS 1001 ('Multi Fibre Arrangement').

2092 They also did not do so in the course of the larger-scale US-China trade conflict unfolding from 2017, see eg Guan 管 Jian 健, '中美贸易争端中的焦点法律问题评析' (Analysis on Key Legal Issues Arising from the Trade Conflicts between US and China) [2018] (3) *Wuda Guojifa Pinglun* 142.

gies in anti-dumping investigations.[2093] Chinese authors claim that almost 100 WTO Members – including Russia, Brazil, Australia, New Zealand and Switzerland – have already recognized China as a market economy, and suggest that negotiations on FTAs can be used to make further progress.[2094] However, the world's most important economies are crucial holdouts.

Flanking recommendations on how the Chinese government should behave vis-à-vis the DSM, Chinese scholars also urge Chinese companies to become more active. First, they should be more aware of the issue and collect supportive data.[2095] Second, they should confidently strive to prove that they are operating under market conditions in China during other Members' anti-dumping investigations.[2096] Third, they should make use of other Members' domestic judicial systems to attack anti-dumping measures.[2097] Liu Yichun[2098] also urged the creation of a new mechanism for coordination between the government and Chinese companies.[2099] Beyond companies, Chinese scholars even address their own community and call for breaking the 'discourse monopoly' of Western international lawyers on WTO reform, and confidently pushing Chinese proposals such as the elimination of 'WTO-plus obligations'.[2100]

V.2.2. Participation in Investment Arbitration

Observations on chronology in the investment field – where there have only been a handful of cases with Chinese participation – are more difficult. Nonetheless, the caesura of the first appearance of actual case law in 2007 (Hong Kong investor) or 2011 and 2012 (Mainland China as host state and

2093 Zhang and Xiao (n 2039) 147; Zhang, Wang and Shi (n 2000) 93; Min Zhao (n 1347) 120.

2094 Zhang and Xiao (n 2039) 143; Min Zhao (n 1347) 120. On China's current FTA strategy and its connection to broader foreign policy goals as well as the so-called 'Belt and Road Initiative' see Jinlong 金龙 Zhao 赵, '我国"一带一路" FTA 战略的路径选择研究' (On China's chosen path regarding a 'One Belt, One Road' FTA strategy) [2016] (12) *Shijie Jingji Yanjiu* 106.

2095 Yanyan Li (n 1223) 61.

2096 Min Zhao (n 1347) 120.

2097 Yanyan Li (n 1223) 61.

2098 Liu Yichun, graduate student at Guangxi Normal University.

2099 Yichun Liu (n 2049) 113.

2100 Zhongfa Ma (n 1941) 152, eg regarding anti-dumping measures on leather shoes, glyphosate and seamless steel pipe.

home state), may be noted at times.[2101] This caesura, the actual appearance of case law, comes only rather late into this study's research period; and only a handful of awards involving China have been rendered, starting even later.

Therefore, the discourse analyzed here is not only one on investment arbitration, but also on China's investment treaty practice more broadly. In this context, it should be recalled – and this indicates movement in the Chinese international law debates before and within this book's research period – that the PRC's BIT practice has been categorized here in four phases.[2102] First, only ad-hoc arbitration on the amount of compensation for expropriation was possible, then ICSID could be approached, then access was broadened and any dispute concerning an investment could be submitted to arbitration, and finally, China's BITs were Americanized with separate sections (or detailed provisions) on ISDS.

The number of pertinent cases in this field is much smaller compared to trade law. Criticism of individual tribunals' decisions, and policy recommendations built thereon, will be noted. Nonetheless, the following subchapters will still mostly concentrate on drawing out overarching trends in relevant Chinese debates.

V.2.2.1. General Attitude – March Towards Liberalism

First, the attitude towards investment treaties, or rather dispute settlement clauses therein, should be explored. A number of authors – including Cai Congyan[2103], Chen Wei[2104], Hu Xiaohong[2105], Huang Shixi[2106], Yang Caixia[2107] and Qin Quan[2108] – narrated the initially restrained practice towards

2101 *Tza* (Decision on Annulment) (n 701); *Ekran Berhad* (n 524); *Ping An Life Insurance* (n 849). A discussion of the case law involving China can be found in Chapter IV.2.1.3.

2102 See Chapters IV.2.1.2.

2103 Cai Congyan, Professor at Xiamen University Law School.

2104 Chen Wei, lecturer at Shanghai Jiaotong University.

2105 Hu Xiaohong, lecturer at Nanjing University.

2106 Huang Shixi, Professor at Shandong University Law School in Jinan, Shandong Province.

2107 Yang Caixia, lecturer at Beihang University Law School.

2108 Qin Quan, PhD Candidate at Université Panthéon-Assas – Paris II.

international investment arbitration and later trend towards liberalism, described in this book.[2109]

Only one author was found explicitly embracing this development already in 2002.[2110] Most others only actively embraced liberal BITs later on, towards the appearance of first case law with Chinese participation. Many scholars then started to support a proliferation of third-generation BITs, and called for specific attention to developing states that had not yet achieved an adequate level of rule of law, and with whom China had a lopsided investment balance.[2111] The examples put forward by Hu Xiaohong in 2009 were the other members of the Shanghai Cooperation Organization (SCO) at the time, ie Russia (new BIT in 2006), Uzbekistan (new BIT in 2011), Kazakhstan, Kyrgyzstan and Tajikistan.[2112]

In recent years, many Chinese scholars have also commented largely favorably on new legal developments regarding BIT clauses – often (co-)proposed by the EU. Dispute settlement provisions in CETA have been described as commendably strengthening host state rights – bringing ISDS 'more under control' of contracting states – as well as transparency, consistency and legitimacy.[2113] Chinese authors have also argued that labor and environmental protection clauses in the US Model BIT 2012 could eventu-

2109 Congyan 从燕 Cai 蔡, '外国投资者利用国际投资仲裁机制新发展反思——国际法实施机制与南北矛盾的双重视角' (Reviewing New Developments in Foreign Investors Use of International Investment Arbitration Mechanisms – Dual Viewpoint of International Law Implementation and North-South Conflict) [2007] (3) *Faxuejia* 102, 108–109; Wei Chen (n 512) 1049–1051, 1056; Xiaohong 晓红 Hu 胡, '中外双边投资协定争端解决机制模式选择——以中国与上合组织成员国间 BITs 为视角' (On the Choice of Dispute Settlement Mechanism Types in China-Foreign Bilateral Investment Treaties – from the Perspective of BITs between China and Shanghai Cooperation Organization Member States) [2009] (3) *Gansu Zhengfa Xueyuan Xuebao* 76; Shixi Huang, 'New Developments' (n 840) 185 [Chinese]; Yang and Qin (n 512) 120.

2110 Ying 瑛 Liu 刘, 'BOT 方式下的争议解决机制与 ICSID 仲裁' (Dispute Settlement Mechanisms under BOT and ICSID Arbitration) (2002) 23 (5) *Faxue Zazhi* 65, 67.

2111 Xiaohong Hu (n 2109) 78–79.

2112 China-Russia BIT 2006; China-Uzbekistan BIT 2011; Xiaohong Hu (n 2109) 76, 78.

2113 Chapter 8 Section F CETA; Tingting 婷婷 Deng 邓, '中欧双边投资条约中的投资者 - 国家争端解决机制———以欧盟投资法庭制度为视角' (Investor-State Dispute Settlement Mechanism in the China-EU Bilateral Investment Treaty – From the Perspective of the EU Investment Court System) [2017] (4) *Zhengzhi yu Falü* 99, Deng Tingting is a lecturer at Central South University in Changsha, Hunan Province; Shixi 世席 Huang 黄, 欧盟投资协定中的投资者-国家争端解决机制——兼论中欧双边投资协定中的相关问题 (Investor-State

ally be accepted by China, and could instigate necessary domestic reforms, while helping make further progress in trade and investment relations with developed states.[2114]

The second question, apart from which kind of BITs the Chinese government should conclude, is how investment arbitration mechanisms are evaluated.

In fact, Chinese scholars' analyses were mainly positive irrespective of whether a more liberal BIT practice was already recommended. Already in 2003, Chen Huihua maintained that investment arbitration via ICSID served to depoliticize conflicts.[2115] Later on, in 2007, Yang Zewei[2116] confirmed this perceived reduction of political risk, and opined that participation in investment arbitration helps attract foreign direct investment.[2117] Hu Xiaohong described ICSID proceedings as largely transparent, and outcomes as predictable.[2118] To Wang Yanzhi[2119], ICSID arbitration had up to

---

Dispute Settlement Mechanisms in EU Investment Treaties – Related Issues in the China-EU Bilateral Investment Treaty) (2015) 37 (5) *Huanqiu Falü Pinglun* 149, 158; Jun 军 Xiao 肖, 中欧 BIT 的投资者-东道国争端解决机制——基于中加 BIT 与 CETA 的比较分析 (The China-EU BIT Investor-Host State Dispute Settlement Mechanism – Comparative Analysis on the basis of the China-Canada BIT and CETA) (2015) 25 (2) *Xi'an Dianzi Keji Daxue Xuebao* 76. Xiao Jun is an Associate Professor at Wuhan University Law School; Section F CETA. On favorably viewed EU moves against treaty shopping see also Yan 燕 Wang 王, 欧盟新一代投资协定"反条约挑选" 机制的改革———以 CETA 和 JEEPA 为分析对象 (Anti-Treaty Shopping Reform Led by EU's New Generation Investment Treaties: Taking CETA and JEEPA as Examples) (2018) 40 (3) *Xiandai Faxue* 156.

2114 Arts 12, 13 Treaty between the Government of the United States of America and the Government of [Country] Concerning the Encouragement and Reciprocal Protection of Investment (2012 US Model Bilateral Investment Treaty) (US Model BIT 2012), US Department of State, 'Bilateral Investment Treaties and Related Agreements' <https://www.state.gov/documents/organization/188371.pdf> (accessed 29 December 2017); Kuiran 岿然 Liang 梁, '美国双边投资协定范本的劳工保护条款分析——兼论其对我国的影响及我国之对策' (Analysis on the Labor Protection Article of the US 2012 BIT Model ———The Influence on and the Countermeasures of China) (2014) 32 (7) *Hebei Faxue* 158, 168.

2115 Huihua Chen (n 2031) 104.

2116 Yang Zewei, Professor at Wuhan University Law School.

2117 Zewei 泽伟 Yang 杨, '跨国能源管道运输的争议解决机制' (The Conflict Resolution Mechanism for Transnational Pipeline Energy Transport) [2007] (12) *Faxue* 84, 91.

2118 Xiaohong Hu (n 2109) 82.

2119 Wang Yanzhi, Associate Professor at Jilin University Law School.

2011 managed to properly balance flexibility and judicialization, and had become an accepted practice for most states.[2120] Huang Shixi detected a further trend in that direction, and Hu Xiaohong remarked on the notable socialization of host states.[2121] Since 2016, Zhang Xiaojun[2122] and Sun Nanxiang[2123] added that de-politicized international investment arbitration could be a good way to tackle NGO actions in host states amounting to illegitimate investment barriers, and Sun Jin praised the fact that up to 40 % of investment arbitrations in 2015 were launched against host states in the developed world.[2124]

The third question is whether Chinese investors and China as a host state should indeed engage in investment arbitration, and proceedings at ICSID in particular – ie not reach a settlement to avoid proceedings with a foreign investor, or have its often at least partly state-owned investors abstain from filing a claim against a host state respectively. This will be tackled after delineating Chinese international law scholars' misgivings about the current system.

V.2.2.2. Criticism – Ambiguous Jurisdiction, Imbalances and 'Legitimacy Crisis'

Almost all criticism of international investment arbitration appears in debates following actual engagement, ie starting with the request for arbitration in *Tza Yap Shum v Peru* in 2007, which may be considered a result of the proliferation of articles on the previously little-discussed topic.[2125]

2120 Yanzhi 彦志 Wang 王, '国际投资争端解决的法律化：成就与挑战' (The Legalization of International Investment Dispute Settlement: Successes and Challenges) (2011) 25 (3) *Dangdai Faxue* 15.

2121 Xiaohong Hu (n 2109) 82; Shixi Huang, 'New Developments' (n 840) 184 [Chinese].

2122 Zhang Xiaojun, Professor at the Southwestern University of Politics and Law.

2123 Sun Nanxiang, PhD Candidate at the Southwestern University of Politics and Law.

2124 Xiaojun 晓君 Zhang 张 and Nanxiang 南翔 Sun 孙, '企业海外投资的非政府性障碍及中国的对策研究' (The Research on Non-Governmental Obstacles in Foreign Investment and China's Strategy) (2016) 38 (1) *Xiandai Faxue* 143, 150; Jin Sun (n 848) 5. For an additional embrace of investment arbitration's important role and effectivity see Tong Qi, 'Reviewing Chinese overseas investors' use' (n 582) 89–90 [Chinese].

2125 *Tza* (Decision on Annulment) (n 701).

From 2008 to 2011, Cai Congyan, Liu Sun[2126], Wang Yanzhi and Zhang Guang[2127] published articles wherein they developed the notion of a 'legitimacy crisis' of international investment arbitration, including ICSID.[2128] Later on, eg Huang Shixi still wrote of 'great controversy' surrounding IS-DS provisions in BITs in 2016. These were supposedly seen as challenging sovereignty regarding managing the public interest.[2129]

V.2.2.2.1. Supposed Ambiguities and Interpretation Issues

Those referring to a 'legitimacy crisis,' built their case almost exclusively on the three most prominent complaints in Chinese discourse on investment arbitration. Two of the three are strongly in line with the two central phase-independent criticisms in the field of trade law.

First, the charge has once again been leveled that the dispute settlement practice in question suffers from underlying norms' supposed ambiguity.[2130] As elaborated on below, this primarily refers to BIT clauses (and

2126 Liu Sun, Professor at Zhongnan University of Economics and Law in Wuhan, Hubei Province.

2127 Zhang Guang, lecturer at NWUPL and PhD Candidate at Zhongnan University of Economics and Law.

2128 Congyan 从燕 Cai 蔡, '风险社会与国际争端解决机制的解构与重构' (Risk Society and the Deconstruction and Reconstruction of International Dispute Settlement Mechanism) (2008) 26 (1) *Falü Kexue* 153, 163; Sun 笋 Liu 刘, 建立国际投资仲裁的上诉机制问题析评 (On Establishing an Appellate Mechanism of International Investment Arbitration) (2009) 31 (5) *Xiandai Faxue* 122; Yanzhi Wang, 'The Legalization' (n 2120) 15, 22 [Chinese]; Guang 光 Zhang 张, '论国际投资仲裁中非投资国际义务的适用进路' (Fulfillment of Non-Investment International Obligations in International Investment Arbitrations) (2009) 31 (4) *Xiandai Faxue* 121, 129. See also later on eg Tong Qi, 'Reviewing Chinese overseas investors' use' (n 582) 89 [Chinese]; Shuling 淑玲 Yi 衣, '国际投资协定一般例外条款探析' (The Analyses of General Exception Clauses of International Investment Agreement) (2016) 31 (3) *Henan Caijing Zhengfa Daxue Xuebao* 106.

2129 Shixi 世席 Huang 黄, '可持续发展视角下国际投资争端解决机制的革新' (Reforming the international investment dispute settlement mechanism from the perspective of sustainable development) (2016) 30 (2) *Dangdai Faxue* 24.

2130 Shixi 世席 Huang 黄, '国际投资仲裁裁决执行中的国家豁免问题' (The Issue of State Immunity in the Enforcement of International Investment Arbitration Awards) (2012) 6 (6) *Qinghua Faxue* 106; Shixi Huang, 'New Developments' (n 840) 177 [Chinese]; Yanzhi Wang, 'The Legalization' (n 2120) 15, 22 [Chinese]; Jingsong 劲松 Yu 余 and Xiaoning 晓宁 Zhan 詹, '论投资者与东道国间争端解决机制及其影响' (Discussing resolution mechanisms for and conse-

their interpretation by arbitral tribunals) on dispute settlement, MFN treatment, FET, and the definition of eg investment.

A large group of academics including Chen Hong[2131], Chen Wei, Huang Shixi, Huang Yueming[2132], Li Qingling[2133], Liang Kuiran[2134], Wang Nan[2135], Yang Caixia, Qin Quan, Xu Shu[2136] and Yu Jingsong, have since about the onset of Mainland China's case law involvement warned about investment arbitration tribunals' alleged tendency to exploit the supposed ambiguity of norms through expansive interpretation.[2137] Tribunals have been accused of disregarding VCLT rules for norm interpretation and ignoring what parties to a certain BIT explicitly negotiated.[2138] This might

---

quences of disputes between investors and host countries) [2005] (5) *Zhongguo Faxue* 175, Yu Jingsong is a Professor at Renmin University Law School in Beijing and Zhan Xiaoning works at the United Nations Conference on Trade and Development (UNCTAD); Jingsong 劲松 Yu 余, '国际投资条约仲裁中投资者与东道国权益保护平衡问题研究' (Research on the Problem of Balancing Investor and Host Country Rights in International Investment Treaty Arbitration) [2011] (2) *Zhongguo Faxue* 133, 142–143; ICSID Convention.

2131 Chen Hong, lecturer at China Southern Normal University Law School in Guangzhou, Guangdong Province, and PhD Candidate at Xiamen University Law School.

2132 Huang Yueming, lecturer at Shenzhen University Law School.

2133 Li Qingling, lecturer at Guangxi Normal University Law School.

2134 Liang Kuiran, PhD Candidate at the University of International Business and Economics in Beijing.

2135 Wang Nan, lecturer at Shenzhen University Law School.

2136 Xu Shu, lecturer at the South China University of Technology Law School.

2137 VCLT; Hong Chen (n 797) 128, 130; Wei Chen (n 512) 1048–1050; Shixi Huang, 'New Developments' (n 840) 184–185 [Chinese]; Shixi Huang, 'Reforming the international' (n 2129) 31 [Chinese], on what should be excluded from 'investment' to avoid the supposed prior 'infinite expansion,' Huang listed inter alia certain licensing agreements and intellectural property rights; Yueming 月明 Huang 黄, 'ICSID 仲裁庭扩大管辖权的途径及其应对 - 从"谢亚深案"切入' (ICSID Tribunals' Ways of Broadening Jurisdiction and Responses – Viewed Through the "Tza Yap Shum Case") [2013] (5) *Huadong Zhengfa Daxue Xuebao* 64, 75; Qingling 庆灵 Li 李, '国际投资仲裁中的缔约国解释：式微与回归' (Contracting state interpretation in international investment arbitration: decline and return) [2016] (5) *Huadong Zhengfa Daxue Xuebao* 132; Kuiran Liang, 'The Dispute Settlement Article' (n 841) 121, 124 [Chinese]; Nan Wang, 'On the Application' (n 840) 120 [Chinese]; Yang and Qin (n 512) 119–120; Shu 树 Xu 徐, '国际投资仲裁庭管辖权扩张的路径、成因及应对' (Path, causes, and responses to international investment tribunals expanding their jurisdiction) (2017) 11 (3) *Qinghua Faxue* 185; Jingsong Yu (n 2130) 133, 142.

2138 See eg Shixi Huang, 'New Developments' (n 840) 184 [Chinese].

concern the preconditions for arbitration, the definition of 'investment' and 'investor,' exhaustion of local remedies, umbrella and fork-in-the-road clauses, but especially arbitration and MFN clauses.

The first of two primary contentions has been that investment tribunals expansively interpret scope of jurisdiction clauses, and was brought forward – inter alia – by Chen Hong, Chen Wei, Huang Shixi and Liang Kuiran. *Tza Yap Shum v Peru* is noted as an 'edifying' example, whereas exclusive use of semantic interpretation to get around the limitation to disputes about the amount of compensation for expropriation was alleged.[2139] China has realized pertinent vulnerabilities, and reacted by changing its investment treaty practice – 'fourth generation' – to align with the American model, as well as including provisions strengthening contracting states' role in treaty interpretation.[2140]

The second major complaint was about arbitrators supposedly making use of vaguely worded MFN clauses to invoke dispute settlement clauses in other BITs, and extend their own jurisdiction. Huang Shixi and Wang Nan underlined that MFN clauses could never replace consent to jurisdiction, and should not be used to determine the latter.[2141] Liang Kuiran recounted the different strands of case law following *Maffezini* and *Plama*, and pointed to diverse opinions in academia, to then also make clear his opposition to MFN application to dispute resolution clauses.[2142] However, state practice in devising MFN clauses already tended towards more limited wording around China's first brush with case law. Moreover, the case law in re-

2139 *Tza* (Award) (n 645); Hong Chen (n 797) 128, 130, who added here that the PRC should clarify that its BITs do not apply to Hong Kong and Macao investors; Wei Chen (n 512) 1048–1050; Shixi Huang, 'New Developments' (n 840) 185 [Chinese]; Kuiran Liang, 'The Dispute Settlement Article' (n 841) 124 [Chinese].

2140 See Chapter IV.2.1.2.5. See also Reinisch (n 544) 115, 117, 119, 174; Hwang and Chang, 'Government of the Lao People's Democratic Republic' (n 545) 521.

2141 Shixi Huang, 'New Developments' (n 840) 184–185 [Chinese]; Nan Wang, 'On the Application' (n 840) 120 [Chinese].

2142 Kuiran Liang, 'The Dispute Settlement Article' (n 841) 128, 131 [Chinese]. See also Hai 海 Tian 田, 论最惠国条款适用于投资争端 解决程序的平等理论困境 (On the Equality Dilemma of Applying the MFN Clause to the Investment Dispute Settlement Procedure) (2018) 16 (3) *Shidai Faxue* 103; *Maffezini* (Award on Merits) (n 823); *Plama Consortium Limited v Republic of Bulgaria*, ICSID Case No ARB/03/24, Award (27 August 2008) ('*Plama* (Award)').

cent years has also trended towards a narrower interpretation of MFN clauses, as – inter alia – in *Ansung v China*.[2143]

Furthermore, commenting on the case *Sanum v Laos*, Huang Shixi criticized the Singaporean Court of Appeal – the arbitral award was subject to judicial review – for supposedly violating the intentions of the parties to the China-Laos BIT 1993 by allowing the Macao company to be subsumed under 'investor' in this case. In Huang's view, both host state trust in investment arbitration and diplomatic relations between host and home state governments are threatened.[2144] Chen Hong already decried that a Hong Kong investor could cite a PRC BIT in *Tza Yap Shum*, supposedly infringing upon Hong Kong's autonomy and self-governance in the realm of international economic relations.[2145]

Moving to clauses that have not been a primary subject of investment arbitrations involving China, Zhao Jun[2146] opined that 'investment' is not consistently defined in international investment agreements, and that tribunals have – while taking diverging approaches since the decisions in *Fedax* and *Salini* – overall tended to expansive interpretations that should solicit the imposition of appropriate limitations.[2147] According to Huang Shixi, host state development has not been sufficiently taken into account in determining whether an 'investment' had indeed been made. Huang would want arbitrators to judge whether the investor has contributed to the host state's GDP, but also social development.[2148]

Furthermore, Wang Yanzhi argued that FET clauses had also been interpreted inconsistently,[2149] creating unpredictability in the system, which he assigned to overly abstract wording, openness to changes in meaning over

---

2143 See also Chapter IV.2.1.3.1.2; *Ansung* (n 814) paras 138–139, 141.

2144 Shixi Huang, 'Inspecting the equitability' (n 923) 144–145 [Chinese]; *Sanum* (Singapore Court of Appeal Judgment) (n 747); China-Laos BIT 1993.

2145 *Tza* (Award) (n 645); Hong Chen (n 797) 128, 130.

2146 Zhao Jun, Associate Professor at Zhejiang University Law School.

2147 Jun 骏 Zhao 赵, '国际投资仲裁中"投资"定义的张力和影响' (The Stretching Force of the Definition of "Investment" in International Investment Arbitrations and Its Impact) (2014) 36 (3) *Xiandai Faxue* 161; *Fedax* (n 513); *Salini Costruttori SpA and Italstrade SpA v Hashemite Kingdom of Jordan*, ICSID Case No ARB/02/13, Decision on Jurisdiction (9 November 2004).

2148 Shixi 世席 Huang 黄, '国际投资条约中投资的确定与东道国发展的考量' (The Determination of Investment and the Consideration of the Host States' Development in International Investment Treaties) (2014) 36 (5) *Xiandai Faxue* 136, 145.

2149 On controvery surrounding the FET principle see also Gallagher and Shan, *Chinese Investment Treaties* (n 34) 106–122, who describe a standoff between

time, and excessive discretion for tribunal interpretation.[2150] Wang thus wrote in support of the enumerated list approach to FET clauses, or even better the comprehensive closed list approach he praised the EU for applying.[2151] The PRC had mostly used independent FET clauses, then included customary international law minimum standards, and in more recent agreements also open enumeration (Article 132 China-Peru FTA 2009, Article 12.5 China-Republic of Korea FTA 2015) and closed enumeration (Article 5 China-Uzbekistan BIT 2011, Article 7 China-ASEAN FTA Investment Chapter 2009).[2152]

---

the 'plain meaning'-approach and equation with the 'international minimum standard' ('IMS'). They call the former difficult to apply when the terms are supposedly 'inherently subjective and therefore lacking in precision' (here they cite UNCTAD), and then expand on contentious debates around whether the IMS is part of customary international law. On FET as an evolving standard see *Azurix Corp v Argentine Republic*, ICSID Case No ARB/01/12, Final Award (14 July 2006) para 368. On FET IMS equation see *El Paso Energy International Company v Argentina*, ICSID Case No ARB/03/15, Award (31 October 2011) para 337. On FET and bad faith see *Mondev International* (n 881). On FET and arbitrariness see *Waste Management Inc v Mexico*, ICSID Case No ARB(AF)/00/3, Final Award (30 April 2004). On FET and legitimate expectations see *International Thunderbird Gaming Corporation v Mexico*, UNCITRAL (NAFTA), Arbitral Award (26 January 2006) paras 147–148. On FET and stability and predictability see *CMS Gas Transmission Company v Argentina*, ICSID Case No ARB/01/8, Award (12 May 2005). For a recent detailed discussion see also *Ioan Micula, Viorel Micula, SC European Food SA, SC Starmill SRL and SC Multipack SRL v Romania*, ICSID Case No ARB/05/20, Award (11 December 2013) paras 665–673.

2150 For supposed progress and the attainment of 'clear benchmarks,' including legitimate expectations, arbitrariness, and denial of justice and due process see Meg Kinnear, 'ICSID and International Investment Treaty Arbitration: Progress and Prospects' in Wenhua Shan (ed), *China and International Investment Law: Twenty Years of ICSID Membership* (Brill 2015) 17. For further deliberations on the subject see also Shotaro Hamamoto, 'Protection of the Investor's Legitimate Expectations: Intersection of a Treaty Obligation and a General Principle of Law' in Wenhua Shan (ed), *China and International Investment Law: Twenty Years of ICSID Membership* (Brill 2015).

2151 Yanzhi 彦志 Wang 王, '国际投资法上公平与公正待遇条款改革的列举式清单进路' (Enumerated list approach to the reform of fair and equitable treatment clauses in international investment law) (2015) 29 (6) *Dangdai Faxue* 148, 157. For supposed FET clause ambiguity, as well as the alleged need to improve clauses on taxation see also Shu 树 Xu 徐, '国际投资仲裁中滥诉防范机制的构建' (Constructing a mechanism to guard against indiscriminate lawsuit in international investment arbitration) [2017] (5) *Faxue* 152, 165.

2152 See also Chapter IV.2.1.2.5; Yanzhi Wang, 'Enumerated list' (n 2151) 157 [Chinese]; Art 132 China-Peru FTA; Art 12.5 China-Republic of Korea FTA; Art 5

V.2.2.2.2. Nature and Legitimacy of Investment Arbitration

Authors such as Cai Congyan, Wang Nan and Wang Yanzhi posited that issues with interpretation had to be viewed in the context of tribunals' failure to recognize the legal nature of investment disputes. Supposedly, the latter were treated as if they were cases of commercial disputes between private companies, not involving sovereign states' behavior under public law.[2153] According to Wang Yan[2154], this then led to misinterpretation of public interest measures, such as measures for the protection of public security and public health.[2155] Thereby, Yu Jingsong maintained that host states have been hindered from protecting 'societal values' and impaired in their development.[2156] Ultimately, Wang Yan wrote that especially developing states lose faith in investment arbitration on account of this.[2157]

Yang Caixia and Qin Quan lamented a new era of 'arbitration without privity'. Opting for international investment arbitration is said to have increasingly become a matter of convenience for investors, while tribunals no longer deem relevant what a host state agreed to in a contract, but rather what is agreed to in investment protection treaties in general, thus maximizing investors' rights in an unprecedented way. Furthermore, they criticized a one-sided right to initiate arbitration.[2158]

In Li Qingling's view, contracting states often underestimated risks to their sovereignty when signing up to international investment arbitration. She argued that one problem was arbitral tribunals' alleged practice of

China-Uzbekistan BIT 2011; Art 7 ASEAN-China Investment Agreement; Gallagher and Shan, *Chinese Investment Treaties* (n 34) 105–138; Patrick Dumberry, 'The Importation of the FET Standard through MFN Clauses: An Empirical Study of BITs' (2017) 32 *ICSID Review* 1.

2153 See eg Congyan 从燕 Cai 蔡, '国际投资仲裁的商事化与"去商事化' (The Commercialization and De-Commercialization of International Investment Arbitration) (2011) 33 (1) *Xiandai Faxue* 152; Yan 燕 Wang 王, '国际投资条约仲裁审查标准之反思' (Reflections on Audit Standards in International Investment Treaties) [2013] (6) *Faxue* 120; Yanzhi Wang, 'The Legalization' (n 2120) 15 [Chinese].

2154 Wang Yan, lecturer at Guangdong University of Foreign Studies.

2155 Yan Wang, 'Reflections on Audit Standards' (n 2153) 120 [Chinese].

2156 Jingsong Yu (n 2130) 142–143.

2157 Yan Wang, 'Reflections on Audit Standards' (n 2153) 129 [Chinese].

2158 Yang and Qin (n 512) 119–120.

building on previous tribunals' interpretations instead of their own.[2159] According to Xu Shu, states might limit or even end the practice of authorizing international investment arbitration, if the supposed trend of tribunals expanding their own jurisdiction goes too far in 'sensitive' cases.[2160]

The second mainstream criticism that is in line with such in the field of trade law, maintained that developing states, here in the sense of being mostly in the role of host states, are supposedly disadvantaged. Several years after China's first case law participations, iterations of this critique shifted further away from a developed state-developing state dichotomy, focusing instead on issues of supposed favoritism towards investors that would concern all host states. Importantly, treaties between developing states significantly proliferated in the 2000s,[2161] as such states increasingly also became capital exporters, and did not bring significant change in treaty practice.[2162]

Huang Yueming, Liang Danni, Liu Sun, Xu Chongli, Xu Shu, Yang Caixia and Qin Quan, Yu Jingsong, and Zhang Guang all perceived a marked imbalance between investors' rights and host state rights.[2163] In Huang Yueming's words, 'what cannot be denied is that [ICSID] is biased in favor of investors'.[2164]

2159 Qingling Li (n 2137) 135, 142, who cites *Waste Management v Mexico*, wherein the tribunal supposedly brought forward a standard defintion of FET under Article 1105 NAFTA by building on *ADF Group Inc v United States of America*, ICSID Case No ARB(AF)/00/1, Final Award (9 January 2003), *Loewen Group Inc and Raymond Loewen v United States of America*, ICSID Case No ARB(AF)/98/3, Award on Merits (26 June 2003), and *SD Myers, Inc v Canada*, UNCITRAL First Partial Award (13 November 2000), as well as *Mondev International* (n 881), while neglecting to make its own interpretation of the NAFTA text; *Waste Management Inc v Mexico*, ICSID Case No ARB(AF)/98/2, Jurisdiction Award (20 June 2000) para 98.

2160 Shu Xu, 'Path, causes, and responses' (n 2137) 206–207 [Chinese].

2161 See Chapter IV.2.1.2.1.

2162 Dolzer and Schreuer (n 523) 7–8.

2163 Yueming Huang (n 2137) 75; Danni 丹妮 Liang 梁, 国际投资协定一般例外条款研究 ———与 WTO 共同但有区别的司法经验 (Researching general exception norms in international investment treaties – common and distinct judicial experiences with the WTO) [2014] (1) *Faxue Pinglun* 100, Liang Danni is an Associate Professor at Sun Yat-sen University Law School; Sun Liu (n 2128) 122; Chongli 崇利 Xu 徐, '晚近国际投资争端解决实践之评判：“全球治理”理论的引入' (Judging the Recent Practice in International Investment Dispute Resolution: Introducing the "Global Governance" Theory) [2010] (3) *Faxuejia* 143, 153; Shu Xu, 'Constructing a mechanism' (n 2090) 164 [Chinese]; Yang and Qin (n 512) 119–120; Jingsong Yu (n 2130) 133; Guang Zhang (n 2128) 129.

2164 Yueming Huang (n 2137) 75.

Yu Jingsong and Zhan Xiaoning added in 2005 that developing states' citizens were allegedly underrepresented at investment arbitration tribunals.[2165] For Cai Congyan, this was to be explained by the international investment arbitration system being the result of the global 'North-South divide', which was supposedly most overtly demonstrated by the case of Argentina. Writing in 2007, Cai held that many developing states saw this as a cautionary tale and mooted a return to exclusive domestic jurisdiction in international investment disputes. Some, like Ecuador, thought about revoking BITs, while Ecuador, Bolivia and Venezuela denounced the ICSID Convention.[2166] By its harshest critics, Wang Yanzhi wrote, the system had by 2011 been termed a new form of colonialism and the epitome of neoliberalism.[2167]

Similar to Latin American states, China had long subscribed to the *Calvo Doctrine* and the 'New International Economic Order', which 'emphasized State sovereignty over natural resources and limited any substantial protection of foreign investment under international law'.[2168] However, policy changes over the last three decades have seen the Chinese leadership leave such positions far behind, as BITs have become progressively more liberal, including broad access to international arbitration.

The third issue put forward in the context of the supposed 'legitimacy crisis' is the lack of an appellate body in international investment arbitration. This has been portrayed in marked and unfavorable contrast with the AB in trade disputes at the WTO DSM. According to Liu Sun, the US has made very positive experiences with appellate mechanisms in domestic in-

2165 Yu and Zhan (n 2130) 175–184.

2166 Congyan Cai, 'Reviewing New Developments' (n 2109) 107–109 [Chinese]; Kuiran Liang, 'The Dispute Settlement Article' (n 841) 122 [Chinese]. For the *Calvo Doctrine* see also Shan, Gallagher and Zhang (n 571) 122, FN 13 where it is diescribed as a 'foreign policy doctrine based on the ideology of Carlos Calvo, an Argentine jurist', focused on 'anti-super-national-treatment.' Calvo viewed weak, developing host states and their citizens as discriminated against by rich, industrialized nations in the investment sphere. Latin American States mostly turned away from the doctrine in the 1990s, but it is 'still alive,' and got some new support in the 2000s through the 'Bolivarian Socialism' of Venzuelas former President Chavez, Bolivian President Morales and others; Sergey Ripinsky, 'Venezuela's Withdrawal From ICSID: What it Does and Does Not Achieve' *International Institute for Sustainable Development* (Winnipeg, 13 April 2012) <https://www.iisd.org/itn/2012/04/13/venezuelas-withdrawal-from-icsid-what-it-does-and-does-not-achieve/> accessed 30 March 2019.

2167 Yanzhi Wang, 'The Legalization' (n 2120) 22–23 [Chinese].

2168 Shan, Gallagher and Zhang (n 571) 122, FN 13.

vestment arbitration that could be emulated. Nonetheless, Liu also warned of the need to guard against resulting excessive duration or cost of proceedings.[2169] Liu opined that deficiencies in investment treaties had led to a proliferation in cases, and the latter to excessive challenges of host state sovereignty.[2170]

Individual other authors complained about insufficient use of alternative dispute resolution methods, and a lack of flexibility in comparison with negotiation or conciliation.[2171] On the latter point, Yang Zewei also held that investment arbitration entailed a higher risk of disturbing regular operations, eg of pipelines. Hence, he called for making use of this option as an *ultima ratio* only.[2172]

Finally, on a very different issue, Huang Shixi cited a European campaign group's 2012 study to argue that a few large law firms dominate the investment arbitration business. Allegedly, neither the IBA conflict of interest guide nor the eligible arbitrators roster in CETA suffice to remedy the issue of arbitrators or their firms also acting as agents of the same parties in different arbitrations.[2173]

V.2.2.3. Recommendations – Identity Shift: From Host State to Home State

V.2.2.3.1. Pre-Engagement – Chinese Views on International Investment Arbitration Ahead of the First Case in 2007

As mentioned above, pertinent articles only proliferated after China actually participated in ICSID proceedings, at least via a Hong Kong investor invoking a BIT concluded by the PRC. Among early authors, Yu Jingsong

---

2169 Sun Liu (n 2128) 122, 129.

2170 Ibid 122.

2171 Jingsong Yu (n 2130) 142–143.

2172 Zewei Yang, 'The Conflict Resolution Mechanism' (n 2117) 91 [Chinese].

2173 Shixi Huang, 'Reforming the international' (n 2129) 33 [Chinese]. See also *IBA Guide to Conflict of Interest in International Arbitration (adopted by resolution of the IBA Council on Thursday 23 October 2014)* (International Bar Association 2014) as well as Art X.25 CETA; Pia Eberhardt and Cecilia Olivet, 'Profiting from Injustice: How Law Firms, Arbitrators and Financiers are Fuelling an Investment Arbitration Boom' *Corporate Europe Observatory* (Brussels, November 2012) <corporateeurope.org/sites/default/files/publications/profiting-from-injustice.pdf> accessed 30 March 2019.

and Zhan Xiaoning, noting the danger to regulatory sovereignty, still recommended that their government convince investors to opt against ICSID by improving local dispute settlement mechanisms as much as possible. However, they already began to promote active participation in reform negotiations, with the system in need of 'perfection'.[2174] Later on, Chen Wei noted a school of thought among Mainland Chinese international lawyers that had put forward the notion that foreign investors actually did not want to make use of ICSID until 2011 on account of the Chinese court system's quality.[2175]

On the other hand, Liu Ying already called for a rather broad position on the range of disputes that could be submitted to ICSID, and also voiced support for consent rules that were not exceedingly strict.[2176] On the question of exhaustion of local remedies, Lan Hua[2177] already advocated a flexible approach.[2178] Moreover, Ceng Huaqun[2179] already highlighted that the PRC was actually in a position of being both one of the largest capital importing and (then still put as 'among developing nations') one of the largest capital-exporting states. Ceng's article also called on the government to pay closer attention to and further strengthen the study of ICSID, as 'one of the most important new developments in international economic law'.[2180]

2174 Yu and Zhan (n 2130) 175–184.

2175 Wei Chen (n 512) 1047–1048.

2176 Ying Liu (n 2110) 67.

2177 Lan Hua, PhD candidate at the Wuhan University International Law Research Institute.

2178 Hua 花 Lan 兰, '用尽当地救济原则与国际投资争议解决' (The Principle of Exhaustion of Local Remedies and the Resolution of International Investment Disputes) (2002) 17 (6) *Henansheng Zhengfa Guanli Ganbu Xueyuan Xuebao* 104, 107.

2179 Ceng Huaqun, Professor at the Xiamen University International Economic Law Research Institute.

2180 Huaqun 华群 Ceng 曾, '国际经济法学要研究新问题' (New Issues Need to be Studied in International Economic Law) (2004) 24 (2) *Faxue Yanjiu* 135.

V.2.2.3.2. Walking a Tight Rope – Chinese Views on International Investment Arbitration as Threat and Protection from 2007

V.2.2.3.2.1. Research and Progress – Steady As She Goes

In parallel to the discourse on trade matters, calls for more research and training have been prominent.[2181] In recent articles published since around the issuing of the first award involving a Mainland investor – *Ping An v Belgium* in April 2015 – Fan Ying[2182] and Yi Shuling[2183] called for research into potential appeals mechanisms in investment arbitration, considering it helpful for ongoing treaty negotiations with the EU and US.[2184] Meanwhile, Zhao Jun and Qi Tong opined that China had already made great strides in studying the use of international investment arbitration, while accumulating practice on both sides against diversified opposing parties and disputing substantive issues very topical to ongoing international investment law debates.[2185] Nevertheless, Chinese scholars continued to underline a further need to hone abilities while gathering more experience on both investment arbitration sides.[2186]

V.2.2.3.2.2. Reforms and Influence – Making the Case

Second – and most intensely in this field – scholars made the familiar case for influencing international legal development, mainly through Chinese

2181 See eg Hong Chen (n 797) 128, 130; Tong Qi, 'Reviewing Chinese overseas investors' use' (n 582) 90 [Chinese]; Yang and Qin (n 512) 119–120.

2182 Fan Ying, Professor at Yantai University Law School.

2183 Yi Shuling, Associate Professor at Yantai University Law School.

2184 *Ping An Life Insurance* (n 849); Ying 静 Fan 樊 and Shuling 淑玲 Yi 衣, 国际投资仲裁监督机制改革问题研究 (Research on International Investment Arbitration Supervision Mechanism Reform) (2015) 33 (2) *Hebei Faxue* 118, 123. On the need to also study investment courts as proposed eg in CETA see also Haitao 海涛 Tang 唐, 欧盟投资者—东道国争端解决机制的改革及我国的应对策略 (EU Investor-State Dispute Settlement Mechanism and Our Country 's Countermeasures) (2018) 33 (3) *Henan Caijing Zhengfa Daxue Xuebao* 145, 154–155.

2185 Tong Qi, 'Reviewing Chinese overseas investors' use' (n 582) 94–95 [Chinese]; Jun Zhao (n 2147) 173.

2186 Kuiran Liang, 'The Dispute Settlement Article' (n 841) 133 [Chinese].

BIT practice.[2187] Following the supposed 'legitimacy crisis' of investment arbitration noted in the preceding sub-chapter, one could have expected a push for retrenchment, abstention from further participation, and reversion to the old BIT model. Instead, Chinese international law scholars called for aiding the system in regaining supposedly lost legitimacy.

On pertinent reasoning, in 2008, Cai Congyan related the need for reform to a change in the societal bases of institutions in the new age of 'risk society' and already praised ongoing change.[2188] Three years later, Wang Yanzhi called for patience with a mechanism that was supposedly still in its infancy.[2189] Since 2014, Chinese scholars have been more open about the direction of change to be achieved.

In Liang Kuiran's words, China's active participation in the ongoing reform of international investment arbitration was to be considered as important as integration with the WTO DSM, and would indeed strengthen Chinese international influence.[2190] Other scholars have – inter alia – suggested that the Chinese government should use the most prominent negotiations, such as those with the EU on the 'Comprehensive Agreement on Investment' (CAI), to shape the future of ISDS.[2191] Furthermore, Beijing should 'go on the offensive' in negotiating the future wording of (quite progressive) labor and environmental protection clauses, and go with reform trends on tax and prudence exceptions, dispute prevention policies, alternative dispute resolution, and a supervisory role of NGOs – should be 'trained' in China – as well as *amicus curiae* briefs. Such steps are – inter

---

2187 See inter alia Yueming Huang (n 2137) 64. For the importance of consistency see Jun 军 Xiao 肖, '国际投资条约的复杂化与多元化 ———晚近国际投资条约发展趋势之辨及我国应对策略' (The Complication and Diversification of International Investment Treaties – Recent Trends and Debates in International Investment Treaty Development and China's Response Tactics) [2014] (5) *Faxue Pinglun* 163.

2188 Congyan Cai, 'Risk Society' (n 2128) 153–154, 162–163 [Chinese].

2189 Yanzhi Wang, 'The Legalization' (n 2120) 22–23 [Chinese].

2190 Kuiran Liang, 'The Dispute Settlement Article' (n 841) 133 [Chinese].

2191 Tingting Deng (n 2113) 111. On China having to grow its influence on global investment rule-making see also Jun Xiao, 'The Complication and Diversification' (n 2187) 169 [Chinese]; Jun Zhao (n 2147) 172; Tong Qi, 'Reviewing Chinese overseas investors' use' (n 582) 96 [Chinese] who emphasizes the role of participation in growing Chinese soft power. On dispute prevention see also Tong 彤 Qi 漆, 论"一带一路"国际投资争议的预防机制 (Discussing the Prevention Mechanism for "Belt and Road Initiative" International Investment Disputes) [2018] (3) *Faxue Pinglun* 79.

alia – intended to improve Beijing's image as well as that of its companies.[2192]

A first pillar of Chinese scholars' recommendations as to how Beijing should proceed in changing its BIT practice, addresses gaining more control over how these treaties are interpreted. Li Qingling urged more 'textual precision' overall, to make BITs more 'self-explanatory.' She also noted options like mandatory consultations on interpretation (see eg Article 12 China-Russia BIT 2006), or required (and potentially binding) joint interpretation by the parties at one party's request (see eg Article 155 China-New Zealand FTA). Li viewed the latter option as a trend, citing also Article 16 Canada-Jordan BIT 2009, and added that issue area (eg taxes) and time limitations could be introduced.[2193] Two further options would be binding interpretations by a permanent interpretation body like in Article 1131 (2) NAFTA (see eg Article 9.7 China-Australia FTA), or the conclusion of subsequent interpretation and application agreements between

2192 Kuiran Liang, 'Analysis on the Labor Protection Article' (n 2114) 168 [Chinese]; Tong Qi, 'Reviewing Chinese overseas investors' use' (n 582) 96 [Chinese]; Zhang and Sun (n 2061) 143. On China having to take into account social, cultural and environmental sustainability in investment treaty relations especially with African, Latin American and Central Asian states see also Shixi Huang, 'The Determination of Investment' (n 2148) 145 [Chinese].

2193 Qingling Li (n 2137) 141–142. For a further call to textual precision see Shixi Huang, 'Reforming the international' (n 2129) 31 [Chinese]. For another recommendation to include joint interpretation clauses akin to Art 155 New Zealand-China FTA see Shuling Yi (n 2128) 111. See also Shixi Huang, 'Inspecting the equitability' (n 923) 145 [Chinese]; Art 12 China-Russia BIT 2006 – Art 12: 'The Contracting Parties shall consult, at the request of either of them, on the matter concerning the interpretation or application of this Agreement. Where either Contracting Party requests such consultation, the other Contracting Party shall give prompt response'; Art 155 New Zealand-China FTA 2008 –
Art 155: '1. The tribunal shall, on request of the state party, request a joint interpretation of the Parties of any provision of this Agreement that is in issue in a dispute. The Parties shall submit in writing any joint decision declaring their interpretation to the tribunal within 60 days of delivery of the request. 2. A joint decision issued under paragraph 1 by the Parties shall be binding on the tribunal, and any award must be consistent with that joint decision. If the Parties fail to issue such a decision within 60 days, the tribunal shall decide the issue on its own account'; Art 16 Agreement Between Canada and the Hashemite Kingdom of Jordan for the Promotion and Protection of Investments (signed 28 June 2009, entered into force 14 December 2009) (Canada-Jordan BIT).

contracting states.[2194] Huang Shixi laid out a specific issue for textual clarity in 2013, arguing that MFN clause application in procedural matters had to be explicitly excluded in the text;[2195] Deng Ruiping[2196] and Dong Weijie[2197] added that more clearly delineated umbrella clauses should be included, taking the issue of subsidiaries into account.[2198]

The second pillar of pertinent recommendations resulted directly from the 2015 defeat of the Chinese investor in *Ping An v Belgium*.[2199] Scholars like Liu Yong[2200] called for BITs – newly negotiated or amended – to be improved by including what he would deem clearer transitional clauses or such on the application of inter-temporal law, using the example of Article 2 (3) in the US Model BIT 2012: '[f]or greater certainty, this Treaty does not bind either Party in relation to any act or fact that took place or any situation that ceased to exist before the date of entry into force of this Treaty'.[2201] Beyond the clarity issue, Sun Jin recommended a policy of

2194 Art 9.7 Australia-China FTA – Art 9.7: 'Committee on Investment – 1. The Parties hereby establish a Committee on Investment that shall meet on the request of either Party or the FTA Joint Commission to consider any matter arising under this Chapter. 2. The Committee's functions shall include: (a) reviewing the implementation of this Chapter; (b) identifying and recommending measures or initiatives to promote and increase investment flows between the Parties; and (c) unless the Parties otherwise agree, conducting the review referred to in Article 9.9. 3. The Committee: (a) shall establish and maintain a list of arbitrators pursuant to Article 9.15.5 and Article 9.15.6; (b) may, pursuant to Article 9.18.2 or Article 9.19, adopt a joint decision of the Parties, declaring their interpretation of a provision of this Chapter and Annex 9-A; (c) may propose amendments to Section B in the light of experience of its operation'; Art 1131 NAFTA; Qingling Li (n 2137) 140, 142.

2195 Shixi Huang, 'New Developments' (n 840) 177, 184–185 [Chinese].

2196 Deng Ruiping, professor at SWUPL.

2197 Dong Weijie, PhD Candidate at SWUPL.

2198 Ruiping 瑞平 Deng 邓 and Weijie 威颉 Dong 董, 论中国双边投资条约中的保护伞条款 (Research on the Umbrella Clause in China 's Bilateral Investment Treaties) (2018) 36 (2) *Hebei Faxue* 10, 22–23.

2199 See Chapter IV.2.1.3.2.1; *Ping An Life Insurance* (n 849).

2200 Liu Yong, Associate Professor at the Zhejiang University of Finance and Economics Law School.

2201 Yong Liu, 'China Ping An' (n 848) 162, 174 [Chinese]. In the Belgium-Luxembourg Economic Union-China BIT 2005 the pertinent clause is Art 10: '1. This Agreement substitutes and replaces the Agreement between the Government of the People's Republic of China and the Belgium-Luxembourg Economic Union on the Reciprocal Promotion and Protection ofInvestments, signed on 4th June, 1984 in Brussels. 2. The present Agreement shall apply to all invest-

drafting new 'replacement' BITs to also explicitly cover 'old' investments.[2202]

In a third main line of argument – which spans debates throughout the post-engagement period – scholars like Cai Congyan, Xu Chongli and Zhang Guang urged their government to actively influence international legal development and help in the supposedly needed process of rebalancing host state and investor rights to allow international investment arbitration to regain legitimacy. According to them, the system needed to once again reflect the reality of host states' obligations beyond investment law. It had to be de-commercialized recognizing investment arbitration's true legal nature, after arbitral tribunals with strong leeway allegedly 'privatized' host states, negating public interest protection.[2203]

This reasoning prompts demands to increase the policy space of host states, mostly through general exception clauses. Yi Shuling described a growing focus on this issue also in recent US, EU and Canadian treaties, and argued that China needed to catch up. Chinese BITs had mostly not included such clauses, introduced 'non-precluded measures' (NPM) to protect basic safety interests with the China-Finland BIT 2004, 'general exceptions' and 'security exceptions' with the China-New Zealand FTA 2008,

---

ments made by investors of either Contracting Party in the territory of the other Contracting Party, whether made before or after the entry into force of this Agreement, but shall not apply to any dispute or any claim concerning an investment which was already under judicial or arbitral process before its entry into force. Such disputes and claims shall continue to be settled according to the provisions ofthe Agreement of 1984 mentioned in paragraph 1 of this Article'; Art 2 (3) Treaty between the Government of the United States of America and the Government of [Country] Concerning the Encouragement and Reciprocal Protection of Investment (2012 U.S. Model Bilateral Investment Treaty) (US Model BIT 2012), US Department of State, 'Bilateral Investment Treaties and Related Agreements' <https://www.state.gov/documents/organization/188371.pdf> (accessed 29 December 2017).

2202 Jin Sun (n 848) 10.

2203 Congyan Cai, 'The Commercialization and De-Commercialization' (n 2153) 152 [Chinese]; Chongli Xu, 'Judging the Recent Practice' (n 2163) 153 [Chinese]; Guang Zhang (n 2128) 129. For the supposed 'commercialization' of judicial review procedures see also Fang 芳 Xiao 肖, 国际投资仲裁裁决司法审查的"商事化"及反思 ———以美国联邦最高法院"BG 公司诉阿根廷"案裁决为例 (Reflections on the "Commercialization" of the Judicial Review of Investment Arbitration Awards – Taking the US Supreme Court's Findings in "BG Group v Argentina" as an Example) [2018] (3) *Faxue Pinglun* 152, 162.

and the first unified general exception clause in Article 33 Canada-China BIT 2012.[2204]

As for case law, Yi lauded the annulment decisions in *Sempra v Argentina* and *Enron v Argentina*, criticizing supposed tribunal reliance on customary international law (Article 25 Draft Articles on State Responsibility) instead of pertinent treaty provisions (Article 11 US-Argentina BIT). One lesson should supposedly be to introduce wording explicitly excluding customary international law in the form of the Draft Articles and GATT-based interpretation.[2205] Yi counseled that new clauses should be clearly 'self-judging,' ie like Article 201 China-New Zealand FTA and not Article 16 (1) China-ASEAN Investment Agreement, in order to allow host states to 'freely move' on emergency responses based on general exceptions and protect pertinent measures from 'rigorous scrutiny' by tribunals.[2206] Investor rights would supposedly remain secured through reputational pressures and

2204 Shuling Yi (n 2128) 112; Art 3 (5), (6) Agreement between the Government of Finland and the Government of the People's Republic of China on the Encouragement and Reciprocal Protection of Investments (signed 15 November 2004, entered into force 15 November 2006) (China-Finland BIT 2004); Arts 200 and 201 New Zealand-China FTA 2008; Art 33 Canada-China BIT 2012.

2205 Shuling Yi (n 2128) 109, 111; *Sempra Energy International v Argentina*, ICSID Case No ARB/02/16, Decision on Annulment (June 29 2010) paras 132–135, 159–165; *Enron Corporation and Ponderosa Assets LP v Republic of Argentina*, ICSID Case No ARB/01/3, Decision on the Application for Annulment of the Argentine Republic (July 30 2010) paras 356–395; Art 25 Draft Articles on Responsibility of States for Internationally Wrongful Acts, in Report of the International Law Commission on the Work of Its Fifty-third Session (2001) UN GAOR 56th Session Supp 10, 43: 'Article 25. Necessity 1. Necessity may not be invoked by a State as a ground for precluding the wrongfulness of an act not in conformity with an international obligation of that State unless the act: (a) is the only way for the State to safeguard an essential interest against a grave and imminent peril; and (b) does not seriously impair an essential interest of the State or States towards which the obligation exists, or of the international community as a whole. 2. In any case, necessity may not be invoked by a State as a ground for precluding wrongfulness if: (a) the international obligation in question excludes the possibility of invoking necessity; or (b) the State has contributed to the situation of necessity'; Art 11 Treaty between United States of America and the Argentine Republic concerning the Reciprocal Encouragement and Protection of Investments (signed 14 November 1991, entered into force 20 October 1994) (US-Argentina BIT 1991).

2206 Shuling Yi (n 2128) 107, 110–111; Art 201 New Zealand-China FTA 2008; Art 16 (1) ASEAN-China Investment Agreement 2009, where the typical 'nothing in this Agreement shall be construed to' is preceded by the limitation '[s]ubject to the requirement that such measures are not applied in a manner which would constitute a means of arbitrary or unjustifiable discrimination between

home state diplomatic protection, as well as clear limitations to the scope of application of general exception clauses and the good faith, non-discrimination and proportionality principles.[2207]

Huang Shixi urged more developing state influence (noting reform proposals by South Africa, Venezuela and Ecuador), framed this 're-balancing' as a sustainable development issue, and called for BITs to either include a general exception on the environment, or separate substantive provisions on the sustainable development principle, or at least a reference in the preamble that could be used in interpretation.[2208] He referenced UNCTAD recommendations to preserve policy space with an eye to the UN's Sustainable Development Goals, and made the link to exhaustion of domestic remedies – giving the host state a chance to avoid 'international liability' and hugely costly awards by remedying 'mistakes' – as well as waiting period clauses.[2209] Yi Shuling added that much could be learned from Chapter 13 EU-South Korea FTA on how to include the principle of sustainable development.[2210]

Still in the spirit of rebalancing, Li Qingling advocated strengthening the domestic remedies side with provisions like Article 14 China-Colombia BIT 2008, on disputes over alleged expropriation through taxation having to first go to the competent national tax authorities.[2211] Huang Shixi urged the redrafting of denial of benefits-clauses to avoid the investor practice of artificially changing 'nationality' via the use of shell or mailbox companies to enjoy the protection of a different BIT. Huang posited that mostly companies from developed states engaged in such activities and that developing states were moved to contemplate withdrawing from investment arbi-

the Parties, their investors or their investments where like conditions prevail, or a disguised restriction on investors of any Party or their investments made by investors of any Party, [...]'.

2207 Shuling Yi (n 2128) 111.

2208 Shixi Huang, 'Reforming the international' (n 2129) 24, 30–31, 34–35 [Chinese].

2209 Ibid 31–32, issue linked to *Vattenfall AB and others v Germany*, ICSID Case No ARB/12/12, Decision pursuant to ICSID Arbitration Rule 41(5) (2 July 2013), which resulted from Germany's *Energiewende*-induced withdrawal from nuclear energy.

2210 Shuling Yi (n 2128) 111; Chapter 13 Free Trade Agreement between the European Union and its Member States, of the one part, and the Republic of Korea, of the other part (signed 6 October 2010, entered into force 1 July 2011) (EU-Republic of Korea FTA 2010).

2211 Qingling Li (n 2137) 142; Art 14 China-Colombia BIT 2008.

tration as a result.[2212] Xu Shu recommended in 2017 that supposed investor abuse should be countered by strengthening preconditions for arbitration, including a fast dismissal procedure with the investor potentially bearing all arbitration fees and a joint contracting state interpretation mechanism, all with strong limitations to avoid states in turn abusing pertinent clauses.[2213]

When proposing a new Model BIT to the Chinese government in 2009, Norah Gallagher and Wenhua Shan[2214] also intended to improve 'the general balance of rights and obligations of the main parties under such treaties.' In adding new clauses 'to safeguard the rights of the host state to regulate foreign investment, and to promote corporate social responsibility,' they quoted the then-Norway Model BIT and the International Institute for Sustainable Development (IISD) Model International Agreement on Investment for Sustainable Development as indicative of the more 'balanced' approach they would suggest.[2215] Since then, the Chinese government has – inter alia – signed and ratified a BIT with Canada, wherein certain recommendations by the authors were included. Most importantly, 1) provisions on ISDS are much more extensive, 2) narrow down which disputes can be submitted, departing from the earlier 'any dispute'-phrasing, 3) require explicit consent and waiver of other remedies by the investor, 4) introduce a time limit of three years from acquiring knowledge of the dispute, and 5) clarify general unconditional consent to international arbitra-

2212 Shixi 世席 Huang 黄, '国际投资仲裁中的挑选条约问题' (The issue of selecting treaties in international investment arbitration) [2014] (1) *Faxue* 62, 72–73. For a more investor interests-focused perspective, though, see also Yong 勇 Liu 刘, "一带一路"投资风险及其法律应对———以"尤科斯诉俄罗斯案"为视角 ("Belt and Road Initiative" Investment Risks and Legal Responses – From the Perspective of the "Yukos v Russia Case") (2018) 40 (1) *Huanqiu Falü Pinglun* 175.

2213 Shu Xu, 'Constructing a mechanism' (n 2090) 152, 164–165 [Chinese].

2214 Shan Wenhua, professor at Xi'an Jiaotong University Law School.

2215 Gallagher and Shan, *Chinese Investment Treaties* (n 34) 386 FN 15, 414, 439–451 (Appendix V); Agreement between the Kingdom of Norway and X for the Promotion and Protection of Investments (draft version 19 December 2007, since then shelved), (Norway Model BIT 2008); International Institute for Sustainable Development, 'International Institute for Sustainable Development (IISD) Model International Agreement on Investment for Sustainable Development – Negotiators' Handbook' (Winnipeg, April 2005) <http://www.iisd.org/library/iisd-model-international-agreement-investment-sustainable-development-negotiators-handbook> accessed 5 January 2018.

tion in accordance with these BIT rules, as well as matters of enforcement.[2216]

A fourth focal point of debates has emerged around the question of whether or not an appeals body in investment arbitrations should be favored. Most scholars agree that an appeals mechanism would enhance consistency in the interpretation and application of international investment law, providing an opportunity to remedy 'mistakes'.[2217] Fan Ying and Yi Shuling have argued that a unified, multilateralized mechanism within ICSID would avoid the fragmentation that would likely result from different appeals bodies within different BIT frameworks.[2218]

However, Deng Tingting cautioned on appeals bodies regarding potential cost and efficiency issues, and argued in favor of a much narrower scope of review than that she perceived with EU proposals.[2219] Xu Shu agreed on costs and a more lengthy process, added that host states could no longer choose arbitrators, and warned of the danger of getting the mechanism wrong and having contracting states 'lose control' due to a 'runaway horse' appellate body.[2220] Both Xu and Huang Shixi added that the process towards both appeals bodies and permanent tribunals would take years, and commended the approach taken in Article 9.23 China-Australia FTA 2015, to give the parties flexibility and space to within three years after the treaty enters into force start negotiating a potential appeals body. According to Huang, the same clause could be included in the CAI with the EU.[2221] Moreover, Huang Shixi noted that ICSID already has rules for annulment and UNCITRAL awards may be followed by appeals to courts.[2222]

2216 Gallagher and Shan, *Chinese Investment Treaties* (n 34) 386–413, 439–451; Arts 20–23, 32–33, Annex C.21 Canada-China BIT 2012.

2217 Fan and Yi (n 2184) 118; Shixi Huang, 'Investor-State Dispute Settlement Mechanisms' (n 2113) 155 [Chinese]; Kuiran Liang, 'The Dispute Settlement Article' (n 841) 133 [Chinese]; Shu Xu, 'Constructing a mechanism' (n 2090) 165 [Chinese].

2218 Fan and Yi (n 2184) 118, 123. For an endorsement of an appeals body see also Yanzhi Wang, 'The Legalization' (n 2120) 22–23 [Chinese].

2219 Tingting Deng (n 2113) 111.

2220 Shu Xu, 'Constructing a mechanism' (n 2090) 165 [Chinese].

2221 Art 9.23 Australia-China FTA 2015; Shixi Huang, 'Investor-State Dispute Settlement Mechanisms' (n 2113) 155, 158 [Chinese]; Shu Xu, 'Constructing a mechanism' (n 2090) 165 [Chinese].

2222 Art 52 ICSID Convention; UNCITRAL Arbitration Rules (n 523); Shixi Huang, 'Reforming the international' (n 2129) 34 [Chinese].

Regarding the less discussed issue of the potential establishment of (a) permanent investment court(s), Deng Tingting cautioned on the EU proposed version, that its rulings might not be considered 'arbitral awards' under Article 1.2 New York Convention.[2223] Xu Shu described the EU as idealistic in its approach for such institutions, and the US as more pragmatic. Moreover, the EU is viewed as struggling to convince others.[2224]

In Xu Shu's eyes, change in treaty practice is made more likely by the trend towards developed and developing states becoming both capital-exporting and importing, and interests thus increasingly aligning. Xu argued that after experiencing the role of the sued host state, the US, Canada and Australia all adjusted their positions.[2225] They supposedly also perceive an imbalance, as well as investors to have abused the system.[2226] Liang Kuiran confirmed this argument, pointing to the US's post-'NAFTA experience' reforms.[2227] Indeed, experiences as respondents in NAFTA cases have led both the US and Canada to change their Model BITs.[2228]

Yang Caixia and Qin Quan additionally counseled improved domestic legislation, warning of the risk of investors making use of 'general' or 'unclear' norms to immediately go to the international level.[2229]

V.2.2.3.2.3. Identity and Engagement – on What Has Changed

Regarding the question of whether China should continue on its new liberal path in BIT drafting and indeed engage with international investment arbitration – while reform efforts are ongoing – the following context is necessary. An important group of authors has indicated that their state's identity in the investment field has been shifting, and likewise the nature of the investment arbitration system.

On China's identity, Cai Congyan and Xu Chongli already maintained in 2007 and 2010, respectively, that their country could no longer be fitted into the 'North-South divide,' that investment arbitration should in general no longer be analyzed along these lines but rather in global governance

2223 Tingting Deng (n 2113) 109; Art 1.2 New York Convention (n 903).
2224 Shu Xu, 'Constructing a mechanism' (n 2090) 165 [Chinese].
2225 Shu Xu, 'Path, causes, and responses' (n 2137) 207 [Chinese].
2226 Shu Xu, 'Constructing a mechanism' (n 2090) 164 [Chinese].
2227 Kuiran Liang, 'The Dispute Settlement Article' (n 841) 123 [Chinese].
2228 See also Gallagher and Shan, *Chinese Investment Treaties* (n 34) 385–386.
2229 Yang and Qin (n 512) 120.

terms, and that the *Calvo Doctrine* needed to be modernized.[2230] Cai still stated that China had a responsibility to think about other developing nations.[2231] In 2013, Huang Yueming confirmed that China was no longer simply a capital importing country, and Wang Yanzhi wrote that a shift from host state to home state was already well under way.[2232] One interviewee in Wuhan also maintained that the PRC's position had obviously changed on account of a marked increase in outward investment.[2233] In 2017, Sun Jin[2234] argued straightforwardly that China had to adopt a 'capital exporting country mindset'.[2235]

Wang Yanzhi still added in 2013 that China was in a transitory position – also still having a rather weak rule of law – and a middle position should be taken, carefully balancing investor and host state rights. To him, the standard of investor protection was too low until and too high after the 1990s.[2236] Huang Shixi, in his analysis of MFN clause interpretations, also portrayed the PRC as in a difficult position, where it is both a large investment destination – and a narrower MFN interpretation would be preferable – and a large foreign investor itself – and a broader MFN interpretation would be preferable.[2237]

On the investment arbitration system having changed, Yu Jingsong held in 2011 that all states, be they developed or developing, are increasingly both capital-exporting and -importing.[2238] Wang Yanzhi described how the harshest detractors want to do away entirely with investment arbitration and have domestic courts take over fully again or at least have an appeals body-role.[2239] Instead, Wang favored reforming supposedly existing 'struc-

---

2230 Congyan Cai, 'Reviewing New Developments' (n 2109) 107–109 [Chinese]; Chongli Xu, 'Judging the Recent Practice' (n 2163) 153 [Chinese] 153.

2231 Congyan Cai, 'Reviewing New Developments' (n 2109) 109 [Chinese].

2232 Yueming Huang (n 2137) 75; Yanzhi 彦志 Wang 王, '中国在国际投资法上的身份转换与立场定位' (Locating China's Changing Identity regarding and Positions on International Investment Law) (2013) 27 (4) *Dangdai Faxue* 131, 131–133.

2233 Author's interview in Wuhan, June 2013.

2234 Sun Jin, legal consultant with the Chinese embassy in the United States (PhD from Wuhan University International Law Institute).

2235 Jin Sun (n 848) 3.

2236 Yanzhi Wang, 'Locating China's Changing Identity' (n 2232) 131–133 [Chinese].

2237 Shixi Huang, 'New Developments' (n 840) 185 [Chinese].

2238 Jingsong Yu (n 2130) 142.

2239 Yanzhi Wang, 'The Legalization' (n 2120) 22 [Chinese].

tural imbalances', 'vagaries' and 'inconsistencies', and giving investment arbitration time to develop and go through a phase of 'trial and error'.[2240]

As a result of such evaluations, Cai Congyan, Chen Wei, Hu Xiaohong, Huang Shixi, Sun Jin, and Wang Yanzhi over the last decade explicitly called for further liberal BIT practice – through the hastened amendment of older and now 'unfit' treaties and conclusion of additional BITs – with broad access to international investment arbitration including at ICSID. They all noted especially important when concluding such treaties with developing states with a weak rule of law.[2241] Li Qingling straightforwardly counseled active participation in international investment arbitration – even as a non-party taking part in hearings – inter alia – as it could help gain more of a voice on legal development.[2242]

Wang Yanzhi underlined that ICSID's value should not be underestimated, and that deficiencies of domestic court systems should not be ignored.[2243] Liu Hua supported this position regarding BITs with developing states, whereas he focused on PRC-African BITs. Within such treaties, ICSID arbitration should be provided for and Chinese investors should learn from previous ICSID cases involving African states, eg regarding legal persons' 'nationality' and make up, and the definition of 'investment' and 'expropriation'.[2244] Writing in 2012, Chen Wei discerned a geographical shift in China's BIT ratifications towards just such jurisdictions.[2245]

While Cai Congyan still wanted to at the same time combat the alleged misuse of international investment arbitration vis-à-vis China and strengthen Chinese domestic courts, Chen Wei saw the aforementioned problem of MFN application already resolved and advised even broader ICSID jurisdiction in future treaties.[2246] After listing certain phenomena in invest-

2240 Ibid 22–23.

2241 Congyan Cai, 'Reviewing New Developments' (n 2109) 107–109 [Chinese]; Wei Chen (n 512) 1067–1068; Xiaohong Hu (n 2109) 82; Shixi Huang, 'The issue of selecting treaties' (n 2213) 73 [Chinese]; Jin Sun (n 848) 3–5, 9; Yanzhi Wang, 'The Legalization' (n 2120) 22–23 [Chinese]. For overhauling the old BIT network and hastening the conclusion of BITs everywhere see also Tong Qi, 'Reviewing Chinese overseas investors' use' (n 582) 95 [Chinese].

2242 Qingling Li (n 2137) 142.

2243 Yanzhi Wang, 'The Legalization' (n 2120) 22–23 [Chinese].

2244 Hua 华 Liu 刘, '通过 ICSID 解决中非之间投资争端的研究' (Research on Resolving China-Africa Investment Disputes through ICSID) (2013) 31 (2) *Zhengfa Luntan* 173.

2245 Wei Chen (n 512) 1067–1068.

2246 Congyan Cai, 'Reviewing New Developments' (n 2109) 107–109 [Chinese]; Wei Chen (n 512) 1067–1068.

ment arbitration that had been criticized by capital importing states, Huang Yueming clarified that she only wanted her government to be aware of these to be able to protect its interests as both a capital importing and exporting power in an informed way.[2247]

Sun Jin additionally recommended that the Chinese government retract its Article 25 (4) ICSID Convention notification, and that it increase its multilateral role in harmonization efforts such as with the 'G20 Guiding Principles for Global Investment Policymaking' adopted at the 2016 summit in Hangzhou.[2248]

In a complete reversal of the earlier conceptualization of China's role within the system, Hu Xiaohong counseled already in 2009, to now even put pressure on developing states (eg Tajikistan) to ratify the ICSID Convention.[2249] Dealing with the members of the SCO, she noted the decidedly low quality of their legal systems, frequent changes to legislation on investment – inter alia through often contradictory presidential and governmental decrees – and many investment barriers, as well as unreliable law enforcement marred by nepotism.[2250] Protection of investor rights should be strengthened by new BITs allowing for international arbitration on many additional highly relevant issues related eg to customs, domestic taxes or administrative permits, which would be especially important in the energy field.[2251] Finally, Hu conceded that the advantage of stronger protection for Chinese investors would naturally entail the disadvantage of creating a headache for China as a host state, but considered this a worthwhile trade.[2252] On potential inner-SCO disputes on energy – seeing as multiple pipelines run from other SCO members to China – Yang Zewei discussed what could be learned from dispute resolution under the *Energy Charter Treaty*.[2253] Sun Jin wrote that participation in that mechanism should be considered.[2254] The exclusive use of diplomatic and political

2247 Yueming Huang (n 2137) 75.

2248 Article 25 (4) ICSID Convention; OECD, 'G20 Guiding Principles for Global Investment Policymaking' (Paris, 2019) <https://www.oecd.org/investment/g20-agrees-principles-for-global-investment-policymaking.htm> accessed 15 November 2019; Jin Sun (n 848) 10–11.

2249 Xiaohong Hu (n 2109) 82.

2250 Ibid 76, 78.

2251 Ibid 81.

2252 Ibid 79.

2253 The Energy Charter Treaty (adopted 17 December 1994, entered into force 16 April 1998) 2080 UNTS 95 (ECT); Zewei Yang, 'The Conflict Resolution Mechanism' (n 2117) 84 [Chinese].

2254 Jin Sun (n 848) 3, 7.

means was in many cases perceived as unsatisfactory. At least one author also mused about a potential new 'One Belt One Road' investment dispute settlement mechanism.[2255]

In Huang Shixi's opinion, concentrating investments on host states that apply the limited state immunity theory in investment arbitration award enforcement, as well as applying it oneself, is also in China's national interest in its new position within the international economic order. While limited state immunity is not yet seen as international customary law, the trend is said to be proceeding in that direction.[2256]

V.2.3. Preliminary Conclusions

The above thorough review of the discourse on trade and investment dispute resolution between 2002 and 2018 allows for several important conclusions.

First, the general attitude towards the role played by the WTO DSM and international investment arbitration tribunals including at ICSID has been overwhelmingly positive. Engagement and compliance were not questioned from the beginning in the trade field, and after actual participation largely also not in the investment field. Chinese scholars interviewed for this study in 2017 held that the PRC should still ramp up participation and comply with decisions in the trade field, even if ongoing cases against the EU and US on anti-dumping price calculation methodologies should be lost (ie DS515 and DS516). However, it should be clarified that none expected this to happen, and more trust is placed in the AB than in Panels.

2255 Lina 丽娜 Zhang 张, "一带一路"国际投资争端解决机制完善研究 (Research on Improvement of the International Investment Disputes Settlement Mechanism under "One Belt One Road" Initiative) (2018) 39 (8) *Faxue Zazhi* 32.

2256 Shixi Huang, 'The Issue of State Immunity' (n 2130) 106 [Chinese]: Huang then goes on to deliberate on the difference between jurisdictional immunity and immunity from execution, whereas giving up the former is said to not mean giving up the latter. Participating in international arbitration supposedly also does not mean that one gives up jurisdictional state immunity, as both need express declarations. Having ratified a pertinent treaty or abandoned state immunity during the arbitral proceedings, ie jurisdictional immunity, does not guarantee implementation that allows getting compensation from a country, which relates to immunity from execution. The PRC still applies absolute immunity theory, courts would require states to expressly give up their immunity.

Recent legal developments in investment law have largely been positively viewed. Scholars have perceived host state rights, transparency and consistency as potentially strengthened through eg dispute settlement provisions in CETA. They have also opined that a Chinese endorsement of labor and environmental protection clauses in the US Model BIT 2012 could aid both necessary domestic reforms and economic relations with developed states.

Second, authors level a series of criticisms that overlap in the most central points. These relate to the supposed ambiguity of norms and its exploitation by tribunals – inter alia – to expand their own jurisdiction, as well as alleged structural imbalances that favor the interests of large developed states and their companies.

In trade law, complaints address – inter alia – the definition of 'public body,' procedures for establishing the amount of compensation, and provisions on evidentiary standards. Most complaints about trade dispute resolution had been expected to become irrelevant through the anticipated end of the applicability of the special anti-dumping price calculation clause in para 15 (a) (ii) Accession Protocol.[2257] Diverging interpretations of para 15 have therefore become the focus of Chinese criticism since 2016. Meanwhile, the general line of argument on more frequent participation in the DSM has not changed, rather Beijing has responded to unwelcome interpretations of para 15 Accession Protocol by the EU and US by immediately launching new DSM cases against the two. However, such activism within the system is to be more assertively flanked by diplomatic efforts geared at making other states abandon alternative anti-dumping price calculation methodologies. On investment law, Mainland scholars – inter alia – criticized the wording and interpretation of MFN clauses and – with emphasis more recently shifting here – jurisdiction clauses.

Third, Chinese international legal scholars' two phase-independent recommendations in both fields of law are to study and 'master the rules of the game', and to become ever more influential in negotiations to reform the institutions and shape them according to Chinese interests. Authors have termed equally important acquiring stronger influence on legal development in investment and trade law, and have especially since 2014 argued that China should be 'on the offensive' in shaping the future eg of ISDS. On BITs, scholars have urged their government to be more 'textually precise' and 'self-explanatory', to include clauses stipulating mandatory contracting party consultation on interpretation or required joint interpreta-

2257 See Paras 15 (a) (ii) and (d) Accession Protocol.

tion or a permanent interpretation body, as well as improved transitional clauses. They have also supported including general exception clauses that would suffice to fulfill the supposed need for broadened policy space.

Fourth, Chinese international law scholars sometimes refer explicitly to national interest, and always implicitly argue on this foundation. Engagement with international dispute resolution mechanisms is no exception. What is crucial is the way scholars interpret Chinese national interests within the context of international adjudication of trade and investment matters. Not only economic growth and development, but also improving the country's international image and gaining institutional influence through integration, have been defined as central to the core national interest of increasing China's relative power position within the international system.

While authors were often skeptical of the mechanisms in question, especially in the early years of the research period, they pragmatically favored engagement if and when deemed in line with the 'desire to regain the status of a world power [rather than] ideological principles'.[2258] That moment arrives when the country's 'identity' (ie home state to host state) and interests change, making expanded participation appear beneficial, but only, when the country is also considered to have readied itself (mainly through familiarization), and readied the 'arena' (ie gained influence on reform).[2259] On investment law, authors appear to be undergoing a further shift in their interpretation of the course most in line with the national interest. While many still advocate balancing host state and investor rights, some already want China to straightforwardly adopt a 'capital exporting country mindset'.[2260]

Fifth, actual Chinese engagement with the WTO DSM and international investment arbitration mostly tracks mainstream scholarly discourse in China. International lawyers counseled mainly passive behavior at the DSM, intense study, and participation as a third party in the early-2000s, and more active participation later on. They recommended a more liberal BIT practice and became increasingly open to actual participation in in-

2258 Ahl, 'China' (n 274) 158.

2259 Author's interviews in Wuhan, June 2013; Wei Chen (n 512) 1067–1068; Shixi Huang, 'New Developments' (n 840) 185 [Chinese].

2260 Yanzhi Wang, 'Locating China's Changing Identity' (n 2232) 131–136 [Chinese]; Jin Sun (n 848) 3, after a PhD at the Wuhan University International Law Institute, Sun Jin serves as a legal consultant with the Chinese embassy in the United States.

vestment arbitration, when investment streams appeared to warrant it. The Chinese government acted accordingly.

In the upcoming phase, outward investment will likely outstrip inward investment, and China's status as a trade power as well as overall global influence will only be strengthened.[2261] This study considers the Chinese government's policies to be influenced by the academic community's interpretations of national interests. With scholars' perceptions and interpretations of national interest – as laid out above – in mind, a proliferation of cases in both trade and investment law appears very likely.

V.3. Territory

When considering the discourse on territorial disputes, clear chronology in the absence of obvious caesurae is replaced by a 'glacial' long-term shift (wherein short-term reverse trends are possible). No clear phases will thus be drawn up and referred to.

The current phase since 2014 is viewed here as a temporary phase of (self-)enforced conformity after the Philippine-initiated South China Sea arbitration.[2262] Bottom-up anger about Manila's 'attack' could be expected, after Chinese citizens had been taught in school and told by state media for decades that the entire South China Sea is inherent Chinese territory.[2263] State and party institutions appeared to oscillate between encouraging and moderating nationalist fervor in public discourse,[2264] but certainly expected the 'patriotic' defense of China's official line from legal

2261 Mainland China is currently rapidly rising through the ranks of the top twelve investor home states. If Hong Kong's numbers are included, it is already number two. Hong Kong has its own BITs, though, and the applicability of China's BITs is still disputed (see discussion on *Tza Yap Shum*).

2262 *The South China Sea Arbitration* (Award on Jurisdiction and Admissibility) (n 1506); *The South China Sea Arbitration* (Award) (n 196); See Chapters II.3.1.4.3 and IV.3.4.

2263 Zheping Huang and Echo Huang, 'China's citizens are livid at the South China Sea ruling because they've always been taught it is theirs' *Quartz* (New York, 14 July 2016) <https://qz.com/730669/chinas-citizens-are-livid-at-the-south-china-sea-ruling-because-theyve-always-been-taught-it-is-theirs/> accessed 16 November 2019.

2264 Shen Lu and Ben Westcott, 'South China Sea: Beijing calls KFC, Apple protests "irrational"' *CNN* (Beijing, 21 July 2016) <https://edition.cnn.com/2016/07/20/asia/china-nationalism-south-china-sea-ruling/index.html> accessed 16 November 2019.

scholars.[2265] Scholars did not want to 1) allow others to gain too much insight into the government's legal thinking, 2) indicate in any way that an eventual award could be even partly respected, or 3) stray from the officially set line of argument,[2266] nor 4) did they want to forego access to new state funding for law of the sea research.[2267] Moreover, they could expect consequences for academic promotions, access to decision-makers and secondment to international organizations.[2268]

However, this book will argue that this is only a temporary state, and that the longer-term shift described herein will continue for multiple overriding reasons. Ultimately, what the Chinese leadership wants is not to get the best out of the international system and not engage with the rest, but rather – through mutual adaptation – to make the entire international legal order work for China. It should be kept in mind that the timeframe for engagement with international adjudication mechanisms for territorial and law of the sea matters is a long-term one. Change started in the 1980s, has already come a long way, and will again continue gradually through the upcoming decade.

To date, the PRC has not participated in contentious proceedings at the ICJ, ITLOS or Annex VII or VIII UNCLOS arbitral tribunals. However, it has engaged with the two courts in limited ways. It has sent judges and other officials to serve there beginning in the 1980s, continuously holding a seat at the ICJ since 1985 and intending to keep it that way – other than the UK, which in 2017 lost its seat for the first time in the ICJ's history.[2269]

Official rhetoric towards the institutions has also grown substantially more positive. While the ICJ's jurisdiction has never been accepted, the Chinese ICJ judge Shi Jiuyong stated in the 1990s that he considered further reservations only necessary when core national interests are at

2265 See Chapter II.3.1.4.3.

2266 See eg Abraham D Sofaer, 'The Philippine Law of the Sea Action against China: Relearning the Limits of International Adjudication' (2016) 15 CJIL 393, 398.

2267 Anthea Roberts, 'China's Strategic Use of Research Funding on International Law' *Lawfare Blog* (Washington DC, 8 November 2017) <https://www.lawfareblog.com/chinas-strategic-use-research-funding-international-law> accessed 30 March 2019.

2268 See also Chapter II.3.1.4.3.

2269 Owen Bowcott, 'No British judge on world court for first time in its 71-year history' *Guardian* (London, 20 November 2017) <https://www.theguardian.com/law/2017/nov/20/no-british-judge-on-world-court-for-first-time-in-its-71-year-history> accessed 30 March 2019.

stake.[2270] Compulsory law of the sea dispute resolution jurisdiction has in certain matters already been embraced in 1996, as the PRC's declaration upon ratification and Article 298 UNCLOS reservation issued in 2006 do not and cannot cover all issues. Chinese scholars have even rather early on embraced their country's responsibility to comply with such compulsory jurisdiction eg concerning 'prompt release'-rules, provisional measures and cases of disputes relating to the deep seabed.[2271]

Since 2008, the PRC has also repeatedly participated in ICJ and ITLOS advisory proceedings,[2272] as well as CLCS proceedings,[2273] showing that China is indeed edging towards more engagement with third-party institutions on the settlement of territorial and law of the sea issues. This kind of engagement also continued in 2017,[2274] after unfavorable rulings in the first contentious case brought against China, *Philippines v China*, had been handed down.[2275] This contentious case came too early for the Chinese leadership, and it would not let its timetable be forced. Non-participation might have had serious drawbacks for the Chinese side, but Beijing sticks to its long-term strategy.

In the following, Chinese international law scholars' overall attitudes towards international adjudication of law of the sea and territorial disputes will be evaluated, main criticisms noted, and policy recommendations laid out, whereas the latter will be split into general recommendations and such on the question of whether, when and how to engage. As there has only been one contentious case with (indirect) Chinese involvement in this field, the South China Sea arbitration, Chinese authors' debates have recently centered somewhat on this dispute. A separate sub-chapter will address pertinent points of criticism.

2270 Wang and Guan (n 499) 73.

2271 See eg Hongxia 红霞 Xie 谢, '国际海洋法法庭若干法律问题的分析' (Analysis of Several Legal Problems Concerning the International Tribunal for the Law of the Sea) [2005] (1) *Heilongjiangsheng Zhengfa Guanli Ganbu Xueyuan Xuebao* 102, 105.

2272 Chapter IV.3.3.1.

2273 Chapter IV.3.3.2.

2274 Chapter IV.3.3.1.4.

2275 Chapter IV.3.4.

V.3.1. General Attitude – From Imperialist Oppressor to Guarantor of Peaceful Dispute Resolution

Laws of the sea and territorial disputes are often interlinked, as eg maritime delimitation might require a decision on sovereignty over certain land features. The legal bases to be considered on that issue are the same regardless which institution were to judge the case. Moreover, regarding disputes covered by UNCLOS, parties can choose whether they want the ICJ, ITLOS or an arbitral tribunal constituted under Annex VII or VIII UNCLOS to rule on the matter.[2276] Chinese discourse on these mechanisms, their general evaluation, criticisms, and policy recommendations, only differ in certain aspects, but generally follow the same trend lines. These institutions will therefore be dealt with in the same chapter.

At the onset of this century, the overall evaluation of the above-listed institutions had already made a quantum leap from the damnation of prior decades. Perceived positive and negative aspects being laid out, the generally constructive and important function of these mechanisms was accepted. However, China's standing aside was still embraced at the beginning of this study's research period, and a certainly cautious and discriminating attitude was retained throughout.

From the distance of (mostly) not yet advocating immediate engagement, Huang Deming[2277] and Zhang Cheng[2278], Nie Hongyi[2279], Pan Junwu[2280], Qu Bo[2281], Wang Yong[2282] and Guan Zhengfeng[2283], as well as Zhao Jingsong[2284] recognized that the ICJ has changed markedly over the preceding decades; in the composition of its workforce, representation of different legal traditions, and successful practice represented in its growing case law. It was highlighted that Chinese citizens represent a growing share of employees of the Court. Developing states were seen to increasingly

2276 Art 287 (1) UNCLOS.

2277 Huang Deming, Professor at Wuhan University Law School.

2278 Zhang Cheng, PhD Candidate at Wuhan University Law School.

2279 Nie Hongyi, PhD Candidate at Tsinghua University in Beijing.

2280 Pan Junwu, Professor at Northwestern University of Politics and Law in Xi'an.

2281 Qu Bo, Professor at Dalian Maritime University.

2282 Wang Yong, graduate student at Eastern University of Politics and Law (later became a Professor there).

2283 Guan Zhengfeng, graduate student at Eastern University of Politics and Law.

2284 Zhao Jingsong, PhD Candidate at Wuhan University International Law Institute.

trust and make use of the ICJ, and to do so with ever-greater success – with *Nicaragua v. United States* taken as one symbol of this shift.[2285]

The ICJ was lauded for developing and applying sensible principles, providing states with authoritative and systematic interpretations thereof, and generally judging a large number of cases fairly.[2286] According to Yao Ying[2287] the court is 'highly effective, cheap, authoritative, executable and more'.[2288] Pan Junwu considered it an 'important guarantee' of peaceful dispute resolution.[2289] He also praised the ICJ's ongoing efforts to encourage negotiations during court proceedings, with negotiations being portrayed by the court itself as the intended primary venue of dispute resolution. Pan would expect an intensification of the trend towards solving disputes judicially should this be realized more broadly.[2290] In recent years, Chinese scholars' attitudes have become slightly more sober, criticizing individual rulings eg on the consistency of treaty interpretation, but remained positive on the ICJ's efforts to retain legal predictability while striving for equitability.[2291]

2285 *Military and Paramilitary Activities in and against Nicaragua* (n 193).

2286 Deming 德明 Huang 黄 and Cheng 成 Zhang 章, '北极海域 200 海里外大陆架划界与北极区域法律制度的建构' (Delimitation of the Outer Continental Shelf Beyond 200 Nautical Miles in the Arctic Region and the Establishment of the Arctic Legal Regime) [2013] (6) *Faxuejia* 161, 171; Hongyi 宏毅 Nie 聂, '国际法院在解决领土争端中的作用及困境评析' (Evaluation of the ICJ's Role and Predicament in Solving Territorial Disputes) (2009) 27 (1) *Hebei Faxue* 1, 4; Junwu 俊武 Pan 潘, '解析国际争端解决机制及其发展前景' (Analyzing International Dispute Settlement Methods and Development Prospects) (2009) 27 (4) *Falü Kexue* 112, 117; Bo 波 Qu 曲, '对大陆架划界的几个问题的思考' (Reflection on Issues of Delimitation of Continental Shelf) (2006) 20 (4) *Dangdai Faxue* 126, 127–129; Wang and Guan (n 499) 75; Jingsong 劲松 Zhao 赵, '中国和平解决国际争端问题初探' (First Exploration of the Issue of China Peacefully Resolving International Disputes) (2006) 24 (1) *Falü Kexue* 97, 102.

2287 Yao Ying, lecturer at Jilin University Law School.

2288 Ying 莹 Yao 姚, '解决中日东海争端的司法路径探析' (Exploring Judicial Methods of Solving the Sino-Japanese East China Sea Dispute) (2011) 25 (3) *Dangdai Faxue* 24 (translation by this author).

2289 Junwu Pan, 'Analyzing International Dispute Settlement' (n 2286) 120 [Chinese].

2290 Ibid 116.

2291 Yao 瑶 Huang 黄 and Xuexia 雪霞 Liao 廖, '国际法院海洋划界的新实践——2014 年秘鲁诉智利案评析' (The Latest Case on Maritime Delimitation by the International Court of Justice – Comments on the Maritime Dispute (*Peru v. Chile*) in 2014) [2014] (1) *Guojifa Yanjiu* 29; Bowen 博文 Xie 谢 and Dong 栋 Xu 徐, '"尼哥领土与海洋争端案"评析及对南海问题的借鉴' (The analysis and assessment of the ICJ Territorial and Maritime Dispute Case and its reference

Concerning ITLOS, Huang Yao[2292] and Liao Xuexia[2293] underlined that states broadly choose the ICJ for a judicial solution of territorial disputes, with ITLOS performing other functions (eg immediate release of detained ships). However, the first delimitation case decided upon by the tribunal in Hamburg – *Gulf of Bengal* (Bangladesh v Myanmar) – has been evaluated positively. Indeed, ITLOS is not only considered to have resolved the long-standing dispute fairly, but also to have meaningfully aided the development of pertinent legal principles, providing guidance for other states, and to have usefully prodded the Continental Shelf Commission to perform its function.[2294] Reviewing the 7 July 2014 award in *Bay of Bengal Maritime Boundary Arbitration* (Annex VII UNCLOS arbitration between Bangladesh and India), Yao Ying soberly deduced positive and negative consequences for China. With an eye to the East China Sea, Beijing should be happy about the reversal in the trend towards single maritime borders. On the other hand, the Tribunal in this case deemed land features low-tide elevations that Yao considered very similar to those in the South China Sea, leading her to predict a negative outcome for China in *Philippines* in 2014, should the tribunal address the status of individual islands.[2295]

On the system of compulsory dispute resolution in the law of the sea under Part XV Section 2 UNCLOS, Chinese international lawyers have recently voiced manifold negative views – or rather on how it has been interpreted – which will be addressed mainly in the next sub-chapter. Criticism was focused on the particular individuals, including the Annex VII tribunal involved in the *Philippines* case, although not on the ICJ, ITLOS or the option of arbitration under Annex VII or VIII UNCLOS as such. On

to South China Sea) (2014) 25 (2) *Zhongguo Haishangfa Yanjiu* 90; Weibin 卫彬 Zhang 张, '国际法院解释领土条约的路径、方法及其拓展' (Ways, methods and development of ICJ interpretation of territorial treaties) (2015) 35 (2) *Faxue Yanjiu* 192.

2292 Huang Yao, Professor at Sun Yat-sen University Law School in Guangzhou.

2293 Liao Xuexia, graduate student at Sun Yat-sen University Law School in Guangzhou.

2294 Yao 瑶 Huang 黄 and Xuexia 雪霞 Liao 廖, 国际海洋划界司法实践的新动向——2012 年孟加拉湾划界案评析 (New Developments in International Maritime Boundary Delimitation Case Law – Analysis of the 2012 Gulf of Bengal Case) [2012] (12) *Faxue* 80, 92; *Delimitation of the Maritime Boundary in the Bay of Bengal* (Bangladesh v Myanmar) (n 1486).

2295 *The Bay of Bengal Maritime Boundary Arbitration (Bangladesh v India)* (n 1822); Ying Yao, 'Comments on the 2014 Bangladesh v India' (n 1515) 159–160 [Chinese].

advisory proceedings, citing *Chagos*,[2296] Song Yan[2297] intimated that the Court should perhaps exercise more caution and restraint on jurisdictional issues, as states may attempt to circumvent contentious proceedings and the consent required therein;[2298] even if, as Wang Shumin[2299] and Wu Haonan[2300] highlighted, objecting states' arguments might not suffice to derogate from the Court's advisory jurisdiction.[2301]

Addressing dispute resolution via the ICJ and ITLOS, Liang Yong[2302] and Yao Ying posited as another advantage that it could always help speed along the possibility of developing hydrocarbon resources in disputed areas. China might win or lose a case, but the hold up through perennial negotiations would find an end.[2303] Furthermore, relations between the involved parties could begin to normalize after a clear end point of the relevant dispute.[2304] Additionally, clear legal regimes could then allow for improved maritime jurisdiction.[2305] Should the PRC not be in control of certain territories or offshore features (islands or rocks) it claims sovereignty over – such as the Diaoyu/Senkaku Islands in the East China Sea – adjudi-

2296 Request for an advisory opinion of the International Court of Justice on the legal consequences of the separation of the Chagos Archipelago from Mauritius in 1965, UNGA 71/292 (22 June 2017) UN Doc A/71/L73.

2297 Song Yan, lecturer at China Foreign Affairs University's International Law Department.

2298 Yan 岩 Song 宋, 国家同意原则对国际法院行使咨询管辖权的限制———兼论"查戈斯群岛咨询意见案"的管辖权问题 (The Restrictions of the Principle of State Consent on the Court's Exercise of Its Advisory Jurisdiction – A Review of the Jurisdictional Issue of Legal Consequences of the Separation of the Chagos Archipelago from Mauritius in 1965) [2018] (1) *Guojifa Yanjiu* 3, 13.

2299 Wang Shumin, professor at Dalian Maritime University Law School.

2300 Wu Haonan, graduate student at Dalian Maritime University Law School.

2301 Shumin 淑敏 Wang 王 and Haonan 昊南 Wu 吴, 国际法院关于"查戈斯群岛从毛里求斯分裂案"的咨询管辖权研究 (Research on the Advisory Jurisdiction of the ICJ in the "Separation of the Chagos Archipelago from Mauritius Case") [2018] (17) *Falü Shiyong* 98.

2302 Liang Yong, lecturer at Fudan University Law School in Shanghai.

2303 Yong 咏 Liang 梁, '从国际法视角看中日东海大陆架划界争端' (Reviewing the Sino-Japanese Dispute over Continental Shelf Delimitation in the East China Sea from an International Law Perspective) [2006] (8) *Faxue* 122, 126; Ying Yao, 'Exploring Judicial Methods' (n 2288) 33 [Chinese]. See also Huang and Liao, 'New Developments in International Maritime Boundary Delimitation' (n 2294) 92 [Chinese], for the case of Myanmar and Bangladesh resource exploitation in the Gulf of Bengal; *Delimitation of the Maritime Boundary in the Bay of Bengal* (Bangladesh v Myanmar) (n 1486).

2304 Ying Yao, 'Exploring Judicial Methods' (n 2288) 33 [Chinese].

2305 Ibid 33.

cation could also serve to disturb another state's (eg Japan's) effective control thereover.[2306] Finally, Pan Junwu claimed that judicial solutions could have a depoliticizing effect compared with negotiations. They could allow the government to 'externalize responsibility', as '[t]he state can use binding ICJ judgments and say to its people: look! We already did all we could, but we are unable to control such a result, this is not our fault, we have to obey the judges' findings'.[2307]

V.3.2. Criticism – The Roots of Caution

V.3.2.1. General Criticism – Surprising Similarities

The central critiques, the later shift towards more technical misgivings related to a purported desire to 'perfect' the legal regime in question, and the eventual representation of new priorities are three crucial points of overlap with the discourse on trade and investment law.

First, the most prominent complaints are once again such about 1) the process of elevating developing states' (and particularly China's) influence at the courts not having been completed, and 2) the respective legal bases being supposedly ambiguous or case law being inconsistent, allegedly creating lamentable legal uncertainty.

Several Chinese international law professors interviewed for this study maintained that ITLOS and ICJ remain somewhat biased either in favor of Western industrialized states or specifically against China.[2308] The narrative of an alleged anti-Chinese bias also appears regarding the Annex VII UNCLOS arbitration *Philippines v China*. Without really supporting their case, Chinese scholars accused expert witness Clive Schofield of all but having committed 'perjury' on the 'island' status of Itu Aba, and the arbitrators of double standards in interpreting evidence of historic rights as well as open tendentiousness after being appointed by the Philippines and then-ITLOS president Shunji Yanai.[2309] The latter point, of course, was the

2306 Ibid 33.

2307 Junwu Pan, 'Analyzing International Dispute Settlement' (n 2286) 117–118 [Chinese] (translation by this author).

2308 Author's interviews in Wuhan, June 2013. See also Ying Yao, 'Exploring Judicial Methods' (n 2288) 33 [Chinese].

2309 Guoqiang 国强 Luo 罗, '论 "南海仲裁案"仲裁裁决的枉法性' (On the injustice of the arbitral award in the 'South China Sea Arbitration') (2016) 30 (6) *Dangdai Faxue* 148, 148–149, 152–153, 154–155. For the notion that initiating the

result of China refusing to participate in the proceedings and UNCLOS regulations on how to proceed in such a case.[2310] No evidence is provided for Mr. Yanai's alleged nefarious role, other than him fulfilling his duties while being a Japanese citizen.

A series of scholars including Cai Gaoqiang[2311], Chen Cong[2312] and Zhang Hongsheng[2313], Jiang He[2314], Luo Guoqiang[2315] and Ye Quan[2316], Ma Deyi[2317], Xue Guifang[2318] and Xu Xiangxin[2319], Yang Qilu[2320], Yang Zewei[2321], Zhang Weibin[2322], and Zou Ligang[2323] and Zhang Kui[2324] all decried the ambiguity of a number of regulations and regimes in the law of the sea. Specifically, they touched upon the archipelago regime and baselines, military activity in Exclusive Economic Zones (hereinafter: EEZs), maritime boundary delimitation (eg obligations ahead of delimita-

case while Yanai was ITLOS President showed that the Philippines were not interested in reaching agreement with China see Xinjun 新军 Zhang 张, '裁判条约中一方不出庭下的"查明管辖权"条款的意义——程序分立视角下对不出庭应对及其法律效果的再考察' (Judging the meaning of 'examining jurisdiction' treaty clauses for cases where one party does not appear in court – re-examination of responses to and legal effects of non-appearance under the perspective of separate procedures) (2017) 11 (2) *Qinghua Faxue* 176, 186–187. For the tribunal not being impartial see also Yongming Jin, 'The Impact and Influence of the South China Sea Arbitration on the Law of the Sea' (2017) 5 *China Legal Science (Zhongguo Faxue)* 82, 101 [English].

2310 See also Chapter IV.3.4.4.2.

2311 Cai Gaoqiang, Associate Professor at Xiangtan University in Xiangtan, Hunan Province.

2312 Chen Cong, Lecturer at the People's Liberation Army University of Science and Technology Military Affairs Law Research and Teaching Section.

2313 Zhang Hongsheng, Director of the People's Liberation Army University of Science and Technology Military Affairs Law Research and Teaching Section.

2314 Jiang He, Associate Professor at Zhongnan University of Economics and Law.

2315 Luo Guoqiang, Professor at the Wuhan University International Law Research Institute.

2316 Ye Quan, Lecturer at Southeast University School of Law.

2317 Ma Deyi, professor at ECUPL.

2318 Xue Guifang, Professor at Shanghai Jiaotong University Law School.

2319 Xu Xiangxin, Kiel University, Germany.

2320 Yang Qilu, Chongqing University of Arts and Sciences.

2321 Yang Zewei, Professor at Wuhan University Law School.

2322 Zhang Weibin, Associate Professor at Anhui University of Finance and Economics Law School in Bengbu, Anhui Province.

2323 Zou Ligang, Professor at Hainan University Law School in Haikou, Hainan Province.

2324 Zhang Kui, lecturer at Changsha University of Science and Engineering University Law School in Changsha, Hunan Province.

tion and the role of sovereignty disputes over islands), the obligation to exchange views under Article 283 UNCLOS, as well as – these are most intensely discussed – historic rights to maritime territory and resources and the distinction between 'islands' and 'rocks' according to Art 121 (3) UNCLOS.[2325] In a rather peculiar line of argument, Luo Guoqiang posited that Annex VII consisting of fewer articles than Annex VI meant that it was not

2325 Gaoqiang 高强 Cai 蔡 and Xu 徐 Xu 徐, '论海洋边界争端与国际海洋法的发展——兼谈中日东海油气争端德解决' (On the Sea Boundary Dispute and the Development of International Law of the Sea – Proposals on resolving Gas Disputes between China and Japan in the East Sea) [2006] (11) *Gansu Zhengfa Xueyuan Xuebao* 39, 47; Cong 聪 Chen 陈 and Hongsheng 红生 Zhang 张, '南海主权争端的法律问题与法律准备' (The Legal Issues and Legal Preparations of the Sovereignty Disputes over the South China Sea) (2009) 27 (12) *Hebei Faxue* 57; He 河 Jiang 江, 国际法框架下的现代海权与中国的海洋维权 (Modern sea power and China's protection of maritime rights and interests in the framework of international law) [2014] (1) *Faxue Pinglun* 92, 97; Guoqiang 国强 Luo 罗 and Quan 泉 Ye 叶, '争议岛屿在海洋划界中的法律效力——兼析钓鱼岛作为争议岛屿的法律效力' (Disputed Islands' Legal Effect in Maritime Boundary Delimitation – Concurrent Analysis of the Legal Effect of the Diaoyu Islands as Disputed Islands) (2011) 25 (1) *Dangdai Faxue* 112; Deyi 得懿 Ma 马, 《联合国海洋法公约》第 283 条交换意见义务: 问题与检视 (On the Obligation to Exchange Views in Article 283 of UNCLOS: Issues and Reflection) [2018] (4) *Zhengzhi yu Falü* 102, 110; Guifang 桂芳 Xue 薛 and Xiangxin 向欣 Xu 徐, '由岛屿维持其本身的"经济生活"标准的界定谈对我国南海岛礁的保护性开发' (The Impact on China's Protective Development of the South China Sea's Islands and Reefs of the Discussion on the Definition of the Standard of Islands and Reefs Being Able to Sustain 'Economic Life' on Their Own) [2013] (6) *Bijiaofa Yanjiu* 63; Qilu 琪璐 Yang 杨, 多视角下我国管辖海域的冲突之研究 (Research from multiple perspectives on conflicts regarding maritime areas under China's jurisdiction) (2018) 36 (3) *Zhengfa Luntan* 118; Quan 泉 Ye 叶, 当事国在海洋划界前的国际法义务之研析 ———兼论南海当事国在划界前之国际法义务 (Analysis of parties' international law obligations before maritime delimitation – on the international law obligations before delimitation of the South China Sea parties) [2016] (6) *Faxue Pinglun* 99; Zewei 泽伟 Yang 杨, '《联合国海洋法公约》的主要缺陷及其完善' (Important Flaws of UNCLOS and Pertinent Remedies) [2012] (5) *Faxue Pinglun* 57; Zewei 泽伟 Yang 杨, '论《海洋法公约》解决南海争端的非适用性' (On Non-Application of the United Nations Convention on the Law of the Sea for Solution to Disputes of South China Sea) (2012) 33 (10) *Faxue Zazhi* 1; Weibin 卫彬 Zhang 张, '海洋划界的趋势与相关情况规则——黑海划界案对我国海域划界的启示' (Maritime Border Delimitation Trends and Pertinent Regulations – the Black Sea Border Delimitation Case and Lessons for China's Maritime Border Delimitation) [2010] (1) *Huadong Zhengfa Daxue Xuebao* 48, 56; Weibin 卫彬 Zhang 张, '《联合国海洋法公约》中"岩礁"的演进解释与南沙群岛问题' (Evolutionary interpretation of 'islands and rocks' in UNCLOS and the Nan-

the focus of the negotiators and left unclear; moreover, that an alleged lack of clarity in delimitation methodology and island classification would point to the drafters aiming at negotiations not an 'imposed' solution.[2326] Luo and Qu Bo even criticized that UNCLOS was drafted and ratified at all considering it to have complicated law of the sea disputes across the globe.[2327]

Jin Yongming[2328] held in 2015 that UNCLOS had already been improved, referring – inter alia – to implementation agreements. Nevertheless, it being a product of compromise, ambiguity was supposedly built in, with further development necessary to address both very different interpretations and new challenges.[2329] As noted in Chapter IV.3.4.4.2, the tribunal in *Philippines* did exactly that. It developed the system further, in a way that befits its function in interpreting UNCLOS. The arbitrators took a crucial first step in clarifying Article 121 (3), which has been the subject of loud disagreement between leading scholars, and they further elucidated the regime of historic rights in the law of the sea.[2330]

On the issue of legal uncertainty, Huang Yao and Liao Xuexia also pointed to contradictory case law, whereas ITLOS' decision in *Gulf of Bengal* is taken as an example. According to them 'the tribunal's legal principles [judicature] in maritime delimitation especially regarding the outer

---

sha Archipelago Issue) (2017) 35 (5) *Falü Kexue* 115, 125; Ligang 立刚 Zou 邹 and Kui 奎 Zhang 张, '岛屿制度与南海海域划界' (The Rules of Islands and Delimitation of the South China Sea) (2011) 26 (5–6) *Henansheng Zhengfa Guanli Ganbu Xueyuan Xuebao* 73, 76.

2326 Guoqiang Lu, 'On the injustice' (n 2309) 150–151 [Chinese].

2327 Guoqiang 国强 Luo 罗, '多边路径在解决南海争端中的作用及其构建——兼评 南海搁放行为宣言' (Legal Principles Used by the International Court when Solving Disputes over Island Sovereignty) (2010) 32 (4) *Faxue Luntan* 1; Bo 波 Qu 曲, '南海周边有关国家在南沙群岛的策略及我国对策建议' (Tactics of South China Sea Littoral States Regarding the Spratly Islands and Recommendations for Countermeasures by China) [2012] (6) *Zhongguo Faxue* 58, 61.

2328 Jin Yongming, researcher at the Law Research Institute of the Shanghai Academy of Social Sciences.

2329 Yongming 永明 Jin 金, 论海洋法的发展与挑战——纪念联合国成立 70 周年 (On the Development and Challenges of the Law of the Sea – In Memory of the 70th Anniversary of the Establishment of the UN) [2015] (3) *Nanyang wenti yanjiu* 1. For UNCLOS as a 'package deal' and balance of interests that had to keep things vague for later clarification see also: Quan Ye (n 2325) 99.

2330 Erik Franckx, 'The Enigma of Article 121, Paragraph 3: The Way Forward?' *Maritime Issues* (14 November 2016) <http://www.maritimeissues.com/law/the-enigma-of-article-121-paragraph-3-the-way-forward.html> accessed 30 March 2019; Art 121 (3) UNCLOS.

continental shelf without 200 nautical miles as described above should not be overestimated', as they are allegedly in violation of ICJ case law (eg *Qatar v Bahrain*) on issues such as islands' effect on maritime boundary delimitation and natural prolongation of the continental shelf.[2331] To Yi Xianhe, the arbitrators failed to live up to consistency requirements also simply because pertinent cases such as *Louisa* and *Southern Bluefin Tuna Case* allegedly only receive 'cavalier' treatment in the awards.[2332]

Adding another point of general criticism of adjudication and arbitration, Qu Bo perceived a lack of flexibility, supposedly particularly important in sovereignty disputes over islands.[2333] Qu also elaborated on the risk that a court judgment might not be implemented due to the losing state's population reacting with aggressive nationalism. A hardline government might be elected or otherwise take power. Negotiations could then have to follow once again and the whole judicial process would have been for naught.[2334]

In a second key parallel with international economic law debates, discourse later shifted towards concerns as to how the system could be 'perfected' by resolving certain legal technical issues. Qu Bo and Zhang Weibin took issue with the standard of proof at ICJ proceedings concerning territorial disputes. According to them, the latter is confused, because there is no clear decision in favor of either civil or common law traditions.[2335] Qu noted additionally that the ICJ tends to delegate evidence collection to the parties. Both issues allegedly dissuade states from engagement. Huang Yao and Liao Xuexia criticized what they perceived as an unclear relationship between the establishment of the limits of the outer continental shelf via the CLCS and the ICJ's adjudication on delimitation issues.[2336] In discus-

2331 Huang and Liao, 'New Developments in International Maritime Boundary Delimitation' (n 2294) 92 [Chinese] (translation by this author); *Maritime Delimitation and Territorial Questions Between Qatar and Bahrain* (n 1741) [104], para 219.

2332 Xianhe (Sienho) Yi (Yee), 'The South China Sea Arbitration' (n 1514) 231.

2333 Bo Qu, 'Tactics of South China Sea Littoral States' (n 2327) 61 [Chinese].

2334 Ibid 61–62.

2335 Ibid 61 [Chinese]; Weibin 卫彬 Zhang 张, '国际法院解决领土争端中证明标准问题' (The Issue of Standards of Proof in ICJ Territorial Dispute Resolution) (2011) 25 (5) *Dangdai Faxue* 131. See also Huang and Liao, 'The Latest Case' (n 2291) 29 [Chinese].

2336 Yao 瑶 Huang 黄 and Xuexia 雪霞 Liao 廖, '论大陆架外部界限的确立与 200 海里以外大陆架划界的关系——以 2012 年尼加拉瓜诉哥伦比亚案为引子' (Discussing the Relationship between Establishing the Limits of the Outer

sions of ICJ practice concerning 'critical date,' Zhang Weibin praised the ICJ's consistency in alleged contrast to arbitral tribunals.[2337]

As for the third main parallel development with discourse on trade and investment law, new priorities might begin to be represented – although this will be more evident through the policy recommendations elaborated upon below – as eg Chen Weidong and Guan Binbin[2338] complained about issues with implementation. More generally, they lamented the fact that UNSC interventions cannot remedy the lack of voluntary compliance with ICJ rulings when the non-compliant state is a veto power. Specifically, they criticized the US's non-compliant behavior.[2339]

V.3.2.2. The South China Sea Arbitration – Recent Flare-up

Following this first case directly involving their country, in many ways Chinese authors accused the Annex VII tribunal of violating requirements already in the system.

V.3.2.2.1. General Criticism and Jurisdictional Matters

First, without making a clear accusation as to which UNCLOS norms this would breach, several Chinese international legal scholars have depicted

---

Continental Shelf and Continental Shelf Boundary Delimitation beyond 200 Nautical Miles – Taking the 2012 Case of Nicaragua v. Colombia as an Introduction) (2013) 27 (6) *Dangdai Faxue* 127, 138, who inter alia refer to *Question of the Delimitation of the Continental Shelf between Nicaragua and Colombia beyond 200 nautical miles from the Nicaraguan Coast (Nicaragua v Colombia)* (Application) [2013] ICJ Rep 2. Since then, there has been a judgment on preliminary objections in this case: *Question of the Delimitation of the Continental Shelf between Nicaragua and Colombia beyond 200 nautical miles from the Nicaraguan Coast (Nicaragua v Colombia)* (Preliminary Objections) [2016] ICJ Rep 100.

2337 Weibin 卫彬 Zhang 张, '国际法院解决领土争端中的关键日期问题——中日钓鱼岛列屿争端关键日期确定的考察' (Critical Date Ascertained by the International Court of Justice in Settling Territorial Disputes: Determining the Critical Date of Diaoyu Islands Dispute between China and Japan) (2012) 34 (3) *Xiandai Faxue* 121, 128.

2338 Guan Binbin, student at Zhejiang Wanli University Law School in Ningbo, Zhejiang Province.

2339 Weidong 卫东 Chen 陈 and Binbin 斌斌 Guan 管, '论国际法院判决在美国的执行' (Discussing the Implementation of ICJ Rulings in the United States) (2008) 22 (6) *Dangdai Faxue* 138, 142–143.

'unilateral' initiation of law of the sea arbitrations as something problematic[2340] – at least according to one scholar, a violation of object and purpose of UNCLOS under an Article 31 VCLT interpretation.[2341] However, of course this is clearly a deliberately provided option under UNCLOS (Annex VII Articles 5 and 9).[2342]

Second, Yu Minyou and Zhang Xinjun lament the disadvantage supposedly suffered by China as the non-appearing party despite requirements on the tribunal under Article 9 Annex VII UNCLOS and Article 25 Rules of Procedure. The arbitrators allegedly did not sufficiently satisfy themselves they had jurisdiction and on the accuracy of facts put forward by the Philippines, and did not take Chinese legal positions put forward outside these proceedings seriously.[2343] According to Jin Yongming, non-appearing states also lack 'reasonable and feasible remedial measures,' because only the same tribunal may be approached – except the parties agree otherwise – if there is controversy about the interpretation or implementation of the award (Annex VII Article 12 UNCLOS).[2344] As noted in Chapter IV.3.4.4.2, it is indeed quite ideal for any lawyer to argue without an opponent, and the tribunal might not be able to rid itself of a certain 'whiff of unfairness' (see Thomas J Schoenbaum) regardless how thoroughly it delved into all potential issues. However, this is the result of a very deliberate decision by the Chinese government, not anybody else, and the tribunal still mounted considerable efforts to ensure that China did not suffer disadvantages.[2345]

Third, it has been mainstream for Chinese authors to claim that the tribunal lacked jurisdiction for manifold reasons. Several scholars argued that there was no dispute between China and the Philippines about the interpretation and application of UNCLOS on the individual submissions

2340 Weibin 卫彬 Zhang 张, '菲律宾诉中国南海争端案的主体适格性问题' (The qualified subject problem in the Philippines v China South China Sea dispute) (2014) 29 (4) *Henan Caijing Zhengfa Daxue Xuebao* 40.

2341 Art 31 VCLT; Guoqiang Lu, 'On the injustice' (n 2309) 150 [Chinese].

2342 Annex VII Arts 5 and 9 UNCLOS.

2343 *The South China Sea Arbitration* (Rules of Procedure) (n 1634) Art 25; Annex VII Art 9 UNCLOS; Minyou 敏友 Yu 余, '评南海仲裁案仲裁庭对我国"断续线"及历史性权利的裁决倾向' (Discussing the tendencies of the arbitral tribunal's ruling on China's 'nine-dash line' and historic rights in the South China Sea arbitration) [2016] (4) *Faxue Pinglun* 83, 90; Xinjun Zhang, 'Judging the meaning' (n 2309) 188 [Chinese].

2344 Yongming Jin, 'The Impact and Influence' (n 2309) 90 [English]; Annex VII Art 12 UNCLOS.

2345 See Chapters IV.3.4.4.2 and IV.3.4.3.1.

Manila made. Zhang Weibin held that the Philippines were not actually an interested party, that they had not suffered any harm and did not have any standing to bring this case.[2346] Jin Yongming added that the Chinese government had not made its position clear as to the status of individual land features in the Spratly Islands, but had rather made claims to maritime zones from what it claims to be an archipelago. In his view, no dispute about island status could therefore have crystallized.[2347] A number of Chinese scholars argued that the tribunal went wrong in 'cutting up' the Spratly archipelago, which they view as endowed with territorial sea, EEZ and continental shelf as a whole.[2348] Exploring this point further, Zhang Weibin maintained that UNCLOS is unclear on the drawing of baselines around mid-ocean archipelagos of non-archipelagic states, whereas he saw many precedents for a straight baseline approach and expected China to bolster that practice and influence international customary law accordingly.[2349]

State practice aside, the tribunal made its interpretation of UNCLOS norms on archipelagos plain, and rightly denied that status to the Spratlys. The Chinese claim for an EEZ and continental shelf around the Spratlys in any case signifies the Chinese position that there is at least one 'island' among them; hence the Philippines could disagree.[2350]

Many Chinese authors also posited that jurisdiction was excluded due to a lacking exchange on claims between the parties before the arbitration (Article 283 UNCLOS).[2351] In Jin Yongming's words, exchanges were only on incidents at sea and conflict prevention, not on the submissions by the Philippines in this case. Citing *Georgia v Russian Federation* and *Gulf of Maine*, Jin critically remarked that negotiations had to be in good faith, and that there had to be a genuine attempt to resolve the concrete subject

2346 Weibin Zhang, 'The qualified subject problem' (n 2340) 40 [Chinese].

2347 Yongming Jin, 'The Impact and Influence' (n 2309) 84, 87–88 [English].

2348 Weibin Zhang, 'Evolutionary interpretation' (n 2325) 125–126 [Chinese].

2349 Ibid 125.

2350 See Chapter IV.3.4.4.2, and also Chapter IV.3.4.2 on disputes about historic rights and rights infringements being evident from diplomatic exchanges.

2351 Guoqiang Lu, 'On the injustice' (n 2309) 150 [Chinese]; Yongming Jin, 'The Impact and Influence' (n 2309) 95–96 [English]; Xinjun Zhang, 'Judging the meaning' (n 2309) 186 [Chinese]; Jiang 江 Zhou 周, 菲律宾在提起诉中国南海争端案之前应履行的法定义务 (Legal obligations to be fulfilled by the Philippines before filing the South China Sea dispute) (2014) 29 (4) *Henan Caijing Zhengfa Daxue Xuebao* 40; Art 283 UNCLOS.

matter through negotiations.[2352] Zhou Jiang argued that such exchanges supposedly had to first, as far as procedural questions go, only address non-compulsory methods, because Article 283 and Article 279 UNCLOS (the requirement to settle disputes peacefully) are both in Section 1 of Part XV UNCLOS. Manila bringing in compulsory methods in such discussions would frustrate appropriate efforts.[2353] However, China itself has not shown any openness to meaningful negotiations, in the sense that such could alter its position in any way.[2354]

Moreover, the general position in Chinese international law scholarship is that the arbitrators were mistaken in not recognizing that jurisdiction had to be barred due to China's Article 298 UNCLOS reservation, as the case supposedly involved excluded disputes over maritime delimitation, historic rights and law enforcement activities.[2355]

On maritime delimitation, Jin Yongming wrote that China's reservation should be interpreted to cover all factors being considered for reaching an equitable solution, which to him includes the effect of maritime features – otherwise the 'integrity and indivisibility of maritime delimitation' will be 'destroyed'.[2356] Jin also thought that Article 299 UNCLOS was rendered meaningless, by the Philippines not first approaching China on whether it would agree to submit a dispute close to its Article 298-reservation to arbitration.[2357] However, rather fundamentally, the tribunal did not see two states with opposing or adjacent coastlines in this case, rendering the pertinent exception moot.[2358]

On historic rights, Zhang Xinjun argued that Article 15 UNCLOS only refers to historic rights of a sovereign quality, but that the Article 298 (1)

2352 Yongming Jin, 'The Impact and Influence' (n 2309) 95–96 [English]; *Gulf of Maine* (n 1483) para 87; *ICERD Application (Georgia v Russia)* (n 1641).

2353 Jiang Zhou, 'Legal obligations to be fulfilled' (n 2351) 39–40 [Chinese].

2354 See *North Sea Continental Shelf Cases* (n 1482) [47] para 85 and this book's Chapters IV.3.4.2 and 3.4.4.2.

2355 Guoqiang Lu, 'On the injustice' (n 2309) 149–150 [Chinese]; Yongming Jin, 'The Impact and Influence' (n 2309) 84 [English]; Weibin Zhang, 'The qualified subject problem' (n 2340) 40 [Chinese]; Xinjun 新军 Zhang 张, '关于菲律宾南海断续线仲裁请求的管辖权问题——《联合国海洋法公约》第 298.1(a)(i)项下的排除和海洋权利之争' (Jurisdictional Objection to the Philippines' Submissions regarding Nine-dash Line: Exclusion of the Dispute concerning Sources of Maritime Entitlements under UNCLOS Article 298.1 (1) (i)) [2016] (2) *Guojifa Yanjiu* 3, 10–11.

2356 Yongming Jin, 'The Impact and Influence' (n 2309) 89–90 [English].

2357 Ibid 90–91.

2358 See Chapter IV.3.4.4.2.

(a) (i) UNCLOS-exception indeed also refers to historic rights of a non-sovereign quality.[2359] Pan Junwu instead considered this issue unclear, and acknowledged jurisdiction over a dispute arising out of overlapping Chinese non-sovereign historic rights claim (ie nine-dash line) and Philippine EEZ.[2360] On military activities, Pan recommended that his government let the military give expression to sovereignty in lieu of law enforcement beyond 24 nautical miles from land features, as compulsory arbitration can in that case be excluded.[2361]

Some scholars went exceedingly far with their critiques on this point. Yu Minyou viewed it as an arbitrary expansion of power that the tribunal would consider a dispute that to him obviously related to maritime delimitation and even territorial sovereignty.[2362] To Jin Yongming, the tribunal went beyond its powers and jurisdiction by determining Taiping Island's status in a 'delimitation in disguise,' and through an excessively stringent interpretation of Article 121 (3) UNCLOS, which in his eyes amounted to a legislative act.[2363] Luo Guoqiang – who in the pertinent article ignores the category of 'low-tide elevations' – also saw the tribunal handing sovereignty over land features to the Philippines 'in disguise' without having or assuming jurisdiction for such a step.[2364] Luo further described using Annex VII UNCLOS procedures to 'go around China's reservation,' as violating 'higher-level legislation' with the help of 'lower-level legislation'.[2365]

Jin Yongming even viewed the arbitrators as going against general principles of international law and jurisprudence by addressing all of these questions related to China's (!) maritime rights, before sovereignty over

2359 Xinjun Zhang, 'Jurisdictional Objection' (n 2355) 10–11 [Chinese]; Arts 15, 298 (1) (a) (i) UNCLOS.

2360 See also Chapters IV.3.4.3.2 and IV.3.4.4.2. See also Junwu 俊武 Pan 潘, '剖析 1982 年《联合国海洋法公约》 中的强制争端解决机制' (Dissecting compulsory dispute settlement in the 1982 UNCLOS) (2014) 32 (4) *Falü Kexue* 193, 197.

2361 Junwu Pan, 'Dissecting compulsory dispute settlement' (n 2360) 199 [Chinese].

2362 Minyou Yu, 'Discussing the tendencies' (n 2343) 90 [Chinese]. On jurisdiction being barred due to the involvement of sovereignty questions see also Yongming Jin, 'The Impact and Influence' (n 2309) 86 [English]; Guoqiang Lu, 'On the injustice' (n 2309) 149, 154 [Chinese].

2363 Yongming Jin, 'The Impact and Influence' (n 2309) 85, 103–104 [English].

2364 Guoqiang Lu, 'On the injustice' (n 2309) 154 [Chinese].

2365 Ibid 149.

land features and maritime delimitation are settled.[2366] Moreover, to Jin, in this case arbitrators making use of their competence – competence regarding Article 298 – reservations the way in which they did:

> (…) will bring unpredictability to exclusionary disputes for states, impair states' rights to freely choose means of dispute settlement of their own accord, damage states' sovereignty and destroy the dispute settlement mechanism of the Convention, thus encroaching on the integrity and authority of the system of the Convention.[2367]

According to Luo Guoqiang, ruling on land reclamation and land features not brought up by the Philippines was an *ultra vires* expansion of jurisdiction, negation of the 'contractual nature' of arbitration, and violation of basic principles of international law.[2368] Luo decried that there is no judicial review or supervisory procedure. He claimed that an arbitral award almost entirely in one party's favor is both unusual and unfair, and that the South China Sea award would be thrown out in domestic US legal proceedings due to the arbitrators' 'obvious favoritism' and intentional 'twisting of facts' and going against object and purpose of the law. He even made a note of criminal liability in some jurisdictions for 'perverting the law in arbitration,' such as represented by the 'relatively advanced norm' in Article 399 PRC Criminal Code.[2369]

An interesting voice in a different direction is Pan Junwu, who emphasized that China 'should realize soberly' that its reservation cannot exclude all disputes from compulsory arbitration – actually the core of UNCLOS dispute settlement, only to be limited under special circumstances – and that such can be initiated unilaterally.[2370] Pan highlighted that even some aspects of Articles 74 and 83 UNCLOS, ie obligations to seek provisional

2366 Yongming Jin, 'The Impact and Influence' (n 2309) 86 [English]. For the assertion that the tribunal supposedly violated basic legal principles see also Guoqiang Lu, 'On the injustice' (n 2309) 148, 156 [Chinese], who writes of 'fundamental principles of international law' (国际法的基本原则, not the Art 38 ICJ Statute term 'general principles of law', 一般法律原则), as well as basic principes of the UN Charter.

2367 Yongming Jin, 'The Impact and Influence' (n 2309) 90 [English].

2368 Guoqiang Lu, 'On the injustice' (n 2309) 150–151 [Chinese].

2369 Ibid 155–156.

2370 Junwu Pan, 'Dissecting compulsory dispute settlement' (n 2360) 193–195, 199 [Chinese]. Contrast this with the categorical statement by Luo Guoqiang that the international legal order being based on states' will means forcing them to accept any tribunal's jurisdiction would be 'obviously unthinkable', see Guoqiang Lu, 'On the injustice' (n 2309) 151 [Chinese].

arrangements and not hamper final agreement, which do not deal with delimitation directly, are not excluded through China's reservation.[2371]

Wang Chongmin put forward another line of reasoning, claiming that the Philippines' own 'Understanding made upon signature [of UNCLOS] and confirmed upon ratification' blocked jurisdiction. Supposedly, this 'understanding,' which is viewed as relating to maritime delimitation, had to be interpreted as an Article 298 UNCLOS reservation under Article 2 (1) and (4) VCLT interpretation. Under Article 298 (3) UNCLOS, then, the Philippines, would have allegedly needed the other party's (ie China's) consent to submit a dispute on a matter it itself had excepted from jurisdiction.[2372] Seeing as the tribunal in *Philippines* did not consider the dispute as one about maritime delimitation, although this different approach would presumably not have helped the Chinese position either.

Furthermore, the almost unison Chinese position has been that jurisdiction was barred under Article 281 UNCLOS due to the parties' supposedly binding agreement in the DOC and other documents to only use negotiations to settle their dispute.[2373] Jin Yongming maintained that the use of the word 'agree' meant that the DOC was legally binding, arguing that while the DOC overall was a political instrument some provisions (including Article 4 on the use of negotiations to settle disputes) could still be binding. He added that the express exclusion of other methods of dispute settlement was not required according to the findings in *Southern Bluefin Tuna*, and that declaring the DOC non-binding would undermine motivation for political agreements and trust-building worldwide.[2374] In a rare dissenting opinion, Pan Junwu noted that the DOC had to still be solidi-

2371 Arts 74 and 83 UNCLOS; Junwu Pan, 'Dissecting compulsory dispute settlement' (n 2360) 195–196 [Chinese].

2372 Arts 2 (1), (4) and 298 (3) VCLT; Chongmin 崇敏 Wang 王, '菲律宾的相关谅解与中菲南海争端案管辖权的关系问题' (The Philippines' Understanding and jurisdiction issues in the China-Philippines South China Sea dispute) (2014) 29 (4) *Henan Caijing Zhengfa Daxue Xuebao* 30, 31–32; United Nations Division for Ocean Affairs and the Law of the Sea, 'United Nations Convention on the Law of the Sea – Declarations made upon signature, ratification, accession or succession or anytime thereafter' <http://www.un.org/Depts/los/convention_agreements/convention_declarations.htm> accessed 30 March 2019).

2373 Weibin Zhang, 'The qualified subject problem' (n 2340) 40 [Chinese]; Chongmin Wang, 'The Philippines' Understanding' (n 2372) 32 [Chinese]; Jiang Zhou, 'Legal obligations to be fulfilled' (n 2351) 40 [Chinese]; Art 281 UNCLOS.

2374 Yongming Jin, 'The Impact and Influence' (n 2309) 93–94, 105 [English]. For another reference to the DOC (Article 4) see Mincai 民才 Yu 余 and Bowei 博

fied and that *Southern Bluefin Tuna* showed the need for a legally binding treaty.[2375] The tribunal convincingly underlined the DOC's and other political agreements' permissive language and purpose.[2376] The Chinese drafters would have had to push for a different agreement, ie a binding COC, if they wanted a different outcome.

V.3.2.2.2. Criticism on the Merits

Fourth, on the tribunal's material decision, Chinese authors used different approaches to defend their government's claim to historic rights in the South China Sea.[2377] Zhang Weibin argued that the tribunal's quashing of the nine-dash-line was supposedly 'invalid', as a clear violation of intertemporal law.[2378] According to Jia Bingbing, historic rights of a non-sovereign quality are mostly not regulated in UNCLOS, but a fact of state practice, claiming they could surely exist outside of the UNCLOS framework. Concretely, he referred to fishing rights – interestingly both artisanal and industrial –[2379] that for Luo Guoqiang amount to 'regional international customary law';[2380] Li Yong[2381] and Zhang Lina[2382] wrote about the 'duality of legal basis' for historic rights including customary international law.[2383]

伟 Li 李, '中国与南海仲裁庭的非正式合作及其效果' (China's informal cooperation with the South China Sea arbitral tribunal and results) [2015] (2) *Xiandai Guoji Guanxi* 46, 52, also citing in support *Southern Bluefin Tuna Cases (Australia v Japan; New Zealand v Japan)* (Award on Jurisdiction and Admissibility) (2000) 23 RIAA 1–57.

2375 Junwu Pan, 'Dissecting compulsory dispute settlement' (n 2360) 199 [Chinese].

2376 See Chapter IV.3.4.2.

2377 See Chapter IV.3.4.3.2 for the decision on this point, and Chapter IV.3.4.4.2 for an approving discussion.

2378 Weibin Zhang, 'The qualified subject problem' (n 2340) 40 [Chinese]; Weibin Zhang, 'Evolutionary interpretation' (n 2325) 115 [Chinese].

2379 Bingbing 兵兵 Jia 贾, '论驳美国国务院《海洋疆界》 第 1 4 3 期有关南海历史性权利论述的谬误' (Refuting the errors in the US State Department's No. 143 'Limits in the Sea' treatise on historic rights in the South China Sea) [2016] (4) *Faxue Pinglun* 76, 82.

2380 Guoqiang Lu, 'On the injustice' (n 2309) 152 [Chinese].

2381 Li Yong, PhD Candidate at Hainan University Law School.

2382 Zhang Lina, professor at Hainan University Law School.

2383 Yong 永 Li 李 and Lina 丽娜 Zhang 张, 论历史性权利法律基础的二重性 (On Dual Nature of Legal Base of Historic Rights) (2018) 36 (2) *Hebei Faxue* 71.

Jia went on to also posit that China would likely be able to provide sufficient evidence to satisfy general international law requirements of open, notorious and effective exercise of authority that is continuous and acquiesced to by foreign states.[2384] Jin Yongming and Luo Guoqiang argued that other historic rights not being explicitly rejected in UNCLOS signified that they were compatible – 'freedom to do what law does not prohibit' – while Jin also claimed that historic rights were actually superior to UNCLOS rights, and that China enjoyed and has exercised such to fishing and navigation.[2385]

Yu Minyou saw an opening to customary international law – and evidence of UNCLOS not being entirely comprehensive – provided by the last sentence of the UNCLOS Preamble: 'Affirming that matters not regulated by this Convention continue to be governed by the rules and principles of general international law'.[2386] He deemed such an opening necessary due to UNCLOS imperfections, and lambasted the tribunal's reasoning in allowing for general international law historic rights in the territorial sea but not the EEZ and continental shelf. To him, such logic distorts the Convention, as the younger rules on the aforementioned broader maritime zones supposedly only lacked direct reference to other norms of international law out of immaturity and a need for further development.[2387] According to Luo Guoqiang, the tribunal supposedly made a decision to only take into account part of the applicable law, which would have to have been authorized by both parties.[2388] Operating more pragmatically with case law, Lei Xiaolu argued that *Eritrea v Yemen* proved that non-sovereign historic rights and EEZ rights may coexist, with no hierarchy being necessary – Tonga's CLCS submission is also referenced.[2389]

2384 Bingbing Jia, 'Refuting the errors' (n 2379) 82 [Chinese].

2385 Yongming Jin, 'The Impact and Influence' (n 2309) 98–99 [English]; Guoqiang Lu, 'On the injustice' (n 2309) 152 [Chinese].

2386 Preamble UNCLOS.

2387 Minyou Yu, 'Discussing the tendencies' (n 2343) 87–88 [Chinese]. See also Xiaolu 筱璐 Lei 雷, '论非主权性历史性权利与专属经济区和大陆架制度的并存与协调' (On the co-existence and coordination of non-sovereign historic rights and the exclusive economic zone and continental shelf) [2016] (3) *Faxue Pinglun* 95, 97, 100. For a pertinent reference to the UNCLOS preamble, and the argument that the tribunal erred grievously in assuming that the drafters intended UNCLOS to cover all of maritime law see also Guoqiang Lu, 'On the injustice' (n 2309) 150–152 [Chinese].

2388 Guoqiang Lu, 'On the injustice' (n 2309) 151–152 [Chinese].

2389 Xiaolu Lei (n 2387) 98–99, 102–103; *Eritrea v Yemen (second stage)* (n 1492) [101–107, 109]; Receipt of the submission made by the Kingdom of Tonga to

To Lei Xiaolu, the tribunal failed to understand that UNCLOS norms were negotiated as coordination with other regimes, and not to decide – which they supposedly could not do – whether these regimes exist. Moreover, According to Lei, international law theory as well as state practice point to non-sovereign historic rights under general international law and UNCLOS EEZ and continental shelf rights being reconcilable. Lei did not view continental shelf rights being *ab initio* as an issue and pointed to sedentary species, which belong to the continental shelf, being potentially open to historic rights according to Judge Oda's separate opinion in *Tunisia v Libya*.[2390]

Despite the lively defense of the Chinese government's position on historic rights, some scholars also recommended during the arbitration that the nine-dash line should be downplayed and emphasis shifted to sovereignty over supposed archipelagos. This has been framed as a rather pragmatic choice of a more promising line of argument.[2391] Moreover, in perhaps something of a climb-down from the previously unclear but potentially more ambitious position, it is now to be clarified that China's historic rights are such to non-exclusive jurisdiction over maritime resources within the nine-dash line.[2392]

On island status, Zhang Xinjun underlined that the scholarly mainstream is supposedly with China on the question of whether any feature in the Spratly Islands is an 'island' under Article 121 UNCLOS.[2393] There is indeed some strong support for the Chinese position, but the issue is hotly debated, and this study favors the interpretation of the arbitrators as the one more in line with object and purpose of UNCLOS.[2394] Zhang Weibin remarked that state practice, eg by Japan, was very broad on 'island' interpretation and saw a double standard.[2395] He also maintained that 'dynamic interpretation' should take into account the impact of technological progress on what could be considered an Article 121-'island'.[2396]

---

the Commission on the Limits of the Continental Shelf (14 May 2009) CLCS. 46.2009.LOS.

2390 Xiaolu Lei (n 2387) 95–97, 99–100, 101–104; *Continental Shelf (Tunisia v Libyan Arab Jamahiriya)* (n 1483) [202] Separate Opinion of Judge Oda, para 73.

2391 Ying Yao, 'Comments on the 2014 Bangladesh v India' (n 1515) 159.

2392 Guoqiang Lu, 'On the injustice' (n 2309) 157 [Chinese].

2393 Xinjun Zhang, 'Jurisdictional Objection' (n 2355) 5 [Chinese].

2394 See Chapters IV.3.4.3.3 and IV.3.4.4.2.

2395 Weibin Zhang, 'Evolutionary interpretation' (n 2325) 126 [Chinese].

2396 Ibid 124.

Leading up to the following sub-chapter on policy recommendations it should be emphasized that Chinese international lawyers have so far stuck close to the government line on non-compliance with the award in *Philippines*.[2397] Zou Ligang and Luo Guoqiang wanted China to provide a detailed explanation (inter alia to the PCA) on why the award could not be implemented, wanted Chinese scholars to pick the award apart, and the entire Chinese society to express its rejection of the award – whatever that would look like.[2398] According to Jin Yongming, the tribunal went beyond its jurisdiction, could not come to correct interpretations also because China's non-participation inhibited fact-finding, and delivered an award so flawed that it could hardly be cited in subsequent case law. China's non-compliance was therefore in service to the 'integrity and authority of the Convention'.[2399] Zhang Weibin wrote that countries calling on China to implement this 'unlawful' award 'can be counted on one's fingers,' while increasingly more governments were embracing the Chinese position. Zhang also thought that the nine-dash line had to be upheld, and that Taiwan was wrong in shifting to only emphasizing an EEZ claim around Taiping Island.[2400]

V.3.3. Policy Recommendations – How to Tame a Dragon

V.3.3.1. General Recommendations – Prepare Yourself and the Arena

In tackling the gargantuan task of engagement with international judicial mechanisms to resolve intricate law of the sea and territorial disputes while keeping tabs on both national and international public sentiment

2397 See eg Yongming Jin, 'The Impact and Influence' (n 2309) 103–104, 107 [English]; Yaqin 雅琴 Wan 万 and Kun 坤 Zheng 郑, '论中国退出《海洋法公约》以抵制南海仲裁案的不可行性' (On the infeasibility of denouncing 'UNCLOS' to boycott the South China Sea arbitration) (2016) 34 (11) *Zhengfa Luntan* 141; Weibin Zhang, 'Evolutionary interpretation' (n 2325) 125–126 [Chinese]; Ligang 立刚 Zou 邹, 中菲南海仲裁案剖析与我国的对策 (Analysis of the China v. Philippines South China Sea arbitration and Chinese countermeasures) [2016] (4) *Fazhi Yanjiu* 3, 7–8.

2398 Guoqiang Lu, 'On the injustice' (n 2309) 156–157 [Chinese], who calls the award 'perverse, vindictive, abusive' and 'a piece of waste paper', in conclusion 'nothing China has to abide by'; Ligang Zou, 'Analysis of the China v. Philippines South China Sea arbitration' (n 2397) 9 [Chinese].

2399 Yongming Jin, 'The Impact and Influence' (n 2309) 103–104, 107 [English].

2400 Weibin Zhang, 'Evolutionary interpretation' (n 2325) 125–126 [Chinese].

and stability, the Chinese international law community favors a proactive yet cautious course. Different mainstream views on engagement and interpretations of importance aside, the principal two lines of action recommended remain the same as in economic matters: study the system and negotiate to change it in your favor.

V.3.3.1.1. Master the Rules – Research & Training

The most prominent point then – among scholars of every stripe in the separate discussion of engagement – is again the emphatic call to action in the field of research and training.[2401] At least one author explicitly called

2401 Chen and Zhang (n 2325) 57; Shoubo 寿波 Feng 冯, 论海洋法中"历史性所有权"的构成要件 (On the Key Components of Historic Title in the Law of the Sea) (2018) 36 (2) *Hebei Faxue* 83, 95–96; Junfeng 俊峰 Gu 古, '和平解决中日东海划界争端的法律程序之纬' (Latitude of Legal Procedures in Peacefully Resolving the Sino-Japanese Maritime Boundary Dispute) [2009] (9) *Gansu Zhengfa Xueyuan Xuebao* 130, 137; Jianqiang 建强 Guan 管, '和平解决东海划界争端之方法探究' (Inquiry of Methods of Peaceful Resolution of the East China Sea Boundary Delimitation Dispute) [2008] (11) *Faxue* 77, 83; Jianqiang 建强 Guan 管, '"南海仲裁案"后续法律应对的关键问题研究' (Studying the key issues in follow-up legal responses to the 'South China Sea arbitration') [2016] (5) *Zhongguo Faxue* 51, 68; Liyu Han, 'The Case Law Applied' (n 1983) 123 [Chinese]; Huang and Zhang (n 2286) 161; He 河 Jiang 江, '和平解决东海争端法律研究' (Legal research on the Peaceful Resolution of the East China Sea Dispute) [2006] (5) *Faxue Pinglun* 84, 89; Yongming 永明 Jin 金, '论南海仲裁案对海洋法的冲击' (On the South China Sea arbitration's impact on maritime law) [2017] (7) *Zhengzhi yu Falü* 116; Luo and Ye (n 2325) 121; Bo 波 Qu 曲, '有效控制原则在解决岛屿争端中的适用' (The Application of the Effective Control Principle in the Resolution of Disputes over Islands) (2010) 24 (1) *Dangdai Faxue* 144; Bo 波 Qu 曲, '国际法院解决岛屿主权争端适用的法律原则' (Legal Principles Used by the International Court when Solving Disputes over Island Sovereignty) (2011) 32 (2) *Faxue Zazhi* 78; Bo Qu, 'Tactics of South China Sea Littoral States' (n 2327) 58–59 [Chinese]; Jie 杰 Song 宋, 从英美实践来看我国参与国际法律事务的有效性问题 (Reviewing the issue of effectivity in China's participation in international legal affairs from the perspective of British and US experience) [2015] (2) *Bijiaofa Yanjiu* 148, 158–159; Xiuwei 秀卫 Wang 王, '我国海洋争端解决的法律思考：《联合国海洋法公约》座谈会观点综述' (Legal Reflections on the Resolution of China's Maritime Disputes: Summary of Viewpoints at the Symposium on 'UNCLOS') [2012] (6) *Zhongguo Faxue* 85; Wang and Guan (n 499) 72, 76, 82; Zhang Weibin, 'Maritime Border Delimitation Trends' (n 2325) 48 [Chinese]; Weibin Zhang, 'Critical Date' (n 2337) 131 [Chinese]; Ligang 立刚 Zou 邹, '南海问题与中国的对策' (The South China Sea Issue and Chinese Countermeasures) (2009) 24 (1)

this 'obligation' the same regardless whether the issue is economic or territorial disputes, regardless whether one is dealing with the WTO DSM or the ICJ.[2402] Among the plethora of authors joining in this chorus one can – inter alia – find Chen Cong and Zhang Hongsheng, Gu Junfeng[2403], Guan Jianqiang[2404], Han Liyu, Huang Deming[2405] and Zhang Cheng[2406], Jin Yongming, Luo Guoqiang and Ye Quan, Qu Bo, Wang Xiuwei[2407], Wang Yong[2408] and Guan Zhengfeng[2409], Zhang Weibin, Zou Ligang and Zhang Kui. Jiang He[2410] viewed Philippine strengths in this regard apparent during the South China Sea arbitration, and urged greater efforts in building law of the sea litigation capacity.[2411]

Qu Bo called upon his government to realize both that international law now regulates ever more facets of international society and has to be used to protect interests, and that it should be held in esteem as the best foundation for dispute resolution.[2412]

Huang Deming, Qu Bo, Wang Xiuwei, Yao Ying, Zhang Weibin and Zhou Zhonghai[2413] all added emphasis on the crucial importance of ICJ and ITLOS case law. Regardless whether participation in proceedings is favored or not, authors considered the two tribunals to be developing legal principles that partly become international customary law.[2414] Han Liyu

---

Henansheng Zhengfa Guanli Ganbu Xueyuan Xuebao 160–161; Zou and Zhang (n 2325) 73.

2402 Liyu Han, 'The Case Law Applied' (n 1983) 132 [Chinese].

2403 Gu Junfeng, PhD Candidate at Xiamen University.

2404 Guan Jianqiang, lecturer at East China University of Politics and Law in Shanghai.

2405 Huang Deming, Professor at Wuhan University Law School.

2406 Zhang Cheng, PhD Candidate at Wuhan University Law School.

2407 Wang Xiuwei, Associate Professor at Hainan University Law School in Haikou, Hainan.

2408 Wang Yong, lecturer at East China University of Politics and Law.

2409 Guan Zhengfeng, graduate student at East China University of Politics and Law.

2410 Jiang He, Associate Professor at Zhongnan University of Economics and Law.

2411 He Jiang, 'Modern sea power' (n 2325) 96–97 [Chinese].

2412 Bo Qu, 'Tactics of South China Sea Littoral States' (n 2327) 64 [Chinese].

2413 Zhou Zhonghai, Professor at China University of Politics and Law in Beijing.

2414 Huang and Zhang (n 2286) 167; Bo Qu, 'The Application of the Effective Control Principle' (n 2401) 151 [Chinese]; Bo Qu, 'Tactics of South China Sea Littoral States' (n 2327) 58 [Chinese]; Wang Xiuwei (n 2401) 82; Ying Yao, 'Exploring Judicial Methods' (n 2288) 33 [Chinese]; Zhang Weibin, 'Maritime Border Delimitation Trends' (n 2325) 54 [Chinese]; Zhonghai 忠海 Zhou 周, '论海洋法中的剩余权利' (The Residual Rights in Maritime Law) (2004) 22 (5) *Zhengfa Luntan* 174.

also reiterated that China has to 'master [the] rules of the game' and referred to ICJ case law and common law countries' practice in particular.[2415]

Qu Bo and Zhang Weibin together with a series of other authors – including Feng Jiehan[2416], Jiang Huiqin[2417] and Gao Fengmei[2418], Jin Yongming, Li Guangyi[2419], Pan Junwu, Xing Guangmei[2420], Yang Zewei, Zhang Lei[2421] and Zhou Jiang[2422] – maintained that this case law (including advisory opinions) and states' record of compliance should be studied, because they can be used in China's favor, can help all states to better understand their own and their counterparts' positions, and can and should be used to inform negotiated solutions.[2423]

2415 Liyu Han, 'The Case Law Applied' (n 1983) 132 [Chinese].

2416 Feng Jiehan, Associate Professor at Wuhan University International Law Research Institute.

2417 Jiang Huiqin, PhD Candidate at China University of Politics and Law Comparative Law Research Institute in Beijing.

2418 Gao Fengmei, PhD Candidate at China University of Politics and Law Comparative Law Research Institute in Beijing as well as Bonn University.

2419 Li Guangyi, Associate Professor at People's Liberation Army Xi'an Institute of Politics.

2420 Xing Guangmei, researcher at the Navy Military Academic Research Institute.

2421 Zhang Lei, lecturer at the ECUPL International Law Institute in Shanghai.

2422 Zhou Jiang, Associate Professor at the Southwestern University of Politics and Law in Chongqing.

2423 Jiehan 洁菡 Feng 冯, '大陆架的权利基础自然延伸与距离标准' (The Basis of the Right to the Continental Shelf: The Principle of Natural Prolongation and the Distance Criterion) (2010) 32 (5) *Faxue Luntan* 24, 25, 28; Huiqin 慧芹 Jiang 姜 and Fengmei 丰美 Gao 高, '第一届比较法北京论坛：南海问题与海洋法治会议综述' (First Comparative Law Beijing Forum: Summary of the Conference on the South China Sea Issue and Maritime Rule of Law) [2013] (6) *Bijiaofa Yanjiu* 113–114; Jin 金 Yongming 永明, '中国拥有钓鱼岛主权的国际法分析' (International Law Analysis of China's Sovereignty over the Diaoyu Islands) (2013) 27 (5) *Dangdai Faxue* 3, 17; Guangyi 广义 Li 李, '东海大陆架划界争端国际法依据辨证' (The International Legal Basis on the Delimitation of the Continental Shelf of the East China Sea) (2005) 19 (3) *Dangdai Faxue* 103, 108–109; Junwu Pan, 'Analyzing International Dispute Settlement' (n 2286) 120 [Chinese]; Bo Qu, 'Reflection on Issues' (n 2286) 126 [Chinese]; Bo Qu, 'The Application of the Effective Control Principle' (n 2401) 151 [Chinese]; Bo Qu, 'Legal Principles Used' (n 2401) 78 [Chinese]; Guangmei 广梅 Xing 邢, '中国拥有南海诸岛主权考' (Study on China's Sovereignty over South China Sea Islands) [2013] (6) *Bijiaofa Yanjiu* 1, 4, 7, 12, 14; Zewei Yang, 'Important Flaws' (n 2325) 58 [Chinese]; Lei 磊 Zhang 张, '加强对黄岩岛有效控制的国际法依据' (Strengthening the International Law Foundation for Effective Control of Huangyan Island) [2012] (8) *Faxue* 67, 69, 73; Weibin Zhang, 'Critical

According to Qu Bo and Song Jie[2424] legal research and ensuing increasingly 'law-based' negotiations have a higher chance of success.[2425] In this vein, they also encouraged their own government to clarify certain positions and their legal content, including historic rights claims within the nine-dash line, and change the language of domestic laws and diplomatic statements to reflect the new 'law-based' approach.[2426]

Scholars of numerous institutions and throughout the research period then followed their own advice and studiously dissected the legal bases and case law of ICJ and ITLOS and the legal principles developed therein. Among such studies evaluating legal principles and their potential use to advance China's interests, one can – inter alia – find those of Cai Gaoqiang and Xu Xu, Chen Weidong and Guan Binbin, Feng Jiehan, Gu Junfeng, Guan Jianqiang, Huang Deming and Zhang Cheng, Huang Yao and Liao Xuexia, Li Guangyi, Luo Guoqiang and Ye Quan, Qu Bo, Song Jie, Wang Chongmin[2427] and Zhang Kui[2428], Wang Yong and Guan Zhengfeng, Yao Ying, Zhang Weibin, Zhang Xinjun[2429] and Zhou Zhonghai.[2430] Chinese

Date' (n 2337) 130–131 [Chinese]; Jiang 江 Zhou 周, '也谈南海断续线的法律性质' (Discussing the Legal Nature of the Dotted Line in the South China Sea) (2013) 31 (5) *Falü Kexue* 130, 133–134.

2424 Song Jie, PhD Candidate at Wuhan University Law School.

2425 Bo Qu, 'Tactics of South China Sea Littoral States' (n 2327) 58 [Chinese]; Jie 杰 Song 宋, '法律视角下的"南海争端"——含义与解决的技术性建议' (The "South China Sea Dispute" from a Legal Perspective – Technical Advice on Meaning and Resolution) (2012) 26 (4) *Dangdai Faxue* 10.

2426 Jie Song, 'The "South China Sea Dispute"' (n 2425) 10 [Chinese]; Yongming Jin, 'The Impact and Influence' (n 2309) 99 [English]. On the need to clarify the historic rights claims as such to non-exclusive jurisdiction see also Guoqiang Lu, 'On the injustice' (n 2309) 148, 157 [Chinese].

2427 Wang Chongmin, Professor at Hainan University Law School in Haikou, Hainan.

2428 Zhang Kui, lecturer at Changsha University of Science and Technology.

2429 Zhang Xinjun, Associate Professor at Tsinghua University Law School.

2430 Cai and Xu (n 2325) 39–43; Chen and Guan (n 2339) 138–143; Jiehan Feng (n 2423) 24; Junfeng Gu (n 2401) 135; Guan Jianqiang, 'Inquiry of Methods' (n 2401) 81–82 [Chinese]; Huang and Zhang (n 2286) 161; Huang and Liao, 'Discussing the Relationship' (n 2336) 127 [Chinese]; Guangyi Li (n 2423); Luo and Ye (n 2325) 112–124; Bo Qu, 'Reflection on Issues' (n 2286) 126 [Chinese] 126, wherein the pertinence of ITLOS and ICJ case law for specific issues is evaluated; Bo Qu, 'The Application of the Effective Control Principle' (n 2401) 144–151 [Chinese]; Bo Qu, 'Legal Principles Used' (n 2401) 78 [Chinese]; Bo 波 Qu 曲, '海洋法中历史性权利构成要件探究' (Exploring Constitutive Requirements of Historical Rights in Maritime Law) (2012) 26 (4) *Dangdai Faxue*

international lawyers particularly sought to use case law to strengthen claims to 'historic rights' to disputed maritime areas.[2431]

Among legal principles developed by the tribunals on maritime boundary delimitation, Chinese scholars have striven to undermine the importance and logic of the equidistance principle, while praising natural prolongation of continental shelves, and generally (ie regarding all maritime zones) solutions according to equitability. Concerning sovereignty disputes over islands, the rising importance of effective control in cases where no 'historic rights' or title through treaty can be proven is noted, the principle often discussed, and the Chinese government called upon to act favorably to the Chinese position in this question should it ever come to pertinent legal proceedings.[2432]

This leads to ancillary recommendations constructed based on the rationale behind the call to carry out research: preparation. Through the principles and case law studied, authors such as Qu Bo and Yao Ying perceived the need to call for not only research and training, but also vigorous efforts in collecting all potential evidence in support of China's claims, be they such that rely on 'historic rights', title through treaty, or effective control.[2433] Jiang Huiqin and Gao Fengmei wanted scholars and officials to cooperate better.[2434] They – as well as Huang Deming and Zhang Cheng, Qu Bo, Wang Xiuwei and Zhang Lei – also recommended improving public education on pertinent matters as well as mobilization of both domestic

3, 3–9; Jie Song, 'The "South China Sea Dispute"' (n 2425) 10 [Chinese]; Chongmin 崇敏 Wang 王 and Kui 奎 Zhang 张, '中国南海 U 形线的法律地位' (A Study on the Legal Status of U-Shape Line in the South China Sea) (2010) 25 *Henansheng Zhengfa Guanli Ganbu Xueyuan Xuebao* 106–109; Wang and Guan (n 499) 73; Ying Yao, 'Exploring Judicial Methods' (n 2288) 24 [Chinese]; Zhang Weibin, 'Maritime Border Delimitation Trends' (n 2325) 48–54 [Chinese]; Xinjun 新军 Zhang 张, '国际法上的争端和钓鱼诸岛问题' (International Law Disputes and the Diaoyu Islands Issue) [2011] (3) *Zhongguo Faxue* 187; Zhou Zhonghai (n 2414) 174–186.

2431 Jie Song, 'The "South China Sea Dispute"' (n 2425) 10 [Chinese].

2432 Cai and Xu (n 2325) 39, 46–47; Jiehan Feng (n 2423) 24; Huang and Zhang (n 2286) 167; Guangyi Li (n 2423) 103; Luo and Ye (n 2325) 112; Bo Qu, 'Reflection on Issues' (n 2286) 126 [Chinese] 126; Bo Qu, 'Legal Principles Used' (n 2401) 81 [Chinese]; Wang and Guan (n 499) 73.

2433 Bo Qu, 'Legal Principles Used' (n 2401) 81 [Chinese]; Ying Yao, 'Exploring Judicial Methods' (n 2288) 33 [Chinese]. Such calls for perfecting evidence collection have continued after the South China Sea arbitral award, see Ligang Zou, 'Analysis of the China v. Philippines South China Sea arbitration' (n 2397) 9 [Chinese].

2434 Jiang and Gao (n 2423) 118.

and international public opinion.[2435] In Wang Yong and Guan Zhengfeng's words, the government has to 'increase people's emotional adaptability to their country being sued and bringing suits in international law'.[2436]

Effective control is then analyzed in connection with the supposed ambiguity of the law of the sea system, leading some such as Xue Guifang and Xu Xiangxin to counsel precautionary steps such as building out or fortifying offshore features in the South China Sea to strengthen Chinese claims to effective control.[2437] A host of Chinese international lawyers – among them Jiang Guoqing[2438], Jiang Youyou[2439] and Lü Zhijun[2440], Qu Bo, Wang Xiuwei, Zhang Lei and Zhang Weibin – supported the need to improve maritime administration, monitoring, and protection of fisheries, environmental protection and resource development. They also wanted to strengthen control of offshore features, increase physical presence there as well as administrative activities concerning and on these features, and symbolic steps to demonstrate sovereignty.[2441] Another group of experts such as Cai Gaoqiang and Xu Xu, Qu Bo and Wang Xiuwei, reminded of the

2435 Huang and Zhang (n 2286) 173; Jiang and Gao (n 2423) 118; Bo Qu, 'Tactics of South China Sea Littoral States' (n 2327) 59 [Chinese]; Wang Xiuwei (n 2401) 78; Lei Zhang, 'Strengthening the international law foundation' (n 2423) 67.

2436 Wang and Guan (n 499) 76.

2437 Xue and Xu (n 2325) 63.

2438 Jiang Guoqing, Professor at China Foreign Affairs University in Beijing.

2439 Lü Zhijun, graduate student at China Foreign Affairs University in Beijing.

2440 Jiang Youyou, graduate student at Renmin University in Beijing.

2441 Guoqing 国青 Jiang 江, Youyou 由由 Jiang 江 and Zhijun 志君 Lü 吕, '"有效控制"原则在领土与海事争端中的适用动向——以国际法院"领土钰海事争端案"(尼加拉瓜诉哥伦比亚)为例' (Trends in the Application of the "Effective Control" Principle in Territorial and Maritime Disputes – Taking ICJ "Territorial and Maritime Dispute" (Nicaragua v. Colombia) as an Example) [2013] (6) *Bijiaofa Yanjiu* 38, 51; Bo Qu, 'The Application of the Effective Control Principle' (n 2401) 151 [Chinese]; Qingtong 清同 Ning 宁, 南海涉外侵权中我国渔业权制度的需求、供给和创新 (Demand, supply and innovation of China's fisheries rights system in the face of foreign infringements in the South China Sea) (2015) 33 (2) *Falü Kexue* 162; Bo Qu, 'Legal Principles Used' (n 2401) 81 [Chinese]; Bo Qu, 'Tactics of South China Sea Littoral States' (n 2327) 66–67 [Chinese]; Wang Xiuwei (n 2401) 78, 85; Lei Zhang, 'Strengthening the international law foundation' (n 2423) 69, 73; Weibin Zhang, 'Critical Date' (n 2337) 131 [Chinese]; Weibin 卫彬 Zhang 张, '南海 U 形线的法律属性及在划界中地位问题' (The Issue of the Legal Attributes and Position in Boundary Delimitation of the U-Shaped Line in the South China Sea) (2013) 27 (2) *Dangdai Faxue* 130, 138.

need to always file protests when other states commit violations.[2442] Yao Ying even favored filing for adjudication or arbitration should negotiations fail in the East China Sea to disturb Japan's effective control.[2443]

On the other hand, limits and supposed abuse of effective control are discussed in terms of other states' claims. The Philippines, supposedly, are estopped from their attempts at 'stealing sovereignty' over land features, wrote Zhang Lei as well as Yao Ying, underlining the importance of a preceding critical date – claims and conflict between the two states allegedly crystallized in 1956 – as well as continuous Chinese protests.[2444] As for Vietnam, Qu Bo argued that it is estopped from gaining sovereignty despite controlling several features, on account of high-ranking North-Vietnamese officials' public statements acquiescing to the Chinese position in the 1950s.[2445] On the other hand, China is supposedly not estopped following its previous silence on the Diaoyu Islands and then-Premier Zhou Enlai's statements on the McMahon Line dividing China and India, because in the former case the critical date favors China and in the latter case the statements are only recounted second-hand by the Indian side.[2446]

V.3.3.1.2. Have a Seat at the Table – Reform & Influence

The second principle line of action recommended by Chinese international lawyers in the fields of trade and investment law is to always be part of negotiations on legal reform. This as well is mirrored in discussions on territorial disputes. The Chinese side expects international law to be fluid here too – eg Zhang Weibin described it as 'constantly developing'[2447] – and takes comfort in the conviction, that international law is shaped by states that are relatively powerful in the international system, ie in the

---

2442 Cai and Xu (n 2325) 48; Bo Qu, 'Legal Principles Used' (n 2401) 81 [Chinese]; Wang Xiuwei (n 2401) 82.

2443 Ying Yao, 'Exploring Judicial Methods' (n 2288) 33 [Chinese].

2444 Ying Yao, 'Comments on the 2014 Bangladesh v India' (n 1515) 158; Lei 磊 Zhang 张, 论有效控制规则视野下中业岛的主权归属 (On sovereign jurisdiction over Thitu Island under the perspective of the effective control principle) (2016) 34 (1) *Hebei Faxue* 68, 74–76.

2445 Bo 波 Qu 曲, 禁反言在国际法中的适用——— 以 领 土 争 端 案 为 例 (Applicability of estoppel in international law – on the case of territorial disputes) (2014) 35 (8) *Faxue Zazhi* 16, 24–25.

2446 Ibid 24–25.

2447 Zhang Weibin, 'Maritime Border Delimitation Trends' (n 2325) 56 [Chinese].

coming decades: China.[2448] It is thus considered of utmost importance to not deny oneself a seat at the table when reforms are negotiated, due to a misguided perception of Chinese national interest and counter-productive isolationist moves.

The Chinese government instead should increase its 'discursive power' and seek to 'perfect' the international legal system in this as in other fields. It should redouble efforts, play a more active role, and gain much greater influence in pertinent reform processes, according to – inter alia – Chen Cong and Zhang Hongsheng, Jiang He, Luo Huanxin, Qu Bo, Wang Yong and Guan Zhengfeng, and Yang Zewei.[2449] Song Jie explicitly posited that active participation has to go beyond Chinese citizens' work at the ILC and ICJ.[2450]

On the law of the sea legal system, Yang Zewei already noted in 2012 that '[f]rom now on the Chinese government should, under the precondition of supporting the purpose and goals of UNCLOS, actively promote the next step of UNCLOS development, and progressively gain a voice in law of the sea development'.[2451] Yang saw opportunities for China to shape this development through support for liberal interpretations of some UNCLOS norms, and the establishment of and participation in the work of review committees, as well as supplementary or regional agreements.[2452] In Jiang He's view, participating in legislation would also mean understanding rules better and having more legally versed diplomats and government lawyers.[2453]

After the awards in the *South China Sea Arbitration*,[2454] Chinese international law academics mostly reinforced this point. Some, like Jin Yongming, connected their diagnosis of supposed 'systemic defects' in the UN-

2448 He Jiang, 'Modern sea power' (n 2325) 92 [Chinese].

2449 Chen and Zhang (n 2325) 57; He Jiang, 'Modern sea power' (n 2325) 97 [Chinese]; Huanxin 欢欣 Luo 罗, 国家在国际造法进程中的角色与功能———以国际海洋法的形成与运作为例 (The role and function of states in international law making processes – taking the formation and operation of the law of the sea as an example) (2018) 38 (4) *Faxue Yanjiu* 53, 67–68; Bo Qu, 'Tactics of South China Sea Littoral States' (n 2327) 67 [Chinese]; Wang and Guan (n 499) 76; Zewei Yang, 'On Non-Application' (n 2325) 1 [Chinese].

2450 Jie Song, 'Reviewing the issue' (n 2401) 158–159 [Chinese].

2451 Zewei Yang, 'Important Flaws' (n 2325) 57 [Chinese] (translation by this author).

2452 Zewei Yang, 'On Non-Application' (n 2325) 1 [Chinese].

2453 He Jiang, 'Modern sea power' (n 2325) 97 [Chinese].

2454 *The South China Sea Arbitration* (Award on Jurisdiction and Admissibility) (n 1506); *The South China Sea Arbitration* (Award) (n 196).

CLOS dispute resolution system with calls for Beijing to play a more active role in promoting reform.[2455] Lei Xiaolu called for 'adjustments' to UNCLOS EEZ and continental shelf norms in line with supposedly international customary law-based non-sovereign historic rights.[2456] For Wan Yaqin[2457] and Zheng Kun[2458] UNCLOS was an important step forward in the 20th century, and another step for the 21st century was needed due to realities like global warming, which supposedly is going to change many 'islands' into 'rocks.' In their view, this will be a particular problem for developing nations, and China should lead them in a reform push on Article 121, as it supposedly did during the negotiations leading up to UNCLOS.[2459]

Guan Jianqiang opined that the authority of the awards in the *South China Sea Arbitration* could be undermined, if most UNCLOS parties support China's position on a given issue, and that a two-thirds majority 'important question' UNGA resolution might be achieved.[2460]

At the same time, Chinese scholars mostly argued that 'denouncing' UNCLOS (Article 317) would do much more harm than good.[2461] Zou Ligang reminded that denunciation does not change past awards' binding force (Article 317 (2) UNCLOS), that others could still launch claims against China for one year (Article 317 (1) UNCLOS), and that UNCLOS is already international customary law, ie pertinent obligations would remain in place (Article 317 (3) UNCLOS). A withdrawal would only exclude China from the negotiations on future norms that it will still be bound by if they also become customary law – important pertinent inter-

2455 Yongming Jin, 'The Impact and Influence' (n 2309) 107 [English]; Yongming Jin, 'On the South China Sea arbitration's impact' (n 2401) 116 [Chinese].

2456 Xiaolu Lei (n 2387) 99.

2457 Wan Yaqin, lecturer at Hanjiang Normal University.

2458 Zheng Kun, lecturer at Hanjiang Normal University.

2459 Wan and Zheng (n 2397) 142.

2460 Art 18 (2) and (3) UN Charter; Jianqiang Guan, 'Studying the key issues' (n 2401) 66–68 [Chinese], who also recommends using the Chinese Society of International Law as a tool to influence counterpart professional organizations around the world.

2461 According to Luo Guoqiang, however, his government should very fundamentally reevaluate the situation and be prepared for both scenarios – remaining inside and leaving – as denunciation is the only available protest and way to eventually end supposed misuse of the system. Not much would supposedly change due to UNCLOS norms mostly being international customary law. In an odd reference, Luo notes that withdrawal from a treaty is not beyond reproach seeing as the UK is doing so regarding the Treaty on European Union. See Guoqiang Lu, 'On the injustice' (n 2309) 148 [Chinese].

ests being seabed resources and polar governance.[2462] Jin Yongming thought that new implementation agreements might be coming, perhaps also on military activities in EEZ.[2463] In the words of Wan Yaqin and Zheng Kun 'a moment's relief can bring endless suffering to come' ('饮鸩止渴'). What they think about is – inter alia – prospective favorable continental shelf delimitation in the East China Sea vis-à-vis Japan, UNCLOS supposedly being a hard-won Chinese achievement for developing nations against Western maritime hegemony, and the need for China to safeguard the image of a responsible power and international legal actor.[2464]

The trend towards emphasizing participation in reform processes concerning international adjudication of maritime and territorial disputes comports with a tendency – in line with developments in the discourse on WTO DSM and ICSID – to review more technical issues. An example would be Song Jie's article on the potential to use counterclaims as a litigation strategy to delay the merits phase, whereas the author favors such tactics.[2465]

More generally on the participation in international legal reform, Yu Minyou maintained that to live up to its new responsibilities as a great power, China had to do more to aid the international legal community in developing a supposedly yet missing 'truly global theory'.[2466] Cai Congyan added that international dispute resolution mechanisms generally needed to regain legitimacy through reform after drastic changes to their societal basis.[2467] According to Yao Ying, China could use the opportunity during the process of such renegotiations to shape other states' image of China into that of a country that supports the international rule of law.[2468]

2462 Ligang Zou, 'Analysis of the China v. Philippines South China Sea arbitration' (n 2397) 8–9 [Chinese]. On there still being a lot of regulatory development outstanding on seabed resource issues, while commercialization is still to come see Yongming Jin, 'On the Development and Challenges' (n 2369) 6 [Chinese].

2463 Yongming Jin, 'On the Development and Challenges' (n 2329) 7–8 [Chinese].

2464 Wan and Zheng (n 2397) 141–142.

2465 Jie 杰 Song 宋, '国际法院司法实践中的反诉问题研究' (Study on the Issue of Counterclaims in International Court of Justice Practice) (2006) 24 (3) *Falü Kexue* 133.

2466 Minyou Yu, 'China's Peaceful Rise and Global Governance' (n 1888) 21–22 [Chinese].

2467 Congyan Cai, 'Risk Society' (n 2128) 163 [Chinese].

2468 Ying Yao, 'Exploring Judicial Methods' (n 2288) 33 [Chinese].

For several scholars – such as Jiang Weiyu[2469], Jin Yongming, Qu Bo, Wang Xiuwei, and Zou Ligang – the advice to contribute to the 'perfection' of international law goes hand in hand with, is one and the same as, or is supposed to have the same effects as, 'perfecting' China's domestic legislation. The latter effort has recently been portrayed as part and parcel of Chinese President Xi Jinping's declared policy of making China a 'maritime power'.[2470] The evident conclusion is that both reform of the national and international legal system was to serve Chinese interests, after China had supposedly been disadvantaged in the past. Ning Qingtong[2471] assertively called for a special Chinese administrative system and law enforcement in the South China Sea to uphold the Chinese legal position despite the adverse rulings in the Annex VII arbitration.[2472]

V.3.3.2. Recommendations on Engagement – A Contested Field

Going beyond the general policy advice regarding rigorous preparation of oneself and the mechanisms that might theoretically be engaged with at some point, there is a very broad spectrum of opinions as to whether, when and how such engagement should indeed materialize. The debate ranges from the abject and definitive rejection of any participation in whatever judicial proceedings concerning territorial disputes to the complete embrace of engagement with all institutions of international adjudication and arbitration already leading up to 2013. The majority of Chinese international lawyers could be found somewhere in between.

However, following the increasing homogenization of the Chinese debate after the initiation of the South China Sea arbitration in 2013, scholars often refrained from discussing the possibility of later adjudication of other law of the sea or territorial matters, projected said possibility further into the future, or connected it to the creation of new judicial

2469 Jiang Weiyu, Professor at East China University of Science and Technology Law School in Shanghai.

2470 Weiyu 伟钰 Jiang 江, '21 世纪海洋开发国际法框架研究' (Study of 21st Century Maritime Exploration under the Framework of International Law) (2004) 25 (9) *Faxue Zazhi* 64, 66; Yongming Jin, 'The Impact and Influence' (n 2309) 99, 108 [English]; Bo Qu, 'Tactics of South China Sea Littoral States' (n 2327) 65 [Chinese]; Wang Xiuwei (n 2401) 86; Ligang Zou, 'Analysis of the China v. Philippines South China Sea arbitration' (n 2397) 10 [Chinese].

2471 Ning Qingtong, Professor at Hainan University.

2472 Qingtong Ning (n 2441) 162.

mechanisms. Overwhelmingly, in all phases the PRC has been deemed to have the best arguments in all territorial disputes discussed, and would be expected to prevail in any given hypothetical case, should the tribunal not be biased.

V.3.3.2.1. Negotiations & Joint Development

Regardless of whether proponents support engagement with international adjudication in this field or not, the Chinese international law community predominantly favors the continuation of negotiations for the time being, although on more law-based terms than this has been the case: in law of the sea matters, UNCLOS-based terms. The latter point has – inter alia – been made by Gu Junfeng, Jin Yongming[2473], Pan Junwu, Wan Yaqin and Zheng Kun, Wang Xiuwei, Yu Mincai[2474], Zhang Xinjun, Zhao Jingsong[2475] and Zou Ligang (in articles with Wang Chongmin, Ye Xinxin[2476] and Zhang Kui).[2477]

2473 Jin Yongming, researcher at the Shanghai Academy of Social Sciences.

2474 Yu Mincai, Associate Professor at Renmin University Law School in Beijing.

2475 Zhao Jingsong, PhD Candidate at Wuhan University International Law Research Institute.

2476 Ye Xinxin, graduate student at Hainan University Law School in Haikou, Hainan.

2477 Junfeng Gu (n 2401) 137; Jin Yongming, 'International Law Analysis' (n 2423) 3 [Chinese]; Junwu Pan, 'Analyzing International Dispute Settlement' (n 2286) 120 [Chinese]; Wang Xiuwei (n 2401) 78; Wan and Zheng (n 2397) 142; Mincai 民才 Yu 余, '论中日东海油气争端的共同开发解决方案' (On The Jointly-Exploited Solution To Sino-Japanese Disputation About The Oil And Gas In East China Sea) (2006) 27 (4) *Faxue Zazhi* 119, 122; Xinjun Zhang, 'International Law Disputes' (n 2430) 190 [Chinese]; Jingsong Zhao (n 2286) 102; Ligang 立刚 Zou 邹 and Chongmin 崇敏 Wang 王, '适用于南海的航行和飞越制度研究' (Study of the Application of the Navigation and Overflight Regime in the South China Sea) (2013) 27 (6) *Dangdai Faxue* 139, 145; Ligang 立刚 Zou 邹 and Xinxin 鑫欣 Ye 叶, '南海资源共同开发的法律机制构建略论' (Brief Introduction to the Structure of the Legal Mechanism of Joint Development of Resources in the South China Sea) [2006] (8) *Faxue* 122; Zou and Zhang (n 2325) 73.

However, after this agreement, ways quickly part. Gao Zhiguo[2478] and Jia Bing Bing[2479], Guo Qiong[2480], Song Jie and Zhou Yimin[2481] all excluded any other course than negotiations.[2482] Qu Bo and Zhang Weibin even rejected multilateral agreements, recommending to exclusively stick to bilateral talks,[2483] Zou Ligang showed himself open to multilateral solutions as well as bilateral ones,[2484] and Luo Guoqiang even claimed that multilateral negotiations should be the clear preference.[2485]

The main advantages of negotiations are different in the eyes of the beholder. Gao Zhiguo and Jia Bing Bing posited that this is the course that is in line with China's UNCLOS responsibilities,[2486] whereas Wang Xiuwei and Zhang Weibin saw the spirit of the PRC-ASEAN joint 'Declaration on a Code of Conduct for the South China Sea' (DOC) upheld.[2487] For Luo Huanxin[2488], territorial disputes are not suited for judicial resolution for several reasons. First, on account of the legal uncertainty resulting from

---

2478 Gao Zhiguo, Executive Director and Senior Research Fellow at the China Institute of Marine Affairs in Beijing, and member of the International Tribunal for the Law of the Sea (from 2008).

2479 Jia Bing Bing, Professor at Tsinghua University Law School in Beijing.

2480 Guo Qiong, lecturer at Lanzhou University.

2481 Zhou Yimin, PhD Candidate at the Party School of the Central Committee of the Chinese Communist Party's International Strategy Research Institute.

2482 Zhiguo Gao and Bing Bing Jia, 'The Nine-Dash Line in the South China Sea: History, Status, and Implications' (2013) 107 AJIL 98; Wei Cui, 'Multilateral Management as a Fair Solution to the Spratly Disputes' (2003) 36 *Vanderbilt Journal of Transnational Law* 799; Qiong 琼 Guo 郭, '新世纪中国和东盟关系的新发展' (New Developments in China-ASEAN Relations in the New Century) [2012] (12) *Lanzhou Xuekan* 1, 1–3; Hailong 海龙 Ju 鞠, '当代南海问题的函数解析 – 兼论两岸关系对我国和平解决南海问题的影响' (Analysis of the Current South China Sea Issue – Including the Impact of Cross-Straits Relations on Our Country's Peaceful Resolution of the South China Sea Issue) [2009] (6) *Dongnanya Yanjiu* 41, 41–45; Jie Song, 'The "South China Sea Dispute"' (n 2425) 10–16 [Chinese]; Yimin 意岷 Zhou 周, '南海争端解决模式分析' (A Model Analysis of Conflict Resolution in the South China Sea) [2011] (7) *Guoji Ziliao Xinxi* 18.

2483 Bo Qu, 'Tactics of South China Sea Littoral States' (n 2327) 58 [Chinese]; Zhang Weibin, 'The Issue of the Legal Attributes' (n 2441) 138 [Chinese].

2484 Ligang Zou, 'The South China Sea Issue' (n 2401) 160–161 [Chinese].

2485 Luo Guoqiang, 'Legal Principles Used' (n 2327) 1 [Chinese].

2486 Gao and Jia (n 2482) 122–123; Zhang Weibin, 'The Issue of the Legal Attributes' (n 2441) 138 [Chinese].

2487 Wang Xiuwei (n 2401) 82; Zhang Weibin, 'The Issue of the Legal Attributes' (n 2441) 138 [Chinese].

2488 Luo Huanxin, PhD Candidate at Peking University Law School.

pertinent mechanisms' flawed construction and operation. Second, due to territorial disputes' allegedly highly complicated nature. Third, because losing such a case might easily inflame nationalist passions.[2489]

Writing before the awards in *Philippines* were handed down, Song Jie maintained that the South and East China Sea disputes could never be submitted to adjudication or arbitration as long as the issue of the status of Taiwan had not been resolved, and core national interests regarding Taiwan might be damaged.[2490] Jiang Huiqin and Gao Fengmei, Zhang Weibin and Zou Ligang added that the negotiation process in these two disputes could be an opportunity for renewed cooperation between Taipei and Beijing, who share the same interests.[2491] Yu Mincai termed negotiations the only realistic option at least in the East China Sea case.[2492] According to Luo Huanxin and Cai Gaoqiang and Xu Xu, another advantage of negotiated solutions is that the PRC can be more magnanimous, maybe giving up on as much as half of its claims. They cited the agreements on land borders with Russia, Myanmar and Vietnam as successful precedents that show how such border settlements can be used to foster trust and improve relations.[2493]

After the awards in the South China Sea arbitration, many Chinese scholars underlined that non-participation, not even to argue against jurisdiction, was the correct decision.[2494] According to Zhang Xinjun, China would have inevitably been drawn into the merits phase as well, would it have appeared in the first phase of the arbitration. Zhang also claimed that the Chinese government still had the opportunity to try and influence jurisdictional findings even without participating in the proceedings.[2495] Guan Jianqiang wrote that some now favored submitting the case to another institution to get a different outcome. He argued strongly against it, because it would violate the government's position against international

2489 Huanxin 欢欣 Luo 罗, '国际法院在解决领土争端中的局限性' (Limitations of Territorial Dispute Resolution at the ICJ) (2010) 25 (11) *Fazhi Luncong* 114, 114–116.

2490 Jie Song, 'The "South China Sea Dispute"' (n 2425) 15 [Chinese].

2491 Jiang and Gao (n 2423) 117–118; Zhang Weibin, 'The Issue of the Legal Attributes' (n 2441) 138 [Chinese]; Ligang Zou, 'The South China Sea Issue' (n 2401) 160–161 [Chinese].

2492 Yu Mincai, 'On The Jointly-Exploited Solution' (n 2477) 119 [Chinese].

2493 Huanxin Luo, 'Limitations of Territorial Dispute Resolution' (n 2489) 119–120. See also Cai and Xu (n 2325) 47–48 for the acceptability of a solution somewhere in the middle of the opposing sides positions.

2494 See eg Yongming Jin, 'The Impact and Influence' (n 2309) 107 [English].

2495 Xinjun Zhang, 'Judging the meaning' (n 2309) 176 [Chinese].

adjudication of territorial disputes, and because ne bis in idem is viewed as influential despite there being no system of precedents.[2496]

A large number of Chinese experts have linked support for negotiations with the suggestion of joint development of resources in disputed territory. This group includes Cai Gaoqiang and Xu Xu, Gu Junfeng, Guo Qiong, Lei Xiaolu, Liang Yong, Yang Zewei, Yu Mincai, Zhang Weibin, Zhang Xinjun and Zou Ligang.[2497] Among precedents to emulate, Yu Mincai cited the cooperation between Kuwait and Saudi Arabia.[2498] Parallel to joint development, some have favored freezing the disputes by eventually concluding a binding 'Code of Conduct for the South China Sea' (COC).[2499] Such a course of action builds on Deng Xiaoping's old maxim of 'Putting Disputes Aside, Developing Together' (搁置争议，共同开发). Commenting after the awards in *Philippines* were rendered, Yang Zewei framed joint development more assertively. According to him, China should preempt new projects in disputed areas between other littoral states and multinational corporations through economic incentives, actively block already agreed projects, and push hard to be included in already substantively ongoing projects.[2500]

2496 Jianqiang Guan, 'Studying the key issues' (n 2401) 65–66 [Chinese], who cites on the ICJ's caution, *Arbitral Award of 31 July 1989 (Guinea-Bissau v Senegal)* (Provisional Measures, Order of 2 March 1990) [1990] ICJ Rep 64, para 14.

2497 Cai and Xu (n 2325) 48; Junfeng Gu (n 2401) 137; Guo Qiong (n 2482) 5; Xiaolu Lei (n 2387) 105; Yong Liang, 'Reviewing the Sino-Japanese Dispute' (n 2237) 128 [Chinese]; Mincai 民才 Yu 余, '论国际法上海洋石油共同开发的概念' (Discussing the Concept of Joint Development of Offshore Oil on the Basis of International Law) [2001] (6) *Faxuejia* 47, 51; Zhang Weibin, 'The Issue of the Legal Attributes' (n 2441) 138 [Chinese]; Xinjun 新军 Zhang 张, '中国周边海域争端处理的程序和实体问题 —— "搁置争议、共同开发"再考' (The Procedures of Dealing with Conflicts in China's Peripheral Waters – Reevaluation of "Putting Disputes Aside and Developing Together") (2011) 23 *Zhongwai Faxue* 1121, 1125–1127; Zou and Ye (n 2477) 122; Ligang Zou, 'The South China Sea Issue' (n 2401) 160 [Chinese]; Ligang Zou, 'Analysis of the China v. Philippines South China Sea arbitration' (n 2397) 10 [Chinese].

2498 Mincai Yu, 'Discussing the Concept' (n 2497) 51 [Chinese].

2499 Ligang Zou, 'Analysis of the China v. Philippines South China Sea arbitration' (n 2397) 10 [Chinese].

2500 Zewei 泽伟 Yang 杨, 海上共同开发的先存权问题研究 (Researching the Issue of Pre-existing Rights in Maritime Joint Development) [2017] (1) *Faxue Pinglun* 121. On China cooperating with multinational companies in exploiting resources in the South China Sea see also Ligang Zou, 'Analysis of the China v. Philippines South China Sea arbitration' (n 2397) 10 [Chinese].

V.3.3.2.2. Adjudication & Arbitration

V.3.3.2.2.1. Criticism of Political Declarations, Negotiations & Joint Development

Readiness to go beyond a commitment to only negotiated solutions stems from different motivations, but certain exasperation with previous attempts at resolution is central for many authors. Liang Yong, Pan Junwu described the potential for solving the pertinent disputes via negotiations as obviously limited, and even thought that the process could be damaging, when parties become more aware of their differences and stances harden.[2501] Yao Ying firstly considered negotiations to often only delay a resolution, and secondly picked apart traditional praise for the resulting agreements based on national interest considerations.[2502] Taking the *Gulf of Tonkin Agreement* with Vietnam as an example, Yao highlighted that what was achieved for the PRC territorially was merely a median line solution with a single maritime boundary for EEZ and continental shelf (ie China gave up on the much touted natural prolongation principle in those negotiations).[2503] According to her, China could achieve more for itself, if it were willing to submit the East China Sea dispute with Japan to the ICJ.[2504] Without necessarily disparaging current attempts at negotiated solutions yet, Luo Guoqiang and Ye Quan, as well as Wang Yong and Guan Zhengfeng, stated that if such attempts do prove futile, there is a need for 'real dispute resolution', including adjudication.[2505]

2501 Yong Liang, 'Reviewing the Sino-Japanese Dispute' (n 2237) 125 [Chinese]; Junwu Pan, 'Analyzing International Dispute Settlement' (n 2286) 113 [Chinese].

2502 Ying Yao, 'Exploring Judicial Methods' (n 2288) 24 [Chinese].

2503 National People's Congress of the People's Republic of China, '中华人民共和国和越南社会主义共和国关于两国在北部湾领海、专属经济区和大陆架的划界协定' (Demarcation Agreement on Territorial Seas, Exclusive Economic Zones, and Continental Shelves in the Gulf of Tonkin between the People's Republic of China and the Socialist People's Republic of Vietnam) (adopted 25 December 2000, entered into force 30 June 2004) <http://www.mfa.gov.cn/chn//pds/ziliao/tytj/t556665.htm> accessed 1 March 2019.

2504 Ying Yao, 'Exploring Judicial Methods' (n 2288) 33 [Chinese].

2505 Luo and Ye (n 2325) 121–123; Guoqiang 国强 Luo 罗, '共同开发"政策在海洋争端解决中的实际效果：分析与展望' (Analysis About The Joint Development Policy And Its Practical Effect In Solving Maritime Disputes: Analysis And Prediction) (2011) 32 (4) *Faxue Zazhi* 14, 17; Wang and Guan (n 499) 75–76.

Leveling much more general criticism, Luo Guoqiang, Nie Hongyi, Yao Ying and Ye Quan took issue with the nature of political declarations – eg the DOC and the 'Common Understanding on the Principles of the East China Sea Issue' – which they deemed too dependent on state parties' enduring voluntary cooperation due to the lack of binding force, hence lacking legal certainty and stability.[2506] Ye Quan, after criticizing other states' supposed unilateral disregard of restraint in the South China Sea, came to explicitly advocate for a legally binding interim agreement, ie the COC, as a safety valve to temper the disputes and a possible catalyst for a later resolution.[2507]

A third focal point of scholars' criticism is the aforementioned slogan of 'Putting Disputes Aside, Developing Together' (搁置争议，共同开发), ie the practice of negotiating joint development zones. Jiang He[2508], Liang Yong, Luo Guoqiang and Ye Quan, and Yu Minyou and Lei Xiaolu[2509] have all considered it to be an interim solution only.[2510] According to Luo Guoqiang, the crux of the issue is the 'lack [of] effective legal guarantees'[2511], as well as other countries' alleged failure to understand and embrace the practice, whereas Jiang Guoqing, Jiang Youyou and Lü Zhijun supported the latter argument.[2512] In any case, Luo held that joint development should only be supplementary and not seen as a stand-alone solution to anything, while it is considered a mistake to think that it always makes economic sense.[2513]

2506 Luo Guoqiang, 'Legal Principles Used' (n 2327) 1 [Chinese]; Hongyi Nie (n 2286) 2–3; Ying Yao, 'Exploring Judicial Methods' (n 2288) 24 [Chinese]; Quan Ye (n 2325) 106.

2507 Quan Ye (n 2325) 106–107.

2508 Jiang He, Professor at the Zhongnan University for Economics and Law, Law School (PhD from Wuhan University Law School).

2509 Lei Xiaolu, researcher at the Colloborative Innovation Center for Territorial Sovereignty and Maritime Rights (PhD from Wuhan University Law School).

2510 He Jiang, 'Legal research on the Peaceful Resolution' (n 2401) 84 [Chinese]; Yong Liang, 'Reviewing the Sino-Japanese Dispute' (n 2237) 126 [Chinese]; Luo and Ye (n 2325) 112; Minyou 敏友 Yu 余 and Xiaolu 筱璐 Lei 雷, '南海诸岛争端国际仲裁的可能性' (Feasibility of International Arbitration of the South China Sea Island Conflict) (2011) 64 (1) *Wuhan Daxue Xuebao* 102.

2511 Guoqiang Luo, 'Analysis About The Joint Development Policy' (n 2505) 14 [Chinese].

2512 Jiang, Jiang and Lü (n 2441) 50; Guoqiang Luo, 'Analysis About The Joint Development Policy' (n 2505) 14 [Chinese].

2513 Guoqiang Luo, 'Analysis About The Joint Development Policy' (n 2505) 17 [Chinese]. See also Guoqiang 国强 Luo 罗 and Chenhong 晨虹 Liu 刘, 历史性水域的性质与协调———以南海断续线内水域为研究对象 (The Nature and

Luo Guoqiang and Ye Quan also considered joint development as not feasible where disputed islands exist in the pertinent area.[2514] Guan Jianqiang[2515] made the point regarding the East China Sea, and Wang Mengdie[2516] and Yu Minyou and Lei Xiaolu made it regarding the South China Sea, that through delaying a resolution of the underlying dispute, joint development actually helped those in control of disputed offshore features. Letting Japan and Southeast Asian nations remain in (effective) control of features in the Diaoyu / Senkaku Islands or the Spratly Islands, and conclude oil and gas exploration agreements with extra-regional energy companies headquartered in powerful states without submitting cases to adjudication or arbitration only made it harder to ever successfully get to a tribunal and prove sovereignty over the respective features.[2517] Yao Ying already referred to 'Putting Disputes Aside, Developing Together' as a maxim of the old leadership generation,[2518] and Wang Yong and Guan Zhengfeng, as well as Yu Minyou and Lei Xiaolu considered it to simply have failed.[2519]

V.3.3.2.2.2. General Preconditions for and Significance of Engagement

Discontent with the outcome of efforts to negotiate a solution to China's territorial disputes has thus been a crucial factor rendering an important group of Chinese international lawyers more open to third-party solutions. Certain skepticism regarding tribunals' unbiased work and potential political influence has been one of the reasons for most of these scholars not to abandon caution.

The majority of those who do not want to limit their country's policy options to negotiations, still want to minimize risks wherever possible, and

---

Adjustment of the 'Historic Waters' – With Respect to the Waters Within the Dashed Line) (2018) 20 (1) *Guoji Luntan* 1, 6.

2514 Luo and Ye (n 2325) 123.

2515 Guan Jianqiang, lecturer at East China University of Politics and Law in Shanghai.

2516 Wang Mengdie, graduate student at Anhui University of Finance and Economics Law School in Bengbu, Anhui Province.

2517 Mengdie 梦蝶 Wang 王, '论南海争端解决的法律方法' (Discussing Legal Methods for the Solution of the South China Sea Conflict) [2012] (7) *Fazhi Bolan* 13; Yu and Lei (n 2510) 8.

2518 Ying Yao, 'Exploring Judicial Methods' (n 2288) 33 [Chinese].

2519 Wang and Guan (n 499) 75; Yu and Lei (n 2510) 6–7.

only gradually engage with international adjudication on territorial disputes. Among the professors interviewed for this study, most were convinced that participation in judicial mechanisms would certainly happen at some point.[2520] Only one of them rejected the notion outright, refused to contemplate any engagement in judicial or arbitral proceedings under any circumstances and regardless how far in the future.[2521] Almost all interviewees considered this merely a question of time and preparation, while one professor expressly stated that at some point in the future 'of course everything can be tried'.[2522] In the literature, Yao Ying confirmed that the PRC should just wait for the right moment.[2523] Huang Yao and Liao Xuexia maintained that the existing case law did not yet inspire sufficient confidence in continuity and predictability, and therefore lobbied for the Chinese government to still wait.[2524] Finally, Jiang He stated that China might take certain other steps along the way, but should only agree to ICJ proceedings on its law of the sea disputes after its judges had become more prominent and its 'peaceful rise' had been accomplished and overall power increased.[2525]

According to Jiang, dispute settlement methods must be chosen in line with power. In 2014 while the South China Sea arbitration was ongoing, he still saw China's level of power indicating a policy of 'negotiations only,' but also wrote that the judicialization of international relations and the trend towards judicial dispute resolution are inevitable, and that sovereignty is relative.[2526]

2520 Author's interviews in Wuhan, Xiamen, Xi'an and Singapore, June and September 2013.

2521 Author's interview in Wuhan, June 2013.

2522 Ibid.

2523 Ying Yao, 'Exploring Judicial Methods' (n 2288) 33 [Chinese].

2524 Huang and Liao, 'New Developments in International Maritime Boundary Delimitation' (n 2294) 92 [Chinese].

2525 He Jiang, 'Legal research on the Peaceful Resolution' (n 2401) 89 [Chinese]. On the need for more Chinese judges see also He Jiang, 'Modern sea power' (n 2325) 98 [Chinese].

2526 He Jiang, 'Modern sea power' (n 2325) 92, 97 [Chinese], who wrote that 'even if it is a superpower, it cannot entirely resist the historical trend of maritime power legazation and become a country outside of the system' (translation by this author). See also Zhao and Wang, 'China's choice to participate' (n 1888) 78 [Chinese], who write that the judicialization trend is irreversible for any country, and that it behoves China as a responsible big power to 'comply with this trnd and actively integrate into international adjudication' (translation by this author).

The expectation has been that over time certain conditions are going to lead to a situation more conducive to Chinese engagement.

First, most interviewees as well as Xu Hao[2527] and Zhao Haifeng expected that the PRC's government, scholars and officials will have familiarized themselves further with the legal bases and case law of, as well as other countries' behavior vis-à-vis, the relevant mechanisms, and will have undergone internationalized training. That is to say they will have complied with the first general recommendation: study and train.[2528]

Second, these same scholars maintained that China will have become more integrated into international society, and gained much more influence on the international legal system (eg via Chinese judges at international tribunals). That is, China will have complied with the second general recommendation: be part of negotiations and increase influence.[2529] Third, Zhao Haifeng added, more experience will have been gathered and confidence built.[2530] Fourth, Zhao Jingsong claimed that the traditional disregard of law in China is receding (while in general, ideational gaps between East and West were deemed much less than in prior decades and very much bridgeable).[2531] Fifth, Zhao Haifeng expected that China's domestic legal system would have been much improved.[2532]

A number of authors implicitly or explicitly admitted to policy proposals on strengthening research and evidence collection as well as participation in international reform negotiations being geared towards raising preparedness. They might counsel negotiations for the moment, but they urged their government to be ready should it eventually have to make use of other facets of UN mandated peaceful dispute resolution, including international adjudication, to protect national interests.[2533]

2527 Xu Hao, lecturer at Guangdong Ocean University Law School in Zhanjiang, Guangdong Province.

2528 Author's interviews in Wuhan, Xiamen, Xi'an and Singapore, June and September 2013; Hao 浩 Xu 许, '南海油气争端解决的法律机制探讨' (Investigation of Legal Mechanisms for the Resolution of the Dispute over South China Sea Oil and Gas) [2008] (5) *Haiyang Kaifa yu Guanli* 71, 73; Haifeng Zhao (n 1132) 12.

2529 Author's interviews in Wuhan, Xiamen, Xi'an and Singapore, June and September 2013; Hao Xu (n 2528) 73; Haifeng Zhao (n 1132) 12.

2530 Haifeng Zhao (n 1132) 12 (translation by this author).

2531 Jingsong Zhao (n 2286) 102.

2532 Haifeng Zhao (n 1132) 12.

2533 Junfeng Gu (n 2401) 137; Junwu Pan, 'Analyzing International Dispute Settlement' (n 2286) 120 [Chinese]; Hao Xu (n 2528) 75; Yu and Lei (n 2510) 11.

Some authors contextualized the significance of actual participation in judicial and arbitral proceedings on territorial issues with discussions on the PRC's 'peaceful rise'. For Cai Gaoqiang, Gu Junfeng, Jiang He and Zhu Tong[2534], the resolution of territorial disputes is a crucial challenge to that concept. China is said to have to go through that rite of passage and eventually be prepared to also use adjudication or arbitration if necessary.[2535]

It is imperative, wrote Yao Ying, that China attains the image of a country that strongly supports the international rule of law.[2536] With this issue in mind, scholars like Jin Yongming have pointed to the threat of China's image being undermined, after the awards in the South China Sea arbitration, and have urged proactive responses.[2537]

Referring to national interest regularly, Cai Gaoqiang and Xu Xu as well as Nie Hongyi, pointed to the importance of soft power gains due to achievements in this field.[2538] Pan Junwu underlined the significance of international pressure and reputational costs, should the country fail in this endeavor and eg not recognize an award or judgment.[2539] Liang Yong and Pan Junwu also thought that the PRC should strengthen the ICJ after the UNGA and the Non-Aligned Movement called for it, and that being the only UNSC veto power summarily rejecting ICJ jurisdiction might hamper influence in the Council and China's overall ascent in the internation-

2534 Zhu Tong, PhD Candidate at Fudan University Law School in Shanghai and lecturer at Lanzhou Jiaotong University International Law Research Institute.

2535 Gaoqiang 高强 Cai 蔡, '论解决南海争端的国际法路径' (Discussing International Law Approaches to Resolving the South China Sea Dispute) (2011) 35 (2) *Xiangtan Daxue Xuebao* 41; Junfeng Gu (n 2401) 137; He Jiang, 'Legal research on the Peaceful Resolution' (n 2401) 89 [Chinese]; Tong 童 Zhu 褚, '论和平解决国际争端中的国家仲裁' (Discussing State Arbitration in the Context of the Peaceful Resolution of International Conflicts) [2012] (11) *Lanzhou Xuekan* 188.

2536 Ying Yao, 'Exploring Judicial Methods' (n 2288) 33 [Chinese]. See also He Jiang, 'Modern sea power' (n 2325) 98 [Chinese].

2537 Yongming Jin, 'The Impact and Influence' (n 2309) 106 [English]. For UNCLOS helping China to establish the image of a good faith and responsible actor that can better integrate into the international system, as well as the threat posed by the South China Sea dispute see also Jieyu 洁宇 Li 李, 论《联合国海洋法公约》 有助于提升中国的软实力 (On how 'UNCLOS' can aid in increasing China's soft power) [2016] (3) *Xin Dongfang* 7.

2538 Cai and Xu (n 2325) 47–48; Hongyi Nie (n 2286) 6.

2539 Junwu Pan, 'Analyzing International Dispute Settlement' (n 2286) 120 [Chinese].

al order.[2540] Moreover, they considered it to be in the self-interest of a new great power to strengthen effective dispute resolution and thus stabilize international order.[2541]

Chinese international law scholars also linked the importance of eventually embracing international adjudication of territorial matters with other international trends. Zhao Haifeng maintained that globalization will inevitably lead to more inter-state disputes,[2542] and Pan Junwu added that modernization of armaments meant that every one of these disputes was more dangerous than used to be the case.[2543] Both of them expected international adjudication to gain in importance constantly and urged authorities in Beijing to re-evaluate their attitude.[2544] Their call for a new openness was echoed by Wang Yong and Guan Zhengfeng, who posited that their government had not yet fully taken into account changes at the ICJ specifically and in the international system generally.[2545]

V.3.3.2.2.3. Engaging to Refute Jurisdiction

In the particular matter of participating only to argue against the legitimacy of the case, the readiness to engage is much higher. Many interviewees wanted China to take part in hearings on admissibility and jurisdiction in the case brought by the Philippines under UNCLOS Annex VII.[2546] Other authors did not want to participate in this way, but did argue in favor of making the Chinese position clear to the tribunal ('informal cooperation') and international society, and providing evidence – as with the later sub-

2540 Yong Liang, 'Reviewing the Sino-Japanese Dispute' (n 2237) 127–128 [Chinese]; Junwu Pan, 'Analyzing International Dispute Settlement' (n 2286) 120 [Chinese].

2541 Junwu Pan, 'Analyzing International Dispute Settlement' (n 2286) 120 [Chinese]. See also Yong Liang, 'Reviewing the Sino-Japanese Dispute' (n 2237) 128 [Chinese].

2542 Haifeng Zhao (n 1132) 12.

2543 Junwu Pan, 'Analyzing International Dispute Settlement' (n 2286) 120 [Chinese].

2544 Haifeng Zhao (n 1132) 12. See also Junwu Pan, 'Analyzing International Dispute Settlement' (n 2286) 120 [Chinese].

2545 Wang and Guan (n 499) 73.

2546 Author's interviews in Wuhan, Xiamen, Xi'an and Singapore, June and September 2013.

mitted *Position Paper.*[2547] Regarding the South China Sea case, Yu Mincai warned that just like the US in *Nicaragua v United States*,[2548] China will get nothing out of denial and non-participation and will not be able to stop the case from going further. Moreover, ultimately it will have to respect whatever decision the tribunal comes to, whether it participated and tried to argue its side or not. However, if it were to engage, it could continue to negotiate with Manila on the sidelines of the arbitration, and favorably influence international public opinion.[2549]

V.3.3.2.2.4. Advisory Opinions

A second step towards engagement could be seen in proposals to seek advisory opinions on the merits of a case. Jin Yongming argued that the ICJ should be approached to provide an opinion on the East China Sea,[2550] and Liu Xuefei counseled the same on the South China Sea.[2551] Authors have generally been more open to adjudication and arbitration in terms of the East China Sea and the dispute over the Diaoyu/Senkaku Islands with Japan, which according to Zhang Xinjun is due to their exasperation with Tokyo's refusal to admit that there is a dispute.[2552] Chinese scholars, such as Li Guangyi, are also liable to take a position different to the general Chinese mainstream in terms of the East China Sea, on what exactly constitutes an 'island' and a 'rock' according to Art 121 UNCLOS.[2553] Concerning the East China Sea, Guan Jianqiang directed criticism also against the US, which allegedly acted illegally and politically irresponsibly by handing the Diaoyu/Senkaku Islands to Japan instead of China decades after the

2547 Weibin Zhang, 'The qualified subject problem' (n 2340) 42 [Chinese]; Yu and Li (n 2374) 46; PRC Position Paper on the South China Sea (n 1507).

2548 *Military and Paramilitary Activities in and against Nicaragua* (n 193).

2549 Mincai 民才 Yu 余, '海洋争端强制仲裁程序及我国的应对策略———以中菲南海争端强制仲裁事件为例' (Compulsory Arbitration Procedures in Maritime Disputes and Our Country's Counter-Strategy – Taking the Example of Compulsory Arbitration in the China-Philippines South China Sea Dispute) [2013] (3) *Fashang Yanjiu* 32, 32–36.

2550 Jin Yongming, 'International Law Analysis' (n 2423) 3 [Chinese].

2551 Xuefei 雪飞 Liu 刘, '国际海洋法法庭与国际法院的咨询管辖比较' (Comparison of the International Tribunal for the Law of the Sea's and the International Court's Advisory Jurisdiction) [2006] (4) *Zhongguo Haiyang Daxue Xuebao* 1, 1–2.

2552 Xinjun Zhang, 'International Law Disputes' (n 2430) 176–190 [Chinese].

2553 Guangyi Li (n 2423) 109.

Second World War.[2554] Washington, held Qu Bo, had succumbed to 'Cold War-thinking', instigating other countries' to enter into conflict with China.[2555] What is more, lamented Zhou Zhonghai, the US has not only refused to ratify UNCLOS, but indeed repeatedly challenged the law of the sea, the UN and the international order as a whole.[2556]

V.3.3.2.2.5. Trial Balloons: Conciliation, Arbitration & Adjudication – New Mechanisms & Special Separate Tribunals

A third stage in the intensity of engagement recommended, is represented by a series of heterogonous policy proposals involving going beyond advisory opinions and employing different strategies to test the waters. One interviewee can only imagine agreeing to a Conciliation Commission like the *Conciliation Commission on the Continental Shelf area between Iceland and Jan Mayen*.[2557] On conciliation, Jiang He merely reminded of the possibility that ITLOS may initiate compulsory conciliation procedures, and otherwise advocated obtaining 'recommendations' through arbitration.[2558]

Among the very few that judge the likelihood and wisdom of participation in either arbitration or adjudication differently, both sides of the argument can be found. Wang Mengdie, Yu Minyou and Lei Xiaolu preferred arbitration as more flexible and supposedly promising even more highly educated professionals judging the dispute.[2559] One scholar interviewed for this study, on the other hand, deemed arbitration potentially more daunting, as an even smaller group of individuals might be even easier to influence politically to China's detriment.[2560]

Luo Chao[2561] as well as Pan Junwu proposed the introduction of a new regional dispute settlement mechanism under the umbrella of the DOC.

2554 Guan Jianqiang, 'Inquiry of Methods' (n 2401) 83 [Chinese].
2555 Bo Qu, 'Tactics of South China Sea Littoral States' (n 2327) 67 [Chinese].
2556 Zhou Zhonghai (n 2414) 185.
2557 Author's interview in Wuhan, June 2013; Conciliation Commission on the Continental Shelf Area between Iceland and Jan Mayen *Report and Recommendations to the Governments of Iceland and Norway* (1981) 20 ILM 797.
2558 He Jiang, 'Legal research on the Peaceful Resolution' (n 2401) 89 [Chinese].
2559 Wang Mengdie (n 2517) 13; Yu and Lei (n 2510) 5–6.
2560 Author's interview in Wuhan, June 2013.
2561 Luo Chao, PhD Candidate at Wuhan University.

Pan reasoned that this could satisfy UNCLOS encouragement on regional structures, and exclude Part XV compulsory dispute settlement.[2562]

Several authors considered ITLOS proceedings less daunting than such at the ICJ. In Zou Ligang's opinion, ITLOS should merely assess the legality of unilateral development of oil and gas fields in and around the Spratlys.[2563] Cai Gaoqiang and Zhu Tong wanted their government to select the bilateral dispute wherein it considered its chances of success highest and file with ITLOS or the ICJ to obtain a precedent.[2564] Cai Gaoqiang also thought that ITLOS could generally be used to test adjudication. If China should lose, he opined, the result could still be challenged at the ICJ.[2565]

Concerning the ICJ, Yao Ying put forward the idea to set up a special separate tribunal akin to the one in *Delimitation of the Maritime Boundary in the Gulf of Maine Area (US v Canada)*. Such a separate tribunal was considered to combine 'the advantages of arbitration and adjudication: it allows for both arbitration-like control of composition, and no need of a separate agreement on procedural rules, [while] the court has specialized administrative staff, court clerks, a seat, facilities and judges, all used by the parties for free during the trial procedures of the case, while there is a stronger guarantee of the implementation of the judgment'.[2566]

V.3.3.2.2.6. Full Embrace – Tackling the Issues Head On

Finally, there are those who do not want to first see about system change and Chinese preparedness, who do not want to gradually try out this or that partial engagement. Guan Jianqiang, Pan Junwu and Zhao Jingsong wrote that China should not limit its arsenal, that it needed to be flexible right away, if it wanted to compete with others that do not do so either, that it would have a higher chance for success in the sense of protecting national interests, if it was open to negotiated agreements, arbitration and

2562 Chao 超 Luo 罗, '南海争端解决机制法律框架初探' (A First Inquiry into Mechanisms under a Legal Framework to Solve the South China Sea Dispute) (2011) 29 (2) *Taiyuan Ligong Daxue Xuebao* 11, 11–12; Junwu Pan, 'Dissecting compulsory dispute settlement' (n 2360) 199–200 [Chinese].

2563 Ligang Zou, 'The South China Sea Issue' (n 2401) 160–161 [Chinese].

2564 Cai Gaoqiang (n 2535) 41; Tong Zhu (n 2535) 188.

2565 Cai Gaoqiang (n 2535).

2566 Ying Yao, 'Exploring Judicial Methods' (n 2288) 33–34 [Chinese] (translation by this author).

adjudication. This course should still be pursued, even though the outcome of adjudication was deemed (as in aforementioned criticism) somewhat unpredictable.[2567] Cai Gaoqiang and Xu Xu already described such a mixed, flexible approach as 'normal' among the world's states.[2568] Zhao Jingsong expected that Chinese reservations against compulsory dispute resolution clauses were going to recede,[2569] and Huang Deming and Zhang Cheng wanted to see the ICJ accepted as a supplementary means for continental shelf delimitation.[2570]

If only particular disputes are discussed, openness to judicial solutions grows. The professors interviewed for this study judged the territorial disputes with India regarding Aksai Chin and Arunachal Pradesh easier to resolve. According to them Chinese international lawyers would have less trouble arguing these cases, and the outcome in these proceedings was more predictable than in such involving the law of the sea. Three interviewees – still reminding of the need to properly prepare, but much less emphatically – were willing to consider a rather short- to medium-term submission of these disputes to any judicial mechanism including the ICJ.[2571]

Regarding the East China Sea, where willingness to engage judicial mechanisms is greater also on account of the PRC's weaker position, projections as to a hypothetical case's outcome are already made. Yao Ying ventured that the ICJ would likely draw a single line for EEZ and continental shelf, would surely take a median line as its starting point, but would then consider coastal length and geographical features. The latter point refers to the Okinawa Trough, which in continental shelf delimitation could, in line with the natural prolongation principle, deliver a border more favorable to China than the median line. In any case, Yao maintained, the Court could not possibly deliver a result that was worse than the status quo, wherein Japan controls the Diaoyu/Senkaku Islands and oil and gas exploration in the East China Sea is largely hampered.[2572]

This readiness to accept a final decision that is less than ideal, because it is still an improvement to the status quo, comports with the described

2567 Guan Jianqiang, 'Inquiry of Methods' (n 2401) 77, 81–83 [Chinese]; Junwu Pan, 'Analyzing International Dispute Settlement' (n 2286) 120 [Chinese]; Jingsong Zhao (n 2286) 102.
2568 Cai and Xu (n 2325) 47.
2569 Jingsong Zhao (n 2286) 102.
2570 Huang and Zhang (n 2286) 171.
2571 Author's interviews in Wuhan, Xiamen and Singapore, June 2013.
2572 Ying Yao, 'Exploring Judicial Methods' (n 2288) 24, 33 [Chinese].

overall return of a pragmatic attitude in China's dealings with international law and its institutions in general.[2573]

This is also reflected in Huang Yao and Liao Xuexia's analysis of ITLOS' decision in *Gulf of Bengal*. The authors criticized several points, such as the tribunal allegedly going against ICJ practice on the importance of islands and natural prolongation, and doubt its jurisdiction for outer continental shelf delimitation. However, they subsequently conceded that 'from the point of view of practical results' the decision was 'fair', ended the countries' dispute as it found both sides' acceptance, and might also spur the Continental Shelf Commission to better perform its function.[2574]

Summing up these deliberations, which show that a shift in discourse is in progress, Zhao Haifeng noted that '[t]hinking of China's constantly developing domestic rule of law, the daily internationalization of training, the fact that more and more international judges are from China, the accumulation of international judicial dispute settlement experience being richer by the day, and especially the growth of China's self-confidence in facing the world's other states and peoples and consistent actions to protect the international rule of law, as well as other factors, a more striking change in China's attitude towards international adjudication is entirely possible'.[2575] In addition, Han Liyu underlined, China already participates in the ICJ's work, has a judge and further citizens fulfilling other functions there. Moreover, as it is part of integrating further into the international system and in line with the PRC's going-out strategy, 'one can trust that following a further broadening of China's participation in international affairs, China might submit certain disputes to the ICJ for resolution'.[2576]

What can be likened to China's identity change in investment law adds to this list of arguments for an already ongoing shift. Within the latter field of law it was from an investor host state to an investor home state, while in the law of the sea the PRC is moving from a developing coastal state to a technologically-advanced state interested in exploiting resources much further afield. Such has been discussed eg by Huang Deming and Zhang Cheng regarding the question of how the Arctic legal regime

2573 See Chapter III.2.2.5.

2574 *Delimitation of the Maritime Boundary in the Bay of Bengal* (Bangladesh v Myanmar) (n 1486); Huang and Liao, 'New Developments in International Maritime Boundary Delimitation' (n 2294) 92 [Chinese].

2575 Haifeng Zhao (n 1132) 12 (translation by this author).

2576 Liyu Han, 'The Case Law Applied' (n 1983) 132 [Chinese] (translation by this author).

should be further developed and what China's pertinent interests are.[2577] Deliberations of this nature are linked with the solidifying free trade leanings discussed in the preceding chapter, and generally growing notions of power projection. Mutually-reinforcing trends might eventually lead the Chinese government to alter its positions on the rights associated with EEZ and continental shelf, particularly concerning free passage, military use and resource exploitation.

V.3.4. Preliminary Conclusions

The discourse among Chinese international lawyers from 2002 to 2018 on the question of engagement with ICJ, ITLOS and arbitral tribunals addressing law of the sea and territorial matters lends itself less to chronological phases than that on engagement with WTO DSM and international investment arbitration. Moreover, it does not come with the 'finality' of the latter, as there has not yet been any participation in ICJ or ITLOS proceedings.

Nonetheless, thorough re-evaluation of the institutions compared with prior decades can be discerned. Chinese scholars grant the ICJ to have changed quite positively in both its composition – as developing states and China in particular are increasingly well represented at the Court through its citizens – and its practice. On the latter point, the legal principles developed – specifically the equitability and natural prolongation principles, and the 'fair' decisions taken, especially since *Nicaragua v. United States* – are lauded and seen as a shift in the right direction.[2578] Increasingly, the ICJ is deemed a guarantor of effective and peaceful dispute resolution in an international order, which to uphold the PRC as a new great power has both a big interest and responsibility.

The overall positive evaluation of the features of ICJ and ITLOS and tone in speaking about them are becoming more akin to those regarding the WTO DSM and ICSID. Similar to the change in China's interests and identity as outward investment flows come to rival inward investment flows, increasing financial and technological capabilities lead to interest in maritime resources worldwide rivaling interest in resources close to home, and interest in power projection further afield rivaling defensive interests along the borders. While attitudes have grown somewhat more sober since

2577 Huang and Zhang (n 2286) 161.

2578 *Military and Paramilitary Activities in and against Nicaragua* (n 193).

2014, overall the ICJ has still been portrayed as laudably working towards both equitability and legal predictability. Even Annex VII UNCLOS arbitrations between other states such as the *Bay of Bengal Maritime Boundary Arbitration* have been pragmatically analyzed for what could (eg trend reversal on single maritime boundaries) and could not (eg definition of low-tide elevations) be used to further China's position. Harshly negative views of the work of the arbitrators in *Philippines v China* are generally focused on the individual tribunal, and not extended to the option or arbitrating such matters, or to the ITLOS or ICJ.

Points of criticism are familiar from analyses of dispute resolution mechanisms in economic matters and their legal bases. Authors mainly point to alleged ambiguities, inconsistencies in case law, a lack of legal certainty and predictability, as well as supposed remnants of bias in favor of Western developed states. On legal uncertainty and UNCLOS, implementation agreements are lauded, but the convention's nature as a product of compromise taken to mean that ambiguity had to be built in. Further development is seen as necessary also on account of perceived new challenges. However, interestingly, analyses of the strongly overwhelming focal issue of debates in the years since 2014 – the South China Sea arbitration (*Philippines v China*) – never concede that the arbitrators in this case probably did more to address uncertainty (eg on island status, archipelagic status, historic rights) than any other recent tribunal. On a supposed anti-Chinese bias, *Philippines v China* is taken as evidence, although it is never convincingly explained why. References are made to the Japanese citizen Shunji Yanai being involved in arbitrator selection as then-ITLOS president, and supposed double standards in evidence interpretation, while the fact that China could have simply participated in the proceedings to avoid the former and address the latter was ignored. In later articles, the discussion of implementation issues shows an ongoing change in priorities.

Policies recommended by the scholars within the scope of this study are those that strongly mirror preparatory phases before (active) engagement with the WTO DSM and international investment arbitration.

First, the government is exhorted to strengthen in any way possible research of pertinent law, teaching on the subjects at academic institutions (eg explicitly building law of the sea litigation capacity), training of officials, and cooperation between academia and authorities, while collecting all possible evidence of potential court cases, comporting in line with legal principles such as effective control, improving legislative work and clarifying claims, as well as mobilizing public opinion. Regarding clarifying China's claims, an interesting shift has been taking place since the awards in

Philippines v China. Authors have started to de-emphasize the nine-dash line, and pivot towards arguments building on supposed 'island groups,' ie archipelagos. While this has been termed a more 'law-based approach,' UNCLOS norms defining 'archipelago' are still being ignored.

Second, experts call on their government to be part of all reform negotiations, and lobby for such on certain points, and to increase its 'discursive power' and influence wherever it can. Efforts are recommended to go beyond Chinese scholars' and judges' work at the ILC, ICJ and ITLOS, and to – inter alia – include a strategic and patiently sustained diplomatic push for a supposedly needed 'next step' in law of the sea development. In justifying the need for reforms, authors refer to new challenges like global warming – supposedly, many 'islands' will become 'rocks'. Chinese scholars overwhelmingly do not want their government to 'denounce' UNCLOS (Article 317), considering benefits to clearly outweigh drawbacks. Instead, Chinese positions are to gain influence by affecting state practice and case law, as well as potentially the establishment of UNCLOS review committees, and adoption of implementation (eg on military activities in the EEZ), supplementary or regional agreements. Reforms should in Chinese scholars' eyes address – inter alia – island status, archipelago status, and bringing EEZ and continental shelf norms in line with supposed customary international law-based non-sovereign historic rights. At the same time, the awards in the *South China Sea Arbitration* are to be undermined diplomatically as well, by collecting explicitly supportive declarations of a majority of UNCLOS parties, and potentially even achieving an two-thirds majority UNGA resolution on an 'important question'.

On actual engagement caution still dominates, but the majority of Chinese international lawyers had explicitly voiced openness to submitting law of the sea and territorial disputes to international adjudication at some point in the future, before debates on this issue were streamlined to support the government's position starting in 2014. It is argued here that the current phase of (self-)enforced homogeneity and conformity is a temporary one, that it is not in line with scholars' previous work, and that previously ongoing trends in their recommendations will resurface and further develop as they impact the policy choices of the next leadership generation. Tellingly, Chinese international lawyers have repeatedly written that 1) sovereignty is relative in a time where 2) no state can resist the judicialization of international relations, that 3) acquiring the image of a supporter of international law is important, and that 4) the manner of engagement depends on the level of systemic power. This belies the point that any similarities with discussions on economic disputes can be discarded, due to a supposed categorical rejection of judicial solutions to such sensitive matters. While this only concerns the *influential elite* of Chinese international law experts, the same process preceded the change of heart in the Chinese government concerning trade and investment disputes. Such a development could very well be echoed in this field.

As repeatedly highlighted by scholars interviewed for this book, this is only a matter of time and influence. As soon as the PRC perceives itself to have obtained a position of sufficient influence on the international (legal) system, and otherwise well prepared – efforts are ongoing and intense – and negotiations fail, a growing number of scholars recommend and expect that third-party solutions will be approached. The preferred policy then is to be the same as with trade and investment disputes, cautious and gradual engagement at first, trying out things such as advisory opinions, picking out certain cases where the chances for success are considered high, choosing a mechanism deemed most promising first, and only then would a comparative proliferation of cases be envisioned. One could argue that this process has already begun with the Chinese government's participation in advisory proceedings initiated by others at the ICJ and ITLOS, as well as its comments on other states' CLCS submissions and own partial CLCS submission (2012). The Philippines' notification in the *South China Sea Arbitration*, then, merely came too early in the process. Chinese scholars did not perceive their country to be ready yet, and would not allow the timetable to be forced. This does not mean that debate patterns throughout the research period do not still mirror those on trade and investment matters, nor that the long-term strategy recommended has changed.

In line with the 'skeptical pragmatism' first developed during China's initial encounter with modern Western international law in late Imperial times, China is open to eventually using all tools at its disposal in the international legal system. The time of categorical rejection of the jurisdiction of international tribunals even in the most sensitive of issues, territory, is over. When this author pressed interviewees for an approximation concerning whether they were thinking of the short, medium or long term when talking about participating in ITLOS and ICJ proceedings, several did not blink or allude to a distant future: the 2020s seemed about right.[2579]

2579 Author's interviews with scholars of Wuhan and Xiamen universities in June and September 2013.

VI. Conclusion – China's Behavior in International Adjudication

VI.1. Imperatives of Greatness – of What 'Has to Be Done'

This study has demonstrated that extensive debates among Chinese international law scholars preceded and informed a series of steps towards gradual PRC engagement with international adjudication.[2580] Modes of engagement have been continually refined and adjusted, with academic debates addressing both very technical micro-level issues and broad questions of overall guidance and 'mission.'

Indeed, before President Xi Jinping arrived at his 2017 call for China to 'guide' global governance that was noted at the beginning of this book,[2581] influential Chinese international law scholars had tightly connected the country's re-emergence as a great power with influence on the international legal order.

Drawing historical comparisons, He Zhipeng argued that influence on and high-level performance within international law was a clear mark of every modern great power and the most important aspect of what he defines as 'soft power.' Citing – inter alia – the Netherlands, Grotius and freedom of the seas, the British Imperial system and colonialism, as well as the post-WWII system of international rules and organizations established under US-leadership, he considered the latter the most effective and also cheapest system of leadership and one for China to learn from. Only the reduction in threat perceptions and long-term influence achieved by 'international law powers' would make China a 'genuine' power.[2582] This chimes with Yi Xianhe's notion that China will not be able to consolidate its successes in the economic and political realm, if it does not also think and act as a 'leader country' in international law.[2583]

2580 See Chapters IV and V.

2581 See Chapter I.1.

2582 Zhipeng He, 'Becoming a Great Power in International Law' (n 2) 148–150, 151, 153, 154. On the importance of both skillful use of and compliance with international law for crucial soft power gains see also Han Yichou, 'Study on China's Strategy' (n 2007) 123–136.

2583 Yuefeng Qi (n 2).

Among supposed preconditions for becoming an 'international law power,' one can find improving international law education, building a strong talent pool of theorists and practitioners, and developing one's own international law theories. Practical abilities would have to be sufficiently strong for active engagement in every field of international law – including maritime and territorial delimitation – and not only in law making, but also in adjudication. Such engagement in international adjudication, in turn, would be necessary to maintain the image of a 'responsible,' 'rule of law power'; and image something crucial in times of global public opinion pressures.[2584]

China's approach could be cautious but it had to be active, it could include refusals to take part in individual cases at certain points in time (ie the South China Sea arbitration) but needed to include a steady move towards more participation – considered clearly preferable to 'out-of-court,' 'indirect,' 'lagging' responses.[2585] This was to say that a nation's life was long; international law behavior creating a good image and keeping cooperation and development opportunities open was key, while the importance of individual cases should not be overestimated.[2586] Yi maintained that China should adopt a dialectical view on international adjudication. Indeed, several WTO cases were lost, but the Chinese economy soared. Even with disputes on territorial or maritime delimitation at the ICJ – eg *Cameroon v Nigeria* – a country may lose on one issue and win on another, while a 'fair' outcome would still be relatively likely. Expectations would have to be realistic, the outlook mature.[2587]

Exclusive reliance on political negotiations and language alone has been deemed problematic – from trade to territorial disputes – in times of an increasingly legalized and judicialized international society. All other means, from political to economic to military, have been classified as mere tempo-

2584 See Zhipeng He, 'Becoming a Great Power in International Law' (n 2) 151; Zhipeng 志鹏 He 何, '国际司法的中国立场' (China's position in international justice) [2016] (2) *Fashang Yanjiu* 45, 52–53.

2585 Zhipeng He, 'China's position in international justice' (n 2584) 53.

2586 Zhipeng 志鹏 He 何, '开放发展与国际法: 风险及应对' (Open Development and International Law: Risks and Countermeasures) (2017) 35 (3) *Zhengfa Luntan* 18–19: 'countries can win battle after battle and still lose wars'. A positive example was seen in how the US and the British Empire handled disputes in the late 19th century *Alabama Claims Arbitration*.

2587 *Land and Maritime Boundary between Cameroon and Nigeria (Cameroon v Nigeria: Equatorial Guinea intervening)* (Judgment) [2002] ICJ Rep 303; Yuefeng Qi (n 2).

rary tools. Meanwhile, making 'full use' of international law, working towards reform from within through norm creation and interpretation, and attaining powers of persuasion, have been judged best suited to protect China's interests in the long term.[2588] While openness and engagement would expose it to risks, such could be reduced through preparation and experience, while risks attached to rejecting engagement were systemic and much harder to overcome.[2589]

VI.2. China and International Adjudication – Different Speeds, Same Direction

This study claims that the PRC as an actor in international adjudication is best understood as a skeptical pragmatist on a historical mission. China has to become a great power again. For that to be realized and consolidated, China has to become a 'leader country' in international law. Progressively engaging more with international adjudication is part and parcel of that. The system has to be engaged as it is and shaped from within. All tools are to be used. At the same time, the Chinese scholarly community and political leadership take pitfalls, commensurate preparation and parallel legislative negotiations to prepare the ground extremely seriously. Engagement will not be rushed. This is a gradual process. Proper time is taken, and Beijing will only take the next step when it feels ready or that it has no choice.

VI.2.1. Round One – Trade Law

This century's first decade saw the PRC submit to international adjudication for the first time. Trade law was first. China joined the WTO, thus recognized the jurisdiction of the WTO DSM, and started to participate in an inflationary number of proceedings.

This was something qualitatively new for the PRC. It showed commitment to and faith in international law to a degree that let it compromise on the 'absoluteness' of sovereignty.[2590] It is a sea change that references to

2588 See Chapter V. See also Zhipeng He, 'Open Development and International Law' (n 2586) 18–19, 24.

2589 Zhipeng He, 'Open Development and International Law' (n 2586) 21–24.

2590 See also eg MD Harpaz, 'Sense and Sensibilities of China and WTO Dispute Settlement' (2010) 44 *Journal of World Trade* 1155, 1156.

supporting norms of international law are now considered legitimate arguments in policy debates.[2591] Some have even diagnosed a new 'aggressive legalism' in East Asia overall (PRC, Japan and Republic of Korea).[2592]

However, for the first five years in the WTO, China remained a rather passive litigant, aimed at finding mutually-agreed solutions where possible ('rule-taker' phase 2001–2006).[2593] Meanwhile, Beijing heeded the two main recommendations by its scholarly community: build litigation capacity and gain influence on legal development.[2594] Capacity building entailed domestic legislative and institutional reforms, incentivizing research, training and coordination between all relevant domestic actors, and garnering experience through frequent third-party participation. Patiently building influence meant taking a more prominent role in the Doha Round (and when it later *de facto* ended, joining or (co-)initiating new multi- and plurilateral negotiations), keeping reform negotiations perpetually ongoing, securing prominent positions for Chinese citizens (eg as AB members and deputies to the WTO director-general), and trusting in the fact and consequences of China's rise in relative power.[2595]

Scholars then considered China ready for, and an expansion of experience gathering to require, ending the focus on settlements.[2596] The PRC indeed began to fight complaints all of the way to the AB and for the first time accepted defeat in international adjudication ('rule-shaker' phase 2006–2008).[2597] Soon enough, the next step was taken, and the government was encouraged to file more complaints itself, and to use the DSM to shape interpretations (especially of China's Accession Protocol) and legal development in the absence of progress in the Doha Round ('rule-maker' phase since 2008).[2598] Views of the mechanism became more whole-heartedly positive, no longer describing membership as something forced upon China, while concerns about enforcement betrayed greater confidence.[2599]

2591 See also Clarke (n 1432) 564.

2592 See eg Saadia Pekkanen, 'The Socialization of China, Japan and Korea (CJK) in International Economic Law: Assessment and Implications' (2010) 104 *Proceedings of the ASIL Annual Meeting* 529.

2593 See Chapter IV.2.2.2.1.

2594 See Chapter V.2.1.3.1.

2595 See also Chapters IV.2.2.1 and IV.2.2.2.4.6.

2596 See Chapter V.2.1.3.2.

2597 See Chapter IV.2.2.2.2.

2598 See Chapters IV.2.2.2.3 and V.2.1.3.2.

2599 See Chapter V.2.1.1.

Cases duly proliferated, China was ever faster to levy complaints when supposed grounds arose, and it stayed the course even when basic assumptions about the trade law system were challenged in the late 2010s. The PRC government and Chinese international lawyers had qualified most complaints about the WTO system with a hopeful view to the year 2016, when a fifteen-year deadline in paragraph 15 (d) of China's Accession Protocol would kick in, and alternative anti-dumping price calculation methodologies would have to be dropped (ie so-called 'non-market economy'-treatment would end). This was seen as a grand caesura, whereafter, Chinese trust in the system would grow further, and case statistics would become more balanced. When the US and EU viewed the supposed deadline differently – also when the US took protectionist steps under the Trump administration from 2017 – China reacted within the system and filed further complaints.[2600] What is more, Chinese scholars interviewed for this study unequivocally stated that China should remain patient and stay the course even if these cases should be lost. Much of the status quo was to now be protected in line with Chinese interests, the AB defended against US attacks, and limited and gradual reforms to be pursued without excessive haste.[2601]

VI.2.2. Round Two – Investment Law

In a second step, the PRC and its companies started to engage in investment arbitration in the 2010s, whereas the number of relevant disputes only rose gradually.

This had been preceded by China agreeing to sign BITs since 1982 ('first generation' BITs), to include the option of arbitration at ICSID from 1990 ('second generation'), and to allow for investment arbitration for all investment disputes instead of just such about the amount of compensation for expropriation from 1998 ('third generation'). From 2008, PRC treaty practice changed further, with 'Americanization' in the sense of – inter alia – including much more detailed provisions or even separate sections on dispute settlement, and further addressing market access ('fourth generation').[2602]

2600 Para 15 (d) Accession Protocol; See Chapter IV.2.2.2.3.8.
2601 See also Chapters V.2.1.3.1.2 and V.2.1.3.2.2.
2602 See Chapter IV.2.1.2.

China's very active conclusion of BITs contrasts strongly with its scarce and only recent engagement in investment arbitration. In the first years of this book's research period, China still refrained from actual engagement. This was in line with a Chinese scholarly discourse less unequivocally positive on judicial mechanisms in this field of law. Central recommendations, meanwhile, to focus on capacity building and gaining influence on legal development, were the same as and deemed just as important as in trade law. Despite an early consensus for liberal BITs, caution was urged on actual participation in arbitration, and attempts to convince foreign investors to refrain from that option.[2603]

From 2007 to 2018, Chinese investors initiated five arbitrations – the first Mainland investor in 2010 – and foreign investors filed three cases against China since 2011. Only five awards have been rendered, with the respective three 'firsts' in 2011, 2015 and 2017.[2604] The caseload has been growing very slowly, while Chinese international lawyers called upon Beijing to assiduously learn the lessons from every case and adapt the country's BITs to avoid supposed surprises and optimize outcomes. At the same time, although Beijing criticized the first awards, discourse turned strongly in favor of participation.[2605]

Over the research period, the PRC underwent a change in identity from 'host state' to 'home state' that was visible in scholarly discourse. Debates shifted from generalized notions of excessive investor rights and a supposed 'legitimacy crisis' in investment law to sober and concrete BIT reform proposals, mostly in line with an 'American' model deemed more amenable to balancing investor rights with space for public interest measures: 'textual precision,' more extensive and narrowed-down ISDS provisions, clearer transition, joint interpretation, and general exception clauses. Some authors even recommended lobbying developing nations to join the ICSID Convention, and mainly using BITs to secure better market access and protection for Chinese investors.[2606]

With the goal of gaining a stronger voice on 'balanced' legal development, Chinese scholars recommended 1) active participation in arbitration, 2) retracting China's Article 25 (4) ICSID Convention notification, as well as 3) making proactive use of high-profile bilateral negotiations (eg on the CAI with the EU) and multilateral processes (eg G20 working groups

2603 See Chapter V.2.2.3.1.
2604 See Chapter IV.2.1.3.
2605 See Chapter V.2.2.3.2.
2606 See Chapters V.2.2.2 and V.2.2.3.2.

and 'Guiding Principles').[2607] Influence should be gained on the future of ISDS, but also substantive clauses, whereas Beijing is urged to go with, and influence from within, trends – inter alia – regarding labor and environmental provisions, the role of NGOs and amicus curiae briefs. Change is considered more likely, both because developed states adjusted positions after experiencing the respondent state role,[2608] and because developing states are more frequently in the capital-exporting role.[2609]

VI.2.3. Round Three – Law of the Sea and Territorial Disputes

The 2020s might very well see China submitting to international adjudication in more politically sensitive matters: law of the sea disputes, including on maritime delimitation, and maybe even territorial disputes. Scholarly discourse shows parallel patterns with such on trade and investment law, and crucial steps in *de facto* participation have been taken since 2008: advisory proceedings at the ICJ and ITLOS, as well as CLCS proceedings on continental shelf delimitation.

Through its ratification of UNCLOS, and despite its later Article 298 declaration, the PRC accepted a certain scope of compulsory dispute settlement for law of the sea matters in 1996. China also for the first time submitted comments in advisory proceedings starting in 2009, both at the ICJ (*Kosovo*, 2009; *Chagos*, 2018) and ITLOS (*Activities in the Area*, 2010; *Sub-Regional Fisheries Commission*, 2013). Moreover, it commented on submissions to the CLCS (Japan, 2008; Vietnam, 2009; Vietnam and Malaysia, 2009), and itself made a partial submission (2012).[2610] While China was not yet ready to participate in contentious proceedings initiated by the Philippines – ie the Annex VII UNCLOS *South China Sea Arbitration*, 2013–2016 – participation in the *Chagos* advisory proceedings demonstrated that the PRC intends to continue on its path of gradual engagement.[2611]

2607 Art 25 (4) ICSID Convention; OECD, 'G20 Guiding Principles' (n 2248).

2608 On changes to international investment treaty practices being likely as 'world economic power relationships' change, as well as 'Western capital exporters' perhaps becoming more defensive in interpretation methodology when faced with 'new economic powers,' see also Wälde, 'Interpreting Investment Treaties' (n 844) 780.

2609 See Chapter V.2.2.3.2.

2610 See Chapter IV.3.3.

2611 See Chapters IV.3.3. and IV.3.4.

Chinese scholars have, within the research period of this study, lauded the ICJ for having changed for the better, and painted a largely positive picture of the work, decisions rendered, and principles developed both by the Court and ITLOS. Representation of developing states, and particularly China, through their citizens has been important.[2612] Harsh criticism of *Philippines v China* has generally been restricted to the tribunal in question.[2613]

Policy recommendations in many ways mirror patterns in trade and investment law in early phases of or before actual participation: increase law of the sea litigation capacity for potential future cases (and collect evidence), improve research, teaching and training, and build cooperation between academia and officials. Authors also adapted arguments after *Philippines v China* in recognition of what had failed to convince (ie de-emphasizing the 'nine-dash line' and historic rights). In a second key overlap, Chinese international lawyers counsel a perpetual reform push supported by efforts to increase China's 'discursive power.' This should entail influence and emphasis on certain state practice – particularly such contravening decisions in *Philippines v China* – and potentially also two-thirds majority UNGA resolutions on 'important questions'. New challenges should be underlined (eg through climate change), and UNCLOS review committees, further implementation, supplementary or regional agreements lobbied for (eg on the definition of 'islands' and 'archipelagos', historic rights, or military activities in the EEZ).[2614]

On actual participation in contentious proceedings caution mostly prevailed in Chinese academic debates, as was the case for a good while on investment law. Nonetheless, a very broad spectrum of opinions unfolded on law of the sea and even territorial issues. Some went as far as recommending immediate full engagement with ITLOS and ICJ. Several (mostly political) developments led to (self-)enforced homogeneous support for the government line of categorical rejection after 2013.[2615] However, it is unlikely that this would suddenly represent the cognitive beliefs of all Mainland Chinese international lawyers. During interviews conducted for this study, the clearly predominant position was that the PRC should be open to submitting law of the sea and territorial disputes to international adjudication at some point in the future. This was again linked both to levels of

2612 See Chapter V.3.1.
2613 See Chapter V.3.2.2.
2614 See Chapter V.3.3.1.
2615 See Chapter II.3.1.4.3.

China's preparedness and of systemic influence and power. Several interviewed professors were willing to approximate a date, namely during the 2020s.[2616]

VI.3. Comparison and Outlook

VI.3.1. A Chinese Path – Not Your Ordinary BRIC

On its way towards becoming a 'leader country' in international law and great power overall, China will closely monitor – inter alia – other large powers' practice in international adjudication. However, importantly, BRICS partners and other large emerging economies are not necessarily indicative of the steps that the Chinese government will take.

Most similarities can be found in trade law, where China has learned and taken heart from Brazil and India's experience and successes. It has sought to emulate aspects of their previous strategies to improve litigation capacity and tactics, as well as joining them in core influence groups in WTO reform negotiations. Only the recently-acceded Russia and disengaged South Africa are less relevant. What sets the PRC most clearly apart – next to its forced focus on its Accession Protocol and lop-sided DSM statistics as a frequent respondent – is its enormous size as a trade power and grand overall ambitions. China has escalated DSM participation in a more linear way than others, filing complaints much more frequently in its most recent phase of engagement, and strategically refraining from filing complaints against anyone other than the US or EU.[2617]

In investment law, China has acted quite differently compared with the other BRICS. It developed the first and largest treaty network, and took the longest time to then actually participate in investment arbitration, demonstrating its dedication to caution and preparedness. Most importantly, China's ambition and convictions regarding the importance of international law engagement have not allow it to join the other BRICS states' restrictive turn over the last decade. This is despite what Chinese scholars and the government in Beijing perceived as several unfortunate case law developments (see eg the debates about *Tza Yap Shum* and *Ping An*). South Africa started to unilaterally terminate its BITs in 2012, India's new Model BIT 2015 severely restricts access to investment arbitration,

2616 See Chapter V.3.3.2.
2617 See Chapter IV.2.2.2.4.

Russia's 2016 guidelines on investment treaties – inter alia – allow for state party consultations that can suspend an ongoing arbitration, and Brazil took investment arbitration out of its treaty drafts to get a first one ratified in 2017. Meanwhile, China has merely recalibrated to gradually shift its BIT practice from the European to the American model.[2618]

On law of the sea and territorial disputes, all BRICS states were reticent to engage, most chose to refuse any participation in at least one contentious case (India: *Pakistani Prisoners of War*; Brazil: *Certain Questions concerning Diplomatic Relations*; Russia: *Arctic Sunrise*), and some also issued diplomatic position papers while proceedings were ongoing in what could be considered indirect participation (India: *Right of Passage*; Russia: *Arctic Sunrise*). China was the last BRICS state to be confronted with contentious proceedings, whereas India and Russia eventually even launched cases themselves (*ICAO Council* and *"Volga"*). Moreover, India has become willing to even settle maritime boundary delimitation through international adjudication (*Bay of Bengal*). Discourse patterns among the *influential elite* of China's international law scholars indicate that the PRC is likely to gradually move from Brazil and South Africa (ie categorical rejection) to Russia (ie cautious and ambivalent testing of the waters) to India (ie more substantial engagement).[2619]

VI.3.2. The Way Forward – Engaging to Rise

This book submits that a common mindset and common concern underlie China's academic discourse and government approach to international adjudication. A 'skeptical pragmatism' with roots in late Imperial times springs from an *image* of international law dominated by two elements: 'something to be wary of' and 'something that needs to be studied and used in China's favor.' This was partly pushed aside in the Republican period in favor of fuller engagement, and in the PRC's first 30 years in favor of outright rejection. Thereafter, the country reverted to a deliberate, cautious engagement with different elements of the international legal system. Scholars recommend comprehensive preparation, pressing for reforms and building influence, and when the time is deemed right, the utilization of all legal tools at the country's disposal.

2618 See Chapter IV.2.1.2.6.

2619 See Chapter IV.3.5.

The dominant concern is to act in line with the 'national interest,' whereas several (often explicit) axioms underlying Chinese authors' work need to be noted. First, Chinese state behavior (and that of other states) in matters of international law should be in line with and is indeed guided by national interests. Second, China's overarching national interest is increasing its relative power within the international system, ie regaining the status of a world power. Third, both economic growth and the 'soft power' that comes from being perceived as 'responsible' contribute to greater relative power. Fourth, maximum flexibility regarding available tools positions a state to best protect its national interests. Fifth, only after preparing oneself, and to a degree the respective tools, can they be sensibly used. Sixth, when the state changes (and its position in the international system does), the tools it should use also change. Accordingly, the prism through which Chinese international lawyers view the subject of this book is how their country should engage with international adjudication to best increase its relative power.

Several strong indications point to the arc on participation bending further towards a fuller usage of international adjudication 'tools.' China is likely to undergo a further economic and technological rise, and concomitant identity shifts as an actor in international relations and international law. Participation in international adjudication is viewed as a key element in becoming an 'international law power,' which in turn is considered central to 'soft power' increases without which the PRC will not be able to attain (much less consolidate) great power status.

Chinese scholars are largely optimistic on the PRC's efforts regarding preparedness and institutional influence; they remain so even after continuing NME treatment in trade law post-2016, and the *South China Sea Arbitration*. Many have maintained that China, also concretely, has more to gain from participation in international adjudication, including protecting newly-ballooning outward investment flows and Chinese IP interests, as well as territorial and maritime border interests vis-à-vis India and Japan.[2620] Authors decidedly do not approach law of the sea and territorial disputes with a fundamentally different mindset – some likely temporary (self-)censorship post-2013 notwithstanding – and discursive patterns are instead in many ways similar to such on trade and investment law.

Some scholars have cautioned against 'worshipping sovereignty' and argued that China has profited more from globalization than anyone

2620 See eg Zhipeng He, 'Open Development and International Law' (n 2586) 16, 28.

else,[2621] while noting that a stable international economic law system had also long been a critical interest of the US.[2622] More 'effective participation' also beyond economic matters is called for, as a sine qua non for gaining influence on normative developments – this includes being less constricted at the ICJ (eg submitting more extensive and less theoretical written comments in advisory proceedings as well as comments on other states' statements).[2623] Next to a proliferation of cases in trade and investment law, a broader spectrum of engagement is to be expected.

In terms of what European and like-minded governments could and should do in response to the described phenomena, the first answer is probably: wait. They should be patient and trust that engagement will improve wherever the stakes in the system rise. Second, they should be open to and even enable a stronger Chinese physical representation at judicial mechanisms, as well as to certain concrete compromises with China in norm interpretation and future legal development, in order to increase trust and a feeling of 'ownership.' Finally, they should refrain from undermining the international legal order themselves, and strengthen coalition building and cohesion around positions they want to defend or newly pursue. Changes driven by the PRC should then remain incremental and such driven by the West should remain possible. If such seemingly simple advice is heeded, the PRC should continue to follow its long-standing self-defined national interest and approach to optimally pursue it, by gradually broadening engagement with international adjudication. This would mean further integration with an international legal order that Beijing would find it increasingly difficult to describe as anything other than China's as well.

2621 Rudan 儒丹 Chen 陈, '解开"囚徒困境"的国际经济法律制度——博弈论方法和中国问题视角' (Resolving "Prisoner's Dilemma" in International Economic Legal System: A Game Theory Analysis from China's Perspective) (2014) 34 (1) *Faxue Yanjiu* 120, 125.

2622 Zhiyun 志云 Liu 刘, '国家利益的层次分析与国家在 国际法上的行动选择' (Analytic Hierarchy of National Interest and Nation's Action Selection on International Law) (2015) 37 (1) *Xiandai Faxue* 139, 143.

2623 Jie Song, 'Evaluating the Effectiveness of China's Participation in International Legal Matters: Lessons from China's Practice in the International Law Commission and the International Court of Justice' (2017) 15 (2) *China: An International Journal* 144, 161, 163.

References

Abbott KW, 'International Relations Theory, International Law, and the Regime Governing Atrocities in Internal Conflicts' (1999) 93 AJIL 361.

—— 'Modern International Relations Theory: A Prospectus for International Lawyers' (2000) 14 *Yale Journal of International Law* 335.

—— and others, 'The Concept of Legalization' (2000) 54 *International Organization* 401.

—— and Snidal D, 'Law, Legalization, and Politics: An Agenda for the Next Generation of IL/IR Scholars', in Dunoff JL and Pollack MA (eds) *Interdisciplinary Perspectives on International Law and International Relations. The State of the Art* (CUP 2013).

Acconci P, 'Most-Favoured Nation Treatment', in Muchlinski P, Ortino F and Schreuer C, *The Oxford Handbook of International Investment Law* (OUP 2008).

Ahl B, *Die Anwendung völkerrechtlicher Verträge in China* (Springer 2009).

—— 'China' in Wolfrum R (ed), *Max Planck Encyclopedia of Public International Law – Volume II* (OUP 2012).

—— 'The Rise of China and International Human Rights Law' (2015) 37 *Human Rights Quarterly* 637.

Ahn D and Messerlin P, '*United States – Anti-Dumping Measures on Certain Shrimp and Diamond Sawblades from China*: never ending zeroing in the WTO?' (2014) 13 *World Trade Review* 267.

—— and Zanardi M, '*China–HP-SSST*: Last Part of Growing Pains?' (2017) 16 *World Trade Review* 159.

Amer R and Schofield CH, 'The Sino-Vietnamese Approach to Managing Border Disputes' (2002) 5 *Maritime Briefings* 29.

Anderson D, 'Peaceful Settlement of Disputes Under UNCLOS', in Barrett J and Barnes R (eds), *Law of the Sea – UNCLOS as a Living Treaty* (The British Institute of International and Comparative Law 2016).

Andreone G, 'The Exclusive Economic Zone', in Rothwell DR and others (eds), *The Oxford Handbook of the Law of the Sea* (OUP 2015).

Asada M, 'Diaoyu/Senkaku Islands' in Wolfrum R (ed), *Max Planck Encyclopedia of Public International Law – Volume III* (OUP 2012).

Attard DJ, Fitzmaurice M and Martínez Guttiérez NA (eds), *The IMLI Manual on International Maritime Law – Volume I: The Law of the Sea* (OUP 2014).

Baldwin DA, 'Power Analysis and World Politics: New Trends Versus Old Tendencies' (1979) 31 *World Politics* 161.

—— 'Interdependence and Power: A Conceptual Analysis' (1980) 34 International *Organization* 471.

Banyan, 'The South China Sea: Troubled Waters' *The Economist* (London, 6 August 2012) <http://www.economist.com/blogs/analects/2012/08/south-china-sea> accessed 1 March 2019.

Bao 包 Yan 艳 and Cui 崔 Riming 日明, '"丝绸之路经济带"框架下中国 – 格鲁吉亚 自由贸易区建设研究' (Studying the Establishment of the China-Georgia Free Trade Area under the Framework of the "The Silk Road Economic Belt") (2017) 45 (1) *Liaoning Daxue Xuebao* 51.

Barkin JS, 'Realist Constructivism', in Morgenthau H, *Politics Among Nations. The Struggle for Power and Peace*. (7th edn, McGraw-Hill 2006).

Barnes R, 'The Continuing Vitality of UNCLOS', in Barrett J and Barnes R (eds), *Law of the Sea – UNCLOS as a Living Treaty* (The British Institute of International and Comparative Law 2016).

Baron D and others, 'ICSID Arbitration Initiated Against China as Negotiations Move Ahead on U.S.-China Bilateral Investment Treaty' (*The National Law Review*, 12 December 2014) <http://www.natlawreview.com/article/icsid-arbitration-initiated-against-china-negotiations-move-ahead-us-china-bilateral> (accessed 30 March 2019).

Baroncini E, 'The Applicability of GATT Article XX to China's WTO Accession Protocol in the Appellate Body Report of the China-Raw Materials Case: suggestions for a different interpretive approach' (2013) 1 (3–4) *China-EU Law Journal* 1.

Barrett J, 'The UN Convention on the Law of the Sea: A "Living" Treaty?' in Barrett J and Barnes R (eds), *Law of the Sea – UNCLOS as a Living Treaty* (The British Institute of International and Comparative Law 2016).

—— and Barnes R (eds), *Law of the Sea – UNCLOS as a Living Treaty* (The British Institute of International and Comparative Law 2016).

Bath V, 'Chinese Companies and Outbound Investment: The Balance between Domestic and International Concerns', in Toohey L, Picker CB and Greenacre J (eds), *China in the International Economic Order: New Directions and Changing Paradigms* (CUP 2015).

—— and Nottage LR, 'Foreign Investment and Dispute Resolution Law and Practice in Asia: An Overview', in Bath V and Nottage LR, *Foreign Investment and Dispute Resolution Law and Practice in Asia* (Routledge 2011).

Bazrafkan A, 'The (R)evolution of Indian model bilateral investment treaty: escaping liability without mitigating risks' (2016) 7 *Jindal Global Law Review* 245.

Beckman R, 'South China Sea: Worsening Dispute or Growing Clarity in Claims?' *RSIS Commentaries no 90* (Singapore, 16 August 2010) <https://cil.nus.edu.sg/publication/south-china-sea-worsening-dispute-or-growing-clarity-in-claims/> accessed 15 March 2019.

Berger A, 'The Politics of China's Investment Treaty-Making Program', in Broude T, Busch ML and Porges A (eds), *The Politics of International Economic Law* (CUP 2011).

—— 'Hesitant Embrace: China's Recent Approach to International Investment Rule-Making' (2015) 16 *Journal of World Investment and Trade* 843.

Bianchi A, *International Law Theories – An Inquiry into Different Ways of Thinking* (OUP 2016).

Bin Liang, *The changing Chinese legal system, 1978-present: centralization of power and rationalization of the legal system* (Routledge 2008).

Bjorklund AK, 'National Treatment', in Reinisch A (ed), *Standards of Investment Protection* (OUP 2008).

—— 'Waiver of Local Remedies and Limitation Periods', in Kinnear M and others (eds), *Building International Investment Law – The First 50 Years of ICSID* (Kluwer Law International 2016).

Blanchard B, 'Duterte aligns Philippines with China, says U.S. has lost' *Reuters* (Beijing, 20 October 2016) <http://www.reuters.com/article/us-china-philippines-idUSKCN12K0AS> accessed 15 March 2019.

—— 'China's defence minister says resolving 'Taiwan question' is national priority' *Reuters* (Beijing, 21 October 2019) <https://www.reuters.com/article/us-china-defence-taiwan/chinas-defence-minister-says-resolving-taiwan-question-is-national-priority-idUSKBN1X003H> accessed 9 November 2019.

Bodde D and Morris C, *Law in Imperial China. Exemplified by 190 Ch'ing Dynasty Cases (Translated from the Hsing-an hui-lan)* (Harvard University Press 1967).

Bohanes J, '*United States – Certain measures affecting imports of poultry from China*: the fascinating case that wasn't' (2012) 11 *World Trade Review* 307.

Bond EW and Trachtman J, 'China-Rare Earths: Export Restrictions and the Limits of Textual Interpretation' (2016) 15 *World Trade Review* 189.

Boundary Department of the Ministry of Interior of the Republic of China, *Map Showing the Location of the Various Islands in the South Sea* (1948).

Bourgeois JHJ, 'China and the WTO Dispute Settlement Mechanism' (2011) 2 *Opinio Juris in Comparatione* 1.

Boute A, 'The Protection of Russian Investments in the EU Energy Market: A Case in Support of Russia's Ratification of the Energy Charter Treaty' (2014) 29 *ICSID Review* 525.

Bowcott O, 'No British judge on world court for first time in its 71-year history' *Guardian* (London, 20 November 2017) <https://www.theguardian.com/law/2017/nov/20/no-british-judge-on-world-court-for-first-time-in-its-71-year-history> accessed 30 March 2019.

Bown CP, 'The Outlook for Market Economy Status for China' *Peterson Institute for International Economies – OpEds* (Washington DC, 12 December 2016) <https://piie.com/commentary/op-eds/trump-says-china-not-market-economy-thats-big-deal> accessed 22 May 2017.

—— and Mavroidis PC, 'One (Firm) Is Noot Enough: A Legal-Economic Analysis of *EC-Fasteners*' (2013) 12 *World Trade Review* 243.

Brewster R, Brunel C and Mayda AM, 'Trade in Environmental Goods: A Review of the WTO Appellate Body's Ruling in *US–Countervailing Measures (China)*' (2016) 15 *World Trade Review* 327.

Brink G, 'South Africa's experience with international trade dispute settlement' in Shaffer GC and Melendez-Ortiz R (eds), *Dispute Settlement at the WTO – The Developing Country Experience* (CUP 2010).

Broches A, 'The Convention on the Settlement of Investment Disputes between States and Nationals of Other States' (1972) 136 *Recueil des Cours* 331.

Bronckers M and Maskus KE, 'China-Raw Materials: a controversial step towards evenhanded exploitation of natural resources' (2014) 13 *World Trade Review* 393.

Brown Weiss E, 'International Law in a Kaleidoscopic World' (2011) 1 AsJIL 21.

Bu Yuanshi, *Einführung in das Recht Chinas: Rechtsstand: September 2008* (CH Beck 2009).

Buckley C and Bradsher K, 'China Moves to Let Xi Stay in Power by Abolishing Term Limit' *New York Times* (New York, 25 February 2018) <https://www.nytimes.com/2018/02/25/world/asia/china-xi-jinping.html> accessed 15 March 2019.

Buga I, 'Between Stability and Change in the Law of the Sea Convention: Subsequent Practice, Treaty Modification, and Regime Interaction', in Rothwell DR and others (eds), *The Oxford Handbook of the Law of the Sea* (OUP 2015).

Bungenberg M and Titi C, 'The Evolution of EU Investment Law and the Future of EU-China Investment Relations', in Shan W (ed), *China and International Investment Law: Twenty Years of ICSID Membership* (Brill 2015).

Busch ML, Reinhardt E and Shaffer G, 'Does Legal Capacity Matter? A Survey of WTO Members' (2009) 8 *World Trade Review* 559.

Butler WE, '"Socialist International Law" or "Socialist Principles of International Relations"?' (1971) 65 AJIL 796.

Caflisch L, 'Unequal Treaties' (1992) 35 *German Yearbook of International Law* 52.

Cai 蔡 Congyan 从燕, '外国投资者利用国际投资仲裁机制新发展反思——国际法实施机制与南北矛盾的双重视角' (Reviewing New Developments in Foreign Investors Use of International Investment Arbitration Mechanisms – Dual Viewpoint of International Law Implementation and North-South Conflict) [2007] (3) *Faxuejia* 102.

—— '风险社会与国际争端解决机制的解构与重构' (Risk Society and the Deconstruction and Reconstruction of International Dispute Settlement Mechanism) (2008) 26 (1) *Falü Kexue* 153.

—— '国际投资仲裁的商事化与"去商事化' (The Commercialization and De-Commercialization of International Investment Arbitration) (2011) 33 (1) *Xiandai Faxue* 152.

Cai 蔡 Gaoqiang 高强, '论解决南海争端的国际法路径' (Discussing International Law Approaches to Resolving the South China Sea Dispute) (2011) 35 (2) *Xiangtan Daxue Xuebao* 38.

—— and Xu 徐 Xu 徐, '论海洋边界争端与国际海洋法的发展——兼谈中日东海油气争端德解决' (On the Sea Boundary Dispute and the Development of International Law of the Sea – Proposals on resolving Gas Disputes between China and Japan in the East Sea) [2006] (11) *Gansu Zhengfa Xueyuan Xuebao* 39.

Cai 蔡 Xue'en 学恩 and Zhang 张 Fakun 发坤, '论 WTO 争端解决机制中的举证责任' (Discussing the Burden of Proof in the WTO Dispute Settlement System) [2003] (6) *Faxue Pinglun* 107.

Caldwell E, 'Social Change and Written Law in Early Chinese Legal Thought' (2014) 32 *Law and History Review* 1.

Calvert J, 'Constructing investor rights? Why some states (fail to) terminate bilateral investment treaties' (2018) 25 *Review of International Political Economy* 75.

Campello D and Lemos L, 'The non-ratification of bilateral investment treaties in Brazil: a story of conflict in a land of cooperation' (2015) 22 *Review of International Political Economy* 1055.

Carlson A, 'Helping to Keep the Peace (Albeit Reluctantly): China's Recent Stance on Sovereignty and Multilateral Intervention' (2004) 77 *Pacific Affairs* 9.

Carter B, 'Is China's economy really the largest in the world?' *BBC News* (London 16 December 2014) <https://www.bbc.com/news/magazine-30483762> accessed 5 January 2019.

Carty A and Lone FN, 'Some New Haven International Law Reflections on China, India and Their Various Territorial Disputes' (2011) 19 *Asia Pacific Law Review* 95.

Ceng 曾 Huaqun 华群, '国际经济法学要研究新问题' (New Issues Need to be Studied in International Economic Law) (2004) 24 (2) *Faxue Yanjiu* 135.

Ceng 曾 Wei 炜, '论国际习惯法在ＷＴＯ争端解决中的适用———以预防原则为例' (On the use of international customary law in WTO dispute resolution – taking the precautionary principle as an example) [2015] (4) *Faxue Pinglun* 109.

CGTN, 'Chinese legal experts refute Philippine claim in South China Sea' (Beijing, 7 May 2016) <https://america.cgtn.com/2016/05/07/chinese-legal-experts-refute-philippine-claim-in-south-china-sea> accessed 1 March 2019.

Chaisse J and Hamanaka S, 'The "Noodle Bowl Effect" of Investment Treaties in Asia: The Phenomenon, the Problems, the Practical Solutions' (2018) 33 *ICSID Review* 1.

Chan PCW, 'A Keen Observer of the International Rule of Law? International Law in China's Voting Behaviour and Argumentation in the United Nations Security Council' (2013) 26 *Leiden Journal of International Law* 875.

—— 'China's Approaches to International Law since the Opium War' (2014) 27 *Leiden Journal of International Law* 859.

Charlotin D and Peterson LE, 'Analysis: In new MERCOSUR Investment Protocol, Brazil, Uruguay, Paraguay and Argentina radically pare back protections, and exclude investor-state arbitration' *IAReporter* (Santa Monica, 4 May 2017 <https://www.iareporter.com/articles/analysis-in-new-mercosur-investment-protocol-brazil-uruguay-paraguay-and-argentina-radically-pare-back-protections-and-exclude-investor-state-arbitration/> accessed 10 November 2018.

Charnovitz S and Hoekman B, '*US–Tyres*: Upholding a WTO Accession Contract – Imposing Pain for Little Gain' (2013) 12 *World Trade Review* 273.

Chen 陈 Binbin 斌彬, 'WTO"蓝箱"规则改革的新进展及我国的对策' (The Recent Advances in 'Blue Box' Rules of WTO and the Countermeasures of China) (2014) 36 (2) *Xiandai Faxue* 139.

Chen 陈 Cong 聪 and Zhang 张 Hongsheng 红生, '南海主权争端的法律问题与法律准备' (The Legal Issues and Legal Preparations of the Sovereignty Disputes over the South China Sea) (2009) 27 (12) *Hebei Faxue* 57.

Chen Deming, 'Chen Deming's Report at the National Working Conference on Commerce and Finance' *Chinese Ministry of Commerce* (Beijing, 21 January 2010) <http://chendeming.mofcom.gov.cn/aarticle/speeches/200801/20080105345233.html> accessed 30 March 2019.

Chen 沈 Hong 虹, '论 ICSID 对涉中国投资条约仲裁的管辖权' (On the Jurisdiction of ICSID Relating to China Investment-Treaty-Based Arbitration) (2011) 32 (7) *Faxue Zazhi* 128.

Chen 沈 Huihua 慧骅, '国家和私人间投资争端解决机制的冲突和协调——兼比较 WTO 与 ICSID 争端解决机制的冲突和协调' (Conflict and Coordination of State-Private Investment Dispute Resolution Mechanisms – Comparing WTO and ICSID Dispute Settlement Mechanisms, Conflicts and Coordination) (2003) 17 (3) *Dangdai Faxue* 104.

Chen Jianfu, *Chinese Law: Context and Transformation* (Martinus Nijhoff Publishers 2008).

Chen 陈 Lihu 立虎 and Zhou 周 Min 敏, '非 WTO 法在 WTO 争端解决中的适用' (Application of Non-WTO Law in WTO Dispute Settlement) (2006) 20 (3) *Dangdai Faxue* 75.

Chen 陈 Rudan 儒丹, '非 WTO 协议"在 WTO 争端解决中的适用' (The Use of 'Non-WTO Agreements' in WTO Dispute Resolution) [2009] (2) *Faxue* 117.

—— '世界贸易组织争端解决实践中的识别冲突问题' (The Problem of Distinguishing Conflicts in WTO Dispute Resolution Practice) [2012] (7) *Faxue* 50.

—— '解开"囚徒困境"的国际经济法律制度——博弈论方法和中国问题视角' (Resolving "Prisoner's Dilemma" in International Economic Legal System: A Game Theory Analysis from China's Perspective) (2014) 34 (1) *Faxue Yanjiu* 120.

—— 'WTO 裁决执行与国家利益实现的潜在背离研究' (On the implementation of WTO findings and potential deviations from the realization of national interests) (2017) 39 (5) *Huanqiu falü pinglun* 177.

Chen 沈 Wei 伟, '论中国双边投资协定中限制性投资争端解决条款的解释和适用' (Discussing the Interpretation and Application of the Restrictive Investment Dispute Settlement Clause in Chinese BITs) (2012) 24 *Zhongwai Faxue* 1046.

Chen 陈 Weidong 卫东, '中美围绕国有企业的补贴提供者身份之争-以 WTO 相关案例为重点' (China-US dispute about the identity of the provider of subsidies to state-owned enterprises – focusing on pertinent WTO cases) (2017) 31 (3) *Dangdai Faxue* 21.

—— and Guan 管 Binbin 斌斌, '论国际法院判决在美国的执行' (Discussing the Implementation of ICJ Rulings in the United States) (2008) 22 (6) *Dangdai Faxue* 138.

Chen 陈 Xin 欣, '论 WTO 争端解决机制对 WTO 农业体制的影响' (Review of the WTO Dispute Settlement Mechanism's Impact on the WTO Agricultural System) (2006) 20 (5) *Dangdai Faxue* 85.

Chen 陈 Yayun 亚芸, 'WTO 争端解决机构法律适用范围争议及原因探析' (Comment on Disputes of Range of WTO Dispute Settlement Mechanism Applicable Law and Reason Analysis) (2015) 33 (6) *Hebei Faxue* 86.

Cheng JYS, 'China's WTO membership and its concern for state sovereignty' (2004) 13 *Journal of Contemporary China* 819.

Cherviatsova A and Yarmysh O, 'Soviet International Law: Between Slogans and Practice' (2017) 19 *Journal of the History of International Law* 296.

Chi Manjiao, 'China's Participation in WTO Dispute Settlement over the Past Decade: Experiences and Impacts' (2012) 15 *Journal of International Economic Law* 29.

—— 'From Ownership-Orientation to Governance-Orientation: An International Economic Law Perspective of China's Shifting Attitudes Towards Resource Sovereignty' (2013) Forschungskolleg Siegen Working Paper 2/2013 <https://www.uni-siegen.de/fokos/publikationen/veroeffentlichungen/fokos_-_working_paper_2013-02_-_chi.pdf> accessed 1 March 2019.

—— 'A Long March towards Compatibility, Coherence and Consistency: the Future of China's Investment Agreements' (2015) 18 *Zeitschrift für Europarechtliche Studien* 373.

—— 'From Europeanization toward Americanization: the shift of China's dichotomic investment treaty-making strategy' (2017) 23 *Canadian Foreign Policy Journal* 158.

Chigara B, 'European/Southern African Development Community (SADC) states' bilateral investment agreements (BITs) for the promotion and protection of foreign investments vs post-apartheid SADC economic and social reconstruction policy' (2011) 10 *Journal of International Trade Law and Policy* 213.

Chimni BS, 'Asian Civilizations and International Law: Some Reflections' (2011) 1 AsJIL 39.

China Academic Journals Database <http://oversea.cnki.net/kns55/brief/result.aspx?dbPrefix=CJFD> accessed 1 March 2019.

China Digital Times, 'CCP Launches Patriotic Education for Intellectuals' *China Digital Times* (Berkeley, 8 August 2018) <https://chinadigitaltimes.net/2018/08/ccp-launches-patriotic-education-for-intellectuals/> accessed 1 March 2019.

China File, 'Document 9: A ChinaFile Translation' (New York, 8 November 2013) <http://www.chinafile.com/document-9-chinafile-translation> accessed 1 March 2019.

China Power Team, 'What does China really spend on its military?' *CSIS China Power* (Washington DC, 28 December 2015, updated 9 October 2018) <https://chinapower.csis.org/military-spending/> accessed 5 January 2019.

Chinese Academy of Social Sciences, '中文核心期刊要目总览（2011 年第六版）' (A Guide to the Core Journals of China (6th edn, 2011) *Chinese Academy of Social Sciences* (Beijing, 10 December 2013) <http://www.cssn.cn/bk/bkpd_zwhxqkymzl/201312/t20131210_900382.shtml> accessed 1 March 2019.

Chinese Ministry of Commerce, 'China FTA Network' <http://fta.mofcom.gov.cn/english/> accessed 30 March 2019.

—— 'List of Bilateral Investment Treaties Concluded by China (Beijing, 12 December 2016)' [Chinese] <http://tfs.mofcom.gov.cn/article/Nocategory/201111/20111107819474.shtml> accessed 30 March 2019.

—— '加强对我国企业海外利益的保障' (Enhancing the protection of Chinese enterprises' overseas investment) (Beijing, 22 October 2014) <http://finance.china.com.cn/news/20141022/2742563.shtml> accessed 30 March 2019.

—— 'The 29th China-U.S. BIT Negotiation Held in Washington, 26 September 2016' (Beijing, 26 September 2016) <http://english.mofcom.gov.cn/article/newsrelease/significantnews/201609/20160901404077.shtml> accessed 30 March 2019.

—— '新形势下中国发力编织自贸区网络' (Under new circumstances, China's weaving of an FTA network gains momentum) (Beijing, 12 June 2017) <http://chinawto.mofcom.gov.cn/article/e/s/201706/20170602589908.shtml> accessed 20 October 2018.

Chircop A, 'The International Maritime Organization', in Rothwell DR and others (eds), *The Oxford Handbook of the Law of the Sea* (OUP 2015).

Chiu Hungdah, 'Communist China's Attitude Toward International Law' (1966) 60 AJIL 245.

—— 'Comparison of the Nationalist and Communist Chinese Views of Unequal Treaties', in Cohen J (ed), *China's Practice of International Law: Some Case Studies* (Harvard University Press 1972).

—— 'Chinese Views on the Sources of International Law (1987) 28 *Harvard International Law Journal* 289.

Chow DCK, *The Legal System of the People's Republic of China in a Nutshell* (West Academic Publishing 2009).

Christol CQ, 'Communist China and International Law – Strategy and Tactics' (1968) 21 *The Western Political Quarterly* 456.

Churchill RR, 'The 1982 United Nations Convention on the Law of the Sea', in Rothwell DR and others (eds), *The Oxford Handbook of the Law of the Sea* (OUP 2015).

—— 'The Exercise of Coastal State Rights on the Outer Continental Shelf Pending Establishment of its Outer Limit', in Barrett J and Barnes R (eds), *Law of the Sea – UNCLOS as a Living Treaty* (The British Institute of International and Comparative Law 2016).

Clarke DC, 'The Chinese Legal System since 1995: Steady Development and Striking Continuities' (2007) 191 *The China Quarterly* 555.

Cohen J (ed), *China's Practice of International Law: Some Case Studies* (Harvard University Press 1972).

—— 'China and Intervention: Theory and Practice' (1973) 121 *University of Pennsylvania Law Review* 471.

Conconi P and Pauwelyn J, 'Trading Cultures: Appellate Body Report on China–Audiovisuals (WT/DS363/AB/R, adopted 19 January 2010)' (2011) 10 *World Trade Review* 95.

Conde Pérez E and Yaneva ZV, 'Unequal Treaties in International Law' (*Oxford Bibliographies*, 30 August 2016) <http://www.oxfordbibliographies.com/view/document/obo-9780199796953/obo-9780199796953-0131.xml> accessed 8 March 2019.

Consulate of the Socialist Republic of Viet Nam in New York, 'Position Paper on the Sovereignty of Viet Nam over the Hoang Sa Archipelago' (New York, 7 July 2014) <http://vietnamconsulate-ny.org/news/2014/07/position-paper-sovereignty-viet-nam-over-hoang-sa-archipelago> accessed 1 March 2019.

Corrales N, 'PH, China to have joint venture in West Philippine Sea – Duterte' Inquirer.net (Manila, 25 July 2017) <http://globalnation.inquirer.net/159003/ph-china-joint-venture-west-philippine-sea-duterte> accessed 15 March 2019.

Cottier T, *Equitable Principles of Maritime Boundary Delimitation – The Quest for Distributive Justice in International Law* (CUP 2015).

Crook JR, 'In re Indus Waters Kishenganga Arbitration (Pakistan v. India). Final Award. At http:// www.pca-cpa.org. Arbitral Tribunal, December 20, 2013' (2014) 108 AJIL 308.

CSIS – Asia Maritime Transparency Initiative, 'Scarborough Shoal' (Washington DC) <https://amti.csis.org/scarborough-shoal/> accessed 1 March 2019.

—— 'Second Thomas Shoal' (Washington DC) < https://amti.csis.org/second-thomas-shoal/> accessed 1 March 2019.

—— 'Occupation and Island Building' (Washington DC) <https://amti.csis.org/island-tracker/> accessed 9 November 2019.

—— 'Updated: Imagery suggests Philippine fishermen still not entering Scarborough Shoal' *CSIS* (Washington DC, 27 October 2016) <https://amti.csis.org/china-scarborough-fishing/> accessed 15 March 2019.

—— 'Update: China's Continuing Reclamation in the Paracels' *CSIS* (Washington DC, 9 August 2017) <https://amti.csis.org/paracels-beijings-other-buildup/> accessed 15 March 2019.

—— 'A Constructive Year for Chinese Base Building' *CSIS* (Washington DC, 14 December 2017) <https://amti.csis.org/constructive-year-chinese-building/> accessed 15 March 2019.

Cui Wei, 'Multilateral Management as a Fair Solution to the Spratly Disputes' (2003) 36 *Vanderbilt Journal of Transnational Law* 799.

Dag Hammarskjöld Library, 'Drafting of the Universal Declaration of Human Rights – Drafting Committee Members' <http://research.un.org/en/undhr/draftingcommittee> accessed 11 December 2018.

Dahlquist J, 'Russia sets out new guidelines for contents of future investment treaties' *IAReporter* (Santa Monica, 26 October 2016) <https://www.iareporter.com/articles/russia-sets-out-new-guidelines-for-negotiation-of-future-investment-treaties/> accessed 3 May 2018.

Davenport T, 'The Archipelagic Regime', in Rothwell DR and others (eds), *The Oxford Handbook of the Law of the Sea* (OUP 2015).

Davis CL and Blodgett Bermeo S, 'Who Files? Developing Country Participation in GATT/WTO Adjudication' (2009) 71 *The Journal of Politics* 1033.

De Jonge A, 'From Unequal Treaties to Differential treatment: is There a Role for Equality in Treaty Relations' (2014) 4 AsJIL 125.

Deng 邓 Ruiping 瑞平 and Dong 董 Weijie 威颉, '论中国双边投资条约中的保护伞条款' (Research on the Umbrella Clause in China 's Bilateral Investment Treaties) (2018) 36 (2) *Hebei Faxue* 10.

Deng 邓 Tingting 婷婷, '中欧双边投资条约中的投资者 - 国家争端解决机制——以欧盟投资法庭制度为视角' (Investor-State Dispute Settlement Mechanism in the China-EU Bilateral Investment Treaty – From the Perspective of the EU Investment Court System) [2017] (4) *Zhengzhi yu Falü* 99.

Dennin JF, *Law & Practice of the World Trade Organization – Commentary Binder 1* (OUP 2007).

De Serpa Soares M, 'Keynote Speech at the International Colloquium on the Five Principles of Peaceful Co-existence and the Development of International Law' (2014) 13 CJIL 481.

Dhar B and Majumdar A, 'Learning from the India-EC GDP dispute: the issues and the process' in Shaffer GC and Melendez-Ortiz R (eds), *Dispute Settlement at the WTO – The Developing Country Experience* (CUP 2010).

Donnan S, Hornby L and Beesley A, 'China challenges EU and US over market economy status' *Financial Times* (London, 12 December 2016) <https://www.ft.com/content/6af8da62-bf5d-11e6-9bca-2b93a6856354> accessed 8 November 2019.

Doshi R, 'Hu's to blame for China's foreign assertiveness?' *Brookings* (Washington DC, 22 January 2019) <https://www.brookings.edu/articles/hus-to-blame-for-chinas-foreign-assertiveness/> accessed 25 January 2019.

Dougherty JE and Pfaltzgraff RLJ, *Contending Theories of International Relations. A Comprehensive Survey* (5th edn, Longman 2001).

Duan Jielong, 'Statement on the Rule of Law on the National and International Levels' (2007) 6 CJIL 185.

Dumberry P, 'The Importation of the FET Standard through MFN Clauses: An Empirical Study of BITs' (2017) 32 *ICSID Review* 1.

Dunoff JL and Pollack MA, 'International Law and International Relations: Introducing an Interdisciplinary Dialogue', in Dunoff JL and Pollack MA (eds) *Interdisciplinary Perspectives on International Law and International Relations. The State of the Art* (CUP 2013).

Dunoff JL and Moore MO, 'Footloose and duty-free? Reflections on European Union – Anti-Dumping Measures on Certain Footwear from China' (2014) 13 *World Trade Review* 149.

Dyer G and Sevastopolu D, 'US strategists face dilemma over Beijing claim in South China Sea' *Reuters* (Washington DC and Hong Kong, 9 July 2014) <https: //www.ft.com/content/b2176dea-0732-11e4-81c6-00144feab7de> accessed 9 November 2019.

Eberhardt P and Olivet C, 'Profiting from Injustice: How Law Firms, Arbitrators and Financiers are Fuelling an Investment Arbitration Boom' *Corporate Europe Observatory* (Brussels, November 2012) <corporateeurope.org/sites/default/files/ publications/profiting-from-injustice.pdf> accessed 30 March 2019.

Eder TS, *China-Russia Relations in Central Asia: Energy Policy, Beijing's New Assertiveness and 21st Century Geopolitics* (Springer 2014).

Eder TS and Mardell J, 'MERICS BRI Tracker' *MERICS* (Berlin, 2019) <https://ww w.merics.org/en/bri-tracker> accessed 30 October 2019.

Elferink AO (ed), *Stability and Change in the Law of the Sea: The Role of the LOS Convention* (Martinus Nijhoff 2005).

Eliasson N, 'Chinese investment treaties: a procedural perspective', in Bath V and Nottage LR (eds), *Foreign Investment and Dispute Resolution Law and Practice in Asia* (Routledge 2011).

—— 'The Chinese Investment Treaty Programme, Jurisdictional Challenges and Investment Planning: The Example of Chinese Outbound Investments in the Natural Resources Sector', in Shan W (ed), *China and International Investment Law: Twenty Years of ICSID Membership* (Brill 2015).

Emmott R, 'China, EU Commission edge towards deal on market economy status' *Reuters* (Brussels, 27 May 2016) <https://uk.reuters.com/article/uk-china-eu-trade-idUKKCN0YI1G0> accessed 8 November 2019.

Espa I and Levy PI, 'The Analogue Method Comes Unfastened – The Awkward Space between Market and Non-Market Economies in EC–Fasteners (Article 21.5)' (2018) 17 *World Trade Review* 313.

European Commission, 'Commission proposes changes to the EU's anti-dumping and anti-subsidy legislation' *European Commission – Fact Sheet* (Brussels, 9 November 2016) <http://europa.eu/rapid/press-release_MEMO-16-3605_en.htm> accessed 22 May 2017.

—— 'EU-China Investment Agreement: Report of the 16th Round of Negotiations' (Brussels, 12–15 December 2017) <http://trade.ec.europa.eu/doclib/docs/2 017/december/tradoc_156520.pdf> accessed 30 March 2019.

Evans D and Shaffer GC, 'Introduction' in Shaffer GC and Melendez-Ortiz R (eds), *Dispute Settlement at the WTO – The Developing Country Experience* (CUP 2010).

—— 'Conclusion' in Shaffer GC and Melendez-Ortiz R (eds), *Dispute Settlement at the WTO – The Developing Country Experience* (CUP 2010).

Evans MD, 'Maritime Boundary Delimitation' in Rothwell DR and others (eds), *The Oxford Handbook of the Law of the Sea* (OUP 2015).

—— 'Maritime Boundary Delimitation: Whatever Next?' in Barrett J and Barnes R (eds), *Law of the Sea – UNCLOS as a Living Treaty* (The British Institute of International and Comparative Law 2016).

Ewing-Chow M, Goh AWS and Patil AK, 'Are Asian WTO Members using the WTO DSU "Effectively"?' (2013) 16 *Journal of International Economic Law* 669.

Fan Jizeng, 'Constitutional Transplant in the People's Republic of China: The Influence of the Soviet Model and Challenges in the Globalization Era' (2015) 2 *BRICS Law Journal* 50.

Fan 樊 Ying 静 and Yi 衣 Shuling 淑玲, '国际投资仲裁监督机制改革问题研究' (Research on International Investment Arbitration Supervision Mechanism Reform) (2015) 33 (2) *Hebei Faxue* 118.

Fang 方 Changping 长平, '中国国际关系理论建设问题和思考' (Establishing a Chinese IR-Theory: Problems and Deliberations) [2005] (6) *Jiaoxue yu Yanjiu* 46.

Feng 冯 Bing 兵 and Huang 黄 Jianqiu 涧秋, '论 WTO 争端解决活动中的法律解释' (Discussing Legal Interpretation in WTO Dispute Resolution Activities) (2002) 20 (1) *Falü Kexue* 76.

Feng Emily, 'China universities accused of ideological weakness' *Financial Times* (London, 19 June 2017) <https://www.ft.com/content/88191d36-54b4-11e7-9fed-c19e2700005f> accessed 1 March 2019.

Feng 冯 Jiehan 洁菡, '大陆架的权利基础自然延伸与距离标准' (The Basis of the Right to the Continental Shelf: The Principle of Natural Prolongation and the Distance Criterion) (2010) 32 (5) *Faxue Luntan* 24.

Feng 冯 Shoubo 寿波, '论海洋法中"历史性所有权"的构成要件' (On the Key Components of Historic Title in the Law of the Sea) (2018) 36 (2) *Hebei Faxue* 83.

Ferrara P, 'Article 296 – Finality and binding force of decisions' in Alexander Proelss (ed), *United Nations Convention on the Law of the Sea – A Commentary* (CH Beck 2017).

Financial Times, 'China fights for market economy status – Beijing had thought trade advantage would come automatically at end of this year' (London, 9 May 2016) <https://www.ft.com/content/572f435e-0784-11e6-9b51-0fb5e65703ce> accessed 30 December 2017.

Franck TM, 'Legitimacy in the International System' (1988) 82 *American Society of International Law* 705.

Franckx E, 'The Regime of Islands and Rocks' in Attard DJ, Fitzmaurice M and Martínez Guttiérez NA (eds), *The IMLI Manual on International Maritime Law – Volume I: The Law of the Sea* (OUP 2014).

—— 'The Enigma of Article 121, Paragraph 3: The Way Forward?' *Maritime Issues* (14 November 2016) <http://www.maritimeissues.com/law/the-enigma-of-article-121-paragraph-3-the-way-forward.html> accessed 30 March 2019.

Friedrich S, *China und die Europäische Union. Europas weltpolitische Rolle aus chinesischer Sicht* (Mitteilungen des Instituts für Asienkunde Hamburg Nr. 321, Verbund Stiftung Deutsches Übersee-Institut 2000).

Fu 伏 Jun 军, 'WTO 外汇争端祖管辖安排：模糊性及其现实理性角' (WTO's Jurisdiction over Exchange Disputes: Vagueness and Rationality) (2007) 29 (5) *Xiandai Faxue* 128.

Gallagher N, 'China's BITs and Arbitration Practice: Progress and Problems' in Shan Wenhua (ed), *China and International Investment Law: Twenty Years of ICSID Membership* (Brill 2015).

—— 'Role of China in Investment: BITs, SOEs, Private Enterprises, and Evolution of Policy' (2016) 31 *ICSID Review* 88.

—— and Shan Wenhua, *Chinese Investment Treaties: Policies and Practice* (OUP 2009).

Gan Nectar, 'China tells its intellectuals to toe the party line' *Inkstone News* (Hong Kong 8 August 2018) <https://www.inkstonenews.com/politics/chinese-communist-party-launches-campaign-enhance-patriotism-among-intellectuals/article/2158744> accessed 1 March 2019.

Gao Henry, 'China on the World Stage: A Trade Law Perspective' (2010) 104 *Proceedings of the ASIL Annual Meeting* 532.

Gao Jianjun, 'The Okinawa Trough Issue in the Continental Shelf Delimitation Disputes within the East China Sea' (2010) 9 CJIL 143.

—— 'The ITLOS Advisory Opinion for the SRFC' (2015) 14 CJIL 735.

Gao Zhiguo and Jia Bingbing, 'The Nine-Dash Line in the South China Sea: History, Status, and Implications' (2013) 107 AJIL 98.

Garwood-Gowers A, 'China's "Responsible Protection" Concept: Reinterpreting the Responsibility to Protect (R2P) and Military Intervention for Humanitarian Purposes' (2016) 6 AsJIL 89.

Gau MST, 'The Agreements and Disputes Crystalized by the 2009–2011 Sino-Philippine Exchange of Notes Verbales and their Relevance to the Jurisdiction and Admissibility Phase of the South China Sea Arbitration' (2016) 15 CJIL 417.

Gautier P, 'The Settlement of Disputes' in Attard DJ, Fitzmaurice M and Martínez Guttiérez NA (eds), *The IMLI Manual on International Maritime Law – Volume I: The Law of the Sea* (OUP 2014).

Gilpin R, *U.S. Power and the Multinational Corporation: The Political Economy of Foreign Direct Investment* (Basic Books 1975).

Glenn PH, *Legal Traditions of the World: Sustainable Diversity in Law* (OUP 2010).

Goldstein J and others, 'Introduction: Legalization and World Politics' (2000) 54 *International Organization* 385.

Gong 龚 Baihua 柏华, '中国影响汽车零部件进口措施"WTO 争端解决案评析' (Evaluation of the WTO DSM Case "Measures Affecting Imports of Automobile Parts") [2006] (11) *Faxue* 101.

Gourevitch P, 'The Second Image Reversed: The International Sources of Domestic Politics' (1978) 32 *International Organization* 881.

Government of India, 'India Model BIT 2015' <https://www.mygov.in/sites/default/files/master_image/Model%20Text%20for%20the%20Indian%20Bilateral%20Investment%20Treaty.pdf> accessed 30 March 2019.

Government of the Russian Federation, 'Decision No 992 – On the conclusion of international treaties of the Russian Federation for the promotion and protection of investments (adopted 30 September 2016)' [Russian] <http://pravo.gov.ru/proxy/ips/?docbody=&prevDoc=102071479&backlink=1&&nd=102412234> accessed 3 May 2018.

Graham E, 'The bolt from The Hague' *The Interpreter* (Sydney, 13 July 2016) <https://www.lowyinstitute.org/the-interpreter/debate/south-china-sea-ruling> accessed 10 November 2019.

Grando MT, *Evidence, Proof, and Fact-Finding in WTO Dispute Settlement* (OUP 2009).

Gray K and Murphy CN, 'Rising powers and the future of global governance' (2013) 34 *Third World Quarterly* 183.

Grossman GM and Sykes AO, 'United States – Definitive Safeguard Measures on Imports of Certain Steel Products (WT/DS259; WT/DS252; WT/DS248; WT/DS249; WT/DS251; WT/DS258; WT/DS254; WT/DS253: DSR 2003:VII, 3117)' (2006) 5 *World Trade Review* 146.

Gu Bin, 'Applicability of GATT Article XX in China-Raw Materials: A Clash within the WTO Agreement' (2012) 15 *Journal of International Economic Law* 1007.

Gu 古 Junfeng 俊峰, '和平解决中日东海划界争端的法律程序之纬' (Latitude of Legal Procedures in Peacefully Resolving the Sino-Japanese Maritime Boundary Dispute) [2009] (9) *Gansu Zhengfa Xueyuan Xuebao* 130.

Guan 管 Jianqiang 建强, '和平解决东海划界争端之方法探究' (Inquiry of Methods of Peaceful Resolution of the East China Sea Boundary Delimitation Dispute) [2008] (11) *Faxue* 77.

—— '"南海仲裁案"后续法律应对的关键问题研究' (Studying the key issues in follow-up legal responses to the 'South China Sea arbitration') [2016] (5) *Zhongguo Faxue* 51.

Guilfoyle D, 'The High Seas' in Rothwell DR and others (eds), *The Oxford Handbook of the Law of the Sea* (OUP 2015).

—— 'Maritime Security' in Barrett J and Barnes R (eds), *Law of the Sea – UNCLOS as a Living Treaty* (The British Institute of International and Comparative Law 2016).

—— 'Article 101 – Definition of piracy' in Alexander Proelss (ed), *United Nations Convention on the Law of the Sea – A Commentary* (CH Beck 2017).

—— 'Article 111 – Right of hot pursuit' in Alexander Proelss (ed), *United Nations Convention on the Law of the Sea – A Commentary* (CH Beck 2017).

—— and Miles CA, 'Provisional Measures and the MV Arctic Sunrise' (2014) 108 AJIL 271.

Guo 郭 Li 雳, 'WTO 争端解决的个案剖析与启示——以美国、印度药品及农用化学品专利保护'纠纷为例 (Case Study and Message on WTO Dispute Resolution – Taking the US-India Pharmaceutical and Agricultural Chemical Products Patent Protection Dispute as an Example) [2002] (4) *Faxue Pinglun* 83.

Guo 郭 Qiong 琼, '新世纪中国和东盟关系的新发展' (New Developments in China-ASEAN Relations in the New Century) (2012) 12 *Lanzhou Xuekan* 1.

Hamamoto S, 'Protection of the Investor's Legitimate Expectations: Intersection of a Treaty Obligation and a General Principle of Law' in Shan W (ed), *China and International Investment Law: Twenty Years of ICSID Membership* (Brill 2015).

Han 韩 Liyu 立余, 'WTO 争端解决程序中的举证责任' (Burden of Proof in WTO Dispute Settlement) (2007) 29 (3) *Xiandai Faxue* 79.

—— 'WTO 争端解决中的案例法方法' (The Case Law Applied in the WTO Settlement) (2008) 30 (3) *Xiandai Faxue* 123.

—— and Gao Henry, 'China's experience in utilizing the WTO Dispute Settlement Mechanism' in Shaffer GC and Melendez-Ortiz R (eds), *Dispute Settlement at the WTO – The Developing Country Experience* (CUP 2010).

Han Xiuli, 'China's First Ten Years in WTO Dispute Settlement' (2011) 12 *The Journal of World Investment & Trade* 49.

—— 'The China–South Africa Bilateral Investment Treaty: National rule of law versus international rule of law' (2017) 24 *South African Journal of International Affairs* 269.

Han 韩 Yichou 逸畴, 'WTO 争端解决机制及其对国家声誉的影响研究' (On the influence of the WTO dispute settlement mechanism on national reputation) (2015) 29 (2) *Dangdai Faxue* 95.

—— 'WTO "免费通行" 现象研究' (On the phenomenon of 'free riding' in the WTO) (2016) 30 (3) *Dangdai Faxue* 138.

—— '中国遵守 WTO 不利裁决的策略及其对国家声誉的影响研究' (Study on China's Strategy of Complying with Unfavorable WTO Rulings and its Impact on National Reputation) (2018) 32 (6) *Dangdai Faxue* 123.

Hancock T, 'China's relentless export machine moves up the value chain' *Financial Times* (Shanghai, 23 September 2018) <https://www.ft.com/content/cdc53aee-bc2e-11e8-94b2-17176fbf93f5> accessed 9 November 2019.

Hanemann T and Huotari M, 'Chinese investment in Europe: record flows and growing imbalances' *Joint report by MERICS and Rhodium Group* (Berlin, January 2017) <https://www.merics.org/en/papers-on-china/chinese-investment-europe-record-flows-and-growing-imbalances> accessed 3 November 2019.

Hanessian G and Duggal K, 'The 2015 Indian Model BIT: Is This Change the World Wishes to See?' (2015) 30 *ICSID Review* 729.

Hansen R and McRae D, 'Reconciling the International and the Domestic: The Reasonable Period of Time under Article 21.3 of the DSU' in Janow ME, Donaldson V and Yanovich A (eds), *The WTO: Governance, Dispute Settlement, and Developing Countries* (Juris Publishing Inc 2008).

Harpaz MD, 'Sense and Sensibilities of China and WTO Dispute Settlement' (2010) 44 *Journal of World Trade* 1155.

—— 'Sense and sensibilities of China and WTO Dispute settlement' in Zeng K and Liang W (eds), *China and Global Trade Governance – China's first decade in the World Trade Organization* (Routledge 2013).

Harrison J, 'The Law of the Sea Convention Institutions' in Rothwell DR and others (eds), *The Oxford Handbook of the Law of the Sea* (OUP 2015).

—— and Morgera E, 'Article 62 – Utilization of the living resources' in Alexander Proelss (ed), *United Nations Convention on the Law of the Sea – A Commentary* (CH Beck 2017).

Hathaway OA and Koh HH, *Foundations of International Law and Politics* (Foundation Press 2004).

Hayton B, 'The Week Donald Trump Lost the South China Sea' *Foreign Policy* (Washington DC, 31 July 2017) <http://foreignpolicy.com/2017/07/31/the-week-donald-trump-lost-the-south-china-sea/> accessed 15 March 2019.

He 何 Zhipeng 志鹏, '走向国际法强国' (Becoming a Great Power in International Law) [2015] (1) *Dangdai Faxue* 148.

—— '国际司法的中国立场' (China's position in international justice) [2016] (2) *Fashang Yanjiu* 45.

—— '开放发展与国际法：风险及应对' (Open Development and International Law: Risks and Countermeasures) (2017) 35 (3) *Zhengfa Luntan* 16.

Head JW and Wang Y, *Law codes in dynastic China: a synopsis of Chinese legal history in the thirty centuries from Zhou to Qing* (Carolina Academic Press 2005).

Hegde VG, 'India and international settlement of disputes' (2016) 56 *Indian Journal of International Law* 1.

Heilmann S (ed), *China's Political System* (Rowman & Littlefield 2017).

—— 'How the CCP embraces and co-opts China's private sector' *MERICS* (Berlin, 21 November 2017) <https://www.merics.org/de/blog/how-ccp-embraces-and-co-opts-chinas-private-sector> accessed 25 June 2018.

Heiskanen V, 'Ménage à trois? Jurisdiction, Admissibility and Competence in Investment Treaty Arbitration' (2014) 29 *ICSID Review* 231.

Hempson-Jones JS, 'The Evolution of China's Engagement with International Governmental Organizations: Toward a Liberal Foreign Policy?' (2005) 45 *Asian Survey* 702.

Henkin L, *How Nations Behave* (Frederick Praeger 1968).

—— *How Nations Behave* (2nd edn, published for the Council on Foreign Relations by Columbia University Press 1979).

Herdegen M, *Principles of International Economic Law* (2nd edn, OUP 2016).

Herz JH, *International Politics in the Atomic Age* (Columbia University Press 1959).

Heuser R, *Einführung in die chinesische Rechtskultur* (Institut für Asienkunde 1999).

—— 'What "Rule of Law"? The Traditional Chinese Concept of Good Government and Challenges of the 21st Century' (2004) 64 *Zeitschrift für ausländisches öffentliches Recht und Völkerrecht* 723.

Ho J, 'Investment Protection under Successive Treaties' (2017) 32 *ICSID Review* 58.

Hobér K, 'MFN Clauses and Dispute Resolution in Investment Treaties: Have we reached the end of the road?' in Binder C and others (eds), *International Investment Law for the 21st Century: Essays in Honour of Christoph Schreuer* (OUP 2009).

—— 'Investment Arbitration and the Energy Charter Treaty' (2010) 1 *Journal of International Dispute Settlement* 153.

Hoekman B and Meagher N, '*China – Electronic Payment Services*: discrimination, economic development and the GATS' (2014) 13 *World Trade Review* 409.

Hoffheimer DJ, 'China and the International Legal Order: An Historical Introduction' (1979) 11 *Case Western Reserve Journal of International Law* 251.

Hong 洪 Dongying 冬英, '以法院文化建设推动司法的改革与发展' (Promoting Judicial Reform and Development through Building Court Culture) [2012] (11) *Faxue* 17.

Hopewell K, 'The BRICS – merely a fable? Emerging power alliances in global trade governance' (2017) 93 *International Affairs* 1377.

Horlick G and Coleman J, 'A Comment on Compliance with WTO Dispute Settlement Rulings' in Janow ME, Donaldson V and Yanovich A (eds), *The WTO: Governance, Dispute Settlement, and Developing Countries* (Juris Publishing Inc 2008).

Horn H, Maggi G, and Staiger RW, 'Trade Agreements as Endogenously Incomplete Contracts' (2010) 100 *The American Economic Review* 394.

Horn H, Johannesson L and Mavroidis PC, 'The WTO Dispute Settlement System 1995–2010: Some Descriptive Statistics' (2011) *Journal of World Trade*, no. 6, 1107.

Howse R, 'Case Comment: China – Measures Affecting the Protection and Enforcement of Intellectual Property Rights' (2011) 10 *World Trade Review* 87.

—— and Teitel R, 'Beyond Compliance: Rethinking Why International Law Really Matters' (2010) 1 *Global Policy* 127.

Hsieh PL, 'Wellington Koo, International Law and Modern China' (2016) 56 *Indian Journal of International Law* 307.

Hsiung JC, *Law and Policy in China's Foreign Relations – A Study of Attitudes and Practice* (Columbia University Press 1972).

Hu 胡 Jiaxiang 加祥, '中国参与 WTO 争端解决机制的实证分析' (Empirical Analysis of China's Participation in the WTO Dispute Resolution Mechanism) [2008] (11) *Faxue* 66.

Hu 胡 Xiaohong 晓红, '中外双边投资协定争端解决机制模式选择——以中国与上合组织成员国间 BITs 为视角' (On the Choice of Dispute Settlement Mechanism Types in China-Foreign Bilateral Investment Treaties – from the Perspective of BITs between China and Shanghai Cooperation Organization Member States) [2009] (3) *Gansu Zhengfa Xueyuan Xuebao* 76.

Huang Cui and Ji Wenhua, 'Understanding China's Recent Active Moves on WTO Litigation: Rising Legalism and/or Reluctant Response?' (2012) 46 *Journal of World Trade* 1281.

Huang Deming, Kong Yuan and Zhang Hua, 'Symposium on China's Peaceful Development and International Law' (2006) 5 CJIL 261.

Huang 黄 Deming 德明 and Zhang 章 Cheng 成, '北极海域 200 海里外大陆架划界与北极区域法律制度的建构' (Delimitation of the Outer Continental Shelf Beyond 200 Nautical Miles in the Arctic Region and the Establishment of the Arctic Legal Regime) [2013] (6) *Faxuejia* 161.

Huang Echo, 'Chinese investment in the US skyrocketed last year' *Quartz* (New York, 3 January 2017) <https://qz.com/876693/chinese-investment-in-the-us-skyrocketed-in-2016/> accessed 3 November 2019.

Huang 黄 Jianqiu 涧秋 and Feng 冯 Bing 兵, '用尽当地救济与 GATT / WTO 争端解决' (Exhaustion of Local Remedies in GATT/WTO Dispute Resolution) [2005] (6) *Faxue Pinglun* 76.

Huang PCC, 'Codified Law and Magisterial Adjudication in the Qing' in Bernhardt K and Huang PCC (eds), *Civil Law in Qing and Republican China* (Stanford University Press 1994).

—— *Civil Justice in China: Representation and Practice in the Qing* (Stanford University Press 1996).

Huang PCC and Bernhardt K (eds), *The History and Theory of Legal Practice in China – Towards a Historical-Social Jurisprudence* (Brill 2014).

Huang 黄 Shixi 世席, '国际投资仲裁裁决执行中的国家豁免问题' (The Issue of State Immunity in the Enforcement of International Investment Arbitration Awards) (2012) 6 (6) *Qinghua Faxue* 95.

—— '国际投资仲裁中最惠国条款的适用和管辖权的新发展' (New Developments Regarding the Application of the Most-Favored-Nation Clause and Jurisdiction in International Investment Arbitration) (2013) 31 (2) *Falü Kexue* 177.

—— '国际投资条约中投资的确定与东道国发展的考量' (The Determination of Investment and the Consideration of the Host States' Development in International Investment Treaties) (2014) 36 (5) *Xiandai Faxue* 136.

—— '国际投资仲裁中的挑选条约问题' (The issue of selecting treaties in international investment arbitration) [2014] (1) *Faxue* 62.

—— '欧盟投资协定中的投资者-国家争端解决机制——兼论中欧双边投资协定中的相关问题' (Investor-State Dispute Settlement Mechanisms in EU Investment Treaties – Related Issues in the China-EU Bilateral Investment Treaty) (2015) 37 (5) *Huanqiu Falü Pinglun* 149.

—— '可持续发展视角下国际投资争端解决机制的革新' (Reforming the international investment dispute settlement mechanism from the perspective of sustainable development) (2016) 30 (2) *Dangdai Faxue* 24.

—— '国际投资仲裁裁决的司法审查及投资条约解释的公正性基于"Ｓａｎｕｍ案"和"Ｙｕｋｏｓ案"判决的考察' (Inspecting the equitability of the judicial review of international arbitral awards and the interpretation of investment treaties based on the rulings in Sanum and Yukos) [2017] (3) *Faxue* 130.

Huang 黄 Yao 瑶 and Liao 廖 Xuexia 雪霞, '国际海洋划界司法实践的新动向——2012 年孟加拉湾划界案评析' (New Developments in International Maritime Boundary Delimitation Case Law – Analysis of the 2012 Gulf of Bengal Case) [2012] (12) *Faxue* 80.

—— '论大陆架外部界限的确立与 200 海里以外大陆架划界的关系——以 2012 年尼加拉瓜诉哥伦比亚案为引子' (Discussing the Relationship between Establishing the Limits of the Outer Continental Shelf and Continental Shelf Boundary Delimitation beyond 200 Nautical Miles – Taking the 2012 Case of Nicaragua v. Colombia as an Introduction) (2013) 27 (6) *Dangdai Faxue* 127.

—— '国际法院海洋划界的新实践——2014 年秘鲁诉智利案评析' (The Latest Case on Maritime Delimitation by the International Court of Justice – Comments on the Maritime Dispute (Peru v. Chile) in 2014) [2014] (1) *Guojifa Yanjiu* 29.

Huang 黄 Yueming 月明, 'ICSID 仲裁庭扩大管辖权的途径及其应对 - 从"谢亚深案"切入' (ICSID Tribunals' Ways of Broadening Jurisdiction and Responses – Viewed Through the "Tza Yap Shum Case") [2013] (5) *Huadong Zhengfa Daxue Xuebao* 64.

Huang Zheping, 'Chinese president Xi Jinping has vowed to lead the "new world order"' *Quartz* (New York, 22 February 2017) <https://qz.com/916382/chinese-president-xi-jinping-has-vowed-to-lead-the-new-world-order/> accessed 24 July 2018.

—— and Huang Echo, 'China's citizens are livid at the South China Sea ruling because they've always been taught it is theirs' *Quartz* (New York, 14 July 2016) <https://qz.com/730669/chinas-citizens-are-livid-at-the-south-china-sea-ruling-because-theyve-always-been-taught-it-is-theirs/> accessed 16 November 2019.

Hufbauer GC and Cimino-Isaacs C, 'Trump Says China Is Not a Market Economy. That's a Big Deal' *Peterson Institute for International Economies – Trade & Investment Policy Watch* (Washington DC, 11 April 2016) <https://piie.com/blogs/trade-investment-policy-watch/outlook-market-economy-status-china> accessed 22 May 2017.

Hughes V, 'The Strengths, Weaknesses, and Future of WTO Appellate Review' in Janow ME, Donaldson V and Yanovich A (eds), *The WTO: Governance, Dispute Settlement, and Developing Countries* (Juris Publishing Inc 2008).

Hung MYV, 'China's WTO Commitment on Independent Judicial Review: Impact on Legal and Political Reform' (2004) 52 *The American Journal of Comparative Law* 77.

Huotari M, Gaspers J and Böhnke O, 'Asserting European interests – How Europe should deal with the question of China's Market Economy Status' *MERICS China Policy Brief* (Berlin, January 2016) <http://www.merics.org/en/press-contact/press-releases/asserting-european-interests.html> accessed 15 March 2017.

Huotari M and others, 'China's Emergence as a Global Security Actor – Strategies for Europe' *MERICS Papers on China no 4* (Berlin, July 2017) <https://www.merics.org/de/papers-on-china/chinas-emergence-global-security-actor> accessed 25 January 2019.

Hurrell A, 'Lula's Brazil: A rising power, but going where?' (2008) 107 *Current History* 51.

Hwang M and Chang A, 'Government of the Lao People's Republic v Sanum Investments Ltd – A Tale of Two Letters' (2015) 30 *ICSID Review* 506.

IBA Guide to Conflict of Interest in International Arbitration (adopted by resolution of the IBA Council on Thursday 23 October 2014) (International Bar Association 2014).

ICJ, 'All Members' <https://www.icj-cij.org/en/all-members> accessed 11 December 2018.

ICJ, 'Declarations recognizing the jurisdiction of the Court as compulsory – India' <http://www.icj-cij.org/en/declarations/in> accessed 1 April 2019.

ICJ, 'List of all cases' <http://www.icj-cij.org/en/list-of-all-cases> accessed 1 March 2019.

ILC, 'Draft on arbitral procedure adopted by the Commission at its fifth session: report by Georges Scelle, Special Rapporteur (with a model draft on arbitral procedure annexed)' (6 March 1958) A/CN.4/113, in II *Yearbook of the International Law Commission* 1.

International Chamber of Commerce, *International Court of Arbitration – Arbitration Rules in force as from 1 March 2017 and Mediation Rules in force as from 1 January 2014* (ICC 2018).

International Institute for Sustainable Development, 'International Institute for Sustainable Development (IISD) Model International Agreement on Investment for Sustainable Development – Negotiators' Handbook' (Winnipeg, April 2005) <http://www.iisd.org/library/iisd-model-international-agreement-investment-sustainable-development-negotiators-handbook> accessed 5 January 2018.

International Seabed Authority, 'Deep Seabed Minerals Contractors' <https://www.isa.org.jm/deep-seabed-minerals-contractors> accessed 1 March 2019.

Italaw, 'India Model BIT 2003' Art 4 (2) <https://www.italaw.com/sites/default/files/archive/ita1026.pdf> accessed 30 March 2019.

ITLOS, 'List of cases' <https://www.itlos.org/cases/list-of-cases/> accessed 1 March 2019.

Jacobs A, 'Realismus' in Schieder S and Spindler M (eds), *Theorien der Internationalen Beziehungen* (UTB 2010).

Janow ME, Donaldson V and Yanovich A (eds), *The WTO: Governance, Dispute Settlement, and Developing Countries* (Juris Publishing Inc 2008).

Japan Times, 'India and China face off in border standoff as fears of all-out military conflict grow' *Japan Times* (Tokyo, 25 July 2017) <http://www.japantimes.co.jp/news/2017/07/25/asia-pacific/india-china-face-off-border-standoff-fears-military-conflict-grow/#.WYcfGNPyhE4> accessed 26 July 2017.

Jervis R, *Perception and Misperception in International Politics* (Princeton University Press 1976).

Ji Wenhua and Huang Cui, 'China's Experience in Dealing with WTO Dispute Settlement: A Chinese Perspective' (2011) 45 *Journal of World Trade* 1.

Jia Bingbing, 'A Synthesis of the Notion of Sovereignty and the Ideal of the Rule of Law: Reflections on the Contemporary Chinese Approach to International Law' (2010) 53 *German Yearbook of International Law* 11.

—— 'The Relations between Treaties and Custom' (2010) 9 CJIL 81.

—— '论驳美国国务院《海洋疆界》 第１４３期有关南海历史性权利论述的谬误' (Refuting the errors in the US State Department's No. 143 'Limits in the Sea' treatise on historic rights in the South China Sea) [2016] (4) *Faxue Pinglun* 76.

Jia Qingguo, 'China' in Watanabe K (ed), *Humanitarian Intervention. The Evolving Asian Debate* (Japan Center for International Exchange, Brookings Institution Press 2003).

Ji 纪 Wenhua 文华 and Jiang 姜 Liyong 丽勇, '中国对和平争端解决的充分参与 - WTO 争端解决中的第三方与中国的参与' (China's Full Participation in Peaceful Dispute Resolution – the Third Party in WTO Dispute Resolution and China's Participation) [2004] (6) *Faxuejia* 27.

Ji 纪 Wenhua 文华 and Huang 黄 Cui 萃, 'WTO 与 FTA 争端解决管辖权的竞合与协调' (Competition, Cooperation and Coordination between WTO and FTA Dispute Resolution Jurisdictions) [2006] (7) *Faxue* 37.

—— '从案例看 WTO 如何处理 RTA 争端管辖权问题' (Analysis on the Jurisdiction Coincidence between the WTO and RTA: Case Study) (2016) 24 (11) *Hebei Faxue* 65.

Jian 健 Guan 管, '中美贸易争端中的焦点法律问题评析' (Analysis on Key Legal Issues Arising from the Trade Conflicts between US and China) [2018] (3) *Wuda Guojifa Pinglun* 142.

Jiang 江 Guoqing 国青, Jiang 江 Youyou 由由 and Lü 吕 Zhijun 志君, '"有效控制"原则在领土与海事争端中的适用动向——以国际法院"领土钰海事争端案"(尼加拉瓜诉哥伦比亚)为例' (Trends in the Application of the "Effective Control" Principle in Territorial and Maritime Disputes – Taking ICJ "Territorial and Maritime Dispute" (Nicaragua v. Colombia) as an Example) [2013] (6) *Bijiaofa Yanjiu* 38.

Jiang 江 He 河, '和平解决东海争端法律研究' (Legal research on the Peaceful Resolution of the East China Sea Dispute) [2006] (5) *Faxue Pinglun* 84.

—— '国际法框架下的现代海权与中国的海洋维权' (Modern sea power and China's protection of maritime rights and interests in the framework of international law) [2014] (1) *Faxue Pinglun* 92.

Jiang 姜 Huiqin 慧芹 and Gao 高 Fengmei 丰美, '第一届比较法北京论坛：南海问题与海洋法治会议综述' (First Comparative Law Beijing Forum: Summary of the Conference on the South China Sea Issue and Maritime Rule of Law) [2013] (6) *Bijiaofa Yanjiu* 109.

Jiang 姜 Liyong 丽勇, '美国在 WTO 争端解决活动中的实践考察和立场研究' (Research on the Positions and Investigation of the Practice of the United States in WTO Dispute Settlement Activities) [2005] (2) *Faxue Pinglun* 134.

Jiang 江 Weiyu 伟钰, '21 世纪海洋开发国际法框架研究' (Study of 21st Century Maritime Exploration under the Framework of International Law) (2004) 25 (9) *Faxue Zazhi* 64.

Jiang 姜 Zuoli 作利, '诚信原则在 WTO 争端解决机制中的适用评析' (On Application of Good Faith in the WTO Dispute Settlement Mechanism) (2010) 32 (1) *Xiandai Faxue* 108.

—— '试论 WTO 争端解决程序中适用盖然性优势证明标准的合理性' (On the Justification of the Evidential Preponderance Standard to Be Applied in WTO Dispute Settlement Proceedings) [2014] (6) *Bijiaofa Yanjiu* 137.

—— '评 WTO 争端解决程序中法律解释的适用法 ———发展中国家的视角' (Reviewing the applicable law in WTO dispute settlement procedures – from a developing country perspective) (2014) 28 (4) *Dangdai Faxue* 131.

Jilin Province Law Society, '何志鹏教授被聘任为外交部国际法咨询委员会委员' (Professor He Zhipeng was appointed as a member of the Foreign Ministry International Law Consultative Committee) *Jilin Province Law Society* (Changchun, 8 March 2017) <http://www.jlfxhw.com/hyfc/2771.jhtml> accessed 10 January 2019.

Jin 金 Xiaochen 晓晨, 'WTO 争端解决机制霞私人诉权的探讨' (Inquiry into Individuals Right to Sue under the WTO Dispute Settlement Mechanism) (2003) 24 (2) *Faxue Zazhi* 31.

—— '国家主权让渡在 WTO 争端解决机制中的发展 - 兼评外经贸部、最高人民法院关于贸易壁垒、反补贴、反倾销的三个规定' (Relinquishing Sovereignty in the Development of the WTO Dispute Settlement Mechanism – Discussion of Three Provisions by the Ministry of Foreign Trade and Economic Cooperation and the Supreme People's Court on Trade Barriers, Anti-Subsidy, and Anti-Dumping) [2003] (2) *Zhengzhi yu Falü* 92.

Jin 金 Yongming 永明, '中国拥有钓鱼岛主权的国际法分析' (International Law Analysis of China's Sovereignty over the Diaoyu Islands), *Dangdai Faxue*, no. 5, 2013, 3.

—— '论海洋法的发展与挑战——纪念联合国成立 70 周年' (On the Development and Challenges of the Law of the Sea – In Memory of the 70th Anniversary of the Establishment of the UN) [2015] (3) *Nanyang wenti yanjiu* 1.

—— 'The Impact and Influence of the South China Sea Arbitration on the Law of the Sea' (2017) 5 *China Legal Science (Zhongguo Faxue)* 82 [English].

Johnson CK, 'Thoughts from the Chairman: Xi Jinping unveils his foreign policy vision' *CSIS* (Washington DC, 8 December 2014) <https://www.csis.org/analysis/thoughts-chairman-xi-jinping-unveils-his-foreign-policy-vision> accessed 3 October 2019.

Johnston AI, *Cultural Realism. Strategic Culture and Grand Strategy in Chinese History* (Princeton University Press 1995).

Jones WC, *The Great Qing Code: A New Translation* (Clarendon Press 1994).

Jones WC, 'The Constitution of the People's Republic of China' in Keller P (ed), *Chinese Law and Legal Theory* (Ashgate/Dartmouth 2001) 147.

Joyner CC, 'International Law is, as International Relations Theory Does?' (2006) 100 AJIL 248.

Ju 鞠 Hailong 海龙, '当代南海问题的函数解析 – 兼论两岸关系对我国和平解决南海问题的影响', (Analysis of the Current South China Sea Issue – Including the Impact of Cross-Straits Relations on Our Country's Peaceful Resolution of the South China Sea Issue) [2009] (6) *Dongnanya Yanjiu* 41.

Jun Qiu, 'The CLCS Modalities for Handling Submissions Involving Disputes and Their Possible Application to the South China Sea' (2015) 14 CJIL 135.

Kahn P and Wälde T, *New Aspects of International Investment Law* (Brill-Nijhoff 2007).

Kaldunski M, 'A Commentary on Maritime Boundary Arbitration between Bangladesh and India Concerning the Bay of Bengal' (2015) 28 *Leiden Journal of International Law* 799.

Kalicki J and Medeiros S, 'Revisiting Brazil's Traditional Reluctance Towards ICSID, BITs and Investor-State Arbitration' (2008) 24 *Arbitration International* 423.

Kaminski G, *Chinas Völkerrecht und Außenpolitik: Historische Grundlagen* (Bastei 1972).

—— *Chinesische Positionen zum Völkerrecht* (Duncker & Humblot 1973).

Karapinar B, 'China's export restriction policies: complying with 'WTO plus' or undermining multilateralism' (2011) 10 *World Trade Review* 389.

Keller P (ed), *Chinese Law and Legal Theory* (Ashgate/Dartmouth 2001).

Kennedy M, 'China's role in WTO Dispute Settlement' (2012) 11 *World Trade Review* 555.

—— 'The Integration of Accession Protocols into the WTO Agreement' (2013) 47 *Journal of World Trade* 45.

Kent A, *Between Freedom and Subsistence: China and Human Rights* (OUP 1993).

Kindleberger CP, *Power and Money: The Politics of International Economics and the Economics of International Politics* (Basic Books 1970).

Kinnear M, 'ICSID and International Investment Treaty Arbitration: Progress and Prospects' in Shan W (ed), *China and International Investment Law: Twenty Years of ICSID Membership* (Brill 2015).

—— and others (eds), *Building International Investment Law – The First 50 Years of ICSID* (Kluwer Law International 2016).

Klein N, 'Who Litigates and Why' in Romano CPR, Alter KJ and Shany Y (eds), *The Oxford Handbook of International Adjudication* (OUP 2014).

Koh T, 'International Law and the Peaceful Resolution of Disputes: Asian Perspectives, Contributions, and Challenges' (2011) 1 AsJIL 57.

Kong 孔 Qingjiang 庆江, '与世贸组织争端解决机制有关的几个问题' (On Certain Issues Regarding the WTO Dispute Settlement Mechanism) (2004) 25 (3) *Faxue Zazhi* 46.

Kontorovich E, 'In re Arctic Sunrise (Netherlands v. Russia). PCA Case No. 2014–02. Merits. At http://www.pca-cpa.org. UN Convention on the Law of the Sea Annex VII Arbitral Tribunal, August 14, 2015' (2016) 110 AJIL 96.

Kopela S, 'Historic Titles and Historic Rights in the Law of the Sea in the Light of the South China Sea Arbitration' (2017) 48 *Ocean Development & International Law* 181.

Koskenniemi M, *The Gentle Civilizer of Nations* (CUP 2001).

Kozyrev V, 'China's Continental Energy Strategy: Russia and Central Asia' in Collins GB and others (eds), *China's energy strategy: the impact on Beijing's maritime policies* (Naval Institute Press 2008).

Kraska J, 'Military Operations' in Rothwell DR and others (eds), *The Oxford Handbook of the Law of the Sea* (OUP 2015).

Krasner SD, *International Regimes* (Cornell University Press 1983).

—— 'Realist Views of International Law' (2002) 96 *Proceedings of the ASIL Annual Meeting* 265.

Krejsa H, 'Rodrigo Duterte's Turn in the South China Sea – Will the Philippines' new president snatch defeat from the jaws of victory?' *The Diplomat* (Tokyo, 15 July 2016) <http://thediplomat.com/2016/07/rodrigo-dutertes-turn-in-the-south-china-sea/> accessed 15 March 2019.

Krisch N, 'Review Essay Legality, Morality and the Dilemma of Humanitarian Intervention after Kosovo' (2002) 16 EJIL 323.

Kroll S, *Normgenese durch Re-interpretation – China und das europäische Völkerrecht im 19. und 20. Jahrhundert*, Göttingen, Nomos, 2012.

Ku J, 'China and the Future of International Adjudication' (2012) 27 *Maryland Journal of International Law* 154.

—— 'China's Ridiculously Weak Legal Argument Against Complying with the South China Sea Arbitration Award' *Lawfare* (Washington DC, 6 June 2016) <https://www.lawfareblog.com/chinas-ridiculously-weak-legal-argument-against-complying-south-china-sea-arbitration-award> accessed 1 March 2019.

—— and Mirasola C, 'The South China Sea and China's "Four Sha" Claim: New Legal Theory, Same Bad Argument' *Lawfare Blog* (Washington DC, 25 September 2017) <https://www.lawfareblog.com/south-china-sea-and-chinas-four-sha-claim-new-legal-theory-same-bad-argument> accessed 15 March 2019.

Kuhn A, 'China Steps Up Crackdown On Liberal Universities' *NPR* (Washington DC, 8 September 2017) <https://www.npr.org/2017/09/08/549549998/china-steps-up-crackdown-on-liberal-universities> accessed 1 March 2019.

Lai KL, *An Introduction to Chinese Philosophy* (CUP 2008).

Lam WWL, 'China's Anti-Graft Campaign in Review' *Jamestown Foundation* (Washington DC, 7 December 2015) <https://jamestown.org/program/chinas-anti-graft-campaign-in-review/> accessed 1 March 2019.

Lan 兰 Hua 花, '用尽当地救济原则与国际投资争议解决' (The Principle of Exhaustion of Local Remedies and the Resolution of International Investment Disputes) (2002) 17 (6) *Henansheng Zhengfa Guanli Ganbu Xueyuan Xuebao* 104.

Lathrop CG, 'Baselines' in Rothwell DR and others (eds), *The Oxford Handbook of the Law of the Sea* (OUP 2015).

Lauterpacht H, *The Development of International Law by the International Court* (Stevens and Sons 1958).

Lee KB, 'Should the Invocation of Paragraph 5(a) of Annex I to the CLCS Rules of Procedure Result in an Automatic Deferral of the Consideration of a Submission' (2014) 13 CJIL 605.

Lee S, 'An Institutional Analysis of Xi Jinping's Centralization of Power' (2017) 26 *Journal of Contemporary China* 325.

Lee YS, *Safeguard Measures in World Trade* (Edward Elgar Publishing 2014).

Lei 雷 Xiaolu 筱璐, '论非主权性历史性权利与专属经济区和大陆架制度的并存与协调' (On the co-existence and coordination of non-sovereign historic rights and the exclusive economic zone and continental shelf) [2016] (3) *Faxue Pinglun* 95.

Leitner K and Lester S, 'WTO Dispute Settlement 1995–2009 – A Statistical Analysis' (2010) 13 *Journal of International Economic Law* 205.

—— 'WTO Dispute Settlement 1995–2016 – A Statistical Analysis' (2017) 20 *Journal of International Economic Law* 171.

Leng Shujie and Wertime D, 'China's Anti-Corruption Campaign Ensnares Tens of Thousands More – Over 100,000 cadres have now been disciplined as part of President Xi Jinping's anti-graft drive' *Foreign Policy* (Washington DC, 9 January 2015) <https://foreignpolicy.com/2015/01/09/chinas-anti-corruption-campaign-ensnares-tens-of-thousands-more/> accessed 3 October 2019.

Lester S, Mercurio B and Davies A, *World Trade Law – Text, Materials and Commentary*, (2nd edn, Hart 2012).

Li 李 Bin 滨, '中国的马克思主义国际关系研究' (Marxist IR-Research in China) in Wang 王 Yizhou 逸舟 (ed), *中国国际关系研究 (1995–2005)* (IR-Research in China 1995–2005) (Beijing Daxue Chubanshe 2006).

Li 李 Dongdong 冬冬, WTO 国民待遇原则在《TBT 协定》适用中的新发展 (The New Development of WTO National Treatment Principle in the Application of TBT Agreement) (2017) 39 (2) *Faxue Luntan* 151.

Li 李 Guangyi 广义, '东海大陆架划界争端国际法依据辨证' (The International Legal Basis on the Delimitation of the Continental Shelf of the East China Sea) (2005) 19 (3) *Dangdai Faxue* 103.

Li 李 Jieyu 洁宇, '论《联合国海洋法公约》 有助于提升中国的软实力' (On how 'UNCLOS' can aid in increasing China's soft power) [2016] (3) *Xin Dongfang* 7.

Li Jing, 'Communist Party orders a course of Marxism for China's universities' *SCMP* (Hong Kong 20 January 2015) <https://www.scmp.com/news/china/article/1682774/communist-party-orders-course-marxism-chinas-universities> accessed 31 December 2018.

Li 李 Qingling 庆灵, '国际投资仲裁中的缔约国解释：式微与回归' (Contracting state interpretation in international investment arbitration: decline and return) [2016] (5) *Huadong Zhengfa Daxue Xuebao* 132.

Li 李 Xianbo 先波 and Zhong 钟 Yuehui 月辉, 'WTO 争端解决机制权力的扩张 - 几类 WTO 争端解决机构管辖的特殊事项' (Aggressive Power Exercised by the WTO Dispute Settlement Mechanism: Several Special Issues Resolved by the DSB) (2005) 19 (6) *Dangdai Faxue* 140.

Li Xiaojun, 'Understanding China's Behavioral Change in the WTO Dispute Settlement System: Power, Capacity, and Normative Constraints in Trade Adjudication' (2012) 52 *Asian Survey* 1111.

Li 李 Xiaoling 晓玲, WTO 补偿实践的动向及其改革启示 (Trend of WTO Compensation Practices and Its Enlightenment on Reform) (2014) 36 (6) *Xiandai Faxue* 157.

Li 李 Yanyan 彦彦, '欧盟反倾销法修改案与 WTO 多边规则的适用' (The case of the EU anti-dumping law amendment and the application of WTO multilateral rules) [2017] (11) *Falü Shiyong* 55.

Li 李 Yong 永 and Zhang 张 Lina 丽娜, 论历史性权利法律基础的二重性 (On Dual Nature of Legal Base of Historic Rights) (2018) 36 (2) *Hebei Faxue* 62.

Li Yongjie, 'Factors to be Considered for China's Future Investment Treaties' in Shan Wenhua (ed), *China and International Investment Law: Twenty Years of ICSID Membership* (Brill 2015).

Liang 梁 Danni 丹妮, '国际投资协定一般例外条款研究 ———与 WTO 共同但有区别的司法经验' (Researching general exception norms in international investment treaties – common and distinct judicial experiences with the WTO) [2014] (1) *Faxue Pinglun* 100.

Liang 梁 Kaiyin 开银, 论 ICSID 与 WTO 争端解决机制的冲突及选择——以国家和私人投资争议解决为视角 (On Conflicts And Choice of Disputes Solving Systems Between ICSID And WTO) (2009) 30 (8) *Faxue Zazhi* 90.

Liang 梁 Kuiran 岿然, '美国双边投资协定范本的劳工保护条款分析——兼论其对我国的影响及我国之对策' (Analysis on the Labor Protection Article of the US 2012 BIT Model ———The Influence on and the Countermeasures of China) (2014) 32 (7) *Hebei Faxue* 158.

—— '美国双边投资协定范本争议解决条款分析——以对 ICSID 仲裁管辖权之认可为视角' (The Dispute Settlement Article of the US 2012 BIT Model ———Its Consent Clause to ICSID Arbitration) (2016) 34 (3) *Hebei Faxue* 121.

Liang Wei, 'China, developing countries, and the Doha agricultural negotiations' in Zeng Ka and Liang Wei (eds), *China and Global Trade Governance – China's first decade in the World Trade Organization* (Routledge 2013).

Liang 梁 Yong 咏, '从国际法视角看中日东海大陆架划界争端' (Reviewing the Sino-Japanese Dispute over Continental Shelf Delimitation in the East China Sea from an International Law Perspective) [2006] (8) *Faxue* 122.

—— 'WTO 框架下碳关税可能引致的贸易争端与解决' (Trade Disputes Possibly Brought About by Carbon Taxes under the WTO Framework and Solutions) [2010] (7) *Faxue* 76.

Lim D, 'Case Comment: Government of the Lao People's Democratic Republic v Sanum Investments Ltd [2015] SGHC 15' *Singapore Law Blog* (Singapore, 10 March 2015) <http://www.singaporelawblog.sg/blog/article/95> accessed 30 March 2019.

Liu Han-Wei and Maughan J, 'China's Rare Earths Export Quotas: Out of the China Raw-Materials Gate, But Past the WTO's Finish Line?' (2012) 15 *Journal of International Economic Law* 971.

Liu 刘 Hua 华, '通过 ICSID 解决中非之间投资争端的研究' (Research on Resolving China-Africa Investment Disputes through ICSID) (2013) 31 (2) *Zhengfa Luntan* 173.

Liu 刘 Sun 笋, 建立国际投资仲裁的上诉机制问题析评 (On Establishing an Appellate Mechanism of International Investment Arbitration) (2009) 31 (5) *Xiandai Faxue* 122.

Liu 刘 Xuefei 雪飞, '国际海洋法法庭与国际法院的咨询管辖比较' (Comparison of the International Tribunal for the Law of the Sea's and the International Court's Advisory Jurisdiction) [2006] (4) *Zhongguo Haiyang Daxue Xuebao* 1.

Liu 刘 Yichun 怡纯, 利用 WTO 争端解决机制维护中国权益探讨 (Discussion on Maintaining China's Rights and Interests by Using the WTO Dispute Settlement Mechanism) (2018) 36 (5) *Zhengfa Luntan* 112.

Liu 刘 Ying 瑛, 'BOT 方式下的争议解决机制与 ICSID 仲裁' (Dispute Settlement Mechanisms under BOT and ICSID Arbitration) (2002) 23 (5) *Faxue Zazhi* 65.

—— and Du 杜 Lei 蕾, 论《中国入世议定书》与 WTO 多边贸易协定的关系——从"中国稀土案"上诉机构报告切入 (Relations between 'China's WTO Accession Protocol' and WTO Multilateral Agreements – Cutting in from the 'China Rare Earts Case' Appellate Body Report) [2015] (1) *Huadong Zhengfa Daxue Xuebao* 25.

Liu 刘 Yong 勇, '"中国平安诉比利时王国投资仲裁案"——以条约适用的时际法为视角' ("China Ping An v. Kingdom of Belgium Investment Arbitration" – From the Perspectve of the Intertemporal Law on Treaty Application) (2016) 38 (4) *Huanqiu Falü Pinglun* 162.

—— "一带一路"投资风险及其法律应对———以"尤科斯诉俄罗斯案"为视角 ("Belt and Road Initiative" Investment Risks and Legal Responses – From the Perspective of the "Yukos v Russia Case") (2018) 40 (1) *Huanqiu Falü Pinglun* 175.

Liu Zhiyun, 'Interdisciplinary Research on International Relations Theory and International Law in China over the Past 10 Years' (2011) 6 *Frontiers of Law in China* 496.

—— '国家利益的层次分析与国家在 国际法上的行动选择' (Analytic Hierarchy of National Interest and Nation's Action Selection on International Law) (2015) 37 (1) *Xiandai Faxue* 139.

Liu 刘 Ziping 子平, 论 GATT 与 GATS 项下义务的累加性 (On the Accumulation of Duties under GATT and GATS) [2015] (1) *Huadong Zhengfa Daxue Xuebao* 35.

Lo Bobo, *Axis of convenience: Moscow, Beijing, and the new Geopolitics* (Chatham House 2008).

Lo CWH, 'Socialist Legal Theory in Deng Xiaoping's China' in Keller P (ed) *Chinese Law and Legal Theory* (Ashgate/Dartmouth 2001).

Lobell SE, Ripsman NM and Taliaferro JW, *Neoclassical Realism, the State, and Foreign Policy* (CUP 2009).

Lodge MW, 'The Deep Seabed' in Rothwell DR and others (eds), *The Oxford Handbook of the Law of the Sea* (OUP 2015).

Low P, 'Developing Countries in the World Trade Organization: What are the Issues?' in Janow ME, Donaldson V and Yanovich A (eds), *The WTO: Governance, Dispute Settlement, and Developing Countries* (Juris Publishing Inc 2008).

Lu Shen and Westcott B, 'South China Sea: Beijing calls KFC, Apple protests "irrational"' *CNN* (Beijing, 21 July 2016) <https://edition.cnn.com/2016/07/20/asia/china-nationalism-south-china-sea-ruling/index.html> accessed 16 November 2019.

Lu Yiyi, 'The Collective Study Sessions of the Politburo: A Multipurpose Tool of China's Central Leadership' *Nottingham: China Policy Institute Briefing Series Issue 27* (Nottingham October 2007) <https://www.nottingham.ac.uk/iaps/documents/cpi/briefings/briefing-27-collective-study-sessions-of-the-politburo.pdf> accessed 1 March 2019.

Lubman SB, *Bird in a Cage: Legal reform in China after Mao* (Stanford University Press 1999.

Luney PRJ, 'Traditions and Foreign Influences: Systems of Law in China and Japan' (1989) 52 *Law and Contemporary Problems* 129.

Luo 罗 Chao 超, '南海争端解决机制法律框架初探' (A First Inquiry into Mechanisms under a Legal Framework to Solve the South China Sea Dispute) (2011) 29 (2) *Taiyuan Ligong Daxue Xuebao* 11.

Luo 罗 Guoqiang 国强, '多边路径在解决南海争端中的作用及其构建——兼评 南海搁放行为宣言' (Legal Principles Used by the International Court when Solving Disputes over Island Sovereignty) (2010) 32 (4) *Faxue Luntan* 1.

—— '共同开发"政策在海洋争端解决中的实际效果：分析与展望' (Analysis About The Joint Development Policy And Its Practical Effect In Solving Maritime Disputes: Analysis And Prediction) (2011) 32 (4) *Faxue Zazhi* 14.

—— '论 "南海仲裁案"仲裁裁决的枉法性' (On the injustice of the arbitral award in the 'South China Sea Arbitration') (2016) 30 (6) *Dangdai Faxue* 148.

—— and Ye 叶 Quan 泉, '争议岛屿在海洋划界中的法律效力——兼析钓鱼岛作为争议岛屿的法律效力' (Disputed Islands' Legal Effect in Maritime Boundary Delimitation – Concurrent Analysis of the Legal Effect of the Diaoyu Islands as Disputed Islands) (2011) 25 (1) *Dangdai Faxue* 112.

—— and Liu 刘 Chenhong 晨虹, 历史性水域的性质与协调———以南海断续线内水域为研究对象 (The Nature and Adjustment of the 'Historic Waters' – With Respect to the Waters Within the Dashed Line) (2018) 20 (1) *Guoji Luntan* 1.

Luo 罗 Huanxin 欢欣, '国际法院在解决领土争端中的局限性' (Limitations of Territorial Dispute Resolution at the ICJ) (2010) 25 (11) *Fazhi Luncong* 114.

—— '国家在国际造法进程中的角色与功能———以国际海洋法的形成与运作为例' (The role and function of states in international law making processes – taking the formation and operation of the law of the sea as an example) (2018) 38 (4) *Faxue Yanjiu* 53.

Lü 吕 Xiaojie 晓杰, '对 WTO 争端解决机制中司法经济原则功能的再思考' (Further Reflections on the Function of the Judicial Economy Principle in the WTO Dispute Settlement Mechanism) (2008) 30 (6) *Huanqiu Falü Pinglun* 81.

Ma 马 Deyi 得懿, 《 联合国海洋法公约》第 283 条交换意见义务: 问题与检视 (On the Obligation to Exchange Views in Article 283 of UNCLOS: Issues and Reflection) [2018] (4) *Zhengzhi yu Falü* 102.

Ma 马 Ran 冉, 'TRIPS 协定之文化思考 ———以文化多样性为视角' (Cultural Thoughts on TRIPS: From the Perspective of Cultural Diversity) (2015) 37 (6) *Xiandai Faxue* 154.

—— WTO 补贴规则视角下中国文化产业财税政策措施探析 (A Study on China's Cultural Industry Financial Measures and Tax Policies in the Framework of WTO Subsidy Rules) (2016) 31 (5) *Henan Caijing Zhengfa Daxue Xuebao* 158.

Ma 马 Zhongfa 忠法, 论条约的整体解释法———以美日欧诉中国稀土等产品出口措施案为例 (On systematic interpretation of treaties – taking the case measures related to the export of rare earths and other products wherein the US, Japan, and EC sued China as an example) (2014) 28 (4) *Dangdai Faxue* 142.

MacCormack G, *The spirit of traditional Chinese law* (University of Georgia Press 1996).

Macfarlane SN, 'The "R" in BRICs: Is Russia an emerging power?' (2006) 82 *International Affairs* 41.

Mahrenbach LC, 'Emerging powers, Domestic Politics, and WTO Dispute Settlement Reform' (2016) 21 *International Negotiation* 233.

Malawer SS, 'Imposed Treaties and International Law' (1977) 7 *California Western International Law Journal* 1.

Marboe I, 'Quasar de Valores SICAV SA and others v The Russian Federation – Another Chapter of the Yucos Affair' (2013) 28 *ICSID Review* 247.

Markus T, 'Article 46 – Use of Terms' in Alexander Proelss (ed), *United Nations Convention on the Law of the Sea – A Commentary* (CH Beck 2017).

Martina M, 'Exclusive: In China, the Party's push for influence inside foreign firms stirs fears' *Reuters* (Beijing, 24 August 2017) <https://www.reuters.com/article/us-china-congress-companies-idUSKCN1B40JU> accessed 25 June 2018.

Martínez Gutiérrez NA, 'Introduction' in Attard DJ, Fitzmaurice M and Martínez Guttiérez NA (eds), *The IMLI Manual on International Maritime Law – Volume I: The Law of the Sea* (OUP 2014).

Matsushita M, Schoenbaum TJ and Mavroidis PC, *The World Trade Organization – Law, Practice and Policy* (2nd edn, OUP 2006).

Mavroidis PC, 'Legal Eagles? The WTO Appellate Body's First Ten Years' in Janow ME, Donaldson V and Yanovich A (eds), *The WTO: Governance, Dispute Settlement, and Developing Countries* (Juris Publishing Inc 2008).

—— and Janow ME, 'Free Markets, State Involvement, and the WTO: Chinese State-Owned Enterprises in the Ring' (2017) 16 *World Trade Review* 571.

McDorman TL, 'Rights and Jurisdiction over Resources in the South China Sea: UNCLOS and the "nine-dash line"' in Jayakumar S, Koh T and Beckman R (eds), *The South China Sea Disputes and Law of the Sea* (Edward Elgar Publishing 2014).

—— 'The Continental Shelf' in Rothwell DR and others (eds), *The Oxford Handbook of the Law of the Sea* (OUP 2015).

McGregor R and others, 'Xi Won't Go' *China File* (New York, 25 February 2018) <http://www.chinafile.com/conversation/xi-wont-go> accessed 31 December 2018.

Mercurio B and Tyagi M, 'China's Evolving Role in WTO Dispute Settlement: Acceptance, Consolidation and Activation' in Herrmann C and Terhechte JP (eds) (2012) 3 *European Yearbook of International Economic Law* 89.

Merrills JG, *International Dispute Settlement*, (4th edition, CUP 2005).

Miller A, 'Politburo Processes under Xi Jinping' *Hoover Institution China Leadership Monitor no 47* (Stanford, 14 July 2015) <https://www.hoover.org/research/politburo-processes-under-xi-jinping> accessed 1 March 2019.

Ministry of External Affairs of India, *Goa and the Charter of the United Nations* (Government of India Press 1960).

—— 'Recent Developments in Doklam Area' (New Delhi, 30 June 2017) <http://www.mea.gov.in/press-releases.htm?dtl/28572/Recent_Developments_in_Doklam_Area> accessed 1 March 2019.

Ministry of Foreign Affairs of Japan, 'Senkaku Islands Q&A' (Tokyo, 13 April 2016) <http://www.mofa.go.jp/region/asia-paci/senkaku/qa_1010.html#q1> accessed 1 March 2019.

Ministry of Foreign Affairs of the PRC, 'International Recognition Of China's Sovereignty over the Nansha Islands' (Beijing, 17 November 2000) <http://www.fmprc.gov.cn/mfa_eng/topics_665678/3754_666060/t19232.shtml> accessed 1 March 2019.

—— 'Foreign Ministry Spokesperson Qin Gang's Response to the International Court of Justice's Advisory Opinion on the Kosovo Case' (Beijing, 23 July 2010) <http://www.fmprc.gov.cn/ce/cemd/eng/fyrth/t719113.htm> accessed 1 March 2019.

—— 'Position Paper of the Governmnt of the People's Republic of China on the Matter of Jurisdiction in the South China Sea Arbitration Initiated by the Republic of the Philippines' (Beijing, 7 December 2014) <http://www.fmprc.gov.cn/mfa_eng/zxxx_662805/t1217147.shtml> accessed 1 March 2019.

—— 'Statement of the Ministry of Foreign Affairs of the People's Republic of China on the Award on Jurisdiction and Admissibility of the South China Sea Arbitration by the Arbitral Tribunal Established at the Request of the Republic of the Philippines' (Beijing, 30 October 2015) <https://www.fmprc.gov.cn/mfa_eng/zxxx_662805/t1310474.shtml> accessed 1 April 2019.

—— '外交部国际法咨询委员会召开第三次全体会议' (The Ministry of Foreign Affairs International Law Consultative Comittee convenes its third plenary meeting) (Beijing, 6 January 2016) <https://www.fmprc.gov.cn/chn//pds/wjb/zzjg/tyfls/xwlb/t1329838.htm> accessed 30 December 2018.

—— 'Statement on the Award of 12 July 2016 of the Arbitral Tribunal in the South China Sea Arbitration Established at the Request of the Republic of the Philippines' (Beijing, 12 July 2016) <http://www.fmprc.gov.cn/nanhai/eng/snhwtlcwj_1/t1379492.htm> accessed 1 March 2019.

—— 'Spokesperson Lu Kang's Remarks on Japanese Foreign Minister's Statement on the Award of South China Sea Arbitration Initiated by the Philippines' (Beijing, 12 July 2016) <http://www.fmprc.gov.cn/mfa_eng/xwfw_665399/s2510_665401/t1380245.shtml> accessed 1 April 2019.

—— 'China Adheres to the Position of Settling Through Negotiation the Relevant Disputes Between China and the Philippines in the South China Sea' (Beijing, 13 July 2016) <https://www.fmprc.gov.cn/nanhai/eng/snhwtlcwj_1/t1380615.htm> accessed 10 November 2019.

—— 'Foreign Ministry Spokesperson Lu Kang's Remarks' (Beijing, 28 July 2016) <http://www.fmprc.gov.cn/mfa_eng/xwfw_665399/s2510_665401/2535_665405/t1385371.shtml> accessed 1 April 2019.

—— 'China and Bhutan Hold 24th Round of Talks on Boundary Issue' (Beijing, 15 August 2016) <http://www.fmprc.gov.cn/mfa_eng/wjbxw/t1389633.shtml> accessed 1 March 2019.

—— 'Foreign Ministry Spokesperson Hua Chunying's Regular Press Conference on October 21, 2016' (Beijing, 21 October 2016) <http://www.fmprc.gov.cn/mfa_eng/xwfw_665399/s2510_665401/t1407743.shtml> accessed 2 July 2018.

—— 'The Facts and China's Position Concerning the Indian Border Troops' Crossing of the China-India Boundary in the Sikkim Sector into the Chinese Territory' (Beijing, 2 August 2017) <http://www.fmprc.gov.cn/mfa_eng/zxxx_662805/P020170802542676636134.pdf> accessed 1 March 2019.

Ministry of Foreign Affairs of the Russian Federation, 'Comment by the Information and Press Department of the Russian Ministry of Foreign Affairs regarding the situation around the Arctic Sunrise' (Moscow, 23 October 2013) <http://www.mid.ru/en/web/guest/kommentarii_predstavitelya/-/asset_publisher/MCZ7HQuMdqBY/content/id/91266> accessed 25 August 2017.

—— 'The Ministry of Foreign Affairs of the Russian Federation on certain legal issues highlighted by the action of the Arctic Sunrise against Prirazlomnaya platform' (Moscow, 5 August 2015) <http://www.mid.ru/en/web/guest/foreign_policy/news/-/asset_publisher/cKNonkJE02Bw/content/id/1639745> accessed 25 August 2017.

—— 'Briefing by Deputy Director of the Information and Press Department Artyom Kozhin' (Moscow, 20 July 2017) <http://www.mid.ru/en/press_service/spokesman/briefings/-/asset_publisher/D2wHaWMCU6Od/content/id/2818579> accessed 25 August 2017.

Ministry of Interior of Taiwan – Maritime Information Service Center, 'Position Paper on ROC South China Sea Policy' (Taipeh, 21 March 2016) <http://maritimeinfo.moi.gov.tw/marineweb/UpLoad/UFile/0000001997/Position%20Paper%20on%20ROC%20South%20China%20Sea%20Policy.pdf> accessed 15 July 2017.

Mitchell AD and Prusa TJ, '*China–Autos*: Haven't We Danced this Dance Before?' (2016) 15 *World Trade Review* 303.

Moellendorf D, 'Treaty Norms and Climate Change Mitigation' (2009) 23 *Ethics and International Affairs* 247.

Mogato M, 'China backs joint energy development with Philippines in disputed sea' *Reuters* (Manila, 25 July 2017) <http://www.reuters.com/article/us-philippines-china-idUSKBN1AA10L> accessed 15 March 2019.

—— Mogato M, Martina M and Blanchard B, 'ASEAN deadlocked on South China Sea, Cambodia blocks statement' *Reuters* (Vientiane, 25 July 2016) <https://www.reuters.com/article/us-southchinasea-ruling-asean/asean-deadlocked-on-south-china-sea-cambodia-blocks-statement-idUSKCN1050F6> accessed 10 November 2019.

Mollman S, 'China is threatening to leave a major UN sea treaty – and there's nothing the US can say about it' *Quartz* (New York, 21 June 2016) <https://qz.com/712170/china-is-threatening-to-leave-a-major-un-sea-treaty-and-theres-nothing-the-us-can-say-about-it/> accessed 11 November 2019.

Monaghan A, 'China surpasses US as world's largest trading nation' *Guardian* (London, 10 January 2014) <https://www.theguardian.com/business/2014/jan/10/china-surpasses-us-world-largest-trading-nation> accessed 5 January 2019.

Moore MO and Wu M, 'Antidumping and Strategic Industrial Policy: Tit-for-Tat Trade Remedies and the China–X-Ray Equipment Dispute' (2015) 14 *World Trade Review* 239.

Morgenthau HJ, *Politics Among Nations. The Struggle for Power and Peace* (Knopf 1948).

—— *Politics Among Nations. The Struggle for Power and Peace* (7th edn, McGraw-Hill 2006).

Moynihan H, 'China's Evolving Approach to International Dispute Settlement' *Chatham House Briefing – International Law Programme* (London, March 2017) 9 <https://www.chathamhouse.org/sites/files/chathamhouse/publications/research/2017-03-29-chinas-evolving-approach-international-dispute-settlement-moynihan-final.pdf> accessed 1 March 2019.

Muller W, 'Beyond History and Sovereignty – China and the Future of International Law' (PhD thesis, European University Institute 2013).

Muniz JDP and Peretti L, 'Brazil Signs New Bilateral Investment Treaties with Mozambique and Angola: New Approach to BITs or "Toothless Lions"?' *Global Arbitration News* (London, 7 April 2015 <https://globalarbitrationnews.com/20150407-brazil-signs-new-bilateral-investment-treaties/> accessed 10 November 2018.

Muró JL, 'The First Ten Years of the Appellate Body and the WTO Dispute Settlement System: A Historical Perspective' in Janow ME, Donaldson V and Yanovich A (eds), *The WTO: Governance, Dispute Settlement, and Developing Countries* (Juris Publishing Inc 2008).

Murphy SD, 'Assessing the Legality of Invading Iraq' (2004) 92 *Georgetown Law Journal* 173.

—— 'WTO Decision Striking Down U.S. Steel Safeguard Measures' (2004) 98 AJIL 179.

Na 那 Li 力 and Zhong 仲 Xinxin 欣欣, '论 WTO 争端解决机制的"司法化"趋势' (Discussing the Trend of "Judicialization" of the WTO's Dispute Settlement Mechanism) (2002) 16 (4) *Dangdai Faxue* 9.

Narlikar A, 'India rising: Responsible to whom?' (2013) 89 *International Affairs* 561.

National Bureau of Asian Research – Maritime Awareness Project, 'Brunei' (Seattle, 2019) <http://maritimeawarenessproject.org/profiles/brunei/> accessed 1 March 2019.

Naughton B, *Growing Out of the Plan: Chinese Economic Reform, 1978–1993* (CUP 1995).

Ndi GK, 'Philippines v China: assessing the implications of the South China Sea arbitration' (2016) 8 *Australian Journal of Maritime and Ocean Affairs* 269.

Neligan M, 'China insurer Ping An files claim for Fortis loss' *Reuters* (London, 24 September 2012) <http://in.reuters.com/article/2012/09/24/pingan-fortis-idINL5E8KO9V520120924> accessed 30 March 2019.

Nguyen HT, 'Vietnam's Position on the Sovereignty over the Paracels & the Spratlys: Its Maritime Claims' (2012) 1 *Journal of East Asia and International Law* 165.

Nie 聂 Hongyi 宏毅, '国际法院在解决领土争端中的作用及困境评析' (Evaluation of the ICJ's Role and Predicament in Solving Territorial Disputes) (2009) 27 (1) *Hebei Faxue* 1.

Ning 宁 Qingtong 清同, '南海涉外侵权中我国渔业权制度的需求、供给和创新' (Demand, supply and innovation of China's fisheries rights system in the face of foreign infringements in the South China Sea) (2015) 33 (2) *Falü Kexue* 162.

Noesselt N, *Die Beziehungen der EU zu China und Taiwan. Hintergründe und Perzeptionen* (Kovac 2008).

—— *Alternative Weltordnungsmodelle? IB-Diskurse in China* (VS Verlag für Sozialwissenschaften / Springer Fachmedien Wiesbaden GmbH 2010).

Nordquist MH and others (eds), *United Nations Convention on the Law of the Sea – A Commentary – Volume II: Articles 1 to 85, Annexes I and II, Final Act, Annex II*, (Martinus Nijhoff Publishers 1993).

—— *United Nations Convention on the Law of the Sea – A Commentary – Volume III: Articles 86 to 132 and Documentary Annexes* (Martinus Nijhoff Publishers 1995).

—— *United Nations Convention on the Law of the Sea – A Commentary – Volume V: Articles 279 to 320, Annexes V, VI, VII, VIII and IX, Final Act, Annex I, Resolutions I, III, IV* (Martinus Nijhoff Publishers 1989).

Noyes, JE, 'The Teritorial Sea and Contiguous Zone' in Rothwell DR and others (eds), *The Oxford Handbook of the Law of the Sea* (OUP 2015).

—— 'In Re Arbitration Between the Philippines and China. PCA Case No. 2013–19. Jurisdiction and Admissibility. At http://www.pca-cpa.org. UN Convention on the Law of the Sea Annex VII Arbitral Triubunal, October 29, 2015' (2016) 110 AJIL 102.

Ochoa-Ruiz N and Salamanca-Aguado E, 'Exploring the Limits of International Law relating to the Use of Force in Self-defence' (2005) 16 EJIL 499.

O'Connell ME, 'New International Legal Process' (1999) 93 AJIL 334.

O'Connor S, 'SOE Megamergers Signal New Direction in China's Economic Policy', *U.S.-China Economic and Security Review Commission – Staff Report* (Washington DC, 24 May 2018) <https://www.uscc.gov/sites/default/files/Research/SOE%20Megamergers.pdf> accessed 25 June 2018.

OECD, 'G20 Guiding Principles for Global Investment Policymaking' (Paris, 2019) <https://www.oecd.org/investment/g20-agrees-principles-for-global-investment-policymaking.htm> accessed 15 November 2019.

Pérez VJT, 'Diplomatic Protection Revival for Failure to Comply with Investment Arbitration Awards' (2012) 3 *Journal of International Dispute Settlement* 445.

Peters P, 'Dispute Settlement Arrangements in Investment Treaties' (1991) 22 *Netherlands Yearbook of International Law* 91.

Petersmann EU, 'Review – Das, Abhijit and Nedumpara, James J. (eds), *WTO Dispute Settlement at Twenty: Insiders' Reflections on India's Participation*, New Delhi, Centre for WTO Studies, and Singapore, Springer, 2016' (2016) 19 *Journal of International Economic Law* 893.

Peterson LE, 'China is sued for the first time in an ICSID arbitration; Malaysian investor, Ekran, had rights to 900 hectares of land for development in China' *IAReporter* (Santa Monica, 26 May 2011) <http://www.iareporter.com.uaccess.univie.ac.at/articles/china-is-sued-for-the-first-time-in-an-icsid-arbitration-malaysian-investor-ekran-had-rights-to-900-hectares-of-land-for-development-in-china/> accessed 25 January 2017.

—— 'China prevails as arbitrators dismiss Korean investor's ICSID claim for non-compliance with BIT's 3 year claims window; MFN argument also fails' *IAReporter* (Santa Monica, 10 March 2017) <http://www.iareporter.com.uaccess.univie.ac.at/articles/china-prevails-as-arbitrators-dismiss-korean-investors-icsid-claim-for-non-compliance-with-bits-3-year-claims-window-mfn-argument-also-fails/> accessed 11 March 2017.

—— 'Investment treaty claim against China is ready to proceed to provisional measures ruling, as three arbitrators are put in place' *IAReporter* (Santa Monica, 8 January 2018) <https://www-iareporter-com.uaccess.univie.ac.at/articles/bit-claim-against-china-is-ready-to-proceed-to-provisional-measures-ruling-as-three-arbitrators-are-put-in-place/> accessed 10 June 2018.

Philips T and Pilkington E, 'No Country for Academics: Chinese Crackdown Forces Intellectuals abroad' *The Guardian* (London, 24 May 2016) <https://www.theguardian.com/world/2016/may/24/academics-china-crackdown-forces-intellectuals-abroad> accessed 1 March 2019.

Polasek M, 'Introductory Note to the Three Decisions on the Stay of Enforcement of an ICSID Award' (2005) 20 *ICSID Review* 581.

Pollack M, 'Political Science and International Adjudication' in Romano CPR, Alter KJ and Shany Y (eds), *The Oxford Handbook of International Adjudication* (OUP 2014).

Potter PB, *The Chinese legal system: globalization and local legal culture* (OUP 2002).

—— 'China and the International Legal System: Challenges of Participation' (2007) 191 *The China Quarterly* 699.

Poulsen LS, 'The Politics of South-South Bilateral Investment Treaties' in Broude T, Busch ML and Porges A (eds), *The Politics of International Economic Law* (CUP 2011).

President of Russia, 'Joint Statement of the BRIC Countries' Leaders' (Moscow, 16 January 2009) <http://en.kremlin.ru/supplement/209> accessed 30 March 2019.

Prieto Muñoz JG, 'Ecuador's 2017 termination of treaties: How not to exit the international investment regime' (2017) 14 *Brazilian Journal of International Law* 178.

Proelss A (ed), *United Nations Convention on the Law of the Sea – A Commentary*, (CH Beck 2017).

Prusa TJ and Vermulst E, 'United States – Definitive Anti-Dumping and Countervailing Duties on Certain Products from China: Passing the Buck on Pass-Through' (2013) 12 *World Trade Review* 197.

—— '*China – Countervailing and Anti-dumping Duties on Grain Oriented Flat-rolled Electrical Steel from the United States*: exporting US AD/CVD methodologies through WTO dispute settlement?' (2014) 13 *World Trade Review* 229.

Putnam RD, *The Comparative Study of Political Elites* (Prentice-Hall 1976).

Qi 齐 Qianqian 倩倩, '确定 WTO 贸易报复形式的法律标准和仲裁实践' (Determining Legal Standards of and Arbitration Practice regarding Modes of WTO Trade Retaliation) [2013] (4) *Bijiaofa Yanjiu* 96.

Qi Tong, 'How Exactly does China Consent to Investor-State Arbitration: On the First ICSID Case Against China' (2012) 5 *Contemporary Asia Arbitration Journal* 265.

—— '论中国海外投资者对国际投资仲裁机制的利用' (Reviewing Chinese overseas investors' use of international investment arbitration) [2014] (3) *Dongfang Faxue* 89.

—— '论"一带一路"国际投资争议的预防机制' (Discussing the Prevention Mechanism for "Belt and Road Initiative" International Investment Disputes) [2018] (3) *Faxue Pinglun* 79.

Qi 齐 Yuefeng 岳峰, '中国应更积极参与国际法治进程——对话外交部国际法咨询委员会委员易显河' (China should actively participate in international rule of law processes – A conversation with member of the Foreign Ministry International Law Consultative Committee Yi Xianhe) *Oriental Outlook* (Shanghai, 28 January 2016) <http://www.lwdf.cn/article_1984_1.html> accessed 10 January 2019.

Qiao 乔 Sheng 生, 'WTO 争端解决机制与我国之因应对策' (WTO's DSM and China's Countermeasures) (2002) 20 (6) *Hebei Faxue* 17.

Qin Julia Ya, 'Trade, Investment and beyond: The Impact of WTO Accession on China's Legal System' (2007) 191 *The China Quarterly* 720.

—— 'Pushing the Limits of Global Governance: Trading Rights, Censorship and WTO Jurisprudence—A Commentary on the China–Publications Case' (2011) 10 CJIL 271.

—— 'Reforming WTO Discipline on Export Duties: Sovereignty over Natural Resources, Economic Development and Environmental Protection' (2012) 46 *Journal of World Trade* 1147.

—— 'The predicament of Chinas "WTO-plus" obligation to eliminate export duties: A commentary on the China-Raw Materials case' (2012) 11 CJIL 237.

—— 'Judicial Authority in WTO Law: A Commentary on the Appellate Body's Decision in *China-Rare Earths*' (2014) 13 CJIL 639.

—— and Vandenbussche H, 'China–GOES (Article 21.5): Time to Clarify the Standard for Price Suppression and Price Depression in AD/CVD Investigations' (2017) 16 *World Trade Review* 203.

Qiu S and Monroe T, 'China exports grow despite U.S. tariffs, but import slump most in nearly three years' *Reuters* (Beijing, 10 June 2019) <https://www.reuters.com/article/us-china-economy-trade/china-exports-grow-despite-u-s-tariffs-but-import-slump-most-in-nearly-three-years-idUSKCN1TB040> accessed 9 November 2019.

Qu 曲 Bo 波, '有效控制原则在解决岛屿争端中的适用' (The Application of the Effective Control Principle in the Resolution of Disputes over Islands) (2010) 24 (1) *Dangdai Faxue* 144.

—— '国际法院解决岛屿主权争端适用的法律原则' (Legal Principles Used by the International Court when Solving Disputes over Island Sovereignty) (2011) 32 (2) *Faxue Zazhi* 78.

—— '海洋法中历史性权利构成要件探究' (Exploring Constitutive Requirements of Historical Rights in the Law of the Sea) (2012) 26 (4) *Dangdai Faxue* 3.

—— '南海周边有关国家在南沙群岛的策略及我国对策建议' (Tactics of South China Sea Littoral States Regarding the Spratly Islands and Recommendations for Countermeasures by China) [2012] (6) *Zhongguo Faxue* 58.

—— 禁反言在国际法中的适用——— 以 领 土 争 端 案 为 例 (Applicability of estoppel in international law – on the case of territorial disputes) (2014) 35 (8) *Faxue Zazhi* 16.

—— '对大陆架划界的几个问题的思考' (Reflection on Issues of Delimitation of Continental Shelf) (2016) 20 (4) *Dangdai Faxue* 126.

Raha UK and Raju KD, 'The Enrica Lexie case at the permanent court of arbitration: an analysis' (2016) 56 *Indian Journal of International Law* 221.

Rahman MM and Ara LA, 'TPP, TTIP and RCEP: Implications for South Asian Economies' (2015) 16 *South Asia Economic Journal* 27.

Rajput A, 'India's shifting treaty practice: a comparative analysis of the 2003 and 2015 Model BITs' (2016) 7 *Jindal Global Law Review* 201.

Ranjan P, 'India and Bilateral Investment Treaties—A Changing Landscape' (2014) 29 *ICSID Review* 419.

—— 'Most favoured nation provision in Indian bilateral investment treaties: A case for reform' (2015) 55 *Indian Journal of International Law* 39.

Ratner SR and Slaughter AM, 'Appraising the methods of International Law: A prospectus for readers' (1999) 93 AJIL 291.

Rayfuse R, 'Regional Fisheries Management Organization' in Rothwell DR and others (eds), *The Oxford Handbook of the Law of the Sea* (OUP 2015).

Reed L and Wong K, 'Marine Entitlements in the South China Sea: The Arbitration Between the Philippines and China' (2016) 110 AJIL 746.

Reinisch A, 'How Narrow are Narrow Dispute Resolution Clauses in Investment Treaties?' (2011) 2 *Journal of International Dispute Settlement* 115.

Reinisch A, Footer, ME and Binder C (eds), *International Law and … – Select Proceedings of the European Society of International Law (Volume V 2014)* (Hart Publishing 2016).

Reisman WM, 'The Government of the State of Eritrea and the Government of the Republic of Yemen' (1999) 93 AJIL 668.

—— and Arsanjani MH, 'Applicable Law under the ICSID Convention: The Tortured History of the Interpretation of Article 42' in Kinnear M and others (eds), *Building International Investment Law – The First 50 Years of ICSID* (Kluwer Law International 2016).

Ren Qing, 'Case Comment: Ping An v Belgium – Temporal Jurisdiction of Successive BITs' (2016) 31 *ICSID Review* 129.

Ren 任 Yuanyuan 媛媛, '论国际仲裁在 WTO 争端解决机制中的嬗变' (On the Evolution of International Arbitration in WTO Dispute Settlement System) (2012) 34 (3) *Faxue Luntan* 126.

Research Center for the Theory System of Socialism with Chinese Characteristics – Chinese Academy of Social Sciences, '争取国际投资规则制定话语权' (Strive for the right to speak on international investment rules) *CPCNews* (Beijing, 2 April 2014) <http://theory.people.com.cn/n/2014/0402/c40531-24801269.html> accessed 30 March 2019.

Reus-Smit C, *The Politics of International Law* (CUP 2004).

Reuters, 'From Africa to South America, China's fishing fleet outstrips the competition' *SCMP* (Hong Kong, 23 February 2018) <https://www.scmp.com/news/china/society/article/2134438/chinas-fishing-industry-dwarfs-rest-worlds-study-suggests> accessed 15 March 2019.

Ripinsky S, 'Venezuela's Withdrawal From ICSID: What it Does and Does Not Achieve' *International Institute for Sustainable Development* (Winnipeg, 13 April 2012) <https://www.iisd.org/itn/2012/04/13/venezuelas-withdrawal-from-icsid-what-it-does-and-does-not-achieve/> accessed 30 March 2019.

Ripsman NM, Taliaferro, JW and Lobell SE, *Neoclassical Realist Theory of International Politics* (OUP 2016).

Roberts A, 'China's Strategic Use of Research Funding on International Law' Law*fare Blog* (Washington DC, 8 November 2017) <https://www.lawfareblog.com/chinas-strategic-use-research-funding-international-law> accessed 30 March 2019.

—— *Is International Law International?* (OUP 2017).

—— 'Crimea and the South China Sea – Connections and Disconnects among Chinese, Russian and Western International Lawyers' in Roberts A and others (eds), *Comparative International Law* (OUP 2018).

Robichez J and Lamartin Montes A, 'A Corte Internacional de Justiça e o Brasil: uma necessária reconciliação' (2016) 9 *Anuario Colombiano de Derecho Internacional (acdi)* 51.

Roe T, Happold M and Dingemans J, *Settlement of Investor-State Disputes under the Energy Charter Treaty* (CUP 2011).

Roessler F, 'Appellate Body Ruling in China–Publications and Audiovisual Products' (2011) 10 *World Trade Review* 119.

Romano CPR, Alter KJ and Shany Y (eds), *The Oxford Handbook of International Adjudication* (OUP 2014).

Rose G, 'Neoclassical Realism and Theories of Foreign Policy' (1998) 51 *World Politics* 144.

Roth AI, 'A Bold Move Forward for Neoclassical Realism' (2006) *International Studies Review*, no. 8, 486.

Rothwell DR and others (eds), *The Oxford Handbook of the Law of the Sea* (OUP 2015).

—— 'Charting the Future for the Law of the Sea' in Rothwell DR and others (eds), *The Oxford Handbook of the Law of the Sea* (OUP 2015).

Ruan Zongze, '"Responsible Protection: Building a Safer World"' (*China Institute of International Studies*, 15 June 2012) <http://www.ciis.org.cn/english/2012-06/15/content_5090912.htm> accessed 20 December 2018.

Rubinina E and Rubins N, 'Russia – Overview of Investment Treaty Programme' *Global Arbitration Review* (London, 21 October 2016) <http://globalarbitrationreview.com/jurisdiction/2000149/russia> accessed 5 May 2017.

Ruskola T, 'China in the Age of the World Picture' in Orford A and Hoffmann F (eds), *The Oxford Handbook of the Theory of International Law* (OUP 2016).

Saggi K and Trachtman JP, 'Incomplete Harmonization Contracts in International Economic Law: Report of the Panel, China – Measures Affecting the Protection and Enforcement of Intellectual Property Rights, WT/DS362/R, adopted 20 March 2009' (2011) 10 *World Trade Review* 63.

Salacuse JW, 'The Emerging Global Regime for Investment' (2010) 51 *Harvard International Law Journal* 427.

Sauvant KP and Nolan MD, 'China's Outward Foreign Direct Investment and International Investment Law' (2015) 18 *Journal of International Economic Law* 893.

Scheuerman WE, *Hans Morgenthau: Realism and Beyond* (Polity 2009).

Schill SW, 'Tearing Down the Great Wall: The New Generation Investment Treaties of the People's Republic of China' (2007) 15 *Cardozo Journal of International & Contemporary Law* 73.

—— 'Maffezini v. Plama: Reflections on the Jurisprudential Schism in the Application of Most-Favored-Nation Clauses to Matters of Dispute Settlement' in Kinnear M and others (eds), *Building International Investment Law – The First 50 Years of ICSID* (Kluwer Law International 2016).

Schlemmer EC, 'An Overview of South Africa's Bilateral Investment Treaties and Investment Policy' (2016) 31 *ICSID Review* 167.

Schoenbaum TJ, 'The South China Sea Arbitration Decision and a Plan for Peaceful Resolution of the Disputes' (2016) 47 *Journal of Maritime Law & Commerce* 451.

Schoernig N, 'Neorealismus' in Schieder S and Spindler M (eds), *Theorien der Internationalen Beziehungen* (UTB 2010).

Schreuer C, 'Investment Arbitration' in Romano CPR, Alter KJ and Shany Y (eds), *The Oxford Handbook of International Adjudication* (OUP 2014).

—— 'The Development of International Law by ICSID Tribunals' (2016) 31 ICSID *Review* 728.

Schreuer CH, Malintoppi L, Reinisch A and Sinclair A, *The ICSID Convention: A Commentary* (2nd edn, CUP 2009).

Schultz T, 'Doing Law and Thinking about Law' (2013) 4 *Journal of International Dispute Settlement* 217.

Schweller R, *Unanswered Threats: Political Constraints on the Balance of Power* (Princeton University Press 2006).

Serapio M and Petty M, 'Philippines' Duterte says pointless discussing South China Sea woes at summit' *Reuters* (Manila, 27 April 2017) <http://www.reuters.com/article/us-asean-summit-idUSKBN17T11J> accessed 15 March 2019.

Serdy A, 'Article 281 – Procedure where no settlement has been reached by the parties' in Alexander Proelss (ed), *United Nations Convention on the Law of the Sea – A Commentary* (CH Beck 2017).

—— 'Article 283 – Obligation to exchange views' in Alexander Proelss (ed), *United Nations Convention on the Law of the Sea – A Commentary* (CH Beck 2017).

Shaffer GC and Melendez-Ortiz R (eds), *Dispute Settlement at the WTO – The Developing Country Experience* (CUP 2010).

Shaffer GC, Badin MRS and Rosenberg B, 'Winning at the WTO: the development of a trade policy community within Brazil' in Shaffer GC and Melendez-Ortiz R (eds), *Dispute Settlement at the WTO – The Developing Country Experience* (CUP 2010).

Shaffer G and Ginsburg T, 'The Empirical Turn in International Legal Scholarship' (2012) 106 AJIL 1.

Shambaugh D, *Beautiful Imperialist: China Perceives America, 1972–1990* (Princeton University Press 1991).

Shan Wenhua (ed), *China and International Investment Law: Twenty Years of ICSID Membership* (Brill 2015).

Shan Wenhua, Gallagher N and Zhang Sheng, 'National Treatment for Foreign Investment in China: A Changing Landscape' (2012) 27 *ICSID Review* 120.

Shaw MN, *International Law* (CUP 2008).

Shen Wei, 'The good, the bad, or the ugly? A critique of the decision on jurisdiction and competence in Tza Yap Shum v. The Republic of Peru' (2011) 10 CJIL 55.

Sheng 盛 Jianming 建明 and Zhong 钟 Ying 楹, 关于 WTO"协商一致"与"一揽子协定"决策原则的实证分析及其改革路径研究 (An Empirical Study of the Principles of Consensus and Single Undertaking in the WTO Decision-making Mechanism and the Path of Reform) (2015) 33 (8) *Hebei Faxue* 45.

Shi 师 Hua 华, '国际贸易争议解决方法的比较研究' (Comparative Study of International Trade Dispute Settlement Methods) (2002) 23 (6) *Faxue Zazhi* 54.

Shi Jiangtao, 'Is Beijing Courting Disaster by Shunning South China Sea Tribunal?' *SCMP* (Hong Kong, 20 June 2016) <https://www.scmp.com/news/china/diplomacy-defence/article/1977418/beijing-courting-disaster-shunning-south-china-sea> accessed 1 March 2019.

Shi 史 Xiaoli 晓丽, '区域贸易协定争端解决机制中的"场所选择条款"探析' (Analysis of the "Choice of Forum Article" in Regional Trade Agreement Dispute Resolution Mechanisms) (2008) 26 (2) *Zhengfa Luntan* 104.

Shi 时 Yewei 业伟, 'WTO 补贴协定中"公共机构"认定标准研究 ———以 DS379 案为例' (Identification Standards for "Public Body" at SCM: Taking Case DS379 for Example) [2016] (6) *Bijiaofa Yanjiu* 135.

Shin HT, 'Annulment' in Kinnear M and others (eds), *Building International Investment Law – The First 50 Years of ICSID* (Kluwer Law International 2016).

Simma B (ed), *The Charter of the United Nations* (2nd edn, OUP 2002).

—— and Paulus AL, 'The Responsibility of Individuals for Human Rights Abuses in Internal Conflict: A Positivist View' (1999) 93 AJIL 302.

Simmons BA, *The International Investment Regime: Sovereignty, Investor Security, and Dispute Settlement Since the 1980s (Straus Institute Working Paper)* (NYU School of Law 2010).

Singh JP, 'Introduction: Emerging Powers and the WTO' (2016) 21 *International Negotiation* 201.

Singh P, 'Sino-Indian Attitudes to International Law: Nations, States and Colonial Hangovers' (2015) 3 *The Chinese Journal of Comparative Law* 348.

Singh ZD, 'After the Hiatus: India-China Border Diplomacy since the 1970s' (2011) 47 *China Report* 83.

Sivakumaran S, 'The Influence of Teachings of Publicists on the Development of International Law' (2017) 66 *International and Comparative Law Quarterly* 1.

Slaughter Burley AM, 'International Law and International Relations Theory: A Dual Agenda' (1993) 87 AJIL 205.

Smith G, 'Chinese Bilateral Investment Treaties: Restrictions on International Arbitration' (2010) 76 *Arbitration* 58.

Sodiqov A, 'Tajikistan Cedes Disputed Land to China' *Jamestown Foundation* (Washington DC, 24 January 2011) <http://www.jamestown.org/single/?tx_ttnews%5Btt_news%5D=37398&no_cache=1#.VaEc5a3tmko> accessed 30 March 2019.

Sofaer AD, 'The Philippine Law of the Sea Action against China: Relearning the Limits of International Adjudication' (2016) 15 CJIL 393.

Song 宋 Jie 杰, '国际法院司法实践中的反诉问题研究' (Study on the Issue of Counterclaims in International Court of Justice Practice) (2006) 24 (3) *Falü Kexue* 133.

—— '法律视角下的"南海争端"——含义与解决的技术性建议' (The "South China Sea Dispute" from a Legal Perspective – Technical Advice on Meaning and Resolution) (2012) 26 (4) *Dangdai Faxue* 10.

—— '从英美实践来看我国参与国际法律事务的有效性问题' (Reviewing the issue of effectivity in China's participation in international legal affairs from the perspective of British and US experience) [2015] (2) *Bijiaofa Yanjiu* 148.

—— 'Evaluating the Effectiveness of China's Participation in International Legal Matters: Lessons from China's Practice in the International Law Commission and the International Court of Justice' (2017) 15 (2) *China: An International Journal* 144.

Song 宋 Yan 岩, 国家同意原则对国际法院行使咨询管辖权的限制———兼论"查戈斯群岛咨询意见案"的管辖权问题 (The Restrictions of the Principle of State Consent on the Court's Exercise of Its Advisory Jurisdiction – A Review of the Jurisdictional Issue of Legal Consequences of the Separation of the Chagos Archipelago from Mauritius in 1965) [2018] (1) *Guojifa Yanjiu* 3.

State Council of the PRC, 'White Paper – China's Peaceful Development Road' <http://www.china.org.cn/english/2005/Dec/152669.htm> accessed 30 March 2019.

State Council Information Office of the People's Republic of China, 'Diaoyu Dao, an Inherent Territory of China' (Beijing, 26 September 2012) <http://www.fmprc.gov.cn/mfa_eng/topics_665678/diaodao_665718/t973774.shtml> accesssed 1 March 2019.

Steinberg RH, 'Overview: Realism in International Law' (2002) 96 *Proceedings of the ASIL Annual Meeting* 260.

—— and Zasloff JM, 'Power and International Law' (2006) 100 AJIL 64.

Stewart TP and others, 'Any Change to China's Non-Market Economy Status Must Be Based on the Criteria Specified under U.S. Antidumping Law' (2005) A Position Paper Prepared for the U.S.-China Economic and Security Review Commission by the Trade Lawyers Advisory Group 18 August 2005 <https://www.uscc.gov/Research/any-change-china%E2%80%99s-non-market-economy-status-must-be-based-criteria-specified-under-us> accessed 5 March 2019.

Sterling-Folker J, 'Realist Environment, Liberal Process, and Domestic Variables' (1997) 41 *International Studies Quarterly* 1.

Strupp M, 'Paracel Archipelago' in Wolfrum R (ed), *Max Planck Encyclopedia of Public International Law – Volume VIII* (OUP 2012).

—— 'Spratly Islands' in Wolfrum R (ed), *Max Planck Encyclopedia of Public International Law – Volume IX* (OUP 2012).

Suarez SV, *The Outer Limits of the Continental Shelf – Legal Aspects of their Etablishment* (Springer 2008).

Sun 孙 Jin 劲, '论构建中国全方位对外投资条约体系' (On Establishing China's Comprehensive Investment Treaty System) [2017] (2) *Guojifa Yanjiu* 3.

Sun Zhiyu, 'Decision-making in the World Trade Organization' in Janow ME, Donaldson V and Yanovich A (eds), *The WTO: Governance, Dispute Settlement, and Developing Countries* (Juris Publishing Inc 2008).

Suse A, 'Old Wine in a New Bottle: The EU's Response to the Expiry of Section 15 (a) (ii) of China's WTO Protocol of Accession' (2017) 20 *Journal of International Economic Law* 951.

Sutter RG, *Foreign Relations of the PRC – The Legacies and Constraints of China's International Politics Since 1949* (Rowman & Littlefield 2013).

Svarverud R, *International Law as World Order in Late Imperial China – Translation, Reception and Discourse, 1847–1911* (Brill 2007).

Sykes AO, 'The Fundamental Deficiencies of the Agreement on Safeguards: A Reply to Professor Lee' (2006) 40 *Journal of World Trade* 979.

Sylvest C, 'Realism and International Law: The Challenge of John H. Herz' (2010) 2 *International Theory* 410.

Symmons C, 'Article 13 – Low-tide elevations' in Alexander Proelss (ed), *United Nations Convention on the Law of the Sea – A Commentary* (CH Beck 2017).

Talmon S, 'The South China Sea Arbitration: Observations on the Award on Jurisdiction and Admissibility' (2016) 15 CJIL 309.

—— 'Denouncing UNCLOS remains option for China after tribunal ruling' *Global Times* (Beijing, 3 March 2016) <http://www.globaltimes.cn/content/971707.shtml> accessed 11 November 2019.

—— 'Article 121 – Regime of Islands' in Proelss A (ed), *United Nations Convention on the Law of the Sea – A Commentary* (CH Beck 2017).

—— 'The South China Sea Arbitration and the Finality of "Final" Awards' (2017) 8 *Journal of International Dispute Settlement* 1.

Tanaka Y, *The International Law of the Sea* (2nd edn, CUP 2015).

Tang 唐 Haitao 海涛, 欧盟投资者—东道国争端解决机制的改革及我国的应对策略 (EU Investor-State Dispute Settlement Mechanism and Our Country 's Countermeasures) (2018) 33 (3) *Henan Caijing Zhengfa Daxue Xuebao* 145.

Tang Shiping, 'Taking Stock of Neoclassical Realism – A Review of: Neoclassical Realism, the State, and Foreign Policy. Edited by Steven E. Lobell, Norrin M. Ripsman, and Jeffrey W. Taliaferro' (2009) 11 *International Studies Review* 799.

Taniguchi Y, Yanovich A and Bohanes J (eds), *The WTO in the Twenty-first Century: Dispute Settlement, Negotiations, and Regionalism in Asia* (CUP 2007).

Tanneberger HG, 'Das Verhältnis der Volksrepublik China zum Völkerrecht – unter besonderer Berücksichtigung der historischen Erfahrungen des Landes mit den sog. „Ungleichen Verträgen" seit dem Frieden von Nanking (1842) und der eigenen Vertragspraxis gegenüber sechs asiatischen Staaten (Afghanistan, Birma, Ceylon, Indonesien, Nepal, Pakistan)' (PhD Thesis, University of Bochum 1974).

Tas D, 'Oil and Gas in the East China Sea: maritime boundaries, joint development and the rule of capture' [2011] (2) *International Energy Law Review* 48.

Tavela Luís D and Fontoura Costa JA, 'Repúblicas bolivarianas e o ICSID: será que o inimigo não é outro?' (2016) XVI *Anuario Mexicano de Derecho Internacional* 189.

Tawil GS, 'Most Favoured Nation Clauses and Jurisdiction Clauses in Investment Treaty Arbitration' in Binder C and others (eds), *International Investment Law for the 21st Century: Essays in Honour of Christoph Schreuer* (OUP 2009).

Taylor I, 'Is Africa Rising?' (2014) 21 *Brown Journal of World Affairs* 143.

Tellis A, 'Morgenthau: Politics as the Struggle for Power' in Morgenthau H, *Politics Among Nations. The Struggle for Power and Peace* (7th edn, McGraw-Hill 2006).

'"The Cairo Declaration," issued 26 November 1943, History and Public Policy Program Digital Archive, Foreign Relations of the United States, Diplomatic Papers, The Conferences at Cairo and Tehran, 1943' (Washington DC, United States Government Printing Office 1961) <https://digitalarchive.wilsoncenter.org/document/122101> accessed 25 October 2019.

The Economist, 'China, Japan and Taiwan: Profit over Patriotism – A new geographical discovery in Asia: a "sea of peace and co-operation"' (London, 19 June 2008) <http://www.economist.com/node/11591458> accessed 1 March 2019.

—— 'Indian, Pakistani and Chinese Border Disputes: Fanatsy Frontiers' (London, 8 February 2012) <https://www.economist.com/node/21517168/all-comments?page=1> accessed 1 March 2019.

—— 'The loyal family – Xi Jinping wants officials to declare allegiance to himself' *The Economist* (London, 6 April 2017) <https://www.economist.com/news/china/21720315-why-it-so-important-him-xi-jinping-wants-officials-declare-allegiance-himself> accessed 15 March 2019.

The Economist Intelligence Unit, 'Bhutan-China border talks offer no progress on broader ties' (London, 23 August 2016) <https://goo.gl/wVn1V8> accessed 1 March 2019.

'Primary Source Document with Questions – "The Potsdam Declaration," issued 26 July 1945' (Columbia University, Asia for Educators 2019) <http://afe.easia.columbia.edu/ps/japan/potsdam.pdf> accessed 25 October 2019.

Thomas WI, *The Child in America* (Knopf 1928).

Tian 田 Hai 海, 论最惠国条款适用于投资争端解决程序的平等理论困境 (On the Equality Dilemma of Applying the MFN Clause to the Investment Dispute Settlement Procedure) (2018) 16 (3) *Shidai Faxue* 98.

Trakman LE, 'China and Foreign Direct Investment: Does Distance Lend Enchantment to the View?' (2014) 2 *Chinese Journal of Comparative Law* 1.

—— 'Geopolitics, China, and Investor-State Arbitration' in Toohey L, Picker CB and Greenacre J (eds), *China in the International Economic Order: New Directions and Changing Paradigms* (CUP 2015).

Tran E, 'China: zero tolerance for academic freedom' *The Conversation* (London, 17 October 2017) <http://theconversation.com/china-zero-tolerance-for-academic-freedom-85200> accessed 30 December 2018.

Treaties between China and Foreign States (by order of the Inspector General of Customs, vol 1, Shanghai 1908).

Treaties between China and Foreign States (2nd edn by order of the Inspector General of Customs, vol 2, Shanghai 1917).

Treves T, 'Maritime Boundary Delimitation' in Rothwell DR and others (eds), *The Oxford Handbook of the Law of the Sea* (OUP 2015).

—— 'Article 290 – Provisional Measures' in Alexander Proelss (ed), *United Nations Convention on the Law of the Sea – A Commentary* (CH Beck 2017).

Wang Alan and others, 'China's new "negative list"' *Lexology* (Beijing, 11 July 2018) <https://www.lexology.com/library/detail.aspx?g=5f3db2d8-3bdb-40e8-a238-de41509373ee&utm_source=lexology+daily+newsfeed&utm_medium=html+email&utm_campaign=lexology+subscriber+daily+feed&utm_content=lexology+daily+newsfeed+2018-07-16&utm_term> accessed 30 March 2019.

Wang 王 Chao 超, '评 WTO 争端解决机构对保障措施中"未预见的情况"的判断' (Reviewing WTO DSM Decisions on Safeguard Measures and "Unforeseen Developments") [2006] (9) *Faxue* 131.

Wang 王 Chenyu 晨于 and He 何 Zhipeng 志鹏, '国际守法文化及近期发展：国际关系司法化' (International Culture of Legal Compliance and recent developments: The Judicialization of International Relations) (2010) 24 (6) *Dangdai Faxue* 133.

Wang 王 Chongmin 崇敏, 菲律宾的相关谅解与中菲南海争端案管辖权的关系问题 (The Philippines' Understanding and jurisdiction issues in the China-Philippines South China Sea dispute) (2014) 29 (4) *Henan Caijing Zhengfa Daxue Xuebao* 30.

—— and Zhang 张 Kui 奎, '中国南海 U 形线的法律地位' (A Study on the Legal Status of U-Shape Line in the South China Sea) (2010) 25 *Henansheng Zhengfa Guanli Ganbu Xueyuan Xuebao* 106.

Wang Guiguo, 'China's FTAs: Legal Characteristics and Implications' (2011) 105 AJIL 493.

—— 'Chinese Mechanisms for Resolving Investor-State Disputes' (2011) 1 *Jindal Journal of International Affairs* 204.

—— 'The New Haven School of Legal Theory from the Perspective of Traditional Chinese Culture' (2012) 20 *Asia Pacific Law Review* 211.

Wang Jie, 'Investor-State Arbitration: Where does China Stand?' (2009) 32 *Suffolk Transnational Law Review* 493.

Wang 王 Jun 军 and Su 粟 Sa 撒, 'WTO 争端解决机制中的救济体系框架及改革问题实证研究' (Empirical Study of the Relief System Framework in the WTO Dispute Settlement Mechanism and Reform Issues) (2014) 28 (3) *Dangdai Faxue* 27.

Wang 王 Mengdie 梦蝶, '论南海争端解决的法律方法' (Discussing Legal Methods for the Solution of the South China Sea Conflict) [2012] (7) *Fazhi Bolan* 12.

Wang Min, 'Statement by H.E. Ambassador Wang Min, Deputy Permanent Representative of China to the United Nations At the 66th Session of the UN General Assembly On Agenda Item 76: Oceans and the law of the sea' *Permanent Mission of the People's Republic of China to the UN* (New York, 6 December 2011) <http://www.china-un.org/eng/gdxw/t884956.htm> accessed 1 March 2019.

Wang 王 Nan 楠, '最惠国待遇条款在国际投资争端解决事项上的适用问题' (On the Application of Most-Favored-Nation Treatment Clause to International Investment Dispute Settlement) (2010) 28 *Hebei Faxue* 120.

Wang 王 Shumin 淑敏 and Wu 吴 Haonan 昊南, 国际法院关于"查戈斯群岛从毛里求斯分裂案"的咨询管辖权研究 (Research on the Advisory Jurisdiction of the ICJ in the "Separation of the Chagos Archipelago from Mauritius Case") [2018] (17) *Falü Shiyong* 98.

Wang Xiaodong and Zeng Ka, 'China and the Doha Round non-agricultural market access (NAMA) negotiations' in Zeng Ka and Liang Wei (eds), *China and Global Trade Governance – China's first decade in the World Trade Organization* (Routledge 2013).

Wang 王 Xiuwei 秀卫, '我国海洋争端解决的法律思考：《联合国海洋法公约》座谈会观点综述' (Legal Reflections on the Resolution of China's Maritime Disputes: Summary of Viewpoints at the Symposium on 'UNCLOS') [2012] (6) *Zhongguo Faxue* 78.

Wang 王 Yan 燕, '国际投资条约仲裁审查标准之反思' (Reflections on Audit Standards in International Investment Treaties) [2013] (6) *Faxue* 120.

—— 欧盟新一代投资协定"反条约挑选" 机制的改革———以 CETA 和 JEEPA 为分析对象 (Anti-Treaty Shopping Reform Led by EU's New Generation Investment Treaties: Taking CETA and JEEPA as Examples) (2018) 40 (3) *Xiandai Faxue* 156.

Wang 王 Yanzhi 彦志, '国际投资争端解决的法律化：成就与挑战' (The Legalization of International Investment Dispute Settlement: Successes and Challenges) (2011) 25 (3) *Dangdai Faxue* 15.

—— '中国在国际投资法上的身份转换与立场定位' (Locating China's Changing Identity regarding and Positions on International Investment Law) (2013) 27 (4) *Dangdai Faxue* 131.

—— '国际投资法上公平与公正待遇条款改革的列举式清单进路' (Enumerated list approach to the reform of fair and equitable treatment clauses in international investment law) (2015) 29 (6) *Dangdai Faxue* 148.

Wang 王 Yong 勇 and Guan 管 Zhengfeng 征峰, '五十五年来中国对国际法院诉讼管辖权的态度之述评' (Review of China's Attitude towards the Litigation Jurisdiction of International Courts over the last Fifty Years) [2002] (3) *Huadong Zhengfa Xueyuan Xuebao* 72.

Wang Zonglai and Hu Bin, 'China's Reform and Opening-up and International Law' (2010) 9 CJIL 193.

Wauters J and Vandenbussche H, 'China – Measures Affecting Imports of Automobile Parts' (2010) 9 *World Trade Review* 201.

Wee SL, 'China's Xi calls for tighter ideological control in universities' *Reuters* (Beijing 29 December 2014) <https://www.reuters.com/article/us-china-universities/chinas-xi-calls-for-tighter-ideological-control-in-universities-idUSKBN0K70TI20141229> accessed 1 March 2019.

Wei Dan, 'Bilateral investment treaties: an empirical analysis of the practices of Brazil and China' (2012) 33 *European Journal of Law and Economy* 663.

—— 'Antidumping in Emerging Countries in the Post-Crisis Era: A Case Study on Brazil and China' (2013) 16 *Journal of International Economic Law* 921.

Wen Jiabao, 'Report on the Work of the Government' *Xinhua* (Beijing, 5 March 2006) <http://wto2.mofcom.gov.cn/article/bilateralvisits/200603/20060301691252.shtml> accessed 30 March 2019.

Whiting AS, *China Eyes Japan* (University of California Press 1989).

Whomersley C, 'The South China Sea: The Award of the Tribunal in the Case Brought by Philippines against China – A Critique' (2016) 15 CJIL 239.

Wilkinson R, 'Conclusions: Emerging Powers in the WTO – Beware the Glass Ceiling' (2016) 21 *International Negotiation* 327.

Willems JY, 'The Settlement of Investor State Disputes and China: New Developments on ICSID Jurisdiction' (2011) 8 *South Carolina Journal of International Law & Business* 1.

Wilson B, 'Compliance by WTO Members with Adverse WTO Dispute Settlement Rulings' in Janow ME, Donaldson V and Yanovich A (eds), *The WTO: Governance, Dispute Settlement, and Developing Countries* (Juris Publishing Inc 2008).

Wilson JL, *Strategic Partners. Russian-Chinese Relations in the Post-Soviet Era* (ME Sharpe 2004).

Winkelmann I, 'Article 122 – Definition' in Alexander Proelss (ed), *United Nations Convention on the Law of the Sea – A Commentary* (CH Beck 2017).

—— 'Article 123 – Cooperation of States bordering enclosed or semi-enclosed seas' in Alexander Proelss (ed), *United Nations Convention on the Law of the Sea – A Commentary* (CH Beck 2017).

Wishnick E, *Mending fences: the evolution of Moscow's China policy from Brezhnev to Yeltsin* (University of Washington Press 2001).

—— 'Russia and the CIS in 2006: Asserting Russian Interests on Korean Security, Energy, and Central Asia' (2007) (1) *Asian Survey* 58.

Wolfrum R, Stoll PT and Kaiser K (eds), *WTO – Institutions and Dispute Settlement* (Martinus Nijhoff Publishers 2006).

World Customs Organization, 'General Rules for the Interpretation of the Harmonized System' <http://www.wcoomd.org/en/faq/~/~/media/B7BC612CEB3B417BB5183841DA7413CB.ashx> accessed 30 March 2019.

WTO, 'WTO Accessions Map' <https://www.wto.org/english/thewto_e/acc_e/acc_map_e.htm> accessed 5 November 2019.

WTO, 'Disputes by Member' <https://www.wto.org/english/tratop_e/dispu_e/dispu_by_country_e.htm> accessed 5 November 2019.

Wu Haitao, 'Statement by Ambassador WU Haitao at the Plenary of the 71st General Assembly under the Agenda Item 73: Oceans and the Law of the Sea' *Permanent Mission of the People's Republic of China to the UN* <www.china-un.org/eng/lghghyywj/smhwj/2016doc/t1422387.htm> accessed 1 March 2018.

Wu 吴 Jiangong 建功, 'WTO 争端解决机制中的不公正性：以发展中国家成员为视角' (Analysis about the Unjust Character of WTO Disputes – Solving System) (2010) 31 (1) *Faxue Zazhi* 142.

Wu Xiaohui, 'Chronology of Practice: Chinese Practice in Public International Law in 2016' (2017) 16 CJIL 547.

Wu Zhanghui, 'International Arbitration for Chinese-Foreign Disputes: Emerging Choices in 2012' (2012) 41 *International Law News* 1.

Xiao 肖 Bing 冰, 'WTO 争端案件中的规则应用差异分析' (Analysis of Differences in Norm Application in WTO Disputes) [2010] (9) *Faxue* 58.

Xiao 肖 Fang 芳, 国际投资仲裁裁决司法审查的"商事化"及反思———以美国联邦最高法院"BG 公司诉阿根廷"案裁决为例 (Reflections on the "Commercialization" of the Judicial Review of Investment Arbitration Awards – Taking the US Supreme Court's Findings in "BG Group v Argentina" as an Example) [2018] (3) *Faxue Pinglun* 152.

Xiao 肖 Jun 军, '国际投资条约的复杂化与多元化 ———晚近国际投资条约发展趋势之辨及我国应对策略' (The Complication and Diversification of International Investment Treaties – Recent Trends and Debates in International Investment Treaty Development and China's Response Tactics) [2014] (5) *Faxue Pinglun* 163.

—— '中欧 BIT 的投资者-东道国争端解决机制——基于中加 BIT 与 CETA 的比较分析' (The China-EU BIT Investor-Host State Dispute Settlement Mechanism – Comparative Analysis on the basis of the China-Canada BIT and CETA) (2015) 25 (2) *Xi'an Dianzi Keji Daxue Xuebao* 76.

Xiao 肖 Wei 威, 'WTO 争端胜诉方"申请授权报复"的程序问题研究' (A Study on the Procedures of WTO Winning Party's Application for Authorization of Retaliation) (2008) 26 (1) *Hebei Faxue* 148.

Xie 谢 Hongxia 红霞, '国际海洋法法庭若干法律问题的分析' (Analysis of Several Legal Problems Concerning the International Tribunal for the Law of the Sea) [2005] (1) *Heilongjiangsheng Zhengfa Guanli Ganbu Xueyuan Xuebao* 102.

Xie 谢 Bowen 博文 and Xu 徐 Dong 栋, '"尼哥领土与海洋争端案"评析及对南海问题的借鉴' (The analysis and assessment of the ICJ Territorial and Maritime Dispute Case and its reference to South China Sea) (2014) 25 (2) *Zhongguo Haishangfa Yanjiu* 90.

Xinhua, 'Education minister warns against "western values" in colleges' *Xinhua* (Beijing, 30 January 2015) <http://www.xinhuanet.com//english/china/2015-01/30/c_133958419.htm> accessed 30 December 2018.

—— 'Xi calls for strengthened ideological work in colleges' *Xinhua* (Beijing, 9 December 2016) <http://www.xinhuanet.com//english/2016-12/09/c_135891337.htm> accessed 31 December 2018.

—— 'BRICS Leaders Xiamen Declaration 2017' *Xinhua* (Xiamen, 4 September 2017) <http://www.xinhuanet.com/english/2017-09/04/c_136583396_2.htm> accessed 30 March 2019.

Xing 邢 Guangmei 广梅, '中国拥有南海诸岛主权考' (Study on China's Sovereignty over South China Sea Islands) [2013] (6) *Bijiaofa Yanjiu* 1.

Xiong 熊 Li 丽, '对 WTO 争端解决机制专家组程序的几点反思' (Some Thoughts on the WTO DSM's Expert Panel Procedure) [2002] (2) *Bijiaofa Yanjiu* 49.

Xu 徐 Chongli 崇利, '国际经济法律秩序与中国的"和平崛起"战略——以国际关系理论分析的视角' (The International Economic Law System and China's "Peaceful Rise" Strategy – From an International Relations Theory Viewpoint) [2005] (2) *Bijiaofa Yanjiu* 79.

—— '晚近国际投资争端解决实践之评判："全球治理"理论的引入' (Judging the Recent Practice in International Investment Dispute Resolution: Introducing the "Global Governance" Theory) [2010] (3) *Faxuejia* 143.

Xu 徐 Quan 泉, 'WTO 争端解决机制下私人诉权之审视' (A Jurisprudential Study of Private Right of Action in WTO Dispute Settlement Framework) (2007) 29 (3) *Xiandai Faxue* 72.

Xu 许 Hao 浩, '南海油气争端解决的法律机制探讨' (Investigation of Legal Mechanisms for the Resolution of the Dispute over South China Sea Oil and Gas) [2008] (5) *Haiyang Kaifa yu Guanli* 71.

Xu 徐 Shu 树, '国际投资仲裁中滥诉防范机制的构建' (Constructing a mechanism to guard against indiscriminate lawsuit in international investment arbitration) [2017] (5) *Faxue* 152.

—— '国际投资仲裁庭管辖权扩张的路径、成因及应对' (Path, causes, and responses to international investment tribunals expanding their jurisdiction) (2017) 11 (3) *Qinghua Faxue* 185.

Xu Xiaoqun, 'Law, Custom, and Social Norms: Civil Adjudications in Qing and Republican China' (2018) 36 *Law and History Review* 77.

Xu 徐 Yunliang 运良, '论协调 WTO 争端解决机制与 RTAs 争端解决机制管辖权冲突的原则' (On Rules About Coordinating Conflicts Between WTO Disputes Solving System And RTAs Disputes Solving System Competence) (2009) 30 (3) *Faxue Zazhi* 136.

Xue 薛 Guifang 桂芳 and Xu 徐 Xiangxin 向欣, '由岛屿维持其本身的"经济生活"标准的界定谈对我国南海岛礁的保护性开发' (The Impact on China's Protective Development of the South China Sea's Islands and Reefs of the Discussion on the Definition of the Standard of Islands and Reefs Being Able to Sustain 'Economic Life' on Their Own) [2013] (6) *Bijiaofa Yanjiu* 63.

Xue Hanqin, 'Chinese Observations on International Law' (2007) 6 CJIL 83.

—— 'Meaningful Dialogue Through a Common Discourse: Law and Values in a Multi-Polar World' (2011) 1 AsJIL 13.

—— and Jin Qian, 'International Treaties in the Chinese Domestic Legal System' (2009) 8 CJIL 299.

Yanai S, 'International Law Concerning Maritime Boundary Delimitation' in Attard DJ, Fitzmaurice M and Martínez Guttiérez NA (eds), *The IMLI Manual on International Maritime Law – Volume I: The Law of the Sea* (OUP 2014).

Yang 杨 Caixia 彩霞 and Qin 秦 Quan 泉, '国际投资争端解决中的无默契仲裁初探' (First Explorations of Arbitration without Privity in International Investment Dispute Settlement) [2011] (3) *Bijiaofa Yanjiu* 108.

Yang 杨 Guohua 国华, 为什么 WTO 是模范国际法 (Why the WTO is Model International Law) [2016] (6) *Guoji Shangwu Yanjiu* 28.

—— 'WTO 上诉机构的产生与运作研究' (On the Creation and Operation of the WTO Appellate Body) (2018) 40 (2) *Xiandai Faxue* 147.

Yang 杨 Guohua 国华 and others, 'WTO 争端解决机制中的磋商程序研究' (Research on the Consultation Procedures in the WTO Dispute Settlement Mechanism) [2003] (2) *Faxue Pinglun* 71.

—— 'WTO 争端解决机制中的专家组程序研究（上）' (Research of the Expert Panel Procedure at the WTO DSM (First Part)) [2004] (3) *Faxue Pinglun* 78.

Yu 余 Fei 菲 and Ma 麻 Guo'an 国安, 'WTO 争端解决机制的司法化历程及我国的对策' (DSM in WTO: Judicial System and China's Countermeasure) (2002) 20 (2) *Hebei Faxue* 26.

Yu 余 Jingsong 劲松, '国际投资条约仲裁中投资者与东道国权益保护平衡问题研究' (Research on the Problem of Balancing Investor and Host Country Rights in International Investment Treaty Arbitration) [2011] (2) *Zhongguo Faxue* 133.

—— and Zhan 詹 Xiaoning 晓宁, '论投资者与东道国间争端解决机制及其影响' (Discussing resolution mechanisms for and consequences of disputes between investors and host countries) [2005] (5) *Zhongguo Faxue* 175.

Yu 余 Li 丽, 'WTO 执行争端次序问题：双边解决和多边完善' (The Issue of Implementing WTO Dispute Sequencing: Bilateral Solutions and Multilateral Improvement) [2007] (2) *Falü Shiyong* 45.

Yu 余 Mincai 民才, '论国际法上海洋石油共同开发的概念' (Discussing the Concept of Joint Development of Offshore Oil on the Basis of International Law) [2001] (6) *Faxuejia* 47.

—— '论中日东海油气争端的共同开发解决方案' (On The Jointly-Exploited Solution To Sino-Japanese Disputation About The Oil And Gas In East China Sea) (2006) 27 (4) *Faxue Zazhi* 119.

—— '海洋争端强制仲裁程序及我国的应对策略———以中菲南海争端强制仲裁事件为例' (Compulsory Arbitration Procedures in Maritime Disputes and Our Country's Counter-Strategy – Taking the Example of Compulsory Arbitration in the China-Philippines South China Sea Dispute) [2013] (3) *Fashang Yanjiu* 32.

—— and Li 李 Bowei 博伟, '中国与南海仲裁庭的非正式合作及其效果' (China's informal cooperation with the South China Sea arbitral tribunal and results) [2015] (2) *Xiandai Guoji Guanxi* 46.

Yu 余 Minyou 敏友, 中国和平崛起与全球治理 (China's Peaceful Rise and Global Governance) [2004] (6) *Faxuejia* 17.

—— '论世贸组织法律救济的特性' (Characteristics of Legal Remedies Provided by the WTO Dispute Settlement Mechanism) (2006) 28 (6) *Xiandai Faxue* 14.

—— '终止不法行为——世贸组织争端解决机制提供的首要救济' (Stopping Illegal Behavior – Principle Remedies Provided by the WTO Dispute Settlement Mechanism) [2006] (6) *Faxue Pinglun* 85.

—— 'WTO 争端解决活动——中国表现及其改进建议' (WTO Dispute Settlement Activities – Some Recommendations for Improvement Put Forward by China) [2008] (4) *Faxue Pinglun* 82.

—— '评南海仲裁案仲裁庭对我国"断续线"及历史性权利的裁决倾向' (Discussing the tendencies of he arbitral triunal's ruling on China's 'nine-dash line' and historic rights in the South China Sea arbitration) [2016] (4) *Faxue Pinglun* 83.

Yu 余 Minyou 敏友 and Chen 陈 Xifeng 喜峰, '论解决 WTO 法内部冲突的司法解释原则（上）' (Discussing Judicial Interpretation Principles on How to Solve Internal Conflicts in WTO Law (First Part)) [2002] (5) *Faxue Pinglun* 78.

—— '论解决 WTO 法内部冲突的司法解释原则（下）' (Discussing Judicial Interpretation Principles on How to Solve Internal Conflicts in WTO Law (Second Part)) [2002] (6) *Faxue Pinglun* 105.

—— 'WTO 争端解决机制中的专家组程序研究（下）' (Research of the Expe Panel Procedure at the WTO DSM (Second Part)) [2004] (4) *Faxue Pinglun* 69.

Yang 杨 Qilu 琪璐, '多视角下我国管辖海域的冲突之研究' (Research from mu ple perspectives on conflicts regarding maritime areas under China's jurisc tion) (2018) 36 (3) *Zhengfa Luntan* 118.

Yang 杨 Zewei 泽伟, '跨国能源管道运输的争议解决机制' (The Conflict Res tion Mechanism for Transnational Pipeline Energy Transport) [2007] (12) *F* 84.

—— '国际社会的民主和法治价值与保护性干预' (Democratic and Rule of Values of International Society and Protective Intervention) (2012) 30 *Falü ue* 41.

—— '《联合国海洋法公约》的主要缺陷及其完善' (Important Flaws of UN and Pertinent Remedies) [2012] (5) *Faxue Pinglun* 57.

—— '论《海洋法公约》解决南海争端的非适用性' (On Non-Application United Nations Convention on the Law of the Sea for Solution to Disp South China Sea) (2012) 33 (1) *Faxue Zazhi* 1.

—— '海上共同开发的先存权问题研究' (Researching the Issue of Pre- Rights in Maritime Joint Development) [2017] (1) *Faxue Pinglun* 121.

Yao 姚 Ying 莹, '解决中日东海争端的司法路径探析' (Exploring Judicial M of Solving the Sino-Japanese East China Sea Dispute) (2011) 25 (3) *Dang ue* 24.

—— '2014 年孟加拉国与印度孟加拉湾划界案评述 ———兼论对中菲南 案的启示' (Comments on the 2014 Bangladesh v India Bay of Bengal b limitation case – On inspiration for the China v Philippines South C arbitration) (2015) 29 (4) *Dangdai Faxue* 149.

Ye 叶 Bo 波, 'WTO 健康和安全争端中的审查标准' (Examination Sta WTO Health and Security Disputes) [2009] (2) *Faxue Pinglun* 90.

Ye 叶 Quan 泉, 当事国在海洋划界前的国际法义务之研析 ———兼论南 在划界前之国际法义务 (Analysis of parties' international law obligati maritime delimitation – on the international law obligations befor tion of the South China Sea parties) [2016] (6) *Faxue Pinglun* 99.

Yi 衣 Shuling 淑玲, '国际投资协定一般例外条款探析' (The Analyses Exception Clauses of International Investment Agreement) (2016) 3 *Caijing Zhengfa Daxue Xuebao* 106.

Yi (Yee) Xianhe (Sienho), 'Notes on the International Court of Justice (Kosovo Advisory Opinion' (2010) 9 CJIL 763.

—— 'The International Law of Co-progressiveness: The Descriptive The Normative Position and Some Core Principles' (2014) 13 CJIL

—— 'The South China Sea Arbitration Decisions on Jurisdiction and Concerns' (2016) 15 CJIL 219.

Yin 尹 Deyong 德永, '试论 WTO 争端解决机构的法律解释权' (On Legal interpretation of the WTO Dispute Settlement Body) (200 *Faxue* 24.

—— and Xi 席 Jing 晶, '论 WTO 争端解决机制中的证据规则（上）' (Discussing Rules of Evidence at the WTO Dispute Settlement Mechanism (First Part)) [2003] (5) *Faxue Pinglun* 86.

—— and Xi 席 Jing 晶, '论 WTO 争端解决机制中的证据规则（下）' (Discussing Rules of Evidence at the WTO Dispute Settlement Mechanism (Second Part)) [2003] (6) *Faxue Pinglun* 92.

—— and Lei 雷 Xiaolu 筱璐, '南海诸岛争端国际仲裁的可能性' (Feasibility of International Arbitration of the South China Sea Island Conflict) (2011) 64 (1) *Wuhan Daxue Xuebao* 102.

—— and Guan 管 Jian 健, '论《中国加入议定书》第 15 条到期后的法律效力' (On the Legal Effect of the Expiration of Article 15 of China's Accession Protocol) (2016) 23 (6) *Shanghai Duiwai Jingmao Daxue Xuebao* 29.

Yu Xingzhong, 'Legal Pragmatism in the People's Republic of China' in Keller P (ed), *Chinese Law and Legal Theory* (Ashgate/Dartmouth 2001).

Zang MQ, 'The WTO Contingent Trade Instruments Against China: What Does Accession Bring?' (2009) 58 *International and Comparative Law Quarterly* 321.

Zelin M, 'The Rights of Tenants in Mid-Qing Sichuan: A Study of Land-Related Lawsuits in the Baxian Archives' (1986) 45 *Journal of Asian Studies* 499.

Zelin M, Ocko J and Gardella R (eds), *Contract and Property in Early Modern China* (Stanford University Press 2004).

Zeng Ka, 'The political economy of developing country antidumping actions against China' in Zeng K and Liang W (eds), *China and Global Trade Governance – China's first decade in the World Trade Organization* (Routledge 2013).

Zeng Ka and Lu Yue, 'Variation in Bilateral Investment Treaty Provisions and Foreign Direct Investment Flows to China, 1997–2011' (2016) 42 *International Interactions* 820.

Zenglein MJ and Kärnfeldt M, 'MERICS Economic Indicators Q1/2018' *MERICS* (Berlin, 24 April 2018) <https://www.merics.org/de/merics-trackers/economic-indicators-q1-2018> accessed 25 June 2018.

Zhang Fusen and Hu Zejun, *Outlines of the Legal System of the People's Republic of China* (Falü Chubanshe 2004).

Zhang 张 Guang 光, '论国际投资仲裁中非投资国际义务的适用进路' (Fulfillment of Non-Investment International Obligations in International Investment Arbitrations) (2009) 31 (4) *Xiandai Faxue* 121.

Zhang Guihong and Feng Yuqiao, 'China's UN Diplomacy: 1971–2011' (2011) 35 *Strategic Analysis* 973.

Zhang 张 Lei 磊, '加强对黄岩岛有效控制的国际法依据' (Strengthening the International Law Foundation for Effective Control of Huangyan Island) [2012] (8) *Faxue* 67.

—— '论有效控制规则视野下中业岛的主权归属' (On sovereign jurisdiction over Thitu Island under the perspective of the effective control principle) (2016) 34 (1) *Hebei Faxue* 68.

Zhang 张 Lina 丽娜, "一带一路"国际投资争端解决机制完善研究 (Research on Improvement of the International Investment Disputes Settlement Mechanism under "One Belt One Road" Initiative) (2018) 39 (8) *Faxue Zazhi* 32.

Zhang 张 Naigen 乃根, '论中国利用 WTO 争端解决机制的对策' (Reviewing China's Policies Regarding the Use of the WTO Dispute Settlement Mechanism) [2003] (1) *Zhengzhi yu Falü* 61.

Zhang 张 Nei 内 and Xiao 肖 Bing 冰, 论《中国加入 WTO 议定书》第 15 条"自动终止条款"的法律效应 (On the Legal Effect of Automatic Terminating Clause of Article 15 in China's Accession Protocol) (2016) 38 (5) *Xiandai Faxue* 141.

Zhang Shu, 'China's Approach in Drafting the Investor-State Arbitration Clause: A Review from the "Belt and Road" Regions' Perspective' (2017) 5 *The Chinese Journal of Comparative Law* 79.

Zhang 张 Weibin 卫彬, '海洋划界的趋势与相关情况规则——黑海划界案对我国海域划界的启示' (Maritime Border Delimitation Trends and Pertinent Regulations – the Black Sea Border Delimitation Case and Lessons for China's Maritime Border Delimitation) [2010] (1) *Huadong Zhengfa Daxue Xuebao* 48.

—— '国际法院解决领土争端中证明标准问题' (The Issue of Standards of Proof in ICJ Territorial Dispute Resolution) (2011) 25 (5) *Dangdai Faxue* 131.

—— '国际法院解决领土争端中的关键日期问题——中日钓鱼岛列屿争端关键日期确定的考察' (Critical Date Ascertained by the International Court of Justice in Settling Territorial Disputes: Determining the Critical Date of Diaoyu Islands Dispute between China and Japan) (2012) 34 (3) *Xiandai Faxue* 121.

—— '南海 U 形线的法律属性及在划界中地位问题' (The Issue of the Legal Attributes and Position in Boundary Delimitation of the U-Shaped Line in the South China Sea) (2013) 27 (2) *Dangdai Faxue* 130.

—— '菲律宾诉中国南海争端案的主体适格性问题' (The qualified subject problem in the Philippines v China South China Sea dispute) (2014) 29 (4) *Henan Caijing Zhengfa Daxue Xuebao* 40.

—— '国际法院解释领土条约的路径、方法及其拓展' (Ways, methods and development of ICJ interpretation of territorial treaties) (2015) 35 (2) *Faxue Yanjiu* 192.

—— '《联合国海洋法公约》中"岩礁"的演进解释与南沙群岛问题' (Evolutionary interpretation of 'islands and rocks' in UNCLOS and the Nansha Archipelago Issue) (2017) 35 (5) *Falü Kexue* 115.

Zhang 张 Xiaojian 潇剑, 'WTO 争端解决机制之利弊得失' (Advantages and Disadvantages of the WTO Dispute Settlement Mechanism) (2003) 15 *Zhongwai Faxue* 222.

—— 'WTO 争端解决机制中的专家决策与公众参与' (Expert Decision and Public Participation in the WTO Dispute Settlement Mechanism) (2007) 25 (3) *Hebei Faxue* 39.

Zhang 张 Xiaojun 晓君 and Sun 孙 Nanxiang 南翔, '企业海外投资的非政府性障碍及中国的对策研究' (The Research on Non-Governmental Obstacles in Foreign Investment and China's Strategy) (2016) 38 (1) *Xiandai Faxue* 143.

Zhang 张 Xinjun 新军, '国际法上的争端和钓鱼诸岛问题' (International Law Disputes and the Diaoyu Islands Issue) [2011] (3) *Zhongguo Faxue* 176.

—— '中国周边海域争端处理的程序和实体问题 —— "搁置争议、共同开发"再考' (The Procedures of Dealing with Conflicts in China's Peripheral Waters – Reevaluation of "Putting Disputes Aside and Developing Together") (2011) 23 *Zhongwai Faxue* 1121.

—— '关于菲律宾南海断续线仲裁请求的管辖权问题——《联合国海洋法公约》第 298.1(a)(i)项下的排除和海洋权利之争' (Jurisdictional Objection to the Philippines' Subissions regarding Nine-dash Line: Exclusion of the Dispute concerning Sources of Maritime Entitlements under UNCLOS Article 298.1 (1) (i)) [2016] (2) *Guojifa Yanjiu* 3.

—— '裁判条约中一方不出庭下的"查明管辖权"条款的意义——程序分立视角下对不出庭应对及其法律效果的再考察' (Judging the meaning of 'examining jurisdiction' treaty clauses for cases where one party does not appear in court – reexamination of responses to and legal effects of non-appearance under the perspective of separate procedures) (2017) 11 (2) *Qinghua Faxue* 176.

Zhang 张 Xinyu 昕宇, '中国—东盟自由贸易区仲裁机制研究' (Research on the Arbitration System of China-ASEAN Free-trade Area) (2010) 28 (6) *Hebei Faxue* 175.

Zhang 张 Yunting 运婷, Wang 王 Hao 皓 and Shi 史 Longxiang 龙祥, 欧美承认中国市场经济地位问题及中国的对策 (The Issue of EU and US recognition of Chinese Market Economy Status and Chinese Countermeasures) [2016] (6) *Guoji Shangwu Yanjiu* 89.

Zhao 赵 Haifeng 海峰, '中国与国际司法机构关系的演进' (Evolution of Relations between China and International Judicial Mechanisms) [2008] (6) *Faxue Pinglun* 3.

—— and Wang 王 Chundong 春栋, 中国参与国际司法的路径选择 (China's choice to participate in international adjudication) [2014] (3) *Xueshu Jiaoliu* 76.

Zhao 赵 Jingsong 劲松, '中国和平解决国际争端问题初探' (First Exploration of the Issue of China Peacefully Resolving International Disputes) (2006) 24 (1) *Falü Kexue* 97.

Zhao 赵 Jinlong 金龙, '我国"一带一路"FTA 战略的路径选择研究' (On China's chosen path regarding a 'One Belt, One Road' FTA strategy) [2016] (12) *Shijie Jingji Yanjiu* 106.

Zhao 赵 Jun 骏, '国际投资仲裁中"投资"定义的张力和影响' (The Stretching Force of the Definition of "Investment" in International Investment Arbitrations and Its Impact) (2014) 36 (3) *Xiandai Faxue* 161.

Zhao 赵 Ke 柯, 'WTO 争端解决机制述评' (Commentary on the WTO Dispute Settlement Mechanism) [2003] (7) *Dangdai Faxue* 124.

Zhao 赵 Min 敏, '从 WTO 的法律规则看中国如何应对市场经济地位的"非市场"阻力' (Reviewing how China should respond to the 'non-market' barrier to market economy status through WTO legal rules) [2017] (2) *Jingji Luntan* 119.

Zhao Xiuwen and Kloppenberg LA, 'Reforming Chinese Arbitration Law and Practices in the Global Economy' (2006) 31 *University of Dayton Law Review* 421.

Zhonghua Liufa (Six laws of China) [1913] (Shangwu yinshuguan 1927).

Zhonghua Minguo Xianxing Fagui Daquan (A Complete Compilation of Current Laws and Regulations of the Republic of China) (Shangwu yinshuguan 1934).

'Zhonghua Minguo Xingfa' (The Criminal Code of the Republic of China), in *Liufa Quanshu (Complete Book of the Six Laws)* (Shanghai faxue bianyi she 1928).

Zhou 周 Jiang 江, '也谈南海断续线的法律性质' (Discussing the Legal Nature of the Dotted Line in the South China Sea) (2013) 31 (5) *Falü Kexue* 130.

—— '菲律宾在提起诉中国南海争端案之前应履行的法定义务' (Legal obligations to be fulfilled by the Philippines before filing the South China Sea dispute) (2014) 29 (4) *Henan Caijing Zhengfa Daxue Xuebao* 38.

Zhou Weihuan and Zhang Shu, 'Anti-dumping practices and China's implementation of WTO rulings' (2017) 230 *The China Quarterly* 512.

Zhou 周 Yanyun 艳云 and Zhou 周 Zhongxue 忠学, "WTO 国家特定规则"的合法性危机及其化解路径 ———基于中国入世议定书中的超 WTO 和负 WTO 规则的思考 (The Legitimacy Crisis of WTO National Specific Rules and its Solution – Reflections on the Rules of "WTO-plus" Rules and "WTO-minus" Rules in Accession Protocol of China) (2018) 33 (2) *Henan Caijing Zhengfa Daxue Xuebao* 160.

Zhou 周 Yimin 意岷, '南海争端解决模式分析' (A Model Analysis of Conflict Resolution in the South China Sea) [2011] (7) *Guoji Ziliao Xinxi* 18.

Zhou 周 Zhonghai 忠海, '论海洋法中的剩余权利' (The Residual Rights in the Law of the Sea) (2004) 22 (5) *Zhengfa Luntan* 174.

Zhu 朱 Guangdong 广东, 'WTO 争端解决中的司法克制及其对我国的启示' (Judicial Restraint in WTO Dispute Resolution and Lessons for China) (2007) 25 (1) *Falü Kexue* 134.

—— '论 WTO 争端解决中的司法克制思想' (On Judicial Restraint in WTO Dispute Settlement) [2007] (1) *Gansu Zhengfa Xueyuan Xuebao* 67.

Zhu Lijiang, 'Chinese Practice of International Law: 2008' (2009) 8 CJIL 493.

—— 'Chinese Practice in Public International Law: 2013' (2014) 13 CJIL 395.

Zhu 褚 Tong 童, '论和平解决国际争端中的国家仲裁' (Discussing State Arbitration in the Context of the Peaceful Resolution of International Conflicts) (2012) 11 *Lanzhou Xuekan* 184.

Zhu 朱 Zhaomin 兆敏, '论世界贸易组织与中国的市场经济地位' (The WTO and China's Market Economy Status) [2015] (9) *Faxue* 88.

Ziegler AR, 'Most Favoured-Nation (MFN) Treatment' in Reinisch A (ed), *Standards of Investment Protection* (OUP 2008).

Ziegler CE, 'Russia and China in Central Asia' in Bellacqua J (ed), *The Future of China-Russia Relations* (University of Kentucky Press 2010).

Zou Keyuan, 'China's U-Shaped Line in the South China Sea Revisited' (2012) 43 *Ocean Development & International Law* 18.

—— 'The South China Sea' in Rothwell DR and others (eds), *The Oxford Handbook of the Law of the Sea* (OUP 2015).

—— 'China's Approach to UNCLOS and its Application to Disputed Issues in the South China Sea' in Barrett J and Barnes R (eds), *Law of the Sea – UNCLOS as a Living Treaty* (The British Institute of International and Comparative Law 2016).

—— and Ye Qiang, 'Interpretation and Application of Article 298 of the Law of the Sea Convention in Recent Annex VII Arbitrations: An Appraisal' (2017) 0 *Ocean Development and International Law* 1.

Zou 邹 Ligang 立刚, '南海问题与中国的对策' (The South China Sea Issue and Chinese Countermeasures) (2009) 24 (1) *Henansheng Zhengfa Guanli Ganbu Xueyuan Xuebao* 158.

—— '中菲南海仲裁案剖析与我国的对策' (Analysis of the China v. Philippines South China Sea arbitration and Chinese countermeasures) [2016] (4) *Fazhi Yanjiu* 3.

—— and Wang 王 Chongmin 崇敏, '适用于南海的航行和飞越制度研究' (Study of the Application of the Navigation and Overflight Regime in the South China Sea) (2013) 27 (6) *Dangdai Faxue* 139.

—— and Ye 叶 Xinxin 鑫欣, '南海资源共同开发的法律机制构建略论' (Brief Introduction to the Structure of the Legal Mechanism of Joint Development of Resources in the South China Sea) [2006] (8) *Faxue* 122.

—— and Zhang 张 Kui 奎, '岛屿制度与南海海域划界' (The Rules of Islands and Delimitation of the South China Sea) (2011) 26 (5–6) *Henansheng Zhengfa Guanli Ganbu Xueyuan Xuebao* 73.

Zuo 左 Haicong 海聪, '论 GATT/WTO 争端解决机制的性质' (Discussing the Nature of the GATT/WTO Dispute Settlement Mechanism) [2004] (5) *Faxuejia* 152.

Translations of Chinese titles and Chinese names of journals are either given as provided by the authors and journals themselves or by this author.